A Grammar of Motives

AND

A Rhetoric of Motives

KENNETH BURKE

A Grammar of Motives

AND

A Rhetoric of Motives

Meridian Books

THE WORLD PUBLISHING COMPANY

CLEVELAND AND NEW YORK

A MERIDIAN BOOK

Published by The World Publishing Company
2231 West 110th Street, Cleveland 2, Ohio
Published simultaneously in Canada by
Nelson, Foster & Scott Ltd.
First Meridian printing August 1962

ACKNOWLEDGMENTS

Portions of *A Grammar of Motives* have previously been published in *Accent, Chimera, The Kenyon Review, The Sewanee Review,* and *View.* And I wish to acknowledge here my indebtedness to the editors of these magazines. I also wish to state my indebtedness to various publishers, editors, and authors for permission to quote from certain copyrighted material; thus: International Publishers, V. I. Lenin's *What Is To Be Done?;* The Macmillan Company, Marianne Moore's *Selected Poems* and *What Are Years?,* and Herbert Read's *Poetry and Anarchism;* The University of Chicago Press, George Herbert Mead's *The Philosophy of the Act* and Otto Neurath's *Foundations of the Social Sciences;* Little, Brown and Company, Ralph Barton Perry's *The Thought and Character of William James;* the University of California Press, Josephine Miles's *Pathetic Fallacy in the Nineteenth Century;* Harcourt, Brace and Company, Inc., I. A. Richards' *Principles of Literary Criticism* and Matthew Josephson's *Jean-Jacques Rousseau;* Peter Smith, Publisher, *Baldwin's Dictionary of Philosophy and Psychology;* the Houghton Mifflin Company, *The Education of Henry Adams,* by Henry Adams; Random House, Inc., Eugene O'Neill's *Mourning Becomes Electra;* Mr. Yvor Winters, *Primitivism and Decadence,* published by Arrow Editions; Mr. Allen Tate, *Reason in Madness,* published by G. P. Putnam's Sons; Mr. Edgar Johnson, *One Mighty Torrent: The Drama of Biography,* published by Stackpole Sons; *The New Republic,* Stark Young's review of Clifford Odets' *Night Music; Partisan Review,* the essay by John Dewey that appeared in the "Failure of Nerve" controversy; *Science & Society,* an article by Lewis S. Feuer on "logical empiricism" and one by K. Ostrovitianov on principles of the Russian economy; *View,* for permission to quote from Parker Tyler; *The New York Times* and Mr. Arthur Krock, for permission to quote a column by Mr. Krock entitled: "Is There a Way to Dispense with Elections?"; *The Virginia Quarterly Review* and M. Denis de Rougemont, for permission to quote from his essay, "The Idea of a Federation," appearing in the Autumn 1941 issue; *The University Review* and the authors, for permission to quote from a series of essays on the theory and practice of literary criticism by R. S. Crane, Norman Maclean, and Elder Olson.

The opening pages of *A Rhetoric of Motives* were previously published in *The Hudson Review,* and some remarks on science and magic are taken from my review of Ernst Cassirer's *The Myth of the State* that appeared in *The Nation*. Otherwise, to my recollection, no portions of the work have been previously published.

I wish to thank the members of my classes at Bennington College, who with charming patience participated in the working-out of the ideas here presented.

And I wish to thank Dr. J. Robert Oppenheimer for the opportunity to spend some very helpful months at the Institute for Advanced Study in Princeton, while making a final revision of the manuscript. Also, during this time, I was fortunate in being able to discuss many of these theories and analyses at the Princeton Seminars in Literary Criticism, then in process of formation.

I regret that I did not have an opportunity to incorporate additions suggested by a six-month sojourn at the University of Chicago where, under the auspices of the College, I presented some of this material.

Many authors of the past and present have contributed to the notions herein considered, in this project for "carving out a rhetoric," often from materials not generally thought to fall under the head. And I wish to make special acknowledgment for permission to quote from the following works still in copyright: Harcourt, Brace and Company, Inc., *Collected Poems* and *Four Quartets* by T. S. Eliot, and *The Meaning of Meaning* by C. K. Ogden and I. A. Richards; Charles Scribner's Sons, George Santayana's *Realms of Being,* and *The Prefaces of Henry James,* edited by Richard Blackmur; Dr. Clyde Kluckhohn, Director of the Russian Research Center, Harvard University, for permission to quote from his pamphlet, *Navaho Witchcraft;* Harvard University Press, the *Loeb Classical Library* translation (by H. Rackham) of Cicero's *De Oratore;* Princeton University Press, Walter Lowrie's translation of Kierkegaard's *Fear and Trembling;* The University of Chicago Press, Austin Warren's *Rage for Order;* Modern Philology, Richard McKeon's essay, "Poetry and Philosophy in the Twelfth Century," which appeared in the May 1946 issue. And to The Mediaeval Academy of America for permission to quote from an essay by the same author, "Rhetoric in the Middle Ages," published in the January 1942 issue of *Speculum;* Longmans, Green and Co., *The Varieties of Religious Experience,* by William James; Schocken Books, Inc., Franz Kafka's *The Castle,* copyright 1946, and Max Brod's *Kafka: A Biography,* copyright 1947; the Oxford University Press, a poem by Gerard Manley Hopkins; The Viking Press, Thorstein Veblen's *The Theory of the Leisure Class;* The Macmillan Company, W. B. Yeats' "Byzantium" in *Winding Stair,* copyright 1933.

K. B.

CONTENTS

A GRAMMAR OF MOTIVES

Introduction: The Five Key Terms of Dramatism   xvii

PART ONE—WAYS OF PLACEMENT

I. CONTAINER AND THING CONTAINED

The Scene-Act Ratio   3
The Scene-Agent Ratio   7
Further Instances of These Ratios   9
Ubiquity of the Ratios   11
Range of All the Ratios   15

II. ANTINOMIES OF DEFINITION

Paradox of Substance   21
Contextual Definition   24
Familial Definition   26
Survey of Terms for Substance   29
Dialectic Substance   33
The Paradox of Purity   35
Dialectic of Tragedy   38
Actus and Status   41
Universal Motives as Substance   43
Intrinsic and Extrinsic   46
The Rhetoric of Substance   51
Two Kinds of Departure   53
The Centrality of Substance   55

III. SCOPE AND REDUCTION

The Representative Anecdote   59
The Way of Creation   62
Act as Locus of Motives   64

The "Grounds" of Creation 69

Pantheism and Ontology 72

Grammatical Steps to Naturalism 74

Circumference 77

Monographic Terms of Placement 85

Monetary Reduction 91

Kinds of Reduction 96

Complexity of a Simple Motive 101

Money as Substitute for God 108

The Nature of Monetary "Reality" 113

Love, Knowledge, and Authority 117

PART TWO—THE PHILOSOPHIC SCHOOLS

I. SCENE

The Featuring of the Terms 127

Scene in General 131

Hobbes 132

Spinoza 137

Alignment of Terms in Spinoza 146

Darwin 152

The Two Great Hellenistic Materialisms 159

Rhetorical and Symbolic Levels 161

II. AGENT IN GENERAL

Idealization 172

Unification 175

Berkeley 177

Hume 181

Leibniz 184

Kant 185

Moral Transcendence in Kant 192

Idealism After Kant 198

Marxism 200

Hegel 202

Communist Manifesto 204

A Dramatist Grammar for Marxism 209

Santayana 214

Imagination 223

III. ACT

Aristotle and Aquinas 227

The "Pathetic Fallacy" 232

"Incipient" and "Delayed" Action 235

Realist Family and Nominalist Aggregate 247

Further Remarks on Act and Potency 252

Psychology of Action 262

IV. AGENCY AND PURPOSE

The Philosophy of Means 275

The Range of Pragmatism 281

Conditions 281

The "Facts" 282

Two Principles of Truth in James 282

Symbolic of Agency 283

Purposive Agencies of Applied Science 286

Ends 287

Modifications of Purpose 292

Purpose in Aristotle 292

Platonist and Neo-Platonist Purpose 293

Physiology of Mysticism 294

Purposiveness in the Negative 294

Unity and the Reflexive 297

Mysticism and Idealism: The Self 299

Images and the "Demonic Trinity" 300

Silence and the Hunt 303

The Mystic "Moment" 305

Mysticism of Means 309

Rationalism and the Verbal Medium 311

Means and Ends of This Grammar 317

PART THREE—ON DIALECTIC

I. THE DIALECTIC OF CONSTITUTIONS

Necessity for Representative Case 323

The Two Circles 325

Terminal as Anecdote 326

Representativeness of Total War 328

The Constitutive and the Admonitory 330

Peace: Constitutive or Directive? 332

Futurism: Religious and Secular 333

Position Epitomized 335

Imagistic and Conceptual Summaries 338

Five Basic Terms as Beginning 340

Meanings of "Constitution" 341

Technical Immunity of "Anarchism" as Ideal 344

"Anarcho-Syndicalism"—the Ideal Organized 345

The Anarcho-Syndicalist "Constitution" 346

A New Constitution for Laissez-faire 349

A Spectrum of Terms Between "Freedom" and "Capitalism" 350

Strategic Choice of Circumference for "Freedom" 354

Money as "God Term" 355

"Principles" and "Reform" 356

Constitutions and the Opponent 357

Constitutions—Addressed by Agents to Agents 360

Constitution-Behind-the-Constitution 362

Shifts in the Locus of the "Representative" 363

The Generalizing of Wishes 365

Limits and Powers of a Constitution 367

Constitutional Tactics of Coleridge's "Pantisocracy" Project 368

Constitutions but Partially Representative 371

Principles of the Conflict Among Principles 373

Constitution Makes Extra-Constitutionality Mandatory 376

Some Degrees of Constitutionality in Every Law 378

"Essentializing" and "Proportional" Strategies of Interpretation 380

Marshall's Argument for Right of Judicial Review 385

Constitutional Unity and Political Diversity 388

Role of the President 391

Political Rhetoric as Secular Prayer 393

War and Collective Nature of "Sacrifice" 394

The Dialectics of Federation 398

II. Dialectic in General

The Transformation of Terms   402
Merger and Division   403
Dialectic of the Scapegoat   406
Per Genus et Differentiam   408
More Variants of Merger and Division   410
The Mind-Body, Being-Nothing, and Action-Passion Pairs   418
The Socratic Transcendence   420
The Temporizing of Essence   430
Dissolution of Drama   440
A Neo-Liberal Ideal   441
Addendum for the Present Edition   443

APPENDIX

A. Symbolic Action in a Poem by Keats   447
B. The Problem of the Intrinsic   465
C. Motives and Motifs in the Poetry of Marianne Moore   485
D. Four Master Tropes   503

A RHETORIC OF MOTIVES

Introduction   521

PART ONE—THE RANGE OF RHETORIC

The "Use" of Milton's Samson   527
Qualifying the Suicidal Motive   529
Self-Immolation in Matthew Arnold   531
Quality of Arnold's Imagery   533
The Imaging of Transformation   534
Dramatic and Philosophic Terms for Essence   537
"Tragic" Terms for Personality Types   539
Recapitulation   540
Imagery at Face Value   541
Identification   543

Identification and "Consubstantiality"   544
The Identifying Nature of Property   547
Identification and the "Autonomous"   551
The "Autonomy" of Science   553
"Redemption" in Post-Christian Science   555
Dual Possibilities of Science   556
Ingenuous and Cunning Identifications   559
Rhetoric of "Address" (to the Individual Soul)   561
Rhetoric and Primitive Magic   564
Realistic Function of Rhetoric   567

PART TWO—TRADITIONAL PRINCIPLES OF RHETORIC

Persuasion   573
Identification   579
Other Variants of the Rhetorical Motive   583
Formal Appeal   589
Rhetorical Form in the Large   593
Imagination   602
Image and Idea   608
Rhetorical Analysis in Bentham   614
Marx on "Mystification"   625
Terministic Reservations (in View of Cromwell's Motives)   634
Carlyle on "Mystery"   638
Empson on "Pastoral" Identification   647
The "Invidious" as Imitation, in Veblen   651
Priority of the "Idea"   656
A Metaphorical View of Hierarchy   661
Diderot on "Pantomime"   666
Generic, Specific, and Individual Motives in Rochefoucauld   669
De Gourmont on "Dissociation"   673
Pascal on "Directing the Intention"   678
"Administrative" Rhetoric in Machiavelli   682
Dante's De Vulgari Eloquentia   691
Rhetoric in the Middle Ages   693
"Infancy," Mystery, and Persuasion   698

PART THREE—ORDER

Positive, Dialectical, and Ultimate Terms	707
Ultimate Elements in the Marxist Persuasion	713
"Sociology of Knowledge" vs. Platonic "Myth"	721
"Mythic" Ground and "Context of Situation"*	727
Courtship	732
"Socioanagogic" Interpretation of Venus and Adonis	736
The Paradigm of Courtship: Castiglione	745
The Caricature of Courtship: Kafka (The Castle)	757
A "Dialectical Lyric" (Kierkegaard's Fear and Trembling)	768
The Kill and the Absurd	776
Order, the Secret, and the Kill	784
Pure Persuasion	791
Rhetorical Radiance of the "Divine"	818
1. HENRY JAMES ON THE DEITY OF "THINGS"	818
2. "SOCIAL RATINGS" OF IMAGES IN JAMES	820
3. RHETORICAL NAMES FOR GOD	822
4. THE "RANGE OF MOUNTINGS"	825
5. ELATION AND ACCIDIE IN HOPKINS	837
6. YEATS: "BYZANTIUM" AND THE LAST POEMS	840
7. ELIOT: EARLY POEMS AND "QUARTETS"	842
8. PRINCIPLE OF THE OXYMORON	848
9. ULTIMATE IDENTIFICATION	852
Index (for both books)	859

A Grammar of Motives

Ad bellum purificandum

To Elizabeth
WITHOUT WHOM NOT

INTRODUCTION: THE FIVE KEY TERMS OF DRAMATISM

WHAT is involved, when we say what people are doing and why they are doing it? An answer to that question is the subject of this book. The book is concerned with the basic forms of thought which, in accordance with the nature of the world as all men necessarily experience it, are exemplified in the attributing of motives. These forms of thought can be embodied profoundly or trivially, truthfully or falsely. They are equally present in systematically elaborated metaphysical structures, in legal judgments, in poetry and fiction, in political and scientific works, in news and in bits of gossip offered at random.

We shall use five terms as generating principle of our investigation. They are: Act, Scene, Agent, Agency, Purpose. In a rounded statement about motives, you must have some word that names the *act* (names what took place, in thought or deed), and another that names the *scene* (the background of the act, the situation in which it occurred); also, you must indicate what person or kind of person (*agent*) performed the act, what means or instruments he used (*agency*), and the *purpose*. Men may violently disagree about the purposes behind a given act, or about the character of the person who did it, or how he did it, or in what kind of situation he acted; or they may even insist upon totally different words to name the act itself. But be that as it may, any complete statement about motives will offer *some kind of* answers to these five questions: what was done (act), when or where it was done (scene), who did it (agent), how he did it (agency), and why (purpose).

If you ask why, with a whole world of terms to choose from, we select these rather than some others as basic, our book itself is offered as the answer. For, to explain our position, we shall show how it can be applied.

Act, Scene, Agent, Agency, Purpose. Although, over the centuries, men have shown great enterprise and inventiveness in pondering matters of human motivation, one can simplify the subject by this pentad of key terms, which are understandable almost at a glance. They need never to be abandoned, since all statements that assign motives can be shown to arise out of them and to terminate in them. By examining them quizzically, we can range far; yet the terms are always there for us to reclaim, in their everyday simplicity, their almost miraculous easiness, thus enabling us constantly to begin afresh. When they might become difficult, when we can hardly see them, through having stared at them too intensely, we can of a sudden relax, to look at them as we always have, lightly, glancingly. And having reassured ourselves, we can start out again, once more daring to let them look strange and difficult for a time.

In an exhibit of photographic murals (*Road to Victory*) at the Museum of Modern Art, there was an aerial photograph of two launches, proceeding side by side on a tranquil sea. Their wakes crossed and recrossed each other in almost an infinity of lines. Yet despite the intricateness of this tracery, the picture gave an impression of great simplicity, because one could quickly perceive the generating principle of its design. Such, ideally, is the case with our pentad of terms, used as generating principle. It should provide us with a kind of simplicity that can be developed into considerable complexity, and yet can be discovered beneath its elaborations.

We want to inquire into the purely internal relationships which the five terms bear to one another, considering their possibilities of transformation, their range of permutations and combinations—and then to see how these various resources figure in actual statements about human motives. Strictly speaking, we mean by a Grammar of motives a concern with the terms alone, without reference to the ways in which their potentialities have been or can be utilized in actual statements about motives. Speaking broadly we could designate as "philosophies" any statements in which these grammatical resources are specifically utilized. Random or unsystematic statements about motives could be considered as fragments of a philosophy.

One could think of the Grammatical resources as *principles,* and of the various philosophies as *casuistries* which apply these principles to temporal situations. For instance, we may examine the term Scene simply as a blanket term for the concept of background or setting *in general,* a name for *any* situation in which acts or agents are placed. In our usage, this concern would be "grammatical." And we move into matters of "philosophy" when we note that one thinker uses "God" as his term for the ultimate ground or scene of human action, another uses "nature," a third uses "environment," or "history," or "means of production," etc. And whereas a statement about the grammatical principles of motivation might lay claim to a universal validity, or complete certainty, the choice of any one philosophic idiom embodying these principles is much more open to question. Even before we know what act is to be discussed, we can say with confidence that a rounded discussion of its motives must contain a reference to *some kind of* background. But since each philosophic idiom will characterize this background differently, there will remain the question as to which characterization is "right" or "more nearly right."

It is even likely that, whereas one philosophic idiom offers the best calculus for one case, another case answers best to a totally different calculus. However, we should not think of "cases" in too restricted a sense. Although, from the standpoint of the grammatical principles inherent in the internal relationships prevailing among our five terms, any given philosophy is to be considered as a casuistry, even a cultural situation extending over centuries is a "case," and would probably require a much different philosophic idiom as its temporizing calculus of motives than would be required in the case of other cultural situations.

In our original plans for this project, we had no notion of writing a "Grammar" at all. We began with a theory of comedy, applied to a treatise on human relations. Feeling that competitive ambition is a drastically over-developed motive in the modern world, we thought this motive might be transcended if men devoted themselves not so much to "excoriating" it as to "appreciating" it. Accordingly, we began taking notes on the foibles and antics of what we tended to think of as "the Human Barnyard."

We sought to formulate the basic stratagems which people employ, in endless variations, and consciously or unconsciously, for the outwitting or cajoling of one another. Since all these devices had a "you and me" quality about them, being "addressed" to some person or to some advantage, we classed them broadly under the heading of a Rhetoric. There were other notes, concerned with modes of expression and appeal in the fine arts, and with purely psychological or psychoanalytic matters. These we classed under the heading of Symbolic.

We had made still further observations, which we at first strove uneasily to class under one or the other of these two heads, but which we were eventually able to distinguish as the makings of a Grammar. For we found in the course of writing that our project needed a grounding in formal considerations logically prior to both the rhetorical and the psychological. And as we proceeded with this introductory ground-work, it kept extending its claims until it had spun itself from an in-tended few hundred words into nearly 200,000, of which the present book is revision and abridgement.

Theological, metaphysical, and juridical doctrines offer the best illus-tration of the concerns we place under the heading of Grammar; the forms and methods of art best illustrate the concerns of Symbolic; and the ideal material to reveal the nature of Rhetoric comprises observa-tions on parliamentary and diplomatic devices, editorial bias, sales methods and incidents of social sparring. However, the three fields overlap considerably. And we shall note, in passing, how the Rhetoric and the Symbolic hover about the edges of our central theme, the Grammar.

A perfectionist might seek to evolve terms free of ambiguity and in-consistency (as with the terministic ideals of symbolic logic and logical positivism). But we have a different purpose in view, one that prob-ably retains traces of its "comic" origin. We take it for granted that, insofar as men cannot themselves create the universe, there must re-main something essentially enigmatic about the problem of motives, and that this underlying enigma will manifest itself in inevitable ambiguities and inconsistencies among the terms for motives. Accordingly, what we want is *not terms that avoid ambiguity,* but *terms that clearly reveal the strategic spots at which ambiguities necessarily arise.*

Occasionally, you will encounter a writer who seems to get great exal-tation out of proving, with an air of much relentlessness, that some phil-osophic term or other has been used to cover a variety of meanings, and who would smash and abolish this idol. As a general rule, when a term is singled out for such harsh treatment, if you look closer you will find that it happens to be associated with some cultural or political trend from which the writer would dissociate himself; hence there is a certain notable ambiguity in this very charge of ambiguity, since he presumably feels purged and strengthened by bringing to bear upon this particular term a kind of attack that could, with as much justice, be brought to bear upon any other term (or "title") in philosophy, includ-ing of course the alternative term, or "title," that the writer would swear by. Since no two things or acts or situations are exactly alike, you cannot apply the same term to both of them without thereby introducing a certain margin of ambiguity, an ambiguity as great as the difference between the two subjects that are given the identical title. And all the more may you expect to find ambiguity in terms so "titular" as to become the marks of a philosophic school, or even several philosophic schools. Hence, instead of considering it our task to "dispose of" any ambiguity by merely disclosing the fact that it is an ambiguity, we rather consider it our task to study and clarify the *resources* of ambiguity. For in the course of this work, we shall deal with many kinds of *transformation*—and it is in the areas of ambiguity that transformations take place; in fact, without such areas, transformation would be impossible. Distinctions, we might say, arise out of a great central moltenness, where all is merged. They have been thrown from a liquid center to the surface, where they have congealed. Let one of these crusted distinctions return to its source, and in this alchemic center it may be remade, again becoming molten liquid, and may enter into new combinations, whereat it may be again thrown forth as a new crust, a different distinction. So that A may become non-A. But not merely by a leap from one state to the other. Rather, we must take A back into the ground of its existence, the logical substance that is its causal ancestor, and on to a point where it is consubstantial with non-A; then we may return, this time emerging with non-A instead.

And so with our five terms: certain formal interrelationships prevail among these terms, by reason of their role as attributes of a common ground or substance. Their participation in a common ground makes for transformability. At every point where the field covered by any one of these terms overlaps upon the field covered by any other, there is an alchemic opportunity, whereby we can put one philosophy or doctrine of motivation into the alembic, make the appropriate passes, and take out another. From the central moltenness, where all the elements are fused into one togetherness, there are thrown forth, in separate crusts, such distinctions as those between freedom and necessity, activity and passiveness, coöperation and competition, cause and effect, mechanism and teleology.

Our term, "Agent," for instance, is a general heading that might, in a given case, require further subdivision, as an agent might have his act modified (hence partly motivated) by friends (co-agents) or enemies (counter-agents). Again, under "Agent" one could place any personal properties that are assigned a motivational value, such as "ideas," "the will," "fear," "malice," "intuition," "the creative imagination." A portrait painter may treat the body as a property of the agent (an expression of personality), whereas materialistic medicine would treat it as "scenic," a purely "objective material"; and from another point of view it could be classed as an agency, a means by which one gets reports of the world at large. Machines are obviously instruments (that is, Agencies); yet in their vast accumulation they constitute the industrial scene, with its own peculiar set of motivational properties. War may be treated as an Agency, insofar as it is a means to an end; as a collective Act, subdivisible into many individual acts; as a Purpose, in schemes proclaiming a cult of war. For the man inducted into the army, war is a Scene, a situation that motivates the nature of his training; and in mythologies war is an Agent, or perhaps better a super-agent, in the figure of the war god. We may think of voting as an act, and of the voter as an agent; yet votes and voters both are hardly other than a politician's medium or agency; or from another point of view, they are a part of his scene. And insofar as a vote is cast without adequate knowledge of its consequences, one might even question whether it should be classed as an activity at all; one might rather call it passive, or perhaps sheer motion (what the behaviorists would call a Response to a Stimulus).

Or imagine that one were to manipulate the terms, for the imputing of motives, in such a case as this: The hero (agent) with the help of a friend (co-agent) outwits the villain (counter-agent) by using a file (agency) that enables him to break his bonds (act) in order to escape (purpose) from the room where he has been confined (scene). In selecting a casuistry here, we might locate the motive in the agent, as were we to credit his escape to some trait integral to his personality, such as "love of freedom." Or we might stress the motivational force of the scene, since nothing is surer to awaken thoughts of escape in a man than a condition of imprisonment. Or we might note the essential part played by the *co-agent,* in assisting our hero to escape—and, with such thoughts as our point of departure, we might conclude that the motivations of this act should be reduced to social origins.

Or if one were given to the brand of speculative enterprise exemplified by certain Christian heretics (for instance, those who worshipped

Judas as a saint, on the grounds that his betrayal of Christ, in leading to the Crucifixion, so brought about the opportunity for mankind's redemption) one might locate the necessary motivational origin of the act in the *counter-agent*. For the hero would not have been prodded to escape if there had been no villain to imprison him. Inasmuch as the escape could be called a "good" act, we might find in such motivational reduction to the counter-agent a compensatory transformation whereby a bitter fountain may give forth sweet waters. In his *Anti-Dühring* Engels gives us a secular variant which no one could reasonably call outlandish or excessive:

> It was slavery that first made possible the division of labour between agriculture and industry on a considerable scale, and along with this, the flower of the ancient world, Hellenism. Without slavery, no Greek state, no Greek art and science; without slavery, no Roman Empire. But without Hellenism and the Roman Empire as a basis, also no modern Europe.
>
> We should never forget that our whole economic, political and intellectual development has as its presupposition a state of things in which slavery was as necessary as it was universally recognized. In this sense we are entitled to say: Without the slavery of antiquity, no modern socialism.

Pragmatists would probably have referred the motivation back to a source in *agency*. They would have noted that our hero escaped by using an *instrument,* the file by which he severed his bonds; then in this same line of thought, they would have observed that the hand holding the file was also an instrument; and by the same token the brain that guided the hand would be an instrument, and so likewise the educational system that taught the methods and shaped the values involved in the incident.

True, if you reduce the terms to any one of them, you will find them branching out again; for no one of them is enough. Thus, Mead called his pragmatism a philosophy of the *act*. And though Dewey stresses the value of "intelligence" as an instrument (agency, embodied in "scientific method"), the other key terms in his casuistry, "experience" and "nature," would be the equivalents of act and scene respectively. We must add, however, that Dewey is given to stressing the *overlap* of these two terms, rather than the respects in which they are distinct, as he proposes to "replace the traditional separation of nature and experience with the idea of continuity." (The quotation is from *Intelligence and the Modern World.*)

As we shall see later, it is by reason of the pliancy among our terms that philosophic systems can pull one way and another. The margins of overlap provide opportunities whereby a thinker can go without a leap from any one of the terms to any of its fellows. (We have also likened the terms to the fingers, which in their extremities are distinct from one another, but merge in the palm of the hand. If you would go from one finger to another without a leap, you need but trace the tendon down into the palm of the hand, and then trace a new course along another tendon.) Hence, no great dialectical enterprise is necessary if you would merge the terms, reducing them even to as few as one; and then, treating this as the "essential" term, the "causal ancestor" of the lot, you can proceed in the reverse direction across the margins of overlap, "deducing" the other terms from it as its logical descendants.

This is the method, explicitly and in the grand style, of metaphysics which brings its doctrines to a head in some over-all title, a word for being in general, or action in general, or motion in general, or development in general, or experience in general, etc., with all its other terms distributed about this titular term in positions leading up to it and away from it. There is also an implicit kind of metaphysics, that often goes by the name of No Metaphysics, and aims at reduction not to an overall title but to some presumably underlying atomic constituent. Its vulgar variant is to be found in techniques of "unmasking," which would make for progress and emancipation by applying materialistic terms to immaterial subjects (the pattern here being, "X is nothing but Y," where X designates a higher value and Y a lower one, the higher value being thereby reduced to the lower one).

The titular word for our own method is "dramatism," since it invites one to consider the matter of motives in a perspective that, being developed from the analysis of drama, treats language and thought primarily as modes of action. The method is synoptic, though not in the historical sense. A purely historical survey would require no less than a universal history of human culture; for every judgment, exhortation, or admonition, every view of natural or supernatural reality, every intention or expectation involves assumptions about motive, or cause. Our work must be synoptic in a different sense: in the sense that it offers a system of placement, and should enable us, by the systematic manipulation of the terms, to "generate," or "anticipate" the various classes of motivational theory.   And a treatment in these terms, we hope to show, reduces the subject synoptically while still permitting us to appreciate its scope and complexity.

It is not our purpose to import dialectical and metaphysical concerns into a subject that might otherwise be free of them.   On the contrary, we hope to make clear the ways in which dialectical and metaphysical issues *necessarily* figure in the subject of motivation.   Our speculations, as we interpret them, should show that the subject of motivation is a philosophic one, not ultimately to be solved in terms of empirical science.

PART ONE

WAYS OF PLACEMENT

I

CONTAINER AND THING CONTAINED

The Scene—Act Ratio

USING "scene" in the sense of setting, or background, and "act" in the sense of action, one could say that "the scene contains the act." And using "agents" in the sense of actors, or acters, one could say that "the scene contains the agents."

It is a principle of drama that the nature of acts and agents should be consistent with the nature of the scene. And whereas comic and grotesque works may deliberately set these elements at odds with one another, audiences make allowance for such liberty, which reaffirms the same principle of consistency in its very violation.

The nature of the scene may be conveyed primarily by suggestions built into the lines of the verbal action itself, as with the imagery in the dialogue of Elizabethan drama and with the descriptive passages of novels; or it may be conveyed by non-linguistic properties, as with the materials of naturalistic stage-sets. In any case, examining first the relation between scene and act, all we need note here is the principle whereby the scene is a fit "container" for the act, expressing in fixed properties the same quality that the action expresses in terms of development.

Ibsen's *An Enemy of the People* is a good instance of the scene-act ratio, since the correlations between scene and act are readily observable, beginning with the fact that this representative middle-class drama is enacted against a typical middle-class setting. Indeed, in this work written at the very height of Ibsen's realistic period, we can see how readily realism leads into symbolism. For the succession of scenes both *realistically reflects* the course of the action and *symbolizes* it.

The first act (we are now using the word "act" in the purely technical sense, to designate the major division of a play, a sense in which we could even reverse our formula and say that "the act contains its scenes")—the first act takes place in Dr. Stockmann's sitting room, a

3

background perfectly suited to the thoroughly bourgeois story that is to unfold from these beginnings. In the course of this act, we learn of a scene, or situation, prior to the opening of the play, but central to its motivation. Dr. Stockmann refers to an earlier period of withdrawal, spent alone in the far North. During his isolation, he had conceived of his plan for the public Baths. This plan may be considered either realistically or symbolically; it is the dramatist's device for materializing, or objectifying, a purely spiritual process, since the plot has to do with pollution and purification on a moral level, which has its scenic counterpart in the topic of the Baths.

Act II. Still in Dr. Stockmann's sitting room. Dr. Stockmann has learned that the Baths, the vessels of purification, are themselves polluted, and that prominent business and professional men would suppress this fact for financial reasons. This opposition is epitomized in the figure of Peter Stockmann, the Doctor's brother. The intimate, familial quality of the setting thus has its counterpart in the quality of the action, which involves the struggle of two social principles, the conservative and the progressive, as objectified and personalized in the struggle of the two brothers.

Act III takes place in the editorial office of the People's Messenger, a local newspaper in which Dr. Stockmann had hoped to publish his evidence that the water supply was contaminated. The action takes on a more forensic reference, in keeping with the nature of the place. In this Act we have the peripety of the drama, as Dr. Stockmann's expectations are reversed. For he learns that the personal and financial influence of his enemies prevents the publication of the article. This turn of the plot has its scenic replica in mimicry involving Peter Stockmann's hat and stick, properties that symbolize his identity as mayor. In false hope of victory, Dr. Stockmann had taken them up, and strutted about burlesquing his brother. But when Dr. Stockmann learns that the editor, in response to the pressure of the conservatives, will not publish the article, it is Peter Stockmann's turn to exult. This reversal of the action is materialized (made scenic) thus:

> PETER STOCKMANN. My hat and stick, if you please. (Dr. Stockmann *takes off the hat and lays it on the table with the stick*. Peter Stockmann *takes them up*.) Your authority as mayor has come to an untimely end.

In the next Act Dr. Stockmann does contrive to lay his case before a public tribunal of a sort: a gathering of fellow-townsmen, assembled in "a big old-fashioned room," in the house of a friend. His appeal is unsuccessful; his neighbors vote overwhelmingly against him, and the scene ends in turbulence. As regards the scene-act ratio, note that the semi-public, semi-intimate setting reflects perfectly the quality of Dr. Stockmann's appeal.

In Act V, the stage directions tell us that the hero's clothes are torn, and the room is in disorder, with broken windows. You may consider these details either as properties of the scene or as a reflection of the hero's condition after his recent struggle with the forces of reaction. The scene is laid in Dr. Stockmann's *study,* a setting so symbolic of the direction taken by the plot that the play ends with Dr. Stockmann announcing his plan to enroll twelve young *disciples* and with them to found a *school* in which he will work for the *education* of society.

The whole plot is that of an internality directed outwards. We progress by stages from a scene (reported) wherein the plan of social purification was conceived in loneliness, to the scene in his study where the hero announces in the exaltation of a dramatic finale: "The strongest man in the world is he who stands most alone." The pronouncement is modified by the situation in which it is uttered: as Dr. Stockmann speaks, he is surrounded by a loyal and admiring family circle, and his educational plan calls not for complete independence, but for coöperation. He is not setting himself up as the strongest man in the world, but merely as one headed in the same direction. And, with the exception of his brother Peter, we may consider his family circle as aspects of his own identity, being under the aegis of "loneliness" since it began so and retains the quality of its ancestry.

The end of the third play in O'Neill's trilogy, *Mourning Becomes Electra,* presents a contrasting instance of the scene-act ratio:

> LAVINIA. (*turns to him sharply*) You go now and close the shutters and nail them tight.
> SETH. Ayeh.
> LAVINIA. And tell Hannah to throw out all the flowers.
> SETH. Ayeh. (*He goes past her up the steps and into the house. She ascends to the portico—and then turns and stands for a while, stiff and square-shouldered, staring into the sunlight with frozen*

eyes. Seth leans out of the window at the right of the door and pulls the shutters closed with a decisive bang. As if this were a word of command, Lavinia pivots sharply on her heel and marches woodenly into the house, closing the door behind her.)

CURTAIN

We end here on the motif of the shut-in personality, quite literally objectified. And the closing, novelistic stage-directions are beautifully suited to our purpose; for note how, once the shutters have been closed, thereby placing before our eyes the scenic replica of Lavinia's mental state, this scene in turn becomes the motivation of her next act. For we are told that she walks like an automaton in response to the closing of the shutter, "as if this were a word of command."

Hamlet contains a direct reference to the motivational aspect of the scene-act ratio. In an early scene, when Hamlet is about to follow the Ghost, Horatio warns:

> What if it tempt you toward the flood, my lord,
> Or to the dreadful summit of the cliff
> That beetles o'er his base into the sea,
> And there assume some other horrible form,
> Which might deprive your sovereignty of reason
> And draw you into madness? Think of it;
> The very place puts toys of desperation,
> Without more motive, into every brain
> That looks so many fathoms to the sea
> And hears it roar beneath.

In the last four lines of this speech, Horatio is saying that the sheer natural surroundings might be enough to provide a man with a motive for an act as desperate and absolute as suicide. This notion (of the natural scene as sufficient motivation for an act) was to reappear, in many transformations, during the subsequent centuries. We find a variant of it in the novels of Thomas Hardy, and in other regionalists who derive motivations for their characters from what Virgil would have called the *genius loci*. There are unmistakable vestiges of it in scientific theories (of Darwinian cast) according to which men's behavior and development are explained in terms of environment. Geopolitics is a contemporary variant.

From the motivational point of view, there is implicit in the quality of a scene the quality of the action that is to take place within it. This would be another way of saying that the act will be consistent with the scene. Thus, when the curtain rises to disclose a given stage-set, this stage-set contains, simultaneously, implicitly, all that the narrative is to draw out as a sequence, explicitly. Or, if you will, the stage-set contains the action *ambiguously* (as regards the norms of action)—and in the course of the play's development this ambiguity is converted into a corresponding *articulacy*. The proportion would be: scene is to act as implicit is to explicit. One could not deduce the details of the action from the details of the setting, but one could deduce the quality of the action from the quality of the setting. An extreme illustration would be an Expressionistic drama, having for its scenic reflex such abstract properties as lines askew, grotesque lighting, sinister color, and odd objects.

We have, of course, chosen examples particularly suited to reveal the distinction between act and scene as well as their interdependence. The matter is obscured when we are dealing with scene in the sense of the relationships prevailing among the various *dramatis personae*. For the characters, by being in interaction, could be treated as scenic conditions or "environment," of one another; and any act could be treated as part of the context that modifies (hence, to a degree motivates) the subsequent acts. The principles of dramatic consistency would lead one to expect such cases of overlap among the terms; but while being aware of them we should firmly fix in our minds such cases as afford a clear differentiation. Our terms lending themselves to both merger and division, we are here trying to divide two of them while recognizing their possibilities of merger.

The Scene–Agent Ratio

The scene-agent ratio, where the synecdochic relation is between person and place, is partly exemplified in this citation from Carlyle's *Heroes and Hero-Worship*:

These Arabs Mohammed was born among are certainly a notable people. Their country itself is notable; the fit habitation for such a race. Savage inaccessible rock-mountains, great grim deserts, alternating with beautiful strips of verdure; wherever water is, there is greenness, beauty; odoriferous balm-shrubs, date-trees, frankincense-trees. Consider that wide waste horizon of sand, empty, silent, like a sand-sea, dividing habitable place from habitable place. You are all alone there, left alone with the universe; by day a fierce sun blazing down on it with intolerable radiance; by night the great deep heaven with its stars. Such a country is fit for a swift-handed, deep-hearted race of men.

The correlation between the quality of the country and the quality of its inhabitants is here presented in quite secular terms. There is a sonnet by Wordsworth that is a perfect instance of the scene-agent ratio treated theologically:

> It is a beauteous evening, calm and free,
> The holy time is quiet as a Nun
> Breathless with adoration; the broad sun
> Is sinking down in its tranquillity;
> The gentleness of heaven broods o'er the Sea;
> Listen! the mighty Being is awake,
> And doth with his eternal motion make
> A sound like thunder—everlastingly.
>
> Dear Child! Dear Girl! that walkest with me here,
> If thou appear untouched by solemn thought,
> Thy nature is not therefore less divine:
> Thou liest in Abraham's bosom all the year;
> And worship'st at the Temple's inner shrine,
> God being with thee when we know it not.

By selecting a religious image in which to convey the purely naturalistic sense of hush, the octave infuses the natural scene with hints of a wider circumference, supernatural in scope. The sestet turns from scene to agent; indeed, the octave is all scene, the sestet all agent. But by the logic of the scene-agent ratio, if the scene is supernatural in quality, the agent contained by this scene will partake of the same supernatural quality. And so, spontaneously, purely by being the kind of agent that is at one with this kind of scene, the child is "divine." The contents of a divine container will synecdochically share in its divinity.

Swift's satire on philosophers and mathematicians, the Laputans in the third book of *Gulliver's Travels,* offers a good instance of the way in which the scene-agent ratio can be used for the depiction of character. To suggest that the Laputans are, we might say, "up in the air," he portrays them as living on an island that floats in space. Here the nature of the inhabitants is translated into terms of their habitation.

Variants of the scene-agent ratio abound in typical nineteenth-century thought, so strongly given to the study of motives by the dialectic pairing of people and things (man and nature, agent and scene). The ratio figures characteristically in the idealist's concern with the *Einklang zwischen Innen- und Aussenwelt.* The paintings of the pointillist Seurat carry the sense of consistency between scene and agent to such lengths that his human figures seem on the point of dissolving into their background. However, we here move beyond strictly scene-agent matters into the area better covered by our term, agency, since the extreme impression of consistency between scene and agent is here conveyed by stressing the distinctive terms of the method, or medium (that is, agency), which serves as an element common to both scene and agents.

The logic of the scene-agent ratio has often served as an embarrassment to the naturalistic novelist. He may choose to "indict" some scene (such as bad working conditions under capitalism) by showing that it has a "brutalizing" effect upon the people who are indigenous to this scene. But the scene-agent ratio, if strictly observed here, would require that the "brutalizing" situation contain "brutalized" characters as its dialectical counterpart. And thereby, in his humanitarian zeal to save mankind, the novelist portrays characters which, in being as brutal as their scene, are not worth saving. We could phrase this dilemma in another way: our novelist points up his thesis by too narrow a conception of scene as the motive-force behind his characters; and this restricting of the scene calls in turn for a corresponding restriction upon personality, or rôle.

Further Instances of These Ratios

The principles of consistency binding scene, act, and agent also lead to reverse applications. That is, the scene-act ratio either calls for acts in keeping with scenes or scenes in keeping with acts—and similarly with the scene-agent ratio. When Lavinia instructs Seth to nail fast the shutters and throw out the flowers, by her command (an act) she brings it about that the scene corresponds to her state of mind. But as soon as these scenic changes have taken place, they in turn become the motivating principle of her subsequent conduct. For the complete embodiment of her purposes functions as a "command" to her; and she obeys it as a response to a stimulus, like a pure automaton moved by the sheer disposition of material factors.

In behavioristic metaphysics (behaviorists would call it No Metaphysics) you radically truncate the possibilities of drama by eliminating action, reducing action to sheer motion. The close of the O'Neill play follows this same development from action to motion, a kind of inverted transcendence. Because of this change, Lavinia's last moments must be relegated to stage directions alone. She does not *act*, she is automatically *moved*. The trilogy did not end a moment too soon; for its close represented not only the end of Lavinia, but the end of the motivating principle of drama itself. The playwright had here obviously come to the end of a line. In his next plays he would have to "turn back." For he could have "gone on" only by abandoning drama for some more "scientific" form. (He might have transcended drama scientifically, for instance, by a collating of sociological observations designed to classify different types of motorist and to correlate them with different types of response to traffic signals.)

We noted how, in Ibsen's drama, the hero's state of mind after his conflict with the townspeople was objectified in such scenic properties as his torn clothing, and the broken windows and general disorder of his study. It is obvious that one might have carried this consistency further in either direction (for instance, spreading it more environmentally, as were we to enlist turbulent weather as an aspect of the scene, or more personally, as were we to enlist facial expressions and postures of the body, which of course the actor does, in interpreting his rôle, regardless of the playwright's omissions). If you took the hero's state of mind as your point of departure here, you could say that the whole scene becomes a mere aspect of the rôle, or person ("agent")— or that the physical body of the agent is itself but "scenic," to be listed among the person's "properties," as with a dwelling that a man had ordered built in strict accordance with his own private specifications, or as theologians see in "body" the dwelling-place of "soul." We observe the same ratio in Swift's account of his Laputans when, to suggest that in their thinking they could be transcendental, or introvert, or extremely biased, but never well balanced, he writes: "Their heads were all inclined, either to the right or to the left; one of their eyes turned inward, and the other directly up to the zenith." But lest our speculations seem too arbitrary, let us cite one more anecdote, this time from a tiny drama enacted in real life, and here reported to illustrate how, when a state of mind is pronounced in quality, the agent may be observed arranging a corresponding pattern in the very properties of the scene.

The occasion: a committee meeting. The setting: a group of committee members bunched about a desk in an office, after hours. Not far from the desk was a railing; but despite the crowding, all the members were bunched about the chairman at the desk, inside the railing. However, they had piled their hats and coats on chairs and tables outside the pale. General engrossment in the discussion. But as the discussion continued, one member quietly arose, and opened the gate in the railing. As unnoticeably as possible, she stepped outside and closed the gate. She picked up her coat, laid it across her arm, and stood waiting. A few moments later, when there was a pause in the discussion, she asked for the floor. After being recognized by the chairman, she very haltingly, in embarrassment, announced with regret that she would have to resign from the committee.

Consider with what fidelity she had set the scene for this pattern of severance as she stepped beyond the railing to make her announcement. Design: chairman and fellow members within the pale, sitting, without hats and overcoats—she outside the pale, standing, with coat over her arm preparatory to departure. She had strategically modified the arrangement of the scene in such a way that it implicitly (ambiguously) contained the quality of her act.

Ubiquity of the Ratios

If we but look about us, we find examples of the two ratios everywhere; for they are at the very centre of motivational assumptions. But to discern them in their ubiquity, we must remain aware of the many guises which the five terms may assume in the various casuistries. In the introduction to his *Discourses,* for instance, Machiavelli complains that people read history without applying its lessons, "as though heaven, the sun, the elements, and men had changed the order of their motions and power, and were different from what they were in ancient times." For our purposes, the quotation could be translated, "as though human agents and both the supernatural and the natural scenes had changed, with a corresponding change in the nature of motives."

Besides general synonyms for scene that are obviously of a background character, such as "society," or "environment," we often encounter quite specific localizations, words for particular places, situations, or eras. "It is 12:20 P.M." is a "scenic" statement. Milton's *L'Allegro* and *Il Penseroso* are formed about a scenic contrast between morning and night, with a corresponding contrast of actions. Terms for historical epochs, cultural movements, social institutions (such as "Elizabethan period," "romanticism," "capitalism") are scenic, though often with an admixture of properties overlapping upon the areas covered by the term, agent. If we recall that "ideas" are a property of agents, we can detect this strategic overlap in Locke's expression, "the scene of ideas," the form of which Carl Becker exactly reproduces when referring to "climates of opinion," in *The Heavenly City of the Eighteenth-Century Philosophers.*

The word "ground," much used in both formal philosophy and everyday speech when discussing motives, is likewise scenic, though readily encroaching upon the areas more directly covered by "agent" and "purpose." We can discern the scenic reference if the question, "On what grounds did he do this?" is translated: "What kind of scene did he say it was, that called for such an act?" Hegelian idealism exploits the double usage (ground as "background" and ground as "reason") by positing "Reason" as the ultimate ground, the *Grundprinzip,* of all history. Thus, whereas historicism regularly treats historical scenes as the background, or motive, of individual developments, Hegel would treat Reason as the background, or motive, of historical sequence in general. Let us not worry, at this point, what it may "mean" to say that "Reason" is at once the mover of history and the substance of which history is made. It is sufficient here to note that such terministic resources were utilized, and to detect the logic of the pentad behind them.

The maxim, "terrain determines tactics," is a strict localization of the scene-act ratio, with "terrain" as the casuistic equivalent for "scene" in a military calculus of motives, and "tactics" as the corresponding "act."

Political commentators now generally use the word "situation" as their synonym for scene, though often without any clear concept of its function as a statement about motives. Many social psychologists consciously use the term for its motivational bearing (it has a range extending from the broadest concepts of historical setting down to the simplified, controlled conditions which the animal experimenter imposes upon his rats in a maze). The Marxist reference to "the objective situation" is explicitly motivational, and the theorists who use this formula discuss "policies" as political acts enacted in conformity with the nature of scenes. However, the scene-act ratio can be applied in two ways. It can be applied deterministically in statements that a certain policy *had* to be adopted in a certain situation, or it may be applied in hortatory statements to the effect that a certain policy *should be* adopted in conformity with the situation. The deterministic usage (in scene-agent form) was exemplified in the statement of a traveller who, on arriving from France under German domination, characterized the politicians as "prisoners of the situation." And the hortatory usage was exemplified when a speaker said that President Roosevelt should be granted "unusual powers" because our country was in an "unusual international situation." In a judgment written by Justice Hugo L. Black, the Supreme Court ruled that it was not "beyond the war powers of Congress and the Executive to exclude those of Japanese ancestry from the West Coast area at the time they did." And by implication, the scene-act ratio was invoked to substantiate this judgment:

> When under conditions of modern warfare our shores are threat-
> ened by hostile forces, the power to protect must be commensurate
> with the threatened danger.

Among the most succinct instances of the scene-act ratio in dialectical materialism is Marx's assertion (cited also by Lenin in *The State and Revolution*), that "Justice can never rise superior to the economic conditions of society and the cultural development conditioned by them." That is, in contrast with those who would place justice as a property of personality (an attribute purely of the *agent*), the dialectical materialist would place it as a property of the *material situation* ("economic conditions"), the scene in which justice is to be enacted. He would say that no higher quality of justice can be enacted than the nature of the scenic properties permits. Trotsky gave the same form an ironic turn when he treated Stalinist policies as the inevitable result of the attempt to establish socialism under the given conditions. That is, you can't get a fully socialist *act* unless you have a fully socialist *scene,* and for the dialectical materialist such a scene requires a high stage of industrial development.

And there is a variant of the usage in Coleridge (in his early libertarian and "necessitarian" period, when he was exalted with thoughts of "aspheterism"). Concerning "Pantisocracy" (the plan of Coleridge, Southey, and their associates to found a communistic colony on the banks of the Susquehanna), he wrote that it would "make virtue inevitable." That is, the colonists were to arrange a social situation of such a sort that virtuous acts would be the logical and spontaneous result of conditions.

As for "act, " any verb, no matter how specific or how general, that has connotations of consciousness or purpose falls under this category. If one happened to stumble over an obstruction, that would be not an act, but a mere motion. However, one could convert even this sheer accident into something of an act if, in the course of falling, one suddenly *willed* his fall (as a rebuke, for instance, to the negligence of the person who had left the obstruction in the way). "Dramatistically," the basic unit of action would be defined as "the human body in conscious or purposive motion." Hence we are admonished that people often speak of action in a purely figurative sense when they have only motion in mind, as with reference to the action of a motor, or the interaction of forces. Terms like "adjustment" and "adaptation" are ambiguously suited to cover both action and sheer motion, so that it is usually difficult to decide in just which sense a thinker is using them, when he applies them to social motives. This ambiguity may put them in good favor with those who would deal with the human realm in a calculus patterned after the vocabularies of the physical sciences, and yet would not wholly abandon vestiges of "animism." Profession, vocation, policy, strategy, tactics are all concepts of action, as are any words for specific vocations. Our words "position," "occupation," and "office" indicate the scenic overtones in action. Our words for particular "jobs" under capitalist industrialism refer to acts, but often the element of action is reduced to a minimum and the element of sheer motion raised to a maximum. (We here have in mind not only certain near-automatic tasks performed to the timing of the conveyor belt, but also many of the purely clerical operations, filing, bookkeeping, recording, accounting, and the like, necessary to the present state of technology.)

When Christ said, "I am the way" (*hodos*), we could translate, "I am the act," or more fully, "I represent a system, or synthesis, of the right acts." *Tao* and *yoga* are similar words for act. And we see how readily act in this sense can overlap upon agency when we consider our ordinary attitude towards scientific method (*met-hodos*), which we think of pragmatically, not as a way of life, or *act* of *being*, but as a *means* of *doing*.

The Greek word for justice (*diké*) was in its beginnings as thoroughly an "act" word as *tao, yoga,* and *hodos*. Originally it meant *custom, usage, manner, fashion*. It also meant *right*. The connection between these two orders of meaning is revealed in our expression, "That sort of thing just isn't done," and in the fact that our word "morality" comes from a Latin word for "custom." Liddell and Scott's lexicon notes that in the *Odyssey* the word is used of mortals, gods, kings, and suitors, referring to their *custom, way of acting, law of being*. After the homogeneous tribal pattern of Greek life (with its one "way" or "justice" shared by all) had dissolved into a political state, with its typical conflicts of property interests, *diké* became a word of the law courts. Hence, in post-Homeric usage, it refers to *legal justice,* the *right* which is presumed to be the object of law. In this form, it could represent a Platonic ideal, that might prevail over and above the real ways of the different social classes. This is the kind of justice that Marx was refuting by a sophisticated reversion to a more "Homeric" usage.

Range of All the Ratios

Though we have inspected two ratios, the five terms would allow for ten (scene-act, scene-agent, scene-agency, scene-purpose, act-purpose, act-agent, act-agency, agent-purpose, agent-agency, and agency-purpose). The ratios are principles of determination. Elsewhere in the Grammar we shall examine two of these (scene-purpose and agency-purpose) in other connections; and the rest will figure in passing. But the consideration of words for "ways" calls for special attention to the *act-agent* ratio.

Both act and agent require scenes that "contain" them. Hence the scene-act and scene-agent ratios are in the fullest sense positive (or "positional"). But the relation between act and agent is not quite the same. The agent does not "contain" the act, though its results might be said to "pre-exist virtually" within him. And the act does not "synecdochically share" in the agent, though certain ways of acting may be said to induce corresponding moods or traits of character. To this writer, at least, the act-agent ratio more strongly suggests a temporal or sequential relationship than a purely positional or geometric one. The agent is an author of his acts, which are descended from him, being good progeny if he is good, or bad progeny if he is bad, wise progeny if he is wise, silly progeny if he is silly. And, conversely, his acts can make him or remake him in accordance with their nature. They would be his product and/or he would be theirs. Similarly, when we use the scene-act and scene-agent ratios in reverse (as with the sequence from act or agent to corresponding scene) the image of derivation is stronger than the image of position.

One discerns the workings of the act-agent ratio in the statement of a former cabinet member to the effect that "you can safely lodge responsibility with the President of the United States," owing to "the tremendously sobering influence of the Presidency on any man, especially in foreign affairs." Here, the sheer nature of an office, or position, is said to produce important modifications in a man's character. Even a purely symbolic act, such as the donning of priestly vestments, is often credited with such a result. And I have elsewhere quoted a remark by a political commentator: "There seems to be something about the judicial robes that not only hypnotizes the beholder but transforms the wearer."

Ordinarily, the scene-act and scene-agent ratios can be extended to cover such cases. Thus, the office of the Presidency may be treated as a "situation" affecting the agent who occupies it. And the donning of vestments brings about a symbolic situation that can likewise be treated in terms of the scene-agent ratio. But there are cases where a finer discrimination is needed. For instance, the resistance of the Russian armies to the Nazi invasion could be explained "scenically" in terms of the Soviet political and economic structure; or one could use the act-agent ratio, attributing the power and tenacity to "Russian" traits of character. However, in deriving the act from the scene, one would have to credit socialism as a major scenic factor, whereas a derivation of the act from the agents would allow for a much more felicitous explanation from the standpoint of capitalist apologetics.

Thus, one of our leading newspapers asked itself whether Hitler failed "to evaluate a force older than communism, more instinctive than the mumbling cult of Stalin—the attachment of the peasant masses to 'Mother Russia,' the incoherent but cohesive force of Russian patriotism." And it concluded that "the Russian soldier has proved the depth of his devotion to the Russian soil." Patriotism, attachment to the "mother," devotion to the soil—these are essentially motives located in the agent, hence requiring no acknowledgement of socialist motives.

There is, of course, scenic reference in the offing; but the stress upon the term, agent, encourages one to be content with a very vague treatment of scene, with no mention of the political and economic factors that form a major aspect of national scenes. Indeed, though our concern here is with the Grammar of Motives, we may note a related resource of Rhetoric: one may deflect attention from scenic matters by situating the motives of an act in the agent (as were one to account for wars purely on the basis of a "warlike instinct" in people): or conversely, one may deflect attention from the criticism of personal motives by deriving an act or attitude not from traits of the agent but from the nature of the situation.

The difference between the use of the scene-act and act-agent ratios can also be seen in the motivations of "democracy." Many people in Great Britain and the United States think of these nations as "vessels" of democracy. And democracy is felt to reside in us, intrinsically, because we are "a democratic people." Democratic acts are, in this mode of thought, derived from democratic agents, agents who would remain democratic in character even though conditions required the temporary curtailment or abrogation of basic democratic rights. But if one employed, instead, the scene-act ratio, one might hold that there are certain "democratic situations" and certain "situations favorable to dictatorship, or requiring dictatorship." The technological scene itself, which requires the planning of a world order, might be thought such as to favor a large measure of "dictatorship" in our political ways (at least as contrasted with the past norms of democracy). By the act-agent ratio, a "democratic people" would continue to perform "democratic acts"; and to do so they would even, if necessary, go to the extent of restoring former conditions most favorable to democracy. By the scene-act ratio, if the "situation" itself is no longer a "democratic" one, even an "essentially democratic" people will abandon democratic ways.

A picturesque effect can be got in imaginative writings by the conflicting use of the scene-act and act-agent ratios. One may place "fools" in "wise situations," so that in their acts they are "wiser than they know." Children are often "wise" in this sense. It is a principle of incongruity that Chaplin has built upon. Empson would call it an aspect of "pastoral."

Here is an interesting shift of ratios in a citation from an address by Francis Biddle when he was Attorney General:

> The change of the world in terms of time and space in the past hundred years—railroad, telegraph, telephone, automobile, movie, airplane, radio—has hardly found an echo in our political growth, except in the necessary patches and arrangements which have made it so extraordinarily complex without making it more responsive to our needs.

Note first that all the changes listed here refer to *agencies* of communication (the pragmatist emphasis). Then, having in their accumulation become scenic, they are said to have had a motivating effect upon our political acts ("growth"). But though the complexity of the scene has called forth "the necessary patches and arrangements" (another expression for "acts"), we are told that there are still unsatisfied "needs." Now, "needs" are a property of agents; hence an act designed to produce a situation "more responsive to our needs" would have its most direct locus of motivation under the heading of agent, particularly if these were said to be "primal needs" rather than "new needs," since "new needs" might best be treated as "a function of the situation." I borrow the expression from a prominent educator, Eduard C. Lindeman, who shortly after the Japanese attack at Pearl Harbor complained of a tendency "to believe that morale will now become a function of the situation and that hence it is less important to plan for education."

The ratios may often be interpreted as principles of selectivity rather than as thoroughly causal relationships. That is, in any given historical situation, there are persons of many sorts, with a corresponding variety in the kinds of acts that would be most representative of them. Thus, a given political situation may be said not to change people in their essential character, but rather to favor, or bring to the fore (to "vote for"), certain kinds of agents (with their appropriate actions) rather than others. Quick shifts in political exigencies do not of a sudden make all men "fundamentally" daring, or all men "fundamentally" cautious, in keeping with the nature of the scene; but rather, one situation calls for cautious men as its appropriate "voice," another for daring men, one for traditionalists, another for innovators. And the inappropriate acts and temperaments simply do not "count for" so much as they would in situations for which they are a better fit. One set of scenic conditions will "implement" and "amplify" given ways and temperaments which, in other situations would remain mere potentialities, unplanted seeds, "mute inglorious Miltons." Indeed, there are times when out-and-out materialistic philosophies, which are usually thought of as "tough," can be of great solace to us precisely because they encourage us to believe in the ratios as a selective principle. For we may tell ourselves that the very nature of the materials with which men deal will not permit men to fall below a certain level of sloth, error, greed, and dishonesty in their relations with one another, as the coöperative necessities of the situation implement and amplify only those traits of character and action that serve the ends of progress.

There is, of course, a circular possibility in the terms. If an agent acts in keeping with his nature as an agent (act-agent ratio), he may change the nature of the scene accordingly (scene-act ratio), and thereby establish a state of unity between himself and his world (scene-agent ratio). Or the scene may call for a certain kind of act, which makes for a corresponding kind of agent, thereby likening agent to scene. Or our act may change us and our scene, producing a mutual conformity. Such would be the Edenic paradigm, applicable if we were capable of total acts that produce total transformations. In reality, we are capable of but partial acts, acts that but partially represent us and that produce but partial transformations. Indeed, if all the ratios were adjusted to one another with perfect Edenic symmetry, they would be immutable in one unending "moment."

Theological notions of creation and re-creation bring us nearest to the concept of total acts. Among the controversies that centered around Lutheranism, for instance, there was a doctrine, put forward by the theologian Striegel, who held that Christ's work on the Cross had the effect of changing God's attitude towards mankind, and that men born after the historical Christ can take advantage of this change.

Here we have something like the conversion of God himself, brought about by Christ's sacrifice (a total action, a total passion). From the godlike nature came a godlike act that acted upon God himself. And as regards mankind, it amounts to a radical change in the very structure of the Universe, since it changed God's attitude towards men, and in God's attitude towards men resides the ultimate ground of human action.

A similar pattern is implicated in the close of Aeschylus's trilogy, the *Oresteia,* where the sufferings of Orestes terminate in the changed identity of the Furies, signalized by their change of name from Erinyes to Eumenides. Under the influence of the "new gods," their nature as motives takes on a totally different accent; for whereas it was their previous concern to avenge evil, it will henceforth be their concern to reward the good. An *inner* goad has thus been cast forth, externalized; whereby, as Athena says, men may be at peace within, their "dread passion for renown" thereafter being motivated solely by "war from without."

Only the scene-act and scene-agent ratios fit with complete comfort in this chapter on the relation between container and contained. The act-agent ratio tugs at its edges; and we shall close noting concerns that move us still farther afield. In the last example, we referred to God's *attitude.* Where would attitude fall within our pattern? Often it is the *preparation* for an act, which would make it a kind of symbolic act, or incipient act. But in its character as a state of *mind* that may or may not lead to an act, it is quite clearly to be classed under the head of *agent.* We also spoke of Christ's sacrifice as "a total action, a total passion." This suggests other "grammatical" possibilities that involve a dialectic pairing of "active" and "passive." And in the reference to a *state* of mind, we casually invite a dialectic pairing of "actus" and "status."

This group of concerns will be examined in due course. Meanwhile, we should be reminded that the term *agent* embraces not only all words general or specific for person, actor, character, individual, hero, villain, father, doctor, engineer, but also any words, moral or functional, for *patient,* and words for the motivational properties or agents, such as "drives," "instincts," "states of mind." We may also have collective words for agent, such as nation, group, the Freudian "super-ego," Rousseau's *"volonté générale,"* the Fichtean "generalized I."

II

ANTINOMIES OF DEFINITION

Paradox of Substance

THERE is a set of words comprising what we might call the Stance family, for they all derive from a concept of place, or placement. In the Indo-Germanic languages the root for this family is *stā*, to stand (Sanscrit, *sthā*). And out of it there has developed this essential family, comprising such members as: consist, constancy, constitution, contrast, destiny, ecstasy, existence, hypostatize, obstacle, stage, state, status, statute, stead, subsist, and system. In German, an important member of the Stance family is *stellen*, to place, a root that figures in *Vorstellung*, a philosopher's and psychologist's word for representation, conception, idea, image.

Surely, one could build a whole philosophic universe by tracking down the ramifications of this one root. It would be "implemented" too, for it would have stables, staffs, staves, stalls, stamens, stamina, stanchions, stanzas, steeds, stools, and studs. It would be a quite regional world, in which our Southern Agrarians might take their stand.

Unquestionably, the most prominent philosophic member of this family is "substance." Or at least it used to be, before John Locke greatly impaired its prestige, so that many thinkers today explicitly banish the term from their vocabularies. But there is cause to believe that, in banishing the *term*, far from banishing its *functions* one merely conceals them. Hence, from the dramatistic point of view, we are admonished to dwell upon the word, considering its embarrassments and its potentialities of transformation, so that we may detect its covert influence even in cases where it is overtly absent. Its relation to our five terms will become apparent as we proceed.

First we should note that there is, etymologically, a pun lurking behind the Latin roots. The word is often used to designate what some thing or agent intrinsically *is*, as *per* these meanings in Webster's: "the most important element in any existence; the characteristic and essential

components of anything; the main part; essential import; purport."
Yet etymologically "substance" is a scenic word. Literally, a person's
or a thing's sub-stance would be something that stands beneath or supports the person or thing.

Let us cite a relevant passage in *An Essay Concerning Human Understanding* (Chapter XXIII, "Of Our Complex Ideas of Substances"):

1. *Ideas of particular substances, how made.* The mind being,
as I have declared, furnished with a great number of the simple ideas
conveyed in by the senses, as they are found in exterior things, or by
reflection on its own operations, takes notice, also, that a certain
number of these simple ideas go constantly together; which being
presumed to belong to one thing, and words being suited to common
apprehensions, and made use of for quick despatch, are called, so
united in one subject, by one name; which, by inadvertency, we are
apt afterward to talk of and consider as one simple idea, which indeed is a complication of many ideas together; because, as I have
said, not imagining how these simple ideas can subsist by themselves,
we accustom ourselves to suppose some *substratum* wherein they do
subsist, and from which they do result; which therefore we call
substance.

2. *Our obscure idea of substance in general.*—So that if anyone
will examine himself concerning his notion of pure substance in
general, he will find he has no other idea of it at all, but only a supposition of he knows not what support of such qualities which are
capable of producing simple ideas in us; which qualities are commonly called accidents. If anyone should be asked, what is the
subject wherein color or weight inheres, he would have nothing to
say but, the solid extended parts. And if he were demanded, what is
it that solidity and extension inhere in, he would not be in a much
better case than the Indian before mentioned, who, saying that the
world was supported by a great elephant, was asked, what the elephant rested on; to which his answer was, a great tortoise; but being
again pressed to know what gave support to the broad-backed tortoise, replied—something, he knew not what. And thus here, as in
all other cases where we use words without having clear and distinct
ideas, we talk like children: who, being questioned what such a
thing is which they know not, readily give this satisfactory answer,
that it is *something;* which in truth signifies no more, when so used,
either by children or men, but that they know not what; and that the
thing they pretend to know and talk of, is what they have no distinct
idea of at all, and so are perfectly ignorant of it, and in the dark.

The idea, then, we have, to which we give the *general* name substance, being nothing but the supposed, but unknown support of those qualities we find existing, which we imagine cannot subsist *sine re substante,* "without something to support them," we call that support *substantia;* which according to the true import of the word, is, in plain English, standing under, or upholding.

The same structure is present in the corresponding Greek word, *hypostasis,* literally, a standing under: hence anything set under, such as stand, base, bottom, prop, support, stay; hence metaphorically, that which lies at the bottom of a thing, as the groundwork, subject-matter, argument of a narrative, speech, poem; a starting point, a beginning. And then come the metaphysical meanings (we are consulting Liddell and Scott): subsistence, reality, real being (as applied to mere appearance), nature, essence. In ecclesiastical Greek, the word corresponds to the Latin *Persona,* a Person of the Trinity (which leads us back into the old argument between the homoousians and the homoiousians, as to whether the three persons were of the same or similar substance). Medically, the word can designate a suppression, as of humours that ought to come to the surface; also matter deposited in the urine; and of liquids generally, the sediment, lees, dregs, grounds. When we are examining, from the standpoint of Symbolic, metaphysical tracts that would deal with "fundamentals" and get to the "bottom" of things, this last set of meanings can admonish us to be on the look-out for what Freud might call "cloacal" motives, furtively interwoven with speculations that may on the surface seem wholly abstract. An "acceptance" of the universe on this plane may also be a roundabout way of "making peace with the faeces."

But returning to the pun as it figures in the citation from Locke, we might point up the pattern as sharply as possible by observing that the word "substance," used to designate what a thing *is,* derives from a word designating something that a thing *is not.* That is, though used to designate something *within* the thing, *intrinsic* to it, the word etymologically refers to something *outside* the thing, *extrinsic* to it. Or otherwise put: the word in its etymological origins would refer to an attribute of the thing's *context,* since that which supports or underlies a thing would be a part of the thing's context. And a thing's context, being outside or beyond the thing, would be something that the thing is *not.*

Contextual Definition

Here obviously is a strategic moment, an alchemic moment, wherein momentous miracles of transformation can take place. For here the intrinsic and the extrinsic can change places. To tell what a thing is, you place it in terms of something else. This idea of locating, or placing, is implicit in our very word for definition itself: to *define,* or *determine* a thing, is to mark its boundaries, hence to use terms that possess, implicitly at least, contextual reference. We here take the pun seriously because we believe it to reveal an *inevitable* paradox of definition, an antinomy that must endow the concept of substance with unresolvable ambiguity, and that will be discovered lurking beneath any vocabulary designed to treat of motivation by the deliberate outlawing of the *word* for substance.

Nor is the perplexity confined to abstruse metaphysical theorizing. Note the Tory usage, for instance, in the expression, "a man of substance," or a man of "standing." Note how readily we shunt here between an intrinsic and an extrinsic reference. For those who admire someone as a man of substance, or standing, have in mind not only his personal traits of character, but also the resources that spring from his environmental connections, the external powers that his position, income, status put at his command, the outside factors that, in backing or supporting him, enable him to make his personal characteristics count. (Another meaning for the Greek *hypostasis,* incidentally, was steadfastness, endurance, firmness.) And when our Southern Agrarians issue a volume entitled *I'll Take My Stand* (their "stand in Dixie"), their claims as to what they *are* get definition in terms of scene, environment, situation, context, ground. Indeed, in the title we can also see another important ambiguity of motive emerging. When taking their stand *in* Dixie, they are also taking their stand *for* Dixie. Their stand *in* Dixie would be a "conditioning" kind of cause; but a corresponding stand *for* Dixie would be a teleological or purposive kind of cause.

In Spinoza we confront the full intensity of the contextual paradox. Indeed, from our point of view, we might translate both his concept of "God" and his concept of "nature" as "the total, or ultimate scene," since he pantheistically held that God and nature are identical. In the Judaic and Christian theologies, since nature was said to have its ultimate ground in God as a person, God was a context for nature, as nature-and-God was the context for man. But Spinoza, in equating God and nature, gave us a concept of nature that could have no scene beyond it. For nature was *everything*—and beyond *everything*, considered as a totality, there could be nothing to serve as its context.

Hence, starting from the Aristotelian notion that a substance, or being, is to be considered "in itself" (*kath auto,* which Spinoza rendered *id quod per se concipitur*), Spinoza went on to observe that nothing less than the *totality of all that exists* can meet this requirement. In Aristotle, each stone, or tree, or man, or animal, could be a substance, capable of being considered "in itself." But Spinoza held that no single thing could be considered "by itself." A distinction between "in itself" and "by itself" might be made here, but the Spinozistic calculus is designed rather to work in the area where the two meanings overlap. Thinking contextually, Spinoza held that each single object in the universe is "defined" (determined, limited, bounded) by the other things that surround it. And in calling upon men to see things "in terms of eternity" (*sub specie aeternitatis*) Spinoza meant precisely that we should consider each thing in terms of its total context, the universal scene as a whole. Only when considering the universe as a whole, and its parts in terms of the whole, would we be making an "intrinsic" statement about substance, since there was but one substance, the universal totality.

And thoroughly in keeping with his contextual strategy of definition, Spinoza explicitly held that all definition is "negation," which is another way of saying that, to define a thing in terms of its context, we must define it in terms of what it is not. And with scholastic succinctness, he formulated the paradox of contextual definition in four words: "all determination is negation; *omnis determinatio est negatio.*" Since determined things are "positive," we might point up the paradox as harshly as possible by translating it, "Every positive is negative."

When we refer to "everything," our reference is indefinite, infinite, undetermined, indeterminate. Hence, to treat of things in terms of "everything" is to treat of them in terms of the infinite. Indeed, since "everything" is the "absolute" (that is, unloosed, absolved, "freed," for I think it is good to remind ourselves of the dramatic meanings lurking behind that strategic metaphysical term) we have here a variant of the so-called "negative theology," which conceived of God as the absence of all qualities; and to see things as contextually "determined" by the "absolute" is thus to see them simultaneously in terms of "necessity" and "freedom." For Spinoza, says Windelband, "the deity is all and thus—nothing." But we should also remember that the deity is equated with nature. Hence, though Spinoza's pantheism was an important step towards naturalism, in itself it had strongly mystical ingredients.

Contextual definition might also be called "positional," or "geometric," or "definition by location." The embarrassments are often revealed with particular clarity when a thinker has moved to a high level of generalization, as when motivational matters are discussed in terms of "heredity and environment," or "man and nature," or "mind and matter," or "mechanism and teleology," where each of the paired terms is the other's "context" in the universe of discourse. To define or locate "man" in terms of "nature," for instance, is to "dissolve" man "into" nature. Hence, the more thorough one is in carrying out his enterprise, the more surely he opens himself to the charge of failing to discuss man "in himself." Historicists who deal with art in terms of its background are continually suffering from the paradox of contextual definition, as their opponents accuse them of slighting the work of art in its esthetic aspects; and on the other hand, critics who would center their attention upon the work "in itself" must wince when it is made apparent that their inquiries, in ignoring contextual reference, frustrate our desire to see the products of artistic action treated in terms of the scene-act, scene-agent, and agent-act ratios.

Familial Definition

However, there is another strategy of definition, usually interwoven with the contextual sort, yet susceptible of separate observation. This is the "tribal" or "familial" sort, the definition of a substance in terms of ancestral cause. Under the head of "tribal" definition would fall any variant of the idea of biological descent, with the substance of the offspring being derived from the substance of the parents or family.

The Christian notion that the most important fact about mankind and the world is their derivation from God is an instance of "ancestral" definition on the grand scale. We find bastardized variants in political doctrines of race supremacy, such as the Nazi "blood" philosophy. The Latin word *natura,* like its Greek equivalent *physis,* has a root signifying to become, to grow, to be born. And the Aristotelian *genus* is originally not a logical, but a biological, concept. We can discern the tribal pattern behind the notion, so characteristic of Greek nationalism, that like causes like or that like recognizes like, as with Democritus' theory of perception. Similarly, there was an *ancestral* notion behind the Platonic theory of forms; in fact, it was this tribal ingredient that recommended it so strongly to the ages of Western feudalism. Each thing in this world had, as it were, an eponym in heaven, a perfect form from which it was derived—and it shared this derivation with all the other members of its class, or genus. And I think we might most quickly understand the mediaeval speculations as to whether universals were "before the thing, in the thing, or after the thing" if we first tried a dramatist translation of the three formulae respectively thus: "Does the tribe give birth to its members (universal *ante rem*), or does the tribe exist in its members (universal *in re*), or is the tribe merely a name for the sum of its members (universal *post rem*)?"

To say yes to the first would make you an extreme mediaeval realist. A realism of this sort was well attuned to feudal collectivism. To say yes to the third would make you a thorough-going nominalist, who treated general terms as mere *flatus vocis,* conventions of speech, and thus moved towards the disintegration of tribal thinking. To say yes to the second would make you an Aristotelian. The motives would be situated in the individual, yet they would be motives common to the species, or tribe, of which it was a member. That is, an individual stone would have motives proper to stones as a class, an individual man motives proper to men as a class, etc. This doctrine came to a head in the Aristotelian concept of the "entelechy," which we might call the individual's potentialities for becoming a fully representative member of its class. However, we need not here give more than a cursory glance at any particular use of the ancestral method. It is sufficient if we can indicate its range.

All told, perhaps the quickest and surest way to find oneself at the centre of the subject would be to ponder the four words, "general," "generic," "genetic," "genitive." Though they are all from the same root, only the third *unambiguously* reveals ancestral connotations. Next removed is "genitive," which refers to either source or possession. But to say that nature is "a part of" God or that man is "a part of" nature would be to use a genitive construction in which one could clearly discern ancestral reference. When we come to "generic," the tribal connotations are beginning more noticeably to fade, as purely biological concepts can be replaced by logical notions of classification. And with "general" this extinction of the familial can be complete. A "family of right-angled triangles in general," for instance, would just about have lost the notion of generation, although we can still, with a little effort, look upon them as a family in the sense that a common set of principles is required for the generating of them.

Similarly, the members of a class derive their *generic* nature from the "idea" of the class in which they are placed. If I make up a classification, for instance, such as "bald-headed carpenters under forty," I shall have "generated" a corresponding class of "objects." These objects (the people who fit the requirements of the class) will be "imperfect copies" of my "idea" or "pure form," since they will all possess other attributes that lie outside the strict definition of the class. This would be the strictly methodological equivalent for Plato's doctrine of archetypes. Thinking in familial terms, Plato looked upon the objects of this world as imperfect replicas of their pure "forms" or "ideas" in heaven.

In sum, contextual definition stresses *placement,* ancestral definition stresses derivation. But in any sustained discussion of motives, the two become interwoven, as with theologies which treat God both as "causal ancestor" of mankind and as the ultimate ground or context of mankind.

And if we were to extend the Stance family by including different roots similar in meaning, we would promptly move into a set of live and dead metaphors ("abstractions") where our five terms, our ratios, and our strategies of definition could be seen emerging in all sorts of places.

For instance, the key philosophic term, sub-ject (in Latin, thrown under) is the companion to the Greek *hypokeimenon* (underlying), a word that can refer to the subject of a sentence, or to the "sub-strate" of the world (the essential constitution of things, hence indeterminately a kind of basis or a kind of causal ancestor). The word can also refer to what is assumed as a ground of argument, in which capacity it serves as a passive for *hypotithemi* (to place or put under, as a base or foundation, to assume as a principle, take for granted, suppose, from the root of which we get such words as theme, thesis, antithesis, synthesis, while a similar development in Latin, from *pono,* to place, gives us position, proposition, opposition, composition, positive, and that neat now-you-see-me-and-now-you-don't metaphysical nuance, "posit," whereby the metaphysician is enabled to discuss the "positing" of principles without being too clear as to what kind of base they are being *placed* upon).

The mention of "substrates" brings us close to a third aspect of definition, the kind we get in projects that discuss the world in terms of the "building blocks" of which it is thought to be composed, as were one to define a kind of house in terms of the materials and operations needed for its construction, or to define an action by reducing it to terms of its necessary motions. But from the dramatistic point of view, we can best observe this strategy later, when we consider the subject of "circumference" (in the sense that the location, or definition, of an act with reference to "the Mississippi valley" as its motivating scene could be said to involve a narrower circumference than its definition in terms of "the United States"). And we shall here pause to survey characteristic forms which the grammar of substance may embody in particular calculi:

Survey of Terms for Substance

Geometric substance. An object placed in its setting, existing both in itself and as part of its background. Participation in a context. Embodied most completely in Spinoza's cult of "Euclidean" relations, logically ("necessarily") derivable from one another. These relations exist all at once, implicitly, though they may manifest themselves, or be made manifest, in various *sequences*. (As soon as certain antecedent steps are taken in the demonstration, certain consequent steps are "inevitable.") The plastic connotations can lead readily into strictly materialistic notions of determinism, as with the novelist, Theodore Dreiser, who professes to view all ultimate motives in terms of "chemism."

Familial substance. In its purity, this concept stresses common ancestry in the strictly biological sense, as literal descent from maternal or paternal sources. But the concept of family is usually "spiritualized," so that it includes merely social groups, comprising persons of the same nationality or beliefs. Most often, in such cases, there is the notion of some founder shared in common, or some covenant or constitution or historical act from which the consubstantiality of the group is derived. Doctrines of creation extend the concept of familial descent to cover the relationship between the craftsman and his product ("the potter and the pot," as with the agent-act ratio).

This in turn moves us closer to purely logical derivations, of actualities from potentialities, of the explicit from the implicit, of conclusions from principles (that is, "firsts"). Plotinus' characterization of God as *to proton* would be a case in point, or Bonaventura's notion of the world's development from *rationes seminales,* an expression clearly combining the ideas of logical and biological descent. The stress upon the informative nature of beginnings can in turn lead us to treat christenings, inaugurations, and the like as aspects of familial substance. There is the girl of high spirits, for instance, who says of herself that she was born during a hurricane, as though the quality of her temper in later life were derived from the quality of the scene prevailing at her birth.

Biologists, in their concern with vital reproduction, necessarily give prominence to concepts of familial substance, in terms for genus and species, cellular structure, and the like. Often they study the responses of organisms at various levels of development, in the expectation that laws of behavior discovered at one level will apply to levels far higher in the scale of complexity. They expect differences, of course, but they also expect the processes at both the higher and lower levels to be "substantially" the same. Thus in an article of biological vulgarization published in one of the "cultural" magazines, a writer observed that, though we may lose confidence in the brotherhood of man, we can still be sure of our consubstantiality in a more inclusive concept of family: "protoplasm" (incidentally, another "first").

Since the taking of nourishment involves a *transubstantiation* of external elements into elements within, we might treat nutritive substance as a combination of the contextual and familial sufficiently notable to deserve a separate designation. Just as the organism dies when deprived of all food, so it will die in part when certain strategic ingredients are absent from its food. Thus, though one might not want to contend that a sufficiency of iodine will make men wise, we can say that a deficiency of iodine will greatly prod them to be stupid. And manganese has been called the chemical of "mother love" because, without manganese, hens won't set. (Similarly, the pituitary has been called the "mother love" gland, since a deficiency of the pituitary hormone in the female is accompanied by "lack of devotion to its offspring.") Modern chemistry prompts us to stress the scenic aspect of the nutritional motive, as the chemist would seek to reduce the efficient principle in both manganese and the pituitary hormone to a common basis. Even a stock to which a scion has been grafted may be considered, from this point of view, as a part of the scion's environment, hence an environmental control upon food supply. For any motivational special factor which is theoretically assigned to the organism (in the sense that a horse and a tiger, a dandelion and a daisy, exemplify in their behavior and development different loci of motion), can be theoretically dissolved into the environmental. If you put a hungry horse and a hungry tiger in a cage together, for instance, you would thereby get not one environment but two, since the tiger would be so drastically momentous an aspect of the horse's environment, and the horse would be a nutrient aspect of the tiger's environment. And any change of nutritive elements such as accompanies glandular transplantations or the injection of hormones is analyzable as a "new physical situation." Dr. Andras Angyal observes in his *Foundations for a Science of Personality*, "A *morphological* distinction between organism and environment is impossible." He also reminds us, "The blood has been called 'internal environment' by Claude Bernard." Accordingly, he employs the concept of a "biosphere" in which "subject (organism)" and "object (environment)" are merged as a single process.

The title of Robert M. Coates's fantasy, *Eater of Darkness,* could be translated: "The agent whose substance is one with the substance of darkness" (though we should next have to make an inquiry into the author's use of "darkness" to discover the special attributes of the term in his particular thesaurus). Totemic rites and the sacrament of the Eucharist are instances where the nutritive emphasis becomes submerged in the notion of familial consubstantiality. "Tell me what you eat, and I'll tell you what you are."

Directional substance. Doubtless biologically derived from the experience of free motion, since man is an organism that lives by locomotion. Frequently, with metaphors of "the way," the directional stresses the sense of motivation from within. Often strongly futuristic, purposive, its slogan might be: Not "Who are you?" or "Where are you from?" but "Where are you going?" Thought in terms of directional substance gained many fresh motives since the Renaissance, and the greater mobility that went with the development from status to contract, alienation of property, the growth of the monetary rationale, and revolutionary innovations in the means of transportation and communication. The directional is also susceptible of conversion from "free" motion into the "determined." Thus, one may "freely" answer a call, yet the call may be so imperious that one could not ignore it without disaster. And statistical treatment of supposedly "free" choices may disclose a uniform response prevailing among the lot.

The directional has encouraged much sociological speculation in terms of "tendencies" or "trends." With such terms, the substantial paradox is not far in the offing. If a man did *not* make a certain decision, for instance, we might nonetheless choose to say that he had a "tendency towards" the decision. Indeed, any tendency *to* do something is, by the same token, a tendency *not* to do it.

The directional is embedded in the very word, "motivation." And we may note four related nuances, or perhaps puns, with corresponding philosophies. Doctrines that reduce mental states to materialistic terms treat *motion* as motive. When an individual's acts are referred to some larger curve, we get *movement* as motive. For instance, individual immigrants came to America as part of a general movement westward. "Movement" in such cases can be either purposive or necessitarian, since one's place in a "movement" is like one's enlistment in a "cause" (and Latin *causa* is defined as: *that by, on account of,* or *through which anything takes place* or *is done; a cause, reason, motive, inducement*). Terminologies that situate the driving force of human action in human passion treat *emotion* as motive. (In his *Principles of Literary Criticism,* I. A. Richards offers a good pun for reducing *emotion* in turn to *motion,* when he proposes that we speak not of the *emotions* aroused in us by art but of the *commotions.*) And one can mystically select the *moment* as motive. Such "moments" are directional in that, being led up to and away from, they summarize the foregoing and seminally contain the subsequent. But in themselves they "just are," being an "eternal present" that has wound up the past and has the future wound up.

All metaphors or generalizations, such as *homo homini lupus,* or "life a pilgrimage," or "the economic man," that treat one order of motivation in terms of a higher order or lower order, are examples of substantiation; and they reveal the paradox of substance in that the given subject both is and is not the same as the character with which and by which it is identified. Such statements about motivating essence, often made in passing and sometimes serving as the midrib of a work, are the stock in trade of imaginative literature. As such, they can be most fully studied under the heading of Symbolic. And much that we have written in *Permanence and Change, Attitudes Toward History,* and *The Philosophy of Literary Form* could be read as an elaboration of this paragraph. The name of any well-developed character in a fiction is the term for a peculiar complexity of motives.

Dialectic Substance

From the standpoint of our present study, all the foregoing types could be considered as special cases of a more inclusive category: dialectic substance. Dialectically considered (that is, "dramatistically" considered) men are not only *in nature.* The cultural accretions made possible by the language motive become a "second nature" with them. Here again we confront the ambiguities of substance, since symbolic communication is not a merely external instrument, but also intrinsic to men as agents. Its motivational properties characterize both "the human situation" and what men are "in themselves."

Whereas there is an implicit irony in the other notions of substance, with the dialectic substance the irony is explicit. For it derives its character from the systematic contemplation of the antinomies attendant upon the fact that we necessarily define a thing in terms of something else. "Dialectic substance" would thus be the over-all category of dramatism, which treats of human motives in the terms of verbal action. By this statement we most decidedly do not mean that human motives are confined to the realm of verbal action. We mean rather that the dramatistic analysis of motives has its *point of departure* in the subject of verbal action (in thought, speech, and document).

A poem, by shifting the imagery of its metaphors, permits us to contemplate the subject from the standpoint of various objects. This effect is dialectical in the sense that we see something in terms of some other. In a more restricted sense, however, the dialectical considers things in terms not of *some* other, but of *the* other. The sharpest instance of this is an *agon* wherein the protagonist is motivated by the nature of the antagonist, as with the situating of socialist motives in resistance to capitalism, or the unifying effect of the Allied Nations' joint opposition to Hitler. There is a grim pleasantry that runs, "Of course we're

Christians—but what are we being Christians *against?*" In earlier days, when the devil enjoyed great personal prominence, he could perform this noteworthy role of agonistic unification which, in our era of humanistic progress, we generally assign exclusively to human vessels.

The ambiguity of external and internal motivation has recently plagued some enemies of Fascism who saw that an effective war against the Fascist nations would require many "Fascist" measures on the part of the Anti-Fascists. As the Irish poet, George Russell, once stated the form of their predicament: "We become the image of the thing we hate." And the great dialectician, Coleridge, has observed that *rivales* are the opposite banks of the *same* stream. And it was dialectically, or dramatically, necessary that the *devil* should be an *angel;* for were he of any less noble substance, the Christian *agonia* would to that degree have fallen short of thoroughness in imagining a common ground on which the two great conflicting motives, good and evil, can join battle.

The most thoroughgoing dialectical opposition, however, centers in that key pair: Being and Not-Being. For the contextual approach to substance, by inducing men to postulate a ground or context in which everything that is, is placed, led thinkers "by dialectical necessity" to affirm that the only ground of "Being" is "Not-Being" (for "Being" is so comprehensive a category that its dialectical opposite, "Not-Being," is the only term that would be left to designate its ground). The Neo-Platonist, Plotinus, carried such thinking to its ultimate limits, in the direction of that "negative theology" whereby the divine substance, as the ground of all that we experience in the material world, could be designated only by the absence of any attributes such as we in our material existence can conceive of. He would evolve a dialectical process that, beginning with material things, in the end had completely transcended its beginnings, thus arriving at a totally immaterial vision of God as an abstract Oneness. Accordingly, in his belief that material existence is estrangement from God, he is said to have been unwilling to name either his parents or his birthplace (the abstract concept of dialectical substance here leading him to proclaim his identity by a *negative* reference to the familial and the geometric).

The process of transcendence may, of course, be reversed. Then the ultimate abstract Oneness is taken as a source, a "first"; and the steps leading up to it are interpreted as stages emanating from it. Or terms that are contextual to each other (such as Being and Not-Being, Action and Rest, Mechanism and Purpose, the One and the Many) can be treated as familially related (as were Being to be derived from Not-Being, Action from Rest, Mechanism from Purpose, the Many from the One). Or, in general, actualities may be derived from potentialities that are in a different realm than the actualities. The most obvious instance of such a derivation would be a naturalistic assertion that the "conscious" is derived from a "pre-Conscious," or that the state of life is derived from a condition of "pre-life." However, many less apparent variants are possible. The human person, for instance, may be derived from God as a "super-person." Or human purpose may be derived from an All Purpose, or Cosmic Purpose, or Universal Purpose, or Absolute Purpose, or Pure Purpose, or Inner Purpose, etc. And instead of a "pre-conscious" as the source or latent form of consciousness, we may have a subconscious or unconscious or "collective unconscious," etc.

The Paradox of Purity

Such pairs are in contrasted orders, with one a transcendence of the other, the one latent or covert, the other patent or overt. And the ambiguities of substance here take a form that we would call the "paradox of purity," or "paradox of the absolute." We confront this paradox when deriving the nature of the human person from God as "super-person," as "pure," or "absolute" person, since God as a super-person would be impersonal—and the impersonal would be synonymous with the *negation* of personality. Hence, Pure Personality would be the same as No Personality: and the derivation of the personal principle from God as pure person would amount to its derivation from an impersonal principle. Similarly, a point that Hegel made much of, Pure Being would be the same as Not-Being; and in Aristotle, God can be defined either as "Pure Act" or as complete repose, a rest that is "eternal, unchangeable, immovable." And Leibniz was able to propose something pretty much like unconscious ideas in his doctrine of the "virtual innateness of ideas." (We might point up the oxymoron here by translating "unconscious ideas" as "unaware awarenesses.")

The painter Kandinsky illustrates our subject when, on the subject of Schönberg's esthetic, he says that, to the uninitiate, the "inner beauty" of music must seem like ugliness. And when discussing Julien Gracq's *Chateau d'Argol,* Parker Tyler comes upon the paradox of the absolute thus:

> In the eighth chapter of the book, Albert and Heide, the woman, follow a road which is said to "symbolize *pure direction.* But looking back, they realize that behind them the avenue seems to peter out and to be blocked by thicket and underbrush. It is a blind alley . . ." Like passage through water, passage through this Hegelian reality is pure direction, meaning that, wherever you turn in it, the way must be created, because behind you, the way has *ceased to be*.

The citation is from the surrealist magazine, *View*, in another copy of which Harold Rosenberg, writing on "the art of escape," says that "in democratic society, this art tends, like all the other arts, to become *Pure.*" And if the fugitive "can combine within himself perfectly all the elements of the art, he will be able to free himself perpetually." The thought suggests the element of "pure escape" that lies at the roots of liberalism. And it suggests the paradox of "pure escape." For in freeing oneself *perpetually*, one would in a sense remain perpetually a prisoner, since one would never have definitively escaped.

With regard to Symbolic, one may expect to encounter the paradox of purity whenever he finds what we have called elsewhere the "withinness of withinness," or the "atop the atop," as when Melville writes in *Moby Dick*: "It was a negro church; and the preacher's text was about the blackness of darkness," or as with the pattern in "The Garden," by Andrew Marvell, when the poet speaks of the mind as

> . . . that ocean where each kind
> Does streight its own resemblance find;
>
> .   .   .
>
> Annihilating all that's made
> To a green thought in a green shade.

And in another issue of *View*, when Parker Tyler is reviewing a manual of judo as though this kind of combat were simply a kind of dance, a "pure" art done for love of the figures involved, not for the utilitarian purpose of victory over an adversary, he states his position in a similar "atop the atop" kind of image. For he sums up his thesis in an image by observing that the high-speed camera has shown us how "a drop of milk falling into a mass of milk creates at the moment a perfectly symmetrical crown, with several points suspended in the air like jewels." His article concludes:

> In the largest sense, Mars is an enemy of Apollo. It is only on the esthetic grounds of fantasy that they may meet and fraternize with each other. So, beyond our capacity to discipline our thoughts in relation to "realities," the instinct of free movement typified by Isadora's dance asserts itself, and we may imagine as eternal, if we like, a drop of American blood being poured into its own mass, and erecting over that precious surface a fragile crown of rubies.

In theological and metaphysical works, we can recognize the paradox of the absolute readily enough. Often, in fact, it is explicitly discussed. But in historicist writings it more easily goes unnoticed. Yet the paradox may be implicit in any term for a *collective* motivation, such as a concept of class, nation, the "general will," and the like. Technically, it becomes a "pure" motive when matched against some individual locus of motivation. And it may thus be the *negation* of an individual motive. Yet despite this position as dialectical antithesis of the individual motive, the collective motive may be treated as the source or principle from which the individual motive is familially or "substantially" derived in a "like begets like" manner. That is, to derive the individual motive from the collective motive would be like deriving the personal principle familially from the super-personal principle, whereas contextually the "super-personal" principle would be the *other* of the personal.

What we are here considering formally, as a paradox of substance, can be illustrated quickly enough by example. A soldier may be *nationally* motivated to kill the enemies of his country, whereas *individually* he is motivated by a horror of killing his own enemies. Or conversely, as a patriot he may act by the motive of sacrifice in behalf of his country, but as an individual he may want to profit. Or a man's business code may differ so greatly from his private code that we can even think of him as a "split personality" (that is, a man of "two substances," or "divided substance"). Or one will find a resistance to people in particular "balanced by" a humanitarian sympathy for mankind in general.

Such histories can be imagined in an endless variety of details. What we are suggesting here is that they all embody a *grammatical form* in accordance with which we should not expect a dualism of motives to be automatically dissolved, as with those apologists of science who believe that in a scientific world ethics become unnecessary. However, to consider these possibilities further, we should move into the areas of Symbolic, involving modes of transubstantiation, rituals of rebirth, whereby the individual identifies himself in terms of the collective motive (an identification by which he both is and is not one with that with which and by which he is identified). At present it is enough to note in a general way how the paradox of the absolute figures grammatically in the dialectic, making for a transcending of one term by its other, and for the reversed ambiguous derivation of the term from its other as ancestral principle.

Dialectic of Tragedy

When things are treated in terms of other things, men may even be said to speak for the dumb objects of nature. Nor are the pronouncements assigned on a purely arbitrary basis. The use of scales, meters, controlled laboratory conditions, and the like, can set up situations in which speechless things can hand down accurate judgments. Men can so arrange it that nature gives clear, though impartial and impersonal, answers to their questions. The dialectical motives behind such methods usually escape our detection, though we get a glimpse of them when Galileo speaks of experimental testing as an "ordeal." Stated broadly the dialectical (agonistic) approach to knowledge is through the *act* of assertion, whereby one "suffers" the kind of knowledge that is the reciprocal of his act.

This is the process embodied in tragedy, where the agent's action involves a corresponding passion, and from the sufferance of the passion there arises an understanding of the act, an understanding that transcends the act. The act, in being an assertion, has called forth a counter-assertion in the elements that compose its context. And when the agent is enabled to see in terms of this counter-assertion, he has transcended the state that characterized him at the start. In this final state of tragic vision, intrinsic and extrinsic motivations are merged. That is, although purely circumstantial factors participate in his tragic destiny, these are not felt as exclusively external, or scenic; for they bring about a *representative* kind of accident, the kind of accident that belongs with the agent's particular kind of character.

It is deplorable, but not tragic, simply to be a victim of circumstance, for there is an important distinction between destiny and sheer victimization. Sheer victimization is not an assertion—and it naturally makes not for vision but for frustration. The victimizing circumstances, or accidents, seem arbitrary and exorbitant, even "silly." But at the moment of tragic vision, the fatal accidents are felt to bear fully upon the act, while the act itself is felt to have summed up the character of the agent. Nor is this vision a sense of cosmic persecution; for in seeing the self in terms of the situation which the act has brought about, the agent transcends the self. And whereas the finality and solemnity of death often leads to the assumption that the tragic vision is possible only at the point of death, we must recognize that dialectically one may die many times (in fact, each time an assertion leads beyond itself to a new birth) and that tragedy is but a special case of the dialectical process in general. In the Hegelian dialectic, for instance, the series of dyings is presented as a gradual progress towards greater and greater self-realization. For spirit has its counterpart in objectification; and by seeing himself in terms of objects, "from them the individual proceeds to the contemplation of his own inner being." (*Philosophy of History*).

We can discern something of the "tragic" grammar behind the Greek proverb's way of saying "one learns by experience"; *"ta pathemata mathemata,"* the suffered is the learned. We can also catch glimpses of a relation between dialectic and mathematics (a kind that might have figured in Plato's stress upon mathematics) in the fact that *mathemata* means both things learned in general, and the mathematical sciences (arithmetic, geometry, astronomy) in particular. A *pathema* (of the same root as our word, "passive") is the opposite of a *poiema* (a deed, doing, action, act; anything done; a poem). A *pathema* can refer variously to a suffering, misfortune, passive condition, situation, state of mind. The initial requirement for a tragedy, however, is an *action*. Hence, by our interpretation, if the proverb were to be complete at the risk of redundance, it would have three terms: *poiemata, pathemata, mathemata,* suggesting that the act organizes the opposition (brings to the fore whatever factors resist or modify the act), that the agent thus "suffers" this opposition, and as he learns to take the oppositional motives into account, widening his terminology accordingly, he has arrived at a higher order of understanding. However, this statement may indicate more of a temporal sequence than is usually the case. The three distinctions can be collapsed into a single "moment," so that we could proceed from one to the others in any order.

A similar grammar (with a similar attenuation of the tragic) may be discerned beneath the scholastic formula, *intelligere est pati,* which we might translate broadly as, "to understand is to be affected by," while remembering however that the deponent verb *pati* contains the following range of meanings: to bear, support, suffer, endure, be afflicted with, pass a life of suffering or privation, permit, experience, undergo, be in a certain state of mind or temper, (and in grammar) to be passive, to have a passive sense, a passive nature. Understanding would be "passive" in the sense that it allowed its way of sizing up things to be moulded by the actual state of affairs. We can best appreciate the dramatistic nature of this realistic formula, which treats of *knowledge* in terms of *action and passion,* by contrasting it with Berkeley's subsequent idealist formula, "to be is to be perceived" (*esse est percipi*) which reverses the direction by treating of *actuality* in terms of *knowledge.*

We may discern a dramatistic pun, involving a merger of active and passive in the expression, "the motivation of an act." Strictly speaking, the act of an agent would be the movement not of one *moved* but of a *mover* (a mover of the self or of something else by the self). For an act is by definition active, whereas to be moved (or motivated) is by definition passive. Thus, if we quizzically scrutinize the expression, "the motivating of an act," we note that it implicitly contains the paradox of substance. Grammatically, if a construction is active, it is not passive; and if it is passive, it is not active. But to consider an *act* in terms of its *grounds* is to consider it in terms of what it is not, namely, in terms of motives that, in acting upon the active, would make it a passive. We could state the paradox another way by saying that the concept of activation implies a kind of passive-behind-the-passive; for an agent who is "motivated by his passions" would be "moved by his being-movedness," or "acted upon by his state of being acted upon."

The Greek verb corresponding to *pati* is *paschein.* Among its more philosophic meanings are: to be actuated by a feeling or impulse, to be influenced by a passion; (and as a technical term of the Stoic school) to be acted upon by outward objects, or to take impressions from them. When Lear complains that he is "more sinned against than sinning," we see the two integral aspects of tragedy, the action and the passion, being dissociated.

Actus and Status

We considered the three Greek words, *poiema, pathema, mathema* (the act, the sufferance or state, the thing learned) because they are at the very center of dialectical motivation. The Greek proverb (*ta pathemata mathemata*) might be said to have merged *poiema* and *pathema* (if, for instance, we translated *ta pathemata* as "the things undergone," an expression that could embrace both the sort of things a person actively encountered and the sort of things that simply befell him). But there is also a way of bringing out *poiema* by itself and merging *pathema* and *mathema*. For *pathema* means not only suffering, but state of mind, condition—and knowledge is a state. Hence, reduced to a dichotomy, the relation could be formalized in terms of "act" and "state" (*actus* and *status*).

The actus-status pair has many possibilities. Often it quite coincides with the action-passion alignment. At other points it diverges from common usage. For though a "passion" and a "state of mind" are much the same, we strongly distinguish between a "political state" and a "political passion." The basic contrast between "motion" and "rest" is a variant of the actus-status pair. The contrast between the dramatic and the lyrical would be another variant (since drama centers in an action, whereas the lyric aims to arrest some one mood or moment). Often the traditional "faith" and "knowledge" pair (*pistis* and *gnosis; fides* and *intellectus*) can be treated as an instance of the same grammatical form, with faith as the act (cf. "an act of faith") and knowledge as the state derived from the act, quite as the tragic hero's *action*, involving his passion, attains its *rest* and *summation* in his *understanding*. From here it is but a brief step to our act-scene pair, inasmuch as the knowledge derived from the act is a knowledge of the act's context, or motivational ground.[1]

[1] Though faith is an act, it is faith in the nature of God as man's ground; hence it also has a strongly scenic reference.

Philologically, the actus-status pair can be used to characterize a major historical development. Consider, for instance, the Greek word for "virtue" (*arete*), and the corresponding Latin, *virtus*. Originally, these words had intensely active meanings. Indeed, *arete* is from the same root as *Ares*, the god of war, and as the Latin words for *art* and military *arms*. "Prowess" would be a good translation for the word in its origins. Gradually the concept of virtue came to place less stress upon action per se, and more stress upon the *potentialities* of action.

We can appreciate the transformation in a word of probably the same etymological origins, "hero." A hero is first of all a man who does heroic things; and his "heroism" resides in his acts. But next, a hero can be a man with the potentialities of heroic action. Soldiers on the way to the wars are heroes in this sense. Their heroism resides in their status as soldiers. Or a man may be considered a hero because he *had done* heroic acts, whereas in his present *state* as a hero he may be too old or weak to do such acts at all. And similarly, the "virtues" may become in the end purely states of mind; or proper attitudes toward God, things, and people; or *not* killing, *not* stealing, *not* coveting, etc.

Sociologically, this movement from actus to status involves *class* substance. It centers about the fact that the different occupational *acts* each have their corresponding *properties*, and out of these differences in properties there develop in time corresponding differences of *status*. Though the spread of occupational classification breaks down the purely tribal nature of a culture, notions of familial substance remain prominent.

Because occupational action requires properties, and because property is not an act but a state, in the social field we can readily observe how a ruling class develops from a stage wherein actus and status are of corresponding importance to a stage wherein the sense of position as an act is slighted and position as a traditional or inherited state is stressed. (Or sometimes we get a new kind of act, not germane to the originating state, as when a nobility, whose privileges grew out of horsemanship in war, turns to pageantry and sport, and may even employ its inherited privileges to hire or command others to fight in its place.) Kingship is originally an act, like heroism. But gradually, as inherited, it becomes a sheer state, the nature of the king's *extrinsic* properties enabling him to be a king by reason of their substantiality alone. He can *be* a king, while commissioning ministers to perform in his stead the kingly acts. (In the mediaeval frame, the primary act, the act of God, is *to be*.) Indeed, the king's holdings may retain him his position as king, investing him with their substance, long after his acts, or his failures to act, have endangered his kingdom. And may we not discern some such grammar behind the Roi Soleil's pronouncement: *"L'état, c'est moi"*? Louis's conception of being, or substance, made it quite natural for him to merge the two meanings of state: the state as a governmental property and the state or property of kingship. The administrative and tax-gathering machinery and the royal domains, we can imagine, could thus be looked upon as an extension of the king's person, a property of his character, like facial traits. In proportion as the quality of a ruling class becomes thus transformed from act to state, we may look for the emergence of a class whose substance centers in a new act.

The actus-status alignment lends itself to another sort of treatment, whereby status is considered as *potentiality* and actus as its *actualization*. That is, in a state there are implicit possibilities, and in action these possibilities are made explicit. But we shall treat of these resources when discussing the potentiality-actuality and implicit-explicit pairs.

Universal Motives as Substance

All gods are "substances," and as such are names for motives or combinations of motives. Polytheistic divinities, besides their personalistic aspects, often represent decidedly geometric, or scenic, kinds of motivation. Indeed, we may even think of local divinities as theological prototypes of contemporary environmentalist, or geographic motives. For to say that a river is a different "god" than a mountain is to say, within the rules of a polytheistic nomenclature, that a river calls for a different set of human actions than a mountain. Whereas the "enlightened" have too often been content to dismiss the pagan gods merely as instances of animistic superstition, the fact is that the complex of social behavior centering about a given "god" was often quite *correct*, in the most realistically biological sense. Thus, insofar as adequate modes of planting and harvesting and distribution are connected with the rites of a given divinity, its name would be the title for a correct summation of motives. However, such concepts of motivation are usually developed to the point where their original reference is obscured, being replaced by motivational concepts peculiar to a special-ized priesthood and to the needs of class domination.

Universal religions, proclaiming some one principle of divinity as the ground of being, have assisted the development of world-wide commerce by enabling the believers, who share in this over-all sub-stance, to retain a sense of one master motive prevailing throughout the world. For the believer in such a universal scheme of motives may go to many different scenes, each with its own peculiar motivational texture, without losing his "hypostasis," the sense of his personal iden-tity and of one "real" motivational substratum underlying it. Scien-tific rationalism can also serve this end, as with the Stoic cosmo-politanism that contributed so signally to the intellectual side of Chris-tianity. Romantic stories of the Westerner, drinking himself to death at some outpost in the tropics, indicate that there *are* local gods (local motives), and that, whereas neither his vestiges of the Christian reli-gion nor his sense of caste permit him to do them formal obeisance, in his dissipation he reveals a distorted response to them. The British official's habit, in the Empire's remotest spots, of dressing for dinner is in effect the transporting of an idol, the vessel of a motive that has its sanctuary in the homeland.

Of course, by the time the monotheistic motive has become embodied in a structure of world empire, it has usually been transformed into its secular analogue, the monetary motive. For the incentive of mone-tary profit, like the One God, can be felt to prevail as a global source of action, over and above any motivations peculiar to the locale. And it serves the needs of empire precisely because it "transcends" religious motives, hence making for a "tolerant" commerce among men whose religious vocabularies of motivation differ widely.

Nonetheless, the greater the diffusion of a motive (be it the One God or the Gold Standard and its later variants) the greater its need to adopt modifications peculiar to specific local scenes. For though a doctrine proclaims a universal scene that is the motivation common to all men whatever their diversities, this "substantial" term must also have "ad-jectival" terms that adapt it to more restricted purposes. We would class as "polytheisms" all terminologies stressing localness of motive (such as nationalism). But we would also recognize that monotheisms (in which we would include any secular title for a universal spring of action, such as "nature" or "the profit motive") can prevail only insofar as they are "incipiently" polytheistic, containing motivational terms ("saints") that break down the universality of the motive into narrower reference.

According to the Marxist calculus, insofar as the world becomes industrialized under capitalism, workers everywhere share the same social motives, since they all have the "factory situation" in common. This is the scene that shapes the workers' acts, and their nature as agents, in conformity with it. Stated in terms of money (the capitalist god, from which are derived men's freedom and their necessity) the motive common to the workers is "wage slavery." It is universal as a motive whenever the means of production are private property, with wages and taxes being paid in symbols rather than in kind. But it divides the over-all capitalist motive into two broad economic classifications, the possessors and the dispossessed, with each status analyzable as a different substance, or contrasting bundle of motives.

Translated dramatistically: the sheer *work* in a factory would not be an *act*. It would be little more than *motion*. And this motion becomes actus only when the workers' status is understood in terms of socialist organization. This act is of revolutionary import since the sheer ownership of the factories is a *state:* hence the property relation becomes increasingly passive, while the proletarian relation becomes increasingly active. However, reversals in keeping with the antinomies of substance complicate the pattern. For the owners' state, in its governmental aspects, is anything but passive. Indeed, the property structure automatically contains an act of expropriation, since the workers receive much less than they produce; and the structure of the state is designed to keep this act of expropriation in force. From this point of view, it is the state that is active, while the workers suffer its action.

The socialist revolution is designed first to reverse the state (during the "dictatorship of the proletariat") and next to abolish it, or let it "wither away." But our grammar would lead us to doubt whether a "state" can ever really "wither away," and least of all in a complex industrial society. Though it may take strategically new forms, we expect the logic of the actus-status pair to continue manifesting itself. The selection of the proletariat as the vessel of the new act that transcends the bourgeois state may or may not be correct as a casuistry, but it violates no law of "grammar." The belief in the withering away of the state, however, does seem to violate a law of grammar. For no continuity of social act is possible without a corresponding social status; and the many different kinds of act required in an industrial state, with its high degree of specialization, make for corresponding *classifications* of status.

Intrinsic and Extrinsic

The treatment of material properties as a "state" brings the actus-status pair in line with the distinction between intrinsic and extrinsic substance, or between motivations within the agent and motivations derived from scenic sources that "support" (or "sub-stand") the agent. In the introduction to his *Philosophy of History*, where Hegel places Matter in dialectical opposition to Spirit, he clearly begins by equating Matter with the extrinsic aspect of substance and Spirit with its intrinsic aspect:

> As the essence of Matter is Gravity, so, on the other hand, we may affirm that the substance, the essence of Spirit is Freedom. . . . Matter possesses gravity in virtue of its tendency toward a central point. It is essentially composite; consisting of parts that *exclude* each other. It seeks its Unity; and therefore exhibits itself as self-destructive, as verging toward its opposite (an indivisible point). If it could attain this, it would be Matter no longer, it would have perished. It strives after the realization of its Idea; for in Unity it exists *ideally*. Spirit, on the contrary, may be defined as that which has its centre in itself. It has not a unity outside itself, but has already found it; it exists *in* and *with itself*. Matter has its essence out of itself; Spirit is *self-contained existence* (Bei-sich-selbst-sein). Now this is freedom, exactly. For if I am dependent, my being is referred to something else which I am not; I cannot exist independently of something external. I am free, on the contrary, when my existence depends upon myself.

However, before he has proceeded very far, remarks on the relation between the potential and the actual lead into the peculiarly Hegelian theory of the State as the vessel of freedom. For the Spirit is free, we are told, and the State is "the perfect embodiment of Spirit." But by the time we arrive at this point, the intrinsic and the extrinsic have begun subtly to change places. One can discern the ambiguity by experimentally shifting the accent in Hegel's formula for the nature of the State. We may say either "embodiment of *Spirit*" or "*embodiment* of Spirit." Or, since "embodiment" is here a synonym for "materialization," we could make the ambiguity still more apparent by rephrasing it as a choice between "materialization of *Spirit*" and "*materialization* of Spirit." For the expression itself is got by the merging of antithetical terms. Hence, when you have put them together, by shifting the stress you can proclaim one or the other as the essence of the pair. Accepting Hegel's definition of Matter, only a State that is the "materialization of *Spirit*" would be "essentially" free. But a State that is the "*materialization* of Spirit" would be the very *antithesis* of freedom (and this was precisely the interpretation given by the Marxist reversal of the Hegelian dialectic).

Indeed, we can take it as a reliable rule of thumb that, whenever we find a distinction between the internal and the external, the intrinsic and the extrinsic, the within and the without, (as with Korzybski's distinction between happenings "inside the skin" and happenings "outside the skin") we can expect to encounter the paradoxes of substance.

Recently, for instance, a "gerontologist," whose specialty is the study of "aging as a physiological process," is reported to have said in an address to a body of chemists:

Aging, like life in general, is a chemical process, and just as chemistry has been able to improve on nature in many respects, virtually creating a new world by reshuffling nature's molecules, so it may be expected that eventually chemistry will learn to stimulate artificially those powers of "intrinsic resistance" to disease with which man is born.

"Intrinsic resistance," you will note, is a concept that situates a motivational source within the body as agent. But the use of chemical means to stimulate this internal motive would involve the transformation of this "intrinsic" motive into an "extrinsic" motive, since it would become but the channel or vessel through which the chemical materials ("scenic," administered "from without") would affect the chemistry of the body. Indeed, since the body is but chemistry, and all outside the body is but chemistry, the very mode of thought that forms a concept of the "intrinsic" in these terms must also by the same terms dissolve it. Everything being chemical, the physiological center of "intrinsic resistance" is but a function of the chemical scene. In fact, insofar as chemical stimulants of the required sort were found, a dependence upon them would be a dependence upon purely *external* agencies. And far from "stimulating" intrinsic resistance, the chemicals should be expected to cause a *weakening* of it, to the extent that the economy of the body grew to require these chemicals. The only place where an intrinsic motive, as a genuinely internal activation, could be said to figure in materialistic medicology is on the occasions when physicians come upon illnesses in which the chances of recovery are felt to depend upon the *mental attitude* of the patient (whether he "wants" to recover). Here one has an intrinsic motive (involving an action) in contrast with such a motive as is supplied by the administering of chemicals (involving sheer motion).[2]

One of the most common fallacies in the attempt to determine the intrinsic is the equating of the intrinsic with the unique. We recall an instance of this nominalist extreme in an essay by a literary critic who exhorted his fellows to discern the quality of a given poet's lines by finding in exactly what way they were distinct from the lines of every other poet (somewhat as advertisements recommending rival brands of the same product play up some one "talking point" that is said to distinguish this brand from all its competitors). Yet the intrinsic value of a poet's lines must also reside, to a very great degree, in attributes that his work shares with many other poets. We cannot define by differentia alone; the differentiated also has significant attributes as members of its class. The heresy that would define human nature solely in terms of some more inclusive category, such as chemistry, or protoplasm, or colloids, has as its over-compensatory counterpart the heresy that would define solely in terms of distinctive traits, actual or imputed. Thus, an article in one of our best magazines is recommended on the grounds that it "applies anthropological method to the diagnosis of our distinctive cultural traits." This is, to be sure, a legitimate limitation of subject-matter for treatment within the scope of one article; but we should be admonished against the assumption that even a wholly accurate description of our culture in terms of its distinctive traits alone could possibly give us a just interpretation of its motives. Indeed, we can discern a variant of the same error in

---

[2] See in appendix, "The Problem of the Intrinsic," as indication of the way in which the quandaries of substance figure in literary criticism.

nationalist and regionalist concepts of motivation as we get in the over-simplifications of literature: the treatment of motivational parts as though they were the motivational whole.

The search for the intrinsic frequently leads to the selection of cal-culi postulating various assortments of "instincts," "drives," "urges," etc. as the motivational springs of biologic organisms in general and of human organisms in particular. Materialistic science prefers this style of vocabulary because it assigns *scenic* terms to motives situated in the *agent;* and scenic words generally seem so much more "real" than other words, even though such lists can be expanded or con-tracted *ad lib.,* quite as suits one's dialectical preferences. Though the treatment of intrinsic motivation in such terms is usually made in good faith, it can also well serve as a rhetorical deflection of social criticism. For instance, if a reformer would advocate important political or social changes on the ground that the present state of affairs stimulates wars, he can be "scientifically refuted" by a calculus which postulates a "combative instinct," or "drive towards aggression," or "natural urge to kill" in all people or certain types of people. For if such motives are intrinsic to human agents, they may be expected to demand expression whatever the social and political structure may be.

When a person has his mind set upon the interpreting of human motivation in a calculus that features an innate "combative instinct" or "natural urge to kill," one may as well accept his decision as a stub-born fact of nature; instead of trying to dispel it, one should try to get around it. Recalling the paradox of substance, for instance, we are reminded that such "drives" or "urges" are like "tendencies" or "trends," which we discussed when on the subject of "directional" sub-stance. And the man who would postulate an "instinct to kill" can be asked to round out his dialectic by postulating a contrary "instinct not to kill." For there is certainly as much empirical evidence that men let one another live as there is evidence that they kill one another. Hence, whenever such words designate motives that may or may not prevail, we can at least insist that they be balanced with their dialectical counterpart. And once the pattern is thus completed, we are able to see beyond these peculiarly "intrinsic" motives to "extrinsic" or "scenic" motives, in the sense of situations which stimulate one rather than the other of the paired motives, as some situations call forth a greater amount of combativeness and destructiveness, whereas other situations call forth a greater amount of coöperation and construction. (There are, of course, complications here that require much more discriminatory calculation than could be got by confinement to such pairings. A certain kind of coöperation is stimulated by war, for instance, both at the time and as the result of new methods which, originally designed for military aggression, can later be adapted for peaceful commercial exchange.)

Spinoza defines substance as "the cause of itself" (*causa sui*). And we can see how this formulation applies to the search for the intrinsic when we contrast supernaturalist and humanist strategies of motivation. Supernaturalist strategies derive the attributes of human substance and motive from God as their ancestral source, whereas humanistic strategies situate the motivational principles within human agents themselves. In brief, humanists assign to man an *inherent* or *intrinsic* dignity, whereas supernaturalists assign to man a *derived* dignity. Any motive humanistically postulated in the agent would be a *causa sui* insofar as it is not deduced from any cause outside itself.

Since agents require placement in scenes, humanism gets its scenic counterpart in naturalism. There is also, of course, a "supernaturalist humanism," but it would be exactly the same as the kind of doctrine we here call simply supernaturalism. And similarly what we here call humanism could be characterized more fully as "naturalistic humanism," or simply "naturalism," as in the following citation from an essay by John Dewey, assigning an intrinsic motive to human nature:

> Naturalism finds the values in question, the worth and dignity of men and women, founded in human nature itself, in the connections, actual and potential, of human beings with one another in their natural social relationships. Not only that, but it is ready at any time to maintain the thesis that a foundation within man and nature is a much sounder one than is one alleged to exist outside the constitution of man and nature.

By placing man and nature together, in dialectical opposition to the supernatural, Dr. Dewey's remarks here somewhat conceal from us the fact that we are shifting between a scenic location for motives and a location within the agent. Only the second kind would be "intrinsic" to people; the other kind would be "derivative" from nature as scene instead of from super-nature as scene. (Both "foundation" and "constitution" are "stance" words, hence capable of merging intrinsic and extrinsic reference.)

It is possible that the reverse perspective so characteristic of Russian ikons may have originated in a theory of the intrinsic, as is indicated in this citation from *The Burlington Magazine* for October 1929 ("Greco: the Epilogue to Byzantine Culture," by Robert Byron):

> It has been suggested that the habit of inverted perspective which the Greeks perpetuated in Duccio and Giotto, derived from the artist's imagining himself within the object portrayed; so that as it progressed in the direction of the beholder it necessarily diminished. Such indeed was the Byzantine vision of form as expressed in terms of light and dark. The head, the arm, was conceived primarily as a dark mass, instead of as a given space to be invested with form by the application of shadow. This principle is explicitly stated in Denys of Fourna's "Guide to Painting" in relation to flesh depiction; and the interest of this instruction lies in the fact that it exhibits the exact converse of the rules for the same process prescribed in mediaeval western manuals such as that of Cennino Cennini.

The notion of "the artist's imagining himself within the object portrayed" would seem to carry the cult of the intrinsic to the point where it exemplifies the paradox of purity, as with the wag who said that only the homosexual man can be the true admirer of women, since he carries his admiration to such an extent that, identifying himself with them, he adopts their very point of view, and thus falls in love with men. For an "intrinsic" observation of women would look, not towards women, but towards men.

The Rhetoric of Substance

The ambiguity of substance affords, as one might expect, a major resource of rhetoric. We can appreciate this by referring again to the citation from Locke, when he says that in speaking of substance "we talk like children: who, being questioned what such a thing is which they know not, readily give this satisfactory answer, that it is *something;* which in truth signifies no more, when so used, either by children or men, but that they know not what; and that the thing they pretend to know and talk of, is what they have no distinct idea of at all, and so are perfectly ignorant of it, and in the dark." For "the *general* name substance" is "nothing but the supposed, but unknown, support of those qualities we find existing." The most clear-sounding of words can thus be used for the vaguest of reference, quite as we speak of "a certain thing" when we have no particular thing in mind. And so rock-bottom a study as a treatise on the nature of substance might, from this point of view, more accurately be entitled, "A Treatise on the Nature of I-don't-know-what." One might thus express a state of considerable vagueness in the imposing accents of a juridic solidity.

We may even go a step further and note that one may say "it is *substantially* true" precisely at a time when on the basis of the evidence, it would be much more accurate to say, "it is not true." And even a human slave could be defined in Christian doctrine as "substantially" free, by reason of qualities which he had inherited "substantially" from his creator. Even in cases where the nature of the case does not justify the usage grammatically, it can be used without strain for rhetorical purposes. What handier linguistic resource could a rhetorician want than an ambiguity whereby he can say "The state of affairs is substantially such-and-such," instead of having to say "The state of affairs *is* and/or *is not* such-and-such"?

There is a similar usage in the expression, "in principle" (a word furthermore that is literally a "first," as we realize when we recall its etymological descent from a word meaning: beginning, commencement, origin). So diplomats can skirt some commendable but embarrassing proposal by accepting it "in principle," a stylistic nicety that was once very popular with the League of Nations. Positivists who would discard the category of substance assert that the only meaningful propositions are those which are capable of scientific proof; and having thus outlawed the conveniences of a substantive rhetoric, they next blandly concede that the scientific proof is not always possible *actually*, but must be possible "in principle"—which would leave them pretty much where they began, except that their doctrine won't allow them to admit it. By this device, we can even characterize as "universally valid" a proposition that may in fact be denied by whole classes of people. As one controversialist has phrased it: "To say that a proposition is valid is to say that *in principle* it can secure the universal agreement of all who abide by scientific method."

Often, of course, this function of language is preserved when there are no such telltale expressions (such as "substantially," "essentially," "in principle," or "in the long run") to make it quickly apparent. For instance, a list of citizens' signatures had been collected for a petition asking that a certain politician's name be placed on the ballot. In court it was shown that some of these signatures were genuine, but that a great many others were false. Thereupon the judge invalidated the lot on the grounds that, the whole list being a mixture of the false and the genuine, it was "saturated" with fraud. He here ruled in effect that the list was substantially or essentially fraudulent. The judgment was reversed by a higher court which ruled that, since the required number of genuine signatures had been obtained, the false signatures should be simply ignored. That is, the genuine signatures should be considered in themselves, not contextually.

Two Kinds of Departure

Since the five key terms can be considered as "principles," and since the margins of overlap among them permit a thinker to consider the genius of one term as "substantially" participant in the genius of another, the ambiguity of the substantial makes it possible to use terms as points of departure in two senses. Thus we may speak in the name of God because this expression is the summation of our thinking. Or precisely because we speak in the name of God, we may be freed to develop modes of thought that lead away from supernaturalism, since absolute conviction about religion might serve as ground for a study of nature. And whereas "naturalism" in its beginnings was a consistent title, referring to man in *nature*, it gradually became transformed into a surreptitiously compensatory title, referring to technological methods and ideals that are almost the antithesis of nature, with nature itself seen in terms of technology and the monetary. Thus, ironically, though much of the resonance in the term "nature" derives from the supernaturalist attitude, which thought of natural law as derivative from the divine, in time the *distinction* between the natural and the divine became transformed into a *contrast* between the natural and the divine. Or, if we think of "God" as the whole and "nature" as a part, we could say that the supernaturalist treated nature as a part *synecdochically* related to the whole, whereas in time naturalism treated this as a *divisive* relation. Or, to adopt a very suggestive usage in Charles M. Perry's *Toward a Dimensional Realism*, the notion of nature as *a part of* God could be converted into the notion of nature as *apart from* God.

But insofar as this divisive emphasis developed, and the secular appeal of "nature" relied less and less upon connotations of the supernatural, "nature" gained resonance from a new source, the romantic reaction against the "unnatural" world progressively created by the technological "conquest" of nature. In this way the selection of "naturalism" as the name for a philosophy of applied science may be *compensatory* rather than *consistent* (somewhat as though one were to call a philosophy "humanistic" because it aimed at the systematic elimination of traits that were formerly considered characteristically human, or as religious doctrines of "personalism" may be formulated, not because the individual person really is in a position of paramount importance, but precisely because he is *not*).

Such tactics of entitling are as legitimate as any other, once the irony has been made explicit. Indeed, philosophies are never quite "consistent" in this sense. All thought tends to name things not because they are precisely as named, but because they are not quite as named, and the name is designated as a somewhat hortatory device, to take up the slack. As others have pointed out, for instance, if the philosophy of "utilitarianism" were wholly correct, there would be no need for the philosophy. For men would spontaneously and inevitably follow the dictates of utility; whereas in actuality the doctrine proclaiming the ubiquity of the utilitarian motive was formulated to serve as a *plea* for the deliberate consulting of the utilitarian motive.

From such ambiguity is derived that irony of historical development whereby the very strength in the affirming of a given term may the better enable men to make a world that departs from it. For the affirming of the term as their god-term enables men to go far afield without sensing a loss of orientation. And by the time the extent of their departure is enough to become generally obvious, the stability of the new order they have built in the name of the old order gives them the strength to abandon their old god-term and adopt another. Hence, noting that something so highly unnatural as technology developed under the name of naturalism, we might ironically expect that, were "technologism" to become the name for "naturalism," the philosophy would be the first step towards a development *away from* technology. And as indication that this is no mere improvising, the philosophy of "operationalism," modeled after technological procedures, embodies a totally different concept of meaning than the one which, we know as a historical fact, figured as an incentive in the *invention* of technological devices and their corresponding mathematical formulae. Hence, if carried out rigorously, it would lead to the *stabilization* of technological operations rather than to the development of new ones. As "naturalism" would lead us, via technology, away from nature, so perhaps "operationalism" might be a way of leading us, in the name of technological operations, away from technology.

It has been said by one of Descartes' editors, John Veitch, that when Descartes questioned an old dogma, rather than attacking it head on, he aimed at "sapping its foundations." And he got rid of traditional principles "not so much by direct attack as by substituting for them new proofs and grounds of reasoning." Veitch also quotes a defender of Descartes who says ironically that his enemies called him an atheist "apparently because he had given new proofs of the existence of God." But these new proofs were in effect new qualifications of God. And in this capacity they subtly changed the nature of "God" as a term for motives, so that those who understood by a God only the character possessing the attributes of the old proofs were justified in calling Descartes an "atheist." Here, subtly, the ambiguous resources in the point of departure were being utilized.

As regards the principles of humanism, we may note that a supernatural grounding of humanism is "consistent" in the sense that a personal principle is ascribed to the ultimate ground of human action. And having thus been put in, it is there for the philosopher to take out, when deriving the principles of specifically human action by deduction from the nature of the universal ground. A naturalistic grounding of humanism, on the other hand, is "compensatory," in that personal agents are placed in a non-personal scene. The first strategy reasons by a "therefore," the second by a "however."

The Centrality of Substance

Contemporary scientific theory, in proposing to abandon the categories of substance and causality, has done speculation a good turn. For it has made clear wherein the difference between philosophic and scientific terminologies of motivation resides. Philosophy, like common sense, must think of human motivation dramatistically, in terms of action and its ends. But a science is freed of philosophic taints only insofar as it confines itself to terms of motion and arrested motion (figure, structure). This convention, almost Puritanical in its severity (surely we should not be far wrong in calling it a secularized variant of Puritanism) has brought about such magnification of human powers that any "objection" to it would have about as much force as an attempt to "refute" Niagara Falls. But such results, however spectacular, do not justify an attempt to abide by the same terminological conventions when treating of human motives. For one could confine the study of action within the terms of motion only by resigning oneself to gross misrepresentations of life as we normally experience it.

Though we here lay great stress upon the puns and other word play in men's ideas of motivation, we do not thereby conclude that such linguistic tactics are "nothing but" puns and word play. Rather, we take it that men's linguistic behavior here reflects real paradoxes in the nature of the world itself—antinomies that could be resolved only if men were able, not in thought, as with the program of Hegelian idealism, but in actual concrete operations, to create an entire universe.

However, strictly for the purposes of our Grammar, we need not defend as much. One might hypothetically grant that the treatment of motives in terms of "action" and "substance" is wholly fallacious, yet defend it as central to the placement of statements about motives. Relinquishing all claims for it as a "philosopher's stone," we might then make claims for it secondarily, as "a philosopher's stone for the synopsis of writings that have sought the philosopher's stone." Men have talked about things in many ways, but the pentad offers a synoptic way to talk about their talk-about. For the resources of the five terms figure in the utterances about motives, throughout all human history. And even the most modern of scientific tracts can be adequately placed only as a development in this long line. From this point of view, terminologies of motion and "conditioning" are to be treated as *dialectical* enterprises designed to *transcend* terminologies of action and substance.

At the very best, we admit, each time you scrutinize a concept of substance, it dissolves into thin air. But conversely, the moment you relax your gaze a bit, it re-forms again. For things *do* have intrinsic natures, whatever may be the quandaries that crowd upon us as soon as we attempt to decide definitively what these intrinsic natures are. And only by systematically dwelling upon the paradoxes of substance could we possibly equip ourselves to guard against the concealment of "substantialist" thought in schemes overtly designed to avoid it. Yet these schemes are usually constructed by men who contemn dialectical operations so thoroughly that, in their aversion, they cannot adequately observe them, and are accordingly prompt to persuade themselves that *their* terminology is not dialectical, whereas every terminology is dialectical by sheer reason of the fact that it is a terminology. If you will, call the category of substance sheer error. Yet it is so fertile a source of error, that only by learning to recognize its nature *from within* could we hope to detect its many disguises from without. Such thoughts apply particularly to Alfred Korzybski's admonitions against Aristotelian "elementalism"; for his aversion leads to so evasive a treatment of the subject that in a very long book he contrives to convey little more than a *negative attitude* towards it.

So, in sum: The transformations which we here study as a Grammar are not "illusions," but citable realities. The structural relations involved are observable realities. Nothing is more imperiously there for observation and study than the tactics people employ when they would injure or gratify one another—and one can readily demonstrate the role of substantiation in such tactics. To call a man a friend or brother is to proclaim him consubstantial with oneself, one's values or purposes. To call a man a bastard is to attack him by attacking his whole line, his "authorship," his "principle" or "motive" (as expressed in terms of the familial). An epithet assigns substance doubly, for in stating the character of the object it at the same time contains an implicit program of action with regard to the object, thus serving as motive.

So, one could, if he wished, maintain that all theology, metaphysics, philosophy, criticism, poetry, drama, fiction, political exhortation, historical interpretation, and personal statements about the lovable and the hateful—one could if he wanted to be as drastically thorough as some of our positivists now seem to want to be—maintain that every bit of this is nonsense. Yet these words of nonsense would themselves be real words, involving real tactics, having real demonstrable relationships, and demonstrably affecting relationships.   And as such, a study of their opportunities, necessities, and embarrassments would be central to the study of human motives.

The design on a piece of primitive pottery may be wholly symbolic or allegorical.   But a drawing that accurately reproduces this design in a scientific treatise would be not symbolic or allegorical, but realistic.   And similarly, even when statements about the *nature of the world* are abstractly metaphysical, statements about the *nature of these statements* can be as empirical as the statement, "This is Mr. Smith," made when introducing Mr. Smith in the accepted manner.

III

SCOPE AND REDUCTION

The Representative Anecdote

MEN seek for vocabularies that will be faithful *reflections* of reality. To this end, they must develop vocabularies that are *selections* of reality. And any selection of reality must, in certain circumstances, function as a *deflection* of reality. Insofar as the vocabulary meets the needs of reflection, we can say that it has the necessary scope. In its selectivity, it is a reduction. Its scope and reduction become a deflection when the given terminology, or calculus, is not suited to the subject matter which it is designed to calculate.

Dramatism suggests a procedure to be followed in the development of a given calculus, or terminology. It involves the search for a "representative anecdote," to be used as a form in conformity with which the vocabulary is constructed. For instance, the behaviorist uses his experiments with the conditioned reflex as the anecdote about which to form his vocabulary for the discussion of human motives; but this anecdote, though notably *informative,* is not *representative,* since one cannot find a representative case of human motivation in animals, if only because animals lack that property of linguistic rationalization which is so typical of human motives. A representative case of human motivation must have a strongly linguistic bias, whereas animal experimentation necessarily neglects this.

If the originating anecdote is not representative, a vocabulary developed in strict conformity with it will not be representative. This embarrassment is usually avoided in practice by a break in the conformity at some crucial point; this means in effect that the vocabulary ceases to have the basis which is claimed for it. The very man who, with a chemical experiment as his informing anecdote, or point of departure, might tell you that people are but chemicals, will induce responses in people by talking to them, whereas he would not try to make chemicals behave by linguistic inducement. And to say that people are "chemicals that talk" is the same thing as saying that people aren't "just chemicals," since chemicals don't talk. It is to confront the paradox of substance in a terminology unsuited to the illumination of this paradox.

Conversely, the notion of chemical affinity about which Goethe organizes his novel of sorrowing love, *Die Wahlverwandtschaften,* is not really the chemicalizing of human substance, but rather the humanizing of chemical substance. For the motive is defined by the action of the characters in a way totally unrepresentative of chemicals; and the situation is not chemical, but thoroughly social. Nothing makes this more quickly apparent than the closing paragraph, where the dead lovers lie buried side by side, surely their nearest approach to a purely chemical condition. Yet the novelist refers to a "peace that hovers over them" and to "the kindred images of angels looking upon them." And what a "gracious moment" it will be, he says, when in the future (*dereinst*) the lovers awaken together.

Subsequently we shall consider at some length this question of the "representative anecdote," itself so dramatistic a conception that we might call it the dramatistic approach to dramatism: an *introduction to* dramatism that is *deduced from* dramatism, and hence gains plausibility in proportion as dramatism itself is more fully developed. For the present it is enough to observe that the issue arises as soon as one considers the relation between representation and reduction in the choice and development of a motivational calculus. A given calculus must be supple and complex enough to be representative of the subject-matter it is designed to calculate. It must have scope. Yet it must also possess simplicity, in that it is broadly a reduction of the subject-matter. And by selecting drama as our representative, or informative anecdote, we meet these requirements. For the vocabulary developed in conformity with this form can possess a systematically interrelated structure, while at the same time allowing for the discussion of human affairs and the placement of cultural expressions in such typically human terms as personality and action (two terms that might be merged in the one term, "role").

The informative anecdote, we could say, contains *in nuce* the terminological structure that is evolved in conformity with it. Such a terminology is a "conclusion" that follows from the selection of a given anecdote. Thus the anecdote is in a sense a *summation,* containing implicitly what the system that is developed from it contains explicitly.

Once we have set seriously to work developing a systematic terminology out of our anecdote, another kind of summation looms up. We might call it the "paradigm" or "prototype."

In selecting drama as our anecdote, for instance, we discover that we have made a selection in the realm of *action,* as against scientific reduction to sheer *motion.* And we thereupon begin to ask ourselves: What would be "the ultimate act," or "the most complete act"? That is, what would be the "pure" act, an act so thoroughly an act that it could be considered the form or prototype of all acts? For if we could have a conception of a consummate act, any less thorough acts could be seen as departures from it, as but partial exemplifications of it. But whatever qualities it possessed clearly, by reason of its nature as an absolute summation, we could then discern dimly in all lesser acts.

What then would be the "pure act" or "pure drama" that one might use as the paradigm of action in general? Such a paradigm or prototype of action, the concept of an ultimate or consummate act, is found in the theologians' concern with the Act of Creation. It "sums up" action quite as the theory of evolution sums up motion, but with one notable difference: whereas one must believe in evolution literally, one can discuss the Act of Creation "substantially," or "in principle."

We shall, then, examine the resources and embarrassments involved in The Creation. And if this seems like a round-about approach to the subject of our chapter, let one ask himself if he could possibly get a more advantageous position from which to observe the aspects of scope and reduction than by beginning with a subject of such comprehensive scope and reducing it.

Before going further, however, we should note that still another kind of reduction (different from both informative anecdote and paradigmatic summation) arises in the dramatist perspective. This is contained in our formula: the basic unit of action is the human body in purposive motion. We have here a kind of "lowest common denominator" of action, a minimal requirement that should appear in every act, however many more and greater are the attributes of a complex act. This is the nearest approach which dramatism affords to the "building block" kind of reduction in materialistic philosophies.

The Way of Creation

In *The Thought and Character of William James,* by Ralph Perry (Vol. II, p. 711) among the letters written by William James to his father there is one in which William is replying to some of his father's theological and ontological speculations. He raises an objection to something his father had written. This objection, he says, "refers to the whole conception of creation, from which you would exclude all arbitrariness or magic." And he continues:

Now I don't see what the word "creation" can mean if this be totally excluded, or what there is to justify its discrimination from pantheism. Creation, emanation, have at all times been opposed to pantheism, immanence; and it is evident from the scorn with which you always mention pantheism that you, too, place a broad gulf between them. The essence of the pantheistic conception, if I understand it, consists in there being a necessary relation between Creator and creature, so that both are the same fact viewed from opposite sides, and their duality as Creator and creature becomes merged in a higher unity as Being. Consequently a conception really opposed to pantheism must necessarily refuse to admit any such ratio as this,—any such external ratio,—so to speak, between them; must deny that each term exists only by virtue of the equation to which it belongs; the Creator must be the all, and the act by which the creature is set over against him has its motive within the creative circumference. The act must therefore necessarily contain an arbitrary and magical element—that is, if I attach the right meaning to those words—undetermined by anything external to the agent. Of course it is impossible to attempt to imagine the *way* of creation, but wherever from an absolute first a second appears, *there* it must be;—and it must be magical, for if in the second there be anything coequal or coeval with the first, it becomes pantheism.[3]

[3] In the immediately following pages we shall have to mull over this passage at considerable length, perhaps even to an extent that will strike the reader as quibbling. These speculations are necessary to the ultimate rounding-out of our position; but they are not necessary to the characterizing and application of the dramatist perspective in general. After the twists and turns which begin at this point, our main line of speculation emerges again on page 74. The reader may have this thought as solace, if these intervening pages greatly worry him. Or he may even skip to page 74.

The pages deal with the halfway stage between doctrines of "the Creation" and doctrines of "Evolution," a stage that is generally called "pantheism," and that marks the area of strategic overlap between terminologies of action and terminologies of motion.

We should not be disturbed if we find this paragraph difficult to follow. After all, the philosopher is here discussing something which he was in no position to report on. Hence, if we attempt to understand his words as information, narration, exposition, we must necessarily find them incomprehensible. For there is nothing here to be understood in the sense in which one might try to understand a report about some event in history. James's discussion of the Creation is not "archaeological." He is not offering a "historical reconstruction." As he himself observes, "It is impossible to attempt to imagine the way of creation," or as some contemporary advocates of physicalist vocabularies might put it: It is impossible to explain the meaning of "the act of Creation" in terms of concrete operations.

Dramatistically considered, there is a tremendous difference between "the Creation" and "the process of Evolution" as motivational summations. One sums up in terms of action, the other in terms of motion. A statement about Evolutionary motion is "true" only if it names events that literally take place. But "the Creation" is "true," as a prototype of action, if it has *the form of the most complete act*. We can come nearest to its kind of "truth," in terms of science, when we think of a composite photograph, which is got by superimposing the portraits of many individuals upon one another. In being a likeness of their "average," it is not literally a likeness of any. The analogy is not quite satisfactory, however, since a concept of "the Creation," as the prototype of action designates not the "average" act, but the logical conclusion of the concept of action (an opponent might rather call it the *reductio ad absurdum* of the concept of action).

Statements about both "Evolution" and "the Creation" are alike in this: despite their reference to matters of sequence, to "befores" and "afters," they are *ontological* statements, statements about *being,* about what *is.* That is, the laws of Evolution *are* such-and-such; and the structure of the Creation *is* such-and-such. For even a fundamentalist who would treat the Creation as an act that *was* would have to agree that the *principles* involved in the act *are.*

We here stand at a moment of great indeterminacy, the watershed moment that slopes down to "being" on one side and "becoming" on the other. It is the ambiguity etymologically present in the Latin, *natura* (and its Greek counterpart, *physis*). For though we came to speak of a thing's "nature" as its essence, the word originally had a genetic or developmental meaning, a reference to *growth* and *birth*.

True, some terminologists would even hold that the laws of becoming themselves become. And this is true in the sense that a new species exemplifies new laws of motion: the particles of matter contained in it behave differently than the particles of matter contained in other species; hence, when this species arises, certain peculiar laws of motion are born, and these laws of motion cease to be when this species becomes extinct. But any such statement about the becoming of becoming ("emergent evolution") can be rephrased as a statement about the "laws" of the becoming of becoming, or as "generalizations" about the becoming of becoming—and this brings us back to the ontological level.

And if even a concept so super-genetic as the evolution of evolution forces us back to an ontological level as soon as we make generalizations about this process of processes, all the more clearly are we found shuttling between being and becoming in the concept of Creation. The shift is between temporal priority and logical priority. The Creation, considered as a prototype of action in our paradigmatic, or summational sense, involves "principles," and these are not historical or temporal "firsts," but logical firsts. They are the kind of "beginnings" that are always. James speaks of an "absolute first," which admonishes us that we here touch upon the paradox of purity. An "absolute" first is the kind of first that both is and is not followed by a second.

In sum: we are discussing the Creation not as a temporal event, but as the logical prototype of an act. Indeed, even if one believed it literally, one would hardly be justified in treating it as a temporal event, since it was itself the positing of time; it was the act that set up the conditions of temporal development; hence a terminology that reduced it to terms of time would lack sufficient scope. Thus, even a literal believer would have to treat it in terms that placed it, rather, at an intersection of time and the timeless—a point at which we place ourselves when we discuss it in terms of those non-temporal firsts called "principles."

Act as Locus of Motives

If one would deny pantheism, James had said, "the Creator must be the all, and the act by which the creature is set over against him has its motive within the creative circumference." And the act must "necessarily contain an arbitrary and magical element . . . undetermined by anything external to the agent." Further, we should note that arbitrariness and magic are equated with novelty, as when James says: "It is impossible to attempt to imagine the *way* of creation, but wherever from an absolute first a second appears, *there* it must be;—and it must be magical, for if in the second there be anything coequal or coeval with the first, it becomes pantheism." Indeed, the Creation as an act of God was a total novelty; and it was magic because, just as the magician would make it seem that he pulls a live rabbit out of an empty hat, so God made *everything* out of *nothing*.

The magician would have us think that he suspends the laws of motion. And God's act likewise "suspended" the laws of motion, though in an absolute sense: that is, upon his originating act depend all the laws of motion which men necessarily accept as the *conditions* of action. Indeed, the analogy suggests the thought that "true" magic prevails *outside* the strict realm of motion, in the area of more-than-motion that we call *action*. The demand for a kind of human magic that violates natural law is then revealed as a superstitious, quasi-scientific ideal. But magic, in the sense of novelty, is seen to exist normally, in some degree, as an ingredient of every human act; for each act contains some measure of motivation that cannot be explained simply in terms of the past, being to an extent, however tiny, a *new thing*.

This consideration could be approached in another way. We have said that a fully-rounded vocabulary of motives will locate motives under all five aspects of our pentad. Yet there is a paradoxical tendency to slight the term, *act*, in the very featuring of it. For we may even favor it enough to select it as our point of departure (point of departure in the sense of an ancestral term from which all the others are derived, sharing its quality "substantially"); but by the same token it may come to be a point of departure in the sense of the term that is "left behind." We see this temptation in the search for an act's motives, which one spontaneously thinks of locating under the heading of *scene, agent, agency,* or *purpose,* but hardly under the heading of *act*.

But if the scene of action is there already, and if the nature of the agent is also given, along with the instrumental conditions and the purposes of action, then there could be *novelty* only if there were likewise a locus of motivation within the act itself, a newness not already present in elements classifiable under any of the other four headings. And in this sense an act has an element of "arbitrariness" or "magic" insofar as it contains a motivational element requiring location under the heading of the term *act* itself.

At this point, we grant, our thinking departs somewhat from that in the James citation. Or rather, there is a strategic ambiguity in the James passage, as when he writes that, if one would avoid pantheism, "the creator must be the all, and the act by which the creature is set over against him has its motive within the creative circumference." If we think of "the Creator" as an "agent," we might contend that the motives of the act are here situated outside the locus of the term *act* and within the locus of the term *agent*. Yet the statement that God's creative act "has its motive within the creative circumference" comes quite close to satisfying our notion that "magic" or "novelty" arises by reason of the motive assignable under the heading of *act* itself. And the requirement is still more fully met if we recall the scholastic definition of God as "pure act."

But what precisely is our point? What are we trying to prove by an example that, we freely grant, cannot be adduced as the literal foundation of an argument? We are reasoning as follows: We are saying that, to study the nature of the term, *act,* one must select a prototype, or paradigm of action. This prototype we find in the conception of a perfect or total act, such as the act of "the Creation." Examining this concept, we find that it is "magic," for it produces something out of nothing. This enables us to equate magic with novelty—and leads us to look for a modicum of magic in every act to the extent that the act possesses a modicum of novelty. This consideration also admonishes us, however, to make a distinction between "true" and "false" magic. "False" magic is a quasi-scientific ideal that would suspend the laws of *motion,* as in the attempt to coerce natural forces by purely ritualistic means. "True" magic is an aspect not of motion but of *action.* And if the motives properly assignable to *scene, agent, agency,* and *purpose* are already given, there could be novelty only if we could also assign motives under the heading of *act* itself. That is, there would be something new intrinsic to the act; and this novelty would be the modicum of motivation assignable under the heading of act rather than under the heading of the other four terms, singly or in combination. There must, in brief, be some respect in which the act is a *causa sui,* a motive of itself.

Up to this point, we have simply followed the implications of the prototype. We have found out something about the term, *act,* as "revealed" by the contemplation of "the Creation." Next we must look about, in the world of experience, to see whether our conclusions make sense. Proverbs in particular might help us; for surely they are in the flatlands, safely distant from the magic mountain (though often we may best understand them if we think of them not just as isolated observations, but as fragments of a vast and complex dialectic structure which the proverbialist discerns not sustainedly and systematically, but in glimpses and inklings).

Proverbs such as *l'appétit vient en mangeant* or *Uebung macht den Meister* seem well suited to our purposes. Skill and habit are derived from the very acts in which they are practiced. Or let us consider some protracted act, such as the writing of a long book, where the act of the writing brings up problems and discoveries intrinsic to the act, leading to developments that derive not from the scene, or agent, or agency, or extrinsic purposes, but purely from the foregoing aspects of the act itself. That is, there is nothing present in the agent or his situation that could have led to the *final* stages of this act, except the *prior* stages of the act itself, and the logic which gradually takes form as the result of the enactment. Or, recalling our *poiemata, pathemata, mathemata* alignment, we can generalize this consideration by noting that, when an act is performed, it entails new sufferances, which in turn entail new insights. Our act itself alters the conditions of action, as "one thing leads to another" in an order that would not have occurred had we not acted.

The mediaeval schoolmen would probably object that we are here confusing "creation" with "generation." In their terminology, only God can create, while his creatures can but generate, as with the parents' generation of offspring or the artist's generation of his art work. However, it is not the purpose of our Dramatism to abide strictly by any one system of philosophic terms that happens to exemplify the dramatist pattern. Rather, it is our purpose to show that the explicit and systematic use of the dramatist pentad is best designed to bring out the strategic moments of motivational theory. Accordingly, at this point, we are more concerned to illustrate the Grammatical scruples than to select one particular casuistry as our choice among them. Philosophies again and again have got their point of departure precisely by treating as a distinction in kind what other philosophies have treated as a distinction in degree, or *v.v.* And we here come upon considerations that permit us to discern a novel ingredient in action, while this ingredient in turn can be equated with the creative.

The Aristotelian God, considered as universal motive, acted upon nature neither as creator nor as generator, but as a motionless inducement to development. The world and its genera and species were considered as eternal, hence not as derivations from God as "pure act." God acted upon nature solely as a goal, somewhat as a desired food might, by lying west of a rational and hungry man, induce him to move towards the west; or as the principles of a perfect art might lead the knowing artist to shape his work as nearly as possible in accordance with them.

The Christian merging of Aristotle's self-enwrapt *eromenon* with the Creator Jehovah (a tribal, tutelary deity made universal), necessarily calls for a drawing of the lines at a different place. In this scheme, stressing plenitude and fertility, God creates and creatures generate. But the Christian terminology also took over the concept of *hexis* (Latin, *habitus;* trained disposition), the term Aristotle uses in his Ethics to name that aptitude in virtues which is acquired by the practice of virtues. And we believe that we are but coming upon the function of this term by a different route when we recognize that the resources of the pentad invite us to locate some motives of action under the heading of Act itself.

There would thus be a modicum of novelty in the act, to the extent that the act could be said to have an ingredient not derivable from any other of the terms. And insofar as the act was derivable from the other terms, it would not possess novelty, but would be a mere unfolding of the implicit into the explicit.

The modicum of novelty in the act would seem to be the element that justified Coleridge's view of poetry as a "dim analogue of Creation." However, that formula was obscured by the idealist stress upon *agent,* as locus of the "shaping spirit of Imagination" by which we give forth that which we receive, since "in our life alone does Nature live." And to glimpse more clearly the independent claims of the term, act, we might better go back to Spinoza who, mediating between the mediaeval and the modern, defined the universal Substance as the "cause of itself." God would thus be perfect action, in that there

would be no motivating principle beyond his own nature (a consideration, incidentally, that enables us to see why Spinoza would equate
God and Nature).

All told, contemplating the Grammar in its simplest aspect, we are
admonished to expect occasions when, in seeking for the motives of an
act, the thinker will in effect locate the motive under the head of Act itself. However confusing the subject may become in the alembications
of theology and metaphysics, it is at least obvious enough on this first
level: That among the resources of the pentad is the invitation to locate
the motives of an act under the head of Act (as with Faust's formula,
Im Anfang war die That).

Do we not see a scruple of this sort behind the Augustinian claim
that God's act of Creation must be wholly without motives? For any
motivation, however slight, would be to that extent a constraint upon
God's will—hence his act would not be wholly free.

But though there are ultimate moments when the substantial, all-
inclusive act, as it were, is derived out of itself, as regards the pentadic
resources generally we must consider rather the transformations
whereby we may deal with this motivational locus in terms of the other
loci. In particular, one might ask, what has become of our scene-act
ratio? And that question will be the subject of our next section.

The "Grounds" of Creation

The Creation, as the ground or scene of human acts, provides the
basic conditions utilized by human agents in the motions by which they
act. In this sense, it represents an ultimate source of motives, though
human agents by their acts may pile up lesser novelties, partial creations which they interpose between themselves and the ultimate
ground, and which become a "second nature" with them, a scene having motivational properties in its own right.

Dramatistically, however, there is an embarrassment as regards God's
constitutive act. James touches upon it somewhat when saying that
it is impossible to imagine the "way" of creation. And we see it more
clearly when we reflect that a "way" is literally a path across some
ground. The symmetry of the pentad requires that even a "first act"
must have been enacted in some kind of "scene" (could we call it a
"pre-first" scene?). If "the Creation" marks the establishment of time

and motion, as conditions that followed from the act, we are prompted to look contextually for a counterpart in timelessness and rest, or familially for some magnitude great enough to produce the universe as its lineal descendant. The concept of God as an agent doesn't quite satisfy the dramatistic necessities, for an agent, like an act, must be placed in some scene.

It has been said of Kant that realistic assumptions were necessary as a way into his system, but once you entered it, you had to abandon them if you would stay there. For, as Windelband puts it, "the conception of the sensibility introduced at the beginning involves the causal relation of being affected by things-in-themselves," yet causality is a category, and according to the doctrine of the Analytic, "categories must not be applied to things-in-themselves." We see here the evidences of a dialectic whereby the point arrived at transcended the point of departure. But one may well expect to find such transformations in a work which was, after all, designed to duplicate the total act of creation itself (except that there would be no operationalist account of the "way," which is an important exception).

Perhaps we should always look for "ladders" of this sort when we are on the subject of "everything," ladders that are used only to attain another level of discourse and that would be an encumbrance if one continued to carry them about with him after he had attained this level. In any case, we might detect the vestiges of such a ladder in the notion of a monotheistic God, which developed out of polytheistic thinking. Polytheistic gods usually did not make "everything." Rather, there was usually some primeval scene, more or less chaotic, that provided the materials out of which the god shaped the motivating conditions of human life. Or rather, he shaped *some* of the motivating conditions, others being supplied by other powers and natures more or less at variance with the purposes of the tutelary deity.

But when one god has risen to such prominence among the gods that he becomes "the" god (taking over, among other things, the role of *destiny* that serves, in polytheistic schemes, as a kind of over-all motivation summing up, or mediating among, the disparate motives of the various gods), theologians attempt to *start* their speculations on this *final* level, abandoning the dialectical ladder by which this level was attained. And here is where the dramatistic embarrassments arise. For whereas the divine agents of polytheism had a scene to contain them and their acts, what are we to do with a god who is himself the ground of everything? When he acts, in what scene does he act?

We may treat the matter summarily by saying simply that he is super-scene, super-act, and super-agent all in one. But in doing so, we thereby fail to appreciate the full pressure of the dramatistic logic. For Christian theology *did* speculate about the "grounds" of God's act, as in the scholastics' argument whether God willed the good because it is good or the good is good because God willed it. The first of these is obviously the more symmetrical from the dramatistic point of view, since it does in effect furnish a scene for the act of the Creation. It was the position upheld by Aquinas, the doctrine of the *perseitas boni* (the "by-itselfness of the good") to which Scotists are said to have objected because it imposed limits upon the freedom of the divine will. We can discern the "scenic" nature of the good, as the principle of God's creation, in Bréhier's statement that Duns Scotus "would avoid the need to admit that there existed outside of God, eternal like him and imposing itself upon him, a sort of *fatum* by which his intelligence and will were guided." (*La Philosophie du Moyen Âge,* p. 387.)

The doctrine that "the good is good because God willed it" points away from dramatistic symmetry and towards the modern centuries of subjectivism and idealism, with their great stress upon the "ego," the "will," and finally the "libido." Among the scholastic upholders of this position, Occam went so far in behalf of God's freedom as to maintain that God might have willed a quite different set of moral laws, even proclaiming as bad what he did in fact proclaim as good, and *v. v.* In effect such doctrines ground the act of the Creation in the term *agent* rather than the term *scene,* for it is derived directly from the will of God, and will is a property of agents.

In contrast, the scenic emphasis in the Thomist doctrine is further revealed by the fact that the Thomists placed the "true" as of higher rank than the "good." This was managed by proclaiming the *rationality* of the good. (That is, as God willed the good because it is good, the good in turn is good because it is rational.) And we can discern the *scenic* factor behind such a concept of rationality if we consider such equations as these: what is, is true; what is true, is rational; what is, is rational. In keeping with such equations the principles of goodness, by having an eternal existence in their own right, would be scenic; and a statement about them, in being a statement about what is, would be a statement about the rational and the true, hence a statement about the scenic.

Sociologically, we may note that the pattern of the controversy corresponded to a poignant political issue of those times. The proposition that God willed the good because it was good represented the mediaeval theory of sovereignty, according to which even the sovereign *obeyed* the laws. And the proposition that the good is good because God willed it represented the newer political theories that were arising with the trend towards absolute central authority. This centralizing trend was marked by great legalistic innovation, in contrast with the former appeal to custom as the arbiter of law. The new methods of production and distribution favored and required this stress upon legalistic innovation, such as could be quickly standardized over comparatively wide areas only if it emanated from a central authority. And in such a state of affairs, since the monarch decreed the laws, the lawful was lawful because the monarch so willed it.

Pantheism and Ontology

We have now discussed three important aspects of "the Creation." We have considered the ambiguity of being and becoming, the equating of "magic" with novelty, and the dramatistic pressure for the formulation of a scene in which Creation, as an act, would be situated. We would now consider the relation between the two alternatives which James mentions: "magic" and "pantheism."

Pantheism is defined in Webster as "the doctrine that the universe, taken or conceived of as a whole, is God; the doctrine that there is no God but the combined forces and laws which are manifested in the existing universe." Its most succinct description is to be found in Spinoza's expression, "God or Nature" (*Deus sive Natura*). In doctrines of "creation, emanation," nature possesses attributes derived from its divine origin, but it is less than God. God does not *need* nature. But in doctrines of pantheism, or immanence, "God" and "Nature" are interchangeable terms. James thus situates the essence of the pantheistic conception "in there being a necessary relation between Creator and creature." In pantheism, he says, both the Creator and the created "are the same fact viewed from opposite sides." And "their duality as Creator and creature becomes merged in a higher unity as Being."

This last word, "Being," gives us our cue. For ontology, according to the dictionary, investigates "the principles and causes of being" (the Greek *onta* means the "things that are"). We may thus readily discern a "pantheistic temptation" in the very nature of ontology as a subject. For if one would treat of "everything" in terms of "being," "being" would then be the over-all concept, the summarizing "god-term," since the word that summed up "everything" would certainly be the god-term, the universal title or all-inclusive epithet to which any less generalized terms would be related as parts to whole. This is how we should interpret James's remark that in pantheism the duality of Creator and creature "becomes merged in a higher unity as Being."

Or we could state it thus: James said of the Creation, "Whenever from an absolute first a second appears, *there* it must be." But to treat of a relation between a first and a second in terms of *being* is to make one step *collapse* into the other, so that one has instead a *simultaneity,* in adopting a point of view whereby the two steps can be treated as "coeval." "The Creation" is not exactly an historical process, since it is not just *in* time and motion, but must be *outside* to the extent that it is the establishment or inauguration of time and motion. But even if one were dealing with a characteristically historical process, one could view it ontologically, or in terms of *being,* only insofar as one viewed it in terms of permanent principles that underlie the process of becoming.

"Principles" are "firsts," but they are "absolute" firsts, not the kind of firsts that require a temporal succession as we go from a first to a second. They just *are*. They have logical, rather than temporal, priority. Hence, to treat of things in terms of their relation to underlying principles is to translate historical sequence into terms of logical sequence (whereby things can "precede" and "follow" one another in a kind of succession that requires no time coördinate). This is why Spinoza's ontology proposes to treat of things *sub specie aeternitatis,* which is to say, in terms of timelessness, or being. But if a first and a second are related "logically," they are by the same token related "necessarily." For a logical relationship, or principle of being, always was, is, and will be; and what always was, is, and will be, *must* be. Whereby ontology merges the "is," the "must be," and the rational.

No aim could be more rational than the desire to find a philosophic language whose order would correspond with the order of things as they are and must be—somewhat as the sequence of letters in a phonetic alphabet corresponds with the sequence of verbal sounds of which these letters are the signs, for though the letters are transposed continually to signalize different sequences of sound, the *relation* between sound and sign is permanent, involving fixed *principles;* and when the notation is adequate, the relation between the sign and the signified is "rational."

But if a first and a second are "necessarily" related, James reminds us, we cannot have arbitrariness and magic. Creator (the first) and creature (the second) thus become "coequal and coeval," in being *ontologically* related (that is, *logically* related in terms of *being*). The second is then related to the first somewhat as conclusions are implicit in premises and premises are implicit in conclusions.

Pantheism would result whenever we went about it thoroughly to translate the "historical" account of the Creation in the book of Genesis (or Becoming) into a "flat," or "simultaneous" equivalent (conceived in terms of ontology, or Being). "In the beginning God created the heaven and the earth" would thus be ontologically translated: "God created the heaven and the earth substantially, in principle."

Grammatical Steps to Naturalism

There are two primary generalizations that characterize the quality of motives: freedom and necessity. And whenever they appear, we may know that we are in the presence of "God-terms," or names for the ultimates of motivation. Doctrines wherein Creator and Creation are not ontologically collapsed into a unity give us a kind of double genesis for motives. Consideration in terms of the *Creation* leads to "necessity" when, in accordance with the logic of geometric substance, all the parts of nature are treated as necessarily related to one another in their necessary relationship to the whole. For "necessity" names the extrinsic conditions that determine a motion and must be taken into account when one is planning an action. And consideration in terms of the *Creator* leads to "freedom" when, in accordance with the logic of tribal substance, men "substantially" derive freedom (or self-movement) from God as its ancestral source. This double genesis allows for free will *and* determinism simultaneously, rather than requiring a flat choice between them. Also, owing to the ambiguity of substance, it permits men to be "substantially" free even when, as regards their natural conditions, they are actually enslaved or imprisoned.

An ancestral source of freedom is in one sense extrinsic to the individual, inasmuch as progenitor is distinct from offspring. Yet origin is intrinsic to the individual in the sense that this genetic or generic fact about his nature is also possessed *within* him (just as members of a given biological species each possess within them, genitively, the substance or motives proper to the species generally). And as regards the geometric logic, when a thing's intrinsic nature is defined as part of a universal whole, the reference here is to a context, hence extrinsic. Formally, the issue figures in metaphysical speculations as to whether relations are internal or external, an ambiguity which, from the dramatist point of view, is implicit in the fact that one can shift between familial and geometric definition, stressing either person (agent) or ground (scene) as a locus of motives.

In pantheistic schemes, the principles of personal (intrinsic) freedom and scenic (extrinsic) determination must collapse into a unity that corresponds to the ontological merging of Creator and Creation. That is, "freedom" and "necessity" become identical, with each definable in terms of the other. Spinoza's pantheism meets this requirement in defining substance as *causa sui,* whereby the concepts of freedom and necessity are merged grammatically in the *reflexive.* The reflexive form satisfies the requirement, putting active and passive together, since one can be simultaneously free and constrained if the constraints are those of one's own choosing, an identification of scene and philosopher-agent that is possible inasmuch as both nature and the philosophy are rational.

Spinoza likewise adopts the expressions, *natura naturans* and *natura naturata* (or "naturing nature" and "natured nature"). Grammatically, we could thus treat the ground term, "nature," (which equals "God") as reflexive in form (though one usually reserves the designation for verbs) having active and passive (the *-ans* and the *-ata*) as its dual attributes. And we note a corresponding grammar in his Cartesian expressions, *res cogitans* and *res extensa,* where "thing" *(res)* would be the reflexive ground, with "thinking" *(cogitans)* as its active voice and "extended" *(extensa)* as its passive voice. So we could speak of nature, or thing, naturing, or thinking—and of nature, or thing, natured or extended. One can discern here the beginnings of the alignment that was to prevail in modern idealism, as the active participle becomes the "subjective" and the passive participle the "objective" (a grammar that is precisely reversed in materialism, where nature in *extension* is treated as the motivational source, while subjective motives are treated as either illusions or reflections).

Or, consider the passages in Aristotle's Physics where he is seeking to establish the number of principles required to account for the changes that take place in the natural world. Here we find a paradigm of grammar in his concern with the reduction of such principles to a pair of opposites, with a possible third term that would be their common ground. Grammatically, these principles are reducible to active, passive, and middle, the concept of self-movement containing active and passive ambiguously in one. Nature, Aristotle says at one point, is like a doctor doctoring himself (a figure that could, if we wanted to translate the universal into medical terms, then give us: doctor doctoring and doctor doctored).

The pantheistic moment in philosophy, by producing a merger of personal and impersonal principles (a merger of personal agent and impersonal scene), can serve well as a bridge leading from theology to naturalism. For theologies are "dramatistic" in their stress upon the personalistic, whereas the terminologies typical of natural science would eliminate the concept of the person, in reducing it to purely scenic terms. Hence, a pantheistic merging of person and scene can add up to the dissolution of the personal into the impersonal along naturalistic lines.

We might sum up the matter thus: *Theologically,* nature has attributes derived from its origin in an act of God (the Creation), but God is more than nature. *Dramatistically,* motion involves action, but action is more than motion. Hence, theologically and/or dramatistically, nature (in the sense of God's Creation) is to nature (in the sense of naturalistic science) as action is to motion, since God's Creation is an *enactment,* whereas nature as conceived in terms of naturalistic science is a sheer concatenation of motions. But inasmuch as the theological ratio between God (Creator) and Nature (Creation) is the same as the dramatistic ratio between action and motion, the *pantheistic* equating of God and Nature would be paralleled by the equating of action and motion. And since action is a personal principle while motion is an impersonal principle, the pantheistic equation leads into the *naturalistic* position which reduces personalistic concepts to depersonalized terms.

If these steps seem to have been too quickly arrived at, let us try approaching the matter from another angle. Indeed, we need not even hang on, but can almost begin anew.

Circumference

This time all we need for our text is a single word from James, his word "circumference," as when he says that, if one would avoid pantheism, "the Creator must be the all, and the act by which the creature is set over against him has its motive within the creative circumference." The word reminds us that, when "defining by location," one may place the object of one's definition in contexts of varying scope. And our remarks on the scene-act ratio, for instance, suggest that the choice of circumference for the scene in terms of which a given act is to be located will have a corresponding effect upon the interpretation of the act itself. Similarly, the logic of the scene-agent ratio will figure in our definition of the individual, insofar as principles of dramatic consistency are maintained.

That is, if we locate the human agent and his act in terms of a scene whose orbit is broad enough to include the concept of a supernatural Creator, we get a different kind of definition than if our location were confined to a narrower circumference that eliminated reference to the "supernatural" as a motivating element in the scene, and did not permit the scenic scope to extend beyond the outer limits of "nature." Or we may reduce the circumference still further, as when we define motivations in terms of the temporally or geographically local scenes that become a "second nature" to us, scenes that may themselves vary in circumference from broad historical situations to the minutely particularized situations of back-stairs gossip.

Now, it seems undeniable, by the very nature of the case, that in definition, or systematic placement, one must see things "in terms of . . ." And implicit in the terms chosen, there are "circumferences" of varying scope. Motivationally, they involve such relationships as are revealed in the analysis of the scene-act and scene-agent ratios whereby the quality of the context in which a subject is placed will affect the quality of the subject placed in that context. And since one must implicitly or explicitly select a circumference (except insofar as he can seem to avoid the predicament by adopting a slung-together terminology that contains a muddle of different circumferences) we are properly admonished to be on the look-out for these terministic relationships between the circumference and the "circumfered," even on occasions that may on the surface seem to be of a purely empirical nature.

Thus, when the behaviorist experiments with animals to discover, under "controlled laboratory conditions," the springs of conduct that operate also in human beings, we consider his experiment fully as important as he does, though for a totally different reason. For we take it to indicate, with the utmost clarity possible, the terministic relationship between the circumscription and the circumscribed. For no matter how much a matter of purely empirical observation it may seem to be, it actually is a very distinct choice of circumference for the placement of human motives. By the very nature of the case it chooses to consider human motives in terms of an animal circumference, an acutely terministic matter, not a matter of merely "empirical observation." And, ironically enough, it is most likely to reveal something about human motives distinctively, only insofar as the conditions established by the laboratory place the animals in a "human" circumference. But though nothing is more distinctly "human" than a scientific laboratory in one sense (for no other species but man is known ever to have made and used one), it is the kind of "humanity" we get in mechanization (a "part of" man that became so poignantly, in industrial routines, "apart from" man). And by the logic of the scene-act ratio, the study of conduct in terms of so mechanistic a scene led to a correspondingly mechanistic interpretation of the act.

This would probably be a good place to repeat that we do not deny the importance of seeking always for "controlled" cases, as anecdotes in conformity with which to form one's terminology for the analysis of human motives. But we maintain that one can avoid the bias of his instruments (that is, the bias of terms too simplist) only if he chooses a *representative* example of an act. Animal experiments have taught us however (we should at least grant them this) that school-teachers like to send animals to school, that physical sadists who have mastered scientific method like to torture animals methodically, and that those whose ingenuity is more psychiatrically inclined like to go on giving the poor little devils mental breakdowns, ostensibly to prove over and over again that it can be done (though this has already been amply proved to everybody's satisfaction but that of the experimenters).

We cherish the behaviorist experiment precisely because it illustrates the relation between the circumference and the circumscribed in mechanistic terms; and because the sharpest instance of the way in which the altering of the scenic scope affects the interpretation of the act is to be found in the shift from teleological to mechanistic philosophies. Christian theology, in stressing the rational, personal, and purposive aspects of the Creation as the embodiment of the Creator's pervasive will, had treated such principles as *scenic*. That is, they were not merely traits of human beings, but extended to the outer circumference of the ultimate ground. Hence, by the logic of the scene-act ratio, they were taken as basic to the constitution of human motives, and could be "deduced" from the nature of God as an objective, extrinsic principle defining the nature of human acts. But when the circumference was narrowed to naturalistic limits, the "Creator" was left out of account, and only the "Creation" remained (remained not as an "act," however, but as a concatenation of motions).

The narrowing of the circumference thus encouraged a shift from the stress upon "final cause" to the stress upon "efficient cause," the kind of cause that would reside not in a "prime mover," but in a "last mover" (as the lever with which a man moves a stone could be called the "last mover" of the stone). We are here in the orbit of the *vis a tergo* kind of cause, prominent in all theories of motivation that stress "instincts," "drives," or other sheerly compulsive properties. Such terminologies attain a particularly thorough form in behaviorism, with its stress upon reflex action and the conditioned reflex, and its treatment of motivation in terms of Stimulus and Response.

Ironically, the dramatistic logic (that is, the logic of the scene-act and scene-agent ratios) here invokes a non-dramatic mode of analysis. For the naturalistic terminology, in eliminating the principles of personality and action from the ultimate ground of motives, leads consistently to ideals of definition that dissolve the personality and its actions into depersonalization and motion respectively. In naturalism there is no Creator; and nature is not an act, but simply "the given."

However, we should add several important modifications to our notions of the movement towards the dissolution of drama. In the first place, we should note that in proportion as Naturalism dropped the principles of personality and action from the *scene,* Humanism compensatorily stressed their presence in men as *agents.* Human personality was not "deduced"; it was simply postulated in men, as part of "the given," quite as the records of our senses are "data." This humanistic stress upon the principle of personality as peculiar to people (who are conceived as set in dialectical opposition to an "impersonal" nature) could lead to a cult of "pure" personality (particularly as an over-compensation for the increasing depersonalization brought about by industrialism, and as a direct response to the vagueness of role that went with the spread of leisure and unemployment). This cult of "pure" personality could in turn attain a "counter-over-compensation" on the part of the materialists, who emphasized the importance of the scenic factor in human personality (since one is a person not "absolutely," but by reason of a *role,* and such a role involves a *situation*). But in materialism the concept of role was narrowed in scope from *acting* to *doing,* until the idea of "vocation" was no wider in scope than the idea of "job." In theories of meaning the movement probably reaches its culmination in Bridgman's "operationalism."

Note that, dialectically, the concept of the "pure" personality itself contained its dissolution as its ultimate destiny. For, by the paradox of the absolute, a "pure" person would be an "im-person." This same paradox is latent even in the theological concept of personality; for God as a super-person is also, by the same token, "impersonal." Hence the monotheistic concept of an all-inclusive God was itself an ambiguous preparation for naturalism, once the circumference was narrowed to omit "God" as a necessary term in motivational statements. And the orbit could be narrowed by reason of a readily understandable procedure in language. For if nature was deemed, as it was by many of the devout, to be a perfect exemplification of God's will, then *nature's* design would accurately represent the design of *God.* Hence, reference to God as a locus of motives would involve an unnecessary duplication of terms—since a statement of motivation in terms of natural structure alone should be sufficient.

That is, if natural structure was the visible, tangible, commensurable embodiment of God's will, one would simply be duplicating his terms if his accounts of motivation had both natural and supernatural terms. The natural terms should be enough, in accordance with the Occamite principle (the keystone of scientific terminologies) that "entities should not be multiplied beyond necessity." And this naturalistic side of the equation had the further advantage of opening the way to test by experiment, as against demonstration by purely verbal manipulation. What was a narrowing of the circumference, as considered from one point of view, was a widening, as considered from another point of view. For naturalistic experimentation was a way of giving Nature itself an articulate voice in the dialectic. When properly used, it could so put questions to Nature that Nature was able to give very definite answers. The strong dramatistic feeling behind such procedures at their inception can be glimpsed in Galileo's reference to the experiment as the "ordeal," a significance that is also in our word "trial," whose bearing upon the attenuated drama of education can be glimpsed somewhat in the expression, "trial and error," as applied to the learning of animals in a maze.

We have spoken of Spinoza's explicit equation, "God or Nature." Note that there was also an implicit equation lurking in the word "design," as when we speak of "God's design" and "Nature's design." In the first case, "design" means "intention." In the second case, it can mean simply "structure"; we could even speak of a "design produced by accident." In this pun there is, accordingly, much the same equation as that explicitly put forward by Spinoza. To make the two meanings explicitly synonymous, as they are allowed to be synonymous in the original ambiguity of the word, we might phrase the corresponding equation thus: "intention or absence of intention," where the "or" means not "the alternative to" but "the same as." Stating the matter with reference to the genitive, Nature's design as "a part of" God's design becomes available to treatment as "apart from" God's design (or otherwise put: the *synecdochically* related part of the divine whole becomes the *divisively* related part).

Such implicit or explicit equations in which distinctions are merged serve historically as bridges from one terminology to another, precisely by reason of the Occamite principle. For if the two terms, or the two aspects of the one term, are taken as synonymous, then one side of the equation can be dropped as "unnecessary." If you say that the laws of electro-chemical transformation are exactly as God would have them, then it follows that their structure represents the will of God. Whereupon, you are invited to treat of motives in terms of these electro-chemical transformations. For why shouldn't you, if their design is to be equated with God's design, plus the fact that their design lends itself to empirical study in the scientific laboratory? Thereupon, almost imperceptibly, the terministic logic has taken you from supernaturalism to "chemism."

Hence, in the course of time, it becomes clear that we have gone from one bank to the other, by reason of an expression that bridged the gulf between them. Often the given writer who first gave vigor to the equation did not, however, intend it as a "bridge" in this historical sense, as a way of abandoning one position and taking up its opposite. Rather he cherished it precisely because this midway quality itself was *his* position, as with that motionless crossing expressed by Wordsworth in his sonnet "Composed upon Westminster Bridge," where the significance of his vision lies in the very fact that he is placed midway between the City of the Living and the City of the Dead, as he sees London transfigured in the early dawn:

> Dear God! the very houses seem asleep;
> And all that mighty heart is lying still!

An equation of two terms hitherto considered unequal can, of course, lead two ways. We can make the "wider" circle of the same circumference as the "narrower" circle either by narrowing the wider, or by widening the narrower. At the close of the middle ages, such equations, or bridging terms, would generally lead from supernaturalism towards naturalism, rather than *vice versa,* precisely because their role as a point of departure came at a time when it was only the supernatural vocabulary that was sufficiently developed to be departed from.

Earlier in this book, we observed that "if all the ten ratios were adjusted to one another with perfect Edenic symmetry, they would be immutable in one unending 'moment.'" That is, the quality of scene, act, agent, agency, and purpose would be all the same, all of one piece; hence there would be no opportunity for a new "beginning" whereby the agent would undertake a different quality of act that might change the quality of himself or of his scene, etc. Thus, there could be no becoming, but only unending being; there could be no *"alloiosis,"* or qualitative change, no development, no origin and destination, no whence and whither, for all the terms would contain what all the other terms contained. We suggested an answer in the consideration that men are capable of but *partial* acts, acts that but partially represent themselves and but partially conform to their scenes. We might now expand our statement in the light of our remarks on the subject of "circumferences."

If the scene-act ratio prevails, for instance, how would it be possible for a man to perform a "good" act in a "bad" situation? Or, by reason of the scene-agent ratio, how could a man be "good" in a "bad" situation? Or, to take a specific case, here is a statement by Stark Young, made in a discussion of Clifford Odets' *Night Music:*

> Can we demand from a dramatist, in an age like ours, scattered, distracted, surging, wide, chopped-up and skimmy, that he provide his play with a background of social conceptions that are basic, sound, organized, prophetic, deep-rooted? Shall he, in sum, be asked to draw the hare of heaven from a shallow cap?

And to this, Mr. Young, in keeping with the genius of the scene-act ratio (and who should implicitly abide by it, if not a dramatic critic?) makes answer:

> The answer is no, we can scarcely demand that. In general we should remind ourselves that there is no reason to ask any theatre to surpass its epoch in solidity, depth or philosophic summation.

There are all sorts of tricks lurking in that one. When we were young, we used to ask one another whether, since we were living in a boring age, it would be possible to write works of art that were not themselves boring or that were not exclusively concerned with boring people in boring situations. Later we found that, whatever the bad character of our age might be, it was not boring. This interpretation of the scene had evidently been a function of our situation as adolescents. Indeed, we discovered that, if no better motives came along, merely the attempt to work one's way out of fear and anger was enough to stave off boredom.

There are all sorts of modifications possible when considering Mr. Young's statement. Surely the dramatic work of Shakespeare, for instance, can be said to "surpass its epoch in solidity, depth or philosophic summation," except insofar as we define the nature of the epoch itself in terms of Shakespeare. But as a matter of fact, Shakespeare has not only "surpassed his epoch" in such properties, but he has surpassed whole centuries, whole populations, whole cultures.

However, it is not our intention here to bring up the many quibbles which Mr. Young's brief statement can invite. We would say only enough to point up the fact that, when confronting such issues, one has *a great variety of circumferences* to select as characterizations of a given agent's scene. For a man is not only in the situation peculiar to his era or to his particular place in that era (even if we could agree on the traits that characterize his era). He is also in a situation extending through centuries; he is in a "generically human" situation; and he is in a "universal" situation. Who is to say, once and for all, which of these circumferences is to be selected as the motivation of his act, insofar as the act is to be defined in scenic terms?

In confronting this wide range in the choice of a circumference for the location of an act, men confront what is distinctively the human freedom and the human necessity. This necessity is a freedom insofar as the choice of circumference leads to an adequate interpretation of motives; and it is an enslavement insofar as the interpretation is inadequate. We might exploit the conveniences of "substance" by saying that, in necessarily confronting such a range of choices, men are "substantially" free.

The contracting and expanding of scene is rooted in the very nature of linguistic placement. And a selection of circumference from among this range is in itself an act, an "act of faith," with the definition or interpretation of the act taking shape accordingly. In times of adversity one can readily note the workings of the "circumferential" logic, in that men choose to define their acts in terms of much wider orbits than the orbit of the adversity itself. The "solace of religion," for instance, may have its roots not in a mere self-deception, whereby one can buoy himself up with false promises or persuade himself that the situation is not bad when it is so palpably bad; but it may stem from an accurate awareness that one can define human nature and human actions in much wider terms than the particularities of his immediate circumstances would permit; and this option is not an "illusion," but a fact, and as true a fact as any fact in his immediate circumstances.

In *The Brothers Karamazov,* Dostoevsky tells how Mitya dreams of a new life with Grushenka, who had "loved him for one hour":

With a sinking heart he was expecting every moment Grushenka's decision, always believing that it would come suddenly, on the impulse of the moment. All of a sudden she would say to him: "Take me, I'm yours for ever," and it would all be over. He would seize her and bear her away at once to the ends of the earth. Oh, then he would bear her away at once, as far, far away as possible; to the furthest end of Russia, if not of the earth, then he would marry her, and settle down with her incognito, so that no one would know anything about them, there, here, or anywhere else. Then, oh then, a new life would begin at once!

Of this different, reformed and "virtuous" life ("it must, it must be virtuous") he dreamed feverishly at every moment. He thirsted for that reformation and renewal. The filthy morass, in which he had sunk of his own free will, was too revolting to him, and, like very many men in such cases, he put faith above all else in change of place. If only it were not for these people, if only it were not for these circumstances, if only he could fly away from this accursed place—he would be altogether regenerated, would enter on a new path.

In brief, he trusted that a new scene would make possible a new act, by reason of the scene-act ratio, and the new act would make a new man, by reason of the act-agent ratio. And he hoped to attain this new structure of motivation by sheer locomotion. Maybe he could have—for the changes he thinks of might very well be sufficiently different in their circumstances to produce in him a correspondingly new bundle of motives. But the mystic Alyosha, we may recall, was in the same scene as his elder brother Mitya; and for him its motivations were entirely different, and precisely because for him it had a different circumference, so that all actions were interpreted in greatly different terms. His terms amounted to a migration in a subtler sense: by a "transcendence," a "higher synthesis," that in effect "negates" the terms of the scene as Mitya interpreted it. For Alyosha's terms implied a wider *circumference*.

Monographic Terms of Placement

Though we have stressed the contrast between theology and behaviorism because it so readily illustrates the "circumferential logic" (that is, the effect of *scope* in a given terminology of motives), we should note that a writer's vocabulary is usually set somewhere between these two extremes. His aims are usually less thoroughgoing, more "monographic," as with the selection of some "thesis." Consider, for instance, the difference between Dante's version of the human drama in *The Divine Comedy*, and a specialized study on *Imperialism, in Relation to the Cult of "Fair Play" and the "Gentleman"*, a treatise which, to our knowledge and to our great regret, has been written by nobody. In such partial tracts, for instance, one man may confine himself to a treatment of the climatic factors in motivation, another may focus upon the effects that some drug has upon the body, another will chart the curve of business cycles, etc.

Any such placement, by the selection of some specialized theme ("theme" is also a member of the Stance family), is a kind of "partial Creation." On a minor scale, and almost imperceptibly, it too is substantive, "constitutive," quite as was God's creative Act. For its terms, in being restricted to the nature of the thesis, will thereby establish a circumference, marking the outer boundaries of the ground that is to be covered. As agent, the writer will have acted creatively—and the motives and motifs featured by his terminology will fix the nature of the constitution which he has enacted.

Thus we may see, in our world of great occupational diversity, even a purely technical or "disciplinary" reason why we should have so much disrelated featuring of motives, ranging from the smallest circumference, local in time, place and purpose (such as, "The man who wrote the letter today in such-and-such a manner in order to get so-and-so to do such-and-such tomorrow") to circumferences marking off all sorts of permanent scenic or materialistic properties (such as planetary influences, hormones, or the means of production), the disposition of which may be continually changing, though the motivational relationships between mover and moved may be said to remain constant if they are stated in terms sufficiently broad.

However, though the great variety of modern instruments provides a special reason for "monographic" treatment of motivational factors, it is true that in any world there will be many and good reasons why we should want, on occasion, to discuss motives in terms of greatly narrowed scope. Ironically, a reference to "man's universal situation" would be too generalized to serve as an explanation of motives for all purposes. Ideally, we might locate an act in a set of widening circles, ranging from the uniquely particularized, through placement in terms of broad cultural developments, to absolute concepts of relationship or ground. It was thus with the eight whorls in the "spindle of Necessity" that, as we are told in the tenth book of *The Republic,* Er saw during his journey beyond the grave; for they were the celestial orbits, and were scooped out and fitted inside one another, like a nest of bowls. But in actuality, such a graduated table of circumferences would be cumbersome and unmanageable. Most circumferences are felt to be, not so much wider or narrower than one another, as merely *different.* We might say that they mark out a circumference by spotlight, while the rest of the stage is left dark.

It may often be the works of wider circumference that give us the faultiest interpretation of a particular motivational cluster. People tend to think that when they speak of "the Universe," they are actually speaking of the Universe—yet "world views" can easily be the narrowest of all in circumference, possibly (to borrow from Windelband) in accordance with a law of formal logic whereby "concepts become poorer in contents or intension in proportion as their extension increases, so that the content *zero* must correspond to the extension *infinity.*" This law also operates in "negative theology," which finds it necessary to define the "Allness" of God in terms synonymous with "nothing" ("infinite," "unending," "incomprehensible," "inexpressible," "invisible," "unknowable," and the like). We must leave for another place (notably our Symbolic) a discussion of the ways whereby such "Allness" or "Nothingness" can nonetheless manage to take on empirical reference, as a stylized replica of the Self. The possibility in its most obvious aspects is indicated by an observation about "man" in *The Education of Henry Adams:* "The universe that had formed him took shape in his mind as a reflection of his own unity."

However, there are respects in which the "monographic" study likewise can lead to a faulty interpretation of motives. Consider, for instance, a well-written little book, *Swords and Symbols, the Technique of Sovereignty,* by James Marshall. Being in the Machiavelli line, in the best sense of the word, it deals with the philosophy of political power, and with the many kinds of disequilibrium that constantly disturb the maintenance of such power. The "motive" of the study dictates its confinement to a circle characterized by such key terms as force, power, threat, police, appetite, fraud, enslavement—concepts that cluster "logically" and "necessarily" about the theme. It is a book that any student of politics could read with attention and respect. Yet, paradoxically, the very limitations inherent in the terms proper to the subject serve to give the thesis an appearance of too great scope. For though the "technique of sovereignty" is in one sense a very narrow theme, in another sense it could be said to embrace the whole world. And whereas the book's universe of discourse quite reasonably and properly invites us to consider only those aspects of power that bear centrally upon the theme, one can derive from the book the feeling that he has been contemplating the very essence of political relations.

The author's genealogy is, briefly: (a) Material needs give rise to ethical values; (b) ethical values give rise to ideologies; (c) out of ideologies, laws are constructed; (d) the sovereign wields these laws (as the principal symbol of political force and power).

The nature of the subject and the method makes it fitting that values and ideas and laws be considered *in terms of* material needs. Indeed, even if we knew it for a fact that ideas and laws and ethical values were derived from heaven, it would still remain proper to the author's universe of discourse that they be discussed in terms of material needs; for the value of such tracts resides precisely in their ability to teach us what important facts can be learned about human motives when considered from the standpoint of such terms.

To be sure, being admonished that there are ways in which temporal priority and logical priority can change places with each other, we should not, for our purposes, want to put a wholly evolutionary interpretation upon the notion that material needs give rise to ethical values. We should say, rather, that in accordance with the structure of the author's terms, the concept of "material needs" is *logically prior* to the concept of "ethical values." That is, whereas the author's position is stated in terms of *historical* sequence, we should want to read the statement more *terministically*—for the relation between material needs and ethical values is not the same kind of purely historicist matter as the mailing of a letter on the fourth and its arrival on the fifth.

No purely temporal sequence can be established here. Obviously, for instance, there is some kind of "prior" ethical faculty in people (even if we would but reduce it to an aspect of language, as were we to agree that the "ethical sense" is but the manipulation of verbal counters). And this potentiality, or latency, or ability to respond to material needs in ethical terms, must be there if the material needs are to have such a formative effect. Hence, for our purposes, we might want to rephrase the concept of genesis here, stating the causal ancestry in accordance with the paradox of substance, thus: "Material needs give rise to ethical values, *in principle*" (and that would be quite accurate, for in some respects they do, and in some respects they don't).

Let us put it this way: let us suppose that one held unquestioningly to a belief in the divine origin of the ethical. Let us further suppose that one considered material needs simply as conditions determining the constantly changing structure of the ethical in different periods of history. Even so, there would be plenty of room for a book such as this, which proposes to make such significant observations about ethical values as can be made when they are seen *in terms of,* or *from the standpoint of,* material needs. Dialectically considered, it is as though the author were at this point to write a dialogue containing a voice, or character, named "Material Needs"—and this fellow, Material Needs, would say the things about ethical values that he can see from his particular position, or point of view, or in his particular perspective (necessarily a restricted perspective, since it represents but one voice in the dialogue, and not the perspective-of-perspectives that arises from the coöperative competition of *all* the voices as they modify one another's assertions, so that the whole transcends the partiality of its parts).

Even if we were to ascribe a supernatural origin to ethics, it would still remain true that one should give Material Needs as accurate a voice as one can, for he has a major contribution to make in any discussion of human relations. And it is quite proper to such a "scientific monograph" as Mr. Marshall's that the ethical should be considered simply in material terms. For the empirical concern with *temporal conditions* is nothing other than a concern with *material de-terminations* (that is, treatment contextually in terms of scene, with scene itself narrowed to a naturalistic circumference).

But there are now many naïve readers of such scientific tracts. And it does not occur to them that a treatment of ethics, sovereignty, power in such terms is, by the very logic of its form, a *partial* treatment. A portion of the dialectic having been "monographically" selected, and made into a monologue that takes up the entire universe of discourse, the reader is prone to take this as a statement covering the essentials of the entire field. That is, instead of reading it as a statement about *ethics as considered in terms of material needs,* it is taken as a statement about *the ultimate origin of the ethical.*

It is when so misread that the very excellence of such a monograph (and we consider this one quite good) can lead to a faulty interpretation of motives. And the area "spotlighted" comes to seem like the entire world, so that what seems like a circumference with wide scope is actually the reduction to a very narrow one.

So far as we can see, this matter of circumference is imbedded in the very nature of terms, and men are continually performing "new acts," in that they are continually making judgments as to the scope of the context which they implicitly or explicitly impute in their interpretations of motives. To select a set of terms is, by the same token, to select a circumference.

The thought suggests a technical reason why one could not "rationally" demonstrate the existence of a personal God, if by "rational demonstration" one means the use of evidence derived solely from examination of the natural scene, rather than an appeal to some kind of "revelation" or "intuition." For one would be required to "demonstrate" the existence of a personal God in terms of an impersonal scene with a circumference that has, by definition, been narrowed to a point where the personal principle has been eliminated. The scene as thus restricted would become, from the thematic or terministic point of view, the "logical ground" of God's existence. God's existence as a person would thus be "grounded" in a scene of naturalistic limits. Nature would in effect be the ground of God, whereas the exactly opposite position was what was to be proved.

On a lesser scale, one may discern the same pattern of embarrassment behind the contemporary ideal of a language that will best promote good action by entirely eliminating the element of exhortation or "command." Insofar as such a project succeeded, its terms would involve a narrowing of circumference to the point where the principle of personal action is eliminated from language, so that an act could follow from it only as a non-sequitur, a kind of humanitarian after-thought. For the principle of personal action would lie completely outside the circumference of the terms. And whatever value such vocabularies may have (as in their possible service to technological development) one could not place great hope in them as an ideal for the definition of human motives. We here observe, as the theologians complain, a linguistic line which, beginning with an ideal that involved the elimination of the super-personal principle, eventually led by the same token to the elimination of the personal principle. Of course, one can always restore the personal principle by a kind of "tiny intuition," in simply proclaiming it as part of the empirically given. But this blanket restitution is not enough in itself, so long as the entire logic and structure of the vocabulary is directed differently.

Monetary Reduction

The concept of scope, or circumference, is particularly relevant as regards the sociology of motives. It is obvious, for instance, that a narrowing of circumference was involved when the rise of industrialism had its reflex in a shift from emphasis upon the rationality of the Good to emphasis upon the regularity of Nature. Or otherwise put, in both monetary and technological rationalisms (the two major interwoven strands of industrial rationalism), we see an "heretically efficient" overstressing of the rationalistic element that was in Christian theology. And this rational element underwent a progressive narrowing of circumference, in proportion as men became more exacting in their attempts to be "empirical," and developed the information and the concepts with which to be "empirical" in this sense.

As the concept of reason in God's order (and note that "order" has much the same ambiguity as we found in "design") could be narrowed, or made more precise, in terms of natural law, so the concern with natural law could become materialism; materialism in turn could be made more circumstantial in evolutionary or historicist ways by a narrowing of the motivational context to various concepts of environment; the general notion of environment, or situation, could be further narrowed to stress specifically the "economic factors"; and by many apologists of capitalist rationalism the orbit of the economic was restricted in turn to the monetary and financial. If one were feeling ironical, he could at this point adapt to his purposes a couplet from *The Dunciad:*

> When reason doubtful, like the Samian letter,
> Points him two ways, the narrower is the better.

And when we have arrived at the stage where the sheer symbols of exchange are treated as the basic motives of human relations, when we have gone from "God's law" to "natural law," and thence to the "market law" that had become a "second nature" with those raised in a fully developed capitalist ethic, we find many pious apologists of the *status quo* who would deduce human freedom itself from the free market, as the only scene from which a free social act could be drawn. They thus attribute to the mechanics of price the position in the genealogy of action once held by no less distinguished a Personage than God Himself, formerly defined as the ground of all possibility.

This narrower, more "humanistic" or "social" genealogy of freedom seemed all the more plausible in proportion as the money motive itself gained poignancy—which it did, not in the sense that men became any more greedy for treasure than they had ever been, but in the sense that the increased use of monetary symbolism as an integral part of the economic process led nations to develop their productive and distributive systems in accordance with the money motive as a rational test. This necessarily meant a "transubstantiation" of money, from its function as an *agency* of economic action into a function as the *ground* or *purpose* of economic action. That is, instead of *using* money as a medium to facilitate the production and distribution of goods, men were moved to produce and distribute goods in response to money as motive.

In proportion as the monetary motivation became a "second nature" to modern man, one was guilty of no mere rhetorical misnomer in proclaiming money the source of freedom. Such a position was a grammatically correct deduction from the conception of scene as narrowed to the circumference of the "monetary situation." The evidence of freedom was obvious. We have in mind not only the liberties available to persons of wealth, but rather a more prevalent condition, a development from that ironical kind of freedom the serf obtained in being freed of his bonds to the land and by the same token being deprived of his rights in the land.

Once the capitalist motive had become the norm, men could "of their own volition" compete with one another for monetary wages; thus they could "freely" perform all sorts of necessary acts, many of which were so new and alien to the traditions of Western culture that they would have seemed wholly irrational as judged by the norms of custom alone. They were equally irrational as judged by the tests of intrinsic satisfaction in the work, and could be rationalized *solely* in terms of the money they earned, however little that might be. Thus, we had the spectacle of free men vying with one another to get work that was intrinsically very unpleasant, with little in its favor but the extrinsic monetary reward; they *volunteered* for tasks that, in previous economic scenes, men could have been induced to perform only by compulsion, as with slaves or convicts, or by such rare motives of voluntary service as are found in personal, familial fealties.

In sum, if you have an unpleasant piece of work to be done, and don't want to do it yourself, in a slave culture you may get this done by force, compulsion, threat. Or in a pious culture you may get it done "religiously," if those who are asked to do the work are moved by such motives as devotion, admiration, sense of duty. But in a capitalist labor market, all that is necessary is for you to say, "Who'll do this for five dollars?"—and men press forward "independently," of their "own free will," under orders from no one, to "voluntarily" enlist for the work.

The money motive also had the advantage of being more nearly neutral than the motives of slavery and religion. For instead of drawing upon feelings so strong as those of fear or devotion, it could motivate merely by presenting an "opportunity." And though the work might "in itself" be drudgery, in time this shortcoming was rectified by the growth of the "amusement industry" to the point where it formed one of the biggest investments in our entire culture. And by going where one chose to be amused, one could enjoy for almost nothing such a wealth of performers, avid to entertain, as was never available to the most jaded of Oriental potentates, however vast his revenues.

Under such conditions the monetary motive, or "market law," really could with some justice replace the reference to God's law as the repository of men's "substantial" freedom, since men could be "substantially" free in willing to obey the necessities of monetary wage and monetary tax (or "price"), *wanting* to do what they *had* to do, uniting "I must," "I ought," and "I will." The noun for this union of necessity, duty, and volition was "ambition." Another such was "enterprise."

Since the religious circumference traditionally provides the basic terms for the tribal or collective motives of a culture ("God" being felt to be "real" insofar as these unifying motives really do make up the most extensive and intensive aspects of men's consciousness) the spread of secularization and rationalistic individualism is "normally" a sure sign of cultural disintegration. But the combination of technological and monetary rationalism transformed these "signs of decay" into trends wholly "progressive." For the fact is that the monetary motive, which stimulated the high development of machinery and was in turn "backed" by the new kinds of production it had so significantly helped to rationalize, could provide an effective technical substitute for the religious motive, as a "symbolic" or "spiritual" ground of social cohesion, a means of "keeping body and soul together."

For if religion is by definition a sort of Rome towards which all roads lead, money likewise has this unifying attribute. As early as Plato, the value of monetary symbolism in promoting the division of labor was recognized, as the hypothetical society in Book II of *The Republic* is soon found to need buying and selling, with "a market-place, and a money-token for purposes of exchange." Dialectically, it is the "homogenizing" principle that, in compensating for heterogeneity, so permits much heterogeneity to arise without disaster. As such it is a kind of lowest common denominator, a public or civic medium that can mediate among an infinity of private motives. We might say that it allows for much heterogeneity without disintegration.

As an abstraction into the terms of which *all* communicative acts could be translated (though not all with equal felicity, the price of a can of beans "translating" better than the price of affection) monetary symbolism provided the equivalent of a rational, monistic, universal centre of reference, such as "God." And as the communion service, wherein men make themselves one by partaking of a substance in common, contains a dialectic of the one and the many, since the rite is social in its emphasis but permits individual appropriation of the sacramental substance, so the philosophy of the market points to the public benefits that follow from individual acquisition. And private appropriation inevitably had social reference: business men could continue "making money" only insofar as they continued to sell goods—and "selling" goods meant *distributing* goods.

The analogy may be pursued even to the extent that the reference to money, like the reference to God, entails a special rationality. Many acts that would be "rational," as tested by the rationality peculiar to the monetary motive, would be "irrational" in its absence. Quite obviously, for instance, it is only by a peculiarly monetary logic that men could have called it a "favorable balance of trade" when they were shipping out of their country goods of greater cost than they were getting back. And consider the many gadgets that it would be irrational for mature men to spend their intensest efforts and the best years of their lives in planning, manufacturing, and selling, if any other but the monetary motive were the standard of judgment. Likewise many acts that might be rational enough if there is no God would be irrational if there is one.

After a society has thoroughly adapted its ways to an economy in which money figures as end rather than means, you may expect its members to carry on a maximum percentage of activities that would seem irrational in any other context. Hence, there must be an increase of occupational anguish (as revealed in suicide, war, and their attenuated variants), not only at the times when, by reason of monetary disorders, economic action is impeded, but also at the times when the money motive is attaining free expression. For at the times of free expression, the over-simplification or rational efficiency of money as motive would frustrate those sides of the human personality or organism adapted to very different tests of value.

The efficiency of money as a rationale of conduct makes it a scientific idiom of reduction which, in the realm of social motives, corresponds to the ideal of Occam's Razor in the realm of physical motives. And this very efficiency would probably be enough to make it self-perpetuating as a motive (in that men who remained discontented with large salaries would seek contentment by still larger salaries); but such self-perpetuation is threatened by problems intrinsic to the nature of money itself, and in response to which money continues to change its nature, regardless of human wishes. And many a legislative act specifically designed to maintain the financial *status quo* serves ironically to hasten its transformations.

For the moment endowing money with a personality, treating it metaphorically as an agent, we could say: Since money acts in a technological scene, by reason of the scene-act ratio, the quality of its action must change with the changing quality of that scene. And by reason of the scene-agent ratio, its nature must change *pari passu* with the nature of the industrial plant that "backs" it; for not rare metals, but economic functions, are the real backing of money. Or considering our paradox of the absolute we could say: Insofar as the monetary motive attains the state of "purity" (as it does in banking and investment, where money is derived from purely symbolic manipulations) we may expect it to become something else as a locus of motives.

Kinds of Reduction

Integral to the concept of scope is the concept of *reduction*. In a sense, every circumference, no matter how far-reaching its reference, is a reduction. A cosmology, for instance, is a reduction of the world to the dimensions of words; it is the world *in terms of* words. The reductive factor becomes quite obvious when we pause to realize that any terminology of motives reduces the vast complexity of life by reduction to principles, laws, sequences, classifications, correlations, in brief, abstractions or generalizations of one sort or another. And any generalization is necessarily a reduction in that it selects a *group* of things and gives them a property which makes it possible to consider them as a *single entity*. Thus, the general concept of "man" neglects an infinite number of particular differences in order to stress certain properties which many distinct individual entities have in common. Indeed, any characterization of any sort is a reduction. To give a proper name to one person, or to name a thing, is to recognize some principle of identity or continuity running through the discontinuities that, of themselves, would make the world sheer chaos. To note any order whatever is to "reduce." To divide experience into hungry and sated moments, into the pleasant and unpleasant, into the before and after, into here and there—even distinctions as broad as these translate the world's infinite particulars into terms that are a reduction of the world; in fact, as per the equating of infinity and zero, terms of such broad scope are perhaps the most drastically reductive of all.

In sum, we have first the reduction of the non-verbal to the verbal. Next, within the verbal, there is the reduction of one terminology to another. Any word or concept considered from the point of view of any other word or concept is a reduction in this sense. One reduces this to that by discussing this *in terms of* that. In this sense, such expressions as "reduced to . . .," "in terms of . . .," and "with reference to . . .," are synonymous. An idealist "reduces the world to ideas" when talking of it *in terms of* mind as its underlying substance. Titles composed of two nouns connected by "and" can quite commonly be read in this light. A title like "Art and Politics," for instance, could be translated, "Art Reduced to Politics," or "Art in Terms of Politics," or "Art with Reference to Politics." Any metaphor is in this broad sense reductive, as it enables us to see one thing in terms of something else (as though we were to give the object a voice, and let it tell what a thing of its nature, and in its position, could observe about the subject). Philosophic equations are in this broad sense reductive, as Berkeley's equating of the "intelligible" with the "sensible" proposes to treat thought in terms of sensation, hence serving as a bridge from rationalism to empiricism (an idealistic bridge, in that sensation in turn was said to be composed of "ideas" grounded in the mind of God).

In this second sense, one can even be said to reduce a "lower" subject to a "higher" one, as Bonaventura, who rated theology as much higher than art, could write "On the Reduction of the Arts to Theology," which we could paraphrase, "The Arts in terms of Theology." But this brings us to the third sense of reduction, as a lowering, a lessening, a narrowing—the difficult spot today, since purely technical conceptions of lowering, lessening, and narrowing can here easily become confused with moral ones.

In recent years, the most drastic manifestation of reduction in this third sense (the sense in which "scope" and "reduction" are flatly contrasted) has been the "debunking" movement, which could be said in general to treat "higher" concepts in terms of "lower" ones, though the pattern is clearly established as far back as the maxims of La Rochefoucauld, which treat "virtues" in terms of "vices" (or what Bentham would call the "extra-regarding" motives in terms of the "self-regarding" motives). Any treatment of a "wider" circumference in terms of a "narrower" circumference would fall generally under the head of reduction in this third sense, as with the location of "consciousness" in terms of "matter," or any other "scientific" metonymies that would define the incorporeal in terms of the corporeal, the intangible in terms of the tangible, and the like. All physicalist, behaviorist, positivist, operationalist ideals of language would be classifiable here, in the technical sense (and some of their opponents would also class them here in the moral sense, on the grounds that the reduction of "spirit" to "matter" is a lowering of caste).

Variants of reduction in this sense are the atomistic vocabularies that would account for entities in terms of the particles of which they are thought to be composed, as one might account for a building in terms of the materials used in its construction. Such atomistic search for the "building blocks" of the universe stresses material cause to the exclusion of final cause. It is somewhat as though one were to "reduce" a game of football to a set of observations about the distribution and movement of masses upon a field, but without any reference whatsoever to such principles of play as one learns from reading the book of rules. The atomistic philosopher's justification would be his contention that there is no cosmic book of rules to read.

We may also note that atomistic reduction is the search for "design" in the narrower sense of that term. And this brings us again to the Occam's Razor, or the "law of parsimony," which plays a central role in the narrowing of circumference. For when two circumferences are matched, it is usually the wider set of terms that will be found to have "multiplied entities beyond necessity." If we say, for instance, that the weight fell because God willed laws according to which the weight would fall when we pushed it, and the wood burned because God willed laws according to which wood burns when we light it, we can quickly become parsimonious enough to say that the weight fell because we pushed it and the fire burned because we lit it. And thereby we have significantly reduced the scope of our motivational terminology.

Or we could state the matter this way: "God" can be omitted from our calculations since it is an invariant term, present as the ground of *all* motives. And we can concentrate upon the search for terms that help us to detect concomitant variations, for it is by the discovery of these that we shall learn how to produce or avoid the specific contexts that serve as de-terminations.

A scientist might happen to believe in a personal God, and might even pray to God for the success of his experiments. In such an act of prayer, of course, he would be treating God as a *variable*. Yet, when his prayer was finished, and he began his experiments, he would now, *qua* scientist, treat "God" as an *invariant* term, as being at most but the over-all name for the ultimate ground of all experience and all experiments, and not a name for the particularities of local context with which the scientific study of conditions, or correlations, is concerned. For scientific experiment would eliminate the personal in every respect in which the concept of the personal means an instance that can be *appealed* to as a variable. That is, the scientist might appeal to God for the *success* of his experiment, but he would not pray to have his experiment prove that the laws of nature had changed since yesterday. Even if God continually changed his mind, the scientist *qua* scientist would aim to discover the *regularities* of each new dispensation. The Marquis de Laplace, whose formulation of the *Mécanique céleste* established the stability of the solar system just about the time of the French Revolution, is said to have told Napoleon that there was no need for a divine agency as an "hypothesis" in his system. The anecdote is at least true "in principle," for it is obvious that "God" would not figure as a term in his equations for the charting of the astronomical motions.

Considered from the strictly logical point of view, to locate the motive of an act by reference to the immediate conditions of the act rather than by reference to the act's motivation "in God," is much the same as to tell a man, who had asked for directions, that Hoboken is across the Hudson from New York City instead of telling him that Hoboken is "in the solar system." Thus, to omit a term from one's calculus of motives because, as an invariant, it can be ignored, is hardly an unreasonable thing to do. But in any case it is clearly a kind of parsimony that automatically reduces the circumference of one's terms. And it can lead to terms that keep getting narrower and narrower, until every term for a state of consciousness has been replaced by a term for the conditions contextual to such a state. The consideration of reduction in this light brings us nearer to such transformations as we described when discussing the antinomies of substance. For instance, because of the fact that an invariant term can readily be omitted from one's calculus, we can begin like the eighteenth-century *philosophes* by postulating certain "constant and universal principles of human nature." Then, precisely because they are everywhere the same, we can drop them from our discussion, and devote ourselves instead to a search for the ways in which these "unchanging principles of human nature" reacted under changing historical conditions. Thereupon, lo! we shall find that we have subtly crossed from one realm into another, in having reduced our universal man to terms of the endlessly shifting historical situations that determine his behavior.

Theological vocabularies of motivation are rarely "perfectionist." Their very stress upon ideals of absolute goodness requires them to be "realistic" in acknowledging the vast number of ways whereby men can fall short of this ideal. The more exacting they are in their concepts of virtue, the more profuse they must be in terms that designate varieties and gradations of vice. However, such vocabularies do provide rich opportunities for rhetorical misnomers that can provide sanctions for iniquity (or, reversing La Rochefoucauld's formula, they can offer ample opportunity to present vices in terms of virtues, as with Molière's religious hypocrite, Tartuffe).

As an attenuated secular variant of this same relation, we have idealizing vocabularies that serve as "eulogistic coverings" for "material interests" (according to Bentham's analysis in his *Tables of the Springs of Action*). And the various "debunking" techniques regularly aim at reductions along Benthamite lines, in disclosing the "material interests" that may lie concealed beneath moralistic euphemisms.

Ironically enough, however, it is reductions of this sort that may be most open to the charge of "perfectionism," albeit a kind of "perfectionism in reverse." For when one puts forward "tough-minded" vocabularies that reduce all motives to pejorative terms (as when a "thinker" appears who tells you that "all men are motivated by nothing but greed and fear," or by "lust for power," etc.), one implies that men can be "perfect exemplars" of some vice or weakness. But human agents cannot be perfect, not even with that inverted perfectionism they might have as total vessels of some weakness or as devotees of some vice, since the scene of their acts is too complex for such ideal simplicity of motivation. The same observation applies, in a lesser degree, with any reduction to simple motives (such as "utility," "comfort," "sex," "hunger," "fear," "wonder," "climate").

At a time when the liars, the stupid, and the greedy seem too greatly in control of a society's policies, philosophies of materialistic reduction may bring us much solace in reminding us that *the very nature of the materials* out of which a civilization is constructed, or in which it is grounded, will not permit such *perfection* of lies, stupidity, and greed to prevail as some men might cause to prevail if they could have their way. For obstructive policies are self-defeating, often ironically hastening the very reforms that these policies were designed to prevent. Sinister interests may have so strong a hold upon the channels of authority, that the people will try their utmost to do what is asked of them, even to the point of destitution, perplexity, and suicide. Yet, even though the people would obey, there is materialistic solace in the thought that the sheer brute materials of the world as it is will disobey. For there are properties of the material order that are grounded in a more basic constitution than any that men can write. These material properties will produce the effects that go with their nature, regardless of how thoroughly the apologists of an outdated order may be equipped to deny this nature, and to so miseducate and misinform that men are trained to draw the lines at the wrong places, interpreting both private and social situations in woefully inaccurate terms. Then it is not by the Courts, but by the constitution of the materials themselves, that false measures will be invalidated.

Complexity of a Simple Motive

In keeping with our distrust of both "perfectionist" and "invertedly perfectionist" motivations, we should feel justified in *never* taking at its face value any motivational reduction to a "simple." As soon as we encounter, verbally or thematically, a motivational simplicity, we must assume as a matter of course that it contains a diversity. Let us consider a "pure" or paradigmatic illustration. Let us set up a hypothetical model of a universe, thus:

The universe, let us say, is a structure of ideas, all interrelated by reason of their common grounding in the mind of God. Though these ideas are distinct, they are all aspects of "the same philosophy," hence they are capable of division into the many while being at the same time consubstantial with the One. In their distinctness, they may be conceived in terms of one another (which they are not), or in terms of their common ground (which they are not). And the attempt to consider them in terms of what they are (namely themselves) is troublesome because they are not wholes, but parts, so that their intrinsic nature depends upon their role in a larger organism. In their distinctness they appear to one another, let us say, as "external" to one another, hence as "objects." Yet we might postulate a simple "motive" common to them all, since they are all parts of one total context. This common motive would be, let us say, their desire to transcend the limits of their distinctness (and the limited points of view that go with it) and to realize that they are all integrally interrelated aspects of the same position. They would recognize that they are all parts of the same sentence, so that the same "meaning" pervades them all.

Yet insofar as the "ideas" were diverse, and perceived one another as different "objects" in different relationship to one another, though they possessed familial consubstantiality by reason of their descent from a common ancestor (or their place in a common context), there would be a very real sense in which they were motivated not identically but diversely. Different things could not be identically motivated, for the differences in their intrinsic nature would involve corresponding differences in relationship to the motivating ground; and this would amount to a difference in the activating properties of the ground itself.

A man cannot be in the same situation as a stone, or even in exactly the same situation as another man—a line of thought which Thomism uses to reconcile the concept of individual free will with the concept of God as universal motive, as per the form translated from Aquinas in Émile Bréhier's *La Philosophie du Moyen Âge,* p. 331: *"Dieu meut tous les êtres selon le mode de chacun."* As regards the imputation of some one *motive* generic to all mankind, the logic of the scene-act relationship would require us to show that all men are in identically the same *situation*. For instance, a reduction of motivation to one essential motive such as "love of power" would require one to show that there is nothing but a "power situation" observable in the human scene. The usual procedure, however, is to acknowledge the existence of other *motives,* but to treat them as in some way derivative, accidental, or unsubstantial, a tactic that would seem less plausible if the speculator were required to show that the corresponding *situations* are similarly derivative from the situation corresponding with the motive he has featured.

Furthermore, although for the purposes of illustration we assume that our hypothetical model of the universe is "correct," even with such "correct" knowledge about these ultimate matters there is room for many different versions of motivation. We have postulated that the "ideas" or parts are motivated by a desire to transcend the limits of their distinctness (and the limited points of view that go with it) and to realize that they are all integrally interrelated aspects of the same position. But there are many ambiguities in this statement, allowing for many different schools of motivational theory, even though there was general agreement on our hypothetical model. One school might stress the ultimate state of consubstantiality as the "significant" feature of the motivation. Another might stress the state of division. A third might situate the strategic factor of motivation in the epistemological miracle whereby the intrinsically related "ideas" appeared to one another as externally juxtaposed "objects." Another might locate the causal ancestry in the dialectical relation between the one and the many, or the quality and the quantity. Another might situate the motivation in some logic of developmental *stages* in the progress towards realization. Others might debate as to whether the desire for realization itself involved intellectual or intuitive methods, or both. Others might attribute different scope or quality to the circumference, or differ as to the hierarchy of circumferences, and so on.

Next let us assume some body of men living in a complex but relatively stable political and economic order. And let us suppose that the philosophy advocated by one of the schools became "implemented" as the authoritative vocabulary for rationalizing this culture's acts, institutions, relationships, and expectancies. Here a new kind of ambiguity would arise. For the vocabulary of the unofficial schools would implicitly or explicitly contain different programs of action with respect to political and economic issues than would the official vocabulary. (In brief, the grammatical resources would take on rhetorical implications.) And such doctrinal differences, when sharpened by their direct or indirect bearing upon the political and economic *agon,* would in time come to be felt not simply as differences, but as antitheses.

We have now carried our hypothetical model of the universe to the point where we confront such motivational ambiguities as are treated particularly in dialectical materialism. Dialectically, the context or ground of the *verbal in general* must be the *non-verbal in general*. But the ground of any particular verbal action must be a complex of verbal and non-verbal factors that can be defined in terms of varying circumference. Hence, more schools may arise, that haggle as to the particular circumference to be selected for particular instances of interpretation. For purely thematic reasons, the analysis may be confined to the verbal alone. But dialectical materialism (like psychologies of the unconscious) may often suggest convincing reasons why apparently thematic limitations are grounded in extrinsic motives.

But surely we have by now traced the matter far enough to suggest why simple vocabularies of motivation can but leave a complexity in the offing, for the diversity of the materials that compose the human situation necessarily involves a corresponding diversity of motives. In this sense, each man's motivation is unique, since his situation is unique, which is particularly obvious when you recall that his situation also reflects the unique sequence of his past. However, for all this uniqueness of the individual, there are motives and relations generic to all mankind—and these are intrinsic to human agents as a class, in that such motives and relations will be different in quality from the motives and relations of any other natures. Motives in this generic sense are titular; that is, they are "single" or "simple" in the way that chapter headings would be, or as is the case with our five terms. And the contents of the chapters which would fill them out by making explicit what the speaker finds implicit in them are "demonstrations" not in the sense of *proof,* but in the sense of *illustrations,* or tautological re-statements having corrective modifiers that indicate the directions which one must take for converting the simplicity back into a complexity.

So, when confronting naturalistic attempts to arrive at intrinsic motivations by reduction to "instincts" or "drives" or "urges" within the organism as a species, upon close analysis you will invariably find that all sorts of "complicating factors" (including external, environmentalist motivations) are referred to, usually without the full awareness of the theorist, who is so intent upon introducing all aspects of his subject *in the name of* his titular terms, that to him all incidental modifiers seem infused by the spirit of their godhead. And since these modifications of his thesis are like adjectives attached to a noun, you can with some justice adopt here a policy of either goodwill or illwill. For it is always a matter of casuistry to decide whether you will treat the modification of a principle as an "extension of" the principle or a "deviation from" it—and so you may decide to treat the modifiers as either "constitutional" or "unconstitutional" variants of the nouns.

Motivations dialectically paired (such as "egoism and altruism," "war and peace," "domination and submission," "experience and nature," "skepticism and animal faith") are to be similarly treated, as titular simplicities which in the writing may become thoroughly and adequately complex, as each of the terms is modified by extensions until sufficient richness is attained. Essentially, the tactics behind all such terms must be referred back to the matter of circumference—for if the substance of the terms is to descend "substantially" through all the line of modifications, it makes a strategic difference what the quality of this original constitutional act may be: whether it be supernatural, naturalistic, or referred to the broader or the narrower aspects of our "second nature." Many a term may be chosen or rejected as titular in the imputing of motives because of the political or programmatic quality which the term happens to possess at the given time and place in history.   That is, there may be Rhetorical motives behind the manipulations of the grammar.   Similarly, the grammar may be shaped to meet the needs of Symbolic, as were purely philosophic theories of power affected by personal problems of potency.

In sum: In any term we can posit a world, in the sense that we can treat the world *in terms of* it, seeing all as emanations, near or far, of its light.   Such reduction to a simplicity being technically reduction to a summarizing title or "God term," when we confront a simplicity we must forthwith ask ourselves what complexities are subsumed beneath it.   For a simplicity of motive being a perfection or purity of motive, the paradox of the absolute would admonish us that it cannot prevail in the "imperfect world" of everyday experience.   It can exist not actually, but only "in principle," "substantially."

The foregoing considerations suggest a sense in which any over-all motive (such as is contained in the formulae, *"ad majorem gloriam Dei"* or *"amor intellectualis Dei"* or *"homo homini lupus"*) could be omitted when imputing the motive of a particular case.   When you have a "Rome" term to which all roads lead, you thereby have as many different variants of the motive as there are roads.   Besides, if you *start* with your Rome term, the process of tracking down the roads that lead *to* it will in effect take you *from* it.   This variant of the substantial paradox (whereby the point of departure in the sense of the inaugurating spirit that will pervade whatever follows becomes the point of departure in the sense of the abandoned) was exemplified by Coleridge in reverse, when he made plans for a poem that was to be called "The Brook" and was to follow the course of a stream from its source to its mouth where, as a broad river, it empties into the sea.   In taking notes for the poem he became interested in writings about the sources of the Nile.   And in meditating upon these he was moved by the imagery not of a forward-flowing but of a backward-turning, or "introversion."   And when he had used the image of a stream in *Biographia Literaria,* he later persuaded himself that it must be flowing uphill.

This is, of course, but another way of coming upon our paradox of substance.   In specifically conceptual terms, the featuring of a single motive will quickly require one to grant that its simplicity operates but "in principle."   Where it is treated simply as an "ideal" the paradox enters at the point where the ideal turns back upon itself. Thus, were we to feature "freedom" or "tolerance," we should eventually have to ask ourselves, as with Mill, whether it would be in conformity with this ideal for us to "force freedom" upon those who resist it (as with "backward peoples" who, having a satisfactory non-monetary economy of their own, resisted the great gift of freedom that the White men brought them, in the form of money and the "free market" and the hut tax that destroyed the primitive economy by requiring the natives to work for money in the White plantations). Similarly the man who would judge by the ideal of "tolerance" alone must confront the embarrassments of trying to decide whether he must by the same token tolerate views that lead to the establishment of intolerance.

Often, however, the aspect of the substantial paradox, whereby the point of departure becomes translated into its betrayal, can lead to more felicitous results. Thus, two men may select totally different points of departure—yet both may, in the course of time, become concerned with modifications of their thought that add up to the abandonment of their starting points. And both may have come upon the *same* roads in the course of their journeys. Still other thinkers, setting out from other points, may come upon this same area of overlap. And so in time, we can build up a realm of reality shared in common, each of us having thus allowed his private point of view to be replaced by a public point of view (which is to say, in effect, that each will have "died" to his private self and been "born into" a public self). Yet whatever may be the degree of alienation that accompanies this development, we can expect to find that the point of departure, in the sense of inaugurating and pervasive spirit, still figures. For the area that all men share in common will be shared by each in accordance with his nature (the nature he expressed in his point of departure), so that the common motive can be again analyzed into different individual motives. (We here have a terministic translation of the Thomist doctrine that God moves all things, but each thing in accordance with its nature.)

Operationalist reductions would abandon over-all points of departure (titles, or "god-terms") so thoroughly as not even to begin with them. Suppose, for instance, that certain of the "ideas" in our hypothetical model of the universe ("ideas" that had the appearance of "objects") were embodied in the materials and operations necessary to the running of an elevator. You might radically change the universal motivation you attributed to these "ideas" in their relation to a common ground, yet you would not have to change your instructions for the running of the car. The instruction reads, let us say: "To move the car forward, place lever 1 in position A." And as related to different titular motivations, we could imagine the instruction figuring thus: "The significant motivating feature of the universe is the ultimate state of consubstantiality among the ideas; 'therefore,' to move the car forward, place lever 1 in position A." Or: "The significant motivating feature of the universe is the state of division among the ideas; 'therefore,' to move the car forward, place lever 1 at position A." Or: "The significant motivating feature . . . etc. is the epistemological miracle whereby the intrinsically related 'ideas' appear to one another as externally juxtaposed 'objects'; 'therefore,' to move the car . . . etc."

Nor is this simply a matter of the shift from a metaphysical to a physical circumference. You may imagine a purely physicalist frame, for instance, such as two different over-all theories as to the nature of electricity, yet along with either of them we could have the instruction: "To light the light, give the knob one half-turn to the right." We are here likewise confronting the Occamite law of parsimony. For even in secular vocabularies one finds statements that are too general for the purpose at hand. Paraphrasing Galileo, we could say that they are "god-terms" which explain too little by explaining too much.

We have spoken previously of respects in which an appositional relationship between the general and the particular, or the collective and the individual, or the "one" and the "many," can become an oppositional relationship. Or, otherwise put, the synecdochic relationship whereby a part can be taken as consistent with the whole (the principle of *omnia ubique* according to which the microcosm is a representative replica of the microcosm) is no longer felt to apply; and instead we encounter the divisive relationship, the genitive transformation of something which is "a part of" a larger context into something which is "apart from" this context. We can see the same conversion in the relation between the terms "genus" and "species." For in the consistent relationship, "species" is a subdivision of "genus"; yet one can see the concepts becoming antithetical when a speaker says: "Don't be so general, be specific."

Applying the same mode of thought to the analysis of personal motives, we often find that the meanings of titular words cannot be accepted at their face value. For every atheist who explicitly denies God, there are a thousand atheists who are church-goers in good standing. The man who will tell you that God is "all-powerful" can also be the man who gives this statement body in not one single sincere act or vigorous image or matured thought throughout his life. Indeed, in the middle ages, when men laid much more stress upon the power of God than we do in an age of technology, philosophers were much given to drawing the line between the things that God could and could not do. Close analysis of contexts would often reveal specific meanings totally at odds with one's catechistic avowals. Such considerations we should consider the equivalent of "operationalist" meanings, when applied to the sphere of personality. We should note, however, that a much wider circumference is involved in the concept of "operations" here. Two men, for instance, may be standing side by side performing the same "operations," so far as the carrying out of instructions is concerned. Yet they are performing radically different acts if one is working for charitable purposes and the other to the ends of vengeance. They are performing the same *motions* but different *acts*.

We have discussed elsewhere (notably in *The Philosophy of Literary Form*) the ways in which such motivational "clusters" can be found in the structure of literary works. They should also be present as equations intrinsic to the structure of any act. That is, as motives behind the structure of either an esthetic or a practical act, there must be an implicit set of evaluations: assumptions as to what kind of act equals heroism, what kind equals villainy, what kind contains the likelihood of reward, of punishment, etc. Such matters are to be treated at some length in the aspect of our study we call the Symbolic.

Money as Substitute for God

Reverting to our hypothetical model of the universe: whatever our philosophy of God and Nature may be, there is the temporal world of a "second nature" that calls for a reduction of circumference to the limits imposed by the "materials." We might still cling to our hypothetical somewhat Berkeleyan model of the world as a structure of "ideas" joined by their common grounding in the mind of God. Yet, within this *total* ideality, we should have to distinguish between the kind of "ideas" that seem like ideas to us and the kind that seem like "objects." And to define situations in terms of such objects would be in effect a reduction to a materialist circumference, as regards "operational" matters, though we still defined the "ultimate reality" as "ideal."

There is one notable difference between the materials of nature and the materials of our "second nature." The materials of our second nature are largely man-made. These accumulations of properties and methods have culminated in the complex of technological inventions that mothered their own peculiar kinds of necessity. And though men have been undergoing fantastic hardships in order to develop and retain these "conveniences," the fact remains that their "materiality" is at the same time an "ideality," in that every invention has been the emanation of some human mind. Nature is "given," but the environments to which we adapt ourselves as to a second nature are the creations of agents. In adapting ourselves to machinery, we are adapting ourselves to an aspect of ourselves. This would be reduction to a higher or a lower circumference, as you prefer, but in either case a reduction.

Since technology, as the primary characterizing feature of our second nature today, is "substantially" human, in accordance with the paradox of substance it can become quite "inhuman." For while the accumulations of the industrial plant are "in principle" the externalization or alienation of intrinsically human virtues, there are many unintended by-products. Many people would vote for cities—but only a few real estate men would vote *explicitly* for slums. (We are not talking of the millions who regularly vote *implicitly* for slums.) The carrying out of any human purpose can be expected to reveal the kind of alienation that accompanies any act of generating or creating, which is an embodiment from within the self, and as such is a representative part that can, by the fact of division, become an antithetical part.

For this externalization of internal aptitudes is different in its state of *being* than in its *becoming*. It is in its *becoming* that technology most fully represents the human agent, since his inventing of it is an *act,* and a rational act. In its state of *being* (or perhaps we might better say its state of *having become*) it can change from a *purpose* into a *problem*. And surely much of the anguish in the modern world derives from the paradoxical fact that machinery, as the embodiment of rationality in its most rational moments, has in effect translated rationality itself from the realm of ideal aims to the realm of material requirements. Few ironies are richer in complexities than the irony of man's servitude to his mechanical servants. For though it is nothing less than an act of genius to *invent* a machine, it is the nagging drudgery of mere motion to *feed* one.

Occupational *diversification* equals by definition occupational *classification,* a splitting of mankind into *classes* that are separated from one another with varying degrees of distinctness and fixity at different periods in history, and with varying degrees of felicity or infelicity in their relationships to one another. And occupational diversity signifies a corresponding motivational diversity. The reader may ask: "Do you mean that, because of occupational classification, all plumbers have a set of social values distinct from those of carpenters, clerks, farmers, teachers, etc., all of which are equally demarcated from one another?"

Perhaps in the early days of the guilds something of this sort could have been noted, though the sense of a common membership in a single Church with a single body of tradition would presumably have supplied the common ground of mediation among the diversity of group motives, with heresy, sect, and schism as evidence of a divisive motivation. But in recent history, with the great occupational fluidity that has accompanied industrial innovation, it would be absurd to look for the most significant aspect of motivation in occupational diversity *per se.* For such a great diversity and fluidity of occupational classifications made it impossible to develop such distinctness of classes as we find, for instance, in the caste system of India. In fact, the present-day jurisdictional disputes among the unions in the United States reveals that the constantly changing methods of technology are continually making new cuts on the bias across the traditional classifications, so that it would be hard for any one to say for a certainty whether a certain new material should be applied by masons, plasterers, or carpenters, and so with a great number of other new products and processes.

Confronting such a state of affairs, we should seek for the significant over-all motivating factor in the nature of the medium by which this great occupational diversity and fluidity, with its almost infinite variety of motives, is "reduced" to a common rationale. And this reduction is made, of course, in terms of money. Monetary symbolism is the "simple," the "god-term," in terms of which all this great complexity attains a unity transcending distinctions of climate, class, nation, cultural traditions, etc.

But reduction to money, we have said, is reduction to a simple, thus to a purity or absolute—and we have said that things in their "pure" state are something else. Hence, in reducing the subject of motivation to a "pure" state, we must warn ourselves against the risk of falling into our own variant of "inverted perfectionism." No human being could be a "perfect" capitalist, since no human being could be motivated by the rationale of money alone.

We may note, however, that the monetary reference is the over-all *public* motive for mediating among the endless diversity of occupational and private (or "preoccupational") motives. We thus encounter from another angle our notion that the monetary motive can be a "technical substitute for God," in that "God" represented the unitary substance in which all human diversity of motives was grounded. And we thus see why it was "grammatically correct" that the religious should fear the problem of money.

Usually this notion of money as the "root of all evil" is taken in a very superficial sense, to indicate the power of money as a "temptation" to dishonest dealings. On the contrary, it is more likely that the diabolic role of money as "tempter" has helped to call forth a whole new gamut of scrupulosities here; and for every ethical defeat in the way of theft or "graft," etc. there must be countless moral victories on the part of men who resisted such temptation. No, any "diabolical" effect in this sense would be a "moralizing" effect, the devil being the dialectical counterpart of God.

Money, as active temptation, could be expected to perform the dialectical role of all such counter-agents in provoking the agent to active combat, hence increasing the realm of scrupulosity (hence leading us from the simplicity of *innocence* into the complexity of *virtue*). And it could probably be said, in this respect, that pecuniary civilizations show a greater range of scruples or "tender-mindedness" (in the way of idealistic, humanitarian attitudes) than is usually the case with realistic "tough-mindedness" of more primitive cultures. Such humanitarian scruples are made possible also by reason of the fact that money, in promoting great *indirectness* or *vicariousness,* has made it possible for great numbers of people to avoid many of the harsher realities entirely. For one need simply pay to have "insensitive" things done by others instead of doing them oneself. Nor is this expedient possible only to the rich. Think how many people eat meat, and how few work in slaughter-houses.

No, where religion is tested by "ethical sensitiveness" and "humanitarianism," the monetary motive has probably added to it rather than subtracted from it. Rather, money endangers religion in that money can serve as universal symbol, the unitary ground of all action. And it endangers religion not in the dramatic, agonistic way of a "tempter," but in its quiet, rational way as a *substitute* that performs its mediatory role more "efficiently," more "parsimoniously," with less "waste motion" as regards the religious or ritualistic conception of "works." And since money thus substitutes technically or scientifically for the godhead as a *public* principle, do we not see the results of this substitution in the fact that Protestantism, arising in response to the growth of occupational diversity, trade, and the necessarily increased dependence upon the use of money, stressed on the contrary the function of the godhead as a *private* principle? For where monetary symbolism does the work of religious symbolism (as a lowest common denominator for mediating among many motives could more efficiently replace a "highest common denomination") the locus of this titular role would have to be placed elsewhere than at the point of public mediation. This was found in the doctrine of communication directly with God.

The humanistic emphasis that arose with the secularization of middle class culture was new not in the sense that humanism itself was new but in the sense that humanism began to undergo a strategic transformation. We might describe this as a change from a "consistent" humanism to a "compensatory" humanism. "Consistent" humanism had placed human personality as the lineal descendant of a "principle of personality" felt to be present in the universal ground. But with the increasingly secular emphasis, the motivations of the universal ground were viewed not in terms of a superhuman personality but in terms of naturalistic impersonality. And human personality was affirmed in dialectical opposition to the quality of the ground. For when the scene was narrowed to a secular circumference, human personality could no longer be "logically *de*duced" familially from the divine personality. But it might be vigorously affirmed simply as an "empirical fact," as part of "the given," in contrast with any new calculus in which the personality was "logically *re*duced" to atomistic, naturalistic terms of impersonality.

At this point a calculus of "therefore" was supplanted by a calculus of "nevertheless." By a change in the tactics of grammar, men ceased to think, "God's personality, *therefore* human personality" and began to think, "nature's impersonality, *nevertheless* human personality," the first pair being related consistently, the second oppositionally. And the experience of an *impersonal* motive was empirically intensified in proportion as the rationale of the monetary motive gained greater authority and organization within the realm of men's "second nature." We may discern these transformations behind the shift from "consistent" religious humanism to the "compensatory" secular humanitarianism of science and money.

The Nature of Monetary "Reality"

Where are we now? We must consider the possible charge that in our discussion of the monetary motive we have ourselves been guilty of "inverted perfectionism." For if money is viewed as a *medium* of exchange, then we have reduced our field of discussion to terms of *agency,* from which we would in turn derive all else as though it were pervaded by the same ancestral spirit.

In the first place, as we noted previously, money is *not a mere agency,* in our civilization, but is a *rationalizing ground* of action. In contrast with the psychosis that would accompany a barter economy, for instance, our monetary economy must be accompanied by a distinctive "capitalist" psychosis. For any important motivational emphasis must have its corresponding emphasis in the thinking of those whose efforts and expectancies are formed with reference to its motivating powers, resources and risks. And we could speak of a "capitalist psychosis" not in the sense of one who thinks that by eliminating capitalism one would eliminate psychosis, but in the sense of one who thinks that, given any pronounced social structure, there will be a "psychosis" corresponding to it. That is, there will be a particular recipe of overstressings and understressings peculiar to the given institutional structure. And the tendency of the culture will be to see everything in terms of this particular recipe of emphases, as the typical apologist of ideal *laissez-faire* capitalism would think "freedom" itself lost if we lost "free market freedom," since he conceived of freedom in these terms.

In this sense, we may legitimately isolate the monetary motive as an essence and may treat many apparently disrelated manifestations as its accidents.   It would not be a primary motive in the sense that it "gave rise to" ethics, philosophy, art, etc. But we could feature it in the sense that its effects could be seen as a significant influence in the ethics, philosophy, art that flourished at a time when it had to be so significantly taken into account (at a time when it rationalized the adoption of new methods, for instance, in contrast with times when the norms of tradition were taken as the major rationalizing test of "right" ways).

In its nature as a "purity" or "simplicity," however, it cannot prevail in this imperfect world.   Hence we must recognize that, even in the heyday of capitalism, the monetary motive is but one member of the "power" family. And the possible transformations here are many. As early as the Calvinistic sanctioning of "usury," it was apparent that a primary aspect of our monetary economy was its stress upon *credit*— and the receiving of credit is *indebtedness*. Thus, in addition to its strongly *futuristic* nature as investment, in its connotations of *owing* it provides a technical normalization of "guilt" or "sin" by converting a religious psychology of "retribution" or "penance" into a commercialist psychology of "ambition."   The fact that the symbolism of debt itself can be manipulated by the resources of accountancy adds further notable convertibilities.   For instance the nature of nationalist integers, formed of abstract relations in keeping with the abstractions of money, makes it readily possible for men to carry out projects that privately enrich themselves while publicly adding to the national debt, as when a "national's" interests abroad are protected by government agencies supported by a tax upon the people as a whole.   We here have simultaneously an apposition of individual and collectivity on the "spiritual" level and an opposition on the practical level.   When "we" get air bases, who is this "we"?

The relations of any one individual to the public medium can be understood only by examining the "clusters" or "equations" in his particular "psychic economy."   In the economy of one man, monetary power may be *compensatory* to some other kind of power (physical, sexual, moral, stylistic, intellectual, etc.).   That is, he may seek by the vicarage of money to "add a cubit to his stature."   But in the economy of another man, monetary power may be *consistent* with one or all of these.   A sense of moral guilt, for instance, or a sense of social inferiority, may "compensatorily" incite one man to seek a fortune, while the same motives may "consistently" prevent another from demanding what his services are worth. Paradoxically, an "anti-social" attitude may sometimes reach expression through the prompt paying of debts, since by the payment one's bonds or obligations would be severed. And the shady promoter may be motivated by a genuine sense of "sociality," to which men instinctively respond in letting themselves be taken in by his "cordiality," a "sociality" and "cordiality" which are not "in principle" dishonest at all, but which he finally "reduces" to the simplified idiom by leaving debts unpaid (that is, by keeping bonds of attachment between him and his creditors).

A wider circle, culminating in thoughts of life and death, may be matched by a narrower circle, culminating in thoughts of solvency and poverty. The two may be so related that each can stand for the other. And so one can seek more and more money, as a symbolic way of attaining immortality. That is, one may thus vicariously seek "more and more life," in the attempt to attain a higher *quality* in terms of a higher *quantity,* for it is easy to think of a "more intense" life in quantitative terms. Conversely, the religious injunction to "live a dying life" can be followed, in an unconscious secular translation, by systematically keeping oneself poor (thus "going to meet" death).

Obviously we could not chart here the many private roads that lead up to, or away from, the monetary Rome. And besides, this phase of our subject more properly falls under the heading of Symbolic. We might in passing, however, refer the reader to André Gide's novel, *The Counterfeiters.* Gide is very discriminating in his ironic appreciation of the ways in which the patterns of religion survive in ingenious secular distortions. He is profoundly, if perversely, a Protestant. In *The Counterfeiters,* the relationships among the important characters are symbolized in monetary terms, as with the lad of homosexual bent, who also ambiguously loves a girl, and as a memento gives her a coin that is counterfeit.

We have said that the rationale of money had much to do with the innovation, specialization, diversification, partialization, and classification of economic motives. For the great changes that the rationale of technological processes and products effected in our "second nature" could not have taken place without a universal idiom to the terms of which all the diversity could be reduced. But clearly we could with as much justice state this ratio the other way round, saying that monetary symbolism could not assume so dominant a role in the rationalization of motives without technological diversity as a ground. Various kinds of occupational diversity (or classification of status) in the past have given us the lineaments of capitalism—but only when symbiotic with applied science could it produce the peculiar kind of motivation that we know as modern capitalism.

This symbiosis of money and technology has made a "double genesis" possible in the imputing of motives, as the thinker may attribute to "capitalism" the aspects of our civilization he dislikes and to "technology" the aspects in which he places his hopes, or *vice versa*. Since both money and technology are objective "powers" existing in history, we might properly expect them to manifest the ambivalence of such powers. Either, that is, should be capable of acting favorably or unfavorably, favorably if properly "discounted," unfavorably when its workings are protected from criticism, as the money motive is piously protected in some quarters by being made synonymous with the national godhead of patriotism, and as the technological motive is protected in other quarters where it is granted immunity in the name of "science" as an absolute good. Also, our very aversion to "talking about money matters" has done much to conceal our understanding of it as a motive, though it is worth noting that this aversion in itself indicates the "godhead" of money, since in formal religions men fear to behold or name lightly their God, or motivational center.

There is an ironic possibility that orthodox capitalism, Fascism, and Communism may all three be variants of the "monetary psychosis" insofar as all three are grounded in the occupational diversity (classification) of technology. In any case Russian Communism was the most "idealistic" of the three, since technology was *willed* there in accordance with Marxist values, rather than being the material ground out of which such values arise. Voluntaristic philosophies would find nothing unusual in this sequence, but it would seem to be a paradox from the standpoint of dialectical materialism.

Though Communist industrialism relies upon financial accountancy, neither Communism nor Fascism will accord to money the primary order of "reality" it possessed for, say, the financial priesthood of capitalism. Shortly after a disastrous hurricane had swept through several northern states, destroying houses, uprooting forests, undermining railroads, and doing much other damage, all "to the value of hundreds of millions of dollars," we recall an article on the stock market page of a New York City newspaper which remarked that, great as the "losses" had been, they were much less than the shrinkage of stock values in a recent market "recession." The whole point of this article was the author's implicit assumption that the two cases were essentially analogous. Note that in the case of the *symbolic* losses of stock market value, the aggregate material wealth of the world had not been diminished one particle. The railroad that had shrunk so in value was exactly the same railroad, with the same equipment, the same trained personnel, the same physical ability to perform useful services. But in the case of the hurricane, much real material wealth had been destroyed. Yet so "instinctively" did this writer think "in terms of" the monetary idiom of reduction, so thoroughly had it become a "second nature" with him, that he made no differentiation whatsoever between these two kinds of "losses." "Spirituality" of this particular sort is lessened under either the explicitly materialist coördinates of Marxism or the realism implicit in the national barter projects of Fascism. Also, the Fascists are able to have a less pious attitude towards monetary symbolism because of their cynical attitude towards the manipulation of symbols in general. And we should note how German Fascism, by centering its attention about industrial empire, was fast approaching a position where it could have destroyed the empire of Britain, which was coming more and more to think of rule in the pure financial terms of The City.

Love, Knowledge, and Authority

It is not a part of our contract here to make final decisions on these many matters. It is enough for the purposes of our Grammar that, when on the subject of reduction in general, we consider the important respects in which both monetary and technological circumferences are themselves reductions and have provoked reductions.

All terminological reductions, when they gain sufficient adherence to form a cultural trend, should probably be ascribed to the stimulating effect which some order of power exerted upon the human imagination during the eras when men first came to recognize and appreciate and develop the resources of this particular power.

There is a sense in which powers are everywhere. According to

Aristotle, Thales believed that "all things are full of Gods." For our purposes this could be interpreted as a recognition of the fact that in everything there is a power, or motive, of some sort. That is, we would interpret it in a broader sense than the notion that "soul is inter-mingled in the whole universe," though Aristotle in his *De Anima* says this is what Thales "probably" meant.

The cult of Prometheus and the rites of the Vestal Virgins must stem from a time when fire was the power, the "new power," that had caught men's fancy, so that they were prompted to construct a whole system of terms about fire as a motive. At this time presumably there came to the fore the vocabularies that treat of motives in terms of fire.

When a weapon or implement or art was said to possess a divine or heroic origin, we would consider this simply as a way of characterizing it as a power or motive in keeping with the terms of definition then available. Thinkers at first would not presumably make up new words for such purposes; they would not proceed like some modern chemist naming some new drug that he had synthesized, or like a manufacturer giving his product a trade name. But they would seek to adapt the tribal terms already in use, perhaps not even being sure themselves to what extent they were giving the term new meanings.

And particularly in view of what we have already noted about the ambiguities whereby concepts of temporal priority and concepts of logi-cal priority can change places, we should propose to translate the state-ment that a certain implement *came from* a power into a statement that this implement was *essentially* a power. That is, we should translate the notion of origin from terms of time to terms of timelessness (terms that consider it *sub specie aeternitatis*). And we should be all the more ready to do this because of the observations we have made about the word "genus," the etymology of which so clearly suggests that even purely logical classes were originally conceived in purely tribal terms, as derivative from ancestral principles. In sum, a statement that an art was descended from a God would be interpretable as a statement that the art was in its nature a power, or motive.

And we should infer that the original conception of the powers or motives in things is not exactly animistic. The evidences of animism which nineteenth-century anthropologists found so profusely among primitive tribes are, to our way of thinking, mainly indications of how thoroughly most of such anthropologists were imbued with the terms typical of nineteenth-century idealist philosophy, so that they *saw* things in these terms.

We should expect, rather, that the basic perception of motives is a perception of things not as possessing the souls and personalities of *agents,* but as being essentially *active.* That is, they were not felt to be *people;* they were felt to be *actions.* If one walks determinedly against a bitter wind, for instance, he feels very definitely that this wind is an *act* against which he is acting, but he does not necessarily feel that the wind is a *person.* The step from thinking of things as powers, or potential actions, to thinking of them as imbued with souls, would seem to come much later, and very probably not until a considerable degree of personal property had arisen, and men could differentiate individual identity from the tribal identity in terms of such "personalty."

Such thoughts would suggest a slight reinterpretation of the "hylozoism" that characterized the Greek "nature philosophers" of the pre-Socratic era. Would it not be more direct to say that these early thinkers saw in nature a *principle of action* rather than "souls" such as post-Christian anthropologists have in mind when they refer to animism. True, the Ionian *"physikoi"* lived in cities stimulated by the commercial enterprise of the Persian Empire; but their way of living was "primitive" as compared with the unnatural ways of modern industrialism. And much later the realism of Plato, in *The Sophist,* brings out the same *activist* rather than *animist* emphasis in the definition of Being as "that which has the power to act or be acted upon."

We can but get glimpses around the corner of the "capitalist psychosis," with its strongly futuristic emphasis, an emphasis so pronounced that an anthropologist (and a very good one) who is himself in the insurance business has made an analysis (and a very good one) of a primitive American Indian language in futuristic terms, stressing the *preparatory* ingredient in the tribal rituals rather than their nature as a mode of *action now.* Ironically, it was our monetary individualism that both invented "animism" and destroyed it (in first attributing to savages the belief in *spirits* rather than the belief in *powers,* and then proving the absurdity of the belief, since a monetary attitude towards manufactured objects transcends their fetishistic nature as aspects of the person).

What we are trying to bring out is this: we do not think merely of a step from the animistic to a conception of an inanimate nature. Instead, we would postulate first a sense of things as *powers* or *acts* (acts potentially or actually). The next stage would be a differentiation into agent and act, so that natural phenomena could come to be divided into two aspects, an invisible soul or agent and a visible material process. Then, when this stage is reached, the world is ready for an enlightened law of parsimony, as men discover that the terms for the agent behind the natural phenomenon duplicate the terms for the natural phenomenon itself. Whereupon the terms for *agent* can be dropped, and the motivational circumference can be reduced simply to terms for the *motion*. For though the original ambiguity could be felt as an act, once agent has been explicitly distinguished and then explicitly eliminated, the orbit of action is thereby reduced to terms of sheer motion. The principle of parsimony, by the way, can be quite clearly discerned in the ancient Greek's ways of saying "It is raining," "It is snowing," etc. Originally he said "the God is raining," or "Zeus is raining." Later he omitted the name for the divine agent (quite as though he had been admonished by Occam not to multiply entities beyond necessity), saying simply, "rains."

Henry Adams' pairing of Virgin and Dynamo clearly suggests two contrasting orders of power. We refer not so much to the contrast between "thirteenth-century unity" and "nineteenth-century multiplicity." Rather, we consider the important matter to be the contrast beween the natural powers and the industrial powers. Ironically, the "supernatural" vocabularies flourished when men's imagination was most powerfully stimulated by the powers of *nature,* while the philosophies that would today label themselves "naturalistic" favor terms taken from the wholly artificial and *unnatural* realm of technological invention and laboratory method.

Is not Adams' pair basic in the sense that it contrasts an order of powers centered about biological generation and an order of powers centered about technological motion? This is, we grant, not quite the way Adams himself draws the line. Rather, his *Education* seems to be a rebirth ritual whereby the author would finally bring himself to see himself in terms of impersonal "force," while renouncing the strongly *familial* sense of his identity (the "eighteenth-century" self) with which his life began. His book traces a kind of attenuated self-immolation. For few people in America could begin life with so pronounced a label of tribal identity as could a member of the Adams family. Yet he describes his quest as the search for a father. And though he was so clearly placed in an heraldic line, he was also the end of a line, for he died childless, the kind of power in terms of which he finally proclaimed his identity being not the powers of generation but the powers of the machine.

Yet, though we would perhaps place a somewhat different interpretation upon Henry Adams' quest than he would have placed upon it himself, is our interpretation of his Virgin and Dynamo pair much different from his? Except for the poignant paragraphs on the death of his sister, when "for the first time in his life, Mont Blanc for a moment looked to him what it was—a chaos of anarchic and purposeless forces," it is not in "nature" that he finds the new powers with whose terms he would identify himself. Rather, it is at the successive world's fairs and international expositions that Adams gets his "education." Of the Chicago Exposition in 1893, we are told that "education ran riot" there. And it is the machinery that impresses him. As he expresses it, "The historical mind can think only in terms of historical processes, and probably this was the first time since historians existed, that any of them had sat down helpless before a mechanical sequence."

And it is in the "great gallery of machines" at the Paris Exposition of 1900, that he found "his historical neck broken by the sudden irruption of forces totally new," forces which he compares and contrasts with the forces of the Christian Cross, on the grounds that both kinds, in their way, have been revolutionary. And while remarking that the historian "cared nothing for the sex of the dynamo until he could measure its energy," he observes:

> Every one, even among Puritans, knew that neither Diana of the Ephesians nor any of the Oriental goddesses was worshipped for her beauty. She was goddess because of her force; she was the animated dynamo; she was reproduction—the greatest and most mysterious of all energies; all she needed was to be fecund.

And so we may say that the Dynamo stands for the man-made forces of *production,* and the Virgin for the natural forces of *reproduction.* The forces of reproduction proceed by growth and decay, the forces of production proceed by the acceleration and deceleration of motion. Growth is by the assimilation of food, motion is by the consumption of fuel.

As regards human motives, the natural, biological, tribal order of food and growth would seem to culminate in the emotion of love. It is the realm of appetites generally, the whole range of desires encompassed by the psychoanalyst's concept of eros or libido. It is the realm of the nursing child, the nursing mother, the cat purring affectionately at the promise of food, sexual coupling, parental affection, feasts, harvests, trodden grapes, spilled cornucopias, the realm of *ubertas*. It is the realm of seasons and of climates. It is the realm that is expressed in the figures of Madonna and Child. But it is also to be seen, say, in the elder Breughel's engraving of Summer, with its avidity of plenty, the many acts and postures of food gathering, the seated peasant guzzling from a jug, his legs sprawling, his codpiece prominent, the woman bearing a laden basket on her head, her face obliterated, as though she were so harvest-minded that her very head had been transformed into the substance of the bounty she was carrying—a fullness everywhere: of generation the generosity.

The technological order of power would seem to represent all that attains its culmination in the faculty of intellection. In its noblest aspects, it is wisdom, reason: *veritas*. But as now reduced to a more restricted realm, it is the order of powers we encounter in the laboratory, the factory, the clinic, the draughting room, the broadcasting studio, the bank vault, the telephone exchange, the department store, the railway terminal, the files and archives. In its nobler aspects, it gives the realm of appetite its true maturity and control.

Yet would not our pair profit much by conversion into a triad? For surely there has been at least one other great order of power that has greatly stimulated men's terminologies of motives: the power of authority, *auctoritas*. Or, seen from another point of view, we could situate this motivational factor in the experience of *slavery*. Though we should want to put a different interpretation than Nietzsche upon the Nietzschean insights, surely we should agree that he is correct in stressing the part played by the motive of servitude in the shaping of the Christian ethic.

Indeed, might we not rightfully say that a most significant feature of the Christian terminology, developed probably from Stoicism, is its way of so merging concepts of servitude and freedom, of obligation and privilege, of obedience and rule, that the free man can be defined in terms of service, and the servant in terms of liberty?

Hence, lying across the order of production and of reproduction (intellection and love), and overlapping upon both, there is the order of authority, stimulating the imagination to think of motives in terms of law, tyranny, freedom, duty, inducement, compulsion, petition, obedience, submission and revolt. And as a term for an order that draws heavily upon the other two orders and is in turn drawn upon by it, "authority" designates it quite well, since the concept of the *auctor* includes both senses of originator, either as progenitor, father, ancestor, and the like, or as inventor, creator, maker, and the like, while out of both senses grows the third sense, the sense of the *auctor* as head or leader, from which we derive our usual meaning for "authority." It is the principle of group cohesion, and of cohesion among groups pitted against the group.

These overlapping areas covered by the terms can unquestionably become areas of conflict. Thus, whereas the contemporary scientific stress upon scenic terminologies of reduced circumference is an embodiment of *veritas,* the resultant cult of sheer correlation, in adding up to a dissolution of act, substance, person, becomes ultimately the antithesis of "love." The powers of fertility are replaced by the technological powers, which are devoid of natural appetite and sexual potency; they have in fact taught us all we know of sterilization.

There is perhaps no strictly logical reason why such an opposition should be felt. In strict logic, perhaps, the "love" and "knowledge" are simply in different planes, rather than being in opposition to each other. But as regards matters of Symbolic, since words have also incantatory effects, inviting men to make themselves over in the image of their imagery, the purely logical implications of reductionist terminologies take on new attributes, when translated into their equivalents in the realm of the imagination. Thus today the conception of man's consciousness as the battleground of supernatural struggles has been typically reduced to the conception of the brain as a battleground of the great motivational struggle between Microbes and Machines (with technology as a pattern for the macroscopic view, and protoplasm for the microscopic). And the cult of authority thus too often becomes an almost hysterical compensation for actual and impending impoverishments.

Indeed, looking back now upon the early theological controversy over the relation between faith and knowledge (*pistis* and *gnosis*), do we not, in the light of our present position in the long historical development from theology to science, begin to see how the Gnostics had triumphed, by implication, in the very setting of the issue? For both "faith" and "knowledge" are kinds of *knowledge;* both are thus strongly scenic in their emphasis. It requires no great gifts of prophecy now to see that the sloganizing of the controversy in terms of a relation between *pistis* and *gnosis* was implicitly a weighting on the side of *gnosis.* We grant, however, that this "prophecy" would be too tenuous if we could not refer to the course of events themselves as our corroboration.

Likewise when considering *justice,* we can readily see a conflict among the terms. Justice is properly under the sign of *veritas,* yet is forever in danger of being lost to a hysterically misused *auctoritas,* as with appeals to nation, class, and race. Or we could say that a truly personal principle is needed in justice, as with the conditions of family authority; but the vast texture of impersonal relations typical of our change from tribal living to the abstractions of the modern state make such conditions impossible. There is little reason to believe that justice is happily apportioned even in primitive clans, though we do find, as in the *Iliad,* much evidence of a pre-political equality, or sense of *personal* equality, which was familial in its origins, with authority vested in the ways of the clan as a whole, and "obeyed" by even the kings. "Justice" under conditions of economic inequality necessarily gravitates between an "ideal" and a rhetorical compensation, since it is not "substantiated" or grounded in the nature of the scene. The *Aeneid* ushers in the period of the Roman emperors by piously thinking of Roman motives in paternal terms *after* the business culture of the expanding Republic had quite obliterated the tribal culture, though the retention of the tribal terminology, throughout the days of the Republic, is clear enough in the name, Conscript Fathers, for the Roman Senate.

Love, Knowledge, Authority: three basic ideals, variously embodied in structures of power, and all liable to such transformations as make of them a mockery. As translated into the terms of social organization, they are necessarily somewhat at odds. But in moments of exaltation, ideally, we may think of them as a trinity, standing to one another in a relation of mutual reënforcement.

Part Two

THE PHILOSOPHIC SCHOOLS

I

SCENE

The Featuring of the Terms

OUR program in this section is to consider seven primary philosophic languages in terms of the pentad, used as a generating principle that should enable us to "anticipate" these different idioms. In treating the various schools as languages, we may define their substantial relationship to one another by deriving them from a common terminological ancestor. This ancestor would be a kind of *lingua Adamica,* an Edenic "pre-language," in which the seeds of all philosophic languages would be implicit, as in the *panspermia* (or confusion of all future possibilities) that, according to some mystics, prevailed at the beginnings of the world.

In our introduction we noted that the areas covered by our five terms overlap upon one another. And because of this overlap, it is possible for a thinker to make his way continuously from any one of them to any of the others. Or he may use terms in which several of the areas are merged. For any of the terms may be seen in terms of any of the others. And we may even treat all five in terms of one, by "reducing" them all to the one or (what amounts to the same thing) "deducing" them all from the one as their common terminal ancestor. This relation we could express in temporal terms by saying that the term selected as ancestor "came first"; and in timeless or logical terms we could say that the term selected is the "essential," "basic," "logically prior" or "ultimate" term, or the "term of terms," etc.

Dramatistically, the different philosophic schools are to be distinguished by the fact that each school features a different one of the five terms, in developing a vocabulary designed to allow this one term full expression (as regards its resources and its temptations) with the other terms being comparatively slighted or being placed in the perspective of the featured term. Think, for instance, of a philosophy that had been established "in the sign of the agent." It must develop coördinates particularly suited to treat of substance and motive in "subjective," or "psychological" terms (since such terms deal most directly with the attributes of agents). Then think of that stage where the philosopher, proud in the full possession of his coördinates for featuring the realm of the *agent,* turned to consider the areas that fall most directly under the heading of *scene.* Instead of beginning over again, and seeking to analyze the realm of scene in terms that had no relation to the terms he had developed when considering the realm of agent, he might proceed to derive the nature of his terms for the discussion of scene from the nature of his terms for agent. This might well, in fact, be the procedure of a thinker who, instead of using a terminology that was merely slung together, felt the logical and aesthetic (and moral!) desire for an internal consistency among his terms. And it would amount to an "agentification" of scene even though the terms for scene were placed in dialectical opposition to the terms for agent. For a scene conceived antithetically to *agent* would differ from a scene conceived, let us say, antithetically to *act* or *purpose,* the genius of the ancestral term surviving even in its negation.

A rival philosophic terminology might propose to abandon this particular system of terms derived from agent, and to feature instead the area of motives covered by our term, scene. Its propounder could maintain that the terms imported from the area of agent were irrelevant or unwieldy as scenic references. However, principles of internal consistency might lead him to undertake imperialist expansions of his own, as were he to treat in scenic terms the areas directly covered by our terms agent or purpose.

These general examples should be enough, for the time being, to indicate what we mean by the featuring of a term. In this section we shall deal with the subject in some detail. But first surveying the entire field at a glance, let us state simply as propositions:

For the featuring of *scene*, the corresponding philosophic terminology is *materialism.*

For the featuring of *agent,* the corresponding terminology is *idealism.*

For the featuring of *agency,* the corresponding terminology is *pragmatism.*

For the featuring of *purpose,* the corresponding terminology is *mysticism.*

For the featuring of *act,* the corresponding terminology is *realism.* *Nominalism* and *rationalism* increase the kinds of terminology to seven. But since we have used up all our terms, we must account for them indirectly.

Historically, nominalism stood in opposition to mediaeval realism. It was the individualistic counterpart of realism's "tribal" or "generic" emphasis. We would here widen the concept so as to include a corresponding "atomistic" movement in any of the other philosophies.

Rationalism is, in one sense, intrinsic to philosophy as a medium, since every philosophy attempts to propound a rationale of its position, even if it is a philosophy of the irrational. But more restrictedly, the term can be applied only to philosophies that treat reason as the very ground and substance of reality, somewhat as though, instead of saying, "a philosophy is a universe," one were to say, "the universe is a philosophy." The fact that rationalism, as a special philosophic strain, converts a *method* (i.e., agency) into a substance might well be the "grammatical reason" why our pragmatists descend from Hegel, who treated reason and world substance as so thoroughly identical that he proposed to recreate all history "in principle" by the sheer exercise of his philosophic method.

The addition of *nominalism* and *rationalism* to our list spoils the symmetry somewhat, for the first (as we extend its meaning) applies to all the other six schools insofar as each of them can have either a collectivistic or an individualistic ("nominalist") emphasis; and the second applies to all in the sense that it is the perfection, or logical conclusion, or *reductio ad absurdum* of the philosophic *métier*. One should also note that a philosophy may be "nominalist" or "rationalist" in one realm without necessarily being so in another—as materialism is usually atomistic in the physical realm, but may be quite collectivistic in the ethical or political realm. Similarly the mystic's merging of the One with the All would often make it difficult to say whether we should call his doctrine collectivistic or atomistic, if we stopped at this point; but there is clearly a great distinction between mystics whose doctrines lead to permanent isolation from other men, and those whose doctrines lead to the founding of religious orders.

The symmetry is also impaired by the fact that there has been much borrowing of terms among the various philosophic schools, so that one cannot always take even key terms at their face value. For instance, we have previously observed that "situation" is a synonym for "scene."

Hence one might take it as a rule that philosophies which account for motivations in terms of "the situation" are "materialistic." But the current prestige of the "situational" approach has led to the term's adoption by other schools. A literary critic who spoke of "the literary situation," for instance, meant not the "objective conditions" under which a writer writes, but the motives peculiar to a writer's medium. What looked "scenic" was here actually "pragmatic," since the writer's medium is an *agency*. And similarly, essayists now often speak of "the human situation" when they seem to have in mind the *motives peculiar to men as men,* a usage that would call for the classifying of the expression under the heading of *agent,* hence giving the *apparently* materialistic usage an *essentially* idealistic application (since, as we have said, idealism features the term agent).

Besides the concealments of misnomer and those due to mutual borrowings among the philosophic schools, there is an internal development that causes the nature of philosophy as an assertion to be lost in the problems of demonstration. That is, as soon as a philosopher has begun to investigate the possibilities in whatever term he has selected as his *Ausgangspunkt,* he finds that the term does not merely create other terms in its image. Also, it generates a particular set of *problems* —and the attempt to solve these problems may lead the philosopher far from his beginnings. It is somewhat, alas! as with the design for a perpetual motion machine. Such a design may have been quite simple in its original conception, but it becomes fantastically complex as the inventor finds that each new wheel or trip or pin or cam which he added to solve his problem gave rise to a new problem, and this in turn suggested the need of some other contrivance, which relieves his former embarrassments only by introducing a new embarrassment of its own.

Indeed, since all the terms of the pentad continually press for consideration, and since it is not possible for us, without contradiction, to recreate in words a world which is itself not verbal at all, we can safely accept it as an axiom that the mere attempt to contemplate persistently the resources of any one term will lead to the discovery of many problems the answers to which will *transcend* the genius of this term. And if a reader comes upon a philosophy after it has been thus sophisticated, he may find himself so caught up in its problems-atop-problems-atop-problems and problems-within-problems-within-problems that he cannot sense the principle of generation behind them. For usually the thinker himself has become similarly intricated.

But with the pentad as a generating principle, we may extricate ourselves from these intricacies, by discovering the kinds of *assertion* which the different schools would exemplify in a hypothetical state of purity. Once this approach is established, problems are much less likely to conceal the underlying design of assertion, or may even serve to assist in the characterizing of a given philosophic work.

Scene in General

In Baldwin's *Dictionary of Philosophy and Psychology*, materialism is defined as "that metaphysical theory which regards all the facts of the universe as sufficiently explained by the assumption of body or matter, conceived as extended, impenetrable, eternally existent, and susceptible of movement or change of relative position." The article also cites Hobbes: "All that exists is body, all that occurs motion." And Paulsen: "The reduction of psychical processes to physical is the special thesis of materialism." Similarly, the *Encyclopaedia Britannica* defines materialism as "the theory which regards all the facts of the universe as explainable in terms of matter and motion, and in particular explains all psychical processes by physical and chemical changes in the nervous system."

These citations make it obvious why one gets a materialistic philosophy by the featuring of our term, scene. We should add, however, that with materialism the circumference of scene is so narrowed as to involve the reduction of action to motion. That is, whether the materialist happens to believe in the existence of a personal God or not, he will employ a materialist vocabulary of motivation insofar as such a personal principle is omitted from the scope of the circumference. Thus the *Encyclopaedia Britannica* remarks: "It may perhaps be fairly said that materialism is at present a necessary methodological postulate of natural-scientific inquiry. The business of the scientist is to explain everything by the physical causes which are comparatively well understood and to exclude the interference of spiritual causes."

In his excellent pamphlet, *Aspects of Scientific Rationalism in the Nineteenth Century,* George de Santillana sums up the situation thus:

In the end, if we want to build up a science and not an animism, we are left with only one choice, which is the historical one: the atom must be quite dead, its substance devoid of all spontaneity.

Hobbes

With Democritus surviving only in fragments (an atomist philosopher who has left us but atoms of his philosophy), perhaps the most thorough and picturesque exemplar of a vocabulary conceived systematically in terms of "extension" is the philosophy of Hobbes, who sums up his materialism vigorously in the opening chapters of his *Leviathan:*

> Nature, the art whereby God hath made and governs the world, is by the *art* of man, as in many other things, so in this also imitated, that it can make an artificial animal.   For seeing life is but a motion of limbs, the beginning whereof is in some principal part within; why may we not say, that all *automata* (engines that move themselves by springs and wheels as doth a watch) have an artificial life?   For what is the heart, but a spring; and the nerves, but so many strings, and the joints, but so many wheels, giving motion to the whole body, such as was intended by the artificer?

Ironically, though Hobbes warns heatedly against the deceptions of metaphor, he is here in effect announcing that his book is to be organized about the metaphor of the machine, in taking it as the *Ausgangspunkt* of his vocabulary.   Next he expands his figure into a proportion: as man is a machine, so the State is a gigantic man.

> Art goes yet further, imitating that rational and most excellent work of nature, man.   For by art is created that great *Leviathan* called a *Commonwealth,* or *State,* in Latin *Civitas,* which is but an artificial man; though of greater stature and strength than the natural, for whose protection and defense it was intended—

whereupon he proceeds to trace such analogies between the human body and the body politic as recall the passages in the opening scene of *Coriolanus,* where Menenius Agrippa tells his parable of "a time when all the body's members / Rebell'd against the belly," and the belly answered its "incorporate friends," the other bodily parts, by showing how they profited in allowing it to remain "idle and unactive" instead of "bearing like labour" with the "other instruments."

That is, like the passage in Shakespeare, Hobbes' comparing of the sovereignty to an "artificial soul," of the magistrates to "artificial joints," of reward and punishment to the nerves, etc. is a figure of speech. But unlike Shakespeare's passage, it is at the same time meant to be taken literally. Or perhaps we should allow for a certain looseness of correspondence between the human body's parts and the political body's parts—but we are certainly meant to interpret the mechanistic vocabulary of human motives literally, as a few more examples can make clear beyond all question.

In the first chapter, "Of Sense," we are told that "The cause of sense is the external body, or object, which presseth the organ proper to each sense." The scenic emphasis is obvious in this reference to "external body, or object," as the motivational source. For the sensory qualities that objects seem to possess "are, in the object that causeth them, but so many several motions of the matter, by which it presseth our organs diversely. Neither in us that are pressed, are they anything else but diverse motions; for motion produceth nothing but motion."

We have cited Mr. De Santillana's reference to the scientific ideal of a "dead" atom. May we not discern a similar motive behind Hobbes' definition of imagination as "decaying sense"? That is, the imagining of things is a *weaker motion* than the sensing of things. "This decaying sense, when we would express the thing itself, I mean fancy itself, we call *imagination,* as I said before: but when we would express the decay, and signify that the thing is fading, old, and past, it is called *memory.*"

Thoughts succeed one another because they are "motions within us," and motions lead into one another. "A *sign* is the evident antecedent of the consequent; and contrarily, the consequent of the antecedent, when like consequences have been observed before; and the oftener they have been observed, the less uncertain is the sign." This statement is meant to offer a mechanistic interpretation of learning and skill. "Besides sense, and thoughts, and the train of thoughts, the mind of man has no other motion; though by the help of speech, and method, the same faculties may be improved to such a height, as to distinguish men from all other living creatures."

In Chapter V he defines reason in terms of addition and subtraction. "When a man *reasoneth,* he does nothing else but conceive a sum total, from *addition* of parcels; or conceive a remainder, from subtraction of one sum from another; which, if it be done by words, is conceiving of the consequence of the names of all the parts, to the name of the whole; or from the names of the whole and one part, to the name of the other part." It is not necessary here to review his arguments for this proposition. For our purposes it is enough to discern the mechanistic genius in such definition, the reduction of reason itself to motion—and we can grasp the full significance of such reduction if we think of a comptometer not as the *product* of a rational man but as a *complete model* of reason itself.

Next, in contrast with the theological grammar of actions and passions, Hobbes undertakes to treat "the passions" themselves in terms of motion. He first distinguishes between "vital" motion (such as the processes of metabolism) and "animal" or "voluntary" motion, "as to go, to speak, to move any of our limbs in such manner as is first fancied in our minds." Since these latter motions "depend always upon a precedent thought of *whither, which way,* and *what,*" Hobbes locates their "first internal beginning" in the *imagination*. And imagination, we must remember, is "but the relics" of motion, "remaining after sense"; it is the kind of motion that, being weaker than the motions of sense, he has called "decaying sense." Such motion of the imagination is imperceptible as motion; "unstudied men do not consider any motion at all to be there"; nonetheless it is there—and "these small beginnings of motion, within the body of man, before they appear in walking, speaking, striking, and other visible actions, are called *endeavor.*"

He next subdivides endeavor into *appetite* and *aversion,* words which "we have from the Latins; and they both of them signify the motions, one of approaching, the other of retiring." He notes the same of the corresponding Greek words *hormē* and *aphormē.* In brief, he contends that we come closer to the real situation here by interpreting such words literally rather than by considering them simply as abstractions or dead metaphors. The appetites and aversions that characterize our endeavors are thus to be considered as real motions toward and "fromward" something. And the chapter proceeds to derive the various passions in terms of these "motions."

There is another passage which illustrates with special clarity the way in which materialism, or reduction to motion, is a treatment of personal motivations in terms of the *scenic,* explaining the *internal* in terms of *external* conditions:

As, in sense, that which is really within us, is, as I have said before, only motion, caused by the action of external objects; but in appearance—to the sight, light and color; to the ear, sound; to the nostril, odor, etc.: so, when the action of the same object is continued from the eyes, ears, and other organs to the heart, the real effect there is nothing but motion, or endeavor; which consisteth in *appetite* or *aversion,* to or from the object moving. But the appearance, or sense, of that motion is that we either call *delight* or *trouble* of mind.

This "motion" of delight, he says, seems to be "a corroboration of vital motion"; and things are called offensive, "from hindering and troubling the motion vital."

From this point on, I must admit, the perfect symmetry of our case is impaired. However, Hobbes's intention is clear enough; namely: the reduction of the will itself to terms of a scene mechanically determined. For he defines will as "the last appetite in deliberating." As I understand his position, one might illustrate it thus: Imagine trying to make a decision in a situation where one felt a conflict of appetite and aversion. If one put his appetite on one side of the balance and his aversion on the other, the balance would tip to whichever side was the heavier. The resulting "decision" would thus follow mechanically from the disproportion in the weight of the conflicting motives. And what we interpreted as an act of the free will would be in reality but the necessary triumph of a stronger motion over a weaker motion. I speak of the symmetry being impaired, however, because precisely at this point we find Hobbes speaking not of "motion" but of "action":

In deliberation, the last appetite or aversion immediately adhering to the action, or to the omission thereof, is that we call the *will,*—the act, not the faculty, of willing. And beasts that have deliberation, must necessarily also have will. The definition of the will given commonly by the Schools, that it is a *rational appetite,* is not good. For if it were, then could there be no voluntary act against reason. For a *voluntary act* is that which proceedeth from the will, and no other. But if instead of a rational appetite, we shall say an appetite resulting from a precedent deliberation, then the definition is the same that I have given here. *Will,* therefore, *is the last appetite in deliberating.* And though we say in common discourse, a man had a will once to do a thing, that nevertheless he forbore to do; yet that is properly but an inclination, which makes no action voluntary; because the action depends not of it, but of the last inclination or appetite.

To some extent, Hobbes here speaks of "action" rather than "motion" simply as a way of avoiding confusion. He is aiming to place a new interpretation upon a subject traditionally discussed in theological rather than mechanistic terms—and he uses the traditional expression as a convenience of discourse. That is, he is talking about a subject that usually goes by the name of "voluntary action," and he designates it accordingly. And if, as we have noted, even mechanics several centuries after Hobbes would speak of a motor's "action" without having the full significance of the term act in mind, we might well expect that Hobbes, so close to the heyday of the dramatistic vocabulary employed by the scholastics, and so close to its esthetic secularization in Elizabethan poetry, would speak now and then of human "actions," particularly in a chapter on human "passions." In any case, the whole point of his philosophy is the explanation of such actions in terms of motion. And even though he refers to the consequences of the will as "acts," his mechanistic reduction of the will itself brings his whole conception quite close to the metaphysics of modern behaviorist psychology (which has likewise literally interpreted the concept of _hormē,_ as evident in its term, "hormone," to name the factors affecting what Hobbes would probably have called "vital motion").

There is another reason for the partial break in symmetry here. We have said that, when a philosopher would feature one of the terms, recreating the others in its image, the original claims of these other terms are nonetheless still in the offing. Now, when one talks of the will, one is necessarily in the field of the _moral;_ and the field of the moral is, by definition, the field of _action_. A billiard ball is neither moral nor immoral, for it cannot act, it can only move, or be moved. We shall return to the matter when we consider the philosophy of Emmanuel Kant, who expended vast ingenuity upon precisely this problem of allowing personal action (moral freedom) in a world of mechanical motion. At the moment it is enough to note that Hobbes, by carrying his theories of mechanism into the moral realm, is necessarily treading upon domains more directly governed by our terms act and agent.

Indeed, he is to go even farther in this direction, for he is to tell us of salvation, "Of What Is Necessary for Man's Reception into the Kingdom of God," a naturally dramatistic concern, as we realize when we recall the Church's drama of salvation. True, he says that "perfect obedience would be enough because the kingdom of heaven is shut to none but sinners; that is to say, to the disobedient, or transgressors of the law." Not even faith in Christ would be necessary, if our obedience were perfect. So we could get to heaven purely by obeying the moral and civil laws with the mechanical accuracy that natural objects exemplify in obeying the laws of motion. Thus the scenic genius is maintained to the end, with as near a symmetry as the pressure of the other terms will permit.

Be that as it may, it was our purpose here to account for the presence of the term action in a philosophy of motion. In part, we say, it was but a loose usage, to designate kinds of "motion" that were traditionally called "actions." And in part it may have been a response to the pressure of the moral category itself, which is essentially dramatic, and may be expected to make its dramatic genius felt even in a philosophy that aims programmatically to transform the dramatic into the mechanical. In brief, there is a purely technical reason why the term, act, should encroach here. For at this point Hobbes is turning from the realm of metaphysics to the realm of politics and ethics. And even were it established that men are pure automata, one might still contend that the realm of political and ethical relations calls "naturally" for treatment in terms of *action*. That is, insofar as ethics is treated *in its own terms*, as a special context of inquiry, rather than being reduced to non-ethical terms, one is pledged in advance to discourse on the subject of action and passion. For that is what the study of ethics is.

Spinoza

Spinoza's naturalistic *Ethics* is central, as seen from this point of view. For could not his basic synonymy, "God equals Nature" (*Deus sive Natura*) be with justice ambiguously translated as "action equals motion"? Again, our translating of God as an "action" word will seem obvious when one considers Kant, who grounds morality (i.e., action) on the three terms, God, freedom, and immortality. Of these three, "immortality" would stand for the nature of the soul, hence serving as a high word for *agent;* and "God" names the kind of scene in which, by the logic of the scene-act ratio, an action would be possible; namely: a scene allowing for human *freedom*. The empirical realm, on the other hand, is for Kant the realm of causality in keeping with the laws of physical motion as defined in Newton's celestial mechanics, in brief the realm of strict *necessity*.

More directly, we could get God as a scenic word for action by recalling again the scholastic formula for God as the ground of all possibility. As for the Spinozist equating of God and Nature, we might best see beyond our contemporary over-naturalistic usage by thinking of "Nature" also in the sense we have in mind when we speak of a person's or a poem's nature. A thing's "nature" is thus necessarily one with the thing. We have found Spinozistic naturalism particularly engrossing, from the dramatistic point of view. For it characterizes to perfection the great watershed moment in Western thought when men were narrowing the scope of their terminologies as *per* the Occamite law of parsimony. Theologically, this amounted to the narrowing of the circumference from a scene comprising both creation and creator to a scene comprising creation alone. And since the creation had already been enacted, such a narrowing of the scenic frame meant in turn simply an examination of the world's *constitution,* a constitution which was just what it was, regardless of whether it had originally been enacted by a divine superagent or was the result of cosmic accident, or was a mere set of *relations without substance.* In other words, even if one still chose to think of it as having originally been *enacted,* it was now to be studied, from without, as a regular concatenation of *events.* Dramatistically this narrowing meant the shift from a poetic or moralistic vocabulary of action and passion to a scientific or mechanistic vocabulary of motion.

The exquisiteness of the Spinozistic terms resides in the fact that his key equation, by our interpretation, serves as a bridge across this gap. In effect, it equates a wider frame with a narrower one. For traditionally "God" is a wider term than "Nature," being the metaphysical scene or ground of Nature's existence. But by proclaiming the two circumferences to be identical in scope, Spinoza leaves you somewhat undecided whether he has naturalized God or deified Nature. The thought readily suggests why pantheism provides a perfect transition from theistic to naturalistic vocabularies of motives. And we can also see why materialists could claim Spinoza as one of themselves, by stressing the Nature side of the equation (as Western thought itself was to do progressively in the following centuries). For "God" as so conceived is a scenic term *par excellence,* and a scenic term of narrowed circumference.

On the other hand, the very fact that Spinoza's naturalism is primarily *ethical* in its stress (in contrast, for instance, with the Galilean physics) invited him to use the vocabulary of action and passion, and not glancingly as with Hobbes at moments when his strict reduction to motion became unwieldy, but formally and systematically, with a whole structure of terms developed in accordance with such dramatistic logic. In fact, one might well derive the entire alignment of terms in Spinoza by putting his word "action" on one side of the ledger and his word "passion" on the other, and treating the doctrines in his *Ethics* as a noble philosophic accountancy whereby, through the cultivation of "adequate ideas," one could transform the passives (of human bondage) into the actives (of human freedom).

Unfortunately, almost as soon as we say this, we must retract somewhat. For if Spinoza would not, like Hobbes, reduce action to motion, he has a non-dramatic ideal of his own, conceived after the analogy of geometry, as in his famous remark at the opening of Book III, where he pledges himself to treat of human actions and appetites as though it were a matter of lines, planes, and solids. This, as he says elsewhere, admonishes us to drop the concept of *purpose* from the philosophy of Nature, since mathematics is concerned not with final causes, but solely with the essences and properties of figures, thereby showing men a different standard of truth than is got by the treatment of the world as an instance of divine purpose. Thus "the reason or cause why God or nature exists, and the reason why he acts, are one and the same"; whereby the concept of *purpose* retreats behind the concept of *rational necessity.* But though action in the full sense of the term is impossible without purpose, leave me the term *Reason* in a philosophy, and you can have *purpose,* so far as the needs of a terminology of action are concerned. For there is purpose enough implicit in the very concept of Reason. Indeed, Reason is as essentially dramatistic a term as Substance, the key word of the entire Spinozistic terminology. Thus, "Reason" too is as transitional a term in Spinoza as is the God-Nature equation itself, and allows for a devoutly purposive surrender to a God whose acts are not *purposive,* but *inevitable.*

Spinoza's opening definitions, defining God or Substance as the *self-caused,* could be said to contain, in telescoped form, what is stated analytically in the *Deus sive Natura* equation. The Latin is *causa sui,* "cause of itself"—and you will note that in this key expression there is both an active and a passive significance. As *cause* it is active. But the self that is thus caused is the object or result or recipient of the cause, hence passive. Hence, God-and-Nature in the totality has, from the purely grammatical point of view, an active and a passive meaning rolled into one.

We encounter the form again in Spinoza's use of the distinction between *natura naturans* and *natura naturata* ("naturing nature" and "natured nature"—or perhaps we could say "the producer" and "the product," though remembering that in Spinoza they are one and the same). If "naturing" is active and "natured" is passive, what grammatically is the third, or ground terms of this expression, "nature"?

When confronting such dialectical embarrassments, I always like to recall a treaty which Fascist Italy made with some of the small neighboring countries. By the fictions of national sovereignty, all the signatories to this treaty were equal in their rights and dignity. By the realities of the political and economic situation, Italy was much the strongest of the signatories, hence able to make her voice heard above the others. And this state of affairs was expressed by the decision that all the signatories were equal, but Italy was "foremost among the equals" (*primus inter pares*). And so, whenever in philosophy I see two terms, of opposite and equal importance, being merged into a third term that will somehow contain the nature of both, I always ask myself: "Which of the two equal terms was foremost?" For I will expect the genius of this term to weight the third term (as Schelling's third term, "subject-object," supposedly "indifferent" to the two terms "subject" and "object" which it combines, is more "subjective" than "objective," even though he would further complicate matters by distinguishing between a "subjective subject-object" and an "objective subject-object").

In Spinoza's case, I would say that, at least as far as human limitations are concerned, though "God" is "active nature" (*natura naturans,* Spinoza's equivalent of the Creator) and God's *modes* (the concatenation of particular things and events we encounter in the vicissitude of history) are "passive nature" (*natura naturata,* his equivalent of the Creation) the essence of this active-passive pair is *active.* The world of God's *modes* (the *substantiae affectiones*) is none other than the world of Hobbes's *motions* (as see Book I, Prop. XXXII, where will and intellect are specifically placed in the category of motion. Hence we see that, at the strategic moment in his God-Nature, or action-motion equation, Spinoza differs from Hobbes in shifting to the *action* side of the pair.

We should here note a further important change which one can arrive at quickly and crudely, in a non-Spinozistic kind of dialectic, in observing that the expression, "causa sui," can be stressed two ways: either "*causa* sui" or "causa *sui*." The first gives us the active interpretation: we act, or are free "insofar as we are the adequate cause of what takes place either within us or outside us." The stress upon *sui* gives us the passive interpretation, of the self as caused—and we are constrained insofar as we are affected by other causes. (*At contra nos pati dico, cum in nobis aliquid fit, vel extra nostra natura aliquid sequitur, cujus nos non nisi partialis sumus causa.*) That is, if we are but the *partial* cause of something, we are constrained or passive to the extent of this partiality. It has already been noted how by putting the active and passive together, Spinoza gets an *active* significance for the over-all concept of Substance or the Absolute Being that embraces all passives as well (the passives or modes being, in fact, but the *parts* of the whole; for Spinoza considers the whole as logically prior to its parts, hence as their cause). But if one thinks simply of the cause and the caused in general, he will quickly see that of the two the term "cause" would contain connotations of action and freedom, while "caused" would contain the connotations of passivity and constraint.

The seventh definition of Book I gives us explicit justification for equating action with freedom and passion with necessity, since Spinoza there defines "free" things and "necessary" or "determined" things quite as he defines active and passive in the above citations from Book III, on the human "affections." Or we might state the matter somewhat non-Spinozistically by saying that the relation of part to whole is always *necessary,* but the necessary can take either "benign" or "malign" forms. We are "free" insofar as our understanding of natural ($=$ rational) necessity leads us to greater virtue (in effect making natural law "benign").

The philosophy as a whole could thus be considered as an enterprise for so changing our attitude towards the world that we can be in the direction of peace rather than in the direction of war. The change is to be prepared by vigorous intellectual means rather than by a mere "change of heart." And to grasp the quality of the freedom of action aimed at, I think it relevant to remember that in the mediaeval terminologies of motives *contemplation* is an act. And although Spinoza's ideas of action are close to the Baconian knowledge-power equation, they are much nearer to the mediaeval ideals of contemplation than to the notions of action that go with our current political, commercial, and technological pragmatisms. The situation of which he considered himself necessarily a part was metaphysical, even theological, transcending the view of motives one gets by consideration merely of contingencies.

The point we were trying to make by our rough shifting of stress might be made still clearer if, instead of *causa sui* as the definition of God ("that whose essence involves its existence"), we used the equivalent expression, "cause of the caused." If then "God" is made to equal *everything* (as the term is treated in Spinoza's pantheistic concept of the universal scene) the "cause" and the "caused" are all *"necessarily"* bound up together, and God's "freedom" as *cause* is one with his *necessary* relation to the *caused*. For, grammatically at least, a cause needs a caused as truly as a caused needs a cause. Hence, we get the equating of freedom and necessity, *God's freedom* being synonymous with the strict *regularity of Nature,* an equation that has given much trouble to those who would use it empirically, without concern for its metaphysical, dialectical, grammatical origins. If God is everything, he both *is free* to be what he is and *must be* what he is. He is free since there is no other cause to constrain him, but by reason of this very freedom he must *necessarily* be himself. In his freedom he is perfect, and what else can the perfect or ultimate be but perfect or ultimate? For that is inevitably its Nature.

However, recalling our earlier concerns with the tactics of the Creation, we might refer again to a passage in Prof. Lovejoy's *The Great Chain of Being*, discussing St. Augustine's reasons for locating the point of origin in God's *will*. Augustine considered as impious any attempt to state God's motives: for if the act of creation had been determined by any motive, even if it but had its ground in the "divine essence," to this extent it would not have been free. To be free, the act must be absolutely unmotivated. Prof. Lovejoy cites from Augustine a sorites that runs:

> Where there is no insufficiency (need, want, lack, *indigentia*), there is no necessity; where there is no defect, there is no insufficiency; but in God there is no defect, hence no necessity.

The whole matter looks so different in Spinoza because of the pantheistic merger whereby he puts God and Nature together in a "necessary" relation. And though he treats God as "logically prior" to the Creation (or in Spinoza's term, the *modes*), opponents of Spinoza have claimed that such strict necessity is really a two-way relationship, so that God's existence as a perfect whole depends upon any single one of the parts.

"Determination" in Spinoza can be best grasped by thinking of it in the most literal sense. A thing is determined insofar as it is limited by the boundaries of other things, determined by whatever outside itself marks its terminations. Spinoza's concern with geometry goes much deeper than the mere borrowing of Euclid's stylistic devices, as when he presents his philosophy *more geometrico* by the use of axioms, propositions, demonstrations, corollaries, scholia, and the like. It is geometrical also in the sense that it is essentially scenic or contextual; indeed, from the terministic point of view, his word for "God" might well be translated "total context." And the world of our everyday finite experience, the world of *positive* things like apples, houses, people, is in the Spinozistic vocabulary a world of "negations," because each such positive thing is *determined,* and the determined is that which has its boundaries marked by other things, in brief by things that this particular thing is *not.* Hence his formula, "all determination is negation." And as an interesting variant of the "negative theology" stemming from the Neo-Platonists, he attributes the use of negative names for God to weaknesses of intelligence and the resultant errors of imagination (for Spinoza, like most philosophers prior to romanticism, placed imagination, and its partner, memory, much closer to sheer brute sensation than to insight or vision). To quote from his treatise *On the Improvement of the Understanding:*

> Since words are a part of the imagination—that is, since we form many conceptions in accordance with confused arrangements of words in the memory, dependent on particular bodily conditions—

there is no doubt that words may, equally with the imagination, be the cause of many and great errors, unless we keep strictly on our guard. Moreover, words are formed according to popular fancy and intelligence, and are, therefore, signs of things as existing in the imagination, not as existing in the understanding. This is evident from the fact that to all such things as exist only in the understanding, not in the imagination, negative names are often given, such as incorporeal, infinite, etc. So, also, many conceptions really affirmative are expressed negatively, and *vice versa,* such as uncreate, independent, infinite, immortal, etc., inasmuch as their contraries are much more easily imagined, and, therefore, occurred first to men, and usurped positive names.

But though finite beings are ultimately to be located in terms of their total context (a context that, being conceived as positive, gives the corresponding conception of finite, determinate things as negative) there is also a device in Spinoza whereby their individual natures can be accounted for. This is the *conatus in suo esse perseverandi,* the endeavor of each being to continue being. Just as the Infinite Substance goes on forever, so every finite or determinate mode of Substance would forever persist in its nature, if its existence were not terminated by the boundaries imposed upon it by other determinate things. In brief, each part would be as eternal as the whole, if it were not for the encroachments of the other parts. Accordingly, insofar as it can be considered in itself, each determinate part seeks by its very nature as a being to endure for ever. We might translate this metaphysical principle into a blunt biological equivalent, thus: Each thing will seek to preserve its nature as long as it can, and will succeed until it is destroyed by factors beyond its control. But though this is the implication of the Spinozist *conatus,* we must remember that he modifies it by placing it in a much wider circumference than a strictly naturalistic reduction of a Darwinian sort.

This concept of the *conatus* performs the function regularly covered by our term *agent.* That is, it gives us the equivalent of a motivational locus situated *within* the individual person or thing, since a thing's being or essence is intrinsic to it. However, the principle is scenically derived, in the sense that it is but a limited application of his definition for the total context, God, Nature, Substance, the Self-Caused, whose essence is identical with its existence (*cujus essentia involvit existentiam*), which is to say that by its very nature it goes on existing.

Thus, we have observed the *scene* function modified first to account for the functions of *act* (in being treated in terms of action and passion), and next to account for the functions of *agent*. Shifting the stress, as a rough approximate we could say that individual things would go on forever in their capacity as parts of the *whole,* but they are restricted in their capacity as *parts* of the whole. The essay *On the Improvement of the Understanding* perhaps, best brings out the conversion of scenic resources to cover the functions of *agency,* as it is concerned with the ways in which the intellect, influenced by *external* causes, "makes for itself intellectual instruments"—and the essay treats of *methods* for improving these instruments. Also, his treatment of good and evil in terms of utility and hindrance respectively has a strongly pragmatist possibility. In the preface to Book IV, he calls good an agency (*medium*); and elsewhere he says that nothing is more "useful" to a man who would live rationally than his fellow-men who are guided by reason. The non-pragmatist nature of the philosophy as a whole, however, is seen in the closing proposition, which defines blessedness (*beatitudo*) not as the reward of virtue (*virtutis praemium*), but as virtue itself. As for *purpose:* it is apparent that the endeavor towards self-preservation provides at least for a stimulus in the purely biological sense, and we shall see that the equating of self-preservation with action and the development of adequate ideas gives us purpose in the rational sense, though the concept of a cosmic purpose is dissolved in the concept of rational *necessity* (as against its reduction to mechanical necessity in Hobbes).

Leibniz, confronting this same embarrassment whereby the notion of a completely rational relation between Creator and Creation dissolves purpose into rational necessity, solved the problem by introducing, along with his *principe de nécessité,* a *principe de convenance,* postulating ideas of *fitness* on the part of God which made God more of a creative agent than a necessary scene, and hence would move us into the areas of idealism proper. But in the preface and seventh definition of Book IV, Spinoza explains how he would reduce even individual human purpose to purely necessitarian terms: for he treats human *ends,* or final causes, simply as *necessary* human *desires.* This formulation, you will note, leads quite readily into the pragmatist interpretation of purpose in terms of *agency,* the recognition of *ends* being in pragmatism but a *means* for man's social and biological adjustment to his needs.

As the concept of the *conatus* is modified by the other aspects of Spinoza's terminology, it has in it something of Stoic grandeur, a high ethical quality that stresses the moral value of *endurance*. Indeed, "endurance" is quite an apt synonym for the Spinozistic *conatus* or "endeavor"; for it possesses both biological and moral meanings, as a term typical of the God-Nature equation should. The Stoics brought out more the idea of *sufferance,* Spinoza suggests rather the will to *survive* one's sufferings, the Stoics thus stressing the *passive* aspect of endurance while Spinoza stresses its nature as *activity*.

Again, we may see how Spinoza's term stands at a watershed moment, for in keeping with his emphasis, "virtue" in Spinoza is equated with *power of action*. His usage does not take us back as far as its original reference (previously discussed) to the power of the warrior; but he does sufficiently redefine the term to conclude from his definition that neither humility nor repentance are virtues, since neither of them is rational, for both involve situations wherein our power of activity is checked. Deprived of its modifiers, such a concept of virtue might be successively transformed until we come to extreme transvaluations of value, as with cults of naturalist expansion, or the characteristically modern impatience with "frustration." But, as modified by all the other key terms in Spinoza's philosophy, the concept leads to the very opposite of the militant: a philosophy of exceptional tolerance, peace, and moderation. And our concern with circumferences of placement should admonish us always to watch, in a given writer, the full orbit of his terms.

Alignment of Terms in Spinoza

Before closing our remarks on Spinoza, we should comment on the fact that, after all these pages, we have hardly mentioned what people seem to note most of all in Spinoza; namely: his relation to the Cartesian dualism, as shown in the distinction between *thought* and *extension*. According to Spinoza, God has infinite attributes; but only two of them are mentioned, the Cartesian mind-body pair. But Spinoza's position at a watershed moment is to be interpreted not merely in terms of the historical streams that have followed him. Admittedly, if we look only at this latter side of the watershed, his reconversion of Descartes' dualism into a monism of one Substance looks central. Leibniz has said: "No substance without action, no body without motion," a formula made to order for our purposes. And the Cartesian dualism was certainly the future in the sense that it led eventually into the subject-object pair of German idealism, and so finally to Hegel's programmatic replacement of "substance" by "Subject." But in its actual proportions his *Ethics,* just as this work is in itself, considered without reference to subsequent developments in history, is as much a *theology* as it is an instance of naturalism; and herein resides its dramatistic stress upon problems of action and passion, rather than the scientist stress upon knower and known (subject and object).

Indeed, if you start trying to trace the alignments in Spinoza's philosophy from the scientist point of view, rather than from the dramatist point of view, thus starting from the mind-body pair rather than the action-passion pair, you will find yourself quickly involved in confusion. Later in the history of philosophy, the problem becomes simple, as mind is flatly equated with the active and body flatly equated with the passive. But Spinoza's philosophic enterprise (in equating *idea* with *ideatum,* the "order and connection of ideas" with the "order and connection of things," and in treating both thought and extension as attributes of God) cuts across this on the bias. The mind, he tells us at the beginning of Book III, is more passive in proportion as it possesses inadequate ideas, and more active in proportion as it possesses adequate ideas. There is in us exactly as much mental activity as there is bodily activity, and exactly as much mental passivity as bodily passivity. Desire is simply the consciousness of bodily appetite. It is man's essence to desire, hence the striving for self-preservation is simultaneously physical and mental. Pleasure is as truly a passive in his system as is pain, the difference being that pleasure accompanies a transition towards greater perfection (it is in the direction of greater reality, or power of action) and pain accompanies a transition towards less perfection. Intellect and will are both passive.

Consequently, there can be no alignment of terms constructed by derivation from the quasi-scientific Cartesian pair (thought and extension). But the alignment constructed about the "pre-scientific" (or "extra-scientific") pair, the alignment sought in accordance with dramatistic admonitions, is almost pat. For instance:

ACTIVE	PASSIVE
self-caused	externally caused
infinite (positive)	finite (negative)
God (Substance)	modes
natura naturans	*natura naturata*
freedom	bondage
(that is free which exists solely by the necessity of its own nature; its actions are determined by itself alone)	(that is constrained which is determined by something external to itself to a fixed and definite kind of existence or action)
existence in itself (eternity)	existence in something else
conceived through itself *	conceived through something else
indivisibility (the whole, One)	division (the parts)
intrinsic	extrinsic
reason and intuition	intellect (except the absolute intellect), will, opinion, imagination
perfection	imperfection (but see qualifying remarks in preface to Book IV)
virtue (= power)	infirmity
good (in harmony with our nature)	bad (contrary to our nature)
useful to man	hurtful to man
determined to actions by reason	determined to actions by emotion
adequate ideas**	inadequate ideas

The list is not exhaustive. And it fails to indicate the third element in the design, the bridging devices for translating us from the bondage of the passions to the sovereignty of action. For such a function there is necessarily an ambiguous term that pontificates by leading into both realms. This function is performed in human agents by the *conatus,* the endeavor (and its corresponding desires) of each man to survive. Since men are necessarily but *parts* of the total divine Substance, the human essence is limited, and our desires are beset by confused and inadequate ideas. To this extent, the desires that characterize our nature

* The stress upon the self, once Spinoza's theological qualifications have been dropped away, can lead into ideals of independence individualistically conceived, and thus eventually into the "self-expression" movements of modern art.

** The mediaeval "principle of generation" is familial in its thinking; the "principle of adequation" is contextual, and as eventually simplified can be seen to lead into the Semanticist ideal of a naming adequate to the named. Spinoza's notion of the adequate, however, is ethical (and with placement in a total context of action), whereas the Semanticist version of the adequate is empirical (as with the word "house" when applied to something that really is a house).

fall on the side of the passions. But insofar as we do acquire adequate ideas, our endeavor can lead to action, power, virtue, perfection, the rational way of life. The terminology pontificates here by allowing for varying proportions of activity and passivity, whereby the human nature can pass from one side of our ledger to the other *paulatim et gradatim*. This locus of transition is, fittingly, treated in the third part of the five-part work. With parts I and II having defined the universal ground out of which this principle of individual conversion is derived, we encounter the derivation itself in the middle part; whereupon we are equipped to consider in parts IV and V its application in transforming bondage into freedom.

Here occurs that remarkable list, "Definitions of the Emotions," (or "affections"), beginning with the statement that "desire is the very essence of man," and constructed about three primary emotions: desire, pleasure, and pain. Here is the most ingeniously scholastic of all scholasticisms: "Love is pleasure, accompanied by the idea of an external cause." The list with its comments contains in itself a whole moral philosophy. The pleasant emotions are treated as transitions towards greater perfection (greater activity), the painful ones as transitions towards less perfection (greater passivity). All told, they are such as Wonder, Contempt, Love, Hate, Aversion, Devotion, Hope, Fear, Confidence, Despair, Joy, Disappointment, Pity, Indignation, Envy, Sympathy.

Only emotions of pleasure can be attributable to the mind as wholly active, and these are summed up as Strength of Character (*Fortitudo*). This is subdivided into Spirit (*Animositas*) and Generosity or group-mindedness (*Generositas*), each of which acts solely in accordance with Reason, the first being directed towards the preservation of one's own being (hence embracing such traits as temperance, sobriety, and presence of mind), while the second aims at the good of others (as with courtesy and mercy). Action, as so conceived, involving as it does the rational consideration of all human necessities in terms of the divine totality, is for Spinoza the same as Piety and Religion.

However, in our zeal to show that the action-passion pair is better able to reveal the structure of Spinoza's thought than the mind-body (*cogitatio-extensio*) pair, we must not go too far. For it is quite true that, in merging the Cartesian dualism back into a monism, Spinoza encountered the *primus inter pares* pattern, and as a result, although he would programmatically treat mind and body as equals, mind comes out with two votes to body's one. For body but represents itself, whereas mind can represent both body and itself. Or otherwise put, there are bodies, ideas of bodies, and ideas of ideas. Or in Spinoza's terms: "In God there is necessarily an idea which expresses the essence of this or that human body *sub aeternitatis specie*." And though we question the value of the mind-body pair in revealing the basic outline of Spinoza's thought, we willingly grant that it must always be considered as the important complicating factor.

Particularly as we move towards the close of the Ethics, we encounter an exaltation much like the Platonist *transcendence* of body. Thus we are told in Prop. XXIII of Book V that "The human mind cannot be destroyed absolutely with the body, but there remains of it something which is eternal." This clearly moves us in the direction of idealism.

However, when we turn to idealism proper, and consider how thorough and strategic the stress upon the function of agent can be, I think we shall see that, by comparison, Spinoza even here is *scenic*. For he is saying always that we have eternity by reason of our natures as parts of a non-personal *whole* (just as, shifting the stress, we perish by reason of our natures as *parts* of a whole). This *contextual* emphasis is always uppermost. His formula for the highest kind of action, the "intellectual love of God," might be grammatically defined as "seeing particulars in their particularity, but remembering always that this particularity is grounded in a total context, and thus is to be understood in terms of this total context." Stated in Spinoza's theological terms it runs: (Book V. Prop. XXIV) "The more we understand particular things, the more we understand God." For (I, XXV, corollary) individual things are nothing but the modes (*modi*) in which God's attributes are expressed in a particular and determinate manner (*certo et determinato modo*).

Perhaps we can appreciate how the scenic emphasis is maintained, even towards the idealistic close of the *Ethics,* if we consider Spinoza's notion of "intuitive knowledge"; for the concept of "intuition" is especially rich in idealistic possibilities. (In fact, the changing values of this word, as we move into romantic philosophy, are as responsive as the changing values of "imagination.") Spinoza distinguished three kinds of knowledge. The first is that of opinion, or imagination, and is inadequate. The second kind is Reason—but higher than Reason stands Intuition, which "proceeds from an adequate idea of the absolute essence of certain attributes of God to the adequate knowledge of the essence of things." (Book II, Prop. XL. Note II). To understand things by this third kind of knowledge is the "highest endeavor of the mind and the highest virtue." Spinoza refers to it as the "eyes of the mind." And it is the kind of knowledge that leads to Spinoza's crowning motive, the intellectual love of God.

Spinoza illustrates the difference in the three forms of knowledge by taking the proportion "1:2::3: ? ." A tradesman, he says, multiplies the second number by the third and divides the product by the first, thus getting 6 as his answer, because he remembers being told to proceed in this way. This would be the lowest form of knowledge, and is the source of error. Or one might proceed in accordance with the demonstration in "the nineteenth proposition of the seventh book of Euclid," concerning the general property of proportionals. This would be the way of Reason. Or we may see the answer at a glance (*uno intuitu*), from the sheer nature of the relation itself (*ex ipsa ratione*).

We shall appreciate the full idealistic possibilities in the concept of intuition when we come to consider the Kantian treatment of knowledge. But note that in Spinoza intuition is derived from *Reason,* the third kind of knowledge being in his system acquired through perfection in the second kind of knowledge—and this second kind of knowledge, or Reason, is thoroughly *scenic*. The first meaning for *ratio* given in Harper's dictionary refers to the reckoning, calculating, and computing of things. Derivatively it came to signify business matters, transactions, affairs. Then respect, regard, consideration for things. Then course, conduct, procedure, manner, method. The conditions or nature of something could be called its *ratio*. Finally we move into such meanings as the faculty of mental action, judgment, understanding, reason. Thence to reasonableness, law, rule, order. And finally, theory, doctrine, system *based* on reason, science, knowledge.

Some of the meanings in the Du Cange *Glossarium Mediae et Infimae Latinitatis* are: thing, authority (*ditio*), ownership, goods, faculties, genus, offspring.

But most important of all for our purposes, one can appreciate the strongly *scenic* significance of Spinoza's usage in particular, by recalling that he equates the *logically* necessary with the *naturally* necessary. Similarly, Spinoza says that God is "naturally prior" (*prior natura*) to his modes where we today would say "logically prior." And though, by the time we reach Rousseau's *Emile,* "nature" itself is transformed from a scene word to an agent word (referring to the principles of growth inherent in human nature), it is obvious that in Spinoza's monistic ways human nature is treated simply as a special case of nature in general, hence a function of scene.

To be sure, when we say that Spinoza derives Intuition from Reason, the dramatistic grammar warns us that any derivation itself is open to two interpretations. As per the paradox of substance, a derivative may be treated as either consistently or divisively derived from its source. By the time we get to Bergson, for instance, it is hard to distinguish a super-rational "intuition" from a sub-rational "instinct." And recall the many early theological battles about the rival claims of "faith" and "knowledge," battles due to a distrust of rational knowledge as being directly inimical to religious insight. Similarly, in contrast with the rationalist claim that intuitive knowledge is the ultimate reward of rational knowledge, we encounter in esthetic theory the "instinctual" artist who, naturally expressive in some medium, resolutely refuses to look a gift horse in the mouth by the study of his craft in conceptual terms. And the psychology books tell of a prodigy who, able to extract cube roots spontaneously (*uno intuitu*) without knowing how he arrived at his results, lost this ability when a kind and helpful savant taught him how to extract cube roots methodically. But any readers sharing the Bergsonian fear that the rational may be the very death of the intuitive are invited at this point to use these very misgivings as an aid toward seeing that Spinoza's position is exactly the opposite of this, though Bergson himself did not think so. The intuition that in his terminology transcends reason is considered not as negating the source which it transcends, but as the ultimate completion or fulfilment of reason.

Darwin

We have observed in Hobbes a nearly symmetrical instance of *scenic* featuring. We could have brought out the encroachment of the *agent* function by examining his theories of monarchy, though he keeps his politics quite scenically infused by defining liberty as "external impediments of motion"; and his famous scenic formula, "the condition of man . . . is a condition of war of everyone against everyone," is stressed as basis of the covenant whereby men submit to a sovereign as a way of getting peace. We have considered Spinoza as a scenic philosopher more ambiguously placed because of the action-motion equation underlying the God-Nature equation.

At first glance, one finds in the doctrines of Darwin a fairly simple instance of the scenic principle, as with this statement at the close of Chapter VI, in *The Origin of Species:*

> It is generally acknowledged that all organic beings have been formed on two great laws—Unity of Type, and the Conditions of Existence. By unity of type is meant that fundamental agreement in structure which we see in organic beings of the same class, and which is quite independent of their habits of life. On my theory, unity of type is explained by unity of descent. The expression of conditions of existence, so often insisted on by the illustrious Cuvier, is fully embraced by the principle of natural selection. For natural selection acts by either now adapting the varying parts of each being to its organic and inorganic conditions of life; or by having adapted them during past periods of time: the adaptations being aided in many cases by the increased use or disuse of parts, being affected by the direct action of the external conditions of life, and subjected in all cases to the several laws of growth and variation. Hence, in fact, the law of the Conditions of Existence is the higher law; as it includes, through the inheritance of former variations and adaptations, that of Unity of Type.

The last sentence here is as nearly perfect an instance of materialism, or reduction to scene, as one could hope for. And Darwin's term, frequently used elsewhere, "accidental variation," is as scenic as is "conditions of existence." Yet it is worth noting, at least, that many of the key terms in Darwin lend themselves readily to appeal by ambiguities of the pathetic fallacy, (an ambiguous personalizing of impersonal events, whereby even so apparently scientific a concept as "adjustment" can refer indeterminately to both actions and motions, as a person may "adjust himself" to a situation by deliberate effort on his part, or the accommodations may be automatic, as with a thermometer's adjustment to a change in temperature). For instance, "adaptation," "competition," "struggle for life," "natural selection," and "survival of the fittest" can all be read and felt as *action* words. Or consider the almost "dramatist" mode of expression in his reference to "one general law leading to the advancement of all organic beings,—namely, multiply, vary, let the strongest live and the weakest die."

Indeed, perhaps in response to the agency-purpose pair which makes readily for a shuttling between *means* and *ends,* we even find him, in explaining his "Natural System" that is "utterly inexplicable in the theory of creation," slipping into references to *purpose.* Thus, when trying to explain why "there is so much beauty throughout nature," and attributing this largely "to the agency of selection," he goes on to say: "Fruit and flowers have been rendered conspicuous by brilliant colors in contrast with the green foliage, in order that the flowers may be readily seen, visited and fertilized by insects, and the seeds disseminated by birds." Yet if I understand his doctrines in their literal application, the flower's use of colors in attracting insects must arise as the result of purely accidental variations, which survived because they happened to attract insects, which in turn happened to make the species more prolific by aiding in the distribution of the pollen.

But, whatever may be the effect of this ambiguity in shaping the appeal of his doctrines on the emotional level, his conscious intention seems purely materialistic: The motions or changes of "conditions" are to be taken as the source of selection among the biologically conditioned motions that make for continuity of type. Some pages later, in answering "miscellaneous objections" to his doctrine, Darwin specifies how very little he would concede to an opponent who was, by our standard, idealistically inclined, and thus wanted to place a strong motivation at the spot covered by the term, agent. Thus:

> Mr. Mivart believes that species change through "an internal force or tendency," about which it is not pretended that anything is known. That species have a capacity for change will be admitted by all evolutionists; but there is no need, as it seems to me, to invoke any internal force beyond the tendency to ordinary variability, which through the aid of selection by man has given rise to many well-adapted domestic races, and which through the aid of natural selection would equally well give rise by graduated steps to natural races of species. The final result will generally have been, as already explained, an advance, but in some few cases a retrogression, in organisation.

Here we see the claims of agent in the offing. Mr. Mivart would obviously make much of them, as in contending that species change their natures through "an internal force or tendency." But Darwin would allow the barest minimum of such internal origination, a mere "tendency to ordinary variability," though even in this slight concession, we see the pressure of *agent*.

In one notable respect, however, the very nature of his subject matter invites a featuring of *agent*, just as we have said that the nature of ethics as a subject matter called for a featuring of *act*. I have in mind the dynastic or heraldic element in his biology itself, as when he considers the future of his evolutionism:

> Our classifications will come to be, as far as they can be so made, genealogies; and will then truly give what may be called the plan of creation. The rules for classifying will no doubt become simpler when we have a definite object in view. We possess no pedigrees or armorial bearings; and we have to discover and trace the many diverging lines of descent in our natural genealogies, by characters of any kind which have long been inherited.

His biology, in brief, invited him to concern himself with *families*. Indeed, his concern even has an "Adamic" pattern, as when he finds cause to assume "that the innumerable species, genera and families, with which this world is peopled, are all descended, each within its own class or group, from common parents." If these families were all families of people, they would be purely and simply *agents*. A biologist's families, however, are families of *organisms*—and organisms might be called a kind of "agent-minus." They might be classed under the term agent to the extent that their behavior has to be accounted for, at least in part, by some purely internal principle of motivation (even though it be but a "tendency to ordinary variability," or a mere power of self-movement on the part of animals). Our Grammar requires this distinction between a motive in some measure intrinsic to living things and the purely scenic explanation for the motions of a bubble rising to the surface. Yet such organisms reflect the same reduction of circumference as we have previously observed with respect to scene. In fact, as per the scene-agent ratio, the turn from agent to organism corresponds to the turn from "Creation" to "Evolution." And by contrast with religions believing in transmigration, orthodox Christianity was always "incipiently evolutionary" because, in addition to the historical elements in the very idea of The Creation itself, Christianity could readily allow that all living things but man be classed as mere automata or organisms, since they were denied the character of agents through being denied the moral freedom that goes with reason.

There is thus a kind of "quasi-idealistic" biology (such as we encounter in much modern genetics, which seeks to control the development of a species by the laws of breeding alone, as with the selecting of seeds from the sturdiest members of a given crop, or by experiments with cross-fertilization). We can detect the idealistic feature here, if we contrast such methods with the materialistic, or scenic methods of those who seek to develop new types by experimenting primarily with changes in external conditions, as with changes in the foods on which the organisms are fed, or the modification of genes by radiation, and the like. There is opportunity for a subtle Grammatical scruple here in looking upon experiments with grafting as materialistic, since the stock may be considered as a kind of environmental condition affecting the nutriment received by the scion grafted upon it. All such lines of effort are obviously scenic in their emphasis, as contrasted with the "idealoid" nature of Mendel's researches into the laws governing the inheritance of "dominant" and "recessive" characters. And laws of inherited characters obviously apply to agents or "agents-minus," practically to the total exclusion of scenic concerns.

Darwin's *Origin of Species* was published in 1859; Mendel published the account of his experiments in 1865. Thus both men wrote midway in the Century of Idealism *par excellence*. All other things being equal, we might expect their biology to be as "idealoid" as the nature of the subject matter permitted. That it would permit a great deal, is evident in the primary stress upon the *familial*, in the work of both the secular Englishman and the Austrian monk. To be sure, Darwin was typical of nineteenth-century English liberalism, in stressing the selective factor of *competition* (which the cloistered priest noticed not at all), and in deriving new species from *individual* variations. The sexual-familial emphasis in Mendel could be treated as the impersonal equivalent of Catholic personalism (one kind of sexual speculation and experiment available to those vowed to chastity and to a sacramental attitude as regards human sexuality).

In keeping with the categorical encouragement which the very nature of biology as a subject holds for the featuring of an "agent-minus," we find Darwin, despite his earlier statement that "Conditions of Existence" is the "higher law," writing in his Conclusion: "The most important of all causes of organic change is one which is almost independent of altered and perhaps suddenly altered physical conditions, namely, the mutual relation of organism to organism." A few pages earlier, in his Recapitulation, he had similarly stated that "the relation of organism to organism is the most important of all relations." And in his first chapter, on "Variation Under Domestication," he had written, "We clearly see that the nature of the conditions is of subordinate importance in comparison with the nature of the organism in determining each particular form of variation;—perhaps of not more importance than the nature of the spark, by which a mass of combustible matter is ignited, has in determining the nature of the flames." But in his later Recapitulation of this same matter, he writes:

> Under domestication we see much variability, caused, or at least excited, by changed conditions of life; but often in so obscure a manner, that we are tempted to consider the variations as spontaneous. Variability is governed by many complex laws,—by correlated growth, compensation, the increased use and disuse of parts, and the definite action of the surrounding conditions.

All told, what is our point? We are trying to specify the exact nature of a great biologist's Grammar, when the nature of the experimental sciences in general calls for a *scenic* stress, yet the study of lineal descent almost inevitably shifts the stress to the motivational functions covered by our term *agent*. Or we might put it this way: In reducing all phenomena to terms of motion, biology is as unambiguously scenic as physics. But as soon as it encounters the subject of *self*-movement, it makes claims upon the areas covered by our term *agent*. We have improvised a solution, for our purposes, by deciding that the biologist's word, "organism," is Grammatically the equivalent of "agent-minus."

As regards Darwin, we have been pointing out how, despite the passages wherein he refers ultimately to "conditions" as the locus of motives, we find in his doctrines an idealistic stress. And we should say that this ambiguity comes to an exquisite focus in his key term, "variability." To illustrate:

Suppose that I wanted to write a work on the filling of vessels. The capacity of vessels to be filled I called their "fillability." My researches would soon convince me that, aside from the mere fact of the containing walls, "fillability" could be explained entirely by *external conditions*.

When it rained, the "fillability" of the vessels was manifest in a rise of their liquid content; in dry weather, there was a cessation of the fill-activity, and a diminution. But now suppose a new situation began to present itself. Suppose I found that sometimes the "fillability" could not be correlated with rainfall. Sometimes there was more fill-activity at times when there had been less rain. So that the contents of the vessels sometimes rose, each at a different rate, even under conditions of drought. That is, suppose they also became filled somewhat independently of conditions. And suppose that I also used my term "fillability" to explain this phenomenon.

I am suggesting that "variability" allows for two quite different meanings, as with the two meanings for "fillability," one referring to a cause *ab extra* and the other to some internal principle of motion. It stands pliantly at the point where scene overlaps upon agent. Because of its affinities with scene, Darwin can use it to explain cases where changing conditions can be correlated with changes in organic structure. But because of its affinities with agent, he can use it to explain cases where variations occur without change of conditions. And particularly when buttressed with his principle of Continuity of Type, it serves this Janus function. For the Conditions of Existence may explain the presence of varieties with functions better suited to conditions prevailing elsewhere.

But we have considered Darwin at sufficient length to show both the scenic logic and the threats to its symmetry in this system which, at first glance, is almost perfectly materialistic. In closing, let us note that a die-hard scenist might save the day for total materialism, by contending that even two daisies living side by side may be living under quite different "external conditions," so that variations in one not found in its brother might be at least hypothetically referrable to external causes. Indeed, the scenic strategy may be applied even *within* the organism itself, since a changed habit on the part of the organism as a whole may be treated as an environmental factor affecting the function of some particular organ, and so leading to its disuse and consequent atrophy. That is, the whole organism can be treated as "environment" for any of its parts.[3]

[3] As for the word "environment" itself, I doubt whether this term, now so characteristic of evolutionary thought, occurs in *The Origin of Species* at all. Various Darwinian terms, in one respect or another its equivalent, are: region, physical conditions, climatal conditions, areas, geographical provinces of the world, period of time, conditions of life or existence, climatal and geographical changes,

The Two Great Hellenistic Materialisms

Of the two great Hellenistic materialisms, each features scene in considering mind as but a finer kind of body, and in contending that as with the body, at death the particles of the soul disintegrate, being scattered among the universal motions. Nevertheless, each of these philosophies has its own particular way of endowing the scene with properties of agent, properties that can then, in accordance with the logic of the scene-agent ratio, be imputed to human agents as deductions from the quality of the ground out of which they arise.

This strategic "pre-agentification" of scene is much less obvious with Epicureanism than with Stoicism; yet it can be found here too, in a term that does for the Epicurean genealogy of motives what "variability" does for Darwinism. I refer to one important trait possessed by the infinite atoms of which the Epicurean universe is said to be composed.

These atoms account for the rise of worlds and of animal forms much as with Darwinian evolution. That is, out of chance atomic combinations many forms arose that could not survive their monstrous unsuitability for the conditions of existence in which they happened to find themselves. But from the atomic seeds many other forms arose that were suited to grow and multiply, the seasonality of their development happening to correspond with the march of the seasons themselves. The stress is upon the accidental here; and in contrast with the Stoic stress upon the action of divine purpose in the creation of the world, Lucretius holds: "Nothing was born in the body that we might use it; but that which is born begets for itself a use."

But from the standpoint of our Grammar it is notable that, although Lucretius thinks of the atomic bodies as possessing different weights and as forever falling through the void, he specifically denies that they could ever have come into contact with one another, were it not for the action of another principle. For he argues that, regardless of their differences in weight, the particles would all fall through empty space at the same rate of speed, and so would remain forever out of touch with one another, except for the presence, within the atomic seeds, of a slight tendency to *swerve*. And in thus swerving, they collide, rebound, and

range, range of time, habitat, surrounding physical conditions, and scenic terms less general in meaning, such as Plutonic rocks, sedimentary formation, Laurentian, littoral.

variously combine, to cause the endless evolution and destruction of worlds, things, and beings.

This slight tendency to swerve or deviate, (L. *clinamen;* Gr. *paregklisis*) this *inclination* arising as a principle of motion *within* the atom, has been looked upon as a break in the symmetry of the atomic scheme. And I guess it is, if we judge it purely from the standpoint of a terminology designed to account for evolution in terms of motion. But the Epicurean physics is the basis for an *ethics.* Hence we are dramatistically admonished to look for the "seeds" of an ethical principle in the physical terminology itself. Or, otherwise stated, we are admonished to examine this "inclination" of the atoms on the possibility that it is a device for transcending sheer motion, and opening towards the wider realm of action and agenthood. Lucretius himself is quite explicit on the subject, when discussing the conclusion that would follow the denial that the atoms swerve of themselves:

> If all motions involve one another, each leading inevitably into the next, and if the first-beginnings of motion do not, by swerving (*declinando*) introduce some new principle to break the bonds of destiny and to keep causes from following causes endlessly, how, I ask, do all living things snatch from fate the power to advance according to the dictates of the will, regulating (*declinamus*) our movements not merely in set response to time and place, but as the mind directs? For unquestionably in these matters the point of origin is in the will, and movements are conveyed from it to other parts of the body. . . . The fact that the mind does not feel an inner compulsion in all its actions, and is not forced to bear and suffer as if in defeat, is due to a tiny swerving (*clinamen*) of the first-principles, not to the set requirements of time and place.

Employing our shift of emphasis as a first rough approximate, we might note that such "clinaminous" or "parenclitic" atoms have this advantage: In their role as *"swerving* atoms" they give us a scenic derivation for human freedom, thereby maintaining the symmetry of the scene-act and scene-agent ratios. But in their role as "swerving *atoms,"* they account for the world on a purely evolutionary basis, without derivation from the divine act of a divine agent. As a result, the terminology is suited to allay the terrors of superstition, by interpreting "acts of God" in terms of sheer motion, and thereby freeing men of the belief that storms, floods, plagues, earthquakes and other natural cataclysms and calamities both public and private are visited upon them by vengeful deities.

The Stoic dialectic, looking upon Nature as the process that giveth and taketh away, pantheistically equates Nature itself with Providence (*pronoia*), and so with Reason, the Will of God, and strict logical Necessity. The principle of moral action is introduced into a universe of necessary motions by an ambiguously "naturalistic" device, in that each thing is required to live according to its nature, and man is by nature rational. This rationality in turn is conceived in political or social terms, all men being intended to serve one another, and all things inferior to man being for the use of man.

As we read Marcus Aurelius from the standpoint of the Grammar, one of the most striking things we notice is the kind of "moral utilitarianism" that arises from the great stress upon the *purposive* factor in the Stoic conception of Nature as a divine plan. The agency-purpose ratio is the same as the integral Grammatical relation between means and ends; and the Stoic teleology clearly shows how this ratio provides a bridge "from Providence to pragmatism," in admonishing the philosopher to ask himself first of all to what use each thing, person, or act should be put. For to say that all things are brought about by God for a purpose, is to say that all things have a *use*. However, such moral pragmatism is still a long way from modern pragmatism as developed under the combined impetus of business and technology. Indeed, we see the Stoic philosopher in the process of *coming upon* the function of agency, but still expressing the position primarily in terms of the starting point, purpose ("Providence"). Marcus Aurelius' role as administrator doubtless had much to do with the incipient pragmatism here, while the condition of the governmental bureaucracy in a time so long prior to modern technology would call for a moral pragmatism rather than for the typical modern intellectualistic brand centering in the philosophy of scientific method.

Rhetorical and Symbolic Levels

Though these Grammatical observations should be enough for our present purposes, they leave unconsidered many important matters that would require examination and demonstration rather in terms of Rhetoric and Symbolic. Simply to illustrate how the other levels impinge upon the Grammatical, I shall add a few observations in the form of mere hypotheses, problems, or undemonstrated propositions:

(1) Note the evidence of working at cross-purposes in Lucretius' *De Rerum Natura*. A poem designed to establish the aloofness of the gods from human affairs begins with a magnificent invocation to Venus, as the all-mother. Though the poem is thus significantly offered in the name of Venus, in one book it strikingly caricatures the effects of love, particularly the errors of judgment provoked by love (in spirit somewhat as the treatment of love in the *Phaedrus* might be if it lacked the second, pious speech on love which Socrates remorsefully offered to make amends for his first impious burlesque).

The theme develops from that of the divine fertility (as exemplified in Venus and her replica, the maternal Earth), to the explanation of all evolution in terms of the seminal principle; but it *ends* when the theme has taken on a sinister quality. For just as there are atomic seeds of things good for man, so there are seeds of disease and death—and the poem closes on a scene of carnage, with a population dying hideously in a plague, and rioting amidst the rites of burial. Something seems to have gone wrong with the *direction* of this poem, at least as regards the philosophic ends of solace. The intention of showing that calamities are not acts of gods leads not to a *medical* treatment of symptoms, but to a *poetic* one, seeking to make the plague as vivid and picturesque as possible, and so building up in one way the disturbing thoughts it is designed to remove in another.

(2) Also, there is much evidence in this poem that the author is in some way goaded. Indeed, on the Symbolic plane, as a likely hunch that may or may not be verified on closer examination, I think one is always justified in looking for tender apprehensions behind the apparent toughnesses of materialist debunking, as Bentham in his childhood had an abnormally intense fear of ghosts, and in adult life developed a critique of language particularly zealous in disclosing kinds of words that named merely fabulous or fictitious entities having but the semblance of reality; or as he aimed to dispel the moral pretense in idealistic words, by treating them in terms of the material interests they cloak, thus translating spirit back into body, which as regards the childhood pattern equalled the transformation of ghosts back into corpses. And similarly, if Lucretius was not goaded, why so monumental an attempt to assure men that the wrath of the gods will pursue them neither in

this life nor in the life hereafter? What unresolved guilt may perhaps reside in this attack upon religions that believe in the punishments of heaven? What was it that would make an Epicurean find in the thought of the soul's mortality the very solace that Christians seek in the thought of immortality?

For one thing, when we contrast the Epicurean ideal of individual aloofness with the Stoic social-mindedness ("Imagine a whole city of Epicureans!" the Stoic Epictetus exclaims incredulously), we see reasons to believe that the Epicurean individualism (which began with the breakdown of the Greek *polis*) did not completely satisfy the needs of justification by socialization. Or better, put it this way: the concept of an aloofness that neither touched worldly things nor could be touched by them attributed to the gods the Epicureans' own ideal way of life. Hence, insofar as the ideal in its human aspect did invite to twinges of conscience (in the avoidance of *civic* responsibilities) the same ideal as a description of the gods assured one that these twinges of conscience were not called for by the *universal* situation.

(A page of Stoicism selected almost at random will be enough to show that the equating of the *civic* and the *universal* was very much in the air, the Stoic preparation for Christianity residing precisely in widening the concept of citizenship from *local* to *metaphysical* dimensions. On the other hand, I most decidedly do not mean to suggest that there was any cause for guilt in the Epicurean doctrine as an invitation to sensual pleasures. Such an interpretation of Epicureanism can be found only in the writings of its opponents. The guilt and sensuality rather would be that of one who thought of his private comfort while there was public work to be done. For the Epicurean ideal was of a pleasant slumber one might enjoy if at the same time he were *thoroughly aware* that he was sleeping. This would be in contrast with the Stoic ideal of a painless insomnia, moral vigilance, a constant watching and waiting which might nonetheless, with the help of rational doctrine, combine universal sympathy and individual apathy—and this moral firmness required of the virtuous was scenically grounded in the Stoics' concept of a universal tension which they name not neutrally but ethically or eulogistically: *"eutonia,"* a "good" tension, which may alas! find its modern equivalent in "hypertension," when the Stoic patience has been made impatient by conditions inviting us to experience in terms of "progress" and "frustration.")

(3) In the case of Lucretius, who was an Epicurean not in the disintegrated culture of a Greek *polis* but in Rome at the time of Cicero, the possibilities of a secret "Epicurean guilt" seem particularly strong, in that Rome was so intensely civic-minded. Besides, there seems to be some basic "problem of the mother" involved in his version of the fertile atoms, as though these uterine principles, from which all living things are derived and to which at death they return, constituted a *philosophic* matrix alternative to that of some *poetic* parent vaguely comprising, all in one: Mother Venus, Mother Earth, and the human mother. (Imagistic bridges are there aplenty for anyone who would show first that fertile Venus and the fertile Earth can be equated, and next that the human body and the earth's body can be equated.) As regards the medium of expression: the opposition shows in his treatment of poetry itself, which he equates with childish things (saying that he writes his doctrine in verse as one uses honey to disguise bitter medicine for children). And when he is on the subject of propitiation rites invented by humans who believe that they have defiled Mother Earth, he calls them mistaken but *beautiful*. (Surely we should not be overstraining matters here to translate: *philosophically* bad but *poetically* good.)

All told, then, there seems to be some clash between the philosophic identity and the poetic one, as exemplified in the change from the Venus-fertility to the fertility of the seminal atoms (the first involving such gods as require propitiation, the second involving such gods as leave men unpersecuted, and the conception of whom invites men to live in their image). And as evidence that the attempted transformation is incomplete, we have the direction of the work itself, ending on the imagery of plague. One might think this an accident, except that it seems such a *fit* ending, powerful and resonant.

It is just possible that the unresolved guilt in this poem has given rise to a remarkable pun, a pun that might go far to explain why, of all Roman battles, the battles with the Carthaginians continued to assume such importance in the popular imagination, long after Carthage was destroyed in the struggles with Rome for economic control of the Mediterranean. I refer to a passage in Book III where Lucretius is explaining how, in accordance with his doctrine, we need worry no more about doom after death than we worried, before our birth, about the possible outcome of the wars with Carthage. The editor of my school text thinks this a particularly effective statement at the time when it was written, since the Punic wars were just beyond the lifetime of Lucretius and his contemporaries, "and marked the most critical period of the Roman state up to his time." But there may be a still deeper linguistic process operating here. I refer to the fact that the Latin word for the Carthaginians is *Poeni,* while the Latin word for the goddesses of vengeance is *Poenae.* In the dative and ablative forms, the two would be exactly the same, *Poenis.* And the word is thus used in Lucretius:

ad confligendum venientibus undique Poenis,

a line which, taken in itself, could be translated, with equal justice, either as "when the Carthaginians were coming to the attack from all sides" or as "when the goddesses of Vengeance were coming to the attack from all sides." There is no doubt that literally the reference is to the Carthaginians. But if we consider it in keeping with such studies of ambiguity as Empson has given us, may we not legitimately hear effects even more resonant than the literal meaning itself? The design in Lucretius' doctrine, deriving life from seeds to which at death it returns, equates the state before birth with the state after death—and the essence of the latter (without Poenae) must well be stated ambiguously as the essence of the former (without fear of Poeni).

(4) As for Stoicism, with such profound sense of civic responsibility as we find in the Meditations of Aurelius, the burden seems to derive from a different source. One could hardly ask for a more thorough attempt at justification by socialization than shows in the diary of this conscientious emperor. Why, then, such down-turning? Why, intermingled with such a profound philosophy of acceptance, affirming so devoutly that the world and all its properties and accidents manifest the nature, will, and reason of God—why of a sudden the almost brutal hatred of the flesh? Why such sudden bursts of impatience in this austere philosophy of patience? All nature being divine, it cannot be purely doctrinal motives that prompts these sudden outcries.

Grammatically, the furthest we need go is this: the *distinction* between the finer rational matter of which mind is composed and the coarser matter of which body is composed may be heightened into a *contrast.* At least, there is always this dialectical possibility of converting the hierarchically related (one term "higher" than another) into the oppositionally related (one term *vs.* the other). But Stoic monism, on purely doctrinal grounds, would seem to require the hierarchic interpretation of the natural order. And I would seek to account for the sudden bursts of fury against the body as resulting, on the Symbolic plane, from the fact that Stoic acceptance was aimed at the *transubstantiation of the excremental,* in attempting to proclaim even the repugnant aspects of the world as essentially divine. As strict an exemplar of the scene-agent ratio as is to be found in all philosophy, equating the human body, the civic body, and the universal body in ways that promote a constant shuttling back and forth among the three, the Stoic burden, the doing of one's duty, seems, on the purely Symbolic plane, to derive from the necessary befouling of the nest implicit in the pantheistic doctrine. Applying shift of accent, we could state the matter thus: in moments of moral exaltation, the result is a scrupulous *"transcendence* of offal." But in moments of misgiving, when the exaltation has collapsed, the result is a "transcendence of *offal."*

(5) Stoicism, of course, covers quite a range of Stoics. And the Stoicism of Epictetus, the manumitted slave, differs greatly in its tone from that of Marcus Aurelius, the ruler of an empire beset by war and decay. And just as in reading the *Meditations* we read the thoughts of a man who, writing in private, never forgot for a moment that he was an emperor, experiencing bondage only in the deeply moral sense of willingly dutiful service in the administering of the commonwealth, so in reading the *Discourses* we read the thoughts of a man who, dictating to a disciple and probably in the presence of many others, never forgot that he was a manumitted slave; or, if he did forget, he forgot only in the sense that he generalized and moralized his change of condition, and so talked always in terms of the Progress (*prokope*) from spiritual slavery to spiritual freedom. In Epictetus, accordingly, there is a kind of lift that one will encounter not at all in the solemn emperor. To hold the highest rank in the world, and to have that rank a burden, is hardly to find much cause for talk of "progress," even in its spiritual translation—and Epictetus' stress upon the ways and means of emancipation becomes, in Marcus Aurelius, an emperor's doctrinal subjection to a political community which he secretly despised, though he repeatedly admonished that any separation from nature or society was an "abscess."

We must remember, however, that the freedman's conception of "progress" differed essentially from its modern pragmatist replica.

when "Providence" has become secularized in terms of investment and utility. The improvement of status that the freedman had in mind was quite alien to the modern "higher standard of living" based upon the acquisition of new commodities, the satisfying of "new needs," by an improvement in one's earning power and buying power. Epictetus laid great stress upon property as the very ground of freedom: but this property was in the possession of Reason and Will, inner powers that are free beyond any tyrant's control. That which is wholly "mine," that in which I am not *subject,* is my power to deal with "impressions" (that is, to philosophically discount any evidences of my misfortune). "Every man's body is a measure for his property, as the foot is the measure for his shoe," said this frail and sickly man who, by reason of the scene-agent ratio, might thus be expected to ask for little. But in the personal power of philosophic deliberation and resignation, every man was a "Senator" (Stoics always being prompt to moralize their politics and politicalize their ethics).

As for the emperor, Matthew Arnold has commented on his struggles against the "feeling of discontent, so natural to the great for whom there seems nothing left to desire or strive for." He then cites the list of indebtednesses with which the diary significantly begins: "I have to thank Heaven that I was subjected to a ruler and a father (Antoninus Pius) who was able to take away all pride from me" . . . etc. But Arnold does not relate this to a previous observation he had made about the dignity of the Stoic ethic, when noting that, as contrasted with the bribes to virtue which Christianity offered by its promises of heavenly reward, Aurelius nobly proclaimed the value of moral service in itself:

> What more dost thou want when thou hast done a man a service? Art thou not content that thou hast done something conformable to thy nature, and dost thou seek to be paid for it, just as if the eye demanded a recompense for seeing, or the feet for walking?

Might not Arnold also have related this superior ethic to his remarks on the "enfeebling" and "deteriorating" effects which the imperial status had upon Aurelius, depriving him of ambitions? The only two ambitions open to a great ruler would be the paranoiac extension of his realm into still wider regions (whereas in actuality the circumference of Roman dominion was contracting), or the improvement of the conditions of his subject. The second course, however, could only amount to service without reward, as administrator, as commander, and as secret moral exhorter. Thus the same imperial conditions apparently offer the same contributions to the concept of virtue without heavenly bribes as to the dispiriting clamps upon ambition.[4]

(6) The spectacle of an emperor's voluntary subjection to the thought of his elders, of his family, of his intimates, and of society, and his pious gratification in the fact that he had so long preserved his sexual purity, recalls a theory that sex repression protects capitalism by serving as a device to dispirit the working classes so that their assertiveness and aggressiveness are inhibited. I know this theory (of Wilhelm Reich) only by hearsay, so I do not know in what ways it is modified and protectively buttressed. But in studying the diary of Aurelius, one does indeed find what is, as judged by modern romantic standards of freedom from "frustration," a ruler who obeys the code of sex repression as devotedly and devoutly and implicitly as he could ever have wished his subjects to do, had he known and subscribed to the Reich theory. Much depends upon the nature of the "equations" here. With a person who treats sexual potency and political power as consistently related, a sexual inhibition would doubtless lead to a political dispiriting. And I would assume that Reich himself shared this equation. But another temperament may be differently organized, treating the cause of political emancipation as a kind of secular religion, for which he might symbolically and sacrificially fit himself by an attitude of chastity, or priestliness, however tough the terms in which this might be conceived. And while it is true that Friedrich Engels had a mistress, it is equally true that Karl Marx disapproved with an almost Puritanic vigor.

However, if you will grant me sufficient reservations, I think that the Reichian doctrine could be applied to this ruler who was, from the moral point of view, as thoroughly subject, and a worker, as an artisan could be. For if you will read his diary carefully, I think you will agree that it is not addressed simply to "himself." We should question whether it is addressed to any one audience, however vague or hypo-

[4] As for the purely family motives involved here, it is notable that Arnold subjected himself as resolutely to a father-principle as we see Aurelius doing in his opening list of indebtednesses, the pattern showing to perfection in Arnold's "Sohrab and Rustum" where, instead of dreaming the typical nineteenth-century dream of Jack the Giant-Killer, the poet dreams of a son slain in combat with a father.

thetical that audience might be. And we should do so for this reason: Stoicism was a highly alembicated dialectic. In its early stages (which survive but in fragments) it seems to have made important contributions to dialectical analysis. And the least we can expect of a dialectician, as of a dramatist, is that he speak in several voices. But the diary being all written in one voice, the variety would show more subtly, in the fact that this voice could address itself to several auditors, more or less distinct from one another, though they all be but private sub-personalities combined in the public office of the one imperial person. Each of these sub-personalities would have its own concerns, hence to an extent its own manner of speech. And one of such nameless and unplaced auditors to whom Marcus Aurelius sometimes addressed himself was a kind of *ideal, philosophy-minded subject* who could, when properly admonished by the diarist, be induced to see things in Stoic terms, yet did not share the social status, political power, and material privileges of the emperor; in fact he was often inclined to grumble at being placed in an inferior and near-destitute condition. Speaking in the firmest Stoic terms, the philosopher-king bade this grumbling subject be content with his lot, on the grounds that the assigning of a lowly position to some men was part of the divine plan, the Providential design of a natural but rational order in which no individual could really suffer so long as his deprivations served the needs of the entire community.

And that he might address this lowly citizen persuasively, thus secretly in his diary, the conscientious emperor gladly imposed upon himself all manner of dispiriting deprivations, seeking to live a kind of life that would be magically an inducement to this other self, himself not as imperial ruler, but as imperial subject. And if the subject could thus by these secret exhortations be persuaded to live accordingly, the prevailing structure of material privileges might be expected to continue. As so modified, I believe I could subscribe to the Reichian theory.

But we have said enough to indicate, even with readers who might disagree with these particular propositions, how the Grammatical area impinges upon the areas of Rhetoric and Symbolic. And though our discussion of the scenic Grammar aims to be representative rather than exhaustive, we should like to end this section by comparing and contrasting two other materialisms, both modern, one powerfully public, the other serenely private, one aggressive, the other retiring, and the

two so different from one another that the adherents of either would
be scandalized to hear the other mentioned in the same breath.   I refer
to the philosophies of Marx and Santayana.   But the fact that each was
strongly affected by German transcendentalism requires that we postpone their consideration until we have examined the functions of the
term, *agent*.

II

AGENT IN GENERAL

IDEALISM, in the Baldwin dictionary, is described thus: "In metaphysics, any theory which maintains the universe to be throughout the work of reason and mind." And elsewhere: "Any theory which seeks the explanation, or ultimate *raison d'être*, of the cosmic evolution in the realization of reason, self-consciousness, or spirit, may fairly claim to be included under this designation. For the end in such a system is not only the result, but—is also the true world-building power." In the *Encyclopaedia Britannica*, an epistemological factor is considered uppermost, as idealism is said to hold that "Apart from the activity of the self or subject in sensory reaction, memory and association, imagination, judgment and inference, there can be no world of objects."

The traits here mentioned are enough to indicate that the unadulteratedly idealistic philosophy starts and ends in the featuring of properties belonging to the term, *agent*. Idealistic philosophies think in terms of the "ego," the "self," the "super-ego," "consciousness," "will," the "generalized I," the "subjective," "mind," "spirit," the "oversoul," and any such "super-persons" as church, race, nation, etc. Historical periods, cultural movements, and the like, when treated as "personalities," are usually indications of idealism.

The variants in esthetic theory stress such terms as "sensibility," "expression," "self-expression," "consciousness" and the "unconscious." The Crocean philosophy has been prominent as a bridge between metaphysical and esthetic idealism. In his preface to *The Portrait of a Lady*, Henry James gives us a characteristically idealistic statement when referring to "the artist's prime sensibility" as the "soil out of which his subject springs" and which "grows" the work of art. Here a book is treated as an act grounded in the author's mind as its motivating scene. The same idealistic pattern is carried into his methods as a novelist, when he selects some "sensibility" who will serve as the appreciative "centre" of his story, and lets the reader follow the story *in terms of* this single consciousness.

Because of its stress upon agent, idealism leads readily into both individual and group psychology. Its close connection with epistemology, or the problem of knowledge, is due to this same bias. For to approach the universe by asking ourselves how knowledge is possible is to ground our speculations psychologistically, in the nature of the *knower*.

Idealization

Sociologically there is an invitation to an idealistic philosophy whenever important human economic relations have become "idealized" or "spiritualized." The Greek word "Moira" is a case in point. It is defined in a modern English dictionary as "the ancient deity who assigns to every man his lot." In this sense it meant Destiny, and was associated with the Three Fates. Consulting a Greek dictionary, however, we find that the word also had a much more realistic significance: a *part* (as opposed to the whole); that which is one's due; a share, or portion (as of a meal). In short, we note the same range between realistic and idealistic senses that we find in our English word "lot" itself.

In its realistic sense, *moira* had a very explicit reference. It referred to the amount that an individual member of the tribe got when things were divided up. "Destiny" or Chance was involved, in that goods incapable of division into exactly equivalent parts were distributed by the drawing of lots, as with the rotation of public office in the Athenian democracy. Hence, one's *moira* was one's proper portion. It was probably never wholly equal, since a man's portion would differ from a child's, etc.; but in the early states of the tribal culture it was relatively near to equality; or inequalities were settled by accident as in a lottery (though the designs of Chance could themselves be felt as "meaningful," a motive in the category not of "motion" but of "action").

In time, however, the development of class distinctions within the tribe subtilized or rarified the concept of lot. Members of different classes would be allotted different *portions*. Such inequalities of portion came to be fixed by tradition rather than being decided anew on each occasion (as with the taking of booty in battle). Hence one's "lot" was decided when he was born into one social class rather than another, a peasant's lot being traditionally different from the king's, etc. In time, therefore, one's "lot" or "portion" might even come to reside in his receiving nothing at all.

In proportion as the word lost its original realistic reference to visible, tangible divisions, we should consider it to have become idealized, or spiritualized. Words of this sort are particularly serviceable when, *unity* having given way to *disunity,* there is a call for *unification.* Hence the idealistic ingredient in Plato's *Republic,* which aims at a *unified* State, founded upon a vision of absolute Good, as a reaction to the individualistic and relativistic teachings of the Sophists.

For the Sophists, defining justice in a more realistic sense, observed that there was a different justice for the rich than for the poor. Etymologically, as we have observed before, the Sophists had the better of the argument, since the Greek word for justice, *dike,* referred originally to a *way of life;* and manifestly there were different ways of life, with correspondingly different values, for the different social classes.

But Plato sought for a "higher" concept of justice, an "ideal" justice that could be conceived as transcending all these different justices. The nature of language, in allowing readily for what Korzybski would call "higher levels of generalization," encourages this search for an "idea" of justice prevailing above and despite the many different "justices," or ways, necessarily embodied in a society that had developed quite a range of economic classes, each with its own properties and proprieties. Dialectically, any conflict between two concepts of justice can be removed by the adoption of a remoter term broad enough to encompass both, as a distinction between farmhouse and palace can be resolved in classing them both as "dwellings."

Justice in such an over-all sense would obviously serve the ends of unification. And insofar as the law courts would "ideally" serve this same role, in aiming at a kind of justice that mediated among the differing ways of differing classes, we can see how the profuse development of law invites to idealistic philosophy. Materialist "debunkers" of such legal idealism can then interpret the "ideal" in terms of its "betrayal"; for "unification" is not unity, but a *compensation for disunity*—hence, any term for "ideal" justice can be interpreted as a rhetorical concealment for *material injustice,* particularly when the actual history of legal decisions over a long period can be shown to have favored class justice *in the name of* ideal justice.

The thought suggests an ironic connection between idealism and the written contract. For before the spread of literacy, a man could break his promise simply by forgetting exactly what he had promised. After the spread of literacy, however, since promises are put unchangeably into writing, the man who would break his promise must hire lawyers to prove that his words no longer mean what they were obviously meant to mean. Such enterprise often requires great "idealization" or "spiritualization," quite as your opponent in a game, if he is neither wrong nor a liar, yet would call your shot "out" when it was *in*, can do so only by being a profound idealist. The courts themselves often come to accept the ingenious misinterpretations proposed by our corporation lawyers such as the legal fiction that financial corporations are persons (thereby deserving the freedom granted to human beings by divine, natural, or Constitutional law). For the judges talk the same language, usually having been corporation lawyers themselves. Hence in time our very notions of reality are affected, since the idealistic fictions have been written into the very law of the land, and the law is our "reality" insofar as it is a public structure of *motives*.

If deception were the only result of the relation between the ideal and the real, ideas would long ago have ceased to deceive. But just as a lie is "creative" in the sense that it *adds* to reality, so there is the powerfully and nobly creative aspect of idealism, since an ideal may serve as standard, guide, incentive—hence may lead to new real conditions. The power of ideas, in such respects, is in the visionary futurism of a Washington or Lenin and their followers, of a Shelley and his public, of a promoter and his investors. And so an *idea* of justice may make possible some measure of its *embodiment* in material situations.

This side of idealism, in fitting it especially to stress the aspect of the agent as *creator,* accounts for the strong idealistic bias in esthetic theories, as with the idealistic Coleridge's view of poetry as a "dim analogue of Creation." True, esthetics came to have as its essential rule the treatment of art in terms of "uselessness." But this seems explainable rather by reason of the fact that the esthetic was conceived in direct opposition to the utilitarianism of business and applied science. And despite the opposition between philosophies of art and the philosophies of the practical, both could be idealistic insofar as business, science, and art all stressed the *innovative*.

Despite their apparent materialism, theories of positive law would likewise fall under the head of idealism. This becomes apparent when we consider that, in accordance with the theory of positive law, constitutions and similar legal enactments are to be taken as the ground by reference to which judgments of legality are substantiated. Such laws and constitutions derive from assemblies whose enactments are taken to represent "the will of the people"—and of course all variants of Rousseau's *volonté générale* are idealistic. The idealistic perspective is further accentuated, in the United States, by the fiction that the will of the people today is consubstantial with the will of the Founding Fathers. Those who established the Constitution are co-agents with those who perpetuate it—and the document itself, considered as a structure of motivations, is a creature of the human will. Hence, though it is a *ground* of action, its essential feature is in its derivation from the attitudes of human *agents*.

When we introduce materialistic considerations, we readily see how idealistic the doctrines of positive law really are. For scenic tests make it apparent that no ground resting in the human will alone can possibly have sufficient circumference to name the important conditions of legality. Any man-made constitution is itself an enactment that takes place in a constitution of a much wider orbit—and a document whose terminology of motives greatly narrows its circumference, as is necessarily the case with a Constitution adopted by some human assembly, repeatedly requires judicial decisions that press for the addition of new terms. These terms are in effect "amendments" to the Constitution, amendments made by "extra-Constitutional" procedures. They are not voted upon by the people or by the legislatures, but are introduced by the Courts. Insofar as they are new terms they introduce new coördinates of motivation. And any judgment which in effect introduces a new *motive* into the Constitution has, to that extent, amended the document. (These remarks, however, anticipate a subject that we shall consider at length in a later chapter.)

Unification

Sociologically, we can also relate the historical development from realism (and its opponent nominalism) to idealism (and its opponent materialism) as a response to the modern proliferations of finance. Indeed, we might almost state it as a cultural law that "realism plus money equals idealism." That is, the tribal pattern of thinking, when broken by the new ways that money promotes, calls for such "unification" as we find in nationalism. The introduction of money as a new term in effect gives to the act of barter a new dimension. And the greater the development of the financial rationale, the greater is the "spirituality" in man's relations to material goods, which he sees less in terms of their actual nature as goods, and more in the "ideal" terms of the future and of monetary (symbolic) profit. And any actual divisiveness in the social body which the inequalities of money intensify, is one more call upon idealistic philosophies of "unification," which can set up group "ideals" (embodied in "laws") to protect private wealth in the name of the commonwealth.

In Emerson's *Nature* there is a passage clearly indicating how the separations of private property are matched by the unifying idealism of country (here esthetically combining connotations of nature, region, and nation):

> The charming landscape which I saw this morning is indubitably made up of some twenty or thirty farms. Miller owns this field, Locke that, and Manning the woodland beyond. But none of them owns the landscape. There is a property in the horizon which no man has but he whose eye can integrate all the parts, that is, the poet. This is the best part of these men's farms, yet to this their warranty-deeds give no title.

It is a type of thinking capable of organizing mighty powers, as men materially in different worlds can be spiritually one.

Technology invites idealistic unification on two major counts. First, like money and in conjunction with money, it makes for diversity and unequal rates of change that require as social corrective the unifying function of ideas and ideals "creatively" at odds with conditions as they look when seen without the idealistic exaltation. And a more technical incentive to idealism derives from the fact that technology, as applied science, invites us to put the major stress upon knowledge. And the problem of knowledge is the epistemological problem, a psychologistic emphasis that falls directly under the head of agent.

Berkeley

But turning now to purely intrinsic considerations, let us examine a representative idealistic philosopher, George Berkeley. For though modern idealist trends emerge with Descartes and Leibniz, and eventually lead into the Big Four of German romanticism (Kant, Fichte, Schelling, and Hegel) it is through the English empiricists Locke, Berkeley, and Hume that the intermediate development is to be traced. Before Berkeley, the doctrines are still largely in formation. After him came Hume, whose brilliant skepticism saddled the school with such burdensome problems that the German Big Four all write like the shifting of cars in a freight yard. But in Berkeley's *Treatise Concerning the Principles of Human Knowledge,* we find the idealistic terminology put forward with as much clarity and directness as in the Hobbesian use of the materialist terminology. And to trace some of its major steps is to see beyond a doubt why idealism is to be considered as a featuring of the term agent, a mode of discourse that gives voice to this term, permitting the term in effect to make an address, with only occasional heckling from the other terms that stand in the offing.

The inquiry begins psychologistically, hence in terms of agent, by questioning the possibility of "abstract ideas," as Locke had defined them in his *Essay Concerning Human Understanding.* Berkeley maintains, for instance, that one cannot conceive of a triangle in the abstract, but must have a picture, more or less accurate, of some visible or tangible triangle. One may, of course, become so familiar with the *word* triangle that he can use it without pausing to imagine some empirical context for the word. But when he pauses and tries to conceive the meaning of which the word may be a sign, he must think of some particular triangle and let it serve as a reference for all triangles. The mere conception of a triangle in the abstract, with no visible or tangible shape whatever, Berkeley asserts to be an impossibility. So similarly with abstract ideas such as extension, color, animal, body.

> And it is equally impossible for me to form the abstract idea of motion distinct from the body moving, and which is neither swift nor slow, curvilinear nor rectilinear; and the like may be said of all other abstract general ideas whatsoever.

Whether or not the reader agrees with this empiricist position, he must grant it is a perfect starting-point for a philosophy that would confront the Known in terms of the *Knower*.

By thus reducing abstract ideas to mere *words*, however, Berkeley is, surprisingly, able to reduce all sensory experience to *ideas*. Or as he puts it:

> It is indeed an opinion strangely prevailing amongst men, that houses, mountains, rivers, and in a word all sensible objects, have an existence, natural or real, distinct from their being perceived by the understanding. But with how great an assurance and acquiescence soever this principle may be entertained in the world, yet whoever shall find in his heart to call it in question may, if I mistake not, perceive it to involve a manifest contradiction. For what are the forementioned objects but the things we perceive by sense? and what do we perceive *besides our own ideas or sensations?* and is it not plainly repugnant that any one of these, or any combination of them, should exist unperceived?

Note that he here makes "ideas" and "sensations" synonymous. Hence the basic Berkeleian equation: To be is to be perceived, *"esse is percipi."* And everything that makes up the "real" world for us must meet this test. We make our way among "ideas." And we learn how to deal with other "ideas," that we can bring about desired situations, which are themselves "ideas," insofar as they are perceived; and insofar as they are not perceived, they don't exist.

Ingeniously reversing the usual application of the Occamite law of parsimony, he points out that no hypothesis of "matter" is necessary to account for experience. *"It is possible we might be affected with all the ideas we have now, though there were no bodies existing without, resembling them.* Hence, it is evident the supposition of external bodies is not necessary for the producing our ideas." Matter, "or the absolute existence of corporeal objects," would "be not even missed in the world, but everything as well, may much easier be conceived without it." With the help of our senses we learn how to vary the sets of "ideas" which we experience, so that we can encounter the desired sensations, or ideas, say, of buying a ticket and taking a train to a particular destination, where, if true sensations or ideas of a successful trip occur, we may expect to encounter the true sensations or ideas of arriving at our desired destination, with its appropriate set of sensations or ideas.

We here sum up briefly a position for which Berkeley argues with considerable thoroughness. One must consult the original if he would do justice to the various steps in the exposition. But whether or not one is convinced by Berkeley's arguments, one must agree that they are statements saying what can be said about "matter" (that is, *scene*) when considered in terms of "ideas" (that is, *agent*). For our purposes here, it is not necessary to review all the stages in Berkeley's argument. What we need is enough to show clearly a functioning of the term agent.

We referred to the creative emphasis in idealism. Though this creative element is often called "the Idea," in the Berkeleian system "ideas" are called inactive; for the active principle is said to reside in a more direct term for agent. "This perceiving, active being is what I call *mind, spirit, soul,* or *myself.*" And "there is not any other substance than *spirit,* or that which perceives." In contrast with materialist reduction to terms of motion, Berkeley holds that "motion is not without the mind." The "ideas" are "unthinking" things, since they are the things that the agent *thinks.* "The very being of an idea implies passiveness and inertness in it, insomuch that it is impossible for an idea to do anything." Thoughts themselves, don't think—hence the thinker is active, the thought is passive. "Things" in the everyday sense, are "collections of ideas," the scenic here clearly being seen in terms of agent:

> Thus, for example, a certain color, taste, smell, figure, and consistence, having been observed to go together, are accounted one distinct thing, signified by the name "apple." Other collections of ideas constitute a stone, a tree, a book, and the like sensible things; which, as they are pleasing or disagreeable, excite the passions of love, hatred, joy, grief, and so forth.

His position is summed up in paragraph 26:

> We perceive a continual succession of ideas, some are anew excited, others are changed or totally disappear. There is therefore some cause of these ideas, whereon they depend, and which produces and changes them. That this cause cannot be any equality or

idea or combination of ideas, is clear from the preceding section. It must therefore be a substance; but it has been shown that there is no corporeal or material substance; it remains therefore that the cause of ideas is an incorporeal active substance or Spirit.

He then proceeds to define a spirit as "one simple, undivided, active being." But though undivided, "as it perceives ideas it is called the *understanding*, and as it produces or otherwise operates about them it is called the *will*." There cannot be any ideas of soul or spirit. For ideas are inactive; hence they could not possibly represent something so different from themselves as the principle of action:

> The words *will, soul, spirit*, do not stand for different ideas, or, in truth, for any idea at all, but for something which is very different from ideas, and which, being an agent, cannot be like unto, or represented by, any idea whatsoever. Though it must be owned at the same time that we have some *notion* of soul, spirit, and the operations of the mind such as willing, loving, hating; inasmuch as we know or understand the meaning of these words.

The distinction between an "idea" and a "notion" may seem a bit tenuous. It depends upon whether one is willing to accept a distinction between the feeling that other *persons* besides oneself exist and the feeling that merely other *bodies* besides one's own exist. For "ideas or sensations" would, by this terminology, be the words for what, in everyday speech, we might call bodies; whereas our conviction that in addition to these bodies there are persons would be a "notion."

Spirit can be perceived, in the empirical sense (not as "notions" but as "ideas or sensations") only in terms of the effects it produces. This formulation allows for empirical evidence of the existence of God, who happily for our purposes is called the "Almighty Agent." In studying the laws of Nature, says Berkeley, we discover that the ideas composing our experience proceed "in a regular train or series, the admirable connection whereof sufficiently testifies the wisdom and benevolence of its Author." What we experience as "things" are to be "considered only as marks or signs for our information." And the natural philosopher should seek "to understand these signs instituted by the Author of Nature." Ideas, spirits, and relations are "all in their respective kinds the object of human knowledge."

"God," then, is Berkeley's equivalent for the ultimate scene, scene as translated into terms of agent. What we experience as "things" are "ideas" which do not cease to be when we cease to think of them, since they are maintained in the mind of God. Though his opponents accuse him of solipsism, this aspect of Berkeley's doctrine would in a Berkeleian's eyes invalidate the charge. *"Esse* is *percipi"* could thus be translated for our purposes: "To be is to be grounded in the term, super-agent." But though the lawfulness of nature is taken as the evidence of God in nature, Berkeley recognizes how his position can lead to a narrowing of circumference:

> And yet this insistent uniform working, which so evidently displays the goodness and wisdom of that governing Spirit whose will constitutes the laws of nature, is so far from leading our thoughts to Him, that it rather sends them wandering after second causes. For, when we perceive certain ideas of sense constantly followed by other ideas and we know this is not of our own doing, we forthwith attribute power and agency to the ideas themselves [that is, to the effects that the "things" of our sensory experience are thought to have upon one another] and make one the cause of another, than which nothing could be more absurd and unintelligible. Thus, for example, having observed that when we perceive by sight a certain round luminous figure we at the same time perceive by touch the idea of sensation called heat, we do from thence conclude the sun to be the cause of heat. And in like manner perceiving the motion and collision of bodies to be attended with sound, we are inclined to think the latter the effect of the former.

Hume

The strategic equating of ideas with sensations naturally leads to a narrowing of circumference. For it invites us to drop the stress upon action and the rational, and to stress rather such mental functionings as fall under the head of motion. Otherwise stated: The Berkeleian idealism served as an important step from rationalism to empiricism by equating "the intelligible" with "the sensible," whereupon in accordance with the law of parsimony the "intelligible" side of the equation could be dropped as an unnecessary duplication, the attention being focused upon the side that lent itself the better to laboratory investigation. Ironically, Berkeley prophesies this very trend in admonishing against it.

In the realm of psychology, the narrowing took place by the develop-ment of the empiricist element in Berkeley's doctrine: namely, the study of "ideas" in terms of "sensations." And the narrowing was ac-complished in the realm of metaphysics by the great skeptic David Hume, with his critique of metaphysics that strongly affected the ideal-istic system of Emmanuel Kant.

Hume's skepticism was particularly drastic, not in the questioning of God, but in the questioning of a *God-term* as basic to secular science as it had been to religion: the concept of *causality*. Let us inspect his *Inquiry Concerning Human Understanding* just enough to specify how he went about this, in following the logic of Locke's and Berke-ley's empiricism.

Beginning psychologistically, he divided "all the perceptions of the mind into two classes or species, which are distinguished by their dif-ferent degrees of force and vivacity." The "less forcible and lively" he called *"thoughts or ideas."* And "all our more lively perceptions, when we hear, or see, or feel, or love, or hate, or desire, or will" he called "impressions." Similarly, the apparently creative power of our mind "amounts to no more than the faculty of compounding, trans-posing, augmenting, or diminishing the materials afforded us by the senses and experience." Our idea of God, for instance, as infinitely intelligent, wise, and good "arises from reflecting on the operations of our own mind, and augmenting, without limit, those qualities of good-ness and wisdom." And where a sense is defective, one can have no idea, as a man born blind can have no idea of colors. In this way, Hume derives ideas from purely sensory impressions. And when we suspect that some term in philosophy is meaningless, for a test "we need but inquire, *from what impression is that supposed idea derived?"*

Applying this test, Hume observes that our idea of cause and effect "is not, in any instance, attained by reasonings *a priori*, but arises en-tirely from experience." Whereas we can advance by pure reasoning from one proposition to another in geometry, we cannot similarly antici-pate what effects will follow a given cause, "for the effect is totally dif-ferent from the cause, and consequently can never be discovered in it." We learn from experience that an unsupported stone will fall. There is no logical way of anticipating such an effect. (Indeed, Hume might have cited here the fact that Galileo's experiments with falling bodies discredited beliefs about motion that had previously been assumed on the basis of reason alone, and by some expert reasoners at that.)

If we were to come into the world with fully developed powers of reason, yet without experiences of fact, we should not know what to anticipate, Hume says.   The principle directing our expectations is a psychological one: *"custom* or *habit."*   "All inferences from experience . . . are effects of custom, not of reasoning."   As a result of custom, the order of our ideas follows the order of nature.   (We can get the point here by contrasting Hume's position with Spinoza's view of a *rationally necessary* connection between the *ordo idearum* and the *ordo rerum*.)   "We only learn by experience the frequent *conjunction* of objects, without ever being able to comprehend anything like *connection* between them."   Habit or custom thus gives rise to a scene-agent ratio on a purely experiential basis, in contrast with the Stoic doctrine of a universal rationality similarly pervading both natural scene and human agents.

In Hume's skepticism the great dramatist cluster of terms (reason, substance, cause, necessity, action, idea, God, Nature, generation, power) is beginning to fall apart.   On the purely Symbolic plane, one might well be justified in examining this placid bachelor's theories as a metaphysical questioning of potency and progeny (dissolving the reality of power and cause by subjecting them to the terms of his empirical quizzicality), as we might similarly examine the theories of that placid bachelor Bentham, who put forward his ideal of a neutral vocabulary.   The ideal of "sterilization" may be indigenous to the patterns of technology.   In any event, at the very least the dethronement of "causality" is the rejection of a term essentially *ancestral* or *parental*, as is similarly the case with the dethronement of reason and the strong stress upon *derivation* that goes with it.   On the Symbolic level, there is a pattern of "race suicide" implicit in the turn from "causality" to the cult of sheer "correlation."   But be that as it may, Hume was certainly correct in contending that there is no purely empirical evidence for concepts like causality, power, necessary connection.   You can observe factual sequences which you choose to interpret as an indication of causality; but you may with as much justice interpret them as indications of a Divine Purpose, so far as the evidence of the senses is concerned.   "Causality" or "power" themselves are not empirically observable, any more than God is. By examining the "impression" of such ideas, we find that it arises merely "from reflecting on the operations of our own minds."

Leibniz

It was this vigilant criticism that awoke Kant from his "dogmatic," or rationalist slumbers. In Germany at that time philosophizing was done mainly under the aegis of Leibniz, whose system still placed great stress upon Substance and necessary logical connection. It was a rationalism of *idealist* cast, however, in that it stressed in substance a psychologistic factor, the nature of entities as *perceptive*, or as endowed with the power to *represent*. The Leibnizian universe was a world of individuals ("monads"), each with its own particular point of view, and "realizing itself" to the extent that the limits of its nature permitted. Indeed, Leibniz' system falls so well under the head of agent that we can clearly see in him the beginnings of our modern psychologies of the unconscious. His "monads" were atom-agents, each developing its own inner potentialities, its own particular range of growth (widest in the case of man) from the implicit to the explicit.

The famous concept of "pre-established harmony" was invented by Leibniz as *deus ex machina* to bring it about that the principle of self-development activating each of the monadic substances does not interfere with the self-development of its fellows. That is, God so adjusted the monads to one another that their development would have the same effect as if they were all mutually constraining or influencing one another. By this pre-established harmony, says Leibniz, it is as though the world were composed of infinite voices, each singing its own particular song, unaware of any other, yet if you could hear them all, you would hear the song of a choir singing in perfect time with all parts in perfect polyphonic relation to one another. Leibniz thus stressed the plurality side of the plurality-unity pair as strongly as Spinoza had stressed the unity side. But God, as the *Monas Monadum*, brought the plurality to a unified head.

This concept also provided for a difference in *degree* rather than in *kind* between God and the lesser monads. And though the infinity of monads represented a corresponding infinity of points of view, these monads were "without windows"—a device that enabled Leibniz to treat them as substances with internal principles of action proper to "things in themselves."

The Kantian idealism, then, encounters the two aspects of the idealist incentive. In the Leibnizian strain were the principles of unification, the powers of the Idea needed for service in the German community of small states, that were separated from one another by cultural traditions and tariff barriers, were feeling the individualism of the rising capitalist tradition, and were accordingly moving in the direction of national union. The Leibnizian idealizing of substance, allowing for a strong individualist emphasis along with an over-all principle of unity, gave exactly the pattern of agent and super-agent that we find in enterprisers and nation. Similarly, the stress upon the Idea allowed for the optimistically developmental, or creatively anticipatory, in short a *futuristic* emphasis (for "unification" implies a gerundive, a "to be unified").

The scientist emphasis is emergent in Leibniz, in that he slants his conception of substance towards *perception* (whereas in its pure scholastic form its primary slant was towards *action*). But it was among the British bourgeois philosophers that the insights provided by the application of science were most clearly perceived. And in Hume Kant encountered the development of idealism in direct response to scientism. (Hume's *Inquiry* opened significantly with a distinction between a philosophy that "considers man chiefly as born for action" and one that considers man "in the light of a reasonable rather than an active being" receiving "from science his proper food and nourishment.") Idealism here had stressed psychology to the point where it came upon a *"problem* of knowledge," leading us to doubt the possibilities of "necessary" truth as regards the world of facts.

Kant

In trying here to consider the complexities of Kant's philosophy, we encounter two difficulties. First we must manage somehow to review it briefly for persons who may not know it at all (so that our review is in danger of being either superficial or confusing). And we may irritate those who do know Kant's philosophy already, but have not approached it from the standpoint of the dramatist Grammar.

We may get around our difficulties somewhat by a subterfuge. Let us imagine ourselves trying to work up a Kantian vocabulary in accordance with the linguistic resources, temptations, and embarrassments we have been studying in these pages.

First, since our system is to show the influence of science, and was written at a time when science was identical with the celestial mechanics of Newton, our terminology must recognize all claims made by a terminology laying down strict laws of *motion*. Yet we are not merely to write a philosophy of physical science. We have also been thinking in the tradition of Leibniz, so we shall want a principle of *action*, an ethical principle wider in scope than the laws of sheer motion. We shall want something to take the place of Leibniz' *principle of sufficient reason*, by which he allowed for *final* causes (*purpose*), in contending that the world of factual experience could only be accounted for if we derived it from God. For no less a cause than God could be great enough to be the source or ground of the creation. However, we shall want our substitute for Leibniz' finalism to be as "scientific" as possible.

We have just been awakened with a jolt. This jolt at first seemed menacing, but on second thought was found to be just what we needed. It was in Hume, and I shall quote it because it significantly introduces one more term than we have watched in Hume so far:

> The bread, which I formerly eat, nourished me; that is, a body of such sensible qualities was, at that time, endued with such secret powers: but does it follow, that other bread must also nourish me at another time, and that like sensible qualities must always be attended with like secret powers? The consequence seems no wise necessary. At least, it must be acknowledged that there is here a consequence drawn by the mind; that there is a certain step taken; a process of thought, and an inference, which wants to be explained. These two propositions are far from being the same, *I have found that such an object has always been attended with such an effect,* and *I foresee, that other objects, which are, in appearance, similar, will be attended with similar effects.* I shall allow, if you please, that the one proposition may justly be inferred from the other; I know, in fact, that it always is inferred. But if you insist that the inference is made by a chain of reasoning, I desire you to produce that reasoning. The connection between these propositions is not intuitive. There is required a medium, which may enable the mind to draw such an inference, if indeed it be drawn by reasoning and argument. What that medium is, I must confess, passes my comprehension; and it is

incumbent on those to produce it, who assert that it really exists, and is the origin of all our conclusions concerning matter of fact.

That request for a "medium" is our cue. Suppose we provide such a medium—and do so in keeping with the genius of our term *agent*. One usually thinks of a medium as something in which an agent acts (scene) or something which an agent uses (agency). But what if we equated it with *the very nature of the agent itself?* Hume has been saying in effect that we can't *see* "causality" or "power" or "necessary connection." How, then, can we arrive at such concepts?

By utilizing a function of our term *agent*, we can transform this problem into a solution. Namely: we can say that people interpret natural sequences in terms of cause and effect not because of something in the natural scene requiring this interpretation, but *because they are the sort of agents that see things in terms of necessary relations*. In this view we do not derive our ideas of cause and effect from experience; all that we can derive from experience is the observation that certain happenings seem likely to follow certain happenings. But our ideas of cause and effect are derived *from the nature of the mind*. You must at least grant that this view would meet Hume's demand for a "medium," and would do so by equating medium with agent.

Another important linguistic resource enters at this point, however. In deriving causality from the realm covered by our term *agent* (whereas heretofore it was considered so thoroughly a property of *scene*), we need not mean *individual* agents. For if we did, the causal principle would still lack universality. That is, it would lack objective reality, being at best like the kind of general opinion that prevailed when all men thought the world was flat. The causal principle need not be assigned to the agent in this sense. Instead, we can *universalize* our concept of agent. We can say that such a way of seeing is not the property of just *your* understanding or *my* understanding but of *"the* understanding" in general.

We have now set ourselves some rich linguistic possibilities, which we shall develop as follows:

First, there is our old action-passion pair. We shall begin with this, dividing our universal agent into two aspects. The "passive" we shall assign to the *sensibility*. Abiding by the grammar of the word "data" (*the given*), we shall view the senses as passive, since they *receive* representations of objects. If only as a grammatical reflex, we shall next look for an "active." And we find it in the *understanding*, which is active in that it performs the act of unification. The senses, for instance, may passively receive a manifold of sense data, a confusion of colors, textures, shapes, etc.—and the understanding may unify all this by a concept, as when, considering that manifold, we say, "It is a house." So we have our first grammatical pair, the senses passively receiving what is "given" to them, and the understanding actively uniting this manifold by a concept. The representations of sense are, in the Kantian terminology, called *intuitions*. As Kant puts it: "Objects are *given* to us by means of sensibility, and it alone yields us *intuitions;* they are *thought* through the understanding, and from the understanding arise *concepts*." But all thought must relate ultimately to the intuitions of sensibility, "because in no other way can an object be given to us." By this last statement we take care of the demands made by empirical science, which must be grounded in the evidence of the senses.

But though we have begun with an active and a passive principle here, we should be disastrously misled if we attempted to characterize our alignment of terms with reference to it as we did in the case of Spinoza. For this philosophy takes its beginning in a *scientist* problem, not the problem of *action*, but the problem of *knowledge*. The vital concern here is with "the object," as perceived through intuition and conceived by the understanding. Let us accordingly center our attention upon the object, to see what momentous linguistic resources we may have for application here.

First, just as we universalized the function of agent, so we shall raise our concern with objects to a high level of generalization. And we shall not inquire into the conditions that make possible our knowledge of this object or that object, but of the "object in general."

Now, the surprising thing about an *object in general* is that you can't distinguish it from *no object at all*. For it is not this object or that object or any other object that you could actually point to in all the world. I realized this when contemplating a chart designed to show the interrelations among the key terms in Kant's *Critique of Pure Reason*. The attempt to represent the appearance of an object in general, in order to show how it was related eventually to an unseen thing-in-itself, led to the embarrassing discovery that such an object in general would be as impossible to represent as would the unseen thing-in-itself that by definition lies beyond the realm of sense relationships.

(Incidentally, lest the reader misinterpret my attitude here, let me add: I believe the true mettle of a philosopher is shown in what he can say about nothing. Any tyro can talk about something. But it takes a really profound thinker to say profound things about nothing. And I hasten to admit that my own five terms are all about nothing, since they designate not this scene, or that agent, etc. but scene, agent, etc. in general.)

If, then, you would talk profoundly and intelligently about the conditions of the possibility of the knowledge of nothing, what *do* you have that you can talk about? You have the *knower*. You can say, for instance, "Whatever an object in general may or may not look like, you can be sure that when you do come across one you are going to have to encounter it in terms of space and/or time." And since you can't here be talking about an object (if you are, what is it?) what you *must* be talking about is the *nature of your own mind*. Your mind is prepared to encounter this object, whatever it may be, in spatial and/or temporal terms. Furthermore, the mind is prepared to expect that the object will be a quantity of some sort (as were it single or plural), that it will have some kind of quality (it will be hard, or light, or sweet, or evanescent, or *something*), that it will be in some relation to other objects in general, etc. These are all requirements that you are mentally prepared in advance to make of the object. Thus they are in the mind, *a priori;* and the object will *necessarily* meet these requirements, since they are the requirements the mind makes of every experienced object. They are *conditions* that the object must meet; and being *mental* conditions, they reside in the *agent* rather than in the *object*. And the locating of such conditions in the agent as medium Kant calls "transcendental." Thus, the difference between "formal" and "transcendental" logic is generated by the fact that the Kantian logic takes its start in a question with which formal logic is not concerned at all. Formal logic deals with *internal* consistency. Transcendental logic, paradoxically enough, arrives at its stress upon agent through a question about scene ("conditions" of knowing).

Still using our readily available linguistic resources, we could put this in another way. We have discussed a tribal, or familial, or parental principle whereby the nature of a thing may be grounded in the nature of the source from which it is derived. Hence, one point of departure will lead to different conclusions than another. And so we can get around the thorough-going empiricist position by distinguishing two starting points, one empirical and the other transcendental.

Thus Kant distinguishes "what begins with" from "what arises out of." "There can be no doubt," he says, "that all knowledge begins with experience," for we can know nothing until we have had experience. "But though all our knowledge begins *with* experience, it does not thereby arise wholly *out of* experience." (*Wenn aber gleich alle unsere Erkenntniss* mit *der Erfahrung anhebt, so entspringt sie darum doch nicht eben alle* aus *der Erfahrung*.) For besides the knowledge we get from impressions, there may be something "which our own faculty of knowledge . . . supplies from itself." Applying the ancestral principle here in ways of our own, you will note that our Kantian structure has contrived to infuse the empirical world with "transcendental" attributes. One can glimpse the kind of resonance this grammar gives us on the Symbolic level, by recalling a recent critic's remark that Carlyle borrowed the vocabulary of transcendentalism to "poetize" the pragmatic and empirical (and though one must admit that Kant's "poetry" here is quite cumbersome, one would be wrong in allowing the occasional scientific pretenses of philosophers to conceal the fact that their basic ways and aims are to be viewed in terms of poetic action).

But look where we now are. We have described intellectual synthesis as "active." Yet what kind of "act" is this? The empirical scene has derived its character from the nature of the agent; but though we have called this action of the mind "spontaneous" and "original," we might just as well have called it "inevitable." It is *compulsory*, lacking the elements of freedom necessary for action. The mind cannot see otherwise than in terms of the categories. To observe is an act, in that one can choose either to observe it or not to observe it. But to observe *in terms of the categories* is not an act in this sense, since we *must* consider it in such terms, whether we choose to observe it or not. Conversely, though the sensibility is "passive," we find space and time called the "forms" of sensibility. And in the tradition from which Western philosophy stems, "form" is the act word par excellence. So the "passive" begins to look as active as the avowedly active. In brief, even though our construction of a Kantian system leads us to conclude that experience derives its appearance from the nature of consciousness (the "I think," or "transcendental synthesis of apperception") this is hardly origination in the moral sense of the term.

Then where are we? Putting together the sensibility (treated in the "Transcendental Aesthetic") and the understanding (treated in the "Transcendental Analytic"), we have encompassed but the world of Newtonian motion, the world of physical science as then conceived in terms of mechanistic determination. There are no "wills," "oughts," "shoulds," or "thou shalt nots" here. There is nothing but an inevitable *is*, a description of conditions as they necessarily *are* for human experience, so that Kant calls them "constitutive," which we could translate "scenic, with circumference narrowed to the scope of motion." It is not materialism, since the scene itself is said to derive its character from a function of the term agent (whereas in pure materialism agent would be derived from scene). And at this stage it is not supernaturalism, since the agent from which the nature of the scene is derived is not a divine super-agent but a kind of universalized human (we might call it a *human mind in general*).

We still have to introduce a principle of action, in the full moral sense of the term. But note that we have not yet drawn upon the resources of two master terms for philosophies of action, "idea" and "reason." So our third section (the "Transcendental Dialectic") will enable us to transcend the empirical-transcendental realm of motion (the "constitutive") by a concern with "ideas of reason," which allow for moral acts (the "regulative").

All told, then, we have:

(a) Intuitions of sensibility (which attain their maximum generalization as pure space and pure time, the two conditions necessary for any sensory representation);

(b) Concepts of understanding (which attain their maximum generalization in the categories, categories we might think of as a questionnaire with a set of blanket questions to be filled in differently in the case of each object, but with the whole set of questions requiring some kind of answer in every case);

(These two together comprise the realm of experience investigated by scientific empiricism, a world conditioned "transcendentally," which is to say conditioned by the conditions of

the mind. The forms of sensibility and categories of understanding, taken together, comprise the scene of narrowed circumference Kant calls the "constitutive.")

(c) Ideas of reason (allowing for the introduction of another principle, the "regulative," that will if properly manipulated permit
us to introduce principles of action into a world of motion).

Moral Transcendence in Kant

It is our job now to place this third step (c) in accordance with the
Grammatical tests of consistency. If ideas are active, the logic of the
scene-act ratio would require that they be derived from a different
scene than the combined empirical-transcendental structure called the
"constitutive." And this we might get by introducing a distinction,
making two meanings grow where but one had grown before. We
might "Desynonymize."

I borrow the word from Coleridge, whose *Biographia Litteraria* is
concerned with desynonymizing two words previously considered synonymous. For *imaginatio* had regularly been taken as Latin equivalent for the Greek *phantasia*. Hence the tendency had been to treat
our derivatives, *imagination* and *fancy*, as synonymous. And Coleridge set about to make a distinction in kind between them. The great
departures in human thought can be eventually reduced to a moment
where the thinker treats as *opposite*, key terms formerly considered *ap-
posite*, or *v.v.* So we are admonished to be on the look-out for those
moments when strategic synonymizings or desynonymizings occur.
And, in accordance with the logic of our ratios, when they do occur, we
are further admonished to be on the look-out for a shift in the source
of derivation, as terms formally derived from different sources are
now derived from a common source, or *v.v.* In the present case, let
us see what we can do if we strategically desynonymize "transcendental" and "transcendent," at the same time remembering grammatical scruples about a corresponding split in derivation. And it would
be all the better if, at the same time as our desynonymizing enabled us
to provide a fitting ground for moral action, it likewise solved a metaphysical problem left by our account of the world of empirical motion.

For according to our account, the world as we experience it is but
a world of *appearances*. The objects of experience, we have said, derive
their appearance from the nature of our minds (as all colors will seem

like shades of but one color if we observe them through colored glasses). But if they are *appearances*, what are they appearances of? Our desynonymizing here will lead us to the answer. The *empirical* realm is the realm of appearances. The *transcendental* realm is the realm that gives things the nature they seem to have in the empirical realm. And the *transcendent* realm will be the realm of things as they are "in themselves," not as empirically conditioned by the conditions of the transcendental.

We have thus arrived at the transcendent realm as a realm of things "in themselves" (that is, with whatever nature they may have intrinsically, not as they are determined by the terms in which we see them). Whereat we might profitably pause to consider the grammar of the intrinsic. It is the puzzle we encountered when discussing the paradox of substance. As soon as one considers things in relation to other things, one is uncomfortably on the way to dissolving them into their context, since their relations lead beyond them. A thing in itself for instance can't be "higher" or "heavier" than something or "inside" or "outside" something, or "derived from" something, etc. For though such descriptions may apply to it, they do not apply to it purely as a thing *in itself;* rather, they are *contextual* references, pointing beyond the thing.

Though Leibniz' notion of "pre-established harmony" among the infinite monads may seem arbitrary, it was designed precisely as a metaphysical solution for the problem of the intrinsic. By means of this invention, he was able to maintain that each monad was a unique substance (hence, capable of treatment in itself, whereas we will recall that Spinoza, noting how each thing was limited by other things, contended that nothing short of *everything considered in its totality* could be treated as substance; for only the universal whole could have no context outside itself to which it would be externally related).

Personally, I do not see that, even if we granted Leibniz his formula, it would wholly solve the problem. For the principle of harmonization derived from God obviously leaves the created substances with a most important external relation, perhaps the most important of all. But in any case, we can know what he was driving at, which is enough for our purpose. If God by a principle of pre-established harmony had so brought it about that every monad could go on realizing its own intrinsic possibilities without reference to any other monad (indeed, if its soul was "windowless" so that it could not even perceive other monads relationally, but represented them intrinsically by representing its own particular point of view), one might treat the monads as independent individuals, each with its own intrinsic principles of self-development, hence each in itself a substance, thereby avoiding the Spinozist merger of the part into the whole.

Be that as it may, I think we may now realize the Grammatical opportunities and embarrassments we encounter as we arrive in our Kantian system at a *transcendent* realm composed of things-in-themselves. Whatever it may be cosmologically, a thing in itself is Grammatically a thing without reference to context. And for our purposes, that is as far as we need go. Grammatically, then, the transcendent realm is a realm of things-without-context, or things-without-relation.

What does that give us? First, note that relations are "determinations." They assign borders (termini) to a thing. A synonym is "conditions," since "conditions" are likewise contextual, as with the conditions of an organism's existence. Without worrying greatly what it may mean in the literal sense, but merely considering the Grammatical resources available here, let us note that, as the empirical realm is the realm of the determined or conditioned, and the transcendental realm is the realm of the conditions that provided the terms (determinations), so the transcendent realm of things-in-themselves would be the realm of the undetermined or unconditioned. Whereupon, lo! we find ourselves in a realm of *freedom!* And so, we have come upon a scene that allows for the possibility of *action*.

The transcendental had transcended the empirical; it had raised us to a level of generalization that "necessarily" unified the world of particulars, infusing the world of particulars with its spirit. And so now in turn the transcendent has transcended the transcendental, thereby infusing the world of determinism with the spirit of freedom (which is another way of saying that we have added to the world of physical motion the possibilities of moral action).

However, since we began our enterprise with all respect for the requirements of empirical science, we have defined knowledge by empirical tests. Knowledge by definition, then, is the knowledge of conditions and relations. It is the knowledge of *appearances*, the knowledge of objects as they necessarily appear when seen in terms of our human categories (the categories of the mind in general). So, by definition, the transcendent realm of the unconditoned things-in-them-selves (the scene that contains the possibilities of freedom) cannot be *known*. Hence, we must restrict the claims we can make about it. But whereas it can't be *known,* it can be *thought about,* for we are now thinking about it.

Modern positivists would question whether this statement has meaning; it is certainly "non-sense" if we interpret that word literally, for it is a statement about a realm *outside* the realm of sensory experience. But if you consider it purely from the standpoint of Grammatical resources, it is obvious that a word as highly generalized as "the conditioned" leaves us with "the unconditioned" as its dialectical opposite, hence as the only term left to be the *ground* or context of the conditioned. And though we certainly cannot *know* this ground, in the scientific meaning which we have given to "knowledge," we can "think" it in recognizing that, *so far as the patterns of human thought are concerned*, the only term that could antithetically match the "conditioned" would be the "unconditioned." And the *unknown* to which we thus refer in so basic a pattern of human thought might be characterized as "thought of."

It is an important spot to haggle over, however, if you are going to haggle at all. For once you let this point go by unquestioned, you give Kant some important advantages. If this realm of the things-in-themselves can be *thought* though not *known*, this limitation upon our claims to knowledge about them applies in reverse to science. Science compels us to admit that things-in-themselves can't be known; but in putting them outside the area of scientific *knowledge*, by the same token we put them outside the area of scientific *refutation* or *denial*. The sources of morality thus lie beyond the reach of the terms proper to the physical sciences (which is but another way of saying that, in this terminology, action cannot be reduced to motion). In his preface to the second edition Kant said: "I must abolish *knowl-*edge, to make room for *belief."* In taking the action out of the scene which he equated with knowledge, he had to make sure that there was still room for an act of faith.

To grant that these unknowns can be thought of, however, is further to allow for a very ingenious verbalism. If they can be thought of, if we can employ our intelligence on them, let us call them the "intelligible." Whereupon, lo! whereas empiricism took its start in equating the intelligible with the sensible, the intelligible is now so named precisely because it *can't* be sensed. Beginning in empiricism, making a line-up that will permit the pursuit of each empirical science in its own terms, we have nonetheless managed to so wangle things that we make allowance for terms beyond the scope of empirical science.

And so, in sum, we have phenomena (appearances, objects as we encounter them in everyday experience) and noumena (the undefined somethings that must lie behind appearances, hence cannot be sensed, but can be considered mentally—*noumena* being a present passive participle from the same root as the Greek *nous*). Such a step from conditioned to the unconditioned, or from things in relation to things-in-themselves, or from the determinate to the indeterminate (in brief, from necessity to freedom) Kant frankly calls "dialectical." With this all would agree. But in so frankly labelling his third section dialectical, he tends to conceal from both us and himself the equally dialectical ingredients in the first two sections. All three involve linguistic operations which, by the very nature of language, transcend the terminology of the senses.

Kant began his inquiry (in the *Critique of Pure Reason*) by considering the "conditions of the possibility" of *knowledge*. But by the end of the book he is concerned with the conditions of the possibility of *action*. Hence his conditional principle of the "as if" (*Als ob*). We cannot *know* that there are God, freedom, and immortality; but we should act *as if* there were. Hence, moral action is rooted in the *ideas* of God, freedom, and immortality. (Unlike sensations and concepts, ideas can have no *empirical* reference. As the understanding uses the materials of sense, so reason uses the materials of the understanding). These ideas thus refer back to the transcendent realm. The moral motive is thus our bond between the realm of necessity (the caused) and the realm of freedom (first causes). We can then round out matters neatly by considering the world of nature as an example of *purpose,* while looking for signs of this purpose not mystically, but scientifically, in the study of natural law. In brief, to find indications of *purpose* behind nature, we shall look for *mechanism* in nature.

Introducing our Grammar here, in a non-Kantian but not anti-Kantian way, I would propose to consider this freedom-necessity, or teleology-mechanism manoeuver thus: Think of an enactment, as with the enacting of a constitution. The enacting is the forming of the

constitution, the constitution is the permanent form left by the enactment.   Let us say that men came together *of their own free will* to enact the constitution.   The resulting document, however, is *not free*.
It must be just what it is.   The clauses are necessarily related to one another in certain ways.   (We need not complicate matters by considering amendments.   To a degree, an amendment simply gives us a new
constitution, which is to say, a new enactment.)   But insofar as we
have one enactment and its corresponding form as a constitution, once
the constitution has been enacted, all the relations among its parts are
necessary.   Or we could think of a poem: the freer and more perfect
the poet was in his craftsmanship, the more "inevitable" would be the
relationships that the parts of his poem bear to one another.   It would
be in this sense that signs of necessity in the phenomenal realm could be
interpreted as signs of freedom in the transcendent or noumenal realm.

And perhaps the quickest way to indicate how "ideals" of action can
be said to transcend empirical conditions would be by a citation from
Book V of Plato's *Republic:*

> The city will be courageous because some of its members maintain
> under all conditions the opinions our legislator taught them about
> the nature of things to be feared and not to be feared.
> And by the words "under all conditions" I mean to suggest that in
> pleasure or in pain, or under the influence of desire or fear, a man
> preserves and does not lose that opinion.

And as for Kant's formula indicating how his principle of action
bridges the two realms of conditioned and unconditioned:

> It does not involve a contradiction to assert on the one hand that
> the will, in the phenomenal realm (of visible action) necessarily
> obeys the laws of nature, and to this extent is *not free;* and on the
> other hand that, as belonging to a thing-in-itself, it is not subject to
> such laws and accordingly *is* free.*

* The entire pattern of thought in the *Critique of Pure Reason* stresses unification.   Even the variety of data available to the intuitions of sense has an
"affinity" in its manifoldness.   This "affinity" I would translate Grammatically
as a gerundive: for if the manifold of sense can be unified by the concepts of
understanding, then there is in this manifold a kind of "to-be-unifiedness" that
one could call an "affinity" among the components of the manifold.   Reason aims
finally at the most unified principle of all, the idea of God as the total unity that
is the ground of all existence.

Idealism after Kant

The thinkable but unknowable noumenal realm, then, was taken as the ground of the phenomenal realm. But we slid over a Grammatical embarrassment. If the phenomenal is the realm of *relationships*, and the noumenal is the realm of things-*in-themselves* (i.e., *without* relationships), just how could there be a bond between the two realms? Otherwise put: If the noumenal is the realm of *freedom* and the phenomenal is the realm of *necessity*, is the connection between the two realms "free" or "necessary"? Kant compromised on a weasel word, saying that the noumenal "influences" the phenomenal. But Fichte grounded his system *wholly* in agent, maintaining that the Kantian thing-in-itself was not necessary. Kant himself had called apperception, or consciousness in general, "the highest principle in the whole

But there is another important unifying principle in Kant: the transcendental imagination, that stands like the keystone in an arch having sensibility at one end and understanding at the other. And in keeping with this, there is an ingenious device called the "schema," which can enable us to shuttle back and forth between intuitions and concepts. For, like intuitions it partakes of the particular; yet like the concept it has generality.

One can expect it to be ambiguous, for it has an ambiguous role to perform, since it must contrive to be homogeneous with two heterogeneous fields. This is managed thus: Suppose I put five dots in a row to represent the concept of "five"; and then seven dots in a row to represent the concept of "seven"; and then, to represent 1,000, instead of going on to make a thousand dots, I say, "You get the idea." That is, you would understand the general rule that you would follow in arriving at the proper image. Because of its function as thus *mediating* between the particular and the general, some commentators have considered imagination in Kant the principle of unification *par excellence*.

And as regards Kant's detailed analysis of the schema, since it does lie in the opposite fields of particularity and generality, would one not be entitled to expect in advance that it itself would have to split into two aspects, each aspect gravitating towards one of the sides? This embarrassment shows up, I think, in the Kantian distinction between "schemata" and "schematism," the "schemata" leaning to the side of the particular, the "schematism" leaning to the side of the general. And, as with the endless subdividing of the atom into ever smaller particles, I am sure that, if we could make our critical instruments sharp enough, we should find it necessary to subdivide "schemata" and "schematism" in turn, finding that each contained in it a particularizing aspect and a generalizing aspect, the "schemata" giving two votes for particular and one for general, the "schematism" giving two votes for general and one for particular.

At least, I offer this hypothesis as solace to the reader for whom Kant's analysis of the schema is alternately revealing and puzzling.

sphere of human knowledge." This placed a high value on the function of agent, but Fichte gave a still higher one, in reducing everything to the Ego and a Non-Ego *derived from* it. In this respect, the pattern is obviously closer to Berkeley than to Kant.

On the Symbolic level, the Nature side of the Spirit-Nature pair in Fichte was born under bad auspices. He apparently evolved his system while contemplating a career alternative to marriage. Fichte is noted for the austerity and consciousness of his doctrines. But his distinction between the I and the Not-I, which gives us in German the *Ich* and the *Nichtich*, happens to produce, for the Not-I, a word pronounced exactly like *nichtig,* the meanings of which are listed in Muret-Sanders as: *unreal, vain, frivolous, empty, hollow, futile, flimsy, transitory, ineffectual, invalid, void,* the adjective itself being derived from the word for nothing, quite like the English *naughty*. We may remember these matters, when reading in an editor of Hegel, Georg Lasson, the complaint that the Ego claims too much in Fichte's scheme, so that too little is left for the Not-Ego.

Since Fichte stressed such thought as would identify the individual ego with the communal ego, we might relevantly cite from Andrew Seth, *The Development from Kant to Hegel:* "In Fichte's own language, everything must 'hang firmly in a single ring, which is fastened to nothing, but maintains itself and the whole system by its own power.'" And Fichte's political theories were presented in the name of a "closed" commercial state (*geschlossener Handelsstaat*), the beginnings of the "autarchic" principle. And in general, there are symbolic ambiguities (or *double-entendres*) in the idealist pattern of externalization, due to the fact that it represents a movement from "inner" to "outer," as from implicit to explicit, from unconscious to conscious, from magma to lava, and thus from visceral to excretory.

In any event, from the time of Fichte the pattern of idealism pure and simple was set. With varying terms, such philosophers as Schelling, Hegel, and Schopenhauer traced the genealogy of the objective world from the subjective, treating nature as an externalization or expression of spirit somewhat as a poem may be called an externalization of the poet. Nature being thus viewed as the incarnation or embodiment of mind, the pattern was edifying in Fichte, esthetic in Schelling, optimistic in Hegel, and pessimistic in Schopenhauer (where the externalizations of the universal *will* are treated not as *assertions* of the agent, but rather like those *involuntary* expressions that the post-Schopenhauer psychologies would call "compulsion neuroses").

Marxism

The Marxian dialectical materialism grows out of idealism by antithesis. Hegel had strongly stressed a *developmental* feature in the expression, externalization, embodiment, or "utterance" (*Äusserung*) of the spirit. The development of the spirit was viewed as objectified through the medium of nature and history. And this process of mediation (*Vermittlung*) led to a much more concrete view of "conditions" than did the high levels of generalization in Kant. Though Hegel constructed an elaborate metaphysical framework for the placement of his historical stages, the stages themselves had to be portrayed by the use of historical detail. And so we got, in effect, a superagent (Spirit) manifesting itself in progressively changing historical conditions (scenes of narrowed circumference). In his *Philosophy of History,* equating World History with Reason, he defines Reason as "Thought conditioning itself with perfect freedom."

Marx materialistically reversed the genealogy here, by deriving the character of human consciousness in different historical periods from the character of the material conditions prevailing at the time. And though I have said that Hegel's treatment of "conditions" is concrete as compared with Kant's, the Marxist treatment of conditions is dazzlingly concrete; and once we look at it we are blinded to any difference between Kant and Hegel in this respect.

Perhaps the change of genealogy is best shown, in its metaphysical proportions, where Lenin, in his *Materialism and Empirio-Criticism* detects the idealistic bias in Machian post-Kantian empiricism, which took its start from the data of *sensation,* a property of agent. In idealism, he says, "sensation is taken as the primary entity." But materialistic science "takes matter as the *prius,* regarding consciousness, reason and sensation as derivative, because in a well expressed form it is connected only with the higher forms of matter (organic matter)."

Up to this point, we have obviously made a simple shift from agent to scene as point of origin. Marxists, however, are not "vulgar materialists," or "mechanical materialists," but *dialectical* materialists. And we might well translate this term as "idealistic materialist." Marx and Engels were "neo-Hegelians" before setting up their philosophic branch as a separate establishment. Hence, if one is to trace his key terms from an heraldic source in scene, and is to do so with good Grammar, there must be some quality of agenthood permeating the scene itself. This is provided clearly enough when Lenin adds to his above remarks: "It becomes possible, therefore, to assume the existence of a property similar to sensation 'in the foundation stones of the structure of matter itself.'"

The metaphysical problem of knowledge retreats into the background, to be replaced by the social problem of action in a society so much of whose resources are both consciously and unconsciously pitted against the fair presentation and examination of the Marxist doctrines. On the metaphysical plane the solution offered is antithetical to that of idealism. Idealism had decided that knowledge was possible because Nature is of the same substance as Thought, hence Thought is able to think it. Dialectical materialism reverses the relation by saying that thought is of the same substance as nature, hence can be a reflection of nature. In Engels' terms: thought and consciousness "are the products of the human brain," and "man himself is a product of Nature." Hence "the products of the human brain, being in the last analysis also products of Nature, do not contradict the rest of Nature but are in correspondence with it."

But though such a doctrine of correspondence allows for the gradual accumulation and perfection of *natural* knowledge, Marxists detect a radical obstruction to *moral* knowledge (an obstruction which can extend also to the realm of natural knowledge). I am aware that I am here presenting the Marxist position in somewhat non-Marxist terms; but to account objectively for the Marxist modifications of idealism, this method is inevitable. In this chapter it is not my purpose at this late date merely to summarize and report on past philosophies. Rather, I am trying to show how certain key terms might be used to "call the plays" in any and all philosophies. My problem at this point is to characterize as accurately as possible the strategy involved in the dialectical-materialist rejection of idealism. And the problem is obviously much more difficult than it would be to characterize an out-and-out shift from idealism to materialism. But dialectical materialism, in its constant call upon human agents, and above all its futuristic stress upon kinds of social *unification,* is intensely idealistic. And it is our task to characterize this *from without,* in over-all terms, rather than in specifically Marxist terms, as a factual report would call for.

In particular, we would consider the role of the "idea" in the Marxist genealogy. We would consider it with relation to the detailed stress upon "conditions" by which Marxists strategically alter the traditional idealistic use of that term. And for the purposes of our Grammar, we must speculate on the exact relation between ideas and the conditions *out of which they arise*—or the other way round, the relation between ideas and the conditions *which they help to bring about,* when acted upon by human agents.

Let us, then, turn to the *Communist Manifesto,* where the symbolic action of ideas is obviously intense. To realize how vigorous this document is as a pronunciamento, one might recall the typical party platform, a hodgepodge of vote-getting devices, as architecturally solid as a false front, slung together by a batch of well-meaning (or at least socially-minded, since politically-minded) party hacks, assembling in back rooms to horse-trade in behalf of the special interests they represent in the name of the national welfare. Let one then turn by contrast to this sturdy Manifesto.

Here are not merely the unsigned I.O.U.'s of the typical sales talk. This document is a *constitution.* For not only is it *regulative,* saying what may be on condition that its offer is accepted. It is soundly *constitutive,* grounding its statement of political principles in statements about the nature of the universal scene (a scene narrowed to naturalistic limits, and defined in particular with relation to the laws and directions of human history). Over and above his fears and prejudices, the true Grammarian should take great delight in the contemplation of this strong document, even though he believed that general adherence to it might entail the loss of all that he holds dear (or at least the loss of all that he holds). But perhaps the handiest way to point it up is to contrast it with the dialectic used by Hegel in his *Philosophy of History.*

Hegel

History, according to Hegel, is the development of Spirit from a state of potentiality to a state of realization, this realization being complete when it has been embodied in concrete details that lead to complete self-consciousness. This historical process is also equated with the process of Reason, and Reason is equated with Freedom. The development of World History itself (its gradual progress from nature to the freedom of self-consciousness) is conceived after a biographical analogy, with Oriental culture corresponding to childhood, Greek culture to adolescence, Roman culture to manhood, and German culture to old age (whereupon the philosopher warns that, although "the Old Age of *Nature* is weakness," that of Spirit is "perfect maturity and *strength*").

Each stage contains inherent contradictions that, as they gradually develop, lead first to great activity and attainment in the forming of a State by which these contradictions are contained. But the State in its vigor expands, and so comes into contact with external factors that lead to the betrayal of its own internal principles. It then begins to disintegrate, though not before having made its contribution to the new culture into contact with which it had been brought by its expansion. Hence with the decay of each stage there emerges the growth of the succeeding stage, which takes place in a different geographical theatre. The dying stage implicitly hands on its degree of spiritual progress to the succeeding stages, until we finally arrive at the culmination and totality of the German stage, as embodied in the German monarchic State. Here secularity, in "gaining a consciousness of its intrinsic worth, becomes aware of having a value of its own, in the morality, rectitude, probity, and activity of man."

Hegel's theory lays quite some stress on the part that human ambitions play in the realizing of World History's "Idea." The subjectivity of human passions is the material which the Spirit uses as means in the enacting of its Universal design. Spirit's way of thus acting through the passions Hegel calls "the cunning of Reason." Individual men do not aim to further the ends of World History. They aim passionately to attain their own private ends, as determined by their own special interests; but in this effort they unconsciously carry out the Will of Providence. "Secular pursuits are a spiritual occupation." In their attempt to further their interests, they develop the State, which is the highest embodiment of *Spirit,* "the Divine Idea as it exists on earth." And since the State's laws are "the objectification of Spirit," one is free in obeying the law (for the will, as Spirit, in changing the law, as Spirit, is obeying itself, hence is independent, hence free). The

State is strongest when conditions are such that private and public interests coincide. A great "World-Historical" Hero, such as Alexander, Caesar, Napoleon, consciously aims only to further his own designs. But being close to the fountainhead of Spirit, he acts when the time is ripe—and in this perfect timing resides his contribution to the development of World History over and above his conscious intentions. The people follow such a leader because they too unconsciously respond to the inner logic of historical development. Spirit is its own aim; World History is the progress of Spirit towards complete self-consciousness, which equals freedom. In sum: "The History of the world is none other than the progress of the consciousness of Freedom." This progress involves an advance to "the *intellectual* comprehension of what was presented in the first instance to *feeling* and *imagination*."

"By the close of day," Hegel says, "man has erected a building constructed from his own inner Sun; and when in the evening he contemplates this, he esteems it more highly than the original external Sun. For now he stands in a *conscious relation* to his Spirit, and therefore a *free* relation." This image symbolizes "the course of History, the great Day's work of Spirit."

Communist Manifesto

The Marxist revision of this dialectic unction opens, with admonitory clangor, in a burlesque of *spirit,* presenting Communism as a *spectre* haunting Europe. (Looking at it thus, I think we can see here something a bit more pointed than a not very fanciful figure of speech. The materialist doctrine that is to be the vessel antithetic to dialectical idealism enters with a mockery of idealism.) Next, the principle of division that for Hegel was benignly contained within the structure of the State is dramatically reinterpreted: "The history of all hitherto existing society is the history of class struggles." Whereupon we confront *conditions,* conceived in terms of reduced temporal circumference:

> Freeman and slave, patrician and plebeian, lord and serf, guild-master and journeyman, in a word, oppressor and oppressed, stood in constant opposition to one another, carried on an uninterrupted, now hidden, now open fight, a fight that each time ended, either in a revolutionary reconstitution of society at large, or in the common ruin of the contending classes.

Thus, where Hegel had said that "Society and the State are the very conditions in which freedom is realized," the materialist revision of Hegel will define the State as a means of coercion, arising in response to a deep social cleavage, and used by a dominant class to maintain the conditions of its domination. It attributes to the *class* structure of society the *bellum omnium contra omnes* which according to Hobbesian materialism, the State is designed to control. And its promise resides in the fact that the dialectic process of class antagonism must be followed through to the point where it leads to its own termination:

> When, in the course of development, class distinctions have disappeared, and all production has been concentrated in the hands of a vast association of the whole nation, the public power will lose its political character. Political power, properly so called, is merely the organized power of one class for oppressing another. If the proletariat during its contest with the bourgeoisie is compelled, by the force of circumstances, to organize itself as a class; if, by means of a revolution, it makes itself the ruling class, and, as such sweeps away by force the old conditions of production, then it will, along with these conditions, have swept away the conditions for the existence of class antagonisms and of class generally, and will thereby have abolished its own supremacy as a class.
>
> In place of the old bourgeois society, with its classes and class antagonisms, we shall have an association in which the free development of each class is the condition for the free development of all.

The entire dialectic thus traces a series of steps whereby each class produces the conditions leading to its overthrow by the class that is to succeed it, until the proletariat, as the ultimate class, produces conditions that lead to its own dissolution as a class. This last step marks the "withering away of the State" that Lenin discusses at some length in *The State and Revolution,* since Marxism agrees with orthodox Christianity, laissez-faire capitalism, and anarchism in its distrust of the State, though for reasons shared mainly by anarchism. The vigorous exertions of Marxist manhood hold out for society the promise of a benign senescence (if we think in sexual terms of this conditioned development from proletarian Dictatorship to a "withering away," a subsidence of the patriarchal State into a non-political state of total freedom).

The Manifesto uses the scene-agent ratio materialistically when asserting that "every change in the conditions" of man's material existence is accompanied by a change in "man's ideas, views, and conceptions, in one word, man's consciousness." In such passages, the idealistic stress upon consciousness or "the Idea" as "creative" gives way to the notion of consciousness as a mere reflection of conditions. "When people speak of ideas that revolutionize society," that is, ideas that act upon society in the idealistic sense of creating important changes in the social structure, "they do but express the fact, that within the old society the elements of a new one have been created, and that the dissolution of the old ideas keeps even pace with the dissolution of the old conditions of existence." Similarly, "the ideas of religious liberty and freedom of conscience merely gave expression to the sway of free competition within the domain of knowledge," an observation similar in spirit to a passage in *Capital,* where Marx refers ironically to "the 'eternal laws of Nature' of the capitalist mode of production."

The Manifesto contains about fifteen references to the role played by "conditions" in the motivating of social change. And the treatment seems to be uniformly scenic. Yet one should also note the tendency to treat cultural expressions in terms of concomitant variation (varying *"pari passu"* with variations in conditions) rather than as an out-and-out *result* of conditions. There is room for ambiguity here, if you want to be especially exacting. Also, the area covered by the term "conditions" can shift considerably, as one might expect of so crucial a concept. Sometimes it applies purely to material things or operations, sometimes to matters more symbolic, such as money and the terms of ownership. But the fact remains that, by and large, the typical idealistic genealogy is slighted. At one point polemically apostrophizing the bourgeois opposition, the Manifesto declares, "Your very ideas are but the outgrowth of the conditions of your bourgeois production and bourgeois property, just as your jurisprudence is but the will of your class made into a law for all, a will whose essential character and direction are determined by the economic conditions of your class." And there is certainly no celebrating of the "creative" factor in Communist doctrine. It is not put forward as "idea," "ideal," or "vision." Indeed, there is a direct attempt to define the doctrine in ways exactly contrary to this:

The theoretical conclusions of the Communists are in no way based on ideas or principles that have been invented, or discovered, by this or that would-be universal reformer.

They merely express, in general terms, actual relations springing from an existing class struggle, from a historical movement going on under our very eyes. The abolition of existing property relations is not at all a distinctive feature of Communism.

All property relations in the past have continually been subject to historical change consequent upon the change in historical conditions.

On the other hand, what are we to make of the fact that the Manifesto itself is an act of propaganda? Implicit in such an act there is certainly the assumption that the ideas contained in it are social *forces,* and that the course of human action, hence the course of human destiny, will be in some degree altered by the diffusion of these ideas. Thus, in the Manifesto's closing challenge, we see what "views and aims" may do, not simply as reflecting conditions, but as guides for the *changing* of conditions: "The Communists disdain to conceal their views and aims. They openly declare that their ends can be attained only by the forcible overthrow of all existing social conditions."

We have still to quote one important reference to our subject. The Manifesto tells of early Utopian socialists who were primarily humanitarian in their concern with the proletariat. "Only from the point of view of being the most suffering class does the proletariat exist for them." So they made plans for improving the lot of the workers, at a time when the economic situation did not as yet provide "the material conditions for the emancipation of the proletariat." For according to the Manifesto, bourgeois methods of production must attain a high degree of development before the political revolution is possible. This is the Marxist equivalent for the Hegelian concern with that critical moment in the development of Spirit when the times are ripe for a great "World-Historical" act. And Lenin's power as a leader resided in his learning to gauge still more accurately just what were the conditions of a "revolutionary situation."

But the Utopians did not think in such terms. So, hoping for conditions that would improve the workers' welfare, they sought "a new social science . . . new social laws . . . to create these conditions." The authors then proceed to comment on these Utopians as follows:

Historical action is to yield to their personal inventive action; historically created conditions of emancipation to imaginary ones; and the gradual, spontaneous class organization of the proletariat to an organization of society specially contrived by these inventors. Future history resolves itself, in their ideas, into the propaganda and the practical carrying out of their social plans.

Surely, here our concerns come to a head. These Utopians are obviously idealists, in relying upon the creative power of the idea to bring about the desired improvements. Their error, we are told, was in ignoring the fact that the class organization of the proletariat must be *spontaneous*. The movement must arise, as our politicians would put it, "from the grass-roots."

But matters are subtler than that. For in his *What Is to Be Done?* Lenin, though against all revision of Marxist doctrine, found it necessary to attack those who would put too much faith in "spontaneity." This greatest of the "professional revolutionaries" said that the task of preparing for the revolution required a triple struggle, "theoretical, political, and economic," under the leadership of a centralized revolutionary party. And against those who relied on "spontaneity" he wrote (International Publishers translation, footnote, p. 71):

> The tasks of the Social-Democrats [at that time the name of the Marxist faction in Russia] are not exhausted by political agitation on the economic field; their task is to *convert* trade-union politics into the Social-Democratic political struggle, to *utilize* the flashes of political consciousness which gleam in the minds of the workers during their economic struggles for the purpose of *raising* them to the level of *Social-Democratic* political consciousness. The Martynovs, however, instead of raising and stimulating the spontaneously awakening political consciousness of the workers, *bow down before spontaneity* and repeat over and over again, until one is sick and tired of hearing it, that the economic struggle "stimulates" in the workers' minds thoughts about their own lack of political rights. It is unfortunate, gentlemen, that the spontaneously awakening trade-union political consciousness does not *"stimulate"* in your minds thoughts about your Social-Democratic tasks!

Here, then, we would seem to confront the "critical moment" in the dialectical materialist theories of motivation. We might now attempt characterizing the motivational structure as a whole.

The scientist stress, of course, adds to Rhetorical effectiveness insofar as the great growth of *technological* power makes science today the best name to conjure with, when invoking *social* powers. The mingling of idealistic and materialistic ingredients due to the fact that this materialistic dialectic was derived from a philosophy of "Spirit" serves well the double purpose of exhortation and polemic; for the idealistic aspects assist party unification, and the materialistic aspects serve well as a critical instrument for disclosing the special interests that underlie bourgeois pretenses to disinterested idealism, impartial justice, and similar universal motives. (Hegel would doubtless have called the brilliant Marxist invective "Thersitism," after Homer's ungainly Thersites who reviled the king.) The patterns of communion, sacrifice, and transcendence involved in party loyalty give Marxism, on the Symbolic level, the great value of a profound social drama, quite as Christianity was formed about the patterns of drama, though the typical Marxist prefers to stress the rational elements of Marxism, while discountenancing explicit recognition of the dramatic rituals implicit in the Marxist eschatology.

From the standpoint of our Grammar, the whole philosophy is essentially ethical rather than scientist, in that its entire logic is centered about an act, a social or political act, the act of revolution, an act so critical and momentous as to produce a "rupture" of cultural traditions:

> The Communist revolution is the most radical rupture with traditional property relations; no wonder that its development involves the most radical rupture with traditional ideas.

A Dramatist Grammar for Marxism

Since the entire concern of Marxist politics prior to the success of the Russian Revolution was with the ways of action necessary to prepare for this culminating act of revolution, I must always see in Marxist terminology Grammatical conditions calling for a rounded terminology of *action,* though the formal development of such a vocabulary was stifled by scientist adherence to a terminology of motion and by the Rhetorical advantages of a vocabulary essentially different from the vocabularies of scholasticism. Marxism here was but continuing the tradition of secular bourgeois philosophers like Locke and Hume, and was in this respect an ironic turning of bourgeois thought against itself.

With the success of the Revolution in Russia, Marxism there becomes an orthodox doctrine, aiming not at revolutionary rejection of an old political structure, but at the acceptance of a new political structure. The change of political conditions put it in a new role; and though its role in other countries is ambiguous, its role in Russia is clearly conservative, aiming at the maintenance of the new State. And even if one still expects the eventual "withering away" of the State, by Marxist doctrine this could not be expected to occur until all varieties of capitalist State had become socialized, and then the change would take place as a simple and gradual cessation of State functioning, not as a revolutionary act.

Already, in Russia prior to the war, the name for the leading post-revolutionary esthetic movement was "Socialist *realism*"—and we take this itself to be evidence of a tendency towards the featuring of *act*, though necessarily an act different from the act of the Communist Manifesto to the extent of the great change in political conditions following the Revolution.

Let us, then, put the matter this way: So far as our dramatistic terminology is concerned, the Marxist philosophy began by grounding *agent* in *scene*, but by reason of its poignant concern with the ethical, it requires the systematic featuring of *act*. On the Symbolic level, it does feature act implicitly but intensely, in having so dramatic a pattern. On the Rhetorical level, its scientist and anti-scholastic vocabulary is needed for purposes of political dynamism (for the use of an ethical terminology would fail to differentiate the doctrine sufficiently from non-secular ways of salvation). But if, as an experiment, you try a systematic development of terms generated from *act*, the entire system falls quickly into place.

So we offer such a tentative restatement of the Marxist doctrine, as formed about the act of class struggle. We are following no particular text, but are trying to restate the Marxist position in general, as it appears when translated into the terms of characterization employed in this book. We freely grant, however, that such a mode of summarization, characterization, and placement is almost ludicrously inapposite, when considered from the Rhetorical point of view. For though we manipulate our terms in keeping with the all important

Marxist emphasis upon class antagonism as the locus of motives, our vocabulary necessarily lacks the partisan vigor that infuses the Marxist rhetoric, and makes the *Communist Manifesto* a masterpiece of challenge. (And as regards rare literary criticism thus rhetorically infused, I submit that the third section of the Manifesto is a masterpiece within a masterpiece.)

> Each social class, insofar as it has a way of life distinct from that of other classes, is distinct in *actus*, hence in *status*.
>
> Its distinctness in status involves a corresponding distinctness in *properties*. ("Properties" here comprising any kind of characteristics: A house is a property, a way of speaking or thinking is a property, even a condition of total impoverishment is, in this usage, a property.)
>
> The properties of a class may become relatively unsuited to the productive forces of the society in which that class is a part.
>
> Yet that class may be a ruling class, and in this capacity may be able to use the State (the status of the society as a whole) to maintain the dominance of its properties. (Insofar as it conceives of reality in terms of its status as a class, rather than in terms of the society as a whole, it will both consciously and unconsciously use the legislative, educational, and constabulary agencies of the State to perpetuate the ways and ideas deemed beneficial to its class.)
>
> From the standpoint of society as a whole, an idea is "active" insofar as it is "adequate" (that is, insofar as it does accurately name the benign and malign properties of that society).
>
> The society must suffer social "passions" insofar as its ideas are "inadequate."
>
> Insofar as any class of that society holds inadequate ideas, the entire society must suffer social passions. But in particular, the society suffers from inadequate ideas of the ruling class, since these are especially reenforced by all the resources of the State.
>
> Insofar as a class maintains inadequate ideas, it has a false view of "reality."
>
> A class's image of reality is false insofar as it is *partial*, representing only the properties peculiar to that class.
>
> A class suffering visible tangible deprivation has a proportionately greater incentive to question the structure of the State than does a class not so suffering.
>
> The agencies of the State, insofar as they represent the properties of a ruling class, prevent the transformation of such passion into action (guided by adequate ideas).

The class thus suffering visible tangible deprivation may transform its passion into action by a revolutionary act designed to change the nature of the State.

In the acts preparatory to this revolutionary act the revolutionary class is guided and represented by a party (a class within a class) whose ideas are active insofar as they are adequate, and are adequate insofar as they correctly name the malign and benign properties of that society.

Insofar as the changes of property relations would produce the desired betterment of society as a whole, the revolutionary effort is rational, hence active.

But the revolutionary act (and its preparation) is irrational, hence a passion, to the extent of the confusions resulting from the real or imaginary dislocations of society involved in revolution.

The revolutionary body can transcend these passions insofar as its ideas are adequate and lead to the success of the revolutionary act.

Insofar as the act succeeds, a new status is established.

Insofar as the new status is common to all members of the society, the society enjoys properties in common.

During the early stages of the new status, it may be necessary to protect by force the new structure of properties, until those who conceive of reality in terms of other properties have changed their ideas or lost their powers of dominion.

The properties of a State are active insofar as the ideas, in being adequate, make possible the desired operation of the society's means of material production and distribution.

Insofar as all members of a society profit by the new status, the passion of class antagonism is transformed into the action of general coöperation.

Insofar as the properties of this new status are named by adequate ideas, there is a common actus, hence a common status.

Insofar as the new properties are inadequately named, conditions are set for the rise of new conflicts.

As regards the requirements of a dramatistic Grammar, we have thus tried to characterize the Marxist doctrine in a somewhat Spinozist fashion, with two notable exceptions. We have "class-angled" [5] Spi-

---

[5] There is an important ambiguity in the concept of "class-consciousness" itself, with one of the meanings much more active than the other. The member of a class may share the thinking (or "consciousness") of his class without awareness that his thoughts have a class character. "Class consciousness" in this sense might, after psychoanalysis, be more aptly termed "class unconsciousness." As Marx has shown, class consciousness in this sense is so unconscious that it inter-

noza's solution of the problem as to when ideas are "active." This gives us a kind of "social realism," as against the treatment suggested by the materialist reversal of idealism. And we have used the notion of property and status in such a way as to modify one's views of the social state following the Revolution. By this usage, one would expect neither the withering away of the State nor the abolition of private property. One would expect merely a change in the nature of State and private property. Orthodox Marxism would, I believe, itself agree with the point about property. In fact, I believe it always has, though the pressures of dialectic opposition have frequently led to an over-statement of the Marxist position in this respect, hence causing undue resistance, both theological and secular, on the part of those who put a "broad interpretation" on the concept of "personal properties." [6]

-----

prets class values as "universal" and "eternal" values. On the other hand, class consciousness may be a deliberately cultivated attitude of class partisanship, as when the proletarian is exhorted to serve his interests as a member of the prole-tariat. Class consciousness in this second sense involves the rationale of Marxist propaganda. Capitalist propaganda has in turn given the concept of consciousness a further twist, as with advertising campaigns to make the public "frigidaire-conscious," or "two-car conscious," and the like. Here the aim is to use words that impose upon the consciousness (the critical faculty) an automatic (uncritical) response.

[6] Since these pages were set into type, I have read the translation of a Russian essay that bears directly upon our present discussion. It is "Basic Laws of Devel-opment of Socialist Economy," by K. Ostrovitianov, and appeared in the Summer 1945 issue of the Marxist quarterly, *Science and Society*.

The author explicitly acknowledges the existence of classes in the present state of Russian socialism: "Our socialist society consists of two basic, non-antagonistic, friendly classes—the working class and the kolkhoz farmers, along with the Soviet intelligentsia."

This would seem implicitly to acknowledge at least three classes. But in any case, class distinctions are here stated as a fact; and to this extent our proposed dramatist revision of Marxism's abolitionist rhetoric would seem corroborated.

As regards the dialectical resources whereby one may stress either the element of competition in coöperation or the element of coöperation in competition, the author's choice is clear. Whereas the basis of capitalist competition is "the savage law of the struggle of one against the other," he says, "the basis of socialist rivalry is the principle of comradely coöperation and socialist mutual aid on the part of the toilers." And "in contradistinction to the politics of bourgeois states, which expresses the interests of the bourgeoisie, which are profoundly contradictory to the interests of the working mass," the Soviet state "expresses the interests of the work-ing class, the farmers and the intelligentsia, the interests of our whole people."

As regards our previous suggestion that even socialist technology requires an over-all monetary motivation, the author recognizes "the need for an accounting of work, which at the stage of socialism is carried out in money form." And he

One ironic misunderstanding (insofar as it is not intentional misrepresentation) on the part of anti-Marxists is the complaint against Marxist "materialism." If you genuinely want to grasp the point of Marxism here, you must add another step. And when you add this step, you find that, precisely where Marxism is most often damned as *materialistic*, is precisely where it is most characteristically idealistic. Marx's most imaginative criticism is directed against the false idealism derived from the concealed protection of materialistic interests. His chapter on "The Fetishism of Commodities and the Secret Thereof," shows how the human personality itself comes to be conceived in the abstract terms of impersonal commodities. And the whole purpose of such materialist criticism is to bring about such material conditions as are thought capable of releasing men from their false bondage to materials.

Irony of ironies, this observation serves well as a transition to the elegant philosophy of George Santayana. For this brand of materialism also grew antithetically out of German transcendentalism. And it was even more explicit than Marxism in stressing the material basis of man's spiritual fulfilment.

Santayana

All told, throughout these pages we have been considering five major aspects of science:

(1) high development of technological specialization
(2) involvement with rationale of money (accountancy)
(3) progressive departure from natural conditions, usually saluted in the name of "naturalism"

---

quotes Stalin: "Money will be with us for a long time, up to the completion of the first stage of communism—the socialist stage of development."

We have also previously spoken of a possible dissociation between "capitalism" and "technology" whereby an anti-capitalist rhetoric can attribute the vices of the money-machine combination to capitalism and the virtues to technology. In internal Soviet apologetics, this pattern is transformed by the use of the distinction between socialism and communism. Socialism thus becomes a comparatively benign monetary system, as contrasted with a malign monetary motive under capitalism. And the elimination of this motive entirely is left to the future (communism, and the withering away of the State). But the article does not discuss the means whereby technology might be managed, at any stage, without monetary accountancy.

(4) reduction of scenic circumference to empirical limits (the rea-
     son why the technological powers that take us farthest from
     natural conditions have been called "naturalistic")
(5) stress upon the "problem of knowledge" as the point of depar-
     ture for philosophic speculation

The modern stress upon the utility of business and science, with a
compensatory counter-stress upon an esthetic of uselessness, was the
analogue, in our wage-society, to Aristotle's stress upon the uselessness
of the higher intellectual activities (which were equated with the free,
the "liberal," in contrast with the utility of slaves). Marxism avoided
the invitations to pragmatism in this situation by the strategic role it
assigned to the class concept. Grammatically, this concept is interesting precisely because we can see its function in making a doctrine of
substance out of a philosophy that would otherwise be purely a doctrine of *means*.

By the class concept, precisely those members of society who might
consider themselves as having nothing but "jobs" at best and often not
even that, are invested with a vocation. In their very deprivation there
is a *status*, made manifest in properties of consciousness pregnant with
futurity. We get here a variant of tribal substance, with the contents
of class consciousness comprising a property shared by all members of
the class. Social status is not a mere means to an end; it is a *way of life*,
hence a *substantial* activity.

Turning from Marx to Santayana with the scientist emphasis in
mind, we miss the tremendous moral admonition of the class concept.
Though you may think that this term played too basic a role in the
structure of the Manifesto, no vocabulary of social temptations is
complete without it. But Santayana's great gifts as a moralist take another shape. And the human relation to material substance is conceived in universalizing or idealizing terms (as regards problems of
class relationship), though Santayana's great stress upon the relation between spirit and nature is likewise an admonition without which no
moral philosophy can be complete. For moral criticism in its totality,
I should think, we should do justice to both the Marxist heckling and
Santayana's cult of contemplation.

Though both of these materialists have their beginnings in the idealist
problem of knowledge, there was an urgency in Marx that Santayana
deliberately sought to dispel. Whatever speculation and investigation

may precede Marxist assertions, there is the pressure to make them serviceable as a Rhetorical inducement to action on the part of people who have slight interest in speculation and investigation *per se*. Santayana, on the other hand, cultivates a *leisurely* approach—and nothing makes one feel this more poignantly than to consider him after Marx. His philosophy of serenity and retirement sounds expensive. As an adolescent, when I first read Santayana, I dreamed of a tourist life in white flannels along the Mediterranean. He still means to me something like that, though more circumstantially accurate: reading in the country, on a mild afternoon, after a bit of gardening, or a slow walk in the woods, perhaps with the sound of friends playing tennis in the distance. (Should the garden not be economically necessary, then it is cultivated on principle.)

Both Marx and Santayana are keen, Marx with the sharpness of a fighter, Santayana with the most astonishing niceties. And his point of departure in the problem of knowledge is not such as one abandons, but the kind that inaugurates. It is an initial spirit pervading all that follows. It takes the form of a systematically cultivated skepticism which is made an integral part of his philosophy.

The scrupulous show of doubt with which many thinkers (particularly since Descartes) begin their essays is usually but an ambiguous way of introducing new assertions under disarming guise. But Santayana undertakes to carry skepticism to the most exacting lengths possible. This is his response to the key scientist question, the problem of knowledge. And it results in his peculiar doctrine of essence (the ideality in his materiality).

The main obstacle to understanding Santayana's doctrine of essence is its simplicity. It is so simple, we are afraid we must have got it wrong. Having extended the areas of doubt as far as possible, he is left with one unquestionable knowledge: that we see what we see. From this point of view, there is no "illusion" in appearances. Appearances are exactly what they are. If equidistant tracks seem to approach each other in the distance, this is the way they really look.

Such perceiving of appearances he calls "intuition." The appearances themselves he calls "essences." These essences are so thoroughly in keeping with the genius of our term *agent,* that they could, if you insist, be the contents of a solipsistic consciousness. There is no device in the realm of immediate, unquestionable knowledge whereby I could prove them otherwise. For if I offer proofs that the world is not my dream, there is no way to prove that I am not dreaming the proofs. Surely skepticism could go no farther. And it does yield a kind of rock-bottom (or rather, airy) certainty: the certainty that appearances are exactly as they appear, that if I think I hear a certain sound I think I hear that sound.

Having thus theoretically restricted knowledge to the idealistic extreme, Santayana turns materialist. He does not propose to leave us thus uncomfortably suspended. He likens his skepticism to the perfect balance that a pendulum might have if it were poised exactly *above* its centre of gravity. And he contrasts it with "animal faith," which he likens to the normal position of a pendulum at rest. This animal faith "posits" the existence of the material world.

We might get the point more easily by putting "supposes" for "posits." The notion of the Ego "positing" a world is a favorite with the German idealists. This Stance word (*setzen*) gains further linguistic effectiveness in German because the word for law (*Gesetz*) so closely resembles the past particle (*gesetzt*). In English we should note the grammatical significance of the direction, from agent to scene. As Santayana uses the concept, we "posit" the existence of the external material world in taking it on *faith*.

This produces an ingenious reversal. The objects of the material world are thus found to *transcend* our knowledge. All we can immediately *know* is that we see what we see. If we assume that there are real objects behind these appearances, and that intuition itself is a material process, we do so by reason of the faith that we have as natural organisms. And we regularly *act* on this faith, in taking measures to attain or to avoid the things we assume to exist outside us and independently of us.

This reversal adds an important qualification to empiricism. For inasmuch as faith is traditionally an *act* word par excellence, at the very start it imbues the world of matter with the connotations of action. Matter, or nature, is thus the world of existence, of the flux, of constant motion; but also it is the world of power, generation, substance; it is the "field of action." For in saying that we must take the existence of matter on faith, Santayana is not questioning its existence. The belief in the reality of matter as a scene external to the self is such an act of faith as biological organisms implicitly exemplify. This material realm, which we thus take on faith, is the realm of rational, scientific knowledge (in contrast with the intuitive or transcendental knowledge in which his skepticism begins). Though truths are essences, they are embodied in this factual world of nature.

Santayana's word for thought or consciousness is "spirit." Hence, in all, he designates four realms of being: matter, essence, spirit, and truth. The significant thing about spirit in his scheme is that he grounds it materialistically, yet locates its actuality in its freedom from material conditions. Using our rough-and-ready shift of emphasis, we might explain the relation thus: One of his definitions of spirit is "the moral fruition of physical life." One could stress the transcendence of the physical in *fruition;* or one could stress the ground of this fruition in the *physical.* I think one will be less bewildered if he keeps this shift in mind; for Santayana celebrates in spirit (and its variant, imagination) its ability to transcend the mechanical flux of nature; yet at the same time he stresses its location in an animal psyche, which depends upon the conditions of material existence. It is by natural order or organization that spirit attains its opportunities for fulfilment. (And I think the same pattern of thought underlies the idealistic ingredient in Marxist materialism, despite the great difference in application.)

We have noted how Marx avoided pragmatism by the concept of class action. Santayana, who was at Harvard at the time when German idealism was being transformed into American pragmatism, clearly shows the pragmatist influence upon his doctrines. Yet he too submerges the pragmatist strain beneath strongly dramatistic patterns. Indeed, his great gifts as ironist, moralist, and literary psychologist are rooted in his explicit and systematic concern with the terminology of action, notably his application of theological thought to the realm of poetic imagination and intuition.

He shows the pragmatist strain in two ways: in equating the realm of matter with utility, and in compensatorily equating the realms of spirit and essence with a meaning directly the opposite. Though the spirit can contemplate essences for themselves alone, and loves to dwell in the realm of essence, the material interests of the organism require it to use its intuitions of essence as *signs.* The animal in the jungle, for instance, catching a sound or scent, interprets it as a sign of food or danger, thereby turning its intuition of essence to use. But the pure intuitions come first—and similarly pure art comes before the conversion of the arts to practical ends (hence the typical idealistic equating of the esthetic with "play," as with Kant's concern with the "free play of the imagination").

It is interesting to observe how, though matter is the scene in which the process of intuition is grounded, the essences which are the content of our intuitions become a kind of scene-behind-a-scene—and we shall try to trace this development, because it is characteristic of the ultimate form which Santayana's dramatism seems to have taken.

Santayana uses the traditional pair of terms: essence and existence. But he gives it elusive twists all his own. Thus, if we flatly contrast existence with essence, it follows by the sheer dialectics of the case that "essences" do not "exist." Nor can existence as such be an essence. In Plato, the world of being (that is, essence) was more real than the world of our everyday experience (which was for Plato the world of appearance). But Santayana has synonymized appearances and essences to the extent that all appearances are essences, though there are many more essences than there are appearances.

While I was puzzling over Santayana's way of distinguishing essence from existence, a six-year-old solved the problem for me when he explained, "There *is* an Easter bunny, but he isn't *real.*" I saw the application immediately: the Easter bunny has a *being,* or *essence,* but he does not *exist.* Or put it this way: there is a *character* called the Easter bunny, since it is distinguished from all other characters; yet the Easter bunny is nowhere to be found in all the realm of material substances. Here clearly is an essence that does not exist.

If it did exist, it would be subject to the flux of existence. It would thus be involved in the world of *relationships,* and of *processes* that require a constant commingling with the particles of matter surrounding it. But in its sheer *character* as Easter bunny it can be contemplated *in itself.* And so similarly, when the essences that we intuit are not interpreted as signs, we consider them *in themselves, immediately.*

Or we may think of the matter this way: Imagine a history of all that ever happened in this world since the beginning of time. Here would certainly be a history of "existence." But in the course of writing this history, let us say that you divided it into periods which you named according to the different stages the world has gone through. Let us assume that you had been quite accurate in thus listing "essences" or characters of each successive stage. Could we say that these characters exist, or ever did exist? What existed at any given time was the particular arrangement of particles comprising the historical flux at that time. It was only these infinite details that existed. The over-all "characters" that they added up to would be "essences" that never existed, hence they are as much characters now as then.

Indeed, whatever character a given stage was to exemplify was that same character even before the existence of the particular combination of particles of which it is the essence. So similarly, whereas Napoleon has ceased to exist, this fact is but an *accident* of Napoleon's essence, which is what it is, just as the character of tomorrow is already "eternal," once we think of eternity as a quality of *being*, in contrast with a quality of *existence*. Then, carrying such thought one step farther, we can people the realm of essence with an infinity of eternal beings that may never have their substantial moment in the fluctuant accidents of existence.

At this final step we suddenly discover that we have come upon a new kind of scene. For the essences are a realm of eternal "possibilities," only a small fraction of which are ever embodied in natural existence. The Easter bunny, for instance, is such a possibility, a universal (since a unique whole), eternally distinct in the realm of essence, though he may never attain embodiment in the flux of nature. And existence itself proceeds by embodying an endless succession of essences (like discrete points on a continuous line), advancing at each moment from character to character. And these successive characters are things-in-themselves, in the sense that each is what it is, without regard for relationships. Similarly, a continuity of flux can be continuity only insofar as it exemplifies the same essence throughout its existence— and this essence would be uniquely itself.

There is an infinity of such essences, and Santayana calls them the "indelible background" for all the transitory facts of nature. He uses the figure of an infinite Koran, prophesying all possible Being, while existence is like an eye that, reading, follows a thin stream of script, as "re-agent" thus selecting one line of possibilities from among the infinite number inscribed in the totality of the eternal essences. Here we find a significant variant of the scribe-script-scroll pattern, as exemplified in Avicebron's *Fons Vitae*. With Avicebron, the scene is matter (the scroll), the act is form (the script), and the agent (the scribe) is

will. In Santayana's variant, the scroll corresponds to the entire immaterial realm of essence; and script and scribe combined equal the
narrow bit of text selected by existence as "re-agent."

Though Santayana is usually classed as a Platonist, his essences have
undergone one notable change from the Forms or Ideas of Plato.
These Platonic essences were above all else *familial*, the principles of
generation. Their very capacity to unify the world of multiplicity
resides in their role as ancestral prototypes, as pure sources from which
all members of their kind are descended, thereby possessing a common
tribal nature. But Santayana's essences are uncompromisingly individual, even individualistic—and without progeny. He explicitly as-
sures us that they are not "seeds." Even the philosophic way of arriving
at them is by a discipline that he likens to a state of chastity prolonged
until late in youth. Their relation to a vocabulary of action is arrived
at by a less "substantial" route than tribal derivation. As matter is
the realm of flux, or motion, the corresponding dialectical role of
essence is that of *rest*. And since this orbit of mechanical motion is
also ambiguously called the "field of action," the kind of rest here indicated is ambiguously both the cessation of motion and the end of
action.

Let us at this point consider the subject purely in itself, regardless of
Santayana. Suppose that you had called the world of mechanical motion the "field of action." You had given an initial plausibility to your
position, since you had introduced this world of motion under the
aegis of "faith," a term essentially active, as in the expression, "an act of
faith." Obviously, you would not thereby get the full value for your
term "action," since it would be confined rather to the limits of purely
biological intention, as with the "action" of a hungry animal stalking
game. If, then, you set up against this pole, as dialectical opposite, a
concept of rest, it would be such rest as equalled the cessation of motion,
and it would ambiguously be such rest as equalled the end of action
(where "end" in turn can refer ambiguously to an ultimate destination
of action either as the point at which action subsides or as the point at
which action attains its purpose).

Let us further suppose that your field of biological action was interpreted pragmatically, as the realm in which the organism puts its
awarenesses to *use*. And you want a wider concept of action, that will
allow for the areas of "free play," where awareness transcends its purely

utilitarian function. How might you proceed, within the usual limits of the dramatist grammar? Or, to put it bluntly, what key dramatist *words* have you left unexploited?

Santayana, at this point, exploits two such words. He calls the area of pure awareness the "actuality" of spirit; and he salutes it for having added a new dimension, that of *the passions*, to the realm of natural mechanisms.

So, all told, we have: (1) an area of the mechanical flux ambiguously called the "field of action"; (2) a correspondingly ambiguous world of rest, that serves as the ground of motion in marking successive stations in the processes of change; (3) an "actuality" of spirit that adds the dimensions of "the passions" to the natural world. Since the ambiguously active area was equated with utility, this second level of activity, the "actuality" of spirit, can thus transcend biological utility at the same time as it introduces the fully dramatic term, *passion*.

What, then, can be the final "end" in such a view? Passion for passion's sake? There is in Santayana's pages much appreciation of the passions that might lead a patchy reader to this conclusion. But there is another, more classically philosophical conclusion available. Recall that we already have an ambiguous concept of end, in our realm of essence. Centering upon this, in the light of spiritual actuality and passion, we can add the fourth step to our alignment of the previous paragraph. We can add to step (2) the qualification that makes it *unambiguously* such kind of rest as is the end of *action*. Thus our line-up would be:

(1)   motion (ambiguously "biological action")
(2)   essence (as its corresponding stasis)
(3)   spirit (dramatic: actuality and passion)
(4)   essence (as end of spirit)

Since biological action was here equated with utility, spiritual action will transcend utility. Being itself a fulfilment, it will love to dwell upon fulfilments. And so, its ultimate delight is in the contemplation of essence, which in the last analysis is a *benign* contemplation of death. The realm of essence is thus ultimately a thanatopsis. And though Santayana draws back at times from the full implications of his doctrine, reminding himself and us that he belongs to the world of rational Greek materialism, it is his serene doctrine of essence that seems most distinctive of him, particularly when we contrast his brand of dramatism with the dramatistic ingredients in Marx. Reading him, we do feel that it might be enough to cultivate the contemplation of essences, simply through love of dwelling in the vicinity of terms at rest and at peace, terms that would serve as much as terms can to guide us through a long life of euthanasia.

The pious Christian was exhorted to "live a dying life." And Santayana, whose skepticism was at every turn able to reproduce religious thought with a difference, finds ways of transforming mortification into an amenity. Though he would present the spiritual delight in essence as a transcending of utility, it seems to have done well by him, even on the purely biological level, attending him from youth into an advanced old age. His philosophy is, however, the exact opposite of a patriarchal one. In his scheme, spirit is powerless. All power is in nature. Nature is to spirit as mother is to child. He thinks as one who is the end of a line; his concern is with culminations; in applying the Aristotelian concept of the entelechy as summational, he eliminates its tribal ingredients as thoroughly as he did in the case of Plato's ideas. Whatever essences in general may be, the essence of his own thought is of a culmination that is a termination. His estheticizing of essence is, in its own way, as pronounced a step away from the familial substance as is the trend of science. But whereas science takes this step by renouncing dramatist terms, Santayana retains them and ingeniously perverts them, while at the same time his romantic cult of neo-classic calm enables him to avoid the agonies of Satanism.

Imagination

In the course of showing how and why idealism is identical with the featuring of the term *agent,* we have incidentally shown how deeply "scientism" has permeated modern thought. One is well advised to look for scientist stress in any terminology that has its start in modern idealism. Thus, although the cult of the "imagination" is usually urged today by those who champion poetry as a field *opposed* to science, our investigations would suggest the ironic possibility that they exemplify an aspect of precisely the thinking they would reject. For our modern views of the imagination come to us *via* the idealist Coleridge from the idealist Kant—and we have already seen the strong scientist bias in the Kantian doctrines.

The autumn, 1944 issue of *The Sewanee Review* contains an essay by Wallace Stevens that is quite to our purposes. Written with all the deftness and subtlety of Stevens' poetry, it speaks of poetry in precisely the idealist cluster of terms we have been examining in this section. The importance of "personality" is stressed. Poetry is derived from an "indirect egotism." "Nervous sensitiveness" is basic, for the poet's morality is "the morality of the right sensation." Poetry is the "spirit out of its own self." There are citations stressing the importance of "temperament." "Kant says that the objects of perception are conditioned by the nature of the mind as to their form." And Mr. Stevens cites a statement by Henri Focillon: "The chief characteristic of the mind is to be constantly describing *itself*."

And the summarizing word for all this typical idealistic cluster is "imagination." The essay places it in dialectical opposition to "reason," thereby going a step beyond Coleridge, whose proportion "imagination : fancy : : reason : understanding," aligned imagination and reason together as against fancy and understanding (while imagination itself was more active, by reason of its *unifying* role). Poetry gives us "an unofficial view of being"; "philosophic truth may be said to be the official view." On the Symbolic level, philosophy and reason here seem equated with the vocational (with office hours), poetry and imagination seem equated with the vacational (after hours). Accordingly, when Mr. Stevens tries to illustrate what he means by poetic imagination, he begins: "If we close our eyes and think of a place where it would be pleasant to spend a holiday . . ."

There are subtle steps in the essay to which I cannot here do justice. In the end, for instance, the poet seems to arrive at a merger of imagination and reason; but not until important changes have been made in both terms by a strategic reference to the Minotaur. This fabulous hybrid apparently represents a joined duality of motives, and here apparently symbolizes the union of a labyrinthine imagination (the "unconscious") with the rationality of a poetic medium developed by deliberate conscious sophistication. The very title gives us further significant data, were it our task here to search for equations on the Symbolic level: "The Figure of the Youth as Virile Poet." This vacational poetry will be a *young* poetry (incidentally, apparently a dangerous ideal for some poets, however great the attainments it stimulated in Mr. Stevens, for elsewhere in the same number of *The Sewanee Review*

Horace Gregory observes: "What American poetry needs most . . . is the courage . . . to mature").

The important point for our present purposes is to note that the key term "imagination" here figures in a theory of poetry that is basically scientist. For poetry is here approached in terms of its search for "truth," as a "view" of reality, as a kind of "knowledge." Thus, Stevens quotes with approval another writer quoting Descartes:

> There are in us, as in a flint, seeds of knowledge. Philosophers adduce them through the reason; poets strike them out from the imagination, and these are the brighter.

Recall that Descartes was as influential as any philosopher in directing the turn from dramatist to scientist terminologies.

Mr. Stevens also quotes from Shelley, whose "Defence of Poetry" is itself interesting in its vacillations between dramatist realism and idealist scientism. There are strong realist ingredients, for instance, in Shelley's concern with the relation between drama and morality. But when Mr. Stevens neared such a subject, as in his remark on the morality of the poet, he ended on the most scientist term of all: "sensation." And the Shelley to whom he refers is the idealist scientist Shelley:

> He says that a poem is the very image of life expressed in its eternal truth. It is "indeed something divine. It is at once the centre and circumference of knowledge."

The figure itself is interesting, for a glance at its past enables us to see it turning scientist. In his *Principles of Nature and Grace*, Leibniz writes:

> God alone has a distinct knowledge of all, for He is the source of all. It has been very well said that as a centre He is everywhere, but his circumference is nowhere, for everything is immediately present to Him without any distance from this centre.

The editor of the Oxford edition (*The Monadology, Etc.*) reminds us that Pascal said the same of the world, while Pascal's editor traces the phrase to Rabelais and earlier writers. Pascal's version was not scientist at all: he simply calls the world an infinite sphere, with its centre everywhere and its circumference nowhere. Leibniz gives it the beginnings of a scientist turn; for though he applies it to God, the remark occurs when he is on the subject of God's *knowledge*. But Shelley, pantheistically merging divinity and poetry into one, similarly brings the poetry and the knowledge together. The next step is to drop from pantheism the *theos*, whereupon, imagination equalling knowledge, one is left with the *pan*: Mr. Stevens' "*mundo* of the imagination."

However, we must watch lest the reader mistake the eagerness of our pursuit for an "indictment" of either Mr. Stevens or of the "scientist" traces in his essay. Indeed, we are hardly in a position to attack "scientism" per se, inasmuch as the present book itself is wholly scientist in its aims. But high among science's obligations is the obligation to recognize its own presence, and to note as far as possible the "perturbations" of its influence upon the orbits of our thoughts. And a notable perturbation of this sort occurs when scientist influences operate undetected in theories of poetic action as is the case with theories of moral action. Indeed, from this point of view, "esthetics" itself is seen to have been predominantly idealist, laying major stress either upon the *expression of the subject* or upon the "object of the imagination," or upon mergers of subject and object. And the Stevens essay, by reason of its very depth and accuracy, enables us to see how such idealist emphasis carries with it a scientist emphasis.

It is particularly important to keep the scientist "heresy" in mind when we are reading so good a statement, by so good a poet, on his own theories of poetry. Insofar as these are expressed scientistically, in terms of *knowledge*, rather than in terms of *action*, dramatism admonishes us that they are to be discounted. The irony is that, whereas the study of esthetics was a typical product of the modern idealistic philosophies, and although, with the weakening of religious certainties, art was often made the very basis of evaluation for all human ways, the typical idealist vocabularies were essentially scientist in their approach to artistic innovation. Precisely at the time when the term "imagination" gained greatly in prestige (in contrast with its low rating in writers as diverse as St. Teresa, Spinoza, and Pascal) theories of art took a momentous step away from the understanding of art as action and towards a lame attempt to pit art against science as a "truer kind of truth." The correct controversy here should not have been at all a pitting of art against science: it should have been a pitting of one view of science against another.

III

ACT

Aristotle and Aquinas

SINCE our entire book illustrates the featuring of act, there is less call for a special section on it.   But let us cite a few passages from the Baldwin dictionary that will sufficiently indicate why scholastic realism should be treated as a speculative enterprise constructed about action as the basic concept.

In Aristotle "things are more or less real according as they are more or less *energeia* (*actu,* from which our 'actuality' is derived)."   In scholastic realism "form is the *actus,* the attainment, which realizes the matter."   "As Saint Thomas says, and as the whole Peripatetic doctrine teaches, *forma per se ipsam facit rem esse in actu* (or, as it is often expressed, *a form is an act*)."   And when discussing the characteristic distinction between existence and essence, the article on Aquinas defines existence as "the act of essence."   Similarly in his comments on Aristotle's *Metaphysics,* Aquinas refers to the soul as the "act of an organic physical body capable of life."   Etienne Gilson's *God and Philosophy* states the matter succinctly in observing that for the scholastics existence is "an act, not a thing."[7]   And when discussing the "Likeness of Creatures" in the *Summa Contra Gentiles,* Aquinas brings out a similar stress, in keeping with the agent-act ratio: "It is of the nature of action that a like agent should produce a like action, since every thing acts according as it is in act" (though he is here using the principle to distinguish between God as cause and human agents as effect, a disproportion whereby "the form of the effect is found in its transcendent cause somewhat, but in another way and another ratio").

The most convenient place I know for directly observing the essentially dramatist nature of both Aristotle and Aquinas is in Aquinas' com-

---

[7] However, *to be* is the act of acts.   Gilson makes much of the fact that the copulative verb is grammatically in the active voice.   Sociologically, we may note how well this identification between act and being served a feudal society built upon the maintenance of fixed social status.

ments on Aristotle's four causes (in pp. 154-163 of the *Everyman's Library* edition). In the opening citation from Aristotle, you will observe that the "material" cause, "that from which (as immanent material) a thing comes into being, e.g. the bronze of the statue and the silver of the dish," would correspond fairly closely to our term, *scene*. Corresponding to *agent* we have "efficient" cause: "the initial origin of change or rest; e.g. the adviser is the cause of the action, and the father a cause of the child, and in general the agent the cause of the deed." "Final" cause, "the end, i.e. that for the sake of which a thing is," is obviously our "purpose." "Formal" cause ("the form or pattern, i.e. the formula of the essence") is the equivalent of our term *act*. This correspondence is more clearly revealed in the earlier dictionary citation that "a form is an act"). We can approximate the equation closely enough if we think of a thing not simply as existing, but rather as "taking form," or as the record of an act which gave it form. Or one may also think of "actualities" legalistically, as the "form" of a constitution is equivalent to the principles involved in its *enactment*.

There is also a negative way of establishing the correspondence between form and act. Recall the scholastic hexameter listing the questions to be answered in the treatment of a topic: Who, what, where, by what means, why, how, when: *quis, quid, ubi, quibus auxiliis, cur, quo modo, quando*. The "who" is obviously covered by *agent*. *Scene* covers the "where" and the "when." The "why" is *purpose*. "How" and "by what means" fall under *agency*. All that is left to take care of is *act* in our terms and "what" in the scholastic formula. Also, the form of a thing was called its "whatness," or *quidditas*.

As for *agency*, Aristotle has this "fifth" cause also in his list; but in accordance with the imperative genius of the purpose-agency (or end-means) ratio, instead of dealing with agency as a special kind of cause, (say, an "instrumental cause") he introduces it incidentally to his discussion of "final" cause. Thus, after the Peripatetic has said that the desire for health may be the end, or final cause, of walking, he goes on to say: "The same is true of all the means that intervene before the end," as "purging, drugs, or instruments" may also be used for the sake of the same end. Thus, though this thinker, whose studies of logic traditionally go under the name of the *Organon* (that is, tool or instrument) omits agency as a fifth kind of cause, he clearly enough takes it into account.

In this brief reference to agency, he also indicates how it overlaps upon our term act. For distinguishing between medicines and walking as the means of health, he says that some means "are instruments and others are actions." One can see the overlap today in our references to scientific "method," which is treated sometimes as a means and sometimes more substantially, as a way of life.

Perhaps a faint indication that Aquinas' "dramatism" is farther along the road towards modern bourgeois idealism than Aristotle's was, is to be seen in Aquinas' tendency to discover the respects in which means might fall under agent as a kind of efficient cause. He here quotes "the theory of Ibn-Sina," according to which there are four varieties of efficient cause. I think one might fairly sum up the lot by saying that they deal with various kinds of "co-agent." But among these four is an *"auxiliary* efficient cause" that differs from the principal agent "in not acting for its own but another's ends":

> Thus, whoever helps a king in war, acts for that which the king intends. This same relation holds between a secondary and a primary cause; for among agents whose nature is to be in a certain order among themselves, the secondary cause acts for the ends proper to the primary cause. The action of a soldier, for instance, is directed to the aims intended by the statesman. An *adviser* differs from a principal agent by laying down the scope and manner of the action. This same relation obtains between the primary agent, acting through his intellect, and the secondary agent—whether this be a physical body or another intelligent being.

This "auxiliary" or "secondary" kind of efficient cause (or co-agent) obviously marks an overlap of agent and agency. And Aquinas leaves it thus wavering, applying either to physical instruments or to persons used as instrumentalities in carrying out the primary intentions of others. Similarly, he applies it either to the partial efficiencies of human beings using means to an end, or to the "universe of nature" as a "secondary agent" that accepts the purpose and manner of its action "from the supreme mind" as "primary agent."

But though the scholastic vocabulary is *essentially* dramatic, I doubt whether we could say that it is *consciously* so. The *direction* was scientist, in moving from the act of faith to the conditions of knowledge. The dramatism was in the *point of departure:* in the Homeric epics and Dionysian dramas that underlay the patterns of Greek thought, and in the drama of salvation that Christianity had constructed about the Bible. Socrates, approaching the world as a moralist, necessarily considered it in terms of action. Reality, he said, was the power to act and to be acted upon. And he was primarily concerned to perfect his "knowledge of the Good"—but though in Plato we may still hear this as "knowledge of the *Good*," even in Aristotle we move towards the alternate emphasis: "*knowledge* of the Good."

Every philosophy is in some respect or other a *step away from* drama. But to understand its structure, we must remember always that it is, by the same token, a step away from *drama*. In Aristotle, the dramatist nature of his vocabulary is well revealed in the fact that it was so well suited to the discussion of drama (in contrast, for instance, with the terminologies of modern science which can at best illuminate drama by their sheer incongruity, as with vocabularies that "debunk" the dramatic elements in men's social and political relations).

Thus, it was not by an added step, but in keeping with the nature of his terminology in general, that Aristotle designated the plot or *action* as the foremost among the six elements of tragedy. For he had written of the physical world itself in terms of active and passive principles, and of natural beings that develop in accordance with the ends proper to their kind. His God, the origin of all motion, was conceived dramatistically, as the *end* of action. By the paradox of the absolute, such "pure act" is like no act at all, being that of an "unmoved mover" in perfect *repose*. Also, in accordance with that same paradox, this "pure act" motivates as a *passive*. For Aristotle's God is not a creator of the world, which has existed from eternity. But he is the goal towards which all worldly forms strive, as the *loved* or *desired* (*eromenon*). But either as pure motionless act or as the loved, God is conceived in terms of action—and this is the perspective that equipped Aristotle to write:

> Tragedy is essentially an imitation not of persons but of action and life, of happiness and misery. All human happiness or misery takes the form of action; the end for which we live is a certain kind of activity, not a quality. Character gives us qualities, but it is in our actions—what we do—that we are happy or the reverse. In a play accordingly they do not act in order to portray the Characters; they include the Characters for the sake of the action. So that it is the action in it, i.e. its Fable or Plot, that is the end and purpose of the

tragedy; and the end is everywhere the chief thing. . . . A tragedy is impossible without action, but there may be one without Character.

Aligning the six elements with our five terms:

Plot would correspond to *act*. *Character* would correspond to *agent* (it is "what makes us ascribe certain moral qualities to the agents"). Whereas the action is the purpose of the play from the standpoint of the audience, *within* the play we should probably assign *purpose* to the third element, Thought (which is shown in all that the characters say "when proving a particular point or . . . enunciating a general truth"). Since Aristotle himself calls Melody and Diction "the means of imitation," they would obviously fall under *agency*. The sixth element, Spectacle, he assigns to "manner" (presumably the *quo modo* of the Latin hexameter quoted above), a kind of modality that we should want to class under *scene,* though Aristotle's view of it as accessory would seem to make it rather a kind of *scenic agency*. It was not until modern naturalism in drama that scene gained its full independence, with the "property man" giving the environmental placement that was regularly suggested in Elizabethan drama, for instance, by the use of verbal imagery. Perhaps "Spectacle" had something of the significance we associate with "sheer pageantry." Aristotle says that the Spectacle, though an attraction, "is the least artistic of all the parts, and has least to do with the art of poetry." We can be affected by a tragedy without a public performance at all; and "the getting-up of the Spectacle is more a matter for the costumer than the poet."

It is obviously the dramatist ingredient in Aristotle's science that makes it unpalatable to the norms of modern technology. His great stress upon the all-importance of "knowledge" we might interpret as a striving *towards* a scene-agent view of the world (a world of lyric agents and impersonal scene). But this striving was either hampered or corrected (depending on your point of view) by the essential featuring of act he had inherited from the Platonist dialectic, which set up a universal motivation of purposive action by deriving all from a *One* that was equated with the *Good*. (The point at which Platonist idealism and Platonist realism overlap.)

Aristotle "neutralized" this doctrine. For he denied to both the Platonist Ideas and his own God any generative function. And the kind of purpose he assigned to natural entities was hardly purpose in the Providential sense of the term.   Though all motion and action are ultimately guided by a desire for the perfection of God, each kind of thing is conceived as striving to be perfectly the kind of thing it is. Teleology as thus modified allowed for much purely inductive study of genera and species.

In his *Psychology* he clearly distinguishes between philosophic and behavioristic definition, noting that we may define anger either as the "desire for vengeance" or in terms of bodily symptoms.   But typically, instead of choosing between them, he favors the kind of inquiry that embraces both.   In our terms, he proposes to keep the terminologies of both motion and action, though his system as a whole gives the preference to action, as revealed in his *Metaphysics,* the field where such choices are brought to a final reckoning.   And it was this stress upon action, of course, that fitted his thought for adaptation by Aquinas, as rationalizer of the Christian drama.

The "Pathetic Fallacy"

As we have said before, however, our difficulties are increased by the fact that motion and action themselves are readily confounded, unless we make an especial effort to distinguish between them.   Aristotle himself, in Book IX of the *Metaphysics,* remarks that "actuality" (*energeia*) in the strict sense "is thought to be identical with movement" and that whereas he equates it with "complete reality," it has "in the main been extended from movements to other things."   If, however, you examine in the Greek dictionaries such root words as *ergon,* you find that the movements signified are clearly those of a *purposive* sort, such as *work* or *deed,* with connotations of *thing* here deriving from the thought of some piece of work fulfilled.   (Similarly two other Greek words for thing, *pragma* and *chrema,* are implicated in verbal roots signifying *to accomplish* and *to use* respectively.   Indeed, viewed from the standpoint of the pentad, "pragmatism" might better have been named "chrematism.")   Only the modern concept of the "erg" can be said to belong unequivocally in the realm of motion alone.

In our passing references to the "pathetic fallacy" as a factor in the motion-action ambiguity, we have somewhat stretched the usual application of the term.   The device in its pure form is considered in a discerning and suggestive little book (*Pathetic Fallacy in the Nineteenth*

Century, by Josephine Miles) which charts the incidence of this figure in representative English poets from Collins to Eliot.

Concerning her inquiry into "the attribution of feelings to things, which Ruskin called pathetic fallacy," Miss Miles defines her subject as follows:

> Since the "powers of human nature" which may be attributed to objects are so varied, I arbitrarily limit them here to the powers of emotion and passion, which are most central to the "pathetic." That is, I count as an instance of the pathetic fallacy every attribution of a named emotion to an object; and the regular signs of emotion, such as tears and laughter, are included. Thus *the trees were gay, the mountains mourned, the proud fields laughed, the hills sadly slept* are all examples.

The device as so defined well illustrates the kind of consistency between "subject" and "object" we would call the scene-agent (or lyric) ratio. We would consider it an instance of the scene-agent ratio because the stress is upon the attribution of personal *feelings,* or *attitudes* (which are properties of *agents*). The moment she thus restricted her inquiry, it was a foregone conclusion that she would slight the more distinctively dramatic ratio, involving consistency of scene and *act*.

Not that we would object to the limitations she has imposed. On the contrary, her very precision in thus defining a standard serves to illumine the area of the action-motion ambiguity lying just beyond the range of her inquiry. Once you include also, for instance, the personalizing of impersonal motions, you have no clear way of knowing when a given motion is personalized and when it is not. By her rules, *the proud fields laughed* is clearly an instance of pathetic fallacy. But if we widened the scope of personalization to include the "actualizing of motion," we might find ourselves ruling, for instance, that *the wheat tossed in the wind* refers to motion, whereas *the wheat tossed its head in the wind* refers to action.

Consider, for instance, the lines which Coleridge quotes from *Venus and Adonis* as an instance of what he means by imagination:

> Look, how a bright star shooteth from the sky,
> So glides he in the night from Venus' eye.

Do shooting stars "move" or "act"? The theory of empathy suggests that even though we might, when asked, say that they simply "move," we attribute action to them when we em-pathetically move with them in our imagination. And this particular star can make a further claim to act, since in its motion across the sky it represents Adonis in his act of departure.

If, in the light of Miss Miles's investigation, you glance through English poetry prior to the era she has charted, you will find a surprising paucity of pathetic fallacies in her restricted sense of the term. Ironically, such formal assigning of human sentiments to the non-human realm seems to have come into prominence precisely at the time when the breach between man and nature was being intensified. But if you examine the poetry prior to this period for examples of the action-motion ambiguity, you will find the incidence quite high indeed. Similarly, Miss Miles finds a notable avoidance of the pathetic fallacy in Eliot. Yet there are many lines such as the reference to "yellow smoke that slides along the street," or "the windings of the violins," or the light that "crept up between the shutters"—and these are indebted to the action-motion ambiguity for much of their power as what Aristotle would call "actualizations."

But it may be asked: Why make so much of the turn from action to motion in the vocabularies of human motivation when in the same breath we testify to the ways in which the distinction is continually being obliterated or obscured?

In the first place, it is important to note any source of ambiguity that has great bearing upon the structure of language in all its levels: Grammatical, Rhetorical, and Symbolic. Thus our concern with the ways of characterization, summarization, and placement requires us to note a point so critical as that watershed moment dividing the dramatistic from the operationalist. The realm of motion is now *par excellence* the realm of instruments. No instrument can record or gauge *anything* in the realm of action ("ideas"), except insofar as the subject-matter can be reduced to the realm of motion.

Our approach forces us to face again the philosophic issue that arose with Cartesian dualism. Many of our best naturalist philosophers seem to be drawing doctrinal sustenance from unrecognized effects of the pathetic fallacy as we have here extended it to cover the action-motion ambiguity. Hence, condemning materialistic reduction, they can speak hopefully of a vocabulary midway between "mind" and "body" (or midway between the terms for the act of "consciousness" and the terms for the scenic "conditions" of those manifestations we call consciousness). We need not dare to say that such a vocabulary cannot be found. We need only say that, whenever it *seems* to be found, you are admonished to be on the look-out for the covert workings of the action-motion ambiguity.

We may finally be forced to recognize, as integral to vocabularies of human motivation, an active or "policy-making" function that is necessarily "nonsense" as tested by our purely technological vocabularies (scenic, scientist, shaped to conform with knowledge of natural behavior—for even if every atom were proved indubitably to possess a "soul," the technologist would have use for it only insofar as it were inanimate, quite as the sales promoter looks for techniques that induce us mechanically and unthinkingly to buy his product). Such a "policy-making" function would be *realistic* when it arises out of tribal experience (as with proverbs). But it tends towards *idealism* in proportion as the derivation is from managerial agents (such as government functionaries); and may often require the correctives of a materialist criticism.

Above all, by sharpening the issue, and thus admonishing ourselves lest *apparently* operationalist vocabularies derive appeal from ingredients *surreptitiously* dramatistic, we prepare the way for the mature development of the dramatistic itself. A slight but undetected ingredient of action can go a long way towards making a flimsy vocabulary of motivation palatable (as is evident from the popularity enjoyed by quasi-scientific "debunkers" in recent years). But once the requirements of linguistic action are contemplated systematically, we become more exacting. We demand a fully worked-out version of the ways of *homo dialecticus,* in contrast with the scraps of dialectical lore now scattered about the literary landscape, with each typical modern verbalizer digging in some one thin vein as though it were a bonanza.

"Incipient" and "Delayed" Action

In his chapter on "Attitudes" in *The Principles of Literary Criticism,* I. A. Richards writes:

> Every perception probably includes a response in the form of incipient action. We constantly overlook the extent to which all the while we are making preliminary adjustments, getting ready to act

in one way or another. Reading Captain Slocum's account of the centipede which bit him on the head when alone in the middle of the Atlantic, the writer has been caused to leap right out of his chair by a leaf which fell upon his face from a tree.

The importance of Mr. Richards' book as a contribution to the analysis of poetry unquestionably centers in his speculations as to how our responses as readers or audience involve such attitudes (which he also calls "imaginal" activities and "tendencies to action"). The symbolic representation of some object or event in art can arouse an added complexity of response in us, he suggests, because it invites us to feel such emotions as would be associated with the actual object or event, while at the same time we make allowance for it as a fiction.

And since we are not called upon to act, no "*overt* action" need take place. In fact, Mr. Richards considers it the sign of intelligence and refinement that we are able thus to leave our impulses in abeyance, at the incipient stage, where they can be contemplated and can thus enrich our consciousness. It is the "stupid or crass person" who habitually responds to his impulses by overt action.

Note, however, that the concept of *incipient* acts is ambiguous. As an attitude can be the *substitute* for an act, it can likewise be the *first step towards* an act. Thus, if we arouse in someone an attitude of sympathy towards something, we may be starting him on the road towards overtly sympathetic action with regard to it—hence the rhetoric of advertisers and propagandists who would induce action in behalf of their commodities or their causes by the formation of appropriate attitudes.

In the sphere of social relations generally, the work of George Herbert Mead has developed with great subtlety and thoroughness this alternative aspect of the incipient. As he puts it in *Mind, Self, and Society,* attitudes are "the beginnings of acts." Indeed, we should not be straining matters greatly if we read his other major work, *The Philosophy of the Act,* as if it were entitled *The Philosophy of the Attitude,* if only we remember that his concern is primarily with the incipient as the *introductory* rather than with the incipient as the *substitutive.* Thus similarly, we would place his valuable treatment of language as "vocal gestures." By such "gestures," he says, we arouse in ourselves the attitudes that language serves to arouse in others; and thereby we adopt the "attitude of the other" in the formation of our moral consciousness.

"I am going on the assumption," he writes, "that action is distinguishable from motion," though action as here conceived does not involve rationality, or even "consciousness of action," but is equated with the internal motivations of an organism which, confronting reality from its own special point of view or biological interests, encounters "resistance" in the external world. And this external resistance to its internal principle of action defines the organism's action. Such a conception, somewhat analogous to Santayana's view of the "field of action," would give us a concept halfway between motion and action. Perhaps, as with our previous improvisation to do with agent, we might call it action-minus. Or rather, "attitude-minus." For when we turn to the higher levels of consciousness we find, according to Mead, that the sense of "self" is developed as the individual learns to foresee the kinds of resistance which external things will put forward if he acts in certain ways. Stating the dialectics of the case in its simplest form, Mead says: "The essential thing is that the individual, in preparing to grasp the distant object, himself takes the attitude of resisting his own attitude in grasping." That is, the individual learns to recognize whether the object will have an elusive or slippery or light or heavy attitude towards his grasp. And "the attained preparation for the manipulation is the result of this co-operation or conversation of attitudes." In studying the nature of the object, we can in effect speak for it; and in adjusting our conduct to its nature as revealed in the light of our interests, we in effect modify our own assertion in reply to its assertion.

A social relation is established between the individual and external things or other people, since the individual learns to anticipate their attitudes toward him. He thus, to a degree, becomes aware of *himself* in terms of *them* (or generally, in terms of the "other"). And *his* attitudes, being shaped by their attitudes as reflected in him, modify his ways of action. Hence, in proportion as he widens his social relations with persons and things outside him, in learning how to anticipate their attitudes he builds within himself a more complex set of attitudes, thoroughly social. This complexity of social attitudes comprises the "self" (thus complexly erected atop the purely biological motives, and in particular modified by the formative effects of language, or "vocal gesture," which invites the individual to form himself in keeping with its social directives). Mead is here applying in ways of his own the pattern of the Hegelian dialectic whereby Spirit is alienated as Nature, and then attains a higher stage of self-consciousness by seeing itself in terms of its Natural other.

In sum: "We are ready to grasp the hammer before we reach it, and the attitude of manipulatory response directs the approach." But the whole situation is complicated by an "arrest" which allows us to take "competing tendencies" into account—as an animal's attitude of desire towards its prey might yet be modified or arrested by an attitude that takes the prey's own resources of defence or escape into account. But however complicated our attitudes may thus finally become, they add up to an attitude that leads to a way of acting. They are but highly alembicated variants of the simple situation wherein "we are ready to grasp the hammer before we reach it, and the attitude of manipulatory response directs the approach."

Alfred Korzybski, in *Science and Sanity,* is concerned with another aspect of the "delayed action." Mead has said:

> The attitude which we, and all forms called intelligent, take towards things is that of overt or delayed response. The attitude which we take towards the contents of mind in their relation to the world is that of explanation.

Korzybski would offer a technique for encouraging the "delayed response." He does not go so far as Richards, who was dealing with a realm of the imagination naturally distinct from the realm of "overt response" (as even when we witness a propaganda play, that might enhearten us to go forth and join some political party, within the conditions of the performance our action is held in abeyance).

Korzybski's concern is primarily with the criticism of man's major social instrument, language. He would agree with Mead that self is largely formed by the effects of society's attitudes in general and our response to "vocal gestures" in particular. He would merely add: "Alas!" He would have it as a rule that we delay every response; and as for our attitudes of explanation, he would advocate the attitude of delayed action precisely because our explanations are askew.

I have made the suggestion that the Marxist Rhetoric, in adopting and adapting the idealistic terminology by which the bourgeoisie had effectively distinguished its slogans from those of feudalism, did not wholly meet the needs of a Grammar, when considered independently of these urgent polemical requirements. There is an analogous difficulty about Korzybski. The "sanity" which is his primary concern is essentially *personal, social and political*. But the "science" in terms of which he interprets it is essentially the science of physics and physiology.

Though Korzybski is always on the track of basic truths, he approaches them through a kind of vocabulary which seems to work better as a Rhetoric than as a Grammar. Since he regularly seeks to translate the problems of action into terms of motion, and since science as so conceived is usually equated with "reality" itself, his explanations in such terms draw upon strongly formed attitudes in us. Hence his doctrine, as so expressed, may have a magically "curative" value, in helping one to convert misgivings into a sense of "knowing."

Korzybski is psychologically acute. Reading his remarks about the "unspeakable level," one gets glimpses into an almost mystical cult of silence. He would systematically sharpen our awareness of that silent moment from which we may derive a truer knowledge, in transcending the level of automatic verbalizations that hide reality behind a film of traditional misnaming. And the moment of delay which he would interpose between the Stimulus and the Response seems to derive its pattern from a sense of that situation wherein, when a person has been thinking hard and long about something, in purely internal dialogue, words addressed to him by another seem to happen twice, as though there were a first hearing and a second hearing, the words being heard first by an outer self, who heard them as words, and then by an inner self who heard them as meanings.

What bothers me always is the conviction that Korzybski is continually being driven by the nature of his keen intuition, to grope beyond the borders of his terminology. He needs a systematic concern with *dialectic*. Indeed, his very key concept, the "consciousness of abstracting," is a haphazardly rediscovered aspect of Neo-Platonism. As such it calls for expansion into a *consciousness of dialectic* in general (a consciousness that would be manifest not merely in a general policy or attitude of skepticism as regards language, but by a *detailed* analysis of linguistic aptitudes and embarrassments). As things now stand, for instance, there is nothing to mitigate our embarrassment on being warned against "two-valued orientations" in the same enterprise that places itself in a two-valued alignment of "Aristotelian" vs. "Non-Aristotelian," or in his distinction between what goes on "inside the skin" and what goes on "outside the skin," or in his flat opposing of "verbal" and "unspeakable" levels.

There is not to this day, nor is there likely to be, a Korzybskian analysis of poetic forms. Nor could a satisfactory one possibly be made without engrafting upon his doctrines a new and alien set of terms and methods. For "semantics" is essentially *scientist,* an approach to language in terms of *knowledge,* whereas poetic forms are kinds of *action.* However, the very incompleteness of his terminology readily allows for the addition of dramatist elements, should any disciple care to pick them up elsewhere and henceforth proclaim them in the name of Korzybskian "semantics." [8]

But whatever may be the shortcomings of Korzybski's "semantics" as a way into the analysis of linguistic forms, any one would be cheating himself who failed to recognize the importance of Korzybski's concern with the abstractive process inherent in even the most concrete of words. His doctrine of the delayed action, as based on the "consciousness of abstracting," involves the fact that any term for an object puts the object in a *class* of similar objects. This logical fact shows in the psychological realm as a situation wherein we see the individual chair not simply as an individual but in terms of its nature as one object in a family of objects.

Thus, we ordinarily sit down in one chair or another, indifferently, assuming that chairs as a class are things to be sat on. But one of Korzybski's greatest triumphs is due to the fact that he does not thus

[8] In brief, the Korzybskian "semantics" is essentially a study of dialectic which is greatly truncated by reason of the fact that it did not formally and systematically recognize its dialectical nature. All enterprises are dialectical which would cure us through the medium of words—and all the more so if their words would cure by training us in the distrust of words. A truly "scientific" cure *ab extra* would be such as corrected a false idea by a drug, glandular operation, and the like. But purely linguistic operations, such as those involved in the use of the "structural differential," are wholly dialectical.

The "structural differential" itself is, to be sure, a mechanical device; but it is merely the kind that *illustrates* a mental process, like Kurt Lewin's "topological" methods for picturing mental states in terms of abstract designs. It illustrates quite graphically *one* dialectical process, the process involving different orders or degrees of abstraction. Mead deals with another, equally important; the seeing of one position in terms of another. Korzybski's favorite words "linguistics" and "semantics" are themselves but other words for dialectic. Indeed, we might define them as "dialectic rediscovered in terms of contemporary science" (which is to say, dialectic rediscovered in terms that constantly hamper the study of dialectic).

consider chairs generically. Being conscious of abstracting, he knows that when we interpret this particular bundle of sense impressions as a "chair," we are considering it not in its particularity, but in terms of an abstraction of "high order." He knows that the abstraction "chair," fails to distinguish between a sturdy chair and a frail chair. And he tells how, in his programmatic awareness that "chair" is an abstraction, on one occasion he sat down on a particular chair with his usual attitude of *delayed* action. And when it turned out to be a frail chair (as the Aristotelians might say, a chair having frailness as one of its "accidents") though it collapsed, the wary savant did not collapse with it; and so he survived to tell the tale, that we might profit from his experience. And so, recalling what we have said about the tragedy of learning: by participation in the Korzybski *mathema,* through the medium of a delayed *poiema* we may avoid a disconcerting *pathema.*

As we have by now become accustomed to expect, the Korzybski concept of "action" itself ranges indeterminately over the areas of both purely physiological movement and critical consciousness, an ambiguity that becomes more unforgivable in proportion as one's terminology of motives aims to be scientistically formed. He follows the usual dialectic pattern whereby he can divide response into both physiological and mental moments, while at the same time admonishing that such dualism must be discounted as a mere convenience of discourse, the reality being a *tertium quid* that has something of both the mental and the physiological, the dialectical conversion of "body" and "mind" into "body-mind" (or in Korzybski's version: the "neuro-semantic").

There are at least three moments here; and if you would pause to examine his position closely at any one of them, you are open to "refutation" insofar as he can jump to one of the other moments and from its point of vantage discover that you are off the subject. But insofar as we can reduce the concept of "delayed action" to its purely physiological moment, note that it must be the very *opposite* of a delay. There must be some particular physiological configuration, some special balance of nerves, muscles, endocrines, and the like, that is the equivalent, in the realm of motion, to this "attitude" of delay in the realm of consciousness, or action proper. Thus, ironically, Korzybski is trying to induce in his patients or students not a "delayed" response, but an unusually *prompt* one. The very split second one becomes aware of a situation, one must remind oneself about the need for "consciousness of abstracting." And he must practice this, until he has firmly established this response in himself, making it almost automatically prompt with him. From the standpoint of action, in the full sense of the term, such a state might properly be considered as a delay—but as regards the bodily *motions,* we must remember that a state of delayed *action* cannot be a corresponding state of delayed *motion.*

In sum, the *action* is delayed precisely because one has trained the body to undergo certain physiological *motions* of a sort designed to forestall the kind of motions ordinarily following such a stimulus when it is received uncritically. The body during the state of delay does not cease to exist. The mental *attitude* of arrest must have some corresponding bodily *posture.* The very delay of action is thus maintained by motions, since the *attitude* of criticism, or delay, or "consciousness of abstracting" must be matched by its own peculiar *physiological* configuration. There is at least as much neural motion going on in the body that hesitates before sitting down as in the body that sits down without hesitation. Mentally to look before one leaps has its equivalent in internal bodily motions quite as leaping does. So we must remember, in hoping for a body-mind (or motion-action, or "neuro-semantic") vocabulary, that the "delay" as regards the norms of action is simply another kind of *promptness,* as regards the norms of motion.

All told, the attitude or incipient act is a region of ambiguous possibilities, as is well indicated in the Latin grammars, where "inceptive" verbs (like *calesco,* grow warm; *irascor,* get angry) are also called "inchoatives," while "inchoate" in turn means "beginning," "partially but not fully in existence," "incomplete," and is now often used as though the writer thought it a kind of metathesis for "chaotic."

Thus, the notion of the attitude as an incipient or delayed action would seem to be a special application of the concept of "potentiality," which in Aristotle's use of the dramatist Grammar was the reciprocal of "actuality." We have tried to show that the attitude is essentially ambiguous, as an attitude of sympathy may either lead to an act of sympathy or may serve as substitute for an act of sympathy. It is thus "potentially" two different kinds of act. In the traditional Aristotelian usage, potentiality is to actuality as the possibility of doing something is to the actual doing of it, or as the unformed is to the formed. In the *Metaphysics,* IX, 8, he says: "Every potency is at one and the same time a potency of the opposite." That which is "capable of being may either be or not be." The term thus shares somewhat the paradox of substance, since the hot is the "potentially" cold. And Aristotle situates the principle of evil in matter not in the sense that matter is essentially evil, but in the sense that it is the realm of potentiality: in being potentially good, matter is by the same token potentially bad. The scientific concept of potential energy lacks the degree of ambiguity one encounters in the potential as applied to the realm of living beings in general and human beings in particular.

The realm of the incipient, or attitudinal, is the realm of "symbolic action" par excellence; for symbolic action has the same ambiguous potentialities of action (when tested by the norms of overt, practical action). Here is the area of thought wherein actual conflicts can be transcended, with results sometimes fatal, sometimes felicitous. But the study of its manifestations will vow us, at every step, to the study of that "attitudinal action" which we have called the dramatistic, but which might also be called the dialectical. We prefer to call it dramatistic because dialectic itself has repeatedly lost tract of its dramatistic origins, when thinkers lay all their stress upon the attempt to decide whether it leads to true knowledge, or when they have so rigidified its forms in some particular disposition of terms (or dogmas) that the underlying liquidity of its Grammar becomes concealed.

Also, in recalling that Mr. Richards speaks of incipient or *imaginal* action, we are reminded that *images* can have the force of attitudes. Hence, when analyzing the structure of a lyric (a form in which there is no act in the full dramatic sense) we may look for a lyric analogue of plot in the progression or development of the poem's imagery. A dramatic or narrative work, for instance, might affect the transubstantiation of a character by tracing his course to and from the abyss, the abyss itself being the realm of transition between pre-abyss and post-abyss identities. A lyric poem might get the same effect by a sequence of stanzas having a different quality of imagery at beginning, middle, and end, with the imagery of the middle section being in some way abysmal. Thus, Shelley's five-stanza "Ode to the West Wind" begins with imagery of that which drives:

> O wild West Wind, thou breath of Autumn's being,
> Thou, from whose unseen presence the leaves dead
> Are driven . . .

In stanza five the poem dwells upon imagery merging the driving and the driven:

> Make me thy lyre, even as the forest is:
> What if my leaves are falling like its own!
> The tumult of thy mighty harmonies
>
> Will take from both a deep, autumnal tone,
> Sweet though in sadness.   Be thou, Spirit fierce,
> My spirit! Be thou me, impetuous one!
>
> Drive my dead thoughts over the universe
> Like withered leaves to quicken a new birth!

And the transition involving this idealistic progress towards identification of individual self with universal spirit takes place in stanza three, through abysmal imagery of *submergence*.   Here the poet meditates upon the ways in which vegetation at the bottom of the sea responds to the agitations on the surface:

> Thou
> For whose path the Atlantic's level powers
> Cleave themselves into chasms, while far below
> The sea-blooms and the oozy woods which wear
> The sapless foliage of the ocean, know
>
> Thy voice, and suddenly grow gray with fear,
> And tremble and despoil themselves: oh, hear!

Through the medium of his sensitive plant, as here submerged, he has added to the West Wind the character necessary for his final identification with it as Spirit.   Actives and passives become one.   An ingredient of *sympathy* is unquestionably implicit in this imagery of submerged vegetation.   But it so happens that the poet also, in a footnote, makes it explicit:

> The phenomenon alluded to at the conclusion of the third stanza
> is well known to naturalists.   The vegetation at the bottom of the
> sea, of rivers, and of lakes, sympathizes with that of the land in the
> change of seasons, and is consequently influenced by the winds which
> announce it.

The final couplet, idealizing the autumn wind as introduction to the season that leads into spring, is presumably the exhilarating result of the transcendent resolution, which encourages the poet to speculate futuristically: "If Winter comes, can Spring be far behind?"

As regards the analysis of poetic forms, the wavering distinction between the attitude as preparation for action and the attitude as substitution for action, involves a similarly wavering distinction between the dramatic and the lyrical. If Aristotle's world is essentially a dramatic one, his God (as a pure act identical with perfect rest) is essentially lyrical. From the dramatic point of view, the moment of arrest that characterizes the attitude is a kind of "pre-act." But the lyrical attitude is rather the kind of rest that is the summation or culmination of action, transcending overt action by *symbolically* encompassing its end.

In drama there is the intense internal debate prior to the moment of decision. Upon the outcome of this debate depends the course of history. But from the lyric point of view, the state of arrest is itself an end-product, a resolution of previous action rather than a preparation for subsequent action (though of course while life is still in progress any culminating stage is but *pro tempore,* and can also be the beginning of a new development).

Mr. Houston Peterson hit upon the happy idea of assembling in an anthology (*The Lonely Debate*) some typical moments of the dramatic arrest. He notes, for instance, what dire events in *Julius Caesar* "are all foreshadowed by that hushed moment in Brutus' garden, when he broods over the waning liberties of Rome," deciding "It must be by his death." And he observes how the tragic destiny that inexorably unfolds in *Macbeth* is decided not with Duncan's murder, "but in that terrifying soliloquy of the first act":

> If it were done when 'tis done, then 'twere well
> It were done quickly.

Here is the moment when the "potential" in the Aristotelian sense of something that may become either this or that is converted into the potential in the mystical or mechanistic sense of the predestined or preformed (as today's decisions are potentially tomorrow's fatalities, as the suicide who has leapt from the bridge is already potentially dead, or as the German proverb, at once mystical and realistic, puts it: *Wer A sagt, muss B sagen*). Yet the very isolating of such momentous soliloquies, and their publication somewhat like a book of lyrics, makes us realize all the more clearly how essentially different they are from lyrics. In fact, we might call them the depiction of such personal situations as *most acutely need* resolution in the lyric state, but drive to action precisely because such resolution is missing.

In contrast with such intense moments of pre-action, recall Wordsworth's sonnet "Composed upon Westminster Bridge." Here we find the perfect lyric mood, marked by the state of arrest in its *culminative* aspect. Here the very process of transition is made motionless: for the imagery is that of a *crossing,* but the crossing just *is,* since the poet stands meditative upon a bridge that by its nature crosses motionlessly from one bank to the other:

> Earth has not anything to show more fair:
> Dull would be he of soul who could pass by
> A sight so touching in its majesty:
> This City now doth, like a garment, wear
> The beauty of the morning; silent, bare
> Ships, towers, domes, theatres, and temples lie
> Open unto the fields, and to the sky;
> All bright and glittering in the smokeless air.
> Never did sun more beautifully steep
> In his first splendour, valley, rock, or hill;
> Ne'er saw I, never felt, a calm so deep!
> The river glideth at his own sweet will:
> Dear God! the very houses seem asleep;
> And all that mighty heart is lying still!

The imagery is of morning, so there is incipience. But it is not the incipience of the internal debate, arrested at the moment of indecision prior to a decision from which grievous consequences are inevitably to follow. Nor is it a retrospective summary. It just *is,* a state of mind that has come to rest by reason of its summarizing nature. It encompasses. We are concerned not with its potentialities, but with it as an end in itself. It has conveyed a *moment of stasis* (we are aware of the pun at the roots of this expression). It envisions such rest as might be a ground, a beginning and end, of all action.[9]

[9] For further applications of the dramatist perspective to lyric forms, the reader is referred to the three essays in the Appendix: "Symbolic Action in a Poem by Keats," "The Problem of the Intrinsic (as reflected in the Neo-Aristotelian School)," and "Motives and Motifs in the Poetry of Marianne Moore," two of which essays were once an integral part of this book in an earlier draft, but were edited somewhat to fit them for magazine publication. Hence, there is in them

Considering *Hamlet* in the light of the ambiguity we have observed in the concept of delayed action, might we not say that the play derives much poignancy from Hamlet's way of transforming the very preparations for action into devices for postponing action? Thus the precautionary steps he takes, in his effort to establish the murderer's guilt beyond question, while they are designed to assist his act of vengeance, threaten to interfere with vengeance. Here Shakespeare nearly dissolved the identity of drama, removing it from the realm of action to a realm of pre-action that would amount to no action. He here stands at the very opposite extreme to that of O'Neill at the close of *Mourning Becomes Electra*. For O'Neill threatens to dissolve drama into behaviorism, as Lavinia ceases to be an agent in becoming a merely automatic Response to a Stimulus; but Shakespeare threatens to dissolve drama into an *excess* of scruples, in making the internal debate not merely the originating motive of the action, but its permanent motif.

Moving into the realm of Rhetoric, we may note how legislatures regularly adopt the "Hamletic" strategy as a way to avoid embarrassing decisions. For if you would forestall final vote on a measure, and would do so in the best "scientific" spirit, you need but appoint a committee empowered to find more facts on the subject. This same Hamletic device (Hamlet being the first great liberal) comes pleasantly to the aid of all savants who would busy themselves in behalf of social betterment without hurting susceptibilities. In keeping with the nature of their specialties, they can gather more data and still more, to aid us in the making of wise decisions. And when the matter has been documented beyond a doubt, they may go on and document it beyond the shadow of a doubt. Assuredly, there will be something for them to do as long as the subsidies last; for no decision in the world's history was ever made on the basis of all the "necessary facts," nor ever will be.

Realist Family and Nominalist Aggregate

We have selected Korzybski's references to the "consciousness of abstracting" as the most important aspect of his doctrine. From the standpoint of dramatistic generation, however, we doubt whether his

some repetition of matters already covered. However, such matters are usually given a somewhat different application in the essays; hence it seemed advisable to leave the text in its present form.

treatment of abstraction is Grammatical enough. He does well in showing that even an apparently concrete word like "table" abstracts and classifies, since it applies to a vast aggregate of possible objects, each different in its particularities from all others of its class. And a word like "furniture" would be a still higher level of abstraction, since it would also include chairs, beds, desks, etc. We might next advance to some such word as "conveniences" or "commodities," and might even arrive at some classification as broad as "things" or "objects," and finally "being."

Korzybski's method here is characteristically scientist and nominalist. It begins with *individual things* as the realities with which language has to deal—and it treats classification as a process of abstraction. According to the Baldwin dictionary, nominalism is "the doctrine that universals have no objective existence or validity." In its extreme form, nominalism holds that universals "are only names (*nomina, flatus vocis*)." That is, they are sheer "creations of language for purposes of convenient communication." The realist Grammar works the other way round: It begins with a *tribal* concept, and treats individuals as participants in this common substance, or element (whereas Korzybski stresses above all else the need for a "non-elemental" approach to language). The realistic pattern thus fitted well with the clan origins of Greek democracy and with the familial patterns of thought in Western feudalism. As we have suggested elsewhere, realism treats individuals as members of a group, whereas nominalism treats groups as aggregates of individuals. Hence our proposal to treat nominalism as linguistically individualistic or atomistic. For whereas realism treats generic terms as names for *real* substances, nominalism treats them as merely conveniences of language. Occam's nominalism, for instance, is distinguished by "the positive assertion that specific individualities, differentiated in themselves, are the real."

Korzybski helps to show how the conveniences of linguistic classification can become drastic inconveniences, leading to such morbid "semantic reactions" as race prejudice whereby many individuals greatly different from one another are lumped together as though their characters were *substantially* the same. Korzybski is continually stressing the need of index figures, to remind us that our word "chair" is a generalizing term for chair$_1$, chair$_2$, chair$_3$, etc. Plato, on the other hand, would treat the perfect idea of a chair as the reality, and would consider individual chairs as imperfectly participating in this essence common to all chairs.

As we have pointed out, in the act there is a *creative* or *generative* feature. It is thus clear that, if one thinks of the world itself as either the result of enactment (Plato) or itself a process of enactment (Aristotle), one begins with an act-genus-generation tie-up which can indicate why, on the Grammatical level, traditional realism favors the term, *act*. One can get the point in a rough way by using in a neutral sense our expression, "acts of God," as it is applied to natural calamities. If all natural events and objects were called "acts of God" (as expressions of the divine intention) we should thus have a world in which act, form, and generation mutually involved one another, since each genus would carry out one line of generation, or actualization. Aristotle got the same relation between genus and act in his uncreated world by his principle of the entelechy, which represented the striving of each thing to be perfectly the *kind* of thing it was.

One should also note that whereas the scientist beginning with "the object" explains abstraction, generalization, classification as a process having to do with *nouns,* a dramatist stress upon act suggests an origin in *verbs*. Words like "run," "go," "do," are likewise abstract and general. No action word refers to just this action and no other. One regularly uses nouns, pronouns, and demonstratives that do thus particularize. Every proper name is of this nature. But verbs are always abstract and generic. And we do well to remember, when trying to generate philosophic methods dramatistically, that a key word of traditional realism was *being* or *essence,* which was no demonstrative noun, but a *verbal* noun, the most abstract and general form of the most abstract and general act.

As to how a thing's *essence* or *quiddity* can become identical with its principle of *action,* let us look at it thus: There is an expression, "He has a way with him," suggesting that the man possesses some quality or aptitude peculiarly his own. Would not this be the very principle of his character, in short his very essence, if we could but define it? Thus Shakespeare "has a way with him"—and this way would be his literary style; and insofar as we can describe it accurately we are describing the essence of Shakespeare as a poet.

And so it is with generic words like "animality" and "rationality" (*animalitas* as the character of man's genus, *rationalitas* as the character of his species). The "whatness" that they name is not merely that of tribal substance; it is also a *way* (that is, a kind of *action*). Rationality is a *way;* as Santayana would say, it is a "life" of reason. Thus, rationa*lity,* as the "essence" of man, is tribal, formal, and an act. (It is formal because it is the guiding principle of such acts as individuate its nature.)

When the ramifications of the term act are developed thus from within, I think we can get a much sounder understanding of the thought-structure than if we approach it purely in terms of "levels of generalization." Indeed, as we pointed out previously, of the four terms, the generic, the genetic, the genitive, and the general, the fourth takes us farthest from the *tribal* patterns in such thinking. Hence, an approach to the generic in terms of the generalized may serve the ends of a polemic analysis conducted from without; but it cannot enable us to "anticipate" the realistic structure by studying the Grammatical principles of its generation.

The *Doctor Subtilis,* Duns Scotus, whose thinking was so ingenious that he was for long accused of all the doctrines against which he contended, stands in an interesting place with relation to the nominalist disintegration of scholastic realism. On its surface, his stress upon the "thisness" (*haecceitas*) of a thing is nominalistic. But Scotus arrives at his concept of thisness by retaining the familial pattern typical of scholasticism. Nominalism was antithetical to the tribal derivation of individuals. Scotus, on the other hand, retains the concept of the tribal, but extends its application in such a way that the individual can be treated as a genus.

Si loquamur realiter, humanitas quae est in Socrate non est humanitas quae est in Platone. That is, if animal is the genus, and mankind the species, Scotus would contend that Socrates has a different "humanity" than Plato. So, to locate the essence of Socrates, we must go a step further, and recognize that it resides in a special *"socratitas."* Our previous exegesis of the essence or quiddity as a "way" should indicate how this thinking differs from straight nominalism. Insofar as a man's acts are characteristic of him, for instance, they are *substantially* related to one another. And the discerning portrait painter might even be able to make us feel how the "accidents" of the man's appearance share in this substantial relationship.

What of contemporary "scientific realism?" Sometimes the term is used, like naturalism, euphemistically for materialism, in referring to ways of thought that stress the motivational importance of scenic factors, in a scene of narrowed circumference. Sometimes it might better be placed as an aspect of pragmatism, in its stress upon science as a means of social adjustment. Sometimes it applies to the field of rhetoric, where it refers to the unmasking of false idealizations (usually a materialist trend, though also at times it may rather be idealism turned against itself). Sometimes, as where it applies to the field of jurisprudence, it combines all these features with a definite sense of the *need* for a stress upon the term act (not merely as a term but as a term from which a whole set of terms would be systematically derived). For the realm of social relations automatically brings up this requirement, though the norms of physicalist science continually encumber efforts in this direction.

As for nominalism, it is "anti-social" only in the purely *Grammatical* sense which we have indicated. That is, if carried out consistently, it obliterates all notions of consubstantiality, however defined, hence obliterating the Grammatical basis of social community. Grammatically, it leaves us with a world of individuals, united only by monetary symbols and the deceptions of an idealistic rhetoric. In practice, nominalists usually temper their philosophies by an humanitarian afterthought advocating "joint action" for some social aim or other.

Human nature being what it is, men can be relied upon to feel themselves consubstantial with enterprises of one sort or another, even though (as with the followers of Korzybski) it be an enterprise devoted to the systematic elimination of the category of substance. Nominalism still enjoys somewhat the privilege it enjoyed in the Middle Ages, when the very firmness of tribal ways allowed for a wide margin of latitude in non-tribal patterns of speculation. The vocabulary of personal and political relations is still dramatistically infused, at least in a piecemeal way, however greatly the *systematic disposition* of such terms may have been impaired by the radical changes in the conditions of living. The powers that now most suggestively strike men's fancy are not in the vital order (of generation); they are in the technological order (of mechanical production). Yet technology itself is an embodiment of essentially human motives. And thus in it there are preserved, though "ungrammatically," the vestiges of a vital grammar, reflecting at least the quality of action defined in Santayana's concept of "animal faith."

Further Remarks on Act and Potency

We must be on guard in these pages lest our zeal in behalf of "dramatism" trick us into taking on more obligations than we need assume for the purposes of this study. We are asserting that dramatist coordinates provide the most direct way into the understanding of linguistic forms. But we are not vowed to uphold any one traditional application of such a grammar. Our appreciation of Aristotle is itself un-Aristotelian; our remarks about Aquinas would not satisfy a Thomist. And so, the pages of this section on Act are not to be read as an argument for any one traditional application of the dramatist grammar, but simply as a review, from the dramatist standpoint, of grammatical principles involved in the attributing of motives. It considers typical dialectical resources that have been used systematically in the past. And because man is essentially in the order of generation, we believe that these same principles will underlie the linguistic forms of the future, though they may be broken into fragments and concealed from view by approaches in terms of knowledge, learning, technological power, conditioning, and the like.

All such scientist approaches have great admonitory value. They provide us with incongruous perspectives that enable us to see mankind from many angles, each of which in its way adds a new "hark ye" to the lore of human relations. But they are all extrinsic, nonsubstantial approaches—and as such are not suited to define man's essentially dramatic nature. They heckle so superbly that many in the audience come to mistake the heckling for the address.

Modern science asks how acts are motivated; but Aristotelian science tells how motions are activated, thus featuring the very term that would now be eliminated. Platonism had left the subject of motivation in the "tribal" stage. In effect Plato treated the genus as the generator of its members (or, as stated in medieval terms, the Platonist universal was *ante rem*). However, the relation of tribal ancestor to individual offspring was transcendent. The individual members of the family existed on earth, in the world of appearances; the pure form or "idea" of the family identity had its eternal being in heaven. The individual members here imperfectly partook of the pure essence there; and in embodying the principles of their form they were enactments in the sense that their motive was intrinsic to their kind. Such transcendent realism differed from Aristotle's more "scientific" brand in that Plato placed the locus of motivation with the heavenly family identity, whereas the Aristotelian "entelechy" resided in the things of sensory experience. "Actuality," says Aristotle, "is prior both to potency and to every principle of change."

Don't forget, however, that Plato equated the divine with the abstract, apparently because both transcend the realm of the senses. Hence, nearly everything that this greatest of dialecticians says of "heaven" can be profitably read as a statement about *language*. And that man cheats himself who avoids Plato because of a preference for purely secular thought. Even the doctrine of the heavenly "archetypes" is sound enough, if read as a statement about the relationship between class names and names for the individuals thus classified by a common essence. And Plato's account of the approach to "divinity" by the processes of dialectic generalizing, particularizing, and transcendence reveals in all thoroughness the abstractive nature of language. This is in contrast with the mere fragment of linguistic analysis which Korzybski would expand into a whole universe of discourse. Korzybski's contribution, we have said, resides in his having said "alas!" to an aspect of linguistic transcendence that Plato considers edifying. But one may doubt whether even this helpful admonition could survive a serious consideration of the Platonist dialectic as a whole.

In one sense, we might call Aristotle's metaphysics of motivation more dialectical than Plato's. Plato used dialectic as a method leading towards the discovery of truth. The dialectic was a means; the truth (knowledge of the Good) was its end. Aristotle finally dropped the dramatic form of the Platonic dialogue. He isolated method as a separate field, in his analysis of formal logic. And he dropped the process of conversational give and take about which Plato organized the stages of an exposition (and which, as we shall show in the last section of this book, was designed to produce a form wherein the end transcended the beginning). This way of development through the coöperative competition of divergent voices was dropped by Aristotle; but he attributed a dialectical structure to the very nature of the universe. He did this by so revising the Platonist conception of the "forms" in their relation to "matter" that the pair went through a series of transpositions. Thus, the forms were conceived as arranged in a hierarchy of being, with the "form" of beings at each level constituting the "matter" of beings at the next higher level. This series was thought to ascend until you arrived at "pure form," the motionless prime mover that moves all else not by being itself moved, but by being loved, the object of desire.

We might state this form-matter relation in terms of the action-motion pair by saying that each order of being constituted the conditions of motion involved in the action of the next higher order. Human action, for instance, depends upon animal motion; animal action depends upon vegetative motion; vegetative action depends upon physical motion. Ordinarily in these pages, however, we have not used the terms in this particular dialectical way, but have confined "action" to the level of human rationality. The inducement to use the terms thus dialectically comes from the need to distinguish animal locomotion from lower orders of motivation, such as physical motion and vegetative growth. Whereupon, we get purely biological action, as with Santayana's "animal faith."

The Aristotelian concept of the pure act as the final cause of all motion possesses possibilities of reversal. The motions *toward* it might be interpreted as motions *derived from* it (that is, final cause might be equated with efficient cause), particularly when Aristotle's God had been taken over by theologians who restored the usual *generative* principle to the concept of divinity. Subsequently, considering God as both a source and a purpose, mystics distinguished alternate moments, with the creation as an *egressus* from God followed by a *regressus* back to God; and then, having thus taken the two motives apart, the mystic could propose that they be conceived as joined together again, the possibilities of reversal in the Aristotelian concept thus being converted explicitly into an oxymoron. Aquinas unites the two directions (God as source and God as purpose) when he says that God is present in things: (1) after the manner of an efficient cause (but "equivocally," as "in the sun is the likeness of whatever is generated by the sun's power"); (2) as the object of an operation is in the operator.

On a purely contextual basis, we could arrive at Aristotle's "unmoved mover" simply by the generalizing of "motion." For the "motionless" would be all that was left to serve as the dialectical counterpart, or "ground," of a concept so comprehensive. No, that is not the only recourse here. Another was to use the macrocosm-microcosm pattern, considering *universal* motion as the ground of *particular* motions. The whole would thus be the ground of the parts; and the parts would synecdochically (by the *omnia ubique* formula) share the nature of the whole.

Another opportunity here has already been touched upon: the kind of ground one gets when considering "matter" as a "substrate" (*hypokeimenon*, the placed-beneath, or "subject"), possessing potentialities that may be variously actualized. Both members of the potentiality-actuality pair, it will be recalled, are tinged by the paradox of substance. Not only does God as pure act take the grammatical form of a *passive* (in being the object of desire). There is a similar reversal of voice implicit in the fact that matter (possessing, in Windelband's phrase, "an impulse to be formed") is characterized as *potency*.

What passivity ever possessed more "active" a name? In its passive role, matter undergoes the shaping activity of form. Yet it partially resists the efforts to shape it. A seed may either grow or rot; in this sense its potentialities are of an either-or sort. But a radish seed possesses solely the potentialities of a radish; and in this sense, its potentialities are foreordained, being related to its actualities as the implicit to the explicit.

The earlier notions of *rationes seminales* were constructed in accordance with the same proportion (implicit is to explicit as potential is to actual). Some mystics similarly viewed the world pantheistically as a development from a *Deus implicitus* to a *Deus explicitus* (nature being God explicit, or God made manifest).

Similarly Leibniz's monads were "possibilities" conceived after the analogy of seeds (and in accordance with a theory of "pre-formation" that thought of seeds as containing, in miniature involution, all the traits that would later evolve into the full-sized plant). Thus "the present is big with the future, the future might be read in the past." And before the soul has clear and distinct ideas, it possesses them "innately" and "virtually." Looking at this pattern in the light of modern psychology, we could rephrase it: "The unconscious is virtually (potentially) the conscious."

The pattern underlies the thinking of the early criminologist, Lombroso. Lombroso had attempted to establish a correlation between criminality and physical traits. For this purpose, he assembled statistics on the measurements of Italian prisoners. Later, he found that many non-criminals exhibited the same traits as he had discovered in his measurements of criminals. He avoided embarrassment by deciding that the non-criminals possessing these same traits were "criminaloid." That is to say, they were found to possess the special inclinations toward crime, though with proper treatment and good fortune these "criminaloid" types might live orderly lives and die at a ripe old age without having committed the crimes prognosticated by their bodies. Despite their good records, he might have called them "substantially" or "potentially" criminals. The same embarrassment was met by legal theorists who situated in *all* men the "potentialities" for committing crime. (Quite true, and if we made it a crime to breathe tomorrow, only a relatively small portion of today's population would manage to remain law-abiding.)

In any case, one could not dismiss this Grammatical point as merely "academic." For the potentiality-actuality pattern is at the bottom of all "scientific" attempts at "prediction" and "control." Lenin, as a "scientific" revolutionary, was involved in this same pattern when trying to decide just what were the sure marks of a revolutionary situation. It is at the bottom of sampling procedures, as with polls of public opinion. And it is implicit in the planning of sales campaigns and the like.

Another variant of the potential figures in the term "tendency." And the social sciences would be cramped fatally if forced to forego this term, or its equivalent. Yet it has that same ambiguity we have noted in the terms, "potential" and "substantial." When we decide, for instance, that a certain group "tends" toward a certain way of acting, we are not embarrassed if this "tendency" remains unactualized. For a mere tendency to do something is also, by the same token, a tendency *not* to do it. Similarly, we may note a "disposition," "predisposition," or "inclination" towards a certain kind of action, without deciding whether such leanings will or will not reach overt expression.

As an interesting instance of such tactics, one might consider the economic theory of Frank Hyneman Knight, propounded in his book, *The Ethics of Competition.* His theory is based upon what I might call an economist's equivalent for the city of God. That is, he begins with the concept of a perfect economic world, obeying ideal market relationships, which in his case are conceived as pure individualistic competition. He is, of course, quite aware that the market in our imperfect world of actuality does not obey the laws of his ideal market, which he sets up as both a technical aid to the description of the actual market and as an ethical norm (a direction towards which he would have the market "tend"). And insofar as the market of actuality does not obey these ideals of pure competition (which notion of purity we should call the "god term" for his economics), he saves the day by noting that it "tends" to.

Next, he observes that "the 'economic' man [as per his theory of ideal competition] is not a social man, and the ideal market dealings of theory are not social relations." And it is the properties of men as social beings (their "imperfections," as judged from the standpoint of the perfect world of ideal competition) that serve to convert the "tendency" of exchange to follow the laws of the ideal market into a "tendency" *not* to follow them.

The author reveals for us another such Janus-term by noting the function of the concept of *"caeteris paribus."* For you may say that A's behavior will reproduce that of B, "all other things being equal," yet you need not be embarrassed if it doesn't, because "all other things never are equal." Hence, the concept of *"caeteris paribus"* matches "tendency" as a locational device. (*"Mutatis mutandis"* would be another.) "All other things being equal," men would behave in accordance with a uniform set of economic laws—but since all other things are never equal, said economic laws cannot serve as adequate for the description of even exclusively economic phenomena. And in the search for the complicating factors, factors that make the *tendency towards* the ideal market synonymous with a *tendency away from* the ideal market, the author abandons economic considerations for sociological ones. His book thus becomes in effect a kind of "conversion" from an economic perspective to a sociological one—which, in this case, since the economic pattern was an "ideal" one and the sociological pattern breaks the symmetry of this ideal, would seem to symbolize, attenuatedly indeed, a Hans Castorp descent from the "magic mountain" to the "flatlands."

We can readily see the difference between the potentiality of "tendencies" and the kind of potentiality imputed in theories of strict determinism, predestination, or the "historically inevitable." The concept of the inevitable "substantially" merges the permanent and the changing, since it accounts for the flux of events by some underlying principle that prevails always. It says in effect not simply that the future *will be,* but that it *is,* since it is *implicit* in the structure of the present. And any group claiming to represent the "inevitable" course of events, as the proletariat in the Marxist view of capitalism's "inevitable" development towards socialism, shares in this substantiality.

The present ease of printing, which makes it almost a necessary condition of the publishing trade that readers turn avidly from one novel to another, without pause for rereading, has led to a corresponding set of esthetic values. Hence the overemphasis upon the element of *surprise* as a factor in esthetic appeal, for "suspense" is now usually conceived in terms of "surprise," despite the fact that one can feel "suspense" in hearing a piece of music with which one is perfectly familiar; and Greek audiences underwent "suspense" when witnessing dramas whose plots were traditional. But suspense is formally more substantial than mere uncertainty of outcome, even when one has "identified himself" with the characters of the fiction. There is a fundamental difference between art on the one hand and competitive sports and games of chance on the other. For we would resent the thought that the outcome of a game might have been settled in advance by collusion among the players. And we would be just as resentful if the outcome of a play depended simply on the toss of a coin or on a last-minute decision of the actors. Even when the ending of a play has been changed, we are satisfied only if the new ending is felt to grow "inevitably" out of the preceding action (though some audiences may be more exacting than others in their notions of the law here).

Admittedly, writers are now able to depend strongly upon the reader's ignorance of a plot's outcome, and to shape their stories accordingly. Cheap production makes it possible to produce literature hygienically, "to be used once and thrown away." But while this condition itself has been made possible by the advance of science, one is wrong when, as is usual today, he tends to explain the essentials of such plots' appeal in scientist terms (as he does when viewing suspense largely in terms of the reader's ignorance).

When we consider both historical and poetic development at once, however, each can throw light upon the other. And taken together, they enable us to see that historic "inevitability" is but the obverse side of dramatic "suspense." For the appeal of both resides in the kind of *substantiality* that comes of *formally* relating all incidents to *one* organizing principle that prevails throughout the diversity of detail. Insofar as either history or the work of art obeys a guiding principle of development, the nature of the motivation at any one point is "substantially" the same as at any other point. The ending is implicit in the beginning. And so, all the changing details are infused by an "eternal now." [10]

Modern views of "probability" fall puzzlingly across this distinction between the "inevitability" kind of potentiality and the "tendency" kind. Sometimes the theory seems to involve assumptions of strict determinism. That is, the outcome is already in the cards, but we don't "know enough" to read the signs correctly, hence must work in an area of probabilities. Probability here would be epistemological rather than ontological. It would be situated not in the nature of things, but in the defects of our instruments. One may estimate the chances of drawing a full house at poker, for instance, and treat this as a statement about his chances of drawing such a hand on the next deal. But if the cards

[10] The concept of "inevitability" may arise in another way, somewhat akin to this, but sufficiently different to consider it as a special route. Consider those speculations on chance, genius, and historical law which Tolstoy has written at the end of *War and Peace*. Naturally, an author who had written a work in which he commanded so many destinies would feel strongly the sense of a divine principle guiding the totality of historical development. Such a feeling would be but the equivalent, in cosmological terms, of his artistic method. Tolstoy points out that, the farther we move from an historical event, the less "freedom" do we see in it, and the more "inevitability." "Freewill is content," he says; "necessity is form." And insofar as we see history in formal terms, the many diversities of individual choice merge into the inevitabilities of a vast movement. He similarly observes that the total absence of freewill equals death. And however something might have been done before it was done, once it is done it is inevitable.

Does not this suggest that we arise to a concept of "inevitability" by seeing present or future things in terms of the *past*? For once something *has been*, it can *now* no longer *have been* any different *then*. The thought suggests a strange paradox whereby Marxism, so strongly *futuristic* in its promises, may ground a sense of *present* substantiality on a way of transcendence derived from a vision that sees in terms of the past. Such would not be an alternative to the "poetic fatalism" we have discussed above. It would simply suggest the possibility of more "thanatoptic" ingredients in our thinking than we usually detect.

We can place this origin for the sense of inevitability more dramatistically by noting that fatalism can be derived from drama since the outcome of the play is known to have been decided before the play begins.

have already been shuffled, this is a purely epistemological computation. Ontologically, his full house is or is not implicit in the order of the cards.

Sometimes probability is taken as a statement about the very substance of the universe itself, which is then thought to face its own future as tentatively as a market operator faces his. Metaphysically, one may legitimately hold to this view. But I have never been able to see how it can logically be said to have been established on a physical basis by the "Heisenberg principle." One may well take it for granted that statements about the nature of the world's substance can never be established any more firmly by instruments than they can by words. At least, since instruments themselves are so fundamentally implicated in language, deriving both their formation and their interpretation from this source, one might well expect in advance that they would be as beset by ultimate dialectical embarrassments as language itself. For though they contrive to eliminate pressures that beset language on the Rhetorical and Symbolic level, they are profoundly Grammatical. And as such, they cannot be expected to get us past the paradoxes of substance.

We might glimpse the full paradox in stating the Heisenberg principle thus: A margin of *indeterminacy* is *inevitable* in measurement. That the determination of a particle's speed would interfere with the determination of its position and *vice versa* seems simply an ultimate refinement, in precision instruments, of the old paradox considered by Zeno, just as in mathematics there is, finally, the principle of discreteness pitted against the principle of continuity. And in any event, even when proclaiming that indeterminacy is inevitably intrinsic to our instruments, there is no logical necessity to conclude from this that the indeterminacy is intrinsic to nature itself. One may hold such a metaphysical view if he prefers. Or one may say that, by the rules of physics, a physicist is not allowed to assume any greater degree of stability than his partially unstable instruments themselves are able to record or verify, though we should not mistake a convention of physics for a statement about ontology. Looking at the matter from the dramatist point of view, we should expect instruments of precision not to avoid the paradox of substance, but to confront it more precisely.

It is not easy to know just when one is deriving potentialities from actualities and the reverse. Thus, in his history of medieval philosophy

Bréhier cites the scholastic proportion: existence is to essence as act is to potency. This alignment would make "essence" synonymous with "matter," if we sought to maintain a strict matter-potentiality equation.

Aristotle, in selecting pure actuality as his God term, resolutely sought to maintain the same pattern throughout, in placing actuality as prior to potentiality. Sometimes he maintained the pattern in a temporal sense, deriving the seed from the mature plant rather than the plant from the seed. Thus "one actuality always precedes another in time right back to the actuality of the eternal prime mover." (*Metaphysics,* IX, 8.) But his theory of the entelechy allowed him to introduce another kind of priority, namely the "principle" involved in a given form. A stage that *follows* another in time may be *prior* "in form and substantiality." That is, man is "prior" to boy because man has already attained its complete form whereas boy has not. Everything that comes into existence moves towards an end. This end is the principle of its existence; and it comes into existence for the sake of this end. This state of completion is its full actuality, and "it is for the sake of this that the potency is acquired." Thus, even with relation to geometry, where we might tend to say that all geometrical propositions exist "potentially" in the geometrical figures, Aristotle reverses the emphasis, stressing rather the fact that these potentialities are discovered by the geometer's activities:

> The potentially existing constructions are discovered by being brought to actuality; the reason is that the geometer's thinking is an actuality; so that the potency proceeds from an actuality; and therefore it is by making constructions that people come to know them (though the single actuality is later in generation than the corresponding potency).

In Greek this mode of thought is aided by the fact that the word for "perfect" is *teleios* (which is also defined as "final," "complete," "completed," "having the attributes of an end"). Hence, we can understand why the prime mover, as "end" of action, should be the "most perfect" being (in Latin, the *ens perfectissimum*). The Greek for "adult" is *teleios aner,* that is, "completed man"—yet the attribute is the same that Greek theologians apply to God, so that a word meaning the "finished" can come to characterize the "infinite." Since an action contains some ingredient of purpose, or end, Aristotle uses the term "entelechy" ("having its end within itself") as synonym for "actuality." Since he classes growth as one species of motion, a being that attains its full development has attained its "end" (whereat one need not decide whether the "end" here is an *aim* or a mere *limit*). As for made things, *poiema* has the same ambiguity, in referring either to a "deed, doing, action, act" or to "anything made or done, a work, piece of workmanship, poetical work, poem"—so that we can look for the "perfection" of the work in the principles of its construction, as embodied in its actual form. The *generic* factor here resides in the fact that the aim is to give the work the form proper to its kind.

Before closing this chapter, let us note how the ratios look, in the light of our discussion. We originally said that the five terms allowed for ten ratios; but we also noted that the ratios could be reversed, as either a certain kind of scene may call for its corresponding kind of agent, or a certain agent may call for its corresponding kind of scene, etc. The list of possible combinations would thereby be expanded to twenty. And the members of each pair would then be related as potential to actual. Thus, a mode of thought in keeping with the scene-agent ratio would situate in the scene certain potentialities that were said to be actualized in the agent. And conversely, the agent-scene ratio would situate in the agent potentialities actualized in the scene. And so with the other ratios.

Otherwise stated: A ratio is a formula indicating a transition from one term to another. Such a relation necessarily possesses the ambiguities of the potential, in that the second term is a medium different from the first. For the nature of the mediated necessarily differs from the nature of the immediate, as a translation must differ from its original, the embodiment of an ideal must differ from the ideal, and a god incarnate would differ from that god as pure spirit.

Psychology of Action

Terms such as "action" and "passion" are, of course, hardly more than chapter-heads, still to be given specific content. Or they are gerundives, indicating that certain blanks on a questionnaire are "to be filled out" according to certain prescribed rules. As we have seen in the case of Spinoza, for instance, "action" and "passion" are but names for bins into which one sorts various kinds of particulars, Spinoza's alignment of the "affections" differing somewhat from that to which any other philosopher would subscribe.

But just as there are relationships among individuals within a State, so there are relationships among States; and similarly, the Grammatical forms can be considered in their relations to one another, over and above the relations prevailing among the many different particulars that may be subsumed under them. A dramatist, for instance, might select any two ethical motives (say: fear and honor), and enact them in the image of particular characters under particular conditions. But the form of the enactment in its *total development* could be *summed up* as the interrelations and transformation of active and passive principles.

A character in a play will not often specifically use the dramatist Grammar. St. Thomas in Eliot's *Murder in the Cathedral* is an exception, owing to Eliot's interest in Dante and theology. Thomas specifically meditates upon human motives in terms of "action" and "passion." [11] Similarly, in *The Dry Salvages,* Eliot specifically considers the action-motion relation, when contrasting supernatural motivation with a state of affairs

[11] The design of the turning wheel that forever turns and is forever still, which Eliot takes as the image for his equating of action and passion, may recall our remarks on "inevitability." If the "dead centre" of the turning wheel were the unchanging substance of the self, then we could explain how the wheel could forever turn and be forever still, since the transformations would all partake of one underlying quality. They would possess what Emerson calls the "tyrannizing unity" of man's "constitution," the principle which man seeks in nature and attains in art. Emerson celebrates it zestfully in the same essay (on *Nature*) in which he wrote:

> Herein is especially apprehended the unity of Nature—the unity in variety—which meets us everywhere. All the endless variety of things make an identical impression. Xenophanes complained in his old age, that, looking where he would, all things hastened back to Unity. He was weary of seeing the same entity in the tedious variety of forms.

The full discussion of the subject belongs rather in the study of symbolic, but since we are trying to indicate, where the opportunity offers, how the different fields overlap, we may note here how "high orders of abstraction," when *personalized,* can become replicas of the "unchanging self," hence a delight insofar as one is pleased with oneself, and a bondage insofar as one would be reborn.

> Where action were otherwise movement
> Of that which is only moved
> And has in it no source of movement—
> Driven by daemonic, chthonic
> Powers,

though the motion here does not remain the neutral kind considered by science, but becomes rather a kind of sinister passion. Usually, the Grammar is left implicit, as when Lear calls himself "more sinned against than sinning," a complex bit of grammar indeed, particularly when we consider the ingredients of passion in the concept of "sinning," that here has the active form.

The Japanese propagandists explicitly used the action-passion grammar when explaining to their people the steady American advances in the Pacific. The Japanese were told they were not to think of the Japanese forces as passively suffering attack, but as actively drawing the enemy closer, so that the eventual counterblow might be more effective. On reading this, one immediately saw the grammatical principle at the basis of German propaganda under conditions of defeat. When they were being pursued across North Africa from the East, for instance, it was explained that their armies were rapidly "advancing Westward." And their retreats in Russia were described as the use of "space as a weapon." Here, on the Rhetorical level, we find the underlying Grammar of the situation implicitly recognized in its explicit stylistic denial.

The examination of the particular way in which any particular writer of imaginative literature exemplifies the grammatical principles would require individual analysis on the Symbolic level. The purposes of this present book, however, require us rather to consider the dialectical resources of terms at a high level of abstraction, such resources as one utilizes when pitting a term like "action in general" against a term like "passion in general."

In discussing the *poiema, pathema, mathema* series, we have noted how you can draw out the grammar into a temporal succession: The action organizes the resistant factors, which call forth the passion; and the moment of transcendence arises when the sufferer (who had originally seen things in unenlightened terms) is enabled to see in more comprehensive terms, modified by his suffering.

Or action and passion may be made simultaneous equivalents, as with the theory of Christian martyrdom, wherein the act of self-sacrifice is identical with the sufferance. In *Murder in the Cathedral,* Eliot shows us this identification arising as a result of the *mathema.* Or rather, the Saint has first suffered temptation *(pathema);* he has detected and resisted this temptation *(poiema);* and the understanding *(mathema)* derived from the trial equips him for martyrdom (which is a new level of action-passion in one). Similarly, we have seen in Spinoza how *mathema* ("adequate ideas") can transform passion into action.

And we should recall here how the Gods, considered as motives, are *par excellence* instances of the dramatist grammar, since they are an active vocabulary for the naming of mental processes and "mechanisms." In proportion as men's sense of *tribal* identity is uppermost, a supernatural vocabulary of motives (either divine or Satanic) is felt adequate. Guilt is a tribal judgment; hence one is being quite "realistic" in attributing remorse to the action of Furies. For they are gods, which is to say, they are tribal motives. And they have external existence (in contrast, for instance, with an individual's sensations). But in proportion as the sense of tribal identity gives way to the sense of individual identity, this "realistic" vocabulary of motives becomes tautological. The sense of guilt is located in the individual; and in explaining it as caused by the Furies one is duplicating the motive. Both "guilt" and "pursuit by the Furies" designate the same condition.

After several centuries of individualism, this development is reversed, as psychologists idealistically begin with the "ego" and treat the tribal motives in terms of a "super-ego." The tribal element is thus reaffirmed (as likewise with Jung's concept of the "collective unconscious"), though the resultant view of psychological mechanisms has necessarily dropped the sense of the human mind as a battleground of supernatural powers. But whereas the grammar of action becomes modified, it remains with us, partly as a mere survival from earlier vocabularies, partly as evidence of man's essential dramatism.

The concept of the "ruling passion" is an instance of a dramatist motivation not directly theological though it was strongly ethical, and showed many vestiges of the Christian pattern. It is at bottom almost an oxymoron, or at least a conceit, as were we to speak of someone's "dominant subjection," or his "sovereign bondage," or his "most commanding weakness."

In *One Mighty Torrent, the Drama of Biography,* Edgar Johnson reviews and discusses this "fascinating theory of the 'ruling passion'" in seventeenth-century biography, a theory that he derives particularly from Tacitus and Theophrastus. Such biographies, he says, were constructed

> upon a deductive scheme of what was consistent for such and such a type to be like, rather than upon detailed observation of what a man was in fact like. Each person, so ran the theory, had one ruling passion, with all the others grouped like vassals round and swaying to its imperious motions.

In *Every Man out of his Humour,* Ben Jonson had already given the term "humour" a similar application. First he observes that the word was originally scenic, referring to a liquid. Next, that there are liquids in the body ("choler, melancholy, phlegm and blood") which are called humours. Here too the usage would fall within our concept of the scenic. Next he explains that the word is metaphorically extended to designate states of mind corresponding to the disposition of the four liquids in the body:

> It may, by metaphor, apply itself
> Unto the general disposition;
> As when some one peculiar quality
> Doth so possess a man that it doth draw
> All his effects, his spirits and his powers,
> In their confluxion all to run one way,—
> This may be truly said to be a humour.

One might choose to see in the passage an adumbration of behaviorism, though only if, at the same time, one recognizes that Jonson's interests are in the opposite direction. He would translate the concept from a materialistic to a dramatist significance. For Jonson's notion of the humour involves a particular kind of dramatic form. The prologue to *Every Man in his Humour* said that comedy deals "with human follies, not with crimes." The dedication of *Volpone* says that "the office of a comic poet" is "to imitate justice." And Jonson carries out the pattern by showing human passions (in this case, "human follies") as inner motives leading to outer actions that in turn lead to the suffering of punishment, a form of plot that Volpone sums up by saying:

> What a rare punishment
> Is avarice to itself!

We have already considered Hegel's variant, in his *Philosophy of History,* where Absolute Spirit is said to *act* by using the blind *passions* of individual men as its medium (a "world-historical individual" thus being one who, in consciously following the lead of merely personal interests and ambitions, unconsciously furthers the designs of the Universal Dialectic).

Much of the action-passion grammar is to be spotted, in liberal writings, beneath references to "freedom" and its opposite. When Aristotle speaks of metaphysics as a liberal art, he conceives of its liberality in contrast with the usefulness or serviceableness of a slave. "As the man is free, we say, who exists for his own sake and not for another's, so we pursue this as the only free science, for it alone exists for its own sake." (I, 2.) And in Book III, Chapter 2, he celebrates it as the "most architectonic and authoritative" science, so authoritative that "the other sciences, like slave-women, may not even contradict it."

"Freedom," as a dialectical term, may be conceived in opposition to *slavery.* Or it may be conceived rather in opposition to *authority.* There is an important psychological distinction between them. Aristotle, in here speaking of freedom, speaks in the role of one who considers himself in the class of free men, in contrast with the class of slaves. He does not conceive of freedom in dialectical opposition to authority; his attitude rather is that of a participant in the authoritative structure. His trade was that of the intellect, in which resided the powers of human action and virtue (through control over the enslaving passions). Aristotle's freedom was not that of protest. It was not negativistic or revolutionary.

But modern freedom, as the slogan of an upstart middle class, was polemic, propagandistic, a doctrine of partial slaves in partial revolt, as with its stress upon service and utility. In proportion as the social values of this rising class became the norm, the original upstart aspect of modern libertarianism was transferred to socialism and anarchism. The propagandistic ingredient in works like *Pilgrim's Progress* and *Robinson Crusoe* (and in general, the novel of middle class *sentiment*) could be dropped. For the development of business had so circumscribed the concepts of practical or moral utility within monetary limits, that the original religious and moralistic vocabulary of bourgeois apologetics became more and more like a sheer Rhetorical evasion of the Grammatical realities. Art now became "useless," a "free play of the imagination," as per the Bourgeois-Bohemian dichotomy. Except among social reformers and revolutionaries, propaganda art was *categorically* decried, for the liberal critic usually insisted that he was against not just "Leftist" propaganda, but *all* propaganda. He was able to hold this position until the recent war against Fascism, when one by one the "pure" artists came forth with some kind of work in which an anti-Nazi or anti-Fascist position was consciously embedded in the very form and style. For it had become too undeniably obvious that political actions and passions are a major aspect of "reality" as now constituted. Where motives are vigorously actual, there are the themes of art.

One can readily become so involved in such controversies on their own terms, that one neglects to place them in terms of their underlying grammatical principles. What is needed is not that we place ourselves "above" the controversies. Rather, we should place ourselves *within* them, by an understanding of their essential grammar. And this result can be attained, according to the present theory, by seeking for vestiges of the dramatistic in modern liberal terminologies that do not directly abide by this Grammar, *concealed beneath synonyms*. Originally, as we saw in Spinoza, the synonyms were explicit. Later, the Grammatical side of the equations is dropped or slighted—and we may thereupon be led to think that modern theories of motives are operating on principles different from those of the earlier Grammar, whereas they are merely different ways of exploiting the same dialectical resources. But for purposes of classification, one must have categories that include all kinds of motivational doctrines. And if such ways of classification are to be substantial, they must name generative principles which the various species have in common. For this reason we would cling as long as possible to the traces of the action-passion alignment; and at the point where we must relinquish it, we would deal with the shift in terms of the action-motion disproportion.

Thus, when considering the vocabulary of that essentially liberal psychology, psychoanalysis, we would look for the common underlying Grammar by classing "frustration," "fixation," "complex," and the like as species of passion; and "adjustment," or "normality" as equivalents of action. "Sublimation" would equal transcendence, and "repression" or "inhibition" would represent a new dialectic of "reason" as the *hegemonikon*, stated in quizzical terms whereas formerly it was stated in terms unambiguously favorable. We do not thereby ask that modern psychology abandon its terms for terms more apparently "Grammatical." Rather, we should ourselves apply such exegesis. For only in this way can we see the true significance of whatever changes may have been introduced into the newer terminologies of motives. It is by such forms designed for bringing out continuities in psychological terminology that we can best locate the *discontinuities,* and thereby be able to know just how religions and secular, ancient and modern, psychologies do square with one another.

As regards normal psychology, McDougall's stress upon the "sentiments" would seem, from this point of view, to require broad placement as another study of "incipient action." For this reason it merits more attention, at least *in principle,* than it now usually gets (having been displaced by psychologies more exclusively scientist in their concerns, as with experiments in perception and learning).

On the other hand, most modern works have departed far from a direct relation to the dramatist grammar. One can see "action" readily enough behind a word like "freedom"; it is more attenuated when we come to "adjustment" (in fact, as we have observed, this term can signify passivity, or sheer motion); we can discern the lineaments of potentiality, or incipient action, in attitudes, images, and sentiments. But often one does best to begin one's analysis the other way round, simply looking for the key terms in a work, inquiring how they are related to one another, and waiting for the dramatist forms to force themselves upon the attention, letting the matter lie in abeyance while one charts the given terms just as they are, on their face. Summarization, characterization, and placement is the general aim. The "tendency" is to summarize, characterize, and place in dramatist terms. But the search for such underlying forms must not lead to a neglect of terminological tactics peculiar to the given work. A particular poem, for instance, might be organized about a single image, variously rami-fied, as theme with variations. It would be enough to discern these developments in themselves, without regard for the possible significance of the image as "incipient action" or "incipient passion." And only when examining the images of the writer's work in its entirety might we come to see the full significance of this image as a symbolic act. (The subject has been considered at some length in our *Philosophy of Literary Form*. We also intend to consider many other aspects of it in our volume on the Symbolic of Motives.)

Considered solely in terms of political power, an "act" would be possible only to a ruler, or to a ruling class. Or, as applied by analogy to the psychology of the individual, an act would be possible only to the part of the soul that enjoyed a corresponding status of authority. At least, that seems to be the ratio at the basis of that *hegemonikon* which the Stoics located in the reason, thus linking the idea of private rule with the idea of public rule by equating reason with authority. Recalling what we have previously said about the nature of modern liberalism, we can grasp the significance of the Stoic's reason-authority equation by comparing it with the partial shattering of that equation in Rousseau.

Rousseau proposed to ground Emile's education in a respect for the "necessity in things" rather than deference to the "caprices" and "authority" of other men. Dependence on things, he said, is the "work of nature." But dependence on men is the "work of society." Dependence on things, "being non-moral, does no injury to liberty." But dependence on men "gives rise to every kind of vice," as "master and slave corrupt each other." It is obvious now how Rousseau's partial dissociating of reason and authority pointed towards the French Revolution. And looking further back, in the light of Rousseau's natural-ism, and still on the Rhetorical level, can we not discern the anti-authoritarian implications in Spinoza's naturalism? It was not merely a position to be considered in itself. It was a *counter*-position (as Spinoza, of course, himself made explicit in his political views disa-greeing with Hobbes).[12]

---

[12] In studying the nature of linguistic action, one must always be on guard for evidence of Rhetorical action embedded in Grammar. A pure scenic approach

As the reason acts, and the body moves, so authorities could act by adopting policies to be carried out by others (who moved as slaves, servants, or assistants). Thus, eventually a "ruling class" (in accordance with the properties of its status) could become transformed from a class that "does" to a class that "does not." It is the development we considered earlier with relation to the actus-status pair. Acts require properties of status; and the "substantiality" of such properties can be inherited independently of the act which was originally their generating principle.

We have already seen how Stoicism led into the Christian paradox, the "revolutionary" transvaluation whereby suffering (the passive) could be treated as an *act* (accounts of martyrdom, for instance, being termed either "passionals" or "acts"). We find this change emerging in Stoicism, with its emphasis upon the moral value of sufferance, and its great humanitarian sympathy with slavery—indeed, its tendency to dwell upon the ways in which all men are slaves and servants (to their appetites, emotions, errors, or to natural or political necessities). Christianity offered a doctrine whereby the subjects were persons, and in their passion were capable not merely of motion, but of action. It permitted one in a way to "will" his subjection—and in so doing it gave him a "substantial" freedom, a "pure" freedom. By the ambiguity of substance, or the paradox of purity, it could call a man free precisely because he was enslaved. And in calling him "substantially" free, in effect it invited him to make himself so in actuality (inviting him to translate his "essential" freedom into its "existential" counterpart, or to proceed from the "form" of freedom to its "materialization"). And by *universalizing* the concept of servitude (so that all

---

errs in stressing this relation at the expense of formal analysis. But one must watch lest the scenic excess lead to the opposite excess, that would eliminate extrinsic reference entirely. Let's remember that, in the long conversation of history, few statements are made simply "in themselves." They are *answers* to other statements. And this function is a part of their intrinsic form. Recently, reading the autobiography of St. Teresa, I was struck by her account of her efforts to establish a complete distrust of herself. Recalling pious exhortations to "put one's faith in God," I suddenly realized that this had been a *dialectical* injunction, as opposition to those who put their faith in *any* human being. In other words, the injunction had not originally meant simply that one should rely upon God; it implied also whom one should *not* rely on. Of a sudden, then, I saw Rousseau's statement in a line of transformations, having St. Teresa's position at one end, and Emerson's cult of "self-reliance" at the other.

men "served," all men "obeyed," all were "patient," as Christians doing the work of the Lord), it could also include the realistic, Aristotelian concept of the free person. For if *all* men are slaves, or better, *servants,* it would be as true to say that *no* men are slaves, "substantially." Hence all would merit a respect for themselves as persons; and it would be wrong to treat men merely as objects of use. Men's servitude to God, law, and other men would be dependent upon a *voluntary* submission to their divinely appointed status. Such a way would make of submission an act and not a mere sufferance. Or better, it made submission an act because sufferance itself was considered an act.

In proportion as the servitude took the form of private enterprise, it endowed the "servants" with material powers. The "passivity" thus did, in the most obvious sense, become active, since ambitions netted results. The "freedom" of universal Christian "servitude," thus in time became transformed into a condition of action, even revolutionary action, particularly since the ideals of *private* wealth could be Rhetorically stated as the ideal of a Christlike *poor* Church.

All told we have, as motivational patterns which psychologies more or less patently realistic might exemplify: the action-passion and actus-status pairs, the action-motion ambiguity, and the potential. These can be variously *individuated* in specific terminologies (as with different schools of psychology, religious or secular, or in the one-time motivational structures of particular biographies, histories, reports, poems, plays, and narrative fictions). Obviously the Grammatical principles here considered can merely suggest the broad categories by reference to which any particular vocabulary of motives would be classed. Such realistic reclamation would enable us to class "ethical" and "scientifically neutral" psychologies together with terms that can be applied to all such terminologies of motives. In brief, all psychologies can, without violence to their subject matter, be approached dramatistically, as vocabularies concerned with the kinds and conditions of action and passion.

Even the most extreme behaviorism would belong here. We refer not only to its dramatistic placement in terms of a narrowed circumference that reduces action to motion. We refer also to the behaviorist concept of "transference." According to this concept, the conditioned response to an object or situation of a certain quality may be transferred to other objects or situations felt to be of the same quality. But this process involves the interpretation and *classification* of signs; and when this is capable of modification by purely linguistic means, as with human beings, it opens up a field of investigation that takes one far beyond the "conditioned reflex" in its simplicity. But though it involves kinds of transcendence and symbolic action that could not be treated in such terms, the need of richer terms can be shown to exist simply by a strict analysis of the elements subsumed under the concept of "transference" itself. For it introduces problems of classification and reclassification that could readily lead to the equating of "adequate" classifications with "action" and the equating of "inadequate" classifications with "passion" (though the two be concealed beneath terms like "adjustment" and "maladjustment").

But one other Grammatical resource of action need be considered briefly, and we can turn to our remaining terms, Purpose and Agency.

In Book I, Chapters 6 and 7 of his *Physics*, we find Aristotle trying to decide "whether the basic principles of nature are two or three or some greater number." As we read on, we see that the matter is purely dialectical, involving the question whether we should reduce nature to a pair of opposites, related as hot and cold, increase and decrease, active and passive, or should postulate a "third something underlying them." He does not make a final choice, being content to observe that, from one point of view, a third term is needed, to serve as the mediating ground of the opposites. But from another point of view, only two are needed, since we can account for change by considering one of the opposites as present or absent; and in this case we should need only it and the underlying principle. As for the underlying substratum itself, we can understand it by analogy:

> It is to any particular and existent substance what bronze is to a completed statue, wood to a bed, and still unformed materials to the objects fashioned from them.

In brief, it is the principle of potentiality which we have already considered.

Looking at this issue from the standpoint of the Grammatical voices, we see Aristotle here asking whether the *active* and *passive* are enough, or whether we may also require a *middle* voice in our Grammar of motives. As a matter of fact, in the Indo-European family of languages, the passive voice is a late development. Originally there were but the active and middle (or reflexive) forms, and the passive developed out of the middle. (In Greek, the conjugations of middle and passive are alike in many tenses.) Prior to its development, passive ideas were expressed actively, but reflexively, in treating the action as directed by the self upon the self. Passive forms probably indicate a high degree of development from actus to status, with a corresponding increase in the sense of mental states.

Once such a development has taken place, however, as it did with the complex vocabulary of sensibility and scruples accumulated by Christianity, the scene is set for "post-passive" kinds of active and reflexive. Writers like Caldwell and Hemingway, for instance, can be sparse in their recital, contenting themselves largely with purely behavioristic narrative, precisely because readers can be relied upon to supply the scruples of themselves. The apparent harshness is thus but a sophisticated variant of sensitivity, perhaps even sentimentality, for the expression of emotions is sentimental in proportion as it is inexact.

But the reflexive, as a mediate relationship, moves us rather in the direction of means; accordingly, it will be considered again when we look at the term, Agency. We have now considered the big three, scene, agent, and act. We shall now consider the remaining two, Agency and Purpose, that draw together in the means-ends relationship. And following that, we shall consider our category of categories, dialectic.

IV

AGENCY AND PURPOSE

The Philosophy of Means

UNDER Pragmatism, in the Baldwin dictionary, we read: "This term is applied by Kant to the species of hypothetical imperative . . . which prescribes the means necessary to the attainment of happiness." In accordance with our thesis, we here seize upon the reference to *means,* since we hold that Pragmatist philosophies are generated by the featuring of the term, Agency. We can discern this genius most readily in the very title, *Instrumentalism,* which John Dewey chooses to characterize his variant of the pragmatist doctrine. Similarly William James explicitly asserts that Pragmatism is "a method only." And adapting Peirce's notion that beliefs are rules for action, he says that "theories thus become instruments," thereby stressing the practical nature of theory, whereas Aristotle had come close to putting theory and practice in dialectical opposition to each other. James classed his pragmatism with nominalism in its appeal to particulars, with utilitarianism in its emphasis upon the practical, and with positivism in its "disdain for verbal solutions, useless questions and metaphysical abstractions."

In one sense, there must be as many "pragmatisms" as there are philosophies. That is, each philosophy announces some view of human ends, and will require a corresponding doctrine of means. In this sense, we might ask wherein "Stoic pragmatism" would differ from "Epicurean," "Platonist," or "Kantian" pragmatisms, etc. But modern science is *par excellence* an accumulation of new agencies (means, instruments, methods). And this locus of new power, in striking men's fancy, has called forth "philosophies of science" that would raise agency to first place among our five terms.

William James, in his book on *Pragmatism,* quotes Papini, who likens the pragmatist stress to the corridor in a hotel. Each room of the hotel may house a guest whose personal interests and philosophic views differ from those of the guests in the other rooms. But all guests use the corridor in common. Pragmatism would thus be a principle of mediation that all philosophies have in common, quite as the instructions for operating a machine are the same for liberal, Fascist, or Communist.

There is a sense, of course, in which this is not so. Two men, performing the same *motions* side by side, might be said to be performing different *acts*, in proportion as they differed in their attitudes toward their work. We might realistically call it one kind of act to run an elevator under a system of private ownership, and another kind of act to run that same elevator, by exactly the same routines, under a system of communal ownership.

Aristotle's concern with logic as the instrument (*organon*) of human reason is "incipiently" pragmatist. But we have already noted that his representative position in a slave culture led to a slighting of agency as we think of it, after the intervening centuries of Christian servitude, business service, and the utility of applied science. We saw how agency failed to attain full rank as a locus of motivation in Aristotle's list of causes (material, efficient, formal, and final). In fact, from the standpoint of the pentad, we might well situate the source of the "non-Aristotelian" element in modern science in the fact that it makes uppermost the very domain of motivation that Aristotle subordinated.

In Aristotle's classification of cause, either a first mover (person, agent) or a last mover (implement, tool, agency) can be classed as an efficient cause. And means are considered in terms of ends. But once you play down the concept of final cause (as modern science does), the distinction between agent and agency becomes sharp. Also, there is a reversal of causal ancestry—and whereas means were treated in terms of ends, ends become treated in terms of means. John Dewey, for instance, lays great stress upon the fact that the formulation of an end may serve as a means of adjustment. And our entire curriculum of vocational training is an instance of agency as ancestor. Thus, because there are cars, some men learn to become automobile mechanics, their conception of a life purpose deriving from the nature of the instrument which they would service. Money, as we have pointed out previously, here figures as the medium that can supply a kind of "absolute purpose" over and above the motives peculiar to each class of instrument.

According to James, the pragmatist evaluates a doctrine by its "consequences," by what it is "good for," by "the difference it will make to you and me," or by its "function," or by asking whether it "works satisfactorily." Having extended Peirce's secular doctrines to include religious utility, he even asks what "menial services" men can require of God. Also, with a disastrous felicity that his opponents were quick to seize upon, he said that the pragmatist looks for the "cash value" of an idea. And if we allow that James was here borrowing a trope from the language of pure capitalism, we see how faithfully the figure retains the stress upon agency, in using a mode of thought according to which a thing's value is tested by its economic usefulness, as tested in turn by its marketability (that is, its function as a means in satisfying desires).

Now that modern pragmatism has flourished long enough to show a curve of development, we can see the incipient pragmatism in Emerson's idealism. His early book, *Nature*, is particularly relevant in this respect, since he is inquiring into the "uses" of Nature. The whole matter is approached much as with the "moral pragmatism" we previously noted in Stoicism:

> Whoever considers the final cause of the world will discern a multitude of uses that enter as parts into that result. They all admit of being thrown into one of the following classes: Commodity, Beauty, Language, and Discipline.

Here, obviously, agency has not yet become the ancestral term, but is seen in terms of universal purpose. Emerson does not even mean by "commodity" quite what the word has come to mean in business English. Here he ranks "all those advantages which our senses owe to nature." He notes how the things of nature "serve" in nature's "ministry to man," and how by the useful arts men serve one another. Later, in the *Over-Soul*, he was to represent the Protestant idealization of the secular by affirming that the world of everyday experience "is one wide judicial investigation of character." Throughout his work, he struggles to see high moral principles behind men's economic acts. And he places modern inventions in this pattern of an idealized utility:

> The poor man hath cities, ships, canals, bridges, built for him. He goes to the post-office, and the human race run on his errands; to the

> book-shop, and the human race read and write of all that happens
> for him; to the court-house, and nations repair his wrongs. He sets
> his house upon the road, and the human race go forth every morn-
> ing, and shovel out the snow, and cut a path for him.

And characteristically, he ends his brief discussion of "commodities"
with the "general remark, that this mercenary benefit is one which
has respect to a farther good. A man is fed, not that he may eat,
but that he may work."

In the love of Beauty, "a nobler want of man is served." Emerson
discusses language as "a third use which Nature subserves to man."
And by the Discipline of Nature he considers the ways in which we
can derive moral improvement from our dealings with the "sensible
objects" of Nature, by "perceiving the analogy that marries Matter and
Mind." Property too, with its "filial systems of debt and credit," performs this moralizing service: "Debt, grinding debt, whose iron face
the widow, the orphan, and the sons of genius fear and hate—debt,
which consumes so much time, which so cripples and disheartens a
great spirit with cares that seem so base, is a preceptor whose lessons
cannot be foregone, and is needed most by those who suffer from it
most." Nature disciplines the will, for "Nature is thoroughly mediate.
It is made to serve." In accordance with this idealizing of agency, we
are told that the ethical character

> so penetrates the bone and marrow of nature, as to seem the end for
> which it was made. Whatever private purpose is answered by an
> member or part, this is its public and universal function, and is never
> omitted. Nothing in nature is exhausted in its first use. When a
> thing has served an end to the uttermost, it is wholly new for an
> ulterior service. In God, every end is converted into a new means.
> Thus, the use of commodity, regarded by itself, is mean and squalid.
> But it is to the mind an education in the doctrine of Use, namely,
> that a thing is good only so far as it serves.

Whether nature has a real existence, or is but a form of thought, he
says, "It is alike useful and alike venerable to me." And imagination
he defines as "the use which the Reason makes of the material world."

We have cited enough to show that in Emerson secular agency is a
function of divine purpose. Obviously, only if we narrow the circumference, by dropping the concept of final cause, could we get to

the true pragmatist stress upon agency as the ancestral term. If we replace Emerson's transcendentalism and James's personalism with Dewey's and Mead's biologism (as in *Experience and Nature* and *Philosophy of the Act*) we find a transitional device that can help us to get farther along in the course from purpose to agency pure and simple. This is in the concept of biologic functioning. That is, the bodily organs are means toward ends; each, insofar as it is functioning properly, carries out the kind of "purpose" for which it is designed; and it serves a use in furthering the survival of the organism. At this level, agencies can be considered without reference to final causes in the theological or personalistic senses; yet in such a view there is no strict *opposition* to purpose. Insofar as the instrumentations of biological adjustment are stressed, we have the pragmatist stress upon agency, while allowing for such a level of "action" as we noted in Santayana's concept of "animal faith."

By this interpretation, pragmatism pure and simple would not be reached until we come to P. W. Bridgman's "operationalism," as described in his *Logic of Modern Physics*. For here we come to a complete treatment of meaning in terms of laboratory instruments. Whatever may have been the purposes of a man who designs such agencies, they themselves are totally without purpose, even in the ambiguously biological sense of the term. We would hardly say that the mercury in the thermometer rises on hot days "in order to" assist the thermometer in the struggle for life, or "in order to" avoid certain discomfitures that it might experience if it did not decide to rise, or even "in order to record the temperature." We treat it purely and simply as an instrument, or agency, that has no intrinsic interest in recording the temperature.

Bridgman has written many studies on the compressibility of gases to high pressure, pressure coefficients of resistance, compressibility of metals as a function of pressure and temperature, the effect of pressure on the rigidity of metals, the effect of pressure on the thermal conductivity of metals, the effect of pressure on viscosity of various liquids, the effect of tension on the electrical resistance of certain abnormal metals—and so on. Obviously, such investigations required a vast battery of meters, gauges, rules, tubes, and sundry other items of laboratory equipment, with strict observance of the procedures or operations involved in their use. Here is *par excellence* a realm of *agencies.* And as philosophers old style would usually pay a tribute to their calling by conceiving of God in ways that, whatever they might tell us about the character of God, told us a lot about the character of the philosophy, so Bridgman pays a tribute to his calling by conceiving of meaning in the strict sense suggested to him by his intensive concern with these agencies. His concern is with the meaning of means.

There are clear adumbrations of this strict position even in James. But Bridgman exemplifies it to perfection, in making a concept synonymous with the corresponding set of operations. A concept of temperature would thus be equated with the actual operations by which one recorded temperature. And strictly speaking, he says, one would have as many concepts as one had sets of operations. (That is, two ways of recording the same temperature would be two concepts.)

The dramatist may tell us that the world's a stage; the sailor might tell us that we're all afloat; a philosopher, having long thought about thinking, might tell us that God is "thought of thought." And so this savant has done well by his instruments, in telling us that concepts are nonsense except insofar as we can define them in instrumental terms. By contrast, we see the strong dramatist ingredient in Mead's concept of the "other" whose attitudes we dialectically include in the internal dialogue of thought and judgment. And the contrast also indicates how thoroughly the stress upon agency fails to notice the demands of the remaining motivational domains. When Bridgman says, for instance, that two different operations for recording the same condition would "in principle" be two different concepts, he expresses himself by the use of a term ("principle") that is possible only to substantialist thought. And were he to ask himself wherein the similarities of operations end and their differences begin, he would find himself involved in all sorts of purely formal problems for the solution of which there can be no such instruments as exist in his laboratories. Indeed, he might even see the instruments themselves as merely one aspect of dialectic, one voice among the several voices whose competitive coöperation is necessary for the development of mature meanings. And when he writes that the world of laboratory experimentation "is not understandable without some examination of the purpose of physics," we must recognize that he is writing about his *purpose in eliminating the concept of purpose,* a state of linguistic affairs which calls for a kind of analysis not possible to his method. Yet it obviously requires consideration, if we are to take his own book seriously; for it represents the *underlying Grammar* of his argument.

Though our laboratory instruments may transcend human purpose, they exist only as the result of human purpose. And we might even say that they can perform satisfactorily without purpose only because they have purpose imbedded in their structure and design. An instrument like a thermometer has its purpose so thoroughly built into its very nature, that it can do its work without purpose, merely by continuing to be itself.

The Range of Pragmatism

Conditions

In philosophers like Aquinas, the concept of "conditions" is highly formal in nature. Kant's "transcendentalism" was the first step towards a more purely historical concept of conditions. For though Kant's conditions were highly generalized, they were distinguished from those of formal logic in being exclusively the conditions of *experience*. (And the condition of conditions, you will recall, was the *unconditioned* realm lying beyond the reach of experience.) Fichte brought us a step nearer to a more particularized notion of conditions in treating the Ego as spiritual source, and the Non-Ego as its material incarnation. This amounts to its translation into a structure of natural conditions.

The movement towards particularization was carried a step further in Hegel, as he traces the particulars of history, but sees them following internal principles of development. It is quite to our purposes that Hegel called the utterance (*Äusserung*) of this internal principle a *mediation* (*Vermittlung*): the expression of itself in a *medium* (a mode of thought which suggests from another angle why idealism is a precursor of pragmatism).

Marx reversed Hegel by treating material, or economic conditions, as formative of spirit (as against the Hegelian genealogy that begins with spirit as source and ground). We have here gone from "God" to "matter" as the condition of consciousness. And the Hegelian pattern of transcendence could be applied by Marxists to account for the development of "higher" forms from "lower" in accordance with the notion that changes in quantity call forth corresponding changes in quality, as at those critical points where a rise in the temperature of water changes it from solid to liquid, and from liquid to gas. But there was a pronounced sense of form pervading Marx's view of history. It was not "pragmatist."

The "Facts"

Essentially pragmatist history enters, I think, with the concept of the "documentary" as the historiographer's ideal. For the documentary facts are the medium with which the historian works; and insofar as he tries to write "pure document," he is placing the major stress upon the medium itself. In this sense such historiography would be a featuring of agency. Avoiding problems of causal ancestry, it would simply record whatever historical events are known to have occurred together.

Lying about the edges of this ideal, there are of course the demands of our other terms. For the historian must in some way seek to characterize, summarize, and place the period with which he is concerned. And in his presentation of an historical era, he is guided by more or less clearly formed notions of its essence (as a character in itself, or as a character in contrast with the character of other times, or as a stage in some historical development). But insofar as he professes to carry out his program, such wider claims of definition must make themselves felt surreptitiously. He must give us essences while disclaiming any such purpose.

Two Principles of Truth in James

Looking again at James from the standpoint of what we have been saying about the concept of "conditions," we find in him a conflict of dramatist and positivist ideals, as revealed in the notion of truth. Kant, while granting that theological meanings could not be proved, had tried to save them negatively by showing that they could not be disproved. Thorough-going positivism, with which James has expressed affinities, would equate meaning with verifiability, hence asserting that a statement capable of neither proof nor disproof is "meaningless."

At the bottom of James's pragmatism seems to lie the Grammatical fact that human acts are not "verifiable" in the way that purely scenic statements are. The "proof" of a human act is in the *doing*. God's acts, however, are different. Insofar as God's acts are the Creation, his actions can be equated with natural events. Hence, as *acts* they are out-and-out *scenic*. And if we say that the island of Manhattan is on the West Coast, we can test the statement by trying to act on the basis of it.

But when you narrow the circumference to humanistic scope, you get two kinds of situation. What A does "from within" as an act, B sees "from without" as an event (that is, a scene). The distinction however is complicated by the fact that A can dialectically consider his own act in terms of B, thus to some extent looking upon it from without; and B can to some extent respond to A's behavior from within, so that it is not felt merely scenically, as a set of signs, but is vicariously *participated in* (or "incipiently imitated") as an *act*.

James's pragmatism, with its stress upon the act of belief, stands midway between the ethical or dramatist sense of act and the positivistist-scientist reduction of the act to terms of sheer events (a behavioristically observed scene). And this midway position is fittingly manifested in terms of *agency*, the function that is essentially *mediatory*. And this concept of agency contains within itself the ambiguity of the two verifications: (1) The verification of an act by an act, as believing is the test of belief: (2) the verification of an act-less *scenic* statement by an act framed in accordance with the scenic statement, as one can test a map by following it in the charting of one's course.

Symbolic of Agency

Instruments are "essentially" human, since they are the products of human design. And in this respect, the pragmatist featuring of agency seems well equipped to retain a personal ingredient in its circumference of motives. But as regards the functioning of Agency on the Symbolic level, we are advised to be on the look-out for a personal principle of another order, stemming from the fact that the human being, in the stage of infancy, formatively experiences a realm of personal utility in the person of the mother. The combination of planning and usefulness that characterizes maternal care apparently suggests the view of "Mother Nature" that we considered in the Hellenistic philosophies and in the incipient pragmatism of Emerson. One might well look for similar motives in James, owing to the devotional ingredient in his brand of pragmatism, for the reference to the "menial services" of our Protector would apply more aptly to maternal attentions than to God.

As we move into more professedly secular varieties of pragmatism, such motivations become more tenuous and dubious. Bridgman, it is true, speaks of the scientist's devotion to his "facts" as something "religious." But though the expression offers grounds for a "hunch," it proves nothing in itself. Perhaps we should have to know what figures or images fleetingly suggest themselves to him when he is at work in his laboratory, or what quality runs through the haphazard reference to his experiments in his conversation, before we could claim that there are "parental" motivations of one kind or another in his morality of science. Yet it is possible that an examination of his writings, undertaken on the purely Symbolic level, might in itself be enough to reveal some such structure.

As regards the Grammatical relation between Agency and Purpose: when translated into sexual terms, it presents an opportunity, on the Symbolic level, for involvement in the relation between the maternal woman and the erotic woman. In coming to sexual maturity, and preparing psychologically to seek a mate, the male during the period of courtship turns from the maternal woman (the principle of utility) to the erotic woman (the principle of purpose, in the form of the *desired*). Insofar as the feminine principle retains maternal aspects, courtship involves symbolic incest; hence, the principle of erotic purpose must "transcend" the principle of maternal utility. A dissociation in the attitude towards woman becomes necessary.

All sorts of possibilities suggest themselves here, particularly when one adds other factors, as when the "pure" poetry of the Art for Art's Sake sort is equated with the sexual, leading to a cult of purely "decorative" women. Obviously, the maternal-erotic dilemma is not solved normally until the woman as wife becomes "useful" on a new level, not directly to the husband (who, by his purpose as wage-earner, has himself become useful, though impersonally), but in her ministering personally to their joint product, the family.

The systematic consideration of such possibilities belongs rather in the Symbolic of Motives. Suffice it here to note that such speculations indicate Symbolic motives behind the thinking of that crabbed old bachelor, Jeremy Bentham, who propounded the philosophy of Utilitarianism, and who visited upon himself a kind of Symbolic castration in his plans for a "neutral" scientific vocabulary for avoiding the "censorious" terms of rhetoric and poetry. His utilitarian theory of language reduces purpose to agency by seeking for the *interests* that correspond to *ideals* (another word for the purposive). And despite his programmatic dislike and distrust of metaphor, in his *Table of the Springs of Action* he calls such idealizing words "eulogistic coverings" or "fig-leaves." All told, his intellectual situation, as with other great Bachelors of Capitalist Liberalism, would seem to be that of one who, arriving at that stage of maturity where the dissociation between the maternal woman and the erotic woman must be confronted, developed a philosophy of utility that could deflect erotic purpose into terms (themselves transformed) of maternal agency. The principle of the erotic could be capitalistically translated, as a rationale of utilitarian enterprise.

And we might well recall that Rousseau begins Emile's education with stress upon the test of usefulness, which he equates with the state of nature prior to society (a perfect parallel to the state of childhood prior to rational awareness of abstract social factors beyond the orbit of the personal). If such usefulness were a "mother principle," we could understand why he himself fell in love with maternal women, even explicitly recognizing this motive in his affair with Madame de Warens, as noted by Matthew Josephson in his *Jean-Jacques Rousseau*, p. 74:

> He found himself for the first time in the arms of a woman, a woman whom he adored. An overwhelming sadness and faintness poisoned the charm of the moment. "Twice, or thrice, as I pressed her passionately to me, I flooded her breast with my tears. *It was as if I were committing incest.*"

Behind the pure Grammar of his educational principle, then, we could discern the pattern of his romances, built about the cataclysmic step from the state of innocence to the state of erotic awakening (when the taboos directed towards the woman as mother become transformed into purpose directed toward the "new" woman).

Stendhal's hero begins similarly with attachment to maternal women, who remain mothers even in their adulterous relations with the hero. In pure capitalism, the transformation from woman-as-agency to woman-as-purpose is effected through the medium of *money* as purpose (money being one kind of "potency"). But the "fires" of Brûlard could not thus transcendently burn, owing to the esthetic distrust of the money motive in the era of *Napoléon le petit* when *enrichissez-vous* was the slogan for the non-esthetic bourgeois.

In pure poetry, perhaps the most magnificent instance of a merging of the maternal and erotic principles (sexual equivalents of agency and purpose) is in Baudelaire's sonnet *La Géante*. Here the disproportion in size between mother and child is idealized as a relation between queen and cat, giantess and poet, mountain and hamlet. The conceit is "evil" because the ratio is maintained in amatory imagery suggesting the attitude of a lover towards his mistress.

On the Symbolic level, there is also the more obvious correspondence, as revealed in the folk puns that refer to the sex organs themselves as instruments, such as tools and weapons. These puns provide bridges that can variously link love, war, and work, thereby greatly complicating the relations between filial and parental principles.

Purposive Agencies of Applied Science

But though Rhetorical and Symbolic factors can surreptitiously re-enforce the appeal of Agency, its prestige derives first from the Grammatical fact that it covers the area of applied science, the area of new power. This relation alone is enough to account for its featuring. And since the requirements of such science favor the elimination of Purpose, or final cause, the means-ends relation provokes a shift to the term nearest of kin, which can supply the *functions* of purpose even when the term is formally omitted as a locus of motives. Since agents act through the medium of motion, the reduction of action to motion can be treated as reduction to Agency, Pragmatism having the advantage over Materialism that *tools* are more "purposive" than *impersonal backgrounds* are, so that the Pragmatist emphasis can more conveniently straddle the action-motion ambiguity.

And of course, the close connection between technological diversification and the monetary motive reminds us that the medium of money also contributes to Pragmatist thinking, quite as James's reference to the "cash-value" of ideas suggested. The ambiguities of personal action and impersonal motion are here too, as with that typical capitalist agency, the stock-market, where the speculative *acts* of the individual trades add up statistically to a *movement* of prices. Such statistical results would themselves be analyzable in terms of *adjustment* rather than *purpose*. Yet this impersonal effect of personal acts in the aggregate, is readily felt not nominalistically, but as the action of a corporate entity. In the financial columns, for instance, we read of a broker who, commenting on the market of that day, said: "It very frankly acts as if it wanted to have an old-fashioned reaction but is afraid to carry it out."

Once Agency has been brought to the fore, the other terms readily accommodate themselves to its rule. Scenic materials become means which the organism employs in the process of growth and adaptation. The organism itself is a confluence of means, each part being at the service of the other parts. Reason becomes a means of adjustment. Empiricism can conform to the genius of Agency, in that the senses play a *mediatory* role, as we likewise come upon the mediatory in reducing everything to *relations*, thus completing the development from Substance to Subject to sheer correlation. Indeed, we seem to be confronting a principle of entropy, as with the second law of thermodynamics, with the distinctions of the various philosophic schools levelling off towards their "heat-death" in Pragmatism (which would be but another way of saying what James had in mind when borrowing Papini's figure of the corridor).

Ends

In the Baldwin dictionary we are told that Mysticism embraces "those forms of speculative and religious thought which profess to attain an immediate apprehension of the divine essence or the ultimate ground of existence." And: "Penetrated by the thought of the ultimate of all experience, and impatient of even a seeming separation from the creative source of things, mysticism succumbs to a species of metaphysical fascination." For it develops an ideal of passive contemplation "in which the distinctions of individuality disappear, and the finite spirit achieves, as it were, utter union or identity with the Being of beings."

Such references to "the divine essence," "the creative source," and "the Being of beings" indicate why we would equate Mysticism with the featuring of our term, Purpose. Often the element of unity *per se* is treated as the essence of mysticism. We should contend, however, that not mere unity, but unity of the individual with some *cosmic or universal purpose* is the mark of mysticism. One realizes this most readily when recalling that scientific philosophies which propose to eliminate "vitalism," "voluntarism," "spiritualism," "animism," "occult powers" and the like from their accounts of motivation regularly herald their attainments as the elimination of "mysticism" and "teleology" (the metaphysician's word for Purpose, or final cause).

Or we may establish the connection between Mysticism and Purpose sociologically by noting that although individual mystics may arise at any period of history, mystical philosophies appear as a general social manifestation in times of great skepticism or confusion about the nature of human purpose. They are a mark of transition, flourishing when one set of public presuppositions about the *ends* of life has become weakened or disorganized, and no new public structure, of sufficient depth and scope to be satisfying, has yet taken its place. Thus, precisely at such times of general hesitancy, the mystic can compensate for his own particular doubts about human purpose by submerging himself in some vision of a *universal*, or *absolute* or *transcendent* purpose, with which he would identify himself. In his chapter on "The Sick Soul" (*The Varieties of Religious Experience*) William James refers to Tolstoy's account of the drought preceding his rebirth. In this period of dire questioning, Tolstoy asked himself: "Is there in life any purpose which the inevitable death awaiting me does not undo and destroy?"

Our investigation promptly becomes complicated, however, by the fact, in accordance with the paradox of substance, that a purpose as thus conceived is so "pure" as to be much the same as no purpose at all, so far as everyday standards are concerned. Just as the mystic oxymoron conceives of a black radiance, a bitter sweetness, a learned ignorance (*docta ignorantia*), etc., so the mystic's "free" union with the All-Purpose becomes much the same as a *compulsion*. Such considerations explain why the psychology of mysticism is close to the psychology of neurosis. For the neurotic's God can be a disguised replica of his compulsion; and in communing with his God, he may by an unconscious subterfuge be but abandoning himself to his own weakness thus stylistically glorified. Also, in identifying the individual with the *All*, Mysticism often makes it hard for us to decide whether the Purpose is essentially collective or nominalist—though on the sociological level we can distinguish between the mystic who lives individualistically and the mystic who serves as the founder or organizer of a monastic order.

The fact that, in mysticism, Purpose is made absolute, always complicates matters by requiring us to lose purpose at the very moment when we find it. For as we have already noted, doctrines of absolute purpose lead into doctrines of mechanism, since the perfect regularity of nature (such as a thoroughly mechanical universe would exemplify) could be taken to indicate the "design" of its Creator.

All told, of the five terms, Purpose has become the one most susceptible of dissolution. At least, so far as its formal recognition is concerned. But once we know the logic of its transformations, we can discern its implicit survival; for the demands of dramatism being the demands of human nature itself, it is hard for man, by merely taking thought, to subtract the dramatist cubits from his stature. Implicit in the concepts of act and agent there is the concept of purpose. It is likewise implicit in agency, since tools and methods are for a purpose—and one of the great reasons for the appeal of pragmatism today, when the materialist-behaviorist reduction of scene has eliminated purpose, may reside in the fact that it retains ingredients of purpose in the very Grammatical function that is often taken as substitute for it. (It is a substitute; but we are suggesting that part of its capacity for such work resides in the implicit retention of what it is often said explicitly to reject.)

One feels this ambiguity particularly when considering the "Something for Itself's Sake" pattern of motivation so characteristic of modern specialization, the pattern that attains its highest level of generality in the "pure" motive of money. Though money is intrinsically a medium, or agency, in banking, gambling, and the "profit motive" generally it becomes translated into purpose, thus giving rise to what the Technocrat Harold Loeb once called the "mysticism" of money.

Similarly, in the esthetic field, doctrines of Art for Art's Sake would seem to fluctuate between the Pragmatic and the Mystical, though we may need some further distinctions here. Since art is a medium, the Art for Art's Sake formula would embody the grammatical form: Agency its own Purpose. One might call pragmatist such doctrines of art as those which hold that art is a means of biological assistance to man, in making for a better adjustment to conditions. Or the use of applied art (such as the "tendentious" art of political propaganda or commercial advertising) could be called pragmatic. But a pragmatist doctrine of art in a deeper sense would be one that applied in the esthetic field the same *form* of thought as had been applied to other activities. Hence, if specialization in the industrial field is considered pragmatic, then by the same token artistic specialization would be pragmatic. Yet such stress upon the medium for its own sake might have no "use-value," except when (as with the *ars gratia artis* of the Hollywood movies) it serves to attract paying customers, and so is indirectly "useful" in "making work" for a vast army of performers, producers, promoters, distributors, and the like. This last sense of the term would bring us before the dilemma we have been considering: whether to call Art for Art's Sake a pragmatist featuring of Agency or a mystic featuring of Purpose.

In any case, we should be on guard against taking the formula itself too seriously. When we look to see how it "behaves" in particular art products, we shall find that it involves the solution, on the Symbolic level, of many complex problems that could not profitably be discussed in terms so broad as either Agency or Purpose. And on the other hand, even when one adopts a rudimentary pragmatist view of art, as in advertising or propaganda, he has but moved the Agency-Purpose ambiguity a step farther along: for we then have to decide whether the financial or political structure which such applied art serves is to be classed as Agency or Purpose. Thus with the Hitlerite cult of the State: was it crass pragmatism (in using the philosophy of the State purely as a rhetoric for inducing the people to acquiesce in the designs of an élite) or crude mysticism (in genuinely looking upon the power and domination of the State as the ultimate end of social life)?

Perhaps, in view of the fact that the term Purpose is so especially susceptible to dissolution, we should be particularly on the look-out for its covert retention even on occasions where it is overtly eliminated. Thus, I once heard a child of five ask: "What are the hills for?" Hearing such a question today, we spontaneously translate it from teleological to evolutionary terms, so that the child is taught to ask instead: "How do the hills come to be?" But may the teleological intent survive vestigially, beneath the evolutionary style of expression? We have heard much of "repression" in recent decades. May there also

be a kind of "Grammatical repression," as we learn to express ourselves in non-teleological forms, while the experience of purpose is at
the very roots of knowledge: for the first sort of thing a child learns is
that way (indeterminately knowledge and action) whereby its random
sounds and random motions are transformed into the purposive. And
as we later learn to superimpose non-purposive forms of thought, to
what extent might the purposive survive?

It is a difficult problem. On the Rhetorical level, we can discount
language behavioristically by comparing what is said with what is
done. But where we are analyzing language intrinsically, we have
only its own appearances to go by. Hence, we must take an expression at its face value, until its own operations give us cause to do otherwise, by revealing some "perturbation" that can only be explained on
the assumption of some hidden gravitational pull. Meanwhile, we
may recall that we surprised teleological expressions in Darwin, forcing their way through his evolutionism, when he was discussing beauty
as sexual incitement. This indicates at least that the evolutionary
thinking was not quite perfected in this high priest of evolutionism,
so that its symmetry could be impaired when he was on a subject so essentially purposive as the erotic.

At least, even when we would take terms at their face value, we may
at least be admonished always to be on the look-out for those points in
a writer's system at which he fails in his pretensions to outlaw the purposive. When the pentadic functions are so essentially ambiguous,
there is always the possibility that one term may be doing service for
another.

We have noted, for instance, how there is a point at which Mysticism
and Materialism become indistinguishable. Both involve a narrowing of motivational circumference. Materialism accomplishes this by
a deliberate elimination of purpose as a term (except for the fact that
the materialist is quite willing to tell you his purpose for eliminating
purpose). Mysticism arrives at somewhat the same result unintention-
ally, in making purpose absolute, and thereby in effect transforming it
into a fatality. Ironically, motivational schemes that would feature it
less may allow it more.

Modifications of Purpose

Purpose in Aristotle

As against the Mystic absolutism, perhaps the most realistic synonym for purpose is the Aristotelian "happiness" (*eudaimonia*). It stands at a level of generalization next beneath Purpose itself. As Aristotle says in Book I, section 5 of the *Rhetoric*: "Men, individually and in common, nearly all have some aim, in the attainment of which they choose or avoid certain things. This aim, briefly stated, is happiness and its component parts." His whole treatment of the "common places" (or typical hopes, fears, and values upon which the orator draws in seeking to affect his audience) takes shape about this motive. Thus, after listing the components of happiness (such as noble birth, children, wealth, good reputation, good physical condition, influential friends), he next observes that the concern of the deliberative orator is with the expedient. For men deliberate "not about the end, but about the means to the end." And since "the expedient is the good," he next proceeds to enumerate men's notions of the expedient and the good in general, as beliefs to which the orator must appeal if he would be persuasive. The purposive is consistently stressed; he defines the good as "whatever is desirable for its own sake, or for the sake of which we choose something else." And further along: "An end is a good." Next he considers the virtues, having defined virtue generally as "a faculty of providing and preserving good things." And so he proceeds to categorize pleasant and unpleasant things, and just and unjust actions, the entire structure of inducements and deterrents deriving its logic from the fact that it successively breaks down the concept of human aim or end into its components, and thence into the various means that men rightly or wrongly think help or hinder the attainment of this end.

The analysis is anything but "mystical." Indeed, it is wholly realistic, involving the usual Aristotelian concern with action, as when he refers human actions to seven causes (*aitia*): chance, nature, compulsion, habit, reason, anger, and desire—showing how these common-places likewise offer resources for the orator to exploit, or in his selection of metaphor, antithesis, and actualization (we might call it "personalization") as the major stylistic devices of the orator. And often his accounts of human character (as with the traits typical of youth and old age) are so dramatistic as to be purely and simply the recipes for *dramatis personae:* the emboldened youngster, and the timid crotchety oldster, with middle age in the mean between these two extremes. We must certainly give due consideration to the fact that the presence of a strongly purposive *ingredient* in the discussion of human motives is not in itself mystical. On the contrary, it is as realistic as the vocabulary of proverbs. Only when purpose becomes *total* does it fit our prescription for mysticism.

Instruments are considered by Aristotle in teleological terms, as their form is said to be derived from the end desired by their users. With living things, the purpose is said to be immanent in their nature, the plant seeking the life proper to vegetation, the animal adding to the vegetative the life of sensation and appetition, while atop these levels of motives, and including them, is the life of reason and moral action that characterizes man and the human community. Accordingly, his *Politics* is constructed about the purposive, as he asserts that every community is formed for the sake of some good, and that the State, as the most comprehensive community, must aim at the highest good.

Similarly, the *Nichomachean Ethics* begins:

> Every art and every inquiry, and likewise every act and purpose, is thought to aim at some good; hence the good has rightly been called that at which all things aim.

Platonist and Neo-Platonist Purpose

This equating of "good" and "purpose" comes nearer to mysticism in Plato, since he likewise equates the Good with the One. And the Neo-Platonists brought this element to the complete stage of the mystic oxymoron, in their dialectic of the Upward Way, as with Plotinus (*Enneads:* Book I, Tractate 3): "Our journey is to the Good, to the Primal-Principle." The Upward Way is much what Korzybski would call a development to higher and higher levels of generalization, or abstraction, until one comes to the principle of Unity (or the "First"). Then the course is reversed: unity is resolved again into particulars. But the particulars, as considered in the descent, are now infused with the spirit of the "First" at which one arrived in the ascent. In one sense, the First is beyond all merely human comprehension, except in the stage of mystic transcendence. But at other times the Neo-

Platonists permit it to be called the Absolute Good, as the nearest approximation possible to human discourse. From the standpoint of our Grammar, we need but consider it as the absolutizing of the concept of purpose, such a First being a principle of Unity quite as a great variety of things otherwise discordant is promptly brought into unity once they are all felt to serve a common purpose.

Physiology of Mysticism

In *Permanence and Change*, speculating on the purely physiological responses involved in the mystic trance, I suggested that:

> the mystic's state of passivity may be a kind of "assertion *in vacuo*," as were all the conflicting nervous impulses to be called into play at once. For instance, since a muscle is moved by the stimulation of a nerve, any *directed* movement such as a practical act would require, would involve the repression of some other nervous impulse. But if the nerves could be stimulated without the accompaniment of muscular movement, even conflicting nervous impulses could proclaim themselves simultaneously. It is at least a possibility that the pronounced sense of unity to which mystics habitually testify involves in the neurological plane some such condition of "pure action," wherein a kind of dissociation between impulse and movement is established, and all the conflicting kinds of nervous impulse may "glow" at once since they do not lead to overt muscular response. Such a possibility would explain why we could choose either the words *pure action* or *total passivity* to describe the state. And it would explain why the sense of attainment that goes with it would be both complete and non-combative, suggesting a oneness with the universal texture as thorough as that which the organism must have experienced during its period of "larval feeding" in the womb.

In brief, I carried the notion of "incipient action" to the point of suggesting that the sense of unity might come from the fact that, in their ambiguously "incipient" stage, even contrary nervous impulses could exist simultaneously, without the necessity for one to repress the other. I would now add that this would amount to a kind of "total purpose," in a transcendent state of "pre-motion."

Purposiveness in the Negative

On the level of purely intellectualistic generalization, what we have is a process whereby the particulars of the world are generalized in terms of a universal purpose (the "Good"), the Upward Way being a process *towards* this principle; and once it has been proclaimed as principle, all the particulars of the world can be derived from it as causal ancestor, hence sharing "substantially" in its nature (or, in our terms, having the nature of copartners in a universal purpose).

When we have thus contrived to detect the ingredient of purpose in Unity, or Totality, we begin to understand how there can be a Mystical strain in Spinoza's stress upon Oneness and Allness, despite his programmatic denial of Universal Purpose. And at this point we can add, to our synonyms for Purpose, another major term in philosophy: the *negative*, as in the mystical *via negativa* of "negative theology."

On the simplest dialectical level, the "First Principle" (as the highest level of generalization) must be endowed with negative attributes (as "infinite," "incomprehensible," "unending," "incorporeal," etc.), by its very nature as highest level of generalization. For it is particulars that have all the attributes of sense; and in proportion as our generalizations broaden in scope, they lose this sensory nature. Hence, the "First" would be something beyond the description of all human experience; we could only say that it does *not* have color, it does *not* have weight, it does *not* have size or shape, etc.

Spinoza, you will recall, proposed at this point to turn things around, treating Universal Substance as the positive, and considering determinate things, the objects of our experience, (the Modes) as the *negation* of this. Hence, his formula that all determination is negation. Accordingly, the applying of negative terms to God does not indicate that God Himself is negative, but only that the human imagination is unable to transcend the limitations of the senses.

In Bergson's semi-pragmatist, semi-mystical *Creative Evolution* there is a discussion of the negative that can be adapted well to our present speculations. As he states it, it is more scientist than it need be. It *should* be dramatist—and we shall make it over dramatistically. Scientistically, Bergson notes that a negative statement, such as "the ground is not damp," really implies some *positive* condition. The ground isn't in a merely negative state of not being damp; actually it is in some positive state, for instance, dry. In the world of nature, there are no negative conditions, but only positive conditions. The only way whereby one can *not be* at one place is for one to *be* at some other place.

The negative, Bergson says, is a function of *desire,* or *expectation,* or *interest.* If I expect an apple, and you give me an orange, then the thing you have given me is *not* an apple. If I want it to be 32 degrees Fahrenheit, and it actually and positively is some other temperature, I may express this state of affairs by saying that it is *not* 32 degrees; but the description of the real condition, aside from my personal interests in the matter, would involve rather the statement as to what the temperature actually is.

I think this is an extremely suggestive notion. And it fits in with a speculation in Coleridge's *Logic,* where Coleridge explains the turning of the head as a sign of negation by suggesting that the gesture arises as with a child which, expecting to be fed one thing, is fed another, and so turns away to avoid the spoon. I think the explanation is at least true "in principle," and where a people has a different gesture to indicate the negative, as I am told the Finns do, I would look for a somewhat different Grammar of the negative, as I believe the Finns have.

The dramatistic revision I would make in Bergson's speculations is to suggest that the origin of the negative should not be sought in such purely *informational* situations. Coleridge's example comes closer, since it involves an *action.* And so I should expect that the negative would originally be the negative of the Decalogue, not an "it is not," but a "thou shalt not," in brief, a *moral* function rather than a *semantic* function. The negative would thus arise in some such usage as this: for the positive, kill; for the negative, kill, at your peril. It would thus in its origin not have the force of a negative at all, but of some *deterrent* positive state. The suggestion is buttressed by the fact that in both Greek and Latin, verbs suggesting fear, apprehension, misgivings, and the like, require negative forms for the positive state. That is, a form like "I fear he will not come" (*vereor ne veniat*) would mean "I fear *lest* he come." And to mean "I fear he will not come," one would have to say, "I fear he will not not-come" (*vereor ne non veniat*). And in accordance with our usual genealogy, we should expect the original *active* meanings *later* to become transformed for purely informational usages.

Of course, from one point of view, we need not try to uphold so much here. It would seem to be enough if one observes that the concept of the One (=good) supplies a principle of purpose which, as highest generalization, would require statement in negative terms. But we hold that such a genealogy does not do quite well enough by the *act*, which is so closely related to the ethical.   And we have pointed out that, as against a mere pattern of ever widening generalizations, there is also a kind of abstraction got through the terms for action itself, as verbs are abstract at their very start.   (One can make up proper nouns; and demonstrative pronouns like "this" and "that" can be made to serve the same particularizing function; but who ever heard of a "proper verb"?)

And so we are trying to suggest that "negative theology" begins in conceptions of fear and apprehension that lie deeper than the purely "semantic" negative, which is "gnostically" superimposed upon the earlier forms (though the great stress upon the problem of evil in Gnosticism itself reveals the close connection between this abstract "science" and the level of motives prior to the domestication of the negative as an instrument of intellectualistic dialectic).   The equating of the "Good" with Purpose is already a step away from this more fearsome religion.   And we are still farther off, once the negative has taken its place as a semantic short-cut for stating situations in terms of our interests rather than stating on each occasion what the situation is positively—and one will appreciate what a convenience this is, if one tries to decide just what any situation is positively, except for the answer to simple questions like temperature when one is looking at a reliable thermometer.

However, though we have here extended our speculations beyond demonstration, we believe this much at least has been established: That the negative of negative theology is another variant of our term, Purpose. And since "the unconditioned" is synonymous with "the condition of conditions," we may often likewise expect to find a subtly transformed Purpose lurking behind concepts of "Totality" or "allness" (which are but other expressions for the Unity which we have already related to Purpose).

Unity and the Reflexive

As for the experience of mystic unity: note that communion is a *unification*. Such a feeling of unity implies the transcending of a *disunity*. Thus, in considering the *psychology* of mysticism, we find ourselves trying to chart a fluctuant situation in which merger and division keep changing places.   And we are continually encountering aspects of the reflexive, as with works like Melville's *Pierre,* where the mystical pattern is expressed in the imagery of incest and self-abuse. Similarly, William James cites one Xenos Clark, who reported an anaesthetic revelation in which he seemed always just about to catch up with himself, so that, if he were but a fraction of a second sooner, he could have kissed his own lips.

The condition described by Xenos Clark might be accounted for neurologically if we assume that the action of the drug intensified the moment of dissociation between the "higher" brain centres and the "lower" vegetative functions so that the "delayed reaction" between the two levels of experience can itself become an experience, where-upon there would be two selves, separated by an appreciable instant. And I believe that the sense of "eternal recurrence" (or its simpler form, the feeling that "this has happened before") has been explained in such fashion.

But there are more purely Grammatical factors operating here like-wise. In the case of a communion with nature, for instance, such an experience can take place only insofar as nature is in some way felt to be a replica of the self, a mighty self repeated in vast transmogrification, so that a doubling of personality is essential to the situation, as with the doubling of motives we already noted in idioms using the gods as terms for motives. And in accordance with the Spinozist pun on sequence, whereby we can translate a temporal priority into logical terms or a logical priority into terms of historical succession, an *essential* dupli-cation could be conceived as a *temporal* duplication. Hence, as with Nietzsche's moment of ecstatic communion with nature, the translation of this feeling into its cosmic replica would yield the doctrine of eternal recurrence.

Or we might state the matter another way: If the structure of lan-guage is essentially human, then a poet or thinker, having gone from the non-linguistic to its replica in linguistic terms, might finally discover in the essence of language, but this time *through* language, the non-linguistic point of origin. And this too would involve a doubling. To be specific: I have suggested, in *Attitudes Toward History,* that the pattern of the wheel forever turning (in Eliot's *Murder in the Cathe-dral*) duplicates the pattern of Eliot's constant transformation of poet into critic and critic back into poet. And by this interpretation the "dead centre" of this wheel is forever still, because it duplicates the permanent aspect of the self underlying these changes.

In *Little Gidding,* this moment of arrest, necessarily but touched upon in the drama, is lyrically contemplated. The four elements are dialectically opposed to the fifth essence, spirit, as fire to Fire. The Midwinter spring in terms of which the Spirit is introduced, is a kind of *transition made permanent.* Or perhaps we might call it the "essence" of transition in the Santayana sense, a character that in itself would just *be* (an intersection of the timeless moment, at once the mind, England, and nowhere, scenically "never and always").

Shelley's poetry suggests a simpler genesis for the sense of eternal recurrence. In "Alastor," for instance, the poet first wanders on foot. Next, the trancelike state of this "passive being" is repeated, with intensification, as he is carried by a boat through further miraculous regions. Then he comes upon a stream, which he addresses:

> O stream!
> Whose source is inaccessibly profound,
> Whither do thy mysterious waters tend?
> Thou imagest my life.

Whereupon, he follows the course of this stream.

It is not hard to see why such a poet should come upon the doctrine of eternal recurrence. If one takes the imagery in its particulars, merely going from point to point along its course, there is no basic recurrence. But as soon as one considers the *quality* behind the imagery, these passive journeyings are seen to be recurrent. Indeed, the journey along the river of one's own life is perhaps a "journey within a journey," as with the song within a song of Coleridge's "Kubla Khan," or Poe's vision of life as a "Dream Within a Dream," or Ezekiel's vision of the wheel within a wheel. No wonder that such a poet would come upon the doctrine of eternal recurrence (a doctrine the reflexive nature of which is further revealed, in Shelley's case, by his preference for the imagery of incest, which in familial terms involves the communing of the self with a self of the same substance, hence a union of the self with the self).

Mysticism and Idealism: The Self

As we go from Purpose to Unity, and from Unity to Self, we see how Mysticism and Idealism reinforce each other. For Self is, of course, directly under the sign of Agent. But it has the same universalized quality, making it a super-self or non-self, that we noticed in the mystic paradox whereby absolute purpose becomes transformed into necessity. Thus in his chapter on Mysticism, James quotes John Addington Symonds' account of a mystical experience:

> It consisted in a gradual but swiftly progressive obliteration of space, time, sensation, and the multitudinous factors of experience which seem to qualify what we are pleased to call our Self. In proportion as these conditions of ordinary consciousness were subtracted, the sense of an underlying or essential consciousness acquired intensity. At last nothing remained but a pure, absolute, abstract Self. The universe became without form and void of content. But Self persisted.

Reading the passage, we see the Mystical ingredients behind the Kantian system, which is rooted in a similar abstract consciousness (the absolute "I think," or "synthetic unity of apperception"), and which includes as essential to the system the concept of teleology revealed through mechanism. We glimpse the relation to that abstract, anonymous person who is the wanderer of Shelley's poems. Indeed, we might well take the vague journeyings as but the verbal equivalent of a universalized first person pronoun. The kind of super-person thus envisaged *beyond* language but *through* language may be *generically* human rather than *individually* human insofar as language is a *collective* product and the capacity of complex symbolic action is distinctive of the human race. Hence, the Self we encounter at the outer limits of language would be a *transcendent* Self, an individual "collectively redeemed" by being apprehended through a medium itself essentially collective. (The matter is further complicated, however, by the fact that the individual himself is largely a function of this collective medium.)

Images and the "Demonic Trinity"

Images may lead to mystical transcendence of the person in generalizing the concept of role to the point where the realistic or dramatistic notion of people in situations retreats behind the pure lyric of imagistic succession. Here we come upon a kind of "pure" personality to match the absence of role that is characteristic of freedom when complete in either leisure or unemployment.

As for images generally, there is no way of knowing in advance what images may be expected to possess a great degree of purposiveness. In the last analysis, our decisions must wait until we have made a detailed analysis of the equational structure in the particular work. But some images more clearly indicate such possibilities. Thus our expressions "vocation" or "calling" derive from the imagery of a voice calling within. Or one would be justified in looking for the essentially purposive in Meredith where he speaks of certain thoughts as being to the thinker like the striking of a bell. Or the imagery, when half asleep, of a door opening or shutting seems to indicate that one can experience different levels of purpose, felt as we feel the differences of purpose in the different rooms of a house. Or change of scene may indicate purpose in indicating change of motive—and so generally with change of associations or associates. Or imagery of knocking may, as admonitory, indicate an obverse kind of purpose: the deterrent, as similarly with imagery of evil eye. Drought and rainfall, famine and plenty, hunger and feast may contain a dialectic of the purposive. All scapegoats are purposive, in aiming at self-purification by the unburdening of one's sins ritualistically, with the goat as charismatic, as the chosen vessel of iniquity, whereby one can have the experience of punishing in an alienated form the evil which one would otherwise be forced to recognize within.

I believe that I once clearly saw, in a child of eight, an instance of the way in which a purpose on the purely bodily level was first expressed in somewhat transcedent terms, in social and moralistic imagery. He told how he had had a dream of urinating, but had awakened just in time to prevent the potential or incipient action of the dream from attaining its literal translation into the actualities of motion. (Need I say: that isn't exactly how he worded it?) As he was talking, the memory of another dream occurred to him: a dream that he was having a month off from school. When I asked about the order of the dreams, he said the dream of urination had interrupted the dream of the vacation from school. He did not himself use this punning word "vacation"; but even so, is it not obvious that the consciousness of the bodily purpose was first imaged in the morally transcendent guise of a release from the controls of the schoolroom, an image of control natural to his level of experience?

The substantial nature of imagery may often produce an unintended burlesque of substance, in drawing upon the ambiguities of the cloacal, where there are united, in a "demonic trinity," the three principles of the erotic, urinary, and excremental. It is thus with the linking of time, the stream of consciousness, and the river—and with Hopkins' humbled vision of himself as "soft sift/ in an hourglass," following his wreck in saying yes "at lightning and lashed rod." Images from the cloacal sources are basic to the "thinking of the body"; and we may expect their privy nature to complicate the capitalist rationale of private property, where matters of monetary income are prominent among the *pudenda,* the bodily and the financial private thus both participating in the mystically secret. The thoroughness and accuracy of mysticism requires that these basic resistances figure in the reckoning. Is not the Hopkins poem built, for instance, about the transcendence that is got in a poetic transformation that takes us from an ambiguous surrender at "lightning and lashed rod" to a clear haven in the divine "lightning and love" (the reference to bodily wreckage in the first phrase having become translated into the incorporeal security of the second)? The relation between imagery and the "thinking of the body" impinges upon neurosis or psychogenic illness in proportion as the correlation between symbolic action and actual motion becomes total, not stopping with the *incipient* bodily agitations which the behaviorist notes as the condition of thought and which were revealed for Richards while reading of the centipede.

We have already considered why the erotic principle is to be considered as purposive. With the other two principles that compose the "demonic trinity" (with its burlesque of "negative theology") the relation is less clear, though their nature as inevitable bodily compulsions would fit them for this role; and the imagery of pollution by which the mystic frequently expresses the sense of drought (as with Eliot's *"Merdes" in the Cathedral,* an *ecclesia super cloacam*) suggests that mystic thoroughness ultimately involves the recognition of the fundamental tabus at the very moment of their transcendence.

Furthermore, in accordance with the cloacal ambiguities, we should be entitled to expect situations where the image of one member in this trinity may serve vicariously for either of the others. Thus, the imagery of rain might on analysis disclose that, besides its function as a transcendent translation of release (as physiologically conceived in terms of urination) it also had the connotations of erotic purposiveness. Of course, one may learn, on a purely social level, that moisture assists the germination of seeds; and the emotional effects of such knowledge may be considered enough in themselves to account for a poet's equating of rain with fertility. But in considering the Grammatical potentialities along the lines of either behaviorism or Yeats's concern with the "thinking of the body," we come upon the possibilities of a more purely internal route of associations. And in accordance with the logic of this route, rain could do imagistic service for erotic purpose in being a transcendent image of release as fundamentally conceived in terms of urination; and urination in turn would be one with the erotic member of the cloacal (demonic, privy) trinity, hence could do service for erotic purposiveness. Similarly, the "excremental" nature of invective or vilification would allow for a translation of erotic purpose from "love" into "war" (whereupon one writer may "commune" with another in the roundabout way of choosing him as specially favored opponent, antipathetically loading him with verbal offal rather than sympathetically showering him with the garlands of fertility).

Silence and the Hunt

Another purely biological motive involved in mysticism derives from the fact that at the very centre of mobility is the purpose of the hunt. Hence the imagery of the desired as that for which we "hunger," so that the quest for prey can become transformed into the erotic quest. Elsewhere (in *The Philosophy of Literary Form*) we have analyzed the opening speech of the Duke in *Twelfth Night* as a subtle instance of such body-thinking, ending on the pun of "hart" and "heart," as objects of the Duke's quest. And in *Emile* Rousseau reflects the same double motivation when advising the hunt as one stage in Emile's education just prior to his concern with a sexual quest. It is designed to delay this very condition into which it ambiguously leads. So thoroughly is our sense of purpose grounded in the expectation of food, that prolonged conditions of frustration may readily lead to digestive disorders, as with disappointments in business or love.

These biological considerations should also suggest why the mystic *silence* has its roots in the purposive. For in the quest one is naturally silent, be it as the animal stalking its quarry or as the thinker meditating upon an idea. Thus, even the utterance of the question begins in the silence of the quest. And we glimpse the profounder motives behind the Socratic questioning, where the essentially *purposive* is transformed

into the liberally *problematic*.   And so in *Hamlet,* whose bepuzzlement
lapses back into silence ("the rest is silence"), following a dissociation
in the development of the plot as a whole whereby Fortinbras takes over
the role of outward quest, in the forthrightness of his role as warrior.

All told, we may note three aspects of the ineffable.   First there is the
"unspeakable level" to which Korzybski is referring when he would
point to things themselves in an attitude of silence, as possessing
attributes not present in their names.   Tribes which have rites of
"desanctification" reveal, in my opinion, the first "mystical" appreciation of this principle.   For the need to "desanctify" the world is
essentially but an appreciation of the fact that all things possess powers
(and sanctity, divinity, or mana are terms for the designating of such
powers).   And the rites of desanctification are designed to mitigate
the intensity of these powers, as things would otherwise be like highly
charged electric wires without insulation.

Though we usually take such rites as perfect examples of "word
magic," I am trying to suggest that word magic is but the failure to
carry through the original insight.   By this notion, word magic has its
origins, paradoxically, not in a naïve belief in the power of words, but
in man's first systematic *distrust* of words.   It began with the sense of
the *ineffable*.   But there were no opportunities to study the subject, or
even to write down one's speculations for others to examine.   Hence,
the insight was easily lost, and deteriorated into magic, particularly as
men's sense of the ineffable could gradually come to be exploited by
the use of charms, so that the original "classless" quest could be transformed into the quest for class privilege.   Whereupon we got the development of a priestly caste, which by word magic obtained goods for itself and for the nobility with which it became allied.

There is also the ineffability of the visceral processes.   No sensation
can be described to someone who has not experienced a similar sensation.   One cannot describe sight to a man born blind.   But a further
step enters here, when these processes themselves, having participated
in the formation of language, are suddenly discovered to have had a
formative effect upon language, and what we had taken as purely
"rational" statements are seen to retain traces of bodily functioning.
If "beauty," for instance, has habitually been considered wholly alien to
the "cloacal," one may be quite horrified at the sudden perception of
the cloacal beneath concerns that one had thought transcendent.   The

fear that often leads to mystical conversions often derives, I think, from sudden perceptions of this sort; and it can be quite disastrous if the insight occurs prior to the development of the critical method which makes a less agitated contemplation of the problem possible. A writer like Freud deserves the eternal respect of mankind because of the profound imaginativeness and methodical skill by which he widened our powers of such meditation.

A third stage involves what I might call the ineffability of linguistic relations themselves. Any level of conscious explications becomes in a sense but a new level of implications. And there thus comes a point where, lacking the protections of method, one must go no farther. Nor is there any good reason why one should, since the methods of linguistic skepticism have been developed far enough to ground the principles of wonder, resignation, tolerance, and sympathy which are necessary for sound human relations—and what we now most need is to perfect and simplify the ways of admonition, so that men may cease to persecute one another under the promptings of demonic ambition that arise in turn from distortions and misconceptions of purpose. With a few more terms in his vocabulary of motives, for instance, the rabid advocate of racial intolerance could become a mild one; and the mild one would not feel the need to be thus intolerant at all. And so human thought may be directed towards "the purification of war," not perhaps in the hope that war can be eliminated from any organism that, like man, has the motives of combat in his very essence, but in the sense that war can be refined to the point where it would be much more peaceful than the conditions we would now call peace.

The Mystic "Moment"

One more aspect of purpose should be added to our list. We have discussed purpose as equatable with Unity, and as a First. The two may often be the same, yet they are not quite the same. And by noting the distinction between them we can throw some light upon the Grammar of the mystic "moment," the stage of revelation after which all is felt to be different.

Riding in an elevator, has one not sometimes got the feeling that a given floor is a different floor when passed on the way up than when passed again on the way down? At such moments a number, like *ten,* becomes a slovenly misnomer; for it means both *nine plus one* and *eleven minus one,* yet the tenth floor is not the "same experience" when approached from above as it is when approached from below.   And if, of course, some important incident had taken place between the time you ascended in the elevator and the time one descended again, you would feel all the more strongly that *eleven minus one* differed essentially from *nine plus one.*   One would proceed from a different "first" than the other.

As translated into terms of capitalist climbing, there is a place in a movie when Jimmy Durante, in the role of an actor in difficulties, is slighted by another actor who thinks himself slated for success.   Jimmy admonishes: You had better be nice to people you pass on the way up; for you may pass them again on the way down.

And so it is with the dialectical principle of the Upward Way. Beginning with the particulars of the world, and with whatever principle of meaning they are already felt to possess, it proceeds by stages until some level of generalization is reached that one did not originally envisage, whereupon the particulars of the world itself look different, as seen in terms of this "higher vision."   The process itself is ordinary enough.   If you had read novels year after year, for instance, approaching each in itself, for whatever entertainment it might afford you, you might next begin to notice that they fell into types or classes. This would be a new level of generalization; and thereafter, when you turned to another book, instead of seeing it simply in itself, you would see it partly at least in terms of your classifications ("detective story," or "historical novel," or "propaganda novel," etc.).   Your view of novels would thus be modified to the extent that your system of generalizations provided you with a new "principle" (that is, "First") for judging or classing them.

The dialectic of the "Upward Way" would carry this process to completion, by extending one's level of generalization to the point of an "Absolute First," and thereafter considering particulars as pervaded with the spirit of this principle.   It is the *Grammar* of rebirth, which involves a moment wherein some motivating principle is experienced that had not been experienced before.   Usually, this dialectic resource takes the form of a generalization carried to the point of some metaphor or image, after which all particulars are seen in terms of it.   Our discussion of Perspective in *Permanence and Change* illustrates many aspects of the method.

In *The Past Recovered,* where Proust is writing of the various moments in his life that all had the same quality (being all in effect *one* moment, in deriving from the same principle) he says that these many occasions in essence one were like a peacock's tail spread out. And the *purposive* aspect of the motivation is revealed, as he continues:

> I drew enjoyment, not only from these colours, but from a whole moment of my life which had brought them into being and had no doubt been an aspiration towards them.

Experience itself becomes mystical when some accidental event happens to be "representative" of the individual, as when a sequence of circumstances follows exactly the pattern desired by him. Hence the mysticism of gambling, where it is hoped that one's "pure purpose" in the pursuit of money will be in perfect communion with the inexorable decrees of fate. It has been suggested that Dostoevsky's sense of guilt had its origin in the fact that he had secretly desired the death of his father, and so was in a sense a vicarious participant in his father's murder. Since his father's murder took place as the result of causes wholly outside the orbit of Dostoevsky's real actions, it would be wholly an accident so far as the son was concerned. But if the psychoanalytic speculation is correct, the father's death would be a "representative" accident so far as the son was concerned. Similarly, the witches in *Macbeth* were representative of Macbeth's inner temptations, and so were a uniting of internal and external motives, since they were also the embodiment of universal fatality. Criminality, as so conceived, is thus mystical in effecting a mock communion of the criminal with the cosmic motives.

In *Crime and Punishment,* Raskolnikov's murder of the two wretched women is mystical since it is a kind of "absolute" act, conceived independently of its conditions. That is, it was not Raskolnikov's intention simply to kill and rob an old woman. This literal act was "representative" of much deeper motives, conceived absolutely. The nearest he comes to describing the ineffable purpose is in his thoughts on Napoleon and the cult of power. He apparently seeks the essence of power, that is, another variant of pure purpose. So that the murder would be representative; and even if he had been another Napoleon, his career would but have been representative of an underlying essential purpose, as with Napoleon's "communion" with fate in his role as a "man of destiny." Raskolnikov struggles to see the absolute "purity" of his crime over and above the revolting conditions of its actuality. He tries to retain his vision of it as an *ideal* transcending any and all material conditions. And perhaps the most startling burlesque of the communion between inner and outer is conveyed by the contrasting of two situations: his listening, outside the door, to the sounds within just prior to the murder; and his listening inside to the sounds without, just after the murder. An intolerable internality has been imposed upon him by the representative moment of the crime itself.

Crime produces a kind of "oneness with the universe" in leading to a sense of universal persecution whereby all that happens has direct reference to the criminal. There is no "impersonality" in the environment; everything is charged with possibilities. And though this is in one sense a painful condition, it is obviously so full that one can understand why men become habitual criminals, once they have come to conceive of living in these terms. Much of the world that would be otherwise neutral is charged with personal reference, thereby having much the quality that Aristotle asks of a dramatic plot, as when he says in the *Poetics:*

> Even matters of chance seem most marvellous if there is an appearance of design in them; as for instance the man who had been responsible for the death of Mitys was killed by Mitys' statue, which fell on him while he was witnessing a public spectacle. Such incidents seem to have a special significance.

And for the criminal, the whole world is thus purposive, so that the experience of criminal guilt in a sense restores the teleological view lost by evolutionism: Every next person may turn out to be the one who knows of his offence or is in pursuit of him. Conversely, a sense of guilt may lead to crime as its representation; and by such translation, a sense of persecution that might otherwise verge upon the hallucinatory can be made thoroughly real and actual.

Hence, as a kind of fragmentary mysticism, there is a tendency to interpret transgression as the moment that expresses a man's "true self," while his better ways are considered as mere "sublimations" of untoward impulses. The thought suggests that even the writings of our debunkers might be trailed back to an original source in mysticism (though usually we can assume a directer genealogy, with debunking as a state of disillusionment resulting from an oversimplified desire to locate purpose in the Unity of the Good).

Mysticism of Means

The "moment" is related to what follows as the implicit is to the explicit, as the order of cards after the shuffle is to their distribution after the deal, as the seed is to the sprout, and the sprout is to the blossom, and the blossom is to the descendant seed. It is the pattern of thought in the mystic doctrine of the relation between the *deus implicitus* and the *deus explicitus* (as with the pantheistic vision of a god whose unfoldment is the world).

There is thus a pragmatist kind of mysticism in Aldous Huxley's doctrine that impure acts must follow from impure means. For the over-stress upon *purpose* leads readily into an overly pointed consideration of all policies in terms of means and ends alone. That is, the terms scene, act, and agent fall away, as we talk simply of purposes and the agencies proper to these purposes. And as an introduction implicitly contains the developments that follow from it, so a stress upon the means, as introduction implicitly containing the end, gives us in effect the relation between means and ends that we noted in the mystic doctrine of the relation between *deus implicitus* and *deus explicitus*. The means would thus, in a sense, be the ancestor of the end. Hence the quality of the end would be implicit in the quality of the means. Hence, only if the means were "pure" in substance, could the result be "pure."

Huxley relies upon such patterns as an argument for pacifism, holding that only by peaceful means can we get peace. The logical conclusion of this doctrine would seem to be that peace as an end is either impossible or unnecessary. For if we could get peace by peaceful means we'd have peace already; and if we couldn't get it by means somewhat short of peace, then there would be no use in our attempting to get it at all.

All means are necessarily "impure." For besides the properties in them that fit them for the particular use to which they are put, they have other properties (properties that would fit them for other possible uses, including hostile uses). And their identity in themselves (as against their identity from the standpoint of some particular use) thus makes them ambiguous from the standpoint of their possible consequences. That is, there is no one end exclusively implicit in them. And thus, from the standpoint of any given end, they are "impure." And we act by a progressive purification of them.

Indeed, from the "dramatistic" standpoint, it would seem wrong to speak of ends as resulting from means. Or rather, we should be reminded that this is a very truncated statement of the case, which would require us to consider the resources and obstacles of scene and agents, while seeking to formulate a whole *hierarchy* of purposes. Agencies being related to purposes somewhat as motion is related to action, a statement when confined to terms of means and end eliminates "act" as a special locus of motives by treating the act simply as means to an end. In a dramatist perspective, where the connotations of "to act" strategically overlap upon the connotations of "to be," action is not merely a *means of doing* but a *way of being*. And a way of being is substantival, not instrumental.

The distinction is ethically of great importance, as a man may deliberately choose a less "efficient" *means* for doing something because it is "his way" (if he is concerned not merely for the successful outcome of the given operation, but also for its performance in keeping with his "character," or norms of his being). In a society like ours, where the pragmatist vocabulary is current, he will probably justify his resistance on the grounds that the rejected method "will not work." But his tests of its successful working covertly include the requirement that it fit his concepts of individual and tribal identity.

Thus, in objecting to socialism, we in America often pragmatically reduced our criticism to the assertion that it "wouldn't work." And when Russia was invaded by the Hitlerite armies, many of us expected that Russia would collapse within a few weeks. But after the quality of Russian resistance had given a stupendous example of socialism's "workability," our rhetoric shifted to the use of Grammatical ingredients more idealist and realist. We decided that, while socialism could apparently "work" in Russia, it is not the "American way."

The more insistently one presses upon such a view, however, the more it tends to become pure mysticism. The "American way" is offered purely and simply as a *purpose*, our *business pragmatism* having thus been transformed into a mystical nationalism. This purpose will be expressed (*äussert, vermittelt*) through one's communion with his country's economic plant—a participation that will in turn be mediated in terms of money, the pure purpose essential to our culture insofar as it is a capitalist culture. We are admonished, however, that in this imperfect world, no man can be moved by this pure motive alone, but must alloy it with the pre-capitalist, non-capitalist, and post-capitalist concerns that, in their totality, compose his nature as a person.

To illustrate purity of purpose in Christian terms, we may take Thomas à Kempis' *Imitation of Christ,* which represents in a thorough form the dialectic of the Upward Way as transformed into the discipline of Christian monasticism. "In all things behold the end," it is written in the first book—and since the following or imitating of Christ, as the principle of purpose, is equated with "the contemning of the world" as the means toward this end, the typical Christian paradoxes follow: "learn now to die to the world that thou mayst begin to live with Christ"; "the profit of adversity"; to "suffer benignly"; "to be a fool for Christ." The steps are not towards higher levels of generalization, but towards the "innerness of Jesu," a stage attained in the third book, which treats "of inward conversation," "of the inward speaking of Christ unto a soul," where the biological inwardness of the quest has been transcended by linguistic utterance; and this form of socialization becomes in turn transcended by its transformation into internal dialogue, which in its turn is externalized, though with the mark of its internality strong upon it.

Rationalism and the Verbal Medium

Three meanings for rationalism are given in the Baldwin dictionary. It is the theory (1) "that everything in religion is to be rationally explained or else rejected"; (2) "that reason is an independent source of knowledge," and has a "higher authority" than sense-perception: (3) that "certain elementary concepts are to be sought," and "all the remaining content of philosophy is to be derived, in a deductive way, from these fundamental notions."

All three of these positions, you will note, contain the same *methodological* stress. And so the three great exponents of modern rationalism, Descartes, Spinoza, and Leibniz, offered respectively a *Discourse on Method,* an *Ethics* presented *more geometrico* after the analogy of

Euclidean demonstration, and "the idea of a universal logic and language" which should be to philosophy what the calculus was to physics. And whereas these earlier rationalists said that the world is rational, Hegel went as much farther in that direction as is possible by saying that the world is Reason.

In its stress upon method, rationalism stands as a forerunner to pragmatism. But the two become dialectically opposed insofar as empiricism became the opponent of rationalism, and pragmatism has aligned itself with empiricism. Here we seem to have contradicted ourselves in two successive sentences. But I think that by adding a few distinctions we can get matters placed satisfactorily enough.

Pragmatism, like empiricism, was particularly opposed to the Leibnizian procedure whereby, beginning with a few fundamental principles, one could spin a vast metaphysical web, in the way that mathematicians can erect highly complex mathematical systems. Leibniz himself being a great mathematician, one can understand why he would apply to words a method that was to prove so fertile in mathematics. But its application to mathematics could lead to idealizations that assist empiricist research, whereas its application to words led to idealizations that transcended materialist testing, and could in fact become sheer word-spinning.

In such procedures, we might say, the end is implicit in the beginning; all conclusions are foregone conclusions, once we have selected our ancestral principles. And whatever may be the relation between past, present, and future in the world itself, Leibniz certainly characterized the ideal of his own writings about the world in saying that the present summed up the past and implicitly contained the future. That is, he was making an accurate statement about the progression of terms in his own books. Rationalism, as so conceived, clearly reveals its affinities with dramatic structure, as it likewise did in its familial stress upon substance and derivation. And by having its answers in advance, rationalism was felt to injure the development of scientific inquiry.

The issue can never be quite clear, because rationalists themselves have progressively contributed to the critique of rationalism, and did much to establish forms of thought (particularly as regards deference to traditional authority) that aided the cause of scientific induction. And the most empirical of scientists depends, in the last analysis, upon the canons of rationality in organizing and interpreting his experiments.

The issue is made clearer, I think, if we consider Santayana's equating of mathematics and dialectic on the grounds that both exemplify the principle of internal development whereby one can begin with a few basic principles and use them to spin a system out of itself. This would lead us to consider all rationalism as essentially dialectical. But we should consider pragmatism and empiricism as likewise instances of the dialectical. And we should distinguish between the typically rationalist dialectic and the typically empiricist dialectic by noting that each features voices neglected by the other.

From the dialectical point of view, for instance, there is nothing "anti-rationalist" in the empiricist position. In accordance with something so thoroughly rationalist or dialectical as the scene-act ratio, we might well expect new experimental conditions to reveal new kinds of behavior. The framing of experiments becomes the translating of our questions into terms that permit inanimate conditions to give intelligible answers. In strict accordance with dialectical principles, we may expect that the laws we discover will "transcend" previous laws, in proportion as the new conditions differ from previous conditions. And *furthermore*, as a corrective on empiricism, we shall be reminded that *our instruments are but structures of terms, and hence must be expected to manifest the nature of terms*. That is, we must always be admonished to remember, not that an experiment flatly and simply reveals *reality*, but rather that it *reveals only such reality as is capable of being revealed by this particular kind of terminology*.

We consider the present venture rationalistic in this dialectical sense. We believe that an explicit approach to language as a dialectical structure admonishes us both what to look for and what to look out for, as regards the ways of symbolic action (and no statement about motives can ever be anything other than symbolic action). The project is also rationalist in seeking, by a rationale of language, to chart methodically the "non-rational" and "irrational" aspects of language (here following that kind of rationalism so superbly developed by a great modern dialectician, Sigmund Freud).

So, either rationalistically or dialectically, we have been spinning five terms into a book, by making their implications explicit. Our analysis itself is empiricist in that it must recognize the respects in which every linguistic structure is a "new thing." It is empiricist in that it must approach experimentally the ultimate problem of the relation between symbolic action and practical conduct. Yet it never permits us to forget that empiricism does not transcend the limitations of vocabulary, but is an especially poignant illustration of such limitations.

Aiming always at reduction, it must admonish continually against the dangers of reduction. Aiming at reduction in a capitalist economy, it must pay particular attention to the rationalism of money. For money provides the reduced circumference of rationality that distinguishes the state of modern enlightenment. It affords a position in terms of which we can transcend the earlier, more personalistic or dramatistic vocabularies of motivation. Yet we can dialectically adopt the terms of these other positions to aid us in seeing beyond the structure of monetary motivations which we might otherwise tend to interpret, not as a *kind* of reality, but as "reality" itself.

But however impersonal may be the relations brought about by the high development of a monetary economy, money itself in its role as a medium or agency contains the humanistic or the personalistic ingredients that we have discerned at the very source of agency. The "inhumanity" of finance, like the "inhumanity" of factory speed-up or technological war, is a peculiarly human invention. Money is essentially "humanitarian," its parable in this respect being the coin tossed to the leper; for it possesses that humanitarian ambiguity whereby one can, through financial charity, give aid to those whom one could not possibly bring oneself to touch in directly personal ministrations. It possesses thus the ambiguity of the attitude, the incipient act.

Putting together what we have said about delayed action, mystic purpose, and the representative moment, may we not see in the withholding (or "postponed consumption") of capitalist investment, the dialectical "moment" of delay translated into capitalist terms, and so drawn out into a long history? Or conversely, since one who invests his money in a title accepts a symbolic instrument in lieu of material goods or services, we could call it an "incipient act" of consumption; and the experience of investment could be said to find in the theory of the delayed or incipient action its corresponding "representative moment."

In its role as symbolic action, investment contrived remarkably to merge principles that must usually be antagonistic to each other: the principles of sacrifice and acquisition. For one denies himself to the extent that he does not consume his bounty in the present, but transforms it into purely promissory, futuristic titles. But we should always remember that this view of money is a much better fit for one stage of capitalism than it is for another. It is particularly serviceable when the economic situation calls for the upbuilding of the primary economic plant, the mills, mines, railroads, and the like which, in their stage of formation, bring denials rather than satisfactions to wide areas of the population. It is a stage of upbuilding that once prevailed during the Puritan upbuilding of capitalism. And we have witnessed it again in the last twenty years of Russia, where the people necessarily acquired little for themselves as individual consumers, while expending their efforts upon the national structure of production, transportation, and defense. But insofar as the basic economic plant is developed, the need becomes rather for consumption than for postponed consumption (though consumption for military purposes rather than consumption of "consumer goods" can postpone the obligations of this condition, which has previously proved so embarrassing to the manipulations of capitalist symbolism).

It is hard to know just what has taken place, in proportion as the motives of guilt and retribution attained "enlightened" secular translation in terms of debt, credit, wages, profit, and the like. The rise of psychoanalysis is, however, clear evidence in itself that men are unequal to the monetary vocabulary of motives in its purity, but can use it only as one might mark his course by a thread through a labyrinth. Even at times when religious symbolism flourished, the basic processes of human psychology were often stated in monetary terms. But in proportion as the monetary terms have become the central vocabulary of motives, not figurative, but public "reality" itself, we may have to read the earlier religious monetary metaphors in a different spirit, using them now rather as passages that indicate to us the possible "overtones" of money which the rationale of accountancy itself must leave out of account. That is, we may find earlier statements where religious concepts of guilt and redemption were explicitly expressed in monetary terms; and we may now examine these for the light they throw upon the patterns of guilt and redemption that may be unexpressed but implicit in our present "rationalist" use of the terms for monetary motivation.

Consider, for instance, the resonance of this citation from St. Ambrose, which we found in a Catholic Catechism:

> The devil had reduced the human race to a perpetual captivity, a cruel usury laid on a guilty inheritance whose debt-burdened progenitor had transmitted it to his posterity by a succession drained by usury. The Lord Jesus came; He offered His own death as a ransom for the death of all; He shed His own Blood for the blood of all.

The complexity of ways in which money, property, the familial, the universal, and the vicarious are interwoven in this passage, with an underlying pre-monetary psychology of personal barter, suggests a whole thesaurus of subtleties in human relationship. Do we not see, here united in a religious view of atonement, the two strands that eventually became dissociated into the rationale of accountancy on the one hand, and on the other the psychoanalytic study of "irrational" guilt?

Revolutionaries often think that their particular revolutions (such as those of capitalism or socialism, or the counter-revolutions that would restore dictators ruling in the name of the Church) can omit one or another aspect of our motivational complexity. The other possibility is that men are "Catholic," "Protestant," and "Scientist," all three in one, though historical conditions at one time or another in their history may induce them to stress one at the expense of the other two. Or, as regards the Big Three in their most abstract forms, men conceive of their world primarily in a dialectic composed of three voices: "Catholic" act, "Protestant" agent, "Scientist" scene. And lying across the three, indeterminately Agent or Purpose, are the various kinds of moneys, or counters, or *symbols* of wealth that have, in the changing situations of history, simultaneously performed both socializing and individualizing functions, and have contributed their terms as voices in the total dialectic by which we develop our vision of reality. In its teleological nature as means and end, money is a direction that greatly multiplies the ways of indirection.

In closing, note that the psychoanalytic concept of *repression* is the *reciprocal* of purpose. If purpose is the cameo, repression is the intaglio. It is a kind of "negative purpose." Consider our notion that the religious vocabulary of motives splits into the material of accountancy on the "rational" side and the material of psychoanalysis on the "irrational" side. Recall also our remarks on negative theology as purposive, centering dramatistically in the God of "thou shalt not." And recall that the "dying life" of the *Imitation* is that of a purpose got by transforming the prohibitions against wordly aims, so negating the negativity of the Commandments as to make them into a positive purpose. Recall also our suggestion that Korzybski recognizes the same principle of transcendence as is found in Plato, except that Plato would say "good" where Korzybski would say "alas!" Do not all these parts all fit together? For "repression" would be "purpose" rephrased in terms of post-Christian liberalism (the liberalism of the "freedman" rather than the liberalism of the ruler). And psychoanalysis would be a secular variant of negative theology, though with an important reversal of attitude whereby the elations of the "dying life" may be looked upon as manifestations of a "death impulse," rather than as a transcending of the worldly. For all the talk of "mechanism" in the Freudian psychology, we may see its underlying dramatistic nature. And we may note that the Freudian system is as fully organized about the concept of the purposive as Aristotle, though adding momentously to our understanding of the dialectic laws whereby the purposive can become moralistically transformed into its negation, with corresponding "sublimations" and "compulsions."

Means and Ends of This Grammar

Our five terms are "transcendental" rather than formal (and are to this extent Kantian) in being categories which human thought necessarily exemplifies. Instead of calling them the necessary "forms of experience," however, we should call them the necessary "forms of *talk about* experience." For our concern is primarily with the analysis of *language* rather than with the analysis of *"reality."* Language being essentially human, we would view human relations in terms of the linguistic instrument. Not mere "consciousness of abstracting," but *consciousness of linguistic action generally,* is needed if men are to temper the absurd ambitions that have their source in faulty terminologies. Only by such means can we hope to bring ourselves to be content with humbler satisfactions, looking upon the cult of empire as a sickness, be that empire either political or financial.

Not that we should avoid the problems of "global" order. On the contrary, we must turn precisely in the direction of a neo-Stoic cosmopolitanism, with ideals of tolerance and resignation to the bureaucratic requirements implicit in the structure of modern industry and commerce. The only alternatives are fanaticism and dissipation. By fanaticism I mean the effort to impose one doctrine of motives abruptly upon a world composed of many different motivational situations. By dissipation I mean the isolationist tendency to surrender, as one finds the issues of world adjustment so complex that he merely turns to the satisfactions nearest at hand, living morally and intellectually from hand to mouth, buying as much as one can buy with as much as one can earn, or selling as much as one can sell, or in general taking whatever opportunities of gratification or advancement happen to present themselves and letting all else take care of itself.

This temptation is always with us, partly because sound common sense admonishes that we should not burden ourselves with problems beyond our powers, partly because this piecemeal approach to life represents to an extent the very attitude of humility that we should seek to cultivate, and partly because it is our inheritance from the days when we were taught that the conditions of the market automatically solved the problems of social welfare, if we but put ourselves wholly and trustingly in the market's hands, as though its workings were a kind of automatic Providence invented by man at God's instigation, so that men could turn from Him to it when seeking motivational guidance.

But do we not rather need both an *attitude* and a *method* of wider scope? The attitude itself would be grounded in the systematic development of the method. The method would involve the explicit study of language as the "critical moment" at which human motives take form, since a linguistic factor at every point in human experience complicates and to some extent transcends the purely biological aspects of motivation. The attitude would be mildly that of "hypochondriasis," a kind of "cultural valetudinarianism," which recognizes that the school of ideas is divisible into both a gymnastic of ideas and a clinic of ideas, and which would assist health by aiming always at the first without forgetting the claims of the second. It would rate men's ability individually and collectively to "keep in trim" as immeasurably higher than the naively perverted religiosity that characterizes our devotion to the ways and means of acquisition.

It would find human foibles a theme for constant contemplation. But it would not make the mistake of thinking that the lore of human foibles stops with the depicting of different personal types in fictions. There is also the *categorized* lore of human foibles, as we find it expressed in proverbs or in moral philosophy. Generalizations about human ways are as essentially humanistic as is the depicting of some particular person acting in some particular way; and they are needed to complete the act of humanistic contemplation. And all this comes to a head in the contemplation of men's linguistic foibles, which can so drastically transform their ways of life.

Remember always that no modern instrument could have been invented, or could be produced, without the use of a vast linguistic complexity. A traffic signal seems very simple, but its production, distribution, and operation requires a set of interlocking linguistic acts that would require a century to trace in their particularity. If we are not to be lost in such a maze of particulars, we must build from the essential humanity of dramatist or dialectic lore in general, considering it as central to the contemplation of the human tragi-comedy.

This work (which would have as its motto *Ad Bellum Purificandum*, or Towards the Purification of War) is constructed on the belief that, whereas an *attitude* of humanistic contemplation is in itself more important by far than any *method*, only by method could it be given the body necessary for its existence even as an attitude. We would thus hold at least that an elaborate analysis of linguistic foibles is justified "in principle." Indeed, the study of linguistic action is but beginning. And we must be on our guard lest the great need for an *attitude* of linguistic skepticism allow us to be content with too hasty a "policy" as regards the nature of language itself. This is too serious a matter for such "dissipatory" approaches to the subject as we find among the contemporary "debunkers." And even serious approaches are invalidated when formed in keeping with the ideals of an uncriticized scientism, which is *too evasive of the dramatistic to make even an adequate preparatory description* of linguistic forms. To contemplate our subject, we must have a terministic equipment that lends itself to such contemplation. Otherwise one has a *principle of aversion* implicit in the very nature of his investigation, as if one hoped to see accurately by partially averting one's gaze. There may be true and false transcendences in language. Or for the sake of the argument, if you will, they are all false. But in any case they *are* transcendences. And we must begin by taking some delight in the contemplation of them as such. By the use of dialectical resources, we shape the versions of human motives that have so greatly much to do with our individual actions and our relations to one another.

Questions of motivation come to a head in questions of substantiation and transubstantiation. And so, in Part III of this book, we shall deal with the dialectic of these two processes. We shall take as our text for substantiation, the theory of Constitutions. And we shall consider transubstantiation as the representative moment of dialectic in general.

PART THREE

ON DIALECTIC

I

THE DIALECTIC OF CONSTITUTIONS

Necessity for Representative Case

THIS closing section is to deal with matters of substance and enactment as they apply to *Constitutions* (another of our Stance words; from
con and *statuere*, to place, set—which is in turn related to *stare*, stand).
It will revolve about the subject of Constitutional principles (or ideals,
or wishes). It will consider the bearing of these principles, or wishes,
upon judicial tactics in the reviewing of legislative enactments. It will
trace the relation between Constitutional principles and the patterns of
litigation. And it will show how the grammar of Constitutional
wishes relates to the rhetoric of political manifestoes and promises (such
as we get in election platforms or a declaration of war aims).

A book On Human Relations being, by the nature of its subject,
to a large extent "idealistic" (since such a book should feature
the relationships typical of *agents*), it is obvious that our analytic instruments must be shaped in conformity with representative idealist
anecdotes. Otherwise the analysis can but lead to misrepresentation.
And such a work, in aiming above all at a set of sub-terms generally
classifiable under the heading of the generic term, *agent*, should be
"idealistic," at least in the sense that it should contribute to the *critique*
of idealism. And a Constitution would be an "idealistic anecdote" in
that its structure is an enactment of human wills.

Originally, I had intended to begin this work with my material on
"The Constitutional Wish," designed as introduction to my material
on rhetorical strategies and symbolic acts. It was to offer a kind of
preparatory groundwork, something "substantial" as a solid point of
departure—for what could be more basic, more "laid down," than the
law? However, I began to realize that this introduction needed in
turn a pre-introduction, to explain exactly why I thought I should begin a study of *human* relations with a study of *constitutional* relations.
And out of this grew a long "Introduction—Concerning Introduc-

tions," in which we considered the problem of a representative anecdote. That is, if one does not select a *representative* anecdote as an introductory form, in conformity with which to select and shape his terms
of analysis, one cannot expect to get representative terms.

To cite from those mostly discarded pages: "One should seek to select,
as representative anecdote, something sufficiently demarcated in character to make analysis possible, yet sufficiently complex in character to
prevent the use of too few terms in one's description (or too few coördinates in one's location, or too few faculties in one's university)."
Elsewhere: "The best example of human relations *in parvo* we could
get would be one having a form sufficiently clear to be contemplated,
yet sufficiently complex to defy simplist description." And: "If you
don't select one that is representative in a good sense, it will function
as representative in a bad sense." (Here we had in mind naturalistic
or simplist anecdotes of one sort or another, such as laboratory experiments with the conditioning of animals, treated as *point de départ* for
the construction of a rudimentary terminology to which complex instances may be "reduced." For if much of service has been got by
following Occam's law to the effect that "entities should not be *multiplied* beyond necessity," equally much of disservice has arisen through
ignoring a contrary law, which we could phrase correspondingly: "entities should not be *reduced* beyond necessity.") And we showed no
great respect for such tactics as those of the materialist who, after telling you, for instance, that "everything is nothing but chemistry," will at
some strategic point advise, "accordingly, let us do such-and-such."
We should consider this as evidence that the speaker had derived his
position from an unhappy choice of anecdote, since one would not
seek to affect the behavior of a chemical by an exhortation—and if he
does believe that effects can be got by exhortation, then he must select
such an anecdote as assists the development of terms for the analysis
of exhortation as such. We, on the contrary, held that, for the analysis of human relations "an idiom should be developed by forming
itself about some anecdote *summational* in character, some anecdote
wherein human relations grandly converge." And one must grant
that a Constitution is summational and converging, yet lends itself to
contemplation as fully as does the statuesque.

I need not detail here the suspense we imposed upon ourselves in
considering and discarding various kinds of anecdote, as a preparation

for our patriotic selection. We dared commend ourselves: "Let the reader grant this in our favor: that in featuring the Constitution as the model for our idiom, we shall have grounded a book On Human Relations upon the very Constitution of our country—and what social philosophy could be more thorough in its patriotism?" It should be enough to note that I treated the anecdote as containing implicitly what the analysis would draw out explicitly—for insofar as one really did form his terms consistently about some "case" he considered typical of his subject, the level of the analysis could rise no higher than the level of the terms. But certain broad considerations underlying the problem of selection should be mentioned, since they cast more light on the motivational grammar.

The Two Circles

First, we rejected "metonymic" anecdotes. That is, considering notions of mind-body parallelism, according to which a given state in consciousness has its corresponding physical state, we rejected the tactics of pure behaviorism which would treat the realm of consciousness in purely physicalist terms. Rather, we held that the relation between these two "parallel" realms should be considered as that between two concentric circles, one of them having a much wider orbit than the other ("consciousness," that is, being related to "matter" as the larger of two concentric circles is related to the smaller).

It is the design one should always have in mind when considering the dialectic of Coleridge. Thus, for him, "understanding" would be a narrower term than "reason": it would in fact be but an aspect of reason, one of its idioms (as "logical argumentation," let us say, would be but a restricted form of "wisdom," or as "technology" or "laboratory method" would be narrower than "science," or as "routine" would be narrower than "method"). In Chapter XXII of the *Biographia,* Coleridge himself uses the figure, observing that "truth and prudence may be imagined as concentric circles."

Obviously, in accordance with our previous remarks on the nature of dialectical counterparts, two realms thus related (as concentric circles greatly differing in circumference) could be treated as being either in apposition or in opposition (as either consistent or compensatory counterparts)—and in Coleridge you will find a shifting between the two usages, though as a general rule his idealistic preferences lead him to treat the smaller circle as a misrepresentation of the larger. We likewise hold that an anecdote, to be truly representative, must be synecdochic rather than metonymic; or, in other words, it must be a *part for the whole* rather than a *reduction of the mental to the physical*. (For more on the distinction between metonymic reduction and synecdochic representation the reader is referred to our article on "The Four Master Tropes," in the appendix of this book.) Thus, if our theme were "communication," we should seek to form our terms about some typical instance of communication, rather than selecting some purely physical mode, as a highway system or telegraphic network.

Terminal as Anecdote

Since we were looking for an anecdote where relations "grandly converge," we did actually consider, as a metonymic anecdote which we set up to be discarded in favor of the Constitution, the example of a railway terminal. The name, "Grand Central," may have secretly moved us to hit upon the expression "grandly converge." And in meditating upon a *terminal* we were certainly quite close to the problem of *terms*. Indeed, this is no mere matter of puns. For instance, we once witnessed, in the most obvious physicalist sense, a representation of walking got by the use of six terms (*termini,* terminals). Six different wires, recording pressures at six different spots on the underside of the foot, were connected with an electrical contrivance that made a graph of these pressures as they were modified in the process of walking. Thus, the "representation" of walking (or more accurately in this case, the "reduction" of walking) as it showed on the graph depended entirely upon the selection of these "terms" and the logic of their interrelationship. Select different "terms" (a different number of them, or differently distributed so that they terminate at different points) and you get a correspondingly different record of the walking process itself. Indeed, judged as a "representation" of walking, the graph derived from the six electric *termini* was a pretty dismal one; however, it was serviceable enough as a purely pragmatic "reduction" of walking, made for comparative purposes (i.e., for comparing the graphs of different gaits, as thus reduced). And though such reductions would have little value as representations of walking, in the sense that Rodin's *Man Walking* might, or even in the sense of Duchamp's *Nude Descending a Staircase,* they might serve well for diagnosing different types of illness or temperament as revealed by different types of gait.

A railway terminal, as our basic anecdote, would have had some value as parable, in reminding us to include dialectical complexities. For with such an example before us, we quickly recognize that great mobility here requires great fixity, since traffic must be coördinated, and this coördination is got by such relatively motionless things as routes, schedules, continuity of personnel, bookkeeping routines and filing systems—while all these set ways would in turn depend upon set ways (the schedules upon the standardizations of the calendar, the personnel upon familistic institutions, and the symbols of accountancy upon a distinct educational pattern). And though much of a man's participation in the patterns of exchange may not be intrinsically interesting, he may find it reasonable to spend his life at such work because of the money it brings him, money in turn found reasonable because of the many organizations whereby the general set of promises, implicit in the money, may be redeemed—quite as, when you drop a coin in one particular kind of slot machine, it will according to its kind yield you certain goods.

All such considerations quickly invite us to develop a highly ramified vocabulary (which would be quite complex, even if we insisted, as materialists, upon deriving all the phenomena of the wider circle, or "ideological superstructure," from the narrower circle, or "economic substructure," as its causal ancestor). But the one great technical advantage of physicalist reduction, its readily observable form, would be lacking, since we are so soon carried beyond the acts of physical routing and exchange. Thus, the clarity of the metonymy would be gone, as we vaguely glimpse an interwovenness of traditions, needs, and expectancies that could not be located in the idiom of our chosen anecdote at all, but would simply lie outside its orbit, and could only be treated bluntly as "complicating factors" (or as "epicycles," to employ the term that Ptolemaic astronomers used for the planetary movements that could not be located integrally until the system of Copernicus).

Representativeness of Total War

And holding that the same sort of objection would apply to all metonymic reductions, we turned to inquire whether we could find "some representative public enactment, to which all members of a given social body variously but commonly subscribe." We required something representative synecdochically (as a part that can stand for the whole). Nor could atomistic reductions serve, for it is the strategy of atomism to reduce the complex to the simple, and the simple cannot be properly said to represent the complex. We wanted a representative part in the sense that the expression about the eyes and mouth of a man could not be called either the totality of the man or the "atomic building-blocks" of which he is constructed, and yet may be said to sum up what he stands for. In primitive communities, for instance, we might have found such a moment of convergence in tribal festivals that were felt by all of the participants to have an integral bearing upon the welfare of the tribe. Such would be totemic rites, symbolic enactments proclaiming group identity, designed to aid success in hunt and war, fertility of crops and women, the exorcising of evil—group modes of invocation and thanksgiving. Obviously, an anecdote of this sort would directly bear upon many elements beyond the materials and conditions of the economic, yet the economic ingredient could not be denied as an important aspect of the total recipe. In the Christian tradition at its heyday, before industrialism had so greatly increased the kinds and number of commodities and the impersonality of their production (stimulating the revolution from intimate, familistic thought in terms of gift and sacrifice, to a more abstract and "enlightened" thought in terms of buying and selling) we might have looked for the focus of public enactment in the communion service.

Unfortunately, in the modern state, with its great diversity of interests and opinions, due to the dispersion of technological and commercial enterprise, the act that comes closest to the totality of tribal festivals and the agape is the act of war. But modern war ("total war") itself is so complex, that we could hardly use it as our representative anecdote until we had selected some moment within war to serve in turn as representative of war. "Modern war in general" would be unwieldy as an anecdote, since it is more of a *confusion* than a *form*.

Our scruples about the tactics of beginnings suggested a still more serious objection. For if we took war as an anecdote, then in obeying the genius of this anecdote and shaping an idiom accordingly, we should be proclaiming war as the essence of human relations. And that choice is too drastic to be taken unless absolutely necessary. Of course, we might take it as our start, with the intention of promptly asserting our independence by abandoning it. But in that case, it would not really be our representative anecdote at all.

However, we couldn't triumph so easily. There may be the most admirable of scruples behind the selection of war as key anecdote. For one thing, if it is the culminative we want, we must grant that war draws things to a head as thoroughly as a suppurating abscess, and is usually, like revolution, the dramatic moment of explosion after an infinity of minute preparatory charges. Being a crisis, it helps criticism. And we must grant the proportion of war in all forms of theoretical or practical enterprises. In fact, when Heraclitus offered "Strife" and "War" as synonyms for his Universal Fire (proclaiming it the causal ancestor and magistrate, "father and king," of all things), was he not but saying, in a forceful way, that history is "dialectical," developing by the give and take of combat? And his very words for War and Strife survive as words for the dialectic in its more agonistic aspects: "polemic" and "eristic."

When Heraclitus proclaimed that "everything flows," he offered an over-all paradigmatic anecdote in terms of which, as a title, all human histories could be grouped. His dictum was a dramatic way of saying: "The principal or ancestral term needed for the characterization of experience is 'change'." His fluent "fire" was itself a kind of irreducible substrate (we could call it the *permanence* of change), an unchanging title or essence for classifying under a single head all kinds of physical combustion, sentimental warmth, emotional fieriness, and logical glow. And when he also tells us that his essential fire is a kind of universal currency or medium whereby "all things are changed for fire and fire for all things as goods for gold and gold for goods," we may recall our passing comments on the relation between doctrinal and monetary currencies; and we may wonder whether, in thus interpreting money in terms of its *mediatory* properties rather than its *competitive* properties, his conception of an essential "fire" like money might also have had, among its motivational attributes, that of celebrating the life of trade.

Such thoughts might justify us in looking for the militarist core in all historic converse, even during times of peace. Whereupon, we had all the more reason for featuring war as an idiom of reduction, in such times, when war was necessarily at the height of a thinker's fashion; and even while our country was still supposedly at peace, we had thousands and thousands of prisoners held in concentration camps (permanent ones: made of granite and steel, like vaults; i.e., our prisons).[13]

The Constitution and the Admonitory

Accordingly, there is a second sense in which war might figure as our introductory. When there is much preparation being made *for* war, we might at least aim to prepare with equal zest *against* it. And war would be as much our idiom in the second case as in the first, except that in the second case war would not be used primarily as a *constitutive* anecdote but rather an an *admonitory* anecdote. That is, an anecdote shaped about war would be designed not so much for stating what mankind *substantially is* as for emphatically pointing out what mankind is *in danger of becoming*.

Where war is used as a constitutive anecdote, the characteristic pattern of thinking would be (with the shadings and transitions omitted): "The universe is substantially war; hence the acts of men, being qualified by the quality of the universal scene, are substantially war; this gamut of war ranges from its attenuated form, in business competition and forensic, to its 'pure' expression in hunt, rape, rapine, and battle."

An attenuated variant of the idiom runs thus: "Men have developed from a competitive situation in nature; hence they are naturally competitive; but their essential competitiveness may, by various economic and/or psychological transformations, be sublimated into coöperation."

---

[13] This passage was originally written before our country was at war. "Concentration camps" here refers figuratively to our "normal" prison population in peace times.

It is an enlightened survival from the recipe of original sin, after having lost many of the ingredients that modified the notion of original sin. But it does have a certain medicinal kind of humanitarianism, as it contends, in effect: "If we begin by saying the very worst thing possible about mankind, we shall have grounds for expecting something better." For if you call all men crooks, you may look for a margin of honesty, insofar as men must fall short of the ideal state of perfect crookedness.

It is often difficult to tell whether this humanitarian pattern is constitutive or admonitory. Where it is constitutive, we repeat that it should not be accepted unless no better idiom could be found. Thus, the reader may for the time being accept it, since we have admittedly not as yet offered a satisfactory alternative. But where it is admonitory, we should note two objections: (1) whatever its serviceability as an idiom of reduction for purposes of moralistic pamphleteering, it cannot be considered as representative, since it has not been concerned with the central problem of representation, and an anecdote about *what one may become* is hardly the most direct way of discussing *what one is*. And (2) it may be doubted whether a purely admonitory idiom can serve even the deterrent role for which it is designed; for it creates nothing but the image of the enemy, and if men are to make themselves over in the image of the imagery, what other call but that of the enemy is there for them to answer?

Thus, many doctrines of "progress," while unable despite their futuristic cast to locate our substance now in terms of any future substance beyond a vague commingling of euphoria, anaesthesia, and euthanasia, were zestful in building up an admonitory image of our warlike past. This they got by tracing our causal ancestry back to mechanism, accident, and the Jungle (the Jungle in turn being conceived in the idiom of our pure competition—an overemphasis that any inspection of the ecological balances in nature might have dispelled, had it not been that our ecologists themselves were trying to ground a few simple theories of small business not merely in the Constitution of the United States but in the very Constitution of the Universe). But all told, we observe the paradox that these doctrines of progress contributed their part to usher *in* precisely the gloom they thought they were ushering *out*. For the only substance represented with any fullness in their statements was that of the warlike past—and so, what we were admonished *against* was just about the only tangible thing there for us to *be*.

Peace: Constitutive or Directive?

The idiom most thoroughly bound to the militaristic starting-point, however, is the one that might seem to be freest of it: pacifism, where the admonition against the threat of absolute *warlike* substance is replaced by the exhortation towards the promise of absolute peacelike substance. An ideal of peace is reasonable enough as a directive, counter to the presence or imminence of war. But the whole matter is over too soon, if we would attempt to treat purely pacifistic coördinates as an idiom of reduction for the location and representation of actual human relations in history. You may, if you will, imagine a spectrum with absolute war at one end and absolute peace at the other, and with all acts in time considered to be lying somewhere along the intervening series of gradations, according to the varying proportions of the two ingredients. But this alone would be too thorough a mode of reduction to represent the many colors of action as they are realistically experienced. The hortatory idiom, like the admonitory idiom, is too *futuristic* for the representation of what secularly *is*. It does nobly what the investor does ignobly, who cannot see a thing in terms of what it yields him as he looks at it, but can see it only in terms of what it might yield him later. In the investor's case, this is of course a financially profitable way of being ungrateful.

And it is mildly so in the case of all futurists, except the Great Futurist, which is a special case, as we were there given a monument, a Great Pacifist Manifesto necessary as commemorative source, a thing stylistically beautiful for what it *is* and not, like a formula, solely for what use it may be put to. Also, the potential, the ideal future, was there proclaimed to be *the very substance of the present* (the Kingdom of Heaven *is* within you)—so that, from the most exactingly visionary point of view, this was not a mere exhortation about what *might be,* but a statement about what *now is* (a statement which, if not lie or irony, is possible only to an author essentially and exceptionally peaceful).

The ideal future was "within," and *now*—the present itself was thus substantially the future; so the Great Pacifist Manifesto was not purely hortatory futurism, as with the pacifist who would consider peace as a *directive for existence* rather than as *mandatory for being*. In Christ's poetry, peace was a substance, *the* substance—and only insofar as one was consubstantial with it was he truly alive. But in the ordinary brands of pacifism, peace is but an ideal, a general direction towards which one should incline when plotting a course—and as evidence that it is not a statement about what *substantially is,* recall that it could be added to any number of statements about substance, thus:

Men are essentially fools
or
Men are essentially crooks
or
Men are essentially automata   } But let's
or   have peace
Men are essentially fighters
or
Men are essentially (suit yourself)

"Peace" here is not an integral-part-of; it is an annex-to. The two statements are not related as axiom and corollary, they are merely juxtaposed like the planks in a political platform.

Futurism: Religious and Secular

In a sense, the doctrine of the Great Futurism had so absorbed futurism that it was much less futuristic than the typical secular variants of the doctrine: all those ways, in the pragmatism and Puritanism of science and business, whereby one *clothes onself* in the severe promises of future yield, *donning* the idealizations of what one would like to be, *dressing up* in the symbols of lien and bond (we mean: *"investing"*). And we must watch this distinction between the directive and the substantial, since there are very fatal moments in human decision that radically alter our notions of purpose precisely because the role of the future is allowed to usurp the role of the present—an illicit substitution that takes place when the ideal is treated as the substantial, or the directive is treated as the mandatory, or the quantity of promises in the wage is treated as a scale to rate the rationality of the act (the last being a particularly crucial moment for industrial capitalism, which requires the expenditure of tremendous effort on work that is intrinsically worthless, and hence would be totally irrational except as tested futuristically, by the promissory nature of pay-day).

We might bring out the contrast in doctrinal tactics between religious futurism and secular futurism thus: Whereas both would merge present and future, religious futurism does so by reducing the future to the present, whereas secular futurism reduces the present to the future. That is, the religious tactic says: Find what now *is* within you, and you have found what will be. The secular tactic says: Find what will bring you promises, and you have found what is worth doing now. Seeing the future in terms of the present, as against seeing the present in terms of the future, has at least this one advantage: that the present *forever is,* whereas the future *forever is not.* The ontological style of religion, as contrasted with the futuristic (admonitory of hortatory) style of naturalism and business, also had the advantage, from the formal point of view, that it did not require one to tack on a humanitarian annex to a scene essentially lacking in personal attributes. In the naturalist strategy, to a bill proclaiming the *what is* to be essentially of one sort, there had to be added a rider legislating that the *what might be* was of essentially a contrary sort. And the greater the indebtedness proclaimed in the bill, the greater was the compensatory inflation in the promissory rider. For without this double-entry system of bookkeeping that countered the malign impersonality of nature with the benign impersonality of institutionalized philanthropy (maintained by "dead hand"), men who had once been of equal worth in the eyes of God would but become of equal worthlessness in the eyelessness of Godlessness.

We can, of course, but speculate vaguely as to just how this mode of thought was carried through. (That is, to what extent the ontological statement was itself futuristic, stylistically rephrasing the optative *"would that it were* so" in the mood of the indicative "It *is* so".) For our immediate inheritance contains several centuries of strongly futuristic thought, developed by the anti-religious, anti-aesthetic, anti-ritualistic pragmatism and utilitarianism of business and technology. We are now idealists all, investors all (even the most impoverished among us), capable only of *glimpsing* a philosophy of Being (while we have gone beyond philosophies of Becoming, into philosophies of the merely About-to-Become, either gerundive or future participle).

To be sure, if those economists are right who contend that the market for long-term investments of private capital is rapidly and permanently dwindling, in proportion as this dwindling progresses the futuristic idiom will come to seem less "natural." For in proportion as financial futurism weakens in the narrower, materialist circle, we may expect a corresponding weakness of futuristic imaginings in the wider, cultural circle. Likewise, the power of the dead hand in permanent bequests to institutions of philanthropic cast will promote such a change, as will also the fixing of a bureaucratic order (as per nepotism in private corporations and permanent employment through civil service in political corporations). In sum: the greatly lowered incidence of futuristic opportunities in the financial realm would alter the nature of the problem to be solved on the cultural level; and a greater stress upon the qualities of the here and now would be the most readily available solution. A major factor operating against this solution, however, should be the extremely fragmentary nature of so many of the occupational acts that go with technological division of labor. The vacational act is now much better rounded than the vocational act, whereby something so material as a means of production would reenforce the Puritan, utilitarian incentives to class the cult of the present-for-itself as dissipation and distraction. The ontological could be restored to the category of vocation only if "mediation" rather than "utility" were taken as the primary characteristic of vocation. Few vocational acts under technology have this character, which can at most be got "after hours," but to trace the ancestry of one's values from the vacational act would be too much like playing golf *pro bono publico*.

Position Epitomized

Meanwhile, it is important that we try to see around the edges of our customary perspective, if we would understand the part that motivational assumptions play in implicitly or explicitly substantiating human decisions, hence in shaping human relations. And related to this, is a still more important reason: When the restricting of investment proceeds without a corresponding change in men's concept of motives, you must get the aggressive futurism of National-Socialist expansion and (or) the balked futurism of would-be business enter- prisers who, deprived of an outlet for their ambitions, and with no other conception of effort to replace these, turn in their disgruntlement to a hatred of Jews, foreigners, Negroes, "isms," etc., as a ritualistic outlet. The reduction of the future to the present may be glimpsed perhaps behind the poet's verdict of posterity. For when he, now suffering neglect, contends that the future will vindicate him, he most assuredly does not mean that his work will later possess some intrinsic quality it now lacks. He means that the recognition of his work in the future is implicit in the quality of the work *now*. And so the present is charged with futurity, as the gun *will* shoot because it *is* loaded.

So, the subject of futurism, introduced as a way of making the necessary distinction between the hortatory-admonitory and the repre- sentative, required us to venture into a concern with the relationship between ontology and history. We pointed out that the anecdote of peace, as a statement about ontology (about the nature of Substance, or *Being*), was much less futuristic than much temporal, financial thinking that is a secular variant of it. We said that Christ was not making a purely directive statement: "Let us have peace," but was proclaiming that Peace was identical with Being, and that Being now *is,* and that only insofar as people were peaceful did they actually partake of Being, and that the promissory must be *now, implicit,* "within you" —while we took the futuristic element here to be a kind of temporalist restatement, translating a doctrine about ontological simultaneity into the parables of historical sequence. And we tried to establish this distinction between the ontological and the futuristic because of the fact that men's judgments are based upon assumptions as to what constitutes the scenic background of their acts.

The quality of the situation in which we act qualifies our act—and so, behind a judgment, there lies, explicitly or implicitly, the concept of a constitution that substantiates the judgment. And by trying to distinguish between Peace as a statement about Being, and Peace as a pacifist, humanitarian exhortation (between ontology and futurism) we came upon relations among indicative, imperative, and optative which, we shall try to show later, have much bearing upon the strategies for the substantiating of values. (At the moment it is enough to recall that men induce themselves and others to act by devices that deduce "let us" from "we must" or "we should." And "we must" and "we should" they deduce in turn from "it *is*"—for only by assertions as to how things *are* can we finally substantiate a judgment.)

As for Peace: when Peace is considered as the Universal Substantive, we can find some valid grounds for considering it as basic anecdote for the discussion of Being. For if history is dialectical, and dialectics is "polemic" and "eristic" (with all the various shades along the spectrum of strife and competition), and if even thinkers so secular as the Marxists would hold that history itself dwindles to a benign impotence insofar as the perfect state of Communism is attained (because, in a perfect state of Communism, there would by definition be no social classifications out of which might arise the conflicts necessary to the dialectic *agon*)—thus even the eschatology of revolutionary history would have its ground in an ontology of peace. And, if the dialectic process is "war," then *any permanent statement* about the dialectic process would be "peace." That is, as the stable, the unchanging, a statement *at rest,* it would be the "technical equivalent" of peace. However, I doubt whether we, as warriors tainted with the "original sin" of the fall from Edenic oneness into the dialectical Babel of conflicting interests, could conceive of such peace as any but the peace of the grave, the *"requiescat in pace"* kind of peace. Indeed, we are so "corrupt" that, when we think of a two-termed dialectic, of Peace and War, we cannot think of the relation as that of "Peace and War at peace," but as "The Struggle Between Peace and War" (with peace as something "to be fought for").

In any event, the world as we know it, the world in history, cannot be described in its particularities by an idiom of peace. Though we may, ideally, convert the dialectic into a chart of the dialectic (replacing a development by a calculus), we are actually in a world at war—a world at combat—and even a calculus must be developed with the dialectics of participation by "the enemy"—hence the representative anecdote must contain militaristic ingredients. It may not be an anecdote of peace—but it may be an anecdote giving us the purification of war.

Men's conception of motive, we have said, is integrally related to their conception of substance. Hence, to deal with problems of motive is to deal with problems of substance. And a thing's substance is that whereof it is constituted. Hence, a concern with substance is a concern with the problems of constitutionality. And where questions of constitutionality are central, could we do better than select the subject of a Constitution and its typical resources as the anecdote about which to shape our terms? Particularly in keeping with out conviction that human relations are at every turn affected by the nature of verbal dialectic, we should welcome so "substantival" an anecdote. And as for its relation to the broadest of all oppositions, such as war and peace, the many and the one, the dialectic of historical change and the calculus of fixed coördinates, the survival of the Constitutional titles or clauses through radical reconstructions of the national situation will give us testimony about the nature of unity and division that serves pretty much as the over-all category for everything, and certainly for human relations.

Imagistic and Conceptual Summaries

Since, however, we had gone from the choice of the Constitution as introductory anecdote to a pre-introduction justifying this choice, and since the draft of the "pre-introduction" was written, in actual fact, later than the draft of the section that was to follow it, we became very self-conscious about the relation between beginnings and endings. A beginning, we observed, should "implicitly contain" its ending—and an ending should be the explicit culmination of all that had flowed from the beginning. But also, there was some kind of almost mystic reversibility here, and the hint of an infinite regress that made us wonder whether we might need a pre-pre-introduction, itself preceded by an introduction, etc. Uneasily, as we found ourselves following the pattern of Coleridge in retracing the course of his Brook, we stated the matter thus:

New sentences, inserted as preparatory to the opening sentence, would have to be preceded in turn by preparations—a process that would require one to write a book backwards, by going on and on, adding one beginning before another, as though the book had been elicited by a relentless cross-examiner, thus:

Q. And why did you begin with this?
A: For such-and-such reason, that logically preceded it.
Q: And why was this reason logically prior?
A. For such-and-such other reason, logically prior to that—etc.

And were you explicitly to write a book in the Q-A form, you would soon find that this pretense of *retracing* your steps, of *going back* to the step-before-the-step-before-the-step, etc., really had all the qualities of a *going forward,* of a *building up,* not like the uncovering of prior assumptions but like the discovering of new conclusions, or "principles." If the book were then written in exactly this same order, the attempt to arrive at the "logically prior" would take such form that the "logically prior" would be the "temporally final."

About this time, reading Richard Wright's *Native Son,* I made some observations very relevant to these quandaries. I noticed that there were *two kinds* of epitomizing in the novel, one imagistic and the other conceptual. That is, the story opens with Bigger's killing of the rat as it comes from behind the wall, an episode that symbolically represents or foreshadows the course of the plot (as Bigger's rebirth will be attained through the killing of the "rat" within himself). But as the story comes to a close we have the summation by lawyer Max, a doctrinal account of Bigger's situation. And this, I realized, was a culmination of the book in the sense that an essayist's last chapter might recapitulate in brief the argument of his whole book.

There was, then, the imagistic source out of which the story flowed; and there was the conceptual summation in which it concluded. There was an "introductory anecdote" and there were final ideological affirmations which might, to intensify our sense of reversibility here, be called a set of "principles" (i.e., "beginnings").

Genetically, however, this statement of the case would not be enough. It is enough *ontologically* (i.e., as a statement about the structure of the book as it stands). But in an article, *How Bigger Was Born,* Wright states that the opening episode was one of the *last* things he added to the book (in other words, he himself, in the course of working through the logic of Bigger's development, *finally* came upon the episodic imagery that would sum Bigger up, or implicitly "name his number"). And as for the conceptual material, the social philosophy which Max propounds, we are told in the same article that the novel was originally of purely narrative cast, a murder story, and that the social (sociological and socialist) interpretations were woven into it afterwards. (Our own version of the matter would be, of course, that the author, after the symbolic committing of the offences through his imaginative identification with Bigger, had thus ritualistically "transcended" the offenses, arriving thereby at a different state, on the critical level, which he then worked back into the book in terms of concept, or doctrine. His role as Marxist critic transcended his role as Negro novelist.)

Five Basic Terms as Beginnings

But while we were thus pondering about the vagaries whereby beginnings and endings may become so indistinguishable (precisely the vagary that must have prompted Aristotle to give us his concept of "final cause" as "prime mover"), we found our pre-pre-introduction actually taking shape. And this we found in the selection of our pentad, as a "final" set of terms that seemed to cluster about our thoughts about the Constitution as an "enactment." (A similar saliency we had found in Maitland's reference to the first British Parliament as being less a "body" than an "act.") And since we had already, in other writings, equated "dramatic" and dialectical," our decision to feature the five terms was accompanied automatically by our decision to use dramatic anecdotes as introductory illustration, with the material on "the Constitutional Wish" assigned to a position as wind-up.

As for the five terms themselves, we found that they needed nothing to proceed them (thus, our uneasy forebodings as to the need for an infinite regress of introductions were suddenly cleared up). They could, in themselves, be stated as a beginning of the "Let there be—and there was" sort. And their justification could *follow,* as one noted their place in the "collective revelation" of common usage, and showed the range of their applicability.

But though *terms* are thus, we now feel, the proper starting point for a presentation, we should still want always to have it borne in mind, particularly in our era, when scientific experiment has so greatly caught our fancy, that the featuring of some particular scientific experiment as crucial is an anecdote implicitly dictating the selection of a terminology. And often, in being startled by the fact that the given experiment is "true," we forget to ask ourselves whether the anecdote is also sufficiently *representative* of our particular subject for it to yield representative terms.

Meanings of "Constitution"

To convey our view of Constitutions, let us now begin, dutifully, by recalling the ordinary dictionary usages:

1. The act or process of constituting; the action of enacting, establishing, or appointing; enactment; establishment; formation.

2. The state of being; that form of being, or structure and connection of parts, which constitutes and characterizes a system or body; natural condition; structure; texture; conformation.

3. The aggregate of all one's inherited physical qualities; the aggregate of the vital powers of an individual, with reference to ability to endure hardship, resist disease, etc.

4. The aggregate of mental qualities; temperament.

5. The fundamental, organic law or principles of government of a nation, state, society, or other organized body of men, embodied in written documents, or implied in the institutions and usages of the country or society; also, a written instrument embodying such organic law, and laying down fundamental rules and principles for the conduct of affairs.

6. An authoritative ordinance, regulation or enactment; especially, one made by a Roman emperor, or one affecting ecclesiastical doctrine or discipline.

Obviously in this list we are dealing with a word that has to do with matters of substance and motive (as one should always consider likely, when a member of the Stance Family is involved). And just as obviously, the word covers all five terms of our pentad. A legal constitution is an *act* or body of acts (or enactments), done by *agents* (such as rulers, magistrates, or other representative persons), and designed (*purpose*) to serve as a motivational ground (*scene*) of subsequent actions, it being thus an instrument (*agency*) for the shaping of human relations.

We shall, of course, focus our attention upon the legal applications of the word. But we cite the other usages to make it apparent that, as is typical of the Stance Family, it readily branches into a whole universe of terms. And in particular we hope that, by recalling this wide range of usages, we shall by comparison not seem to be interpreting the notion of a Constitution too broadly in the much narrower list of instances we treat under this head.

The dictionary itself, after the fifth usage (we are quoting from Webster's Revised Unabridged), pauses to remind us:

> In England the Constitution is unwritten, and may be modified from time to time by act of Parliament. In the United States a constitution cannot ordinarily be modified, except through such processes as the constitution itself ordains.

And behind this distinction we may glimpse two relations between law and custom: first, law as the mere codification of custom (a relation such as we detect in the expression, "That sort of thing just isn't done," which would construct a precept for the future by obedience to the past as already constituted); and second, law as innovative, as a device for the transformation of customs. In a given instance, of course, it is difficult to decide exactly which of these functions, the conservative or the innovative, a given legal enactment or judicial decision is performing. For when a new situation arises, the treatment of it in terms of past fictions may often have a very radical effect, whereas a corresponding adoption of new coördinates would have made for a temperance of response that in the end would have perpetuated the old ways longer. For instance, the revolutionary changes in the living conditions of America since the adoption of the Constitution were mostly the work of men who hired expensive legal talent to get their *innovations* sanctioned in the name of *tradition*.

A constitution is a *substance*—and as such, it is a set of *motives*. There are constitutions of a purely natural sort, such as geographical and physiological properties, that act motivationally upon us. We are affected by one another's mental constitutions, or temperaments. A given complex of customs and values, from which similar customs and values are deduced, is a constitution. And we may, within limits, arbitrarily set up new constitutions, legal substances designed to serve as motives for the shaping or transforming of behavior.

Even in the case of the British Constitution, which is an undefined accumulation of customs, laws, and judicial interpretations, certain charters formulated along the way stand out with greater prominence, as featured acts, more thoroughly culminative or representative or critical than the general body, such as the Magna Carta wrested from King John in the early thirteenth century, the Petition of Right at the beginning of the seventeenth century, and at the close of the century the Bill of Rights confirming the results of Cromwell's Revolution. As for the United States, the Declaration of Independence is as typical of constitutional tactics as is the Constitution itself, in proclaiming a common substance, or motivational basis, for the rebellious colonies.

At an earlier time, when the style of secular law was closer to that of religious law, and the notion of legal precedent was interwoven with the anecdotes of past living, either historical or legendary, the Old Testament and the Talmud were an accumulated Constitution, and the Mosaic code a representative feature. The New Testament would figure here as a new act, a Constitution that, whatever its continuity with the traditions from which it emerged, had the quality of a discontinuity (as a son, encountering influences alien to his father, might continue the father's training in ways that were, in the father's eyes, an alienation)—and a representative feature, a summarizing or culminating moment, would be the Sermon on the Mount.

However, we must not take on too many burdens. For present purposes, we need merely note that the law of pagan Rome, whatever religious qualities it may have had for Stoic administrators, with their attitude towards the state as a religious body, was felt by the Christians as an alien act, not *their* representative act; and the secular-religious dissociation was not merged again until the triumph of Christianity as a state religion under Constantine (a merger in which Augustine played a major role stylistically). Over the centuries, this theocratic re-association was again gradually dissociated, with faith and knowledge changing their relationship, step by step, from that of complementary counterparts to that of antagonist counterparts.

The typical political platform may be thought of as a kind of flimsy and ephemeral constitution, a set of motivations slung together for the needs of the moment. For the most part, political platforms are best analyzed on the rhetorical level, as they are quite careless grammatically. Also, there is a form, the political tract, which has the properties of both constitutions and platforms. In upholding or attacking some political or social philosophy, which is treated with some degree of thoroughness and complexity, the political tract will necessarily, in the course of its exposition, propound a theory of social action (of substance and motivation) that justifies us in classing such works as constitutional variants.

In fact, it was in the attempt to review two books of this sort that we first found ourselves confronting what we consider the typical properties of constitutions. The books are *Poetry and Anarchism,* by Herbert Read, and *Marxism: An Autopsy,* by H. B. Parkes. And perhaps the handiest way to lead us into the kind of analysis we would develop here, is to explain the problems we encountered in the course of trying to chart the structures of these books.

Technical Immunity of "Anarchism" as Ideal

In considering the Read book, we found ourselves confronting the following situation: The author began by a claim of immunity. He said that he would assert certain social ideals, of anarchistic cast; he would, he said, put these forward as a "vision." And he insisted that his critics, in examining this vision, were not entitled to reject it on the ground of its "impracticality," since practicality is not the proper test of visions.

The "vision," it seemed as we progressed with the reading, had a great many aspects that contradicted one another. We were sure that, in order to enjoy some of the promises proclaimed in the author's vision of ideal anarchy, you would have to forego others. Yet we did not see how we could legitimately raise objections on this score, for we had to admit that the author was justified in his claim that a "vision" was immune to such tests. One might even, in one's "vision," quite properly include among his batch of ideals, or promises, a clause to the effect that in this hypothetical world of pure intention, or pure futurity, all contradictions would be reconciled. And that would be a very noble ideal, an ideal well worth holding. To be sure, it would not be "practicable"—but ideals are never practicable; indeed, they are *by definition* something that you don't attain; they are merely *directions* in which you aim. (You can't hit "North," for instance, though you may hit a target placed to the north of you.)

As for contradictions, we had to admit that each ideal is like a sovereign state, proclaiming and maintaining its identity independently of other sovereign states. And we conceded that, ideal anarchy being by definition a state of affairs in which the lion and the lamb shall lie

together, implicit in the very nature of such a project there is an un-
written clause to the effect that in this realm all contradictions are to be
reconciled; hence it would simply be irrelevant to concern oneself with
contradictions at all. For ideal anarchy is, like Christ's vision, the
vision of a world in which contradictions merge. Anarchy, as the
ultimate extreme of individualism, would be a state of absolute continuity approached through a state of absolute discontinuity.

The thought of Christ's vision reminded us that there is a test
applicable to visions: the test of moral grandeur and stylistic felicity.
And we began to evaluate Mr. Read's vision on this count, comparing
and contrasting it with some of the Great Manifestoes, such as the
Decalogue, The Sermon on the Mount, the various proclamations of
rights in the British Constitution, the Declaration of Independence, and
the vigorously muscular "pre-Constitution" that Marx and Engels laid
down for Communism (a document that is, to be sure, explicitly concerned with tests of practicability, but would not figure from this point
of view if treated as a "vision").

"Anarcho-Syndicalism"—the Ideal Organized

However, while we were grudgingly and laboriously changing our
terms of analysis to the kind deemed proper for the appreciation of a
"vision," we began to notice a new development in Mr. Read's book.
The subject became modified. And instead of merely enunciating a
vision of ideal anarchy, the author went on to propose the kind of social
and political organization by which this ideal could be embodied. In
this rebirth, the subject fittingly transformed its name, being no longer
merely "anarchism," but "anarcho-*syndicalism*."

When we confronted this new, hyphenated term, we realized that the
second member of the pair was of a different order than the first
member. For only the first member was "ideal," thus enjoying the
immunity to questions of practicability that goes with the ideal, or
heavenly. The second was a "worldly" term; and thus, like all worldly
terms, it dealt with a realm to which tests of practicability do very
rigorously apply. The term, "Anarchism," we might say, is the
Sermon on the Mount stage in Mr. Read's church; but with the term,
"syndicalism," he moves into the epistolary, Pauline realm of organizational problems, involving elections, membership drives, finances,

and the like. If we think of the hyphenated terms as "counterparts," we find them related as "soul" and "body." And though, in the realm of the soul, the lion and the lamb may lie down together, in the realm of the body the lion either eats the lamb or starves. We know, in brief, that the realm of the body is the realm of "contradictions." Hence, as soon as Mr. Read endowed his vision with a body, he sacrificed his claims that his book should be considered purely on the ideal level.

In sum, in "anarchism" we have an *ideal* term, in "syndicalism" we have a *practical* term—and what we can treat in the former realm as ideal mergers, we must consider in the latter realm as practical contradictions. In the former realm, no compromise is necessary. In the latter realm you encounter the necessity to compromise at every turn. For not only must you, in the process of embodying some one ideal, frustrate the embodiment of some other ideal that points in a different direction; but also, in the mere act of embodying any ideal at all, you are "translating" it into another and "inferior" idiom—and this "translation" may, as per the *"traduttore traditore"* formula, be treated as either a "copy" or a "betrayal" of the original.

This is not the place in which to discuss all the important deployments of Mr. Read's book. By our interpretation, the hyphenated term, "anarcho-syndicalism" is an oxymoron. The first member refers to a spiritual state that is *free of organizational hazards* through being *free of organization,* and the second member refers to the *kind of social organization* through which this happy state would be attained. Hence, all told, the hyphenated pair would, by our way of thinking, add up to something like "disorganized organization."

The Anarcho-Syndicalist "Constitution"

The transformations that the argument undergoes make it difficult to chart the dialectical alignments briefly. But we might try conveying the general quality of Mr. Read's approach. While granting that "form, pattern, and order are essential aspects of existence," he holds that "in themselves they are the attributes of death." This would seem to give us a dialectic of Being vs. Having-Become, with the "unformed" or "to be formed" as "life" and the "formed" as "death." And when he says that "In order to create it is necessary to destroy; and the agent of destruction in society is the poet," we find "destruction," usually a "death" word, redeemed as a bringer of life (an equation typical of Futurism, but "re-Christianized"; for though the Futurists celebrate war and cruelty, Mr. Read celebrates his destructiveness differently, saying: "Peace is anarchy").

The basic pattern of the book involves the equating of poetry, anarchism, syndicalism, in opposition to such institutional structures as church, business, the state, and parties of professional politicians. He would have a world related not authoritatively, as father and sons, but in the true equality of brotherhood. And he would define the anarchist as the "man who, in his manhood, dares to resist the authority of the father," including here the rejection of the leader principle which involves "a blind unconscious identification of the leader and the father." (This rejection, and the destruction of institutional structures interwoven with the parental symbolism would, presumably, be done peacefully. At least, this would be the "ideal." Poetry is here viewed in terms of the "permanent revolution," minus the political application which Trotsky gave to the term. But for our purposes, the crucial moments in the book are to be seen in the difference between the author's handling of the relation between "poetry" and "business" and his handling of the relation between "imagination" and "reason."

We are told that "the doctrinaire civilizations which are forced on the world—capitalist, fascist and marxist—by their very structure and principles exclude the values in which and for which the poet lives." And in considering the suicide of the revolutionary Russian poet, Mayakovsky, he writes of poetic development thus:

> The essential process is that of a seed falling on fertile ground, germinating and growing and in due course reaching maturity. Now just as certainly as the flower and the fruit are implicit in the single seed, so the genius of a poet or painter is contained within the individual. The soil must be favourable, the plant must be nourished; it will be distorted by winds and by accidental injuries. But the growth is unique, the configuration unique, the fruit unique. All apples are very much alike, but no two are exactly the same. But that is not the point: a genius is the tree which has produced the unknown fruit, the golden apples of Hesperides. But Mayakovsky was a tree which one year was expected to produce plums of a uniform size and appearance; a few years later apples; and finally cucumbers. No wonder that he finally broke down under such an unnatural strain!

To ask that a poet become anything so naked as a cucumber tree is, I admit, to place him under a terrific strain. Mayakovsky himself, we might recall, left a suicide note in which he referred to a "Love boat smashed against mores," and on this point Mr. Read writes:

> Obviously there was a love affair, but to our surprise there were also the *mores*—the social conventions against which this love-boat smashed. Mayakovsky was in a special sense the poet of the Revolution: he celebrated its triumph and its progressive achievements in verse which had all the urgency and vitality of the event. But he was to perish by his own hand like any miserable in-grown subjectivist of bourgeois capitalism. The Revolution had evidently not created an atmosphere of intellectual confidence and moral freedom.

One may, of course, put many interpretations upon this event. One may note that the kind of mentality best adapted to flourish at the most liquid stages of a Revolution is hardly likely to be equally adapted to the later period of greater crystallization and organization. And one may wonder whether Mr. Read is not asking more of life than it can give in his assumption that a Revolution should not go through various stages and finally settle into some kind of relatively fixed organizational pattern, with its *mores* (though I have been told that, in this particular case, even the husband of the woman with whom Mayakovsky was in love condoned their affair, since he was a close friend of the poet and a great admirer of his verses, but the poet suffered because of his conflicting attachments to both the friend and the wife).

In any event, we have been quoting to indicate that Mr. Read treats poetry and the world's business as in *opposition* (and by poetry, he means not merely a poetic *attitude,* but the actual *body* of the work done by producing poets). But when he discusses reason and imagination, he treats them as "balancing" each other (even going so far, in fact, as to speak of the "rule of reason," which seems to us the smuggling of a highly incongruous term into an anarchistic project—for if you allow of anarchist "rule," I should think you would by the same token bring back state and *mores,* hence also fathers and leaders). Or, to quote once more:

> I balance anarchism with surrealism, reason with romanticism, the understanding with the imagination, function with freedom. Happiness, peace, contentment—these are all one and are due to the per-

fection of the balance. We may speak of these things in dialectical terms—terms of contradiction, negation, synthesis—the meaning is the same. The world's unhappiness is caused by men who incline so much in one direction that they upset this balance, destroy the synthesis. The very delicacy and subtlety of the equilibrium is of its essence; for joy is only promised to those who strive to achieve it, and who, having achieved it, hold it lightly poised.

To draw this all together: we note that the first pair, poetry and business, confronting one another in the practical world, are conceived as in *conflict,* whereas these other pairs confront each other as in *equilibrium.* (Indeed, in a more rigorously conducted argument, we might even be able to hammer the alignments into such symmetrical shape that "imagination" would be the idealistic equivalent of "poetry" and "reason" the idealistic equivalent of structure, organization, rational order, methods of accountancy and proof, etc., in short, the equivalent of "rule," which is to say, "authority.") And it was this distinction, as a development implicit in Mr. Read's hyphenated term, that struck us as particularly relevant to the tactics of Constitutions. A constitution may, for instance, propound a set of generalized rights or duties, and all these may be considered as a grand promissory unity, a *panspermia* in which they all exist together in perfect peace and amity. Yet when, in the realm of the practical, a given case comes before the courts, you promptly find that this *merger* or *balance* or *equilibrium* among the Constitutional clauses becomes transformed into a *conflict* among the clauses—and to satisfy the promise contained in one clause, you must forego the promise contained in another.

A New Constitution for Laissez-faire

With Mr. Parkes's book, we found this distinction between the ideal and the practical taking a variant form. His book is an argument against Marxism, undertaken from the position of a modified *laissez-faire.* Mr. Parkes did not present his material as a "vision," hence we were at no point called upon to consider it without regard for matters of contradiction. But when we tried to make a diagram of the alignments, so as to know just where the battle was being fought, we found a situation as follows:

First, we noticed that the concept of *laissez-faire* underwent an important alteration, as the author distinguished between "negative" and "positive" *laissez-faire*. "According to the doctrines of eighteenth-century liberalism the functions of the state were negative; it must maintain order by preventing individuals from injuring each other. For the state to issue positive commands, dictating to individuals what they must do, was tyranny." And the author would now have us give to *laissez-faire* this positive emphasis, though in a modified form. To get the pattern underlying this concept, let us define "negative" *laissez-faire* as "hands-off." Then "positive" *laissez-faire* would be "hands off, with a measure of hands-on." (This interpretation is, of course, offered without consulting the author.) Obviously, we have here, phrased as a distinction between positive and negative, an ambiguity of the "potential" or "substantial" sort; hence, proposals of a distinctly hands-on sort can be recommended in the name of hands-off. Under the head of positive liberalism, for instance, Mr. Parkes proposes that the concept of property rights should be extended to include the property rights of every worker in his job. It is a proposal I have myself subscribed to (in *Attitudes Toward History*); but it never occurred to me that such a *universalizing* of the concept of property rights, assured by government interference, could be treated under the head of *laissez-faire,* or "hands-off." As indeed it could not, without flat misnomer, if the author had not proposed his transitional term, "positive" *laissez-faire,* which we, in order to make its form apparent, would call "hands-off *à la* hands-on." The author's purpose, he says, is to reform the practice of capitalism, "not to abandon the principles." And since he would thus preserve the same *substance,* it is understandable that he might strive to retain the same *name* for that substance (or rather, its same *good* name, as tested by the criteria of the liberalism to which his book is addressed).

A Spectrum of Terms Between "Freedom" and "Capitalism"

In attempting to clarify the alignment of the author's key terms, we found a spectrum of such terms, ranging in a graded series from "freedom" on the pure, heavenly, idealistic side, to "capitalism" on the impure, worldly, practical side. The major members of this series seemed to be arranged in a delicately differentiated set of modulations, thus:

On one side, we have freedom, against which there is nothing to be said. It is the ideal term. On the other side, we have the practical, or organizational term, capitalism, against which the author frequently says almost as much as the Marxists (perhaps even more, since the Marxist dialectic requires that capitalism be saluted as a necessary and beneficial stage in the cultural sequence, relatively "progressive" in its destruction of feudalism, and relatively "reactionary" only in its resistance to modern socialism). The major terms intervening between these two are: humanism, *laissez-faire,* free market, the price system (i.e., money), and industrialism. Thus the whole series would be:

freedom
humanism
laissez-faire
free market
price system (money)
industrialism
capitalism

Let us examine these terms by first considering their resources without reference to the actual uses to which the author might put them.

"Freedom," you will note, is the "God" term, since God alone is conceivable as *wholly* free. "Freedom," as the dialectical counterpart of "necessity," may be treated as either in *op*position *to* "necessity" or in *ap*position *with* "necessity." Or, if you divide "necessity" into two terms, one impersonal ("law") and the other personal ("authority" or "dictatorship"), you could treat "freedom" as in apposition with some kind of natural law and in opposition to some kind of leadership or bureaucratic control. For instance, freedom could be in apposition with the laws of the "natural" workings of the free market in goods or ideas, and in opposition to dictatorial or monopolistic interference with such "spontaneous" adjustments. The early liberal slogan calling for a "government by laws rather than a government by men" is an off-shoot of this distinction.

Next adjoining "freedom" comes "humanism." The human is the area of the "substantially" free. Accordingly, "humanism" may be treated as a philosophic attitude that retains the God-term ambiguously. It is a stepping-down of the God-term, a confinement to a narrower circumference, a translation into an idiom that may be treated either as having retained something of the pure original or having lost it by reason of defects in the material (defects which, according to the theological doctrines that shaped the development of Western humanism, were themselves an outgrowth of freedom, since the defects were derived from the fall of man, and man had fallen because his "substantial" freedom had also included the possibility that he could carry freedom to excess).

The next adjoining term, *laissez-faire,* restricts our circumference still further. Indeed, we are here in a marginal area ambiguously covering both the ideal and the organizational. As a principle, ("live and let live") the term is quite ideal. Yet it also refers to various institutional devices for translating the perfection of this ideal into the more or less imperfect world of practical approximations. We could obviously, without violating the orthodox resources of the term, slip back and forth between these two quite different meanings; and conversely, we could treat a given approximation (or deviation) either as a "betrayal" of the ideal or as the retention of the ideal "substantially."

As we move to the next adjoining term, "free market," we are brought more definitely into the purely organizational area. Not wholly, to be sure, for the epithet, "free," is a bridge that can lead us back to heavenly or Edenic origins, though these origins are quite eliminated from the companion term "market." "Free market" is, just ever so faintly, an oxymoron, as would become clearer if we stopped to realize that at the very basis of the concept is the notion of a *labor* market, i.e., a market where men's ability to work for others is bought and sold. A slave market is also a market in which man's ability to work for others is bought and sold. And where a free labor market is the general economic scene in which men must economically act, it is obvious that the *ability* to sell one's services (or one's partial servitudes) is also synonymous with the *need* to sell one's services. Now, a need is not "freedom," but "necessity," and a necessity not *from within* but *from without*. A necessity *from within* can be equated with freedom, as Spinoza contended, since in accordance with necessity so conceived one "must" follow the laws of his own internal development, which would equal freedom, as per Mr. Read's poetic tree prior to the time when political leaders demanded that it give forth cucumbers. But a necessity *from without* is compulsion. And when a need to sell one's services is *imposed upon* one, the market to this extent would be not a "free" market, but a "slave" market.

However, at this point let us look at the next adjoining term, "money" (or, in Mr. Parkes' preferred equivalent, the "price system"). And let us note that, by the introduction of money as motive, the "substantial" freedom is retained. For once man has learned to transcend the material aspect of goods and services by perceiving them in terms of the money motive, then the criterion of the market has become a "second nature" with him. The market motive is then not merely scenic; it is not felt as an alien and outward compulsion (as it is felt, for instance, by members of a primitive African tribe who are forced, by the hut tax, to abandon their non-monetary tribal economy and to solicit work on the white man's plantations in order to get the cash which the requirements of the new economic scene impose upon them). The market motive is also "personal," a spontaneous rationale of conduct *within* the agent. Thus, the medium of money translates the labor market from a "slave" market into a "free" market.

The next adjoining word on our list is "industrialism"—and then, finally, "capitalism." These are terms for subjects wholly in the practical realm, hence terms which, in all strictness, should be treated ambivalently, or ironically, from the ethical, or evaluative point of view, as their placement in "this imperfect world" should endow them with qualities good, bad, and indifferent. In Western history, it is impossible to deal with one of these terms without implying the other.

But we should note that behind "industrialism" (and behind capitalist accountancy) lies another key term, "science," which we should also have included in our list, but which we omitted because of an awkwardness in assigning it a place in the series. For though "industrialism," as "applied science," is a worldly, organizational term, there is behind it "pure science," which carries us directly back to our God-term. For "science," as the study and discovery of "laws," is directly concerned with "necessity," and "necessity" is as divine as "freedom," being its reflex. Though "applied science" may lack the spiritual attributes of "pure science," as a member of the same family it may retain these qualities "substantially"; and its devices and routines compose a material body that is always there to help us appreciate the vast amount of intelligence and imaginativeness ("free" attributes) that lie behind the formulation and utilization of scientific laws (somewhat as religious dogma, which is sometimes said to conceal religious insight behind its rigidities and formalisms, may on the other hand be said to preserve a firm structure of forms that maintains the continuous possibility of true understanding, since everything is there in the semi-darkness, laid out in perfect formation, and it will gleam the moment a sudden light is thrown upon it).

Strategic Choice of Circumference for "Freedom"

We refer the reader to Mr. Parkes's book, if he would decide in detail just how the author chooses to exploit these resources. Our primary interest here is not in giving a full report of the book, but in considering the grammatical relations inherent in the key terms which the author selects as the coördinates for his calculus of human relations. So we shall here attempt to treat only of the aspects that bear most directly on Constitutional tactics.

Though noting that the humanist valuation of freedom is related historically to theological doctrine, Mr. Parkes simply takes this value as part of the socially given, considering it sufficiently well grounded through being grounded in a great and representative tradition. He might also have derived his value from purely naturalistic motivations (that is: an organism that lives by locomotion must desire conditions that allow a primitive "freedom of motion"; and in the evaluations of human speech, this strong preference would be fittingly conceptualized as "love of freedom-in-general," a standard that would be the ideal counterpart of the practical interests). But had he deduced his value from either the theological or the naturalistic circumference, he could not so easily have carried out his tactical aim to present "freedom" and the "free market" as synonymous. For there is no "market" in either heaven or the state of nature—hence, if freedom were ancestrally situated in either of these sources, we could treat the free market as but one idiom among many for translating the "ideal" into practical equivalents. And even if we asserted that it is, by and large, the best idiom, no one could claim by the same token that it is the best idiom for every occasion—for no idiom enjoys such categorical and universal supremacy.

Mr. Parkes avoids these embarrassments by beginning with a social circumference, a traditional cult of freedom which has become a part of our second nature. And since another tradition, the monetary motivation or rationale of pricing, has become a part of our second nature, he thus has, all woven together and supporting one another: freedom, quantitative or monetary pricing, and the controlling laws of the free market (which cease to be a "free" government by law, and become instead a tyrannical government by men, insofar as private monopolies or public dictatorships usurp the legal function of control).

In discussing the free market, Mr. Parkes neglects to treat the ways in which the conception of the free market involved the conception of a free *labor* market. We can't know why he made this omission; but we can note that, having made it, he has a less difficult job in presenting his own proposals in the name of *laissez-faire*. For if a worker would be guaranteed property rights in his job, there must be a vigorous governmental interference and control in the administrative policies of private business—and such "positive" *laissez-faire* would seem more of a misnomer if we were forced to realize that it was designed to "preserve the principles" of the free market by destroying the free market at a most strategic point, the free *labor* market.

Money as "God Term"

In the stress he places upon the price system, or monetary motivation, as a device for rationalizing the structure and trends of the free market, we probably come upon the crucial moment in his concept of substance. Money would be, in the technical sense, his "God term." For a God term designates the ultimate motivation, or substance, of a Constitutional frame. And as we have previously noted how the ambiguities of substance cause extrinsic and intrinsic motivation to merge, we note that when men respond to the laws of the market and its price system as second nature, the qualities of the *scene* are thereby *internal* to the *agent*. Thus, a migration of workers moving from one scene to another in response to a hope of better wages would, however great the social dislocations it produced, be motivated by "free will," in contrast with a transference of population decreed by a dictator or some central planning agency. There are, of course, more complex notions of freedom than this (notions according to which such a migration would be treated as hardly more than a compulsion), but they would not figure here. The slogan here would seem to be: Where one can volunteer, there one is free.

Another indication that this is his "God term" is in the fact that, in the name of the freedom got by the workings of the market, he strongly attacks the rival Marxist God, or substance, "inevitability." Thinking along Spinozistic lines, Marx had arrived at the divine word, "freedom," through its divine counterpart, "necessity." Science is "free" in discovering the "laws" of nature—hence the Marxist formula: "freedom is the knowledge of necessity." Men innovate, or act, but according to law. A class, in "fulfilling its historic destiny," is "free" inasmuch as it is doing what it *wants* to do; that is, in its internal motivation it fulfills the role imposed upon it *ab extra* by the scene and by its place in the total dialectic. But only the proletariat enjoys a freedom uncontaminated by illusion; in its enslavement it is, like the person of the early Christian slave, "substantially" free, for nothing but the truth can set it free, whereas other classes must protect their interests by a partial avoidance of the truth, inasmuch as they enjoy their rights at the expense of others. The proletariat, as *primus inter pares,* is "substantially" free because it can, or must, both represent itself and be the representative vessel or logical culmination of the total dialectic. This is the doctrine, as I understand it, though I am aware that many a Marxist would complain at the theological tone I have given to my summary. But I think I can thus make it apparent why I feel justified in saying that Mr. Parkes attacks the doctrine as a rival God, representing in its grounds for the destruction of the market a causal ancestry directly opposed to Mr. Parkes's doctrines of motivation.

"Principles" and "Reform"

Mr. Parkes's other major proposal to preserve the principles by reforming the practice would aim at a spot as strategic as the free labor market. For he would also end the free money market. (We are using "free" in the traditional *laissez-faire* sense: free of government interference.) Here too, while showing the traditional liberal distrust of strong central government, he somewhat incongruously calls for a strengthening of government authority to "force down the rate of interest to the appropriate economic level."

"It is improbable," he says, "that this can be accomplished by any means short of direct government control of the banking system." And when proposing to alter the conception of property rights by extending them to cover the property rights of a worker in his job, he had acknowledged that such changes would be "revolutionary in their implications." Thus, he would drastically change the traditional conception of the free market at its two most vital spots: the labor market and the money market. And he can presumably feel justified in presenting this program as the reform of capitalist practice rather than the abandonment of its principles by reason of an ambiguity lurking in the notion of "reform." If we say that a sinner "reforms," we mean that he simply gives up his sins and returns to the traditional norms of action. In this sense, a monopolistic capitalist would "reform" if he gave up the exploitation of his monopoly and abided by the traditional "principles" of free competition. But if one calls it a "reform" to change these principles themselves, introducing government control at the two most consequential spots in the structure (spots so strategic that a whole new set of implications would follow from the change), is not one rather using "reform" in the sense of "transform"? And a transformation is a change in substance or principle, a qualitative shift in the nature of motivation. The old motivation could then be said to be "substantially" retained only in the rhetorical sense, as when we say that something is "substantially so" because it is *not* so.

Constitutions and the Opponent

Constitutions are agonistic instruments. They involve an enemy, implicitly or explicitly. We may glimpse their mere beginnings, for instance, in the rites whereby a new sovereign, on his accession to authority, swore an oath promising to obey and enforce the traditional tribal laws, or customs. This implied the inimical possibility that the sovereign might do otherwise. Later, men began to exact more specific promises of their sovereigns, promises that were directed against possible abuses of authority which they would anticipate and forestall. Out of this arose written charters or grants, containing explicit assurances against unwanted eventualities of one sort or another. In all such projects, the attempt is made, by verbal or symbolic means, to establish a motivational fixity of some sort, in opposition to something that is thought liable to endanger this fixity.

In *The Philosophy of Literary Form,* footnote on pp. 109-111, we try to show how shifts of authority, from the Crown to representative government, and thence to modern monopolies, dialectically affected the interpretation of the promises, or principles, in the United States Constitution. Similarly, Mr. Parkes is being quite "Constitutional" in setting up his theory of motivation by reference to an opponent motivation. For what a Constitution would do primarily is to *substantiate an ought* (to base a statement as to *what should be* upon a statement as to *what is*). And in our "agonistic" world, such substantiation derives point and poignancy by contrast with notions as to what should not be.

Logically, of course, we should go from substance to command; but in *proposing* a Constitution we reverse this process, going from command to substance, and thereby trying to so frame the statement of substance that it implies or contains the command (which can then be "deduced" from it by judicial interpreters). Thus, in an article on "The Development of Logical Empiricism," by Lewis S. Feuer (*Science and Society,* Summer 1941), in which the author traces the development of neo-positivist theory through various "slogans" in response to shifts in the scene of world politics (giving us a picture of these austere philosophers veering under situational pressures as with the "party lines" of political factions), we glimpse the "constitutional logic" of substantiation operating:

> With the spread of fascism, however, logical empiricism became an article for export. A new slogan now tended to supersede "physicalism," the slogan "the unity of science." Although opinions differed as to the logical meaning of this expression, there was no disagreement that it was the goal of empiricism. Sociologically speaking, the import of the slogan was the "unity of the intellectual class." Confronted by the anxieties of insecurity, the empiricist proposed that scientists join together in their culture-circle and gather collective solace from their closed ranks. Coöperation with the labor movement was not a meaningful alternative within the bourgeois perspective. The "unity" of science was not, however, without economic consequences, for it conveyed the ethical imperative that universities abroad should provide jobs for the scholars who were leaving their native lands. It was at this juncture that the mating of logical positivism with American pragmatism took place. The child of the union was, after some deliberation, provided with the less sectarian name,—"logical empiricism."

Here we see a new "ought" substantiated by a group of thinkers most of whom would abandon the category of "substance" completely and would confine themselves solely to the tactics of "pointing" and "description."

In Mr. Parkes's case, the use of Marxism as the dialectical competitor coöperating in the pronouncements of his Constitution (or structure of motivation) points up quite readily for us the relation between ideals and practices. For he may thereby contrast the perfections of capitalism's other-worldliness (the ideals of pure *laissez-faire*) with the imperfections of the Marxist world (the organizational aspects of Marxist parties and the problems of Russia during the interregnum of dictatorship). Or, otherwise put: Where he by his criteria finds a Communist practice wrong, he may say that *the error derives from the principle;* but where he finds a capitalist practice wrong he may say that *the error derives from a departure from the principle.* This may, if you insist, be the case. But the issue could be intelligently discussed only from a perspective with coördinates beyond those of either the Marxist "inevitability" or the *laissez-faire* "freedom"—and such a perspective would frustrate Mr. Parkes's purposes, since it would be an alternative to the perspective of *laissez-faire* which he would celebrate.

As for the shift between the ideal and the organizational, like the shift between Mr. Read's visionary anarchism and his organizational syndicalism, we can cite a passage from *The Friend,* Essay IV, where Coleridge notes a similar pattern. He is discussing Edmund Burke, who considered policies in terms of "principles" and "expediency" (holding that a policy should be so framed as to embody permanent "principles," but should take the realities of a given temporal situation into account). Coleridge writes:

> Let me not be misunderstood. I do not mean that this great man supported different principles in different areas of his political life. On the contrary, no man was ever more like himself. From his first published speech on the American colonies to his last posthumous tracts, we see the same man, the same doctrines, the same uniform wisdom of practical counsels, the same reasoning and the same prejudices against all abstract grounds, against all deduction of practice from theory. The inconsistency to which I allude, is of a different kind: it is the want of congruity in the principles appealed to in different parts of the same work; it is an apparent versatility of the

principle with the occasion. If his opponents are theorists, then everything is to be founded on prudence, on mere calculations of expediency; and every man is represented as acting according to the state of his own immediate self-interest. Are his opponents calculators? Then calculation itself is represented as a sort of crime. God has given us feelings, and we are to obey them;—and the most absurd prejudices become venerable, to which these feelings have given consecration.

All told, what are we trying to get at here? We have been considering "ideals" or Constitutional "principles" much as we previously considered "attitudes." That is, as terms bearing upon motivation, they contain the ambiguities of the "substantial" and "potential." Both the Read book and the Parkes book, by propounding "constitutions" in the name of freedom, themselves enjoy maximum freedom of argument, hence were chosen by us as particularly challenging to analysis. The search for alignments in the Parkes book led us into a less clearcut outline than that of the Read book, which was organized in keeping with the like genius of the term, "anarcho-syndicalism." But we have tried to show how, despite the variants, a similar form prevails here, as the author confronts the "evils" of Marxism with the "virtues" of capitalism ("virtues" which are not situated in "capitalism" *per se;* indeed, capitalism is said to have sinned against them; but the other terms are repositories of these virtues, so that we can retain by reference to the repository terms, the principles that are dimmed in terms of capitalist practice). We are not trying to "review" these books. We have been trying to abstract their tactics as "Constitutions."

Constitutions—Addressed by Agents to Agents

Now, a Constitution, as a "substance" (hence, as a structure of motivation) propounds certain desires, commands, or wishes. It is "idealistic," as we use the term, in that such attributes are properties of the term *agent.* Indeed, in actual point of fact, a Constitution is addressed by the first person to the second person. In propounding a Constitution, "I" or "we" say what "you" may or should and may not or should not do. If a Constitution declares a right "inalienable," for instance, it is a document signed by men who said in effect, "Thou shalt not alienate this right."

Two important factors tend to make us forget this idealistic factor in Constitutions, their nature as a document addressed by persons to persons. In the first place, the persons to whom the clauses are addressed must necessarily change with the course of history. In adopting Constitutions, men may impose commands not only upon others (as the signers of our Constitution imposed the principles of alienable property upon the future, and sought to balance them with the principles of "inalienable rights"), but they may also impose commands upon themselves which we could analyze by saying that in their present person they address commands to their future person. Further, a command, when it is subscribed to, may be framed with reference to one kind of sovereignty, but by the nature of language it survives to be interpreted under conditions when there is another kind of sovereignty; hence, in the new situation, the command cannot possibly be addressed as it was originally. Thus, many of the commands in the United States Constitution owe their wording to charters originally wrested from kings ruling by tradition and divine right, yet as they are read today they cannot be so addressed, but must be interpreted as addressed either to a government elected by ballot or to some new kind of sovereignty perpetuated by tradition and lying outside the direct control of the ballot (the great business corporations, for instance).

This vagueness of address helps greatly to make us forget that commands are addressed. They may be addressed "to whom it may concern," which is a cross between "everybody" and "nobody," and so vague an address can seem like no address at all. Moral commands were imposed upon Everyman, but to each as a private individual; hence the Mosaic commands are phrased in the singular. But moral commands fail to strike us as addressed in proportion as we lose a sense of direct communication between God and creature; and this loss, ironically enough, was itself heightened by theological doctrine, as God's commandments were also said to be imprinted in natural law, and natural law was not, like God, a "person," hence could not address us. That is, commands grounded in natural law merged the *what must be* in the *what is*. And thus, whereas an "inalienable" right is really a *gerundive,* a right "not to be alienated," the term assumes the grammar of a much more substantial form, a right "that *cannot* be alienated" (since the "nature of things" would make this "impossible"), a futuristic, idealistic form thus being given the appearance of a scenic, ontological concept, as if it were a statement about "inevitable" structure.

In idealistic individualism, the matter of address could be overlooked by another route. The agent could, as with Mr. Read's "vision," simply propound a list of *wishes,* where the stress upon the will of the visionary ("*I* want such-and-such") could help one forget what his statement implies, ("*You* must do such-and-such if I am to get what I want"). Indeed, in such case, the implied form probably is: "We want such-and-such—i.e., all men of good will want such-and-such—and my statement represents them, as it will represent you also, dear reader, if you agree with me."

Constitution-Behind-the-Constitution

In any case, be one's statement consciously a command or merely some kind of wish in which he hopes others will participate, in having to do with the will of representatives, it is typically under the aegis of our term, agent; yet in laying down the "environment" for future acts, a Constitution is *scenic.* However, no human Constitution can constitute the whole scene, since it itself is an enactment made in a given scene and perpetuated through subsequent variously altered scenes. Since, by reason of the scene-act ratio, the quality of the Constitutional enactment must change *pari passu* with changes in the quality of the scene in which the Constitution is placed, it follows that a complete statement about motivation will require a wider circumference, as with reference to the social, natural, or supernatural environment in general, the "Constitution behind the Constitution."

Actually, however, "positive" law has tried to uphold the fiction that the Constitutional enactment itself is the criterion for judicial interpretations of motive. It would abandon "natural law" or "divine law" as criteria, looking only to the Constitution itself and not to any scientific, metaphysical, or theological doctrines specifying the nature of the "Constitution behind the Constitution" as the ultimate test of a judgment's judiciousness. And since it is simply impossible to so confine the circumference of the scene in which occurs the given act that is to be judged, i.e., since an act in the United States has not merely the United States Constitution as its background, but all sorts of factors originating outside it, the fiction of positive law has generally served to set up the values, traditions, and trends of business as the Constitution-behind-the-Constitution that is to be consulted as criterion. In effect, therefore, the theory of "positive law" has given us courts which are the representatives of business in a mood of mild self-criticism.

Such researches as those of Beard remind us that the Constitution was framed and adopted in a period of reaction; the Revolutionary exaltation of the era in which the Declaration of Independence was enacted had passed; and the time for retraction and consolidation was on. And such expressions of the popular will as found their summation in Shays's Rebellion clearly revealed that, where debtors were in a majority and creditors in a minority, the potential "badness" of popular sovereignty was no mere metaphysical quibble. The Constitution was a capitalist Constitution. "It is a striking feature of American constitutional guaranties," says the *Encyclopaedia of the Social Sciences* (IV, 254) "that with the exception of the Thirteenth Amendment, which protects against peonage, they afford protection only against the possibility of abuse of governmental power and not against the possibility of capitalist exploitation." And not even the Thirteenth Amendment need be excepted here, since exploitation by peonage is more feudal than capitalistic, and this particular command arose in dialectical response to the feudal forms of the Southern plantation system. The irony here is that, with the weakening of the feudal participant in the definition of rights (a weakening of course that got its major blow in the elimination of the Crown as the centre of government and the placing of popular sovereignty in its stead) "rights" that were once asserted in dialectical opposition to feudal authorities would now be asserted in opposition to the authority of the people's government itself.

Shifts in the Locus of the "Representative"

Whereas, in the heyday of feudal thought, the nobility is considered to be the "representative" class (the class in which the society's values culminate) in the course of further social development such "distinction" becomes felt as a "contrast." A "fall" has occurred, and the "representative" part has become the "divisive" part, with an antagonistic part (or rival class) laying claim to greater representativeness, and conceiving of these claims in opposition to the nobility. So long as the nobility still figures as the vessel of sovereignty, rights of the opposing class can be defined with reference to such resistance. But when the nobility is abolished, its function as a dialectical participant in a contrary concept of rights necessarily ends; there is a new scene; and the enactments that derived their significance from the old scene must change accordingly.

Thus, the rights that had been enunciated as *group rights, belonging to "the people" as a class in dialectical opposition to the crown and the crown's administrators as a class,* became the rights of men as *individuals, in dialectical opposition to men as a group.* The Rousseau theory of the relation between the individual and the group had followed the microcosm-macrocosm pattern. The *volonté générale* was the macrocosmic aspect, and individuals were identified as microcosmic participants in this common substance. So long as this common substance was defined with relation to a common *external* enemy (the feudal sovereign whose opposition the people communally shared), it was easy to consider any individual member of the popular antagonist as a consubstantial part of the popular antagonism as a whole. But when the coöperating member in this *agon,* the monarch, had been removed, his vital contribution to the definition of popular essence was gone (for of primary importance in the locating of what one *is,* is the locating of what one is *against*). As a result, we got a different notion of the individual: not the individual as an *integral* part of the popular whole, but the individual as a *divisive* part of the popular whole.

Unheralded, even unnoticed, another "fall" had taken place. And instead of the individual as microcosmic replica of the popular macrocosm, we got the individual *against* the group, men *against* society, business enterprise *against* its own government. And the Court, in keeping with this individualistic perspective, repeatedly nullified the effect of laws passed in strict accordance with the theory of popular sovereignty (i.e., nullified not the laws of a *disobedient* government, as were the legislatures to pass laws in defiance of the majority's wishes, but the laws of an *obedient* government enacting laws that the majority itself favored).

These nullifications were based on reference to the "principles" enacted in the Constitution itself. Hence, what we are trying to do here is to suggest that the nature of "principles" themselves might merit closer study.   And we are suggesting that a document, arising at a given period in history, should not be treated (if we are to understand its nature as an *act*) simply as though its "principles" were something eternal, for eternal things do not have a beginning, and these did.   We may perhaps rescue universality here—but only by a much more round-about way.

Considering the Constitution, then, as an enactment arising in history, hence a dialectical act, we find something like this: Thrust A (the will of the monarch) had called forth parry A_1 (the "rights" of the people). A document is formed that memorializes or perpetuates this parry. And it survives, in its memorialization, after the role of the opponent whose thrust called forth this parry has been removed.   What, then, is the parry in answer to, when in the course of time a new opponent, with his own different style of thrust, has arisen to take the place of the former opponent?

The design can be easily pictured.   Imagine a statue of two fencers, the one lunging forward with his sword aimed at the shoulders.   And the other fencer raising his sword to deflect the flow.   Imagine next that, in the course of historic change, one of this pair is lost.   Only the figure of the parrier remains, with his sword obviously raised to ward off a thrust at the shoulders.   Imagine next a change to a new form of duelling.   And some sculptor portrays this new opponent, a man let us say with a pistol.   And now imagine some academician trying to fit the posture of the swordsman's parry to the posture of the man with the gun.   Or, if that seems too incongruous, imagine the statue of a swordsman this time thrusting at the groins; and imagine attempting to see in the memorialized parry an *eternal* parry, a *universal* parry, quite as fit to meet the second thrust as it was to meet the first.

The Generalizing of Wishes

There is, however, a sense in which a "principle," even thus arising historically and by partisanship, can be considered eternal or universal. This is so when the principle is raised to a sufficiently high level of generalization.   The strategy is then couched in terms sufficiently general to serve as a response to the "human situation" in general.

And even partial or partisan experiences can be "universal" in the sense that all human relations are so, hence such experiences are typical of all men.

If one prays for rain, his prayer is adapted to drought. If one prays for clearing, his prayer is adapted to cloudburst. But if one prays for "welfare" or "security," he has a "higher order" of prayer, prayer at a sufficiently high level of generalization to serve in situations as different as drought, cloudburst, earthquake, pestilence, and debt. Thus, to say of a Constitution (we are quoting a tribute that has been paid to the Constitution of the United States) that "its unchanging provisions are adaped to the infinite variety of the changing conditions of our national life," is to say that it contains some very highly generalized wishes, wishes so generalized that they can be "adapted to" living conditions almost inconceivable to the Founding Fathers who thus so ably wished in our behalf more than a century and a half before our times.

One can thus see "Constitutional" tactics at work grandly, in such a formula as Christianity's golden rule, a prescription so universalized that, like God, it applies to every man uniquely. For every man will conceive in ways peculiar to himself just exactly what he would have done unto him. Hence, this precept can have a precise meaning to him that it could have to no other man. However, if he would obey the rule, he will find that it is like a question to be answered—and since to a general question we can give a general answer, for all the particularities of his notions as to what he would have done unto him, he can conceive of such a policy more broadly, in terms of "justice," or "frankness," or "kindliness," etc. The "principle" itself (it is the *lex talionis* translated from the style of the threat into the style of cajolery) had to be couched in highly generalized form, if Christianity was to qualify as a world religion that would unite under a common cultural constitution the many tribes, with unique rules of conduct, which had been brought into contact by trade and empire. We might think of it as a chapterhead, with each tribe filling out the chapter in details peculiar to the tribe (until in time the body of Christian thought had become comparatively fixed, with a structure of evaluations applicable to the culture as a whole). And similarly with our secular Constitutions, men might lay down a "principle" of liberty (that is, the wish for liberty, or the command, "let there be liberty")—and this would be so generalized a chapterhead that men long afterwards could go on, filling out the chapter differently, interpreting in the light of wholly new situations (new scenes that must give correspondingly new meaning to the clause or slogan or chapterhead, which by the nature of the printed word had long outlasted the scene in which it was enacted, and thus had outlasted the particular opponents who had contributed to its meaning in that scene).

Limits and Powers of a Constitution

There is, of course, a sense in which a human Constitution is an act of supererogation. Imagine, for instance, an Ideal Constitution for Students, that claimed for students the "inalienable right to solve all their problems, whatever these might turn out to be." Obviously, if the student has a problem that he can't solve, he will derive no help from the guaranty in his ideal Constitution. And if he has a problem that he can solve, he needs no Constitutional guaranty. It is in this sense that the right to the "pursuit of happiness" is supererogatory. The "pursuit of happiness," as a motive, is embedded in the Constitution-beneath-the-Constitution—though such a slogan might be of moment in implying the adoption of secular values as against religious values, i.e., a different notion as to what happiness is and how it is to be attained—as were it to be attained, for instance, through a stress upon commercial activity rather than through a stress upon aesthetic or religious practices. Insofar as our Constitution is a Constitution for small business, then in proportion as the conditions favoring such kinds of enterprise drop away, the Constitution willy nilly "abolishes itself." The change of scene makes it inevitable that the enactments become new enactments.

Constitutions are of primary importance in suggesting what co-ordinates one will think by. That is, one cannot "guaranty" a people any rights which future conditions themselves make impracticable; and whatever the limits and resources of liberty in the future may be, if they are there, they need no Constitutional guaranty; but Constitutions are important in singling out certain directives for special attention, and thus in bringing them more clearly to men's consciousness. During the era of the New Deal, for instance, we saw attempts to introduce the "principle" or "directive" of "private economic security without private property" into a Constitution that lacked such a co-ordinate. And it is interesting that this principle of individual security had to be approached through the collectivist coördinates in the document, such as "public emergency" and "national welfare." The socialization of losses, whereby government subsidy had protected private property, became somewhat extended to the point where government subsidy protected private poverty. The state of the population made it necessary; the state of the banking structure made it viable. A capitalist motivation that distributes by money made it reasonable, since only by having the wherewithal to purchase does one stay strictly within the bounds of a money economy.

A Constitution is "binding" upon the future in the sense that it has centered attention upon one calculus of motivation rather than some other; and by thus encouraging men to evaluate their public acts in the chosen terms, it serves in varying degrees to keep them from evaluating such acts in other terms. In this sense we could say that not only Marxist and Fascist calculi of motives, but also all individual and group psychologies, and all naturalistic, metaphysical, and theological theories of motivation, are "un-Constitutional."

Constitutional Tactics of Coleridge's "Pantisocracy" Project

If a man is pushed over a cliff, his descent is not an act; it is a natural event. But if, during his descent, he clutches at something to break his fall, this clutching for a purpose however futile is an act. This substantival (motivational, or "Constitutional") distinction between the human act and the physical event was a basic concern with Coleridge, both in his poetry and in his moral theorizing. He phrased it as a distinction between "motive" and "impulse." If one did exactly as he wished, spontaneously, purely because he so felt, he would be acting from "impulse." If one arrested this spontaneity in any way, he would be acting from "motive." In some contexts Coleridge used "motive" much as Bentham used the word "interest." To write a poem for money, for instance, would be a "motivated" act rather than an "impulsive" one—and the two could be merged only insofar as the poem was written without a single concern with monetary interests but happened to be so constructed that it had a market value.

Coleridge's works show a shifting dialectic with regard to this motive-impulse relationship. At some points, the two are considered after the analogy of our two-circles pattern. Motives, interests, expediencies are treated as the more restricted idiom, but concentric with the wider idiom of impulse. At other points, the two become divisively related, the narrower circle being an antagonist of the wider circle. Judged as a Constitutional wish, his "Pantisocracy" project (an early Utopian enterprise envisioning a Communist colony on the banks of the Susquehannah) was designed to solve the problem by so constructing a society that virtue would be "inevitable." This would be attained, he felt, by the socializing of property, since such "aspheterism" would remove partisan interest as a motive of action.

A solution possibly hysterical is offered in the critical moment of "The Ancient Mariner" where the Mariner impulsively blesses the water-snakes (blessing them "unaware" and proclaiming them beautiful that is, in essence blessable, whereby the command and the obedience would be one—for if one wanted to bless something which was blessable, there would be no problem of virtue). It was a moment that greatly annoyed our great expert in virtue, Irving Babbitt (who held that this could not be a virtuous act because it had no "inner check"). At best, we might say, it could be an innocent act, an Edenic act, an act of oneness—but it could be so only prior to the "fall," and the Ancient Mariner on the contrary is a guilt-laden moralist.

In "Aids to Reflection" we find Coleridge offering in advance his comment on Babbitt's objection, since Coleridge would probably have considered Babbitt's notion of the "inner check" closer to a Stoic position than a Christian one. "The Stoic," Coleridge writes, "attaches the highest honor (or rather attaches honor solely) to the person that acts virtuously in spite of his feelings, or who has raised himself above the conflict by their extinction." But Christianity "instructs us to place small reliance on a virtue that does not begin by bringing the feelings to a conformity with the commands of the conscience. Its especial aim, its characteristic operation, is to moralize the affections. The feelings, that oppose a right act, must be wrong feelings. The act, indeed, whatever the agent's feelings might be, Christianity would command: and under certain circumstances would both command and commend it— commend it as a healthful symptom in a sick patient; and command it, as one of the ways and means of changing the feelings, or displacing them by calling up the opposite."

If Coleridge's "Christian," then, would attain wholeness in his virtuous act ("Faith is a total act of the soul" *The Friend,* Essay XV), he cannot do the good merely because he *ought* to; he must also *want* to. The commanded and the commended must be identical (a difficult merger to coach, as per the formula, *velle non discitur*). If the snakes represented temptation, we should get a secretly subversive solution to the problem of the total act. It would have the *form* of the Christian strategy in translating the *lex talionis* into the golden rule. That is: it would convert a "negative" style into a "positive" style. But beneath this form, it would be furtively diabolical. For it would bless temptation, proclaiming temptation to be substantially blessed, whereby the response to its *com*pulsiveness could become transubstantiated into an *im*pulsiveness. It would be somewhat as though the man, pushed over the cliff, were to make his descent an act by willing that he continue to descend, so that the impulse "from within" would be one with the motive "from without."

However, Coleridge's hope for spontaneous virtue and the total act (a hope basic to both his Pantisocracy project and his radical reconstitution of temptation in "The Ancient Mariner") is obviously an ideal incapable of realization in an imperfect world. The very *wish* for wholeness is derived from partiality—hence could only be attained through the unity of all men with one another and all mankind with the universe. We must aim at congregation by devices making for segregation—*peace* is something we must *fight* for. The more perfect the end, the correspondingly more imperfect the means. If one could get peace by peaceful means, there would be no peace left to get: peace would be here already. We may, it is true, modify the conditions of fighting (forensic competition, for instance, may replace competition by force—but rhetorical sway and logical cogency are dialectical, or agonistic, in that they require the coöperation of an opponent, though this opponent but take the attenuated form of a "problem" to be solved). Some means are so much more "peaceful" than others as to seem, by comparison with them, to be "peacefulness" itself. And we should always seek to select these means farther along towards peace on the peace-war spectrum. It is wrong, however, to consider them as *essentially* peaceful. And there is a real sense in which brute force is less thoroughly militant than poetry or philosophy, since its expression is so crude and superficial, and can only be said to go to the depths of a man because there is a stupid modern habit of thinking that a few easily aroused forms of fury and vengeance constitute the "depths" of mankind. One might with much more justice complain that we today are suffering from a woeful inferiority in the quality of "the enemy." "Evil" has become reduced to brute masses of explosive, with a few rudimentary processes of misrepresentation (got by organized control of the news). By such crass simplifications, people are *emptied* rather than *filled*—and their wars are more like the clashes of automata than the combat of men profoundly locked in a wrestling match that has an infinity of holds.

Constitutions But Partially Representative

But if the total act cannot be attained in a partial world, even in the case of a work enjoying the efficiencies of a private enterprise (as Coleridge's Pantisocracy dream did somewhat and his "Ancient Mariner" still more), it can be still less thoroughly attained in a document attesting to a public act. For it must be representative of a vast and complex social body. So that, even when it was enacted, many men could at best participate in the act vicariously through their representatives as drafters and signatories. While, as research has shown, even at the time, a large proportion of the citizenry did not participate, even thus vicariously.

We should certainly not deny that vicarious enactment is possible. Even an event, caused wholly from without, can be an act, if one wills the event. If a man prognosticates a natural calamity, for instance, and comes to have such a vested interest in his modes of diagnosis as to require the calamity (as vindication of his judgment) he is a vicarious conspirator in the calamity.[14] Or an accident, killing a person one should love but does not, may become representative, and thereby cause feelings of remorse. But though vicarious enactment, through representatives appointed by either vote or destiny, can occur, it can occur for

---

[14] There is a surprising moment, bearing on this, in the movie, *A Man to Remember,* where the audience is greatly gratified at the news that many children are sick and dying of infantile paralysis, so gratified in fact, that, at the performance we saw they broke into applause. The hero had foretold the epidemic, and was in disgrace with the medical authorities for rebelling against their ordinances and taking steps in his community to forestall the outbreak. Hence the audience's impulsive satisfaction on being told that the epidemic had struck the surrounding communities while the children of the hero's community were spared. The calamity vindicated his judgment and his rebellion.

all only insofar as all are united. Even the Declaration of Independence could not be a total act, owing to the large proportion of Tories (many of whom resisted it through an admirable sense of loyalty to the traditional modes of sovereignty). But its dialectic function as a rejoinder to the Crown did make it a representative act for diverse groups unified by the sharing of a single opponent (their consubstantiality thus being defined dialectically, by reference to a contrary term,—totemic communion got if not by a love-feast, by what they ate in common, then at least by a hate-feast, by what they vomited in common—or if the figure seems too extreme, we may think of the king's tea rejected, and of the communal sense implicit in the unified turn to a substitute). But, as we have noted, when the Constitution was drafted, this "second state of Eden" had passed. We call it a second state of Eden, or Eden once removed, because rebellion against the Crown was an act of *division,* hence technically a "fall," but it was a majority division, hence from its own standpoint a unity. But in its very act of abolishing the monarch, it abolished the very term by which it had been unified. And the Constitution was concerned with a new division, the rights of "minorities."

Recently, as we have said, the rise of monopolies has begun to produce a new opponent, thus calling for a corresponding reinterpretation of rights. For a long time the vessels of the business philosophy were felt to be representative of the nation's ways (the *businessmen's* justice served as *everybody's* justice). The business class seemed culminative, as nobility had previously done. However, in proportion as some businesses emerged above the others, it became dubious whether they should be considered as the synecdochic part or as the divisive part. And though the monopolists use all the resources of finance, tradition, and journalistic indoctrination to perpetuate the earlier terminology in accordance with which their role would be interpreted as culminative rather than divisive, their very function as a new form of administration assigns them a crucial role in the dialectical redefinition of Constitutional rights. Only by subsidizing inaccuracy (translating popular education into popular miseducation) can this rising kind of administration henceforth prevent the appreciation of the change that should take place in the concepts of authority and rights.

The rise of monopolies may have one important feature, from the moralistic point of view. Their emerging function as sovereigns provides a stronger incentive for "liberty" to be thought of as a *group* wish, rather than as an *individualistic* wish. And there correspondingly emerges a stronger incentive for the great majority of the people to conceive of their interests collectively in opposition to the economic sovereignty of the monopolists. A Hitler or a Mussolini may be encouraged at such a point, since he centers the collective attitudes in a single person, who can then *appear* culminative while functioning divisively, as a colleague of the monopolists.

Principles of the Conflict Among Principles

We have said enough to make it apparent in what way we would equate "principles" with terms having a volitional element, such as "ideals," "commands," or "wishes." To insert the "principle of equality" into a Constitution is to utter a hope that men may become equal or may continue to be equal. It obviously would proclaim their equality *within* the Constitution as a way of counteracting some kind of inequality *outside* the Constitution (or within the wider circumference of the Constitution-beneath-the-Constitution). "Principles" in this sense are a decreeing of substance, hence a decreeing of motives (and they thereby open the avenues to the ambiguities of substance, whereby those who are called equal "substantially" or "in principle" may be so called because they are not, and new inequalities would be encouraged to develop precisely because the given terminology of motivation introduced a bluntness where a discrimination was needed).

An "ideal" being by definition something that is beyond attainment, and a "wish" referring to a state of affairs that is at least beyond attainment at the time, we can understand why men might salute an actual inequality in the name of "equality in principle." However, we have also called these principles "commands"—and a command, when it is rational, is something capable of being obeyed, or incapable of being disobeyed with impunity. "Commands," as "laws," are more "substantial" than wishes; they say not "would you?" but "you must"; and by this "mandatory" style, so the legal fiction goes, the Constitution, or "Substance," which the Founding Fathers enacted in an act of will, imposes the wishes of the Founders upon the Courts, which must obey them as commands.

Note, however, that there is another meaning of "principle" figuring here, and that much confusion often arises from our failure to make this distinction. A Constitution is but a partial act; the only truly total act would be the act of a Supreme Founding Father who founded the Universal Substance, the Constitution-beneath-the-Constitution, the scene in which the Constitution of 1789 was an enactment, and the motivational circumference of which extends far beyond the motives featured and encouraged by the local calculus that has formally governed our public relations for the last century and a half. And the fact that every single act done within the jurisdictional borders of the United States has involved motives that lie partially within and partially beyond the factors named in the Constitution, gives rise to another use of the term "principles." Here the term refers to the judicial standards developed from the fact that the Constitution, as a necessarily very limited calculus of motives, must be used as the basis of reference, in courts of law, for the judgment of acts more widely or richly motivated.

We have noted, for instance, that ideals, or wishes, need not be consistent with one another. One might, for instance, wish for the right to gamble and one might also wish for security in one's gambling. In themselves, these are contradictory wishes, since gambling by definition involves an element of risk; and if this risk is eliminated, it is not gambling, but a sure thing. Yet one might wish for both dispensations nonetheless. Or, at least, one could enact a document in which both wishes stood side by side. One could even quite consciously work out his calculus of wishes by pitting each wish against a contradictory wish, and by further wishing that these wishes, as contradictory extremes, might counterbalance one another to produce the happy medium. Or one could make up a Constitution as our politicians often make up their political platforms, by deciding how many influential groups there were whose suffrage was needed and introducing planks that would please each group, regardless of their bearing upon the planks introduced to please the other groups—and then all present could sign their names to the lot.

And thus, we could also consider as "principles," the formulae for treating the state of mutuality or contradiction among the ideals or wishes, as revealed by the problem of arriving at judgments in specific practical cases. Thus, in the *volitional* sense, any clause announcing a right or an obligation would be a Constitutional "principle." But in the *necessitarian* sense, any statement would be a "principle" if it signalized a logical or practical conflict between clauses, or defined a procedure for arriving at "Constitutional" judgments despite such conflicts.

Let us consider, for instance, the "principle" (in the second sense) that is implicit in the very name of our nation, which signifies a *plurality* acting as a *unity* (the pattern that is also quite accurately reproduced in the device, *"e pluribus unum"*). As a union of states, we can accent our nation either as "The United *States*" or "The *United* States." The first accent would give us the Jeffersonian stress upon states' rights; the second would give us the Hamiltonian stress upon national federation. "Ideally," as in the name of our country and in the pattern of its thoroughly accurate device, we can have both wishes (or "principles" in the first sense) at once. But practically, a law which grants greater powers to one member of this pair deducts proportionately from the powers of the other member. And we should note this effect as a "principle" in the second sense (not a "wish" but an *inevitable fact* about the relationships between elements in the Constitution as affected by contact with the demands of the Constitution-beneath-the-Constitution). And as an attendant principle in the second sense, we could next note how, as a result of this relationship between the ideal motives of the Constitutional scene and the actual motives of the historical scene, when the ideal merger is converted into the practical division, a Court can sanction a law in the name of plurality (states' rights) or refuse to sanction the same law by judging it in the name of unity (national federation). Or, conversely, the Court could refuse to sanction a law in the name of plurality or could sanction the same law by judging it in the name of unity.

In sum: There are principles in the sense of wishes, and there are principles in the sense of interrelationships among the wishes. Principles as wishes are voluntary or arbitrary, inasmuch as men can meet in conference and decide how many and what kind of wishes they shall subscribe to. But once you have agreed upon a list of wishes, the interrelationships among those wishes are necessary or inevitable. A public right, for instance, "necessarily" implies a private obligation or a private jeopardy; a private right "inevitably" implies a public obligation or a public jeopardy. Confronting such a situation, you could, "of your own free will," draw up a Constitution that merely proclaimed a set of public rights and a set of private rights (or a set of public and private obligations); but in doing so, you would have made it "mandatory" that, in all specific cases, a conflict must arise out of these implications.

Constitution Makes Extra-Constitutionality Mandatory

Judicial theorists often would contend it is the wishes in a Constitution that are mandatory upon the Court. This is in keeping with the genius of the term, "Constitution," as a word for "substance" or "ground" which imposes the quality of its motivation upon all acts enacted within its circumference (the circumference, in such cases being considered coextensive with the span of time in which the Constitution is accepted as the law of the land). But actually, where a Constitution contains a set of wishes more or less at odds with one another, what would really be "mandatory" upon a Court in such circumstances (if this Court is taken to have the right of judicial review of all legislation) would be a "demand" that the Court decide which of the wishes is to be granted and which of the wishes is to be ignored. In other words, where the attempt to carry out the wishes of a Constitution in specific legal cases involves a conflict between Constitutional wishes, what is really mandatory upon the Court is a *new act,* an act of *arbitration,* a partly *voluntary* or *arbitrary* choice decided upon by the Court. Were there no conflict among the wishes proclaimed in a Constitution, it would then obviously be mandatory upon the Court simply to see that its decisions obey the wishes of the document. But where wishes are in conflict (or otherwise put, where the sovereign ideality of the "confluence" or "balance" or "panspermia" of all the wishes must be translated into the idiom of practical *contradictions*) the interrelationships among the wishes impose a new kind of command upon the Court: a command not simply to see that the wishes of the Constitution are fulfilled, but rather to decide which wishes shall be given preference over others.

"Substance" and "motivation" are convertible terms (*Wechselbegriffe*); hence, it is indeed a Constitution of some sort, with its circumference of some sort, that motivates an act in the country where an arbitrarily proclaimed Constitution is the law of the land. But the total motivation of any act (including a Court's act of judgment) must be derived from substance in its total scope, not merely in the restricted range laid down by the document—and it is from this wider area, rather than from the document, that the Court must draw its motivations for arbitrating contradictions within the document.

Indeed, an oration designed to do none other than to celebrate the wisdom and justice of a Constitution would have to go outside the Constitution for reasons. Otherwise, such an oration could be but a tautological restatement of the Constitution itself, not a testimony offering proofs or arguments why the document is good. And if the oration did aim to do more than merely restate, it would be "un-Constitutional" at least in the sense that it was "extra-Constitutional," since it would derive arguments from reference to a wider orbit of motivation, involving some concept of a Constitution-beneath-the-Constitution (as were one to praise the Constitution because of its assistance in helping us to develop modern technology). Similarly, when a Constitution contains a batch of wishes which, as applied to specific practical cases, are found to be variously at odds, were the Court to be as explicit about its motivation as Courts are supposed to be, it would have to formulate a theology, or a metaphysics, or a physics, or at least a philosophy of history as the ground of its decisions. In other words, to be as explicit about its motivations as a Court should be, the Court would have to undermine the very theory of positive law upon which its whole function is based.

There is another very important sense in which Constitutions do have a mandatory effect, however. A written Constitution, which is continually referred to as a basis of decision, is a *calculus* of motives. It is a terminology, or set or coördinates, for the analysis of motives. Thus, when such a vocabulary for the treatment of motives is, by public consent or acquiescence, given far greater authority than any other vocabulary of motivation, oddly enough such a Constitution must, by the very nature of the case, *enforce* a great measure of intellectual tolerance and extra-Constitutional speculation. For by being so obviously restricted or simplified a calculus of motives, it practically *compels* men to put forward alternative calculi, of different focus or wider circumference. In this way, particularly, a positive Constitution "guaranties" freedom of religious belief, as a calculus of wider circumference (explicitly derived from a set of doctrines about the Constitution-beneath-the-Constitution) could not. A religious doctrine of motivation, for instance, could not provide the basis of such tolerance—

for it explicitly refers matters of motivation to pronouncements about
substance in the Constitution-beneath (or behind)-the-Constitution,
involving substance in terms of the "total" circumference. And whatever substance, or "Constitution," in this wider sense, may be, it *is*
"mandatory." Insofar as the "positive" Constitutions in the West have
been business Constitutions, thus in effect making the "religion of
business" the partially proclaimed and partially unproclaimed circumference of the Constitution-beneath-the-Constitution, positive law
here also contributed to religious tolerance, since the perspective of
business makes it reasonable for one to tolerate an infidel if he works for
low wages or is a good-paying customer. Tolerance fostered by
business, however, departs in proportion as the substance of business
itself is endangered by untoward developments in the Constitution-
beneath-the-Constitution, and by persons or parties who are rightly or
wrongly felt to be the vessels or causes of these developments. Hence
the businessman distrusts, first of all, the Marxist, since the Marxist
substance would replace the business substance. He has no essential
objection to Fascism—only his fear that he may not be one of the
"insiders" who get the profits of Fascist coördination.

Some Degree of Constitutionality in Every Law

Insofar as a good job of wishing is done in a Constitution (that is, if
the document contains an assortment of both public and private rights
and obligations) there is one sense in which it becomes almost impossible for a legislature to propose a law in defiance of Constitutional
guaranties. The law that frustrates one wish in the Constitution will,
by the same token, gratify another. The given law, for instance, may
propose confiscatory measures that further restrict the rights of private
property; but in so doing it may further the general welfare, or act in a
state of national emergency, or make for greater equality, or regulate
inter-state commerce; or, at the very least, it may invoke the right of
police powers granted to the government.

Imagine, for instance, a recipe of wishes. The recipe calls for an
egg, two cups of flour, a level tablespoonful of baking soda, and salt to
taste—etc. A legislature proposes a law that falls under the title of
eggs. The Court may then either imply its sanction under the title of
eggs, or imply its nullification under the title of flour, baking soda, or

salt. And even if it is a law that falls under the title of salt, the provision "salt *to taste*" requires a new act of arbitration to decide whether there is too much salt or too little.

Where there is a recipe of wishes, variously related to one another, existing as sovereign states in the ideality and generality of the Constitutional document, but requiring the partial exclusion of one another when they are applied to particular cases, then note that specific measures could not properly be called either Constitutional or un-Constitutional. That is, they would not be wholly and unambiguously one or the other. But in being Constitutional from the standpoint of some one Constitutional principle, they would by the same token be un-Constitutional if considered solely in terms of some opposing principle.

In such a state of affairs, it is obvious that if the Court selects but *one* principle by which to test the legislative measure in question, and considers the matter in terms of this alone, it has simply not confronted the issue. If it wishes to sanction the measure, it can do so in the name of the appropriate wish. If it wishes to nullify the measure, it can do so in the name of a different wish. To say that the decision, under such circumstances, was "mandatory" upon the Court would be to put a "broad interpretation" indeed upon the concept of the mandatory.

In the early years of the Republic, many Judicial decisions were substantiated in the name of the "higher law," which was an idealized way of referring to those aspects of the Ultimate Scene here called the "Constitution-beneath-the-Constitution." However, after a few decades when a sufficient number and *variety* of precedents had been amassed, the Court could ground its choice of "mandatory" decisions in a corresponding choice of precedents, by selecting the particular kind of precedent that best substantiated, or rationalized, the favored decision. Reference to precedent could thus *function* as reference to the extra-Constitutional scene; but in *appearance* such decisions were purely *internal* to the traditions of Constitutional law.

The ironic fact about reference to precedent is that, in a nation whose scenic conditions were changing constantly, one might well expect precedent to count most if used *in reverse*. That is, one might adduce precedents to justify the *opposite* kind of decision now, on the grounds that the scenic conditions are now so different from those when the precedent was established. However, "higher law" and the precedents based upon it referred not to changing material conditions, but to the kind of "immutable scene" that could be idealized and generalized in terms of "eternal truth, equity and justice."

"Essentializing" and "Proportional" Strategies of Interpretation

Constitutional theory has generally swung between "strict constructionists" and "broad constructionists," with the two schools changing places on occasion, (as Jefferson, a strict constructionist, adopted the contrary principle when seeking Constitutional authority for the Louisiana Purchase). But we might make a distinction between the "essentializing" and the "proportional" that would cut across this on the bias. The essentializing strategy would be that of selecting some one clause or other in the Constitution, and judging a measure by reference to it. The proportional strategy would require a more complex procedure, as the Court would test the measure by reference to *all* the wishes in the Constitution. That is, the Court would note that the legislation in question would be wholly irrelevant to certain of the wishes, would wholly gratify one or some, would partially gratify others, and would antagonize the rest. And its judgment would be rationalized with reference to this total recipe. The aim would be to state explicitly a doctrine of *proportions*.

The proportional method would also require explicit reference to a *hierarchy* among the disjunct wishes. To be sure, the wishes, in their pure ideality, are all "sovereign states" or "independent individuals," all of equal importance; but as applied to practical cases some of the wishes must be more important than others. Or some one of them must be more important at one time in history than at another time in history. And since the Constitution itself does not specify priority among the wishes, does not state which among these equals shall be "foremost," then the Court must make these decisions for itself, its judgment being a "new act," so far as the Constitution is concerned. And this act would lie outside the Constitution, being motivated by the Court's views of the Constitution-beneath-the-Constitution (as indeed the Constitution itself justifies, since the notion of a "state of emergency" obviously requires reference to a supporting, extra-Constitutional scene into which the Constitution has survived as an enactment). An explicit rationalization of such a decision would certainly involve a statement as to the Court's grounds of preference among the wishes.

Let us illustrate the difference as it shows through an article by Arthur Krock, "Is There a Way to Dispense with Elections?" (*The New York Times,* September 18, 1941). He writes:

> Some enthusiastic trumpeters for a "truly all-out" rearmament effort have been heard in Washington to propose that the Congressional elections of 1942 be dispensed with. They purport to find executive authority to do this in the war powers of the President, which they contend will be in full operation by November of next year; and legislative authority in Section 4, Article I, of the Constitution to achieve the same result if that method should be preferred, prophesying that the present Supreme Court majority would protect either device.

> Their animating idea is that bipartisan Congressional contests will promote further national disunity and paralyze the rearmament program in an even greater degree than was done by the third term campaign of 1940. If, because of the proclaimed "unlimited emergency," the President sees national peril in holding the elections, he should—so argue these zealots—continue the present Congress by executive order or ask the legislators for a law. . . .

> This correspondent today consulted several students of the Constitution and the statutes in an effort to discover how the elections could be called off if the Administration so desired. He could not find one who was able to develop a constitutional or statutory base for such a move. But it is interesting to record that several, mentioning Charles Evans Hughes's comment that the Constitution means what the high justices say it means, suggested that if public opinion should be favorable, or the President determine—as Lincoln did concerning habeas corpus—that the emergency required it, made-to-order means could be produced and solemnly called legal.

The issue is reducible to this: Article I of the Constitution specifically provides that members of the House "shall be chosen every second year by the people of the several States" and that Senators shall be elected for a term of six years. Section 4 of Article I permits the States to prescribe the "times, places and manner of holding elections" for Congress unless Congress chooses to alter them, which it may do "at any time." Of these two clauses, every reasonable person would surely select the first as prior, unless he had ulterior motives for doing otherwise. That is, he would take it that the second would not justify the modification

of elections to such an extent that it changed the term of tenure stipulated in the first.   When we come to the matter of national emergency,
however, we confront a much less tenuous problem in priority.   There
certainly can be situations in which an election would be ill-timed, as
regards the welfare of the country—and if such a situation arises,
which would be "more Constitutional": should the government fulfil
its obligation to hold the elections at the stipulated time, or should it
claim its rights to act as best it may in behalf of the general welfare?
If the Constitution specifically stated that the clause fixing tenure of
office is under all circumstances to be given priority over the clause
granting the President extraordinary rights in times of emergency,
there would be no question.   But since no such hierarchy is specified,
the Court's decision must be a new act.

The Constitution itself justifies the President's recourse to extraordinary acts when an extraordinary situation prevails in the Constitution-
beneath-the-Constitution (perhaps this is even a supererogatory grant,
since the nature of the scene-act ratio would seem to make it "inevitable"
that acts be out of the ordinary when the scene is out of the ordinary,
as with the fictions of Constitutionality made by many European governments in exile during the Nazi invasion.   But in any case, were
Congress to pass a law postponing the elections, or were the President
to make a proclamation of this sort, by reason of his powers in war
time, then the Court would be using the "essentializing" strategy if, for
instance, it simply noted that Article I stipulated the terms of tenure
and that the measure was "un-Constitutional" because it violated these
stipulations.   But the Court would be using the "proportional" strategy if it explicitly rationalized its decision by proclaiming a hierarchy
among the Constitutional wishes and judging the *"relative* Constitutionality" of the measure accordingly.

We see an attempt to avoid the proportional strategy in the principle
that all rights not specifically granted to the federal government are
reserved to the States.   But the proportional strategy is implicit in the
change of policy that came over the Court under the impact of the New
Deal.   This change amounted to an "interpretative revolution" in
the sense that, whereas private rights and States rights had previously
enjoyed a higher rating among the hierarchy of wishes, they were now
deposed in favor of the wishes granting power to the central govern-

ment. Or we could state this more analytically by saying that the earlier granting of private rights to public corporations, in accordance with the legal fiction that they were "persons" with the properties of persons, had encouraged the development of these corporations to the point where it resulted in the "depersonalization," or rightlessness and rolelessness and propertylessness, of many citizens as the inevitable dialectical reflex.

The revolution in the Court's hierarchy of judgments was a partial response to the growing tendency to treat the popularly elected government as a "corporation of corporations," and to endow it with a "personality" having rights to match the "personal" rights of the business corporations. Hence the complaints that we were getting "personal government," that we were sacrificing our traditional "government by law" for "government by men," that we were becoming more prone to the "leader principle" in looking to the President as the human person in whom would be vested the increased personalization of the government in its role as the "corporation of corporations." The Court, as finally affected by the New Deal psychology, was more inclined to grant the rights to the government as a person which it had once restricted to private individuals and business corporations as persons.

Now, it is a Judge's role to be judicious; and since the proportional mode of judgment would obviously be more judicious than the essentializing mode, one will find traces of this mode throughout the whole course of Judicial Review. However, there are many factors that have as constantly favored the essentializing mode. For one thing, nineteenth-century thinking is one grand gallery of rival essentializations. The law of parsimony came into its very own; if entities had once been multiplied beyond necessity, it would be truer to say that now they were *reduced* beyond necessity. The increasing complexity, giving rise to a compensatory cult of simplification, made "essentializing" seem the most "natural" mode of thought. "It all boils down to this" . . . etc. —an excellent direction in which to move, but a very bad one if arrived at by shortcuts. Further, the dialectics of the law court itself encourages a Justice to make his decisions in its image. Since attorneys for both plaintiff and defendant spontaneously sharpen and substantiate their antagonism by featuring the particular Constitutional wish that seems most serviceable for their purposes, they supply a dramatic inducement for the Court to decide the issue on the basis of the *particular* wishes the antagonists had isolated as their rules of combat. Also, the natural sympathies of the Judges with one or another trend of material interests would make them lean towards the essentializing strategy, since their own judgment was, after all, itself a plea, requiring justification by Constitutional reference, quite as did the pleas of the barristers. Accordingly, the efficiency of the essentializing method had as much in its favor with them as with the barristers.

You could hardly think of anything less judicious than the patterns of litigation; yet they are precisely the patterns of experience that the Justice confronts during every moment of his office—so we find as a judicial replica of the split between plaintiff and defendant, a split of the Court into majority decision and minority decision, with each "Judicial faction" invited to justify its decision as "effectively" as possible by featuring the wishes that would provide maximum plausibility for that decision. Furthermore, since the Constitutional principles or ideas, by their very nature as generalizations, are expressions which can give no indications as to "where you draw the line" in specific cases, one can show that any measure leads to damnation, by the mere expedient of following out its possible implications.

That is, any one of the Constitutional principles would lead to an absurd state of affairs, if enforced independently of all the other principles that modify it; and similarly any proposed legislative measure may be found to contain ominous implications, if we extrapollate such implications in a straight line, without reference to all the other factors, in law and custom, that would correct or check such a simple development. Columnists, doing the Court's work in advance, have often made themselves highly serviceable in certain quarters by thus essentializing and extrapollating the implications of some measure, which they feature in isolation, without reference to the modifying and corrective factors. It is the method used by all cartoonists to make us laugh; it is a method that can be used by our judges on and off the bench to make us tremble. And since the implications of a new measure are certainly something about which a Court could legitimately concern itself, such resources for the solemn production of "judicial cartoons" are there for pointing up the essentializing mode.

Marshall's Argument for Right of Judicial Review

Let us go back to the decision by Chief Justice Marshall in which the Court's right of review is established. He writes:

> If two laws conflict with each other, the courts must decide on the operations of each. So, if a law be in opposition to the constitution; if both the law and the constitution apply to a particular case, so that the law, disregarding the constitution; or conformable to the constitution, disregarding the law; the court must determine which of these conflicting rules governs the case: this is the very essence of judicial duty. If then, the courts are to regard the constitution, and the constitution is superior to any ordinary act of the legislature, the constitution, and not such ordinary act, must govern the case to which they both apply.

The Justice then proceeds by selecting as a test case, not one of the more generalized wishes, such as the Bill of Rights, the general welfare clause, or the granting of police powers or control of interstate commerce; instead, he selects a thoroughly specific clause, which is not fully representative of the issue:

> There are many other parts of the constitution which serve to illustrate this subject. It is declared, that 'no tax or duty shall be laid on articles exported from any state.' Suppose, a duty on the export of cotton, of tobacco, or of flour; and a suit instituted to recover it. Ought judgment to be rendered in such a case? Ought the judges to close their eyes on the constitution, and only see the law?

The Justice is here discussing precisely the kind of case which, by our approach, would require the use of the "proportional" strategy. For he is establishing the right of the Court to pass upon the "constitutionality" of a legislative measure—and in accordance with our thesis, this should be discussed not in terms of constitutionality or unconstitutionality, but in terms of relative constitutionality. Indeed, by our thesis, there are so many generalized wishes in the Constitution, that it would be very difficult for Congress to pass a law wholly un-Constitutional; for the law in question would probably be in accord with at least *one* clause, particularly if this clause were conceived as existing independently of all the other clauses.

Yet note that there seems no occasion for a "proportional" treatment. Even more, the "essentializing" treatment seems to be the only one appropriate to the issue as so presented. A law establishing an export duty would obviously have direct bearing on a clause prohibiting export duty. Hence, unless the Constitution is amended, a law establishing an export duty would run flatly counter to this particular wish. And the Chief Justice had overwhelming good reason on his side, in such cases, not only to choose the Constitution as the highest public motivation or "supreme law of the land," but what is more relevant to our purposes here, to test the validity of the given law by the essentializing strategy, with reference to the specific relevant clause.

We must recall, however, that the same Justice established precedents of broad interpretation, whereby a clause may be interpreted to cover not merely what it *explicitly* lays claim to cover, but also what, in the Court's opinion, it *implies*. This allowance was necessary, particularly in view of the fact that the pace of the industrial revolution (with all the changing modes of relationship and action that went with it) was producing a constant change of situation; and in proportion as the situational context that gave meaning to a clause at the time of its pronouncement underwent change, an almost infinite procession of new amendments to the Constitution would have been necessary unless the Courts were allowed to interpret according to the "spirit" rather than the "letter." Our own analysis of Constitutional principles as generalized wishes would force us to admit that a *strict* interpretation of "principles" is simply a contradiction in terms.

However, although broad interpretation is inevitable insofar as a wish uttered prior to experience with a given new situation is to be taken as a wish relevant to that situation, the tenth article of the Bill of Rights utters a contrary wish:

> The powers not delegated to the United States by the Constitution, nor prohibited by it to the states, are reserved to the States respectively, or to the people.

To interpret a clause in terms of its "implications" is, if this clause delegates powers to the national government, to interpret it as granting powers that it does not grant. For one can't delegate "implications" to anybody. Nor can one reserve them to anybody. They are "inalienable," though their inalienability is not grounded in the Constitutional substance, but in the substance supporting that substance, in the nature of existence itself (the Constitution-beneath-the-Constitution).

And more ironically still, in the very clause in which rights not delegated to the national government are reserved (i.e., the clause attempting to establish Constitutional grounds for literal interpretation), we find an ambiguity requiring an improvisation on the part of judges: for the phrase, "reserved to the States respectively, or to the people," gives us an "or" that may treat "the States" and "the people" as either in *ap*position or in *op*position. The more idealized a statement is, the broader will be its area of possible relevance; hence the greater its demand for new juridical acts, in deciding what weight shall be laid upon "implications." Otherwise put: in broad interpretation, such as a concern with "implications" involves, it gets down to a matter of "where you draw the line"—and no document that did our willing for us more than a century and a half ago can will the point at which our representatives today shall draw the line.

The point I am trying to make is this:

In order to make the case for Judicial Review as effective as possible, the Chief Justice, in his role as an advocate, selected a case where a new law would be in flat contradiction with a wish in the Constitution. Hence, the only issue was that of a conflict between the Constitution and the new measure. And he could present the Court's rulings as made mandatory upon the Court by the explicit motivations proclaimed in the Constitution. The important omission, from our point of view, is this: the Justice does not here ask what relationships prevail among the generalized wishes, or ideals, in the Constitution itself, and whether they too, when embodied in specific practices, might come in conflict with one another. Instead, he selects a kind of case in which a law clearly either *is* or *is not* Constitutional. And he can present his judgment as one that the Constitution makes mandatory.

However, a broad interpretation, involving a concern with "implications" and a decision as to "where you draw the line," is not "mandatory." It is "free," so far as the Constitution is concerned. It is a new act. Indeed, it is a kind of Constitutional Amendment made by the Court, without waiting for the unwieldy processes of amendment prescribed in the Constitution. And once you recognize that, as regards the more generalized grants and guaranties in the Constitution, (with undefined private rights confronted by undefined public powers), the implications of one clause can be extrapollated to the extent where they encroach upon the implications of another, then you realize that the proportional method, involving a hierarchy among the clauses, is the only one that a Justice could use in the great majority of cases. In brief, the same Justice who established the right of Judicial Review introduced principles of free interpretation that would call for a different kind of Judicial Review than the kind he cites. As an advocate of Judicial Review, he employs the essentializing tactics of a litigant—but once the right was established, the Court found itself constantly facing situations calling for a kind of judiciousness not claimed by the Chief Justice at all. These would require modes of rationalization alien to the patterns of litigation, and based upon the explicit recognition of the Court as a free agent, set free of the "mandatory" by reason of the ambiguities and contradictions arising from the nature of the Constitution itself, as a batch of generalized and variously related wishes.

Constitutional Unity and Political Diversity

The clauses of a Constitution would be "substantially" related insofar as we could show that they develop out of one another, as with the propositions of Euclidean geometry. A common essence would pervade the lot, as something from which all the parts radiated, and it is in this respect that the essentializing strategy of interpretation would be relevant. Thus, it would seem fair to characterize our Constitution as essentially a capitalist Constitution, but one that points beyond capitalism (since there are no limitations whatsoever placed upon the range of wishes that can be covered by amendment).

Theological, metaphysical, or naturalistic terminologies may, with varying degrees of plausibility, appear to embrace the total circumference of motivation. But our capitalist Constitution could not possibly pretend to such thoroughness. Indeed, whereas the theological, metaphysical, or naturalistic constitution is the scene (of varying scope) in which a human act takes place, a political constitution is itself an act. And though such an act, in establishing an arbitrary set of motives, becomes in turn the scene of subsequent acts, this quasi-scenic property does not take away its essential character as an enactment of human wills, an enactment that goes on being reënacted each time its principles are reaffirmed (or goes on being reënacted in effect, as a kind of "act by default," insofar as any who would withhold their active assent do not proclaim an active dissent).

Thus, when we speak of the relation between a Constitution and a Constitution-beneath-the-Constitution, we are really dealing with the relation between a political act and a non-political or extra-political scene. And when the framers of the Constitution (or more accurately, the framers of The Enactment that would be the Basis or Ground of Future Enactments) referred to states of "emergency" that might arise, they were obviously recognizing the fact that a human constitution, in contrast with a constitution laid down by God or nature, could not be total. Scenes might arise of such a sort that the wishes enacted in the document would be irrelevant acts.

There is even a sense in which one might even say that, since the establishment of the Constitution, every single day has been a day of emergency, ranging from very grave emergency to emergencies more or less limited or attenuated. Or in other words, every single day has been a day in which the particularities of the scene required some manner of new decision involving motivational ingredients not treated in the Constitutional calculus.

Just as the patterns of litigation are reproduced in the pattern of minority and majority decision on the part of the Supreme Court, so Constitutional wishes have their replica in Party Promises, often the most disparately assembled Constitutions of all, motivations-for-the-nonce: political platforms. And these platforms, as verbal acts of preparation, have regularly manifested the dual nature of preparations, either in leading towards the promised political act or in serving as prayerful substitute for it. As a Constitution can, by reason of ideality, stylize a conflict of material interests as a diversity of principles or a reciprocation of rights, so a political party will, quite as a matter of course, sling together a platform containing promises for each class of voters. Though the party could carry out some of these promises only by violating other promises, the politicians can be "idealistic" or "visionary" enough during the campaigning stage to play down this stylistic matter, except when discussing the platform of the opposition.

Political coalition (uniting the contingently or accidentally related rather than the integrally or substantially or constitutionally related) is got by two methods of compromise. In the *bloc* system, there are a great many factions, each with a very definite and fairly self-consistent platform, its promises usually too accurately attuned to the interests of some one group of voters for general acceptance by other groups of voters. When there is a great number of factions, no one faction can control a majority of the votes, hence various temporary coalitions among the *blocs* must be formed after the election. And since each group in the coalition must make concessions to the other groups in order to get concessions in return, at this stage the clarity and definiteness of the campaign promises must necessarily give place to what you may call either "intelligent compromise" or "betrayal," as you prefer.

Or you may assemble much bigger parties, as we do in the United States, by platforms that themselves represent a coalition of various factions (usually geographically distinguished). It is customary to ridicule Hitler's 25-point program, by noting how the promises in the various clauses would cancel one another if seriously translated into the realm of practical interests. Yet this was a "coalition" platform such as is quite the norm of United States politics. (Whereat we may recall that the Founders of our nation expected us to have a one-party government, with elections involving primarily the choice of individual administrators. Hence, the whole party structure developed outside the provisions of the Constitution. And Washington's grave misgivings, in his Farewell Address to the nation, reflect simply his disturbance at the rise of the party system which we have since been taught to take as the norm, and even as our glory.)

Behind the various legislative factions in turn, are the lobbies that represent local pressure groups of varying size and strength and that employ varying degrees of publicity and secrecy (with the secrecy usually more candid than the publicity). In these extra-legislative or "pre-legislative" bodies, there is a plurality of interests adding up to a pure babel of fractional and factional motivations so much at odds with one another that Congress as a body cannot possibly yield to them all, though each has its individual Congressmen that would.

How ironically far we are here removed from the "Edenic" state of the Constitutional wishes in their sovereign ideality may be glimpsed in the typical businessmen's convention held at Washington. The businessmen, as a national body, pass a resolution strongly in favor of decreased government expenditure. But, being in the national capital, each member individually, as representative of his local interests, visits his Congressman to urge upon him that he do all in his power to get a larger federal grant for local projects. Thus the businessmen's ideal unitary wish becomes the exact opposite of their divisive practical wishes.

Role of the President

The President, as head of a party hoping for reëlection, seeks to act as the happy resultant of these many contradictory motives. The platform on which he was elected is usually a replica of the Constitution, containing promises for everybody—but since his acts as national executive translate such matters from the realm of ideal "balances" to that of practical "contradictions" where "differing ideals" become "conflicting interests," he finds himself continually confronting a multitude of piecemeal situations at odds with one another. His problem then is, like that of any ruler, to find some unitary principle from which all his major policies may consistently radiate. In brief, his problem is to find for himself and his party a "substance" or "constitution," of varying duration. And a slogan, as motive, serves here, either as an honestly ancestral title from which the specific policies may descend, or as a rhetorical misnomer that gives at least the appearance of substance.

In the person of Franklin Delano Roosevelt, our country surely found the politician most thoroughly and competently at home in such exigencies as we have been considering. It is even conceivable that his illness contributed substantially as an important motive shaping the quality of his understanding, and thence the quality of his acts. For during the period of the attack and the slow recovery, he must have experienced most poignantly and forcibly a distinction between action and motion, since he could act only by proxy, through enlisting the will and movements of others. Thus, even down to the purely physiological level, he must have learned to make peace with a kind of dissociation between impulse and response rarely felt by men whose physical motions are in more spontaneous or naïve relation to their thinking. Hence, it is conceivable that from this dissociation could arise a more patient attitude towards motives outside one's direct control than other men would naturally have. And from this could arise a sharpening of the administrative sense, which is decidedly that of acting by proxy, and utilizing the differences among the agents through whom one acts.

But this would take us beyond grammatical and rhetorical matters, into the areas of symbolic speculation.

And in any case, we should note this: Whatever private motives may have contributed to Roosevelt's sense of tactics, a man in his position who would want to think of himself as in some measure a free agent and not a mere "servant" of either the public or some one class or group among the public, could retain this role only insofar as he had strong opposing groups with which to work. While there are fairly equal weights at both ends of a seesaw, the "candlestick" at the center can swing things this way or that by redistributing his own weight; but if the weights are made greatly unequal, then the candlestick is but "prisoner" to the pull of the heavier weight. It is doubtless for this reason that the President, as an astute political tactician, so often refused to go as far towards the weakening of labor organizations as the general public, under the "education" of the press, seemed willing to have him go. Let labor unions be weakened beyond a certain extent, by either the manufacturing interests or their own internal dissensions, and the President's own ability to act would be impaired, since he needed labor as one of his "reflexes." "Discord" in this sense would be his only means of personal harmony (assuming that harmony requires in some measure freedom of action). Nor is this statement inconsistent with the fact that, in moments of exasperation, he could wish a plague on both the houses.

For here we confront the unity-diversity paradox all over again, as we see that a President who would strive to unify a democratic nation must not unify it too well. That is, if the material situation itself contains vast conflicts of interests, he must keep all the corresponding voices vocal. Yet at the same time he must seek to find some over-all motive, or situation, as would be got in some slogan featuring a common goal or a common enemy. These we had, first, in "The New Deal" motif, and next in "All-Out Aid to the Democracies." The measures for the first were justified on the grounds that the nation was in an emergency like that of war; so were the measures for the second. It was almost as though the metaphorical usage of the first time served as incantatory preparation that brought about the reality the second time.

Political Rhetoric as Secular Prayer

However, we must note some ironies here, due to the nature of political rhetoric as a secular variant of prayer. Imagine that you, as President, were about to put through Congress some measure that would strongly alienate some highly influential class. What would be the most natural way for you to present this matter to the public? Would you not try, as far as is stylistically possible, to soften the effects of the blow? You would try to be as reassuring as possible. Thus you might say: "Really, the proposed measure is not so drastic as it seems. Those men who are so afraid of it should look at things more calmly, and they'll understand how it will actually benefit them in the end. It is really a measure of partial control, done for their own good." And the more drastic the measure is in actuality, the more natural it would be for the politician to present it in a way that would allay fears and resentment.

Imagine, on the other hand, that the public had been clamoring for such a measure, but you as President did not want to be so drastic. In fact, if the measure did what the public wanted it to do, it would alienate some very influential backers of your party. In this case, you would try to put through a more moderate measure—but you would make up the difference stylistically by thundering about its startling scope. One could hardly call this hypocrisy; it is the normally prayerful use of language, to sharpen up the pointless and blunt the too sharply pointed. Hence, when Roosevelt, some years ago, came forth with a mighty blast about the death sentence he was delivering to the holding companies, I took this as evidence on its face that the holding companies were to fare quite favorably. Otherwise, why the blast? For if something so integral to American business was really to be dissolved, I was sure that the President would have done all in his power to soften the blow, since he would naturally not go forth courting more trouble than he would be in for already. To use language consistently in such cases, rather than for stylistic refurbishment, would seem almost like a misuse of language, from the standpoint of its use as a "corrective" instrument. And I think that a mere treatment of such cases in terms of "hypocrisy" would be totally misleading: it would be not judicious, but litigious.

However, this stylistic or rhetorical factor gives rise to many ironies.

The collective emphasis of the early Roosevelt period, for instance, did much to reinvigorate the individualistic trends to which such official ideologists as Tugwell were bidding farewell. This "collectivism" was more like the extension of individualism into new areas, as the federal recognition of unemployment opened new avenues of private career. And even the Tennessee Valley development was designed to be as much a boon to private property and private business as to the nation at large. Indeed, when the Roosevelt administration began, the country was quite prepared for socialization of the banking structure. Even a large proportion of the bankers themselves were willing; for their banks were insolvent, and one thing that our capitalists are always willing to socialize is a loss. Yet it was precisely here that Roosevelt's "collectivism" made its most important contribution to individualism, in that he drew upon the government credit, not to introduce a new collectivistic step (as his ideologists interpreted his moves) but to underwrite the traditional modes of private investment insofar as the changes in the situation itself permitted. And since banking is the very essence of a monetary economy, the whole logic of his administration followed from this act, which really was "constitutive." For in a capitalist economy, a decision about banking is a decision about the very core of motivation, and in its substantiality it is the ancestor of a whole family of policies.

War and Collective Nature of "Sacrifice"

A truly collectivistic movement would have shifted the locus of motivation by changing the concept of wealth. To illustrate our meaning by an extreme example: We have a truly collectivistic motive when a group is content to live in private hovels, while deriving great and enduring satisfaction from the thought that some magnificent public building, such as a church or school, is "theirs." A genuine change from individualism to collectivism as a motive would involve such a shift in the locus and definition of wealth, just as the shift from feudalism to capitalism presented the cult of individual wealth as a demand for a "poor church." When the retreating Russians destroyed their great power dam at Dnieprostroy, an American reporter in seeking to explain for his readers in America the significance of the dam to the people of Russia, said that it was an outstanding landmark such as the

Empire State Building is to New Yorkers. So consistently had the propaganda of our press played down the value of our great public constructions and played up the value of private constructions, in contrast with the stress upon the all-importance of public construction in Russian propaganda, that the reporter was probably right in comparing a public works project there to a private real estate promotion here. Even where the mood is so highly collectivistic as in the Americans' attachment to their local baseball team, we have but a vicarious or symbolic sociality here, since these teams are all privately owned businesses which but have the *mask* of public institutions.

Perhaps the one public institution that is generally spared invidious comparison with private models in the steady propaganda of our press is the military. I have never heard it said that we should let out our wars to private contractors, so far as the recruiting of a fighting force itself is concerned, though of course we are encouraged to find a place for the private contractor at every other stage of equipment and action. I do not think that this is due simply to the fact that a mercenary army would be too expensive. It would obviously be hard to get many men who would face maiming or death in war for a few dollars a month, if their inducement to work were placed on a purely capitalistic basis, as a monetary reward for the private's enterprise. But there is also the fact that, since business had become identified with all the constructive acts in our society, business itself was willing to consider the purely destructive function of "defense" as its dialectical opposite. And as the two-worlds distinction between church and state gradually became replaced by the two-worlds distinction between private business and public business, businessmen were jealously apprehensive whenever government threatened to encroach upon the constructive side of the equation. As a consequence, the press, in propagandizing for business, constantly strove to present any increase in the public debt as a menace to our entire civilization, when such increases were made in order to build up the wealth of the nation as a whole; and it propagandized strenuously against the notion that a government might, like public business itself, keep its books in a way that treated such improvements as new assets to balance the new liabilities—and the press ceased its alarm only when the constructive acts of the government were dropped to a minimum while the expenditures for purely destructive purposes rose fabulously. In brief: the same editorializing which foresaw national disaster when the government was spending billions for economically useful goods lapsed into calm approval when the same government began calling for scores of billions for armaments, which are from the purely economic point of view, as a contribution to the world's total wealth, a dead loss.

Indeed, ironically enough, this same press found it highly edifying to call for greater "sacrifice" on the part of the people; which presumably means that the business class it represents found the idea similarly edifying. Yet, translated into purely monetary equivalents, such "sacrifice" on the part of the people could only mean a lowering of consumption, which is to say a decreased market for the businessmen themselves, insofar as they were engaged in any business but the war business.

However, insofar as they can succeed in changing over their plants for the war business, this particular embarrassment is removed. While, furthermore, once the situation has become thoroughly a war situation, it so permeates the whole scene that many an act formerly an act of peace becomes secondarily an act of war: the growing and transportation of foods, for instance. And now, at last, an important contradiction has been taken out of capitalism, thus:

In capitalism, under normal peace-time conditions, the worker possessed a dual role. As a wage-earner he was feared; at times of strikes he was quite systematically slandered; and the attempt was always made to keep his salary at a minimum. Yet this same man was also a customer. And as a customer, or wage-spender, he was subjected to an incessant campaign of cajolery and flattery. He was given, for a few cents a copy, papers or periodicals that cost as much as thirty or forty cents a copy, all for the purpose of wheedling his attention, or his inattention, in behalf of sellers. On the radio, he was treated to all sorts of blandishments, given more entertainment than a jaded Oriental monarch. And these were his two fabulously different roles: one as an object of great distrust, and even vilification; the other as an object of almost abject courtship.

On the other hand, in proportion as you turn to a war economy, this incongruity drops away. The ideal worker then becomes the one who produces a maximum and consumes a minimum. He no longer needs to be courted as a private consumer, since the public market for war goods takes care of the consumption factor. From then on, a one-direction logic is possible: to shrink the market for consumption goods and proportionately increase the production of destruction goods. From this standpoint, alas! a war economy is quite "rational."

We may now circle back to the matter of collectivism. For note that, although capitalism as a war economy "makes sense" in that the contradiction between the wage-earning and wage-spending role is eliminated, what has happened to your individualist motive? Obviously, when you are asking that individuals produce much more and receive much less, you cannot present this in terms of the individualistic incentive. You must, indeed, present it in terms of "sacrifice." But sacrifice *for what?* Capitalism itself has too thoroughly trained people acquisitively for them to retain in very vigorous form the earlier religious belief in the spiritual value of sacrifice *per se*.

An individual sacrifice must be presented in terms of a public benefit. An individual impoverishment must be presented in terms of public wealth. An individual risk in terms of group security. In other words, for the conditions of a war economy, as for the conditions of warfare itself, we need a *collectivistic* motive, which will be shared by all except the war profiteers and the empire-builders of big business.

To say as much is to realize the magnitude of the problem. The orthodox philosophy of capitalism involves precisely the opposite kind of dialectic. In the capitalist dialectic, as per Adam Smith, individual aggrandizements are made synonymous with public benefits. Though Christians have a record of much turbulent fighting, Christianity is a philosophy of peace. In the Adam Smith vision of peace, people would be too busy amassing things to stop and fight over them. And the more they amassed as individuals, the more this would add up as total wealth for the society as a whole. Here there would be neither need nor room for a concept of individual sacrifice for the collective good— individual and collectivity being in apposition, not opposition.

Yet in a war situation, i.e., under a war motive, you must so alter the dialectic that individual sacrifice equals collective good. A mere "investment psychology" is not enough here. That is, it would not be enough to contend that, by sacrificing now one may hope for rewards later. For one thing, we had been told that even a small increase in the public debt would ruin the future, even though that increase in debt was largely an investment in national welfare and economic resources; what then could we expect of an incomparably larger debt, expended on armaments that could bring us positive economic returns only if we used them to despoil other peoples of their wealth, precisely the kind of Fascist plundering we are supposed to be arming *against?*

Hitler, by his attacks upon democracy, helped give us democracy as a slogan. But "democracy" is not public wealth or public power. It has been one of the ideals, or means, implicated in the amassing of wealth as we have known it in the past. But it cannot serve as a compensation for private loss, since we have been taught that its value resided precisely in the resources it provided for the man of ability to recover from private loss.

As a result, the motive of "All Out Aid to the Democracies" was vague. Insofar as it asked men to undergo personal sacrifice, a compensatory concept of collective wealth was needed. The Fascists and Hitlerites provided this compensatory concept in the promise of booty. That is, when the wars were over and the period of sacrifice ended, all citizens would profit by the resources taken from other peoples. And these resources would be taken by the people as a whole. Our incentive, on the other hand, was the promise of return to an economic order which was already proving unworkable. In a sense, the "democracies" propose a more "reactionary" solution than the Fascists.

In Russia, we see evidence of an almost fanatical will to sacrifice as individuals in behalf of the public good—yet without the Hitlerite motive of booty. We know that this incentive derives from the collectivistic point of view. But in America, our propagandists feared to adopt this motive, even in cynicism, even for purposes of deception. For it was feared that, were the mildly collectivist slogans of the New Deal to be refurbished this time, while reinforced by the collectivist quality of a war situation, their "potentialities" as incantatory imagery inviting us to make things in its image would this time really bring about the end of "business as usual." Accordingly, Roosevelt dropped all policies except those of the "win the war" sort, deeming it enough that, for the time being, the war as grand collectivist consumer solved the problem of our great productivity.

The Dialectics of Federation

We might end this section, by a kind of *aria da capo,* in considering an essay, "The Idea of a Federation," by Denis de Rougemont (*The*

Virginia Quarterly Review, Autumn 1941). The author being Swiss, he considers the possibility of an international federation in the light of Swiss experience "as an inheritor of the oldest federalist tradition—six and a half centuries."

It is the old problem of unity and diversity, as we have discussed it with relation to our own Constitution. And the author would have us work towards a "federalist philosophy" for uniting all the world's sovereign states, while attempting to avoid a "system." For any system, he says, even if it is called federalist,

> is unitary in essence, and therefore anti-federalist. It is so in spirit, and it will therefore be fatally so in its application. The true federalism is the absolute opposite of a system, which is always conceived in the brain and centered about one abstract idea. I should even define federalism as a constant and instinctive refusal to make use of systematic solutions.

A "system," presumably, would require some kind of "educating and organizing hegemony," which is precisely what the idea of a federation must avoid. And as against notions of a systematic *Gleichschaltung,* in a federation differences must be cherished:

> For it is not superficial or partial similarities (language, race, geographical vicinity) which are federated, but essential differences, which reveal themselves as complementary. It should no longer be said: "Let us renounce what sets us apart and underline what forms a bond between us." For it is precisely on the basis of recognized and legitimate differences and diversities that fruitful unions are formed.

And he likens federation to "a marriage, and not an economic, military, and geometrical alignment."

The author here passes over things a bit too swiftly for our purposes. For though we grant that the kind of spiritual or cultural differences he has in mind may be treated as "complementary," we would consider that marriage a feeble one indeed in which the husband and wife were not bound together in a community of economic interests—and where economic interests are at odds, such differences are not "complementary" but "antagonistic." There was perhaps a bit of prestidigitation in thus quickly bracketing the "economic" with the "military" and "geometrical." And owing to this particular distribution of his terms, the author is able to treat the whole subject on somewhat too "spiritual" a plane.

However, the author does very clearly reveal the difference between a federalist dialectic and a centralizing one, each constituted of a distinct political substance. And in one passage much to our purposes, he writes:

> Let us here introduce a new concept: the essential paradox of federalism, which means taking seriously the expression "union in diversity." Unitary or totalitarian systems are easy to conceive and to carry out: it is enough for them to crush opposition. But federalism implies the vitality of a large number of opposing elements and their harmonization. That is the whole problem.
>
> The word "federalism," in Switzerland, has in our day taken on among conservatives the limited and inaccurate meaning of the autonomy of the canton or district and the systematic opposition to central authority. To be a "federalist," in French Switzerland especially, is to reject on principle whatever proceeds from Berne, the capital of the confederation. This amounts to a kind of local nationalism. On the other hand, the German word corresponding to federation—*Bund*—emphasizes only the central union. When we speak of federalism, we ought to mean both the union and the autonomy of the parts that are united; both *one for all* and *all for one,* the two parts of our ancient Helvetian motto.

A good statement of the case, but hardly a "new concept." Rather, we find it well explored by Coleridge—and before him, it was a key emphasis of Leibniz. In an article on Surrealism (New Directions: 1940), we have applied it to Coleridge's distinction between "fancy" and "imagination" thus:

> Coleridge, as a dialectician, knew that there must be a concept of "one" behind a concept of "many," or a concept of "many" behind a concept of "one." Each implies the other. However, a radical difference in stress, or accent, is possible here. You may emphasize unity in *diversity,* or you may emphasize *unity* in diversity. If you emphasize *unity* in diversity, you get the effect that Coleridge called "imagination." If you emphasize the unity in *diversity,* you get what he called "fancy." It was the use he made of the Leibnizian dialectic, of unity and plurality, an idealist dialectic that is with us even in the name of our nation, "The United States," which is to

say, "The Unity of Plurality," or *"e pluribus unum"* (a dialectic that our Supreme Court is also at home with, as it may sanction or discredit a law either from the standpoint of the *nation as a whole* or from the standpoint of *states' rights,* which is to say that it can give either *imaginative* decisions or *fanciful* ones, depending upon whichever of the opposed principles it prefers to use in the given case).

DIALECTIC IN GENERAL

The Transformation of Terms

BY DIALECTICS in the most general sense we mean the employment of the possibilities of linguistic transformation. Or we may mean the study of such possibilities. Though we have often used "dialectic" and "dramatistic" as synonymous, dialectic in the general sense is a word of broader scope, since it includes idioms that are non-dramatistic.

One may study the possibilities of linguistic transformation in general (as with our analysis of the possibilities inherent in the pentad). Or one may study particular instances of linguistic transformation (as with the critic describing the developments in some one work of art).

The use of the pentad as a generating principle somewhat resembles the Kantian transcendentalism in one respect. Kant was concerned with the necessary forms of experience; and similarly the pentadic ratios name forms necessarily exemplified in the imputing of human motives.

As regards the analysis of particular forms: one looks for key terms, one seeks to decide which terms are ancestral and which derivative; and one expects to find terms possessing ambiguities that will bridge the gulf between other terms or otherwise serve as developmental functions. One seeks to characterize the *dis*position and the *trans*position of terms.

For the discussion of dialectic in the most general sense, we shall consider dialectic under three heads:

(1) Merger and division. (There may be a state of merger, or a state of division, or developments from either state to the other.)

(2) The Three Major Pairs: action-passion, mind-body, being-nothing.

(3) Transcendence. (Transcendence likewise may be either a state or a development. Non-representational art, for instance, may be a state of transcendence with respect to representational art, as the

artist thereafter dwells in the contemplation of relatively disembodied forms. But within the fixity of this stage, the particular things he paints will have development, quite as the lyric, while arresting some mood or attitude and making it the entire universe of discourse, yet has progression rather than mere succession.)

Other definitions of dialectic are: reasoning from opinion; the discovery of truth by the give and take of converse and redefinition; the art of disputation; the processes of "interaction" between the verbal and the non-verbal; the competition of coöperation or the coöperation of competition; the spinning of terms out of terms, as the dialectician proceeds to make explicit the conclusions implicit in key terms or propositions used as generating principle (the kind of internal development that distinguishes mathematical systems); the internal dialogue of thought, as with the inward way of Thomas à Kempis, or as with ratiocination and calculation generally; or any development (in organisms, works of art, stages of history) got by the interplay of various factors that mutually modify one another, and may be thought of as voices in a dialogue or roles in a play, with each voice or role in its partiality contributing to the development of the whole; or the placement of one thought or thing in terms of its opposite; or the progressive or successive development and reconciliation of opposites; or so putting questions to nature that nature can give unequivocal answer. An ever closer approximation to truth by successive redefinition is sometimes offered as the opposite of the dialectical method, or such "spiraling" may very well be taken as the example *par excellence* of dialectic. All these definitions are variants or special applications of the functions we shall consider under our three headings.

Merger and Division

In the *Phaedrus,* Socrates describes the principle of merger as "the comprehension of scattered particulars in one idea." And on the principle of division, he says that the dialectician must learn to carve an idea at the joints, "not breaking any part as a bad carver might." And of both principles, in sum:

I am a great lover of these processes of division and generalization; they help me to speak and think. If I find any man who is able to see unity and plurality in nature, I follow him, walking in his steps as if he were a god. And those who have this art, I usually call dialecticians.

In evolutionary thought, the simplest instance of the two principles is Spencer's formulation of a progressive development from homogeneity to heterogeneity.

In his section on the Transcendental Dialectic (in the *Critique of Pure Reason*) Kant contrives to turn the merger-division two-ness into a three-ness by introducing a third principle that partakes somewhat of both the others. Merger in its simplicity he calls the principle of genera or "homogeneity." The unity of nature is assumed, he says, in the Occamite law of reduction according to which "principles must not be multiplied beyond necessity (*entia praeter necessitatem non esse multiplicanda*)".

But in contrast with those half-dialecticians who would seek only a rational reduction to unity, he also formulates a counter-principle, the principle of diversity or "specification," admonishing us that varieties must not be reduced without due caution (*entium varietates non temere esse minuendas*). Kant is exemplifying this notion of specification when, in his introduction to the second edition, he writes: "Rather than enlarging the sciences, we merely disfigure them when we lose sight of their respective limits and allow them to merge with one another."

The principle of specification is particularly applicable, as regards the subject of this book, to terminologies of motives that attempt to treat of ethical issues in exclusively non-ethical terms, or of verbal action in terms of non-verbal motion, or of human motives generally in terms of non-human entities, such as the learning processes of lower animals, or the physiology of endocrine secretions, and the like. In brief, we violate the principle of specification when our terms for the examination of one field are got by simple importation from some other field.

Kant's third formula is a principle of "continuity" that, in bridging the opposition of the other two principles, partakes somewhat of both. It leads to what Lovejoy would call the "great chain of being": the principle that the step from kind to kind is by a gradual increase of diversity. As Arthur Lovejoy points out, the scholastic notion of a continuous series of beings, extending without an hiatus from the highest to the lowest forms of life, involves a contradiction. For such complete continuity would not allow for a series of species, but would run them all into one. It would be a gradual slope rather than a succession of specific steps such as we get in a hierarchy of biological classification. And may we not see a similar ambiguity in the third Kantian principle?

When he is discussing what one could call the *dialectics* of mathematics (in *The Handmaiden of the Sciences*), Eric T. Bell notes the shifts between the mathematics of continuity and the mathematics of discreteness. Here in mathematical translation is the merger-division pair, its members still confronting each other as they did in the days when Zeno showed how the dialectic of discrete, ordered points was at odds with the dialectic of continuous motion. Bell notes that in the past, continuity has been the fashion at some times, discreteness at others. And at present, he observes, the two are "inextricably knotted together in one gorgeous confusion." Our present traditional frame of logic, he says, does not permit us "to imagine a third basic pigment, which shall be neither continuous nor discrete." But in reading of this logical dilemma as regards the dialectic of mathematics, can we not at least use it to reveal the *necessary* ambiguity in Kant's third dialectical principle? For is it not a concept which, if translated into an exact mathematical counterpart, would be the *tertium quid* for bringing merger and division together in a formula that is in some respects neither and in some respects both?

In brief, we again confront a variant of the Grammatical need for a third term that will serve as the ground or medium of communication between opposing terms. And whatever logical problems such a third term may give rise to, we are being logical in feeling the need for it. Similarly, we may expect to find such ambiguous or pontificating thirds strongly at work in dialectic on the Rhetorical and Symbolic levels.

The paradox of substance contains something of all three principles. The offspring is "substantially one" with the parent: its history thus being a development from merger (during the Edenic conditions of the foetus in the womb) to division (at the first "biological" revolution," experienced by the offspring at the time of parturition; the "birth trauma" due to the bursting of the bonds that has been made necessary by the growth of the foetus to the point where the benign circle of protection, the "enclosed garden," had threatened to become a malign circle of confinement); and its status as offspring of *this* parent rather than *that* keeps it consubstantial with the familial source from which it was derived. So we have here, in another form, the ambiguity of starting points, which may be considered either as the inaugurating moment (the introduction that will contain implicitly all that is to follow explicitly) or as the point abandoned (inasmuch as the offspring becomes a new bundle of motivations peculiar to itself). Or, recalling another formulation: that which was "a part of" the parent has become "apart from" the parent; yet it may, from the familial point of view, still be considered consubstantial with its ancestral source. Seen in this light, metaphysics might be described as an attempt to decide which propositions we should connect with a "therefore," which we should connect with a "however," and which with sheer "and."

Dialectic of the Scapegoat

When we examine the "scapegoat mechanism" in these terms, we find it a very clear example of the three principles. For the scapegoat is "charismatic," a vicar. As such, it is profoundly consubstantial with those who, looking upon it as a chosen vessel, would ritualistically cleanse themselves by loading the burden of their own iniquities upon it. Thus the scapegoat represents the principle of division in that its persecutors would alienate from themselves to it their own uncleanlinesses. For one must remember that a scapegoat cannot be "curative" except insofar as it represents the iniquities of those who would be cured by attacking it. In representing *their* iniquities, it performs the role of vicarious atonement (that is, unification, or merger, granted to those who have alienated their iniquities upon it, and so may be purified through its suffering).

All told, note what we have here: (1) an original state of merger, in that the iniquities are shared by both the iniquitous and their chosen vessel; (2) a principle of division, in that the elements shared in common are being ritualistically alienated; (3) a new principle of merger, this time in the unification of those whose purified identity is defined in dialectical opposition to the sacrificial offering.

Criminals either actual or imaginary may thus serve as scapegoats in a society that "purifies itself" by "moral indignation" in condemning them, though the ritualistic elements operating here are not usually recognized by the indignant. When the attacker chooses for himself the object of attack, it is usually his blood brother; the debunker is much closer to the debunked than others are; Ahab was pursued by the white whale he was pursuing; and Aristotle says that the physician should be a bit sickly himself, to better understand the symptoms of his patients. The same pattern of thought is rephrased by W. H. Auden, with our characteristically modern conversion of the valetudinarian principle from the gymnastic to the clinical: "Every brilliant doctor hides a murderer."

The Christian dialectic of atonement is much more complex than this, hence includes many ingredients that take it beyond the paradigm we are here discussing. Here we are concerned rather with the kind of scapegoat seen in the Hitlerite cult of Anti-Semitism. Here the scapegoat is the "essence" of evil, the *principle* of the discord felt by those who are to be purified by the sacrifice. Note also that the goat, as the principle of evil, would be in effect a kind of "bad parent." For the alienating of iniquities from the self to the scapegoat amounts to a *rebirth* of the self. In brief, it would promise a conversion to a new principle of motivation—and when such a transformation is conceived in terms of the familial or substantial, it amounts to a change of parentage.

We have here introduced another principle (previously considered in these pages): the pun on sequence, which allows for an ambiguous shuttling between concepts of logical priority and concepts of temporal priority. "Essences" or "principles" are among the logically prior, as an essence is logically prior to its accidents, or as a principle is logically prior to the instances of its workings. Hence the ancestral nature of the scapegoat as vessel of vicarious atonement. And by the same token the scapegoat can possess the divinity of a sacrificial king, since gods too are terms for the essence of motivation, as a tribe that regulates its life about the seasonal fluctuations of a river may sum up the whole complex of tribal motivations in the concept of a river god, which would be the "essence" of the tribal adjustments to the stream's behavior and utility.

As an essence of motivation, the scapegoat is a concentration of power, hence may possess the ambiguities of power, which may be for either good or evil until that stage of religious development is reached where power is dissociated into good and evil principles. This stage was more complete in the Manichaean heresy than it is in orthodox Christianity, which sees in Lucifer a fallen *angel,* and which proclaims the divinity in Jesus by a revolutionary redefinition of the figure whom His crucifiers had classed with criminals. In the Christian dialectic of atonement, the vicarious sacrifice Who took upon Himself the burdens of the world thus retains the ambiguities of power only in the sense that He suffered calumny.

The Hitlerite Anti-Semitism as scapegoat principle clearly reveals a related process of dialectic: unification by a foe shared in common. On the purely Grammatical level, this is reducible purely to the antithetical nature of "dialectical" terms, like "freedom," "perfection," or the terms for social movements, that derive their significance from their relation to opposite terms. One can best see their nature by contrasting them with terms like "house" or "apple," which require no counter-words like "anti-house" or "un-apple" to define them.

Where the principle of division is frustrated, as it was in Germany after the Allied victories began making it impossible for Hitlerism to assert itself in further expansion as a "master race" conquering the "Semitic" enemy, the discords must again be faced *within*. Hence the mood of self-destruction (called "honor") which led the Nazis to prolong the war even when it was apparent that such prolongation could but add to the sufferings of Germany itself. "Honor" was the name for the fact that, insofar as ritual transference of guilt feelings to the scapegoat is frustrated, motives of self-destruction must come to the fore.

Per Genus et Differentiam

Returning to the two principles in their simplicity, we have them in the traditional scholastic concept of definition *per genus et differentiam,* or in Coleridge's opposing of unity and multeity. The stress upon the principle of division is seen in theories of literary criticism that would attribute the excellence of a work to the respects in which that work is unique. Thus one critic maintained that to characterize the "beauty" in Marlowe we should find wherein his work is distinct from that of other dramatists. And similarly, advocates of esthetic nationalism or regionalism would situate the essence of esthetic motivations in the factors thought peculiar to that nation or region. Yet obviously, Marlowe's greatness also draws upon the effectiveness of esthetic principles that he shares with other great dramatists, (or even with inferior dramatists, for there are necessary principles of drama embodied in the works of both good dramatists and bad, as poet and poetaster may be alike in that they both derive some measure of appeal by exemplifying the rudimentary principles of prosody involved in a sonnet). And the appeal of national or regional art to readers outside the local circumference of motives embodied in its production must obviously involve respects in which the work embodies artistic principles generically.

The excessive cult of the three dramatic unities seems to have derived from an overstress upon the principle of division, or specification. For Aristotle, proceeding to define drama *per genus et differentiam,* in an essay that also originally contained a treatment of the epic, rightly pointed out the stricter canons of unity in drama, as compared with the epic. But later, the section on the epic was lost—and theorists seized upon these specifications without reference to the epic, in dialectical opposition to which they were originally stated. As defined with reference to the epic, the distinction is quite sound. The epic was quite loose in its treatment of the three unities (of time, place, and action), whereas even now the drama is relatively strict. It is by ignoring the generic context of such specifications that the French theorists arrived at such excessive reverence for these canons.

The Scotist stress upon the principle of thisness (*haeccëitas*), the particular way of the individual thing, does not in itself require the nominalist overstress that would see in a thing's uniqueness the totality of its characters. *Haeccëitas* should be thought of rather as the third stage in characterization, as one begins with generic characters, next notes the specific ones, and *only then* determines the respects in which the individual entity is unique. Its character would be a merger of all three.

The principle of merger, on the other hand, is overstressed when our reduction to generalizations causes us to overlook specifications. For there are always ways whereby, in searching for the "essence" of a thing, we can consciously or unconsciously choose to seek either the "specific" essence or the "generic" essence.

Thus we may define man as an animal, or even as a bundle of chemicals, thereby "reducing" our definition to wholly generic terms. Surprisingly, such stress upon *generic* definition of man's essence co-exists today with an equally intensive stress upon man's *specific* essence; but the two methods continue in isolation from each other, so far as conscious method is concerned.

When Aristotle defined man as a rational animal, he defined *per genus et differentiam,* with "animal" designating the generic and "rational" the specific. But note that our vocabularies of technology and finance derive wholly from man's "specific" essence—since money and machinery are *exclusively human* attributes. No such motives exist in nature, outside of human invention. And they provide that withinness-of-withinness or atop-the-atopness that is so characteristic of human thought, as with tools for making tools, money for making money, or Aristotle's view of God as thought of thought. (Similarly, Kant says that only man reads signs *as signs.*)

To see man in terms of money and technology, as when we "efficiently" construct a rationale of human motives about either of these terminologies, is thus in a sense to reduce the subject of motives "perfectionistically." For we treat an *aspect* of human motivation as the very *essence* of human motivation, thereby in effect asking that man's generic essence be reduced to the specific essence. Ironically enough, though we no longer *formally* accept it that man in his specific essence is "rational," we *informally* place much more stress upon the rational than Aristotle did, when we consider human motives in the reduced (scientist) terms of technology or finance alone. And we uncritically recognize the inadequacies of our definition by a compensatory "discovery" of man as "irrational." That is, when the specific essence has been so strictly reduced, the generic essence is rediscovered in terms correspondingly askew. And so, in our shifting between the pure animality or chemicality of man, and the pure pragmaticality of man, we reëncounter, ironically disguised, the traditional mode of definition. But in the dialectical naiveté due to our neglect of the fact that the language of *science* is a *language* of science, we usually fail to recognize that we are but reënacting piecemeal and without method the very ways of definition that we so often reject as "purely verbal."

More Variants of Merger and Division

A recent interesting example of the unity-multeity dialectic is to be seen in Otto Neurath's *Foundations of the Social Sciences,* where he carries the principle of division to such an extent that he speaks not merely of an individual Cromwell, but of a "pluri-Cromwell," and would set over against this extremely nominalist position an "oceanic feeling" that begins with the generic approach (the principle of merger), as when he writes:

> We suggest not starting with the antithesis: living being and the environment (as bio-ecology does), but starting with what may be called a "synusia" composed of men, animals, soil, atmosphere, etc. I am here using the term 'synusia' in analogy with the term 'symbiosis,' and I hope that the old theological use of the word will not mar our argument. . . .

Such a "synusia," he says, "may present a kind of cohesiveness, i.e., continuance of some relations." And this "aggregational program" has its counterpart "in some metaphysical speculations, e.g., in what is called 'Holism' ('Ganzheitslehre,' etc.)."

A more fanciful variant of the merger principle (atop division) occurs in a dialectical exercise by Coleridge, a *Theory of Life,* wherein he simultaneously describes and exemplifies the dialectic process. Discussing the relation between flowers and insects, he writes:

> The insect world, taken at large, appears as an intenser life, that has struggled itself loose and become emancipated from vegetation, *Florae liberti, et libertini!* If for the sake of a moment's relaxation we might indulge a Darwinian flight, though at the risk of provoking a smile, (not, I hope, a frown,) from sober judgment, we might imagine the life of insects an apotheosis of the petals, stamina, and nectaries, round which they flutter, or the stems and pedicles, to which they adhere. Beyond and above this step, Nature seems to act with a sort of free agency, and to have formed the classes from choice and bounty. Had she proceeded no further, yet the whole vegetable, together with the whole insect creation, would have formed within themselves an entire and independent system of Life. All plants have insects, most commonly each genus of vegetables its appropriate genera of insects; and so reciprocally interdependent and necessary to each other are they, that we can almost as little think of vegetation without insects, as of insects without vegetation. Though probably the mere likeness of *shape,* in the *papilio,* and the papilionaceous plants, suggested the idea of the former, as the latter in a state of detachment, to our late poetical and theoretical brother; yet a something, that approaches to a graver plausibility, is given to

this fancy of a flying blossom; when we reflect how many plants depend upon insects for their fructification.

In this notion of insects and flowers as part of a single system (so that the insect is a kind of "flying blossom") the principle of merger is uppermost, though in this essay as a whole the dialectic traces a series of progressive differentiations, with each higher level of existence transcending the next lower level, by including it while at the same time exemplifying a new principle of motivation.

In *Creative Evolution,* Bergson offers a variant that, whatever doubts one may have of it as a description of nature, well illuminates the ambiguities of sympathy and antipathy we have considered with reference to the scapegoat. He is contemplating the fact that the *Ammophila Hirsuta* in attacking the caterpillar in which it is to lay its larva, usually contrives to paralyze the caterpillar without killing it. He suggests that this ability is derived from "a *sympathy* (in the etymological sense of the word)" between the *Ammophila* and its victim. Hence it does not need to acquire, by a process of trial and error, its knowledge how to paralyze without killing. Its sense of the caterpillar's vulnerability comes *from within,* since both the attacker and the victim are parts of the same system (or "duration") so that it knows how to hurt the other somewhat as it might know how to hurt itself. The principle of merger in Bergson is thus regularly localized in his views of instinct and intuition (which is a kind of super-intellectual instinct). And the intellect represents the principle of division, as with his "cinematographical" analogy. According to this analogy, the continuity of motion (or "duration") which we instinctively sense is analyzed by intellectual concepts into a succession of disconnected steps or stages, as the movement of the actors in a motion picture is photographed by a series of stills, with an unphotographed hiatus between each exposure and the next.

Coleridge suggests some purely formal terms for distinguishing varieties of the merger and division principles. Beginning with oneness, or identity, he writes:

> But as little can we conceive the oneness, except as the mid-point producing itself on each side; that is, manifesting itself on two opposite poles. Thus, from identity we derive duality, and from both together we obtain polarity, synthesis, indifference, predominance.

Suppose that we began, for instance, with a concept like "the good." It would subdivide into "good" and "evil," as with "duality". The "polarity" of these terms would reside in the fact that the concept of each involves the other. Their "synthesis" might be found in some "higher level" generalization, like "morality," which unites both. Or it might be got by an act or power ambivalent in its effects. "Indifference" would reside in a ground term "beyond the opposites," as with a non-moral or "extra-moral" or "sub-moral" concept that neutralized both. Or there might be a "predominance" of one over the other.

Perhaps we might also add "succession" (as a history may develop from either term to the other, with a different significance in the two orders). Another variant of succession would be "alternation."

A variant of predominance would be "substitution". We have in mind the dialectical resource whereby, if paired terms are made equal, one of them may come to do service for both, as the Spinozist equating of "God" and "nature" prepared the way for the naturalist dropping of "God" as an unnecessary term. Or when confronting opposed terms, the thinker may see in one of them the essence of the pair, as with Augustine's view that only the good really exists, with evil as a mere deficiency. The position is almost reversed in many modern tendencies to take the dyslogistic term as real and primary, and to see the eulogistic term as illusory and derivative. A case in point is Thurman Arnold's picture of human rationalizations as a pageantry erected above a set of human motivations that are essentially "psychiatric."

The principle of identity itself is perhaps most succinctly illustrated in Jehovah's sentence: "I am that I am." One can see how it immediately suggests possibilities of expansion, since the *am* invites to the discussion of God as a *being,* which term in turn calls for some variant of non-being. Or the Spinozist statement of identity in his definition of substance as *Causa sui,* invites to expansion in terms of cause and caus~ (freedom and necessity).

Or an identity like the theme of a play is broken down ~ into principles of opposition which in their variants com~ municate by a neutral ground shared in common. ~ we to situate the "identity" of *Othello* in the ~ should immediately find it subdividing, in a~ erties of love, into love as the essence o~ relation and hate as the essence of the Othello-~

be considered "consubstantial" with Othello in that he represents the principles of jealousy implicit in Othello's delight in Desdemona as a private spiritual possession. Iago, to arouse Othello, must talk a language that Othello knows as well as he, a language implicit in the nature of Othello's love as the idealization of his private property in Desdemona. This language is the dialectical opposite of Othello's; but it so thoroughly shares a common ground with Othello's language that its insinuations are never for one moment irrelevant to Othello's thinking. Iago must be cautious in leading Othello to believe them as *true:* but Othello never for a moment doubts them as *values.*

We can grasp the point by contrasting the assumptions behind the entire play with such notions of material and spiritual property as might prevail among the peasants of polyandrous Tibet. Or we could state the matter formally by recalling the dialectic formula quoted by Coleridge: *inter res heterogeneas non datur oppositio,* a notion that he also expresses by observing that *rivales* are opposite banks of the *same* stream. Iago's goatish imagery works upon Othello by suggesting Cassio in his place; and this puts Othello beside himself, in leading him to experience his own relations exclusively from without rather than from within. In the image of Cassio as his successful rival, motives within himself become alienated. The effect is all the more brutal in that, as thus considered only from without, many of the important modifications in the relations between Othello and Desdemona are eliminated—and Othello now sees Desdemona in terms of this greatly reduced idiom, wholly lacking in possibilities of idealization.

The principle of identity, as carried into the realm of discourse, always leads to a localizing in some term which has potentialities of its own. Thus we noted that Jehovah's words, "I am that I am," implicitly contain the equating of God with being. Or one might also have chosen to develop the words idealistically, in the featuring of the "I" as the essence of the identity. The whole matter leads us into the strategic choice between synonymizing and desynonymizing that momentously affects a writer's key terms. For we may stress either ʼe element that two terms have in common or those respects wherein ʋ are distinct. And if they are ancestral terms, different perspectives be generated from such beginnings, as a slight deflection at the may show as a vast one at the circumference.

to treat two terms as differing in degree is to exemplify the principle of merger (as with Hume's treatment of "impressions" and "ideas" as respectively "more lively" and "less lively" perceptions). And we exemplify the principle of division when treating such pairs as differences in kind (as with Kant's distinction between concepts and ideas). The Hegelian *Insofern* (like Spinoza's *quatenus*) offers a basic resource here—as Hegel says of something white, cubical, and tart that *insofar as* it is white it is not cubical, *insofar as* it is white and cubical it is not tart, etc. "Shakespeare *qua* Englishman" draws the line differently than "Shakespeare *qua* poet"—and such resources permit us to *divide speculatively* the *empirically indivisible*. Thus is made possible the Socratic way of thought whereby the artist *as artist* can be said to be interested only in the perfection of his art; the ruler, *as ruler,* can be said to be interested only in the good of his subjects; and "in what he prescribes, the physician, *insofar as* he is a physician, considers not his own good but the good of the patient; for the physician is also a ruler having the human body as a subject, and is not a mere money-maker." In sum, one's initial act in choosing "where to draw the line" by choosing terms that merge or terms that divide has an anticipatory effect upon one's conclusions.

Eric Bell discusses a similar aspect of dialectic in his remarks on the importance of the way in which the mathematician "sets up" his equations, when confronting the situation that is to be "idealized" in mathematical terms. And in his *Procedures of Empirical Science,* Victor F. Lenzen treats of the same dialectical resource when discussing the "partition between object and observer," as affected by the use of instruments. Citing Bohr, he notes that if one taps an object with a stick held firmly in the hand, "the stick is an apparatus that may be viewed as part of the observer." (Note the term "part of," which here gives us merger.) But if the stick is held loosely, the stick itself becomes the perceived object, "and the partition is between stick and hand." (The stick here is "apart from" the observer.)

There is a card trick that illustrates to perfection the strategic importance of the shifts between the principles of merger and division. Let us say that you hid the Jack of Hearts, and your problem is, by leading questions, to bring your audience to the selection of this card.

The leading questions follow an order of decreasing generalization, and so shift between merger and division. Let us say that the Jack of Hearts is always kept implicit in the various orders of generalization.

Thus, you first ask: "Name the four suits." The answer is: "Spades, clubs, hearts, and diamonds." Then you ask: "Select two of them." If the answer is, say, "Hearts and clubs," your next question is, "Now select one of these." But if the answer had been, say, "spades and clubs," the Jack of Hearts would be excluded. And in that case, you would say instead: "That leaves hearts and diamonds. Now select one of these." Similarly, if hearts are selected, you "merge" with the choice, and proceed: "Now name the four highest cards in that suit." But if diamonds are named, you "divide," saying instead: "That leaves hearts. Now name the four highest hearts." Next you call for a selection of two among the four, again using whichever principle serves to keep the Jack of Hearts implicit in the choice. Then you call for a selection of one. If the Jack is named, you produce it. If the other card is named, you say, "That leaves the Jack," and produce it.

When thinkers shift between their therefore's and their however's, are they not following a like procedure? Or between synonymizings and desynonymizings. Or between distinctions in kind and distinctions in degree.

We previously mentioned (on page 254) Aquinas' distinction between the univocal and the equivocal. An "univocal" derivation of the world from God as its efficient cause would be like that of offspring from parent: an exact reproduction in kind ("as when man reproduces man"). But the relation is "equivocal" as when the work bears the character of the workman (as when "an agent is present to that upon which it acts"). The work, as the effect, "pre-exists virtually in the efficient cause" (the workman). An agent as such is perfect (being actual); but the matter upon which an agent acts is imperfect (being potential). Hence "to pre-exist virtually in the efficient cause is to pre-exist . . . in a more perfect degree." Hence, in such equivocal derivation, God as cause is more "eminent" than the world as effect.

Such a course from God to His Creation can, by our interpretation, collapse into a blunt distinction between the start and the finish— whereupon we confront the paradox of substance, and can say that a world derived "substantially" from God both is and is not like its divine ground. But, of course, the paradox in its simplicity is greatly modified, and even concealed, by the steps that are thus interposed. And in a similar spirit, theologians can shift between "merger" and "division" tactics in choosing on some occasions to reason from human experience to the divine and on other occasions to consider God and man as fundamentally different. To use the former method alone (as with reasoning in formal logic) would lead to pantheism; to use the latter method alone encourages a stress upon "conditions" that, when Occamistically truncated, leads to materialism.

The dialectical principles of merger and division are clearly apparent in any systems of *classification,* be they the formal and explicit classifications of the sciences or the classificatory structure implicit in the "equations" of a poem. Though scientific classification is often considered to possess a kind of non-verbal or extra-verbal "reality," its essentially *dialectical* nature is obvious in Lenzen's remark that "Classification is founded on the similarities between things and events; it is based upon the fact that things are similar in specific respects and dissimilar in others." And as for the classification of "events": though "events" themselves are often said to be "constitutive of reality," we appreciate the essentially dialectical nature of an event when Lenzen lists as examples of events "a flash of lightning, an eclipse of the sun, an earthquake, the birth of a living being," all of which are capable of being carved at many different joints, while we are further told that "In daily life and qualitative science an event may extend through an appreciable duration, but for precision an event is idealized as the occurrence of properties at an instant."

Even so apparently "factual" a matter as correlation depends upon the place at which our concepts draw the line between merger and division; and the dialecticians of mathematics can derive "invariance" as a function of their symbols, though the fruitful use of this dialectical resource is not taken as proof that invariants exist in nature. Whether or not invariants exist in nature, they *do* exist in language, since any generalization that applies to a whole series of transformations is invariant with respect to that series.

The language of poetry has this same classificatory nature, and the analysis of "equations" on the Symbolic level is intended to reveal it; but it is usually left implicit. The concrete vocabulary used in proverbs may conceal from us their essentially *classificatory* nature. But actually, proverbs comprise a moralistic frame of concepts so highly generalized that incidents unlike in every particular circumstance can be classed together under the same proverbial head. Both the king and the peasant, for instance, might have an experience that led each to say,

"One man's meat is another man's poison." This would be the proverbial heading under which each classified his experience. It would be the "invariant" element common to both experiences. Yet the two experiences could be as distinct in their particulars as the differences between their two ways of life.

The thought suggests what we mean by treating imagery as classificatory. For instance, if a book were constructed about action in two contrasted scenes, one featuring imagery of the country and the other imagery of the city, we could treat each of these scenes as the generalization that classified all the details of action taking place in it. Similarly, a man with a tic, as with an eye that twitches when certain things are said, thereby gives us, in a bodily image, the evidences of a classification. For the tic reveals that he feels an emotional element in common among a series of events that, to men with other points of view, would not seem thus closely classifiable together. It testifies to the merger, within the individual psyche, of matters that for others would be divided.

On the Rhetorical level, the merger-division shift draws upon the fact that any *distinction* is liable to sharpening into a *contrast,* and any contrast may be attenuated into the form of a distinction. At the time of French hegemony on the continent of Europe, for instance, French thought placed much stress upon the *universal* aspects of human motivation. The Germans on the other hand got for themselves a kind of "symbolic autonomy" by stressing the *distinctness* of the various cultural strains. It was a kind of art-gallery principle, involving an appreciation of different cultural traditions somewhat as one might appreciate different traditions of painting, or different types of human personality, valuing each for itself, in its cultural sovereignty, without necessarily choosing among them. Yet the position had implicit in it a declaration of independence from French hegemony (stated in terms of "universal" man). And in time it developed into the militance of a cultural *contrast,* as when used to reënforce Nazi expansionism.

Mind-Body, Being-Nothing, and Action-Passion Pairs

The mind-body, being-nothing, and action-passion pairs generalize the first major steps usually taken towards the localizing of identity. That is, the principles of merger and division apply to all thought; the mind-body, being-nothing, and action-passion pairs, singly or in combination, variously overlapping, and variously manipulated, will be found to figure in any statement which embodies the principles of merger and division specifically. Their scope as generalizations is only slightly less broad.

The resources of the mind-body pair are obvious. The members of the pair can be treated as in apposition or in opposition, or as sharing a relation in which one member is primary and the other derivative, or as aspects of an underlying reality that is the ground of both, etc. Since either of the terms can be taken to represent the other, physicalist or idealist reductions are readily available. And Rhetorically, by shifting from one member of the pair to the other, one has the opportunity to "idealize" his own cause while "materializing" that of his opponents.

The being-nothing pair has its most prevalent form in the essence-existence pair, with either member of the pair being capable of selection as the "reality." Thus Plato situates the reality in *being*, the appearance in *existence*; but Santayana's variant of Platonism would situate the *substantial* nature of things in the flux of existence, while "essences" are such characters as existing things share with non-existents. Or in historicist frameworks, the pair may take the form of a distinction between the *becoming* and the *having-become*. Here the vital principle that gives form is equated with becoming; and the formed is equated with the fossilized, as a state of having-become.

The principles of merger and division can readily figure here, as when being is equated with the one, and becoming with the many (though of course the principles of the one and the many may be considered in apposition rather than in opposition, as with the microcosm-macrocosm pattern whereby any part of the universe is taken as representative of the whole (*omnia ubique*). Or we may move into the Eleatic paradoxes, as with the dialectician Zeno, "who has an art of speaking which makes the same things appear to his hearers like and unlike, one and many, at rest and in motion," as Socrates says in the *Phaedrus*.

In any given work, the pairs usually merge and divide in many ways, depending upon the particular interests that set the course for that given work. And once you have localized a form, the requirements of this particularized logic come to the fore. The action-passion pair, for instance, may be localized as the peace-war pair, or as coöperation and

competition.   Or if the active principle is equated with mind and the
passive principle with body, we may find ourselves working rather with
a faith-knowledge or act-scene pair.   Or action and passion may
become indistinguishable, as with a pair like love and war, or the
Wagnerian pair, love and death.   Theories of psychogenic illness seem
to be a commingling of the action-passion and mind-body pairs.   The
principle of evil is usually equated with division ("Legion"); yet there
can also be malign unities, and we know how nations can be unified by
resistance to a common enemy.

Reviewing briefly, let us recall that the action-passion pair, as used
directly, gives us the resources of actus and status (the agent's status
residing in the *properties* that go with his act).   And such sub-stance
in properties leads us into considerations for linking the Stance family
of terms with the Power family.   And acts become scenic in that
enactments survive as *constitutions*.

Theories of the development from implicit (sometimes equated with
the "unconscious") to explicit (the "conscious") can be treated as
variants of the action-passion terminology, owing to their bearing upon
the potentiality-actuality relation.   But here obviously we are moving
close to the third aspect of our subject: *alloiosis,* transformation,
transcendence.

The Socratic Transcendence

We have said that a distinction can become a contrast.   This takes
place when some part formerly treated synecdochically, as representative of the whole, becomes divisive with reference to the whole of
which it was a part.   Thus a class that represents the culmination of a
society's purposes may, under changing scenic conditions, gradually
arrive at the point where its act (and therefore its status) is no longer
representative of the new conditions in their totality.   The actus and
status that were formerly representative thus become antithetical (as
with the position of the nobility, which had represented a culmination
of the feudal society, but became antithetical to the society of trade
except insofar as they adapted themselves to the new conditions, themselves becoming *embourgeoisés*).

In any event, it is obvious that the transformation from the merger of
the representative role to the division of the antithetic role represents a

change of *principle*.   A critical point has been passed; a new quality of
motivation has been introduced.   The moment of crisis in transcendence involves a new motive discovered en route.

Such an introduction of a new motive may often look like a break
in continuity, particularly when it is exemplified in the form of a change
in the character of some figure in a fiction.   And surprisingly enough,
though Jowett devoted so great a portion of his life to the translating
and interpreting of Plato, he fails to deal with the nature of transcendence or transformation as embodied in Plato's dialogues.   That is,
whereas he fully recognizes the Platonic *doctrine* of transcendence, he
does not analyze the dialogues themselves as *acts* of transcendence.
For not only do they *plead for* transcendence; they are themselves so
formed that the end transcends the beginning.   Thus, in his Analysis
of the *Republic*, Jowett writes:

> Or a more general division into two parts may be adopted; the
> first (Books I-IV) containing the description of a State framed gen-
> erally in accordance with Hellenic notions of religion and morality,
> while in the second (Books V-X) the Hellenic State is transformed
> into an ideal kingdom of philosophy, of which all other govern-
> ments are the perversions.   These two points of view are really op-
> posed, and the opposition is only veiled by the genius of Plato.   The
> Republic, like the Phaedrus, is an imperfect whole; the higher light
> of philosophy breaks through the regularity of the Hellenic temple,
> which at last fades away into the heavens.   Whether this imperfec-
> tion of structure arises from an enlargement of the plan; or from the
> imperfect reconcilement in the writer's own mind of the struggling
> elements of thought which are now first brought together by him;
> or, perhaps, from the composition of the work at different times—
> are questions, like the similar question about the Iliad and the Odys-
> sey, which are worth asking, but which cannot have a distinct answer.

Similarly, in his Introduction to the *Phaedrus,* Jowett questions "the
notion that the work of a great artist like Plato could not fail in unity,
and that the unity of a dialogue requires a single subject."   He says
that the dialogue is not "a style of composition in which the requirement of unity is most stringent."   The double titles in several of the
dialogues, he says, seem to indicate that Plato made no attempt at a
"severer unity."   He notes that some dialogues have digressions only
remotely connected with the main theme.   And:

The Republic is divided between the search after justice and the construction of the ideal state; the Parmenides between the criticism of the Platonic ideas and of the Eleatic one or being; the Sophist between the detection of the Sophist and the correlation of ideas.

And he concludes that we should not expect to find one idea pervading a whole work, but several, "as the invention of the writer may suggest or his fancy wander." If each dialogue were devoted to the development of a single idea, there would be no controversy "as to whether the Phaedrus treated of love or rhetoric." But "like every great artist he gives unity of form to the different and apparently distracting topics which he brings together." He "works freely," and is not supposed to have worked out a perfect outline before he begins. He "fastens or weaves together the frame of his discourse loosely and imperfectly."

Yet throughout these comments, Jowett was in a sense quite accurate. He has characterized the process of transcendence as it looks from without, rather than as it looks from within. For as seen from without, the change from one level of discourse to another would be a kind of jolt or inconsistency, a somewhat random or opportunistic juxtaposition of partially disrelated subjects. Yet as seen from within, this change of levels would be precisely what the dialogue was designed to trace. For a Platonic dialogue is not formed simply by breaking an idea into its component parts and taking them up in one-two-three order (the purely scholastic aspect in Aristotle's method of exposition). A Platonic dialogue is rather a process of *transformation* whereby the position at the end transcends the position at the start, so that the position at the start can eventually be seen in terms of the new motivation encountered en route.

Considering a dialogue thus, as the development through a series of levels, we find that Jowett's summary of the Phaedrus reveals its structure perfectly, so perfectly that it is hard to see why he could fail to draw the proper conclusions from his own description:

The subjects of the Phaedrus (exclusive of the short introductory passage about mythology which is suggested by the local tradition) are first the false or conventional art of rhetoric; secondly, love or the inspiration of beauty and knowledge which is described as madness; thirdly, dialectic or the art of composition and division;

fourthly, the true rhetoric, which is based upon dialectic; fifthly, the superiority of the spoken over the written word. The continuous thread which appears and reappears throughout is rhetoric; this is the ground into which the rest of the Dialogue is inlaid. . . . The speech of Lysias, and the first speech of Socrates are examples of the false rhetoric, as the second speech of Socrates is adduced as an instance of the true. But the true rhetoric is based upon dialectic, and dialectic is a sort of inspiration akin to love; they are two aspects of philosophy in which the technicalities of rhetoric are absorbed. Thus the example becomes also the deeper theme of discourse. The true knowledge of things in heaven and earth is based upon enthusiasm or love of the ideas; and the true order of speech or writing proceeds according to them. Love, again, has three degrees: first, of interested love corresponding to the conventionalities of rhetoric; secondly, of disinterested or mad love, fixed on objects of sense and answering, perhaps, to poetry; thirdly, of disinterested love directed towards the unseen, answering to dialectic or the science of the ideas. Lastly, the art of rhetoric in the lower sense is found to rest on a knowledge of the natures and characters of men, which Socrates at the commencement of the Dialogue has described as his own peculiar study.

Does not Jowett's own summary make it apparent that the themes of love, rhetoric, and dialectic are here all parts of a single series? Lysias' speech on love, which is read with naïve admiration by Phaedrus, is trivial. It is built about a conceit, the proposition that Lysias should gain his suit not because he is a lover but because he is a non-lover, and the non-lover will never cause the beloved the many disturbances that a lover would. Socrates lifts the dialogue to a higher level in using the same conceit as Lysias, but developing it with examples of much deeper moral significance. His next speech transcends this in turn, by abandoning the terms which Lysias had set for the discussion. It is an impassioned celebration of love; and it is dialectically matured by systematic subdivision into the kinds of love, and by the matching of Eros with Anteros. When Socrates has finished, he proceeds to point out the superiority of this speech over the other two. He thereby raises the dialogue to a fourth level: the abstract appreciation of the formal principles that had been embodied in his speech. This involves a discussion of dialectic in general—and the last level is reached when Socrates rounds out this discussion by a celebration of the spoken word as superior to the written word.

Why does this round out the whole dialogue? Why is it the ultimate step that in a sense enables us of a sudden to see down, as through an interior shaft, to the place where we had started, far below, and to see it now in terms of the place at which we had arrived? I would interpret the matter thus:

At the opening of the dialogue there had been reference to a "feast of discourse." We might be content simply to call such an expression a metaphor, and think no more of the matter. But when we consider it from the standpoint of the Platonic theories, I think we can see in it much more than a metaphor. It is not merely a "metaphor." It is a *juncture of two levels.* "Feast" is on the level of bodily appetite. Yet not quite. For the element of *sociality* in a feast introduces an ingredient of motivation beyond that of sheer animal hunger. And "discourse" completes this pattern of transcendence—for the feast of words that accompanies the banquet involves bodily appetite in only a most roundabout way, as one most enjoys his food and digests it best when his general attitude towards the world is that of a "healthy appetite." We may again recall the modern theories of psychosomatic medicine that illustrate the principle in reverse, as with the doctrine that digestive disorders, even to the extent of ulcers, may derive from a sense of insecurity or disappointment. For in the "thinking of the body," the primary expectancy is that of food; hence digestive disorders may well result when mental insecurity is metonymously reduced to its equivalent in purely physiological terms.

Since love is similarly appetitive, we have a cluster of *food, love, hunger, enjoyment* experiences functioning at the roots of purpose. And recalling Plato's *Symposium,* we see a certain deeper justice in discourses on love on the occasion of a banquet (a pattern which in our less eloquent society, is often exemplified more modestly by the comfortable interchange of ribald jokes).

And so, I propose to interpret the dialogue, not as a sequence of parts somewhat disrelated to one another and given a tolerable semblance of unity by the sheer literary tact of the writer; but I would interpret it as leading, step by step, from the sheer bodily appetite of the "non-lover" who would possess the beloved without even the rudiments of sentiment, up to the stage of purely verbal insemination. In brief, the dialogue is a "way" from sexual intercourse to the Socratic intercourse of dialectical converse.

We generally use too few terms when interpreting the concept of "Platonic love." Thus, turning to the dictionary, I read that Platonic love is "a pure, spiritual affection, subsisting between persons of opposite sex, unmixed with carnal desires, and regarding the mind only and its excellences;—a species of love for which Plato was a warm advocate." In the first place, there is nothing to be gained by overlooking the fact that Socrates was *not* talking about love "subsisting between persons of the opposite sex." The Athenians' charge against Socrates, as *corruptor juventutis,* involved his relations with young men. It was with these young men that Socrates carried on his dialectic intercourse, with its educational insemination.

And it is the living, *spoken* word that would be the completest form of love, as thus transformed into the corresponding interlockings of verbal interchange. Socrates complains that once a speech is written down, its possibilities of dialectical accommodation are ended. It must present the same wording to all sorts of people. And then he turns to the principle of the seed, embodied in the spoken word of knowledge which has a living soul, as the garden in which it is sown by a skilled husbandman. The garden of letters, he says, exists at its best in this "serious pursuit of the dialectician," who

> finds a congenial soul, and then with knowledge engrafts and sows words which are able to help themselves and him who planted them, and are not unfruitful, but have in them seeds which may bear fruit in other natures, nurtured in other ways—making the seed everlasting and the possessors happy to the utmost extent of human happiness.

In his poem "The Mother of God," Yeats startlingly applies the pattern to Christian symbolism, in referring to Mary's conception of the Logos as received "through the hollow of an ear," in keeping with a Byzantine notion as to the way in which the Annunciation, or receiving of the word, took place.

Does not this view give us a deeper insight into the nature of Plato's thought than is got by too pruriently pure an interpretation of Platonic love? We see its relation to the whole theory of abstraction that pervades Platonist thought. We see exactly how the transcendence *begins* in the bodily, and may even *return* to the bodily, though with the difference that new terms have been discovered en route, so that new principles are introduced. The third oration is the turning point of the dialogue. Following it, the restricted terminology of the first and second orations is permanently discredited. But could we also say that steps four and five similarly discredit the third stage? I think not. Socrates has spoken too eloquently in honor of Eros. And it is left as a profound motive, by which any one may expect to be moved on occasion. But along with it, as its purely socialized equivalent, is the universal converse of dialectic.

There are two acts representative of each situation, though by the paradox of substance they may readily merge into one, as the "essential" is one, and thus continually resists the attempt to divide it clearly into a "good" and a "bad." And the distinction further tends to be obliterated by the dialectical fact that either of such two extremes is ultimately stated in terms of the other, their differences partaking in a common ground of indifferences. But insofar as the separation is maintained, there would be a representative action and a representative passion (which latter, in a secular terminology, would amount either to a representative illness or a representative crime). The transcending "essence" of a situation would, in brief, tend to manifest the defect of its qualities, at least as regards heresies which efficiently tracked down such unwieldy possibilities at a sacrifice of balance. Thus the slaying of the ruler is the act representative of the democratic situation. And "pride" is a kind of "blanket" offense, representative of the human situation in general.

Biologically, Greek love was an offence, since its fruitfulness would not be that of tribal progeny. It was thus the "representative crime" of the Athenian enlightenment, the practice that corresponded in the realm of transgression to the pedagogy of Socratic intercourse in the realm of the transcendent and ideal.

Socrates was thus accused of the "representative" transgression. And whatever may have been the realities of the case in the literal sense, the structure of the *Phaedrus* shows that he was a "corruptor of youth" in the transcendental sense. He was thus resigned to the hemlock, since "impiety" was the "logical conclusion" of his austere philosophy as it would seem when reduced metonymically to the simplest biological terms.

Ironically, then, this theorist of transcendence was the victim of a transcendence transcended. On this one occasion at least the fellow-

citizens who cast their judgments against him were themselves transcending. For the homosexual love which lay at the basis of their
educational system was most fully and nobly represented in the ideals
of Socratic intercourse. Hence in selecting Socrates as their victim,
they were choosing the thinker who represented the very *essence* of the
cultural trends away from tribalism. They could not have been more
accurate. Doubtless they were for the most part simple fellows who,
insofar as homosexual love attracted them at all, were content with boy
favorites, as with the practice of Greek army officers casually but frequently mentioned in Xenophon. But they were sensitive enough to
know when they had come upon the very *essence* of such practices.
And it resided of course in the Socratic doctrines of transcendence
whereby "corruption" was transformed into a "saving of souls," an
ambiguity that Mann recovers when the Aschenbach of *Death in
Venice* commingles expressions from the *Phaedrus* in his conscientiously corrupt contemplation of young Tadzio. A process that had
thus been translated from the bodily to the spiritual, they (the lumber-
ing citizenry) translated back again. In punishing him, they were
punishing the biological transgression implicit in their enlightenment
itself, which was in every way tending to transcend the thinking proper
to them as a tribal integer. He was their properly "representative"
victim, their properly chosen vessel. And so thoroughgoing a searcher
after essence was bound to feel that their choice of him was "essentially"
correct.

In sum: His version of the dialectic, as attested in the *Phaedrus,* had
the ambivalence of the potential. It was either a *transcendence* of
homosexuality or a transcendence of *homosexuality*. Being in the latter aspect "biologically guilty," it was transgression against the principles of the tribe. It was thus essentially "impious," quite as charged.
And in the light of what we have said about the vicarious atonement
through the scapegoat, we need not be deterred by the thought that
those who judged against him were incipiently implicated in his guilt.
Indeed, we assume that this was a contributing motive in their judgment against him.

Thus Socrates died that Plato and Aristotle might live. Out of his
death, Plato was enabled to reconstruct a tribal emphasis idealistically
atop the enlightened break-down of the tribal culture. The steps from
the *Phaedrus* to the *Republic* to the *Laws* form a dialectic series in them-

selves: the first motivated by a dissolution of the tribal in its traditional, realistic, "pre-enlightened" state; the second reclaiming the tribal concept on a "higher" level, in the form of an idealistically constituted State; the third brought down to the *business* of legislation, almost a Benthamite kind of project.

As for Aristotle, whose work is like a final revision of Plato, adjusting to one another the *conclusions* in which the Socratico-Platonist heuristics had terminated, he too could without strain transcend the original tribal patterns of thought which the Socratic dialectic had "impiously" surpassed. His strangely infertile god, a principle of the *loved* rather than a principle of generation, was in this respect sufficiently non-tribal to serve as the basis of a Hellenistic imperialism that extended far beyond the tribal orbit, though it was finally merged with the tribal deity, Jehovah, in the new more "spiritualized" Christian concept of the tribal, which allowed for the catholic inclusion of all men in one family.

We have spoken of the *Republic,* placing it midway between the *Phaedrus* and the *Laws.* If one examines it from the standpoint of its nature as a "way," I think one will find that it is a process whereby an *economic necessity* is transformed into a *moral purpose.* We begin by observing how injustice develops *pari passu* with the increase of economic specialization. Such occupational diversity, we are told, makes for the break-down of the original tribal homogeneity into a corresponding diversity in ways of living.[15] And by a series of transformations involving the search for an ideal of justice that will prevail over and above all the many divergencies, we reach the conclusion that justice resides in each man's readiness to do that for which he is best fitted. Here, you will note, you are back at much the same diversified situation with which you began. The development is now repeated grandly, as you are taken on the Upward Way to a vision of the One (a principle of Unity which, as we observed in our discussion of Purpose, Plato equates with the purposive concept of the Good). And when you return to the world of diversity, you consider it in terms of the new principle encountered en route, whereupon it is viewed in a transcendent light. And what the transcendence amounts to in this case is the addition of moral terms that solve a technical problem

---

[15] Recall our previous remark that the Greek word for "justice" (*dike*) is also the word for "way" in the sense of what we today might call "pattern of life" or "class morality," etc.

(the breakdown of the tribe into a condition of great occupational diversity). The philosopher will devote himself to the welfare of the State, whose diversity is now infused for him with his vision of the One.

In all that we have been saying about transcendence, it is easy to see why Plato, as dialectician, was so attracted to mathematics as a dialectical discipline. For in both the Platonist and neo-Platonist versions of transcendence, the dialectician begins with the particulars of the senses, with the images of imagination—and he subjects these to progressive transformations whereby their sensory diversity is thoroughly lost in generalization, the structure being completed in the vision of the One (which we might call the Title of Titles). When reading accounts of mathematical progress, and of the ways in which images, or metaphors, guided the development of mathematical formulae,[16] we can readily see why mathematics should be treated as an aspect of dialectic.

One might, for instance, conceive of electricity after the analogy of a river, and thereby arrive at formulae for ohms, volts, and amperes, corresponding to the strength, speed, and volume of the current in a river bed. Other aspects of electricity, however, would suggest other metaphors, which in turn acquired corresponding mathematical formulation. And finally, as men began to work with these formulations themselves, complicating them with the help of still other metaphors, or modifying them in terms wholly intrinsic to mathematics, the entire procedure resulted in a body of formulations beneath which lay a whole jumble of disjunct imagery, more bewildering than any mystic's oxymoron or any Surrealist's assemblage of forms from different orders of experience. That is, in effect, a way of carrying out the dialectician's ideal: the use of imagery to transcend imagery.

And surely Faraday's search for a mathematical formula that would reduce all forms of energy to one expression is, in effect, an embodiment of the Platonist movement towards the One, which we would call the Title of Titles. Such a formula would be a perfect "god-term," inas-

---

[16] *Aspects of Scientific Rationalism in the Nineteenth Century,* by George de Santillana, contains a very clear review of the ways in which imagery guided mathematical formulation. Indeed, both this essay and its companion piece, Edgar Zilsel's *Problems of Empiricism* are recommended highly as works that at every point bear succinctly on the subjects considered in this book. And we originally included a section (later omitted for exigencies of space) which attempted a partial translation of these two excellent studies into the language of "dramatism."

much as it had, through a dialectic operation lasting through two thousand years and carried on by many voices, progressed through imagery to the complete transcending of imagery. Still it would not be quite the end, for it would not quite have led through language to the transcending of language, since mathematics is but a special case of language. But as regards the relation between such transcendent use of the principle of merger and its relation to the principle of division, even though we might in a sense say that such a universal reduction as Faraday's would provide the generic formula for all motivation, we should note that any such summarizing term would necessarily be dispensed with, in any statement about specific motivational problems, or even specific mathematical problems. For whatever its value as a generalization about the nature of nature, it would be of no value for particular problems requiring description in particular terms. Or, in the personal realm, it would not be of value for describing the disposition of factors to be considered by a particular person trying to reach a decision about a specific matter of human relations. Only its "spirit" might be present in such instances. In another way, its very nature as a generalization, or summation, or title of titles, would lay it open to the same objection that Galileo raised to the name of God as an explanation of natural causes, since in explaining everything it would explain nothing.

The Temporizing of Essence

Because of the pun whereby the logically prior can be expressed in terms of the temporally prior, and *v.v.,* the ways of transcendence, in aiming at the discovery of *essential* motives, may often take the historicist form of symbolic *regression*. That is, if one is seeking for the "essence" of motives, one can only express such a search in the temporal terms of imaginative literature as a process of "going back." And conversely, one given to retrospect, as Proust in his "remembrance of things past," may conceptualize his concern as a search for "essence."

This double vocabulary for the expression of essence is, I think, a basic factor to be watched continually if one would know how to translate back and forth between logical and temporal vocabularies. And many statements that might otherwise seem worthless, depending upon the kind of language you favor, can be readily reclaimed by such discounting.

In his *Foundations of the Social Sciences,* for instance, Otto Neurath proposes that we should drop the "cause-effect phraseology," and should use instead the "growing-out-of phraseology." That is, instead of saying that certain causes produce certain effects, we should follow the example of some savages who speak of some things as "growing out of" other things, or "arising from" them, or "coming out of" them. Such a change of phraseology would obviously reduce to terms of temporal sequence the parent-offspring relation that we have noted where ancestry is stated in causal terms. "The whole cause-effect phraseology," he says, "seems to be rooted in some older assumptions." ("Rooted in," you will note, is another of his proposed emendations. If we replaced it by an expression like "derived from," we might have a usage which would satisfy both temporalist and essentialist at once, as each could read it in his own way.)

The only way in which I would want to change Mr. Neurath's suggestions would be to interpret them differently. And I would advise one to read carefully this section of his pamphlet for added hints as to the ways in which essentialist and temporalist thought can be convertible. In the light of such speculations consider, for instance, a doctrine like Freud's borrowing of Darwin's theory of the "primal horde," as explained in his *Totem and Taboo,* and in *Group Psychology and the Analysis of the Ego.* If you recall that Darwin's evolutionism vowed him to a wholly historicist vocabulary, you will begin by taking it for granted that Darwin could not possibly state a theory of essence in his characteristic terms except by attributing to this essence some stage of existence in the past. And Freud, in response to the Darwinian vocabulary, would be led to a similar mode of expression. Hence, if you take the theory of the "primal horde" as a statement about *existence* rather than about *essence,* you find it proved or disproved by anthropological research.

Anthropologists seem to have done it quite a lot of damage. There seems to be no evidence that any such "primal horde" ever existed. But if we interpreted the concept as a statement about *essence,* we might find it quite usable despite the anthropologists' discrediting of it. For it may well be that the human relation which the concept of the primal horde designates really is *essential* to some social structures, such as the society of his own day which Freud was studying. Indeed, do we not see Freud himself attempting to rescue the concept as "essentially" true, despite its existential discrediting? Thus he writes in his chapter on "The Group and the Primal Horde":

> In 1912 I took up a conjecture of Darwin's to the effect that the primitive form of human society was that of a horde ruled over despotically by a powerful male. I attempted to show that the fortunes of this horde have left indestructible traces upon the history of human descent; and, especially, that the development of totemism, which comprises in itself the beginnings of religion, morality, and social organization, is concerned with the killing of the chief by violence and the transformation of the paternal horde into a community of brothers. To be sure, this is only a hypothesis, like so many others with which archaeologists endeavour to lighten the darkness of prehistorical times—a 'Just-So Story,' as it was amusingly called by a not unkind critic (Kroeger); but I think it is creditable to such a hypothesis if it proves able to bring coherence and understanding into more and more new regions.

At the end of this citation, we see clearly what the historicist vocabulary here lets Freud in for. His analysis of the patriarchal family convinced him that certain kinds of rivalry and allegiance are essential to it. But to state this belief in historicist terms, he had to assume: (a) that such a condition had existed in its purity in some past era, and (b) that the lineaments of this original extreme form were still observable as more or less attenuated survivals. When the theory was attacked by anthropologists, he still wanted to retain it, and for a good reason: for whatever doubts one might cast upon the pattern of the primal horde as an *existent,* he needed the concept as a term in his description of the family *essence.*

And may we not see the same principle at work, though more subtly, in the Platonist doctrine (as in the *Meno*) that knowledge is innate in us, remembered from a past existence? Might this doctrine be a somewhat "storial" way of saying that there is certain *essential* knowledge, or that there are fixed *principles* of knowledge?

Similarly, the doctrine of "original sin" could be converted from historical terms (i.e., the "historical" terms of legend) to essentialist terms, if we translated it as "essential sin" (that is, man as "essentially a transgressor"). And we could then clearly see Freud dealing with the same "essential" situation, though in non-theological terms, when in his *Reflections* he sees behind the injunction, "Thou shalt not kill," man's lineal descent from a long line of murderers. But murder is not essential to man just in this temporally derivative sense. It is essential in that it is the "logical conclusion" or "reduction to absurdity" of vituperation and invective. This condition exists *now*. Indeed, I felt it when witnessing the genuine dismay that many of Roosevelt's bitter enemies revealed at the news of his death. I recalled the psychoanalytic theory (previously mentioned in these pages) that Dostoevsky had been disastrously unsettled by his father's death, since he had vicariously participated in this death by secretly willing it. And when, reversing our application of time to essence, we recall that magical prophecy aimed to bring about events by solemnly proclaiming that they would come to pass, we might also recall the great "concern" which Roosevelt's opponents at the last election constantly showed about his health. I do not mean that there is a single one of them who would have killed him. I mean simply that his sacrifice was demanded, as the logical conclusion of their own position. His death was "representative" of their antagonistic attitude. And when it came, they were perhaps more deeply shocked than was the case with many of his devoted followers, for whom his spirit would still live on, since for them his death was likewise a resurrection. For his followers his death was a sacrifice ennobling the cause that, thus revivified, would survive him.

Ibsen's *Peer Gynt* offers us an exceptionally good opportunity to observe the workings of the time-essence ambiguity. For here the plot is explicitly concerned with Peer's search for his true self (that is to say, his essence). And since drama necessarily takes the form of "story," the approach to essence is conveyed in temporal, or "storial" terms.

Peer Gynt is the third of the poetic satires that preceded Ibsen's turn to realistic social drama. The first, *Love's Comedy,* attacked the community's insensitivity to the values of individualist, idealist love. The second, *Brand,* ennobles the cause of reform as personalized in a priestly, sacrificial figure. The third satirizes what Ibsen considered characteristic trivialities of the Norwegian character.

But there are important complications. For the paradox of substance operates strongly in Ibsen's plays. Thus, in *The Wild Duck,* Ibsen seems to accept many of the attitudes he most strongly condemned in *An Enemy of the People;* for *The Wild Duck* shows us the reformer from the standpoint of his opponents, quite as *An Enemy of the People* had shown us the opponents from the standpoint of the reformer. There is here a dialectical shift from the voicing of one position to its opposite. Or rather, though both positions are voiced in both plays, the dramatist's sympathies have changed sides, at least within the special conditions of the fiction. And similarly, before Ibsen had finished with the character of *Peer Gynt,* it had greatly transcended its original purely satiric intent. In fact, as we shall show, a close analysis of its imagery will reveal that Peer ends as a replica of the Christ-child.

There seems to run through Ibsen's work an attempt to distinguish, not conceptually but in terms of dramatic action, between an "egoist" and an "individualist." Both in a sense stand alone. But whereas the loneliness of the egoist is selfish, and may thus even take the form of an easy-going sociality, the loneliness of the individualist is that of one who is willing to sacrifice himself for the good of mankind, and who may thus outrage society by *acting alone* in behalf of some *social ideal.* But the distinction is difficult to maintain in its purity, particularly when it is made in terms of action. For egoist and individualist have a neutral ground of attributes shared in common. There are many respects in which these two concepts, even if desynonymized, again become synonymous. Hence one may expect to find ambivalences in Ibsen's portraying of the two types.

The ambiguities responsible for Peer's translation seem to derive in great part from the motives we have been considering with respect to the masculine problem of dissociating the maternal woman from the erotic woman (the problem of distinguishing one's responses to woman as mother from one's responses to woman as the object of courtship). *Peer Gynt* performs a notable role in Ibsen's own development, since it marks the turn from verse to the realistic prose of his problem plays. Where verse and prose become thus motivationally contrasted, we are justified in looking for evidences of precisely such stock-taking as comes with the turn from the maternal to the erotic. For verse, as thus contrasted, is usually set in the familial or "pre-political" cluster of motives (a cluster coadunating the parental, the religious, and the poetic). Hence it in itself may be taken as indicative of a conservative principle lying deeper than the accidental properties of reform which Ibsen may be advocating. A profound inventory is taking place here. And the character whose development must meet these demands is bound to become so laden with ritualistic functions that he is translated far beyond the role of purely social satire.

The ambiguities are complicated by Ibsen's own vocation as a playwright who, in the nature of the case, would possess great aptitude at fabrication, and much responsiveness to the ways of prevarication. Hence, Peer's glibness as a spinner of fantastic tales (a teller of lies that in a deeper sense are true) amounts to a playful idealizing of the playwright's own vocation. And that again would be enough to translate Peer to a "sacrificial" level, as a personal embodiment, however dubiously, of the writer's devotion to his craft. Accordingly, the character as thus finally developed sums up a sufficient complexity of motives to make his very vices attractive, somewhat as with our complex response to the transgressions of Falstaff.

In brief, then, *Peer Gynt* depicts a character in search of his identity. This quest of essence centers in the need to "desynonymize" Peer's responses to the maternal and erotic principles. The desynonymizing is not completed, but instead the erotic woman is idealistically transformed into the maternal woman. Peer's search for essence is thus depicted in terms of a return to the mother. Solveig, who was to be his wife, becomes instead his spiritual mother, replacing his real mother in whose death he had magically participated. Peer is thereby transformed, having found a new principle of motivation. This transformation is expressed in terms of dramatic substance as Peer's grounding in a new parentage. And now, to indicate the major steps in this transformation:

Note that the play begins with Peer as story-teller, inventing tall tales which he tells his mother, to explain his recent absence. But we should take this opening anecdote much more seriously than Peer does, for it wholly symbolizes his situation. Peer is obviously outgrowing his mother's powers to restrain him. Indeed when, a little later, she tries to strike him as if he were still a child, he playfully picks her up and carries her, protesting helplessly. Peer has become too big for the nest. However, the story he tells, to account for his recent absence indicates what form the new motivation has taken. For he tells of having seized a buck reindeer by the horns, of being carried high up on the mountains, of how the buck finally plunges from a cliff towards the water far below, and of how Peer saw in the water the reflection of himself and the buck rising to meet him in his fall.

In sum: breaking free of the earlier, familial identity (going from merger to division), sensing a new purpose as symbolized in the hunt, Peer is carried by the horned buck (a potency). And the mounting and the fall is in its design reflexive, ending as Peer, carried to a fall by this powerful buck, meets the reflection of himself. The pattern incidentally suggests a "problem" at the very centre of Ibsen's individualism; for Peer, in finally dividing from the familial identity with which he had been merged, is here seen to fall into the self. Hence, though Ibsen in his later plays repeatedly seeks for ways in which the individualistic motive can be resocialized (by enlistment in some cause), Peer's story indicates that in its inception it took the pattern of a potency whereby the fall involved encounter with the self. Later the pattern will be repeated in Peer's encounter with the Boyg, who introduces himself as "Myself." The Boyg is so shapeless that when Peer attempts to attack him, there is nowhere to strike, and Peer falls to biting his own arms. As we shall see, this Boyg plays a momentous role in motivating Peer's way of life.

The reindeer theme belongs as essentially to this story as the theme of the two horses belongs to Socrates' talk of love in the *Phaedrus*. It is a power theme, and appears at several important stages in Peer's development. First, when Peer is carried over the cliff to his encounter with the self; next, in Peer's carrying of his mother where, as she struggles helplessly, he plays that he is the Reindeer and she is Peer (whereupon he puts her on the roof, where she is afraid of falling). When he meets Solveig, he likens her to a reindeer that "grows wild when summer's approaching."

There are many women in *Peer Gynt* who appeal to Peer, as it were, in their "pure sexuality." Indeed, the whole thesaurus of amative responses seems to be composed of: the maternal principle; the reflexive; sheer sexual appetite without affection (as when he mounts the hill with another man's bride; when he goes with the three girls who, lacking boys, would play with trolls; and when later, as elderly "prophet," he is the dupe of his transient interest in Anitra)[17]—and finally, Solveig, the one woman he would love with affection. But when Solveig

---

[17] These women, possessing almost the "pure" sexuality of prostitutes, are also close to the reflexive. For their attraction acts upon Peer Gynt's absolute male selfhood, as such an absolute would be expressed in terms of a relation to woman.

comes to live with him in his newly built forest hut with reindeer horns over the door, he remembers the Boyg's injunction, "Go roundabout." And as Solveig waits to welcome him inside the hut, instead of entering he begins his wanderings.

This is a five-act play. Act III ends appropriately on his mother's death. It is significant timing. Solveig, the one woman whom he could court with affection, has come to live with him. As she calls him, he remembers the Boyg's injunction to go roundabout. If, as we have said, Solveig is to be not simply his beloved, but a new mother-principle, his mother Aase is henceforth superfluous. So Peer's first "roundabout" episode is his return home, where he sits on his sick mother's bed and plays that he is driving her to a party given by Saint Peter in heaven. During the make-believe, she is dying; when he has finished, she is dead. I invite the reader to examine carefully this final scene of the third act, to see whether he can agree with me that Peer has "playfully" participated in her death, thus almost bringing it about, by imitative magic. And in any event, from the standpoint of the development as a whole, if we are right in saying that Solveig is to be the "new mother," Aase becomes superfluous the moment that Solveig enters Peer's cabin to be his woman. And since all the incidents of the plot are but scenic replicas of Peer's own transformations of character, his first "roundabout" approach to Solveig is appropriately his presence at the death of Aase.

Act IV is concerned with Peer's wanderings: the first movement in his search for his essence. Near the end of this act, after he has been deceived by Anitra, he makes an observation much to our purposes. "I have made mistakes," he says; "but it's comforting to realize that my mistakes were the result of the role I had assumed." (He had assumed the role of a prophet.) "It wasn't I myself that made the mistakes." In brief, he is distinguishing between a "scenic" motivation, derived from the *situations* in which he found himself, and such *essential* motivations as an idealist like Ibsen would locate in the Agent, or personality. And then comes the resolve that clearly formulates in temporal terms his search for his essence:

> Suppose I become a travelling scholar, and make a study of past ages? I believe that's the thing for me! I always liked history, and recently I've improved my knowledge. I'll trace the story of mankind. I'll float like a feather on the stream of history. And I'll live

the old days over again, like in a dream. . . . The Past shall be a
lock, and I have the key to it. I'll abandon the sordid ways of the
present.

Significant timing again: immediately after this resolve, the scene
shifts to a hut in a forest in the far north of Norway, where Solveig,
now middle-aged, tells us in a song that she still waits for Peer's return.

It is not necessary, for our purposes, to follow all the steps of Peer's
return, after the incident where the inmates of an insane asylum
(where "each shuts himself in a cask of self") had crowned Peer "the
Emperor of Self." But it is worthy of note that, having at one point
likened himself to an onion, he peels off the successive layers until nothing is left, whereupon the voice of Solveig is heard. And his encounters with the buttonmoulder, who brings up such embarrassing
questions about his lack of identity, are "regressive" in a double sense:
both as regards the problem of essence with which they are explicitly
concerned, and as regards the fact that Peer, when a child, had pre-
tended to mould buttons (ambiguously tin or gold) with an old
casting-ladle.

Peer, through lack of a real self, is to be returned to the buttonmoulder, to be dissolved and recast into a new person. Twice the
buttonmoulder has called for him, twice Peer has managed to put him
off. And then, with the buttonmoulder waiting for him at the next
crossroads, Peer comes upon Solveig, now an elderly woman:

> PEER GYNT. Tell me, then—where was my real self, complete and
> true—the Peer who bore the stamp of God upon his brow?
> SOLVEIG. In my faith, in my hope and in my love.
> PEER GYNT. What are you saying? It is a riddle that you are speak-
> ing now. So speaks a mother of her child.
> SOLVEIG. Ah, yes; and that is what I am; but He who grants a pardon
> for the sake of a mother's prayers, He is his father. (*A ray of light
> seems to flash on* PEER GYNT. *He cries out.*)
> PEER GYNT. Mother and wife! You stainless woman! Oh, hide
> me, hide me in your love! (*Clings to her and buries his face in her lap.
> There is a long silence. The sun rises.*)

And the curtain descends with Solveig singing a lullaby. The buttonmoulder is again heard saying that he will meet Peer at the next crossroads. But Solveig's lullaby has the last word: "I will rock you to sleep
and guard you! Sleep and dream, my dearest boy!"

Has not Peer here at the last found his identity again in the maternal woman? And since he had gone on his wanderings at the very moment when Solveig had first come to his hut, she is the Virgin Mother, who has conceived him as an idea derived from God. He is, in brief, translated to the role of the Christ-child, whose conception was an Annunciation. And his essence resides in merger with this spiritualized maternal grounding, which simultaneously transforms the wife back into a mother and replaces his real mother and his drunken wandering father by a new and ideal parentage.

Despite the vast difference in particulars, we can discern in Proust the same shuttling between temporal and essential terms. And whereas through many volumes the search for essence is novelistically expressed in terms of a prolonged reminiscence, the final volume culminates essayistically in a non-temporal doctrine of essence, as exemplified in the Proustian theory of art. Here one will find many of the typical devices we have considered in these pages. Above all, there is the cult of the moment, with its peculiar synthesizing quality. Moments separated in time are linked outside of time, their community being idealistically grounded in a transcendent self that is neither present nor past, but lies outside of both by reason of its ability to experience the present in terms of the past.

Proust's attentiveness (or in his word, "aspiration") suggests a variant of that "looking forward to looking back" we have elsewhere noted in Shelley. That is, he singles out for appreciative description those moments which he will remember at some later moment. They will not be remembered because they were observed; rather, they were observed because they would be remembered. And their fulfilment as terms for the designation of essence occurs when some later moment is felt to partake of their same quality. His attentiveness at these first encountered is thus the adumbration of an eventual return to them, when later moments are to be defined in terms of them as prototype (a "first edition" for Proust being the particular edition in which he first read any given work).

But we have said enough to illustrate the nature of the time-essence ambiguity as it is reflected on the level of Symbolic. Rhetorically, this ambiguity prepares the way for "temporizing," as a person who is against some policy *absolutely* may assert simply that he is objecting to it *now*. Each time the conditions change, he can rephrase his objections accordingly, by stating them in terms of the new conditions. He thus need never defend his position categorically; and in fact, by thus temporizing he may recruit on a day-to-day basis allies who would be against him if he upheld his position in the absolute. Few men are absolute pacifists, for instance; but nearly all men are against war at any particular time, and the pacifist can get them to *function* as his allies by translating his categorical beliefs into the terms of ever-changing conditions. The search for one constant interest underlying a faction's shifts of policy (as with the doctrine of *Zweck im Recht*) is thus seen to be an attempt at the discernment of an *essential* motive beneath the particular appearances of many *temporized* motives.

Dissolution of Drama

All told, dialectic is concerned with different levels of *grounding*. It may be arrested after but a brief excursion, hardly more than a half-formulated enumeration of the most obvious factors in a situation. But whatever the range of the enterprise, the procedure is in general thus: Encountering some division, we retreat to a level of terms that allow for some kind of merger (as "near" and "far" are merged in the concept of "distance"); then we "return" to the division, now seeing it as pervaded by the spirit of the "One" we had found in our retreat.

Even on the purely Grammatical level, the process can lead to surprising results. In the case of our pentad, for instance, after having stressed the need for the functioning of all five terms in rounded vocabularies of motives, we summed up our position as "dramatistic"—whereupon of a sudden we discovered that our terms had collapsed into a new title that had, as its only logical ground, the "non-dramatistic." Thus we have two kinds of scene: one designating a function *within* the pentad, another designating a function *outside* the pentad; for a term as highly generalized as the "dramatistic" calls for the "non-dramatist" as its sole contextual counterpart. And the fact that one of these usages "transcends" the other may be concealed by the fact that we can refer to either of them by the same word, scene.

What, then, has happened to the genius of our pentad, which has thus dissolved before our very eyes? (Similarly, Korzybski must sometimes wonder what happened to his admonitions against "two-valued orientation," when they are finally summed up as an opposition between "Aristotelian" and "Non-Aristotelian," a "two-valued orientation" if we ever saw one.)

The "dramatistic" itself must have as its context a grounding in the "non-dramatist." The permanent structure of interrelations prevailing within the pentad would be "principles of development" that could not themselves develop (though they could be progressively discovered). So there is a point at which the dramatist perspective, defined in terms of its contextual opposite, must "abolish itself" in the very act of its enunciation. But though this eventuality is inevitable, one must be continually coming upon it, if he would retain an intrinsic appreciation of linguistic structures. A terminology that "begins where others left off" is not in a different order of linguistic resources and embarrassments, though it may contrive to conceal its true nature and conditions until we approach it intrinsically, in dramatistic terms.

The four ways in which drama is dissolved have been considered elsewhere. But it may be appropriate to list them here:

(1) Drama is dissolved by the turn from dramatic *act* to lyric *state*. This is not to be considered a dissolution in the full sense, since *status* is a reciprocal of *actus*.

(2) Drama is dissolved by terminologies that reduced action to motion.

(3) Drama is dissolved by philosophies of "dramatism," as with our present work. We use coördinates derived from the contemplation of drama, yet our use of them is non-dramatic.

(4) Drama is dissolved by philosophies of "super-drama."

By "super-drama" we refer, of course, to the way whereby a monotheistic god, in being treated as a "super-person," becomes "*im*personal." Such impersonality is in effect a dissolution of the person, a dramatistic paradox that makes it readily clear why scholastic theology could prepare the way for the secular terminologies of science.

A Neo-Liberal Ideal

So much for the Grammar of Motives. As we have said, our primary purpose has been to express towards language an *attitude* embodied in a *method*. This attitude is one of linguistic skepticism, which we synonymize with linguistic appreciation, on the grounds that an attitude of methodical quizzicality towards language may best equip us to perceive the full scope of its resourcefulness.

This Grammar is of course designed for reading independently of the Rhetoric and Symbolic. The Rhetoric and Symbolic are required, if one would examine *in detail* the ways in which the Grammatical resources are employed for the purposes of persuasion and self-expression; but the present book has already indicated how these other areas impinge upon the Grammatical and bear upon its logic.

All told, in this project directed "towards the purification of war," the Grammar should assist to this end through encouraging tolerance by speculation. For it deals with a level of motivation which even wholly rival doctrines of motives must share in common; hence it may be addressed to a speculative portion of the mind which men of many different situations may have in common. The Rhetoric, which would study the "competitive use of the coöperative," would be designed to help us take delight in the Human Barnyard, with its addiction to the Scramble, an area that would cause us great unhappiness could we not transcend it by appreciation, classifying and tracing back to their beginnings in Edenic simplicity those linguistic modes of suasion that often seem little better than malice and the lie. And the Symbolic, studying the implicit equations which have so much to do with the shaping of our acts, should enable us to see our own lives as a kind of rough first draft that lends itself at least somewhat to revision, as we may hope at least to temper the extreme rawness of our ambitions, once we become aware of the ways in which we are the victims of our own and one another's magic.

Such, then, are the "moralistic" reasons for the enterprise. They are offered in the firm belief that a kind of "Neo-Stoic resignation" to the needs of industrial expansion is in order. For better or worse, men are set to complete the development of technology, a development that will require such a vast bureaucracy (in both political and commercial administration) as the world has never before encountered. Encountering a "global" situation, to what extent can we avoid the piecemeal response of dissipation (that is content simply to take whatever opportunities are nearest at hand) and the response of fanaticism (that would impose one terminology of motives upon the whole world, regardless of the great dialectic interchange still to be completed)? To what extent can we confront the global situation with an attitude neither local nor imperialistic? Surely, all works of goodwill written in the next decades must aim somehow to avoid these two extremes, seeking a neo-liberal, speculative attitude. To an extent, perhaps, it will be like an attitude of hypochondriasis: the attitude of a patient who makes peace with his symptoms by becoming interested in them. Yes, on the negative side, the "Neo-Stoicism" we advocate would be an attitude of hypochondriasis. But on the positive side it would be an attitude of appreciation. And as regards our particular project, it would seek delight in meditating upon some of the many ingenuities of speech. Linguistic skepticism, in being quizzical, supplies the surest ground for the discernment and appreciation of linguistic resources.

Addendum for the Present Edition

With regard to the Dramatistic pentad (act, scene, agent, agency, purpose), I have found one modification useful for certain kinds of analysis. In accordance with my discussion of "attitudes" (in the section on "'Incipient' and 'Delayed' Action," pp. 235-47), I have sometimes added the term "attitude" to the above list of five major terms. Thus, one could also speak of a "scene-attitude ratio," or of an "agent-attitude ratio," etc. "Agency" would more strictly designate the "means" (*quibus auxiliis*) employed in an act. And "attitude" would designate the manner (*quo modo*). To build something with a hammer would involve an instrument, or "agency"; to build with diligence would involve an "attitude," a "how."

I have also found that it is sometimes useful to differentiate the ratios by the order of the terms. For instance, by a "scene-act ratio" one would refer to the effect that a scene has upon an act, and by an "act-scene ratio" one would refer to the effect that an act has upon a scene. The Supreme Court would be exemplifying a "scene-act ratio" in deciding that emergency measures are admissible because there is a state of emergency. And we should be exemplifying an "act-scene ratio" in fearing that an arms race may lead to war. At still other times, however, there is merely a state of conformity between scene and act, without any notion of cause and effect. For instance, in Joseph Conrad's novel *Victory* a volcano erupts precisely at the time when the plot attains its maximum degree of agitation. Yet one could not properly say either that the erupting volcano caused the story to erupt, or *vice versa*.

Incidentally, one might note that all the ratios are essentially analogies. That is, by a "scene-act ratio" we mean that the nature of the act is implicit, or analogously present, in the nature of the scene, etc.

APPENDIX

SYMBOLIC ACTION IN A POEM
BY KEATS

W E ARE here set to analyze the "Ode on a Grecian Urn" as a viaticum that leads, by a series of transformations, into the oracle, "Beauty is truth, truth beauty." We shall analyze the Ode "dramatistically," in terms of symbolic action.

To consider language as a means of *information* or *knowledge* is to consider it epistemologically, semantically, in terms of "science." To consider it as a mode of *action* is to consider it in terms of "poetry." For a poem is an act, the symbolic act of the poet who made it—an act of such a nature that, in surviving as a structure or object, it enables us as readers to re-enact it.

"Truth" being the essential word of knowledge (science) and "beauty" being the essential word of art or poetry, we might substitute accordingly. The oracle would then assert, "Poetry is science, science poetry." It would be particularly exhilarating to proclaim them one if there were a strong suspicion that they were at odds (as the assertion that "God's in his heaven, all's right with the world" is really a *counter*-assertion to doubts about God's existence and suspicions that much is wrong). It was the dialectical opposition between the "aesthetic" and the "practical," with "poetry" on one side and utility (business and applied science) on the other that was being ecstatically denied. The *relief* in this denial was grounded in the romantic philosophy itself, a philosophy which gave strong recognition to precisely the *contrast* between "beauty" and "truth."

Perhaps we might put it this way: If the oracle were to have been uttered in the first stanza of the poem rather than the last, its phrasing proper to that place would have been: "Beauty is *not* truth, truth *not* beauty." The five stanzas of successive transformation were necessary for the romantic philosophy of a romantic poet to transcend itself (raising its romanticism to a new order, or new dimension). An abolishing of romanticism through romanticism! (To transcend romanticism through romanticism is, when all is over, to restore in one way what is removed in another.)

But to the poem, step by step through the five stanzas.

As a "way in," we begin with the sweeping periodic sentence that, before the stanza is over, has swiftly but imperceptibly been transmuted in quality from the periodic to the breathless, a cross between interrogation and exclamation:

> Thou still unravish'd bride of quietness,
>   Thou foster-child of silence and slow time,
> Sylvan historian, who canst thus express
>   A flowery tale more sweetly than our rhyme:
> What leaf-fring'd legend haunts about thy shape
>   Of deities or mortals, or of both,
>   In Tempe or the dales of Arcady?
> What men or gods are these?   What maidens loth?
> What mad pursuit?   What struggle to escape?
>   What pipes and timbrels?   What wild ecstasy?

Even the last quick outcries retain somewhat the quality of the periodic structure with which the stanza began.   The final line introduces the subject of "pipes and timbrels," which is developed and then surpassed in Stanza II:

> Heard melodies are sweet, but those unheard
>   Are sweeter; therefore, ye soft pipes, play on;
> Not to the sensual ear, but, more endear'd,
>   Pipe to the spirit ditties of no tone:
> Fair youth, beneath the trees, thou canst not leave
>   Thy song, nor ever can those trees be bare;
>   Bold Lover, never, never canst thou kiss,
> Though winning near the goal—yet, do not grieve;
>   She cannot fade, though thou hast not thy bliss,
>   Forever wilt thou love, and she be fair!

If we had only the first stanza of this Ode, and were speculating upon it from the standpoint of motivation, we could detect there tentative indications of two motivational levels.   For the lines express a doubt whether the figures on the urn are "deities or mortals"—and the motives of gods are of a different order from the motives of men.   This bare hint of such a possibility emerges with something of certainty in the second stanza's development of the "pipes and timbrels" theme. For we explicitly consider a contrast between body and mind (in the contrast between "heard melodies," addressed "to the sensual ear," and "ditties of no tone," addressed "to the spirit").

Also, of course, the notion of inaudible sound brings us into the region of the mystic oxymoron (the term in rhetoric for "the figure in which an epithet of a contrary significance is added to a word: e.g., *cruel kindness; laborious idleness*"). And it clearly suggests a concern with the level of motives-behind-motives, as with the paradox of the prime mover that is itself at rest, being the unmoved ground of all motion and action. Here the poet whose sounds are the richest in our language is meditating upon *absolute* sound, the *essence* of sound, which would be soundless as the prime mover is motionless, or as the "principle" of sweetness would not be sweet, having transcended sweetness, or as the sub-atomic particles of the sun are each, in their isolate purity, said to be devoid of temperature.

Contrast Keats's unheard melodies with those of Shelley:

> Music, when soft voices die,
> Vibrates in the memory—
> Odours, when sweet violets sicken,
> Live within the sense they quicken.
>
> Rose leaves, when the rose is dead,
> Are heaped for the beloved's bed;
> And so thy thoughts, when thou art gone,
> Love itself shall slumber on.

Here the futuristic Shelley is anticipating retrospection; he is looking forward to looking back. The form of thought is naturalistic and temporalistic in terms of *past* and *future*. But the form of thought in Keats is mystical, in terms of an *eternal present*. The Ode is striving to move beyond the region of becoming into the realm of *being*. (This is another way of saying that we are here concerned with two levels of motivation.)

In the last four lines of the second stanza, the state of immediacy is conveyed by a development peculiarly Keatsian. I refer not simply to translation into terms of the erotic, but rather to a quality of *suspension* in the erotic imagery, defining an eternal prolongation of the state just prior to fulfilment—not exactly arrested ecstasy, but rather an arrested pre-ecstasy.[1]

Suppose that we had but this one poem by Keats, and knew nothing of its author or its period, so that we could treat it only in itself, as a series of internal transformations to be studied in their development from a certain point, and without reference to any motives outside the Ode. Under such conditions, I think, we should require no further observations to characterize (from the standpoint of symbolic action) the main argument in the second stanza. We might go on to make an infinity of observations about the details of the stanza; but as regards major deployments we should deem it enough to note that the theme of "pipes and timbrels" is developed by the use of mystic oxymoron, and then surpassed (or given a development-atop-the-development) by the stressing of erotic imagery (that had been ambiguously adumbrated in the references to "maidens loth" and "mad pursuit" of Stanza I). And we could note the quality of *incipience* in this imagery, its state of arrest not at fulfilment, but at the point just prior to fulfilment.

Add, now, our knowledge of the poem's place as an enactment in a particular cultural scene, and we likewise note in this second stanza a variant of the identification between death and sexual love that was so typical of 19th-century romanticism and was to attain its musical monument in the Wagnerian *Liebestod*. On a purely dialectical basis, to die in love would be to be born to love (the lovers dying as individual identities that they might be transformed into a common identity). Adding historical factors, one can note the part that capitalist individualism plays in sharpening this consummation (since a property structure that heightens the sense of individual identity would thus make it more imperiously a "death" for the individual to take on the new identity made by a union of two). We can thus see why the love-death equation would be particularly representative of a romanticism that was the reflex of business.

Fortunately, the relation between private property and the love-death equation is attested on unimpeachable authority, concerning the effect of consumption and consummation in a "mutual flame":

[1] Mr. G. Wilson Knight, in *The Starlit Dome,* refers to "that recurring tendency in Keats to image a poised form, a stillness suggesting motion, what might be called a 'tiptoe' effect."

So between them love did shine,
That the turtle saw his right
Flaming in the phoenix' sight;
Either was the other's mine.

Property was thus appall'd,
That the self was not the same;
Single nature's double name
Neither two nor one was called.

The addition of fire to the equation, with its pun on sexual burning, moves us from purely dialectical considerations into psychological ones. In the lines of Shakespeare, fire is the third term, the ground term for the other two (the synthesis that ends the lovers' roles as thesis and antithesis). Less obviously, the same movement from the purely dialectical to the psychological is implicit in any imagery of a *dying* or a *falling* in common, which when woven with sexual imagery signalizes a "transcendent" sexual consummation. The figure appears in a lover's compliment when Keats writes to Fanny Brawne, thus:

I never knew before, what such a love as you have made me feel, was; I did not believe in it; my Fancy was afraid of it lest it should burn me up. But if you will fully love me, though there may be some fire, 'twill not be more than we can bear when moistened and bedewed with pleasures.

Our primary concern is to follow the transformations of the poem itself. But to understand its full nature as a symbolic act, we should use whatever knowledge is available. In the case of Keats, not only do we know the place of this poem in his work and its time, but also we have material to guide our speculations as regards correlations between poem and poet. I grant that such speculations interfere with the symmetry of criticism as a game. (Criticism as a game is best to watch, I guess, when one confines himself to the single unit, and reports on its movements like a radio commentator broadcasting the blow-by-blow description of a prizefight.) But linguistic analysis has opened up new possibilities in the correlating of producer and product—and these concerns have such important bearing upon matters of culture and conduct in general that no sheer conventions or ideals of criticism should be allowed to interfere with their development.

From what we know of Keats's illness, with the peculiar inclination to erotic imaginings that accompany its fever (as with the writings of D. H. Lawrence) we can glimpse a particular bodily motive expanding and intensifying the lyric state in Keats's case. Whatever the intense *activity* of his thoughts, there was the material *pathos* of his physical condition. Whatever transformations of mind or body he experienced, his illness was there as a kind of constitutional substrate, whereby all aspects of the illness would be imbued with their derivation from a common ground (the phthisic fever thus being at one with the phthisic chill, for whatever the clear contrast between fever and chill, they are but modes of the same illness, the common underlying substance).

The correlation between the state of agitation in the poems and the physical condition of the poet is made quite clear in the poignant letters Keats wrote during his last illness. In 1819 he complains that he is "scarcely content to write the best verses for the fever they leave behind." And he continues: "I want to compose without this fever." But a few months later he confesses, "I am recommended not even to read poetry, much less write it." Or: "I must say that for 6 Months before I was taken ill I had not passed a tranquil day. Either that gloom overspre[a]d me or I was suffering under some passionate feeling, or if I turn'd to versify that exacerbated the poison of either sensation." Keats was "like a sick eagle looking at the sky," as he wrote of his mortality in a kindred poem, "On Seeing the Elgin Marbles."

But though the poet's body was a *patient,* the poet's mind was an *agent.* Thus, as a practitioner of poetry, he could *use* his fever, even perhaps encouraging, though not deliberately, esthetic habits that, in making for the perfection of his lines, would exact payment in the ravages of his body (somewhat as Hart Crane could write poetry only by modes of living that made for the cessation of his poetry and so led to his dissolution).

Speaking of agents, patients, and action here, we might pause to glance back over the centuries thus: in the Aristotelian grammar of motives, action has its reciprocal in passion, hence *passion* is the property of a *patient.* But by the Christian paradox (which made the martyr's action identical with his passion, as the accounts of the martyrs were called both Acts and Passionals), *patience* is the property of a moral *agent.* And this Christian view, as secularized in the philosophy of romanticism, with its stress upon creativeness, leads us to the possibility of a bodily suffering redeemed by a poetic act.

In the third stanza, the central stanza of the Ode (hence properly the fulcrum of its swing) we see the two motives, the action and the passion, in the process of being separated. The possibility raised in the first stanza (which was dubious whether the level of motives was to be human or divine), and developed in the second stanza (which contrasts the "sensual" and the "spirit"), becomes definitive in Stanza III:

> Ah, happy, happy boughs! that cannot shed
>   Your leaves, nor ever bid the Spring adieu;
> And, happy melodist, unwearied,
>   For ever piping songs for ever new;
> More happy love! more happy, happy love!
>   For ever warm and still to be enjoy'd,
>   For ever panting, and for ever young;
> All breathing human passion far above,
>   That leaves a heart high-sorrowful and cloy'd,
>   A burning forehead, and a parching tongue.

The poem as a whole makes permanent, or fixes in a state of arrest, a peculiar agitation. But within this fixity, by the nature of poetry as a progressive medium, there must be development. Hence, the agitation that is maintained throughout (as a mood absolutized so that it fills the entire universe of discourse) will at the same time undergo internal transformations. In the third stanza, these are manifested as a clear division into two distinct and contrasted realms. There is a transcendental fever, which is felicitous, divinely above "all breathing human passion." And this "leaves" the other level, the level of earthly fever, "a burning forehead and a parching tongue." From the bodily fever, which is a passion, and malign, there has split off a spiritual activity, a wholly benign aspect of the total agitation.

Clearly, a movement has been finished. The poem must, if it is well-formed, take a new direction, growing out of and surpassing the curve that has by now been clearly established by the successive stages from "Is there the possibility of two motivational levels?" through "there are two motivational levels" to "the 'active' motivational level 'leaves' the 'passive' level."

Prophesying, with the inestimable advantage that goes with having looked ahead, what should we expect the new direction to be? First, let us survey the situation. Originally, before the two strands of the fever had been definitely drawn apart, the bodily passion could serve as the scene or ground of the spiritual action. But at the end of the third stanza, we abandon the level of bodily passion. The action is "far above" the passion, it "leaves" the fever. What then would this transcendent act require, to complete it?

It would require a scene of the same quality as itself. An act and a scene belong together. The nature of the one must be a fit with the nature of the other. (I like to call this the "scene-act ratio," or "dramatic ratio.") Hence, the act having now transcended its bodily setting, it will require, as its new setting, a transcendent scene. Hence, prophesying *post eventum,* we should ask that, in Stanza IV, the poem *embody* the transcendental act by endowing it with an appropriate scene.

The scene-act ratio involves a law of dramatic consistency whereby the quality of the act shares the quality of the scene in which it is enacted (the synecdochic relation of container and thing contained). Its grandest variant was in supernatural cosmogonies wherein mankind took on the attributes of gods by acting in cosmic scenes that were themselves imbued with the presence of godhead.[2]

Or we may discern the logic of the scene-act ratio behind the old controversy as to whether "God willed the good because it is good," or "the good is good because God willed it." This strictly theological controversy had political implications. But our primary concern here is with the *dramatistic* aspects of this controversy. For you will note that the whole issue centers in the problem of the *grounds* of God's creative act.

Since, from the purely dramatic point of view, every act requires a scene in which it takes place, we may note that one of the doctrines (that "God willed the good because it is good") is more symmetrical than the other. For by it, God's initial act of creation is itself

[2] In an article by Leo Spitzer, *"Milieu* and *Ambiance*: An Essay in Historical Semantics" (September and December 1942 numbers of *Philosophy and Phenomenological Research*), one will find a wealth of material that can be read as illustrative of "dramatic ratio."

given a ground, or scene (the objective existence of goodness, which was so real that God himself did not simply make it up, but acted in conformity with its nature when willing it to be the law of his creation).   In the scholastic formulas taken over from Aristotle, God was defined as "pure act" (though this pure act was in turn the ultimate ground or *scene* of human acting and willing).   And from the standpoint of purely dramatic symmetry, it would be desirable to have some kind of "scene" even for God.   This requirement is met, we are suggesting, in the doctrine that "God willed the good *because* it is good." For this word, "because," in assigning a reason for God's willing, gives us in principle a kind of scene, as we may discern in the pun of our word, "ground," itself, which indeterminately applies to either "place" or "cause."

If even theology thus responded to the pressure for dramatic symmetry by endowing God, as the transcendent act, with a transcendent scene of like quality, we should certainly expect to find analogous tactics in this Ode.   For as we have noted that the romantic passion is the secular equivalent of the Christian passion, so we may recall Coleridge's notion that poetic action itself is a "dim analogue of Creation."   Keats in his way confronting the same dramatistic requirement that the theologians confronted in theirs, when he has arrived at his transcendent act at the end of Stanza III (that is, when the benign fever has split away from the malign bodily counterpart, as a divorcing of spiritual action from sensual passion), he is ready in the next stanza for the imagining of a scene that would correspond in quality to the quality of the action as so transformed.   His fourth stanza will concretize, or "materialize," the act, by dwelling upon its appropriate ground.

> Who are these coming to the sacrifice?
> To what green altar, O mysterious priest,
> Lead'st thou that heifer lowing at the skies,
>   And all her silken flanks with garlands drest?
> What little town, by river or sea shore,
>   Or mountain built with peaceful citadel,
>   Is emptied of this folk, this pious morn?
> And, little town, thy streets for evermore
>   Will silent be; and not a soul to tell
>   Why thou art desolate, can e'er return.

It is a vision, as you prefer, of "death" or of "immortality." "Immortality," we might say, is the "good" word for "death," and must necessarily be conceived in terms of death (the necessity that Donne touches upon when he writes, ". . . but thinke that I / Am, by being dead, immortall"). This is why, when discussing the second stanza, I felt justified in speaking of the variations of the love-death equation, though the poem spoke not of love and *death,* but of love *for ever.* We have a deathy-deathless scene as the corresponding ground of our transcendent act. The Urn itself, as with the scene upon it, is not merely an immortal act in our present mortal scene; it was originally an immortal act in a mortal scene quite different. The imagery, of sacrifice, piety, silence, desolation, is that of communication with the immortal or the dead.[3]

Incidentally, we might note that the return to the use of rhetorical questions in the fourth stanza serves well, on a purely technical level, to keep our contact with the mood of the opening stanza, a music that now but vibrates in the memory. Indeed, one even gets the impression that the form of the rhetorical question had never been abandoned; that the poet's questings had been couched as questions throughout. This is tonal felicity at its best, and something much like unheard tonal felicity. For the actual persistence of the rhetorical questions through these stanzas would have been wearisome, whereas their return now gives us

[3] In imagery there is no negation, or disjunction. Logically, we can say, "this *or* that," "this, *not* that." In imagery we can but say "this *and* that," "this *with* that," "this-that," etc. Thus, imagistically considered, a commandment cannot be simply a proscription, but is also latently a provocation (a state of affairs that figures in the kind of stylistic scrupulosity and/or curiosity to which Gide's heroes have been particularly sensitive, as "thou shalt not . . ." becomes imaginatively transformed into "what would happen if . . ."). In the light of what we have said about the deathiness of immortality, and the relation between the erotic and the thought of a "dying," perhaps we might be justified in reading the last line of the great "Bright Star!" sonnet as naming states not simply alternative but also synonymous:

> And so live ever—or else swoon to death.

This use of the love-death equation is as startlingly paralleled in a letter to Fanny Brawne:

> I have two luxuries to brood over in my walks, your loveliness and the hour of my death. O that I could take possession of them both in the same moment.

an inaudible variation, by making us feel that the exclamations in the second and third stanzas had been questions, as the questions in the first stanza had been exclamations.

But though a lyric greatly profits by so strong a sense of continuous-ness, or perpetuity, I am trying to stress the fact that in the fourth stanza we *come upon* something.   Indeed, this fourth stanza is related to the three foregoing stanzas quite as the sestet is related to the octave in Keats's sonnet, "On First Looking Into Chapman's Homer":

> Much have I travell'd in the realms of gold,
>   And many goodly states and kingdoms seen;
>   Round many western islands have I been
> Which bards in fealty to Apollo hold.
> Oft of one wide expanse had I been told
>   That deep-brow'd Homer ruled as his demesne;
>   Yet did I never breathe its pure serene
> Till I heard Chapman speak out loud and bold;
>
> Then felt I like some watcher of the skies
>   When a new planet swims into his ken;
> Or like stout Cortez when with eagle eyes
>   He stared at the Pacific—and all his men
> Look'd at each other with a wild surmise—
>   Silent, upon a peak in Darien.

I am suggesting that, just as the sestet in this sonnet, *comes upon a scene,* so it is with the fourth stanza of the Ode.   In both likewise we end on the theme of silence; and is not the Ode's reference to the thing that "not a soul can tell" quite the same in quality as the sonnet's reference to a "wild surmise"?

Thus, with the Urn as viaticum (or rather, with the *poem* as viati-cum, and *in the name* of the Urn), having symbolically enacted a kind of act that transcends our mortality, we round out the process by com-ing to dwell upon the transcendental ground of this act.   The dead world of ancient Greece, as immortalized on an Urn surviving from that period, is the vessel of this deathy-deathless ambiguity.   And we have gone dialectically from the "human" to the "divine" and thence to the "ground of the divine" (here tracing in poetic imagery the kind of "dramatistic" course we have considered, on the purely conceptual plane, in the theological speculations about the "grounds" for God's creative act). Necessarily, there must be certain inadequacies in the conception of this ground, precisely because of the fact that immortality can only be conceived in terms of death. Hence the reference to the "desolate" in a scene otherwise possessing the benignity of the eternal.

The imagery of pious sacrifice, besides its fitness for such thoughts of departure as when the spiritual act splits from the sensual pathos, suggests also a bond of communication between the levels (because of its immortal character in a mortal scene). And finally, the poem, in the name of the Urn, or under the aegis of the Urn, is such a bond. For we readers, by re-enacting it in the reading, use it as a viaticum to transport us into the quality of the scene which it depicts on its face (the scene containing as a fixity what the poem as act extends into a process). The scene *on* the Urn is really the scene *behind* the Urn; the Urn is literally the ground of this scene, but transcendentally the scene is the ground of the Urn. The Urn contains the scene out of which it arose.

We turn now to the closing stanza:

> O Attic shape! Fair attitude! with brede
>   Of marble men and maidens overwrought,
> With forest branches and the trodden weed;
>   Thou, silent form, dost tease us out of thought.
> As doth eternity: Cold Pastoral!
>   When old age shall this generation waste,
>   Thou shalt remain, in midst of other woe
> Than ours, a friend to man, to whom thou say'st,
>   'Beauty is truth, truth beauty,'—that is all
>   Ye know on earth, and all ye need to know.

In the third stanza we were at a moment of heat, emphatically sharing an imagery of loves "panting" and "for ever warm" that was, in the transcendental order, companionate to "a burning forehead, and a parching tongue" in the order of the passions. But in the last stanza, as signalized in the marmorean utterance, "Cold Pastoral!" we have gone from transcendental fever to transcendental chill. Perhaps, were we to complete our exegesis, we should need reference to some physical step from phthisic fever to phthisic chill, that we might detect here a final correlation between bodily passion and mental action. In any event we may note that, the mental action having departed from the bodily passion, the change from fever to chill is not a sufferance. For, as only the *benign* aspects of the fever had been left after the split, so it is a wholly benign chill on which the poem ends.[4]

I wonder whether anyone can read the reference to "brede of marble men and maidens overwrought" without thinking of · "breed" for "brede" and "excited" for "overwrought." (Both expressions would thus merge notions of sexuality and craftsmanship, the erotic and the poetic.) As for the designating of the Urn as an "Attitude," it fits in admirably with our stress upon symbolic action. For an attitude is an arrested, or incipient *act*—not just an *object,* or *thing.*

Yeats, in *A Vision,* speaks of "the diagrams in Law's *Boehme,* where one lifts a paper to discover both the human entrails and the starry heavens." This equating of the deeply without and the deeply within (as also with Kant's famous remark) might well be remembered when we think of the sky that the "watcher" saw in Keats's sonnet. It is an internal sky, attained through meditations induced by the reading of a book. And so the oracle, whereby truth and beauty are proclaimed as one, would seem to derive from a profound inwardness.

Otherwise, without these introductory mysteries, "truth" and "beauty" were at odds. For whereas "beauty" had its fulfilment in romantic poetry, "truth" was coming to have its fulfilment in science, technological accuracy, accountancy, statistics, actuarial tables, and the like. Hence, without benefit of the rites which one enacts in a sympathetic reading of the Ode (rites that remove the discussion to a different level), the enjoyment of "beauty" would involve an esthetic kind of awareness radically in conflict with the kind of awareness deriving from the practical "truth." And as regards the tactics of the poem, this conflict would seem to be solved by "estheticizing" the true rather than by "verifying" the beautiful.

Earlier in our essay, we suggested reading "poetry" for "beauty" and "science" for "truth," with the oracle deriving its *liberating* quality

---

[4] In a letter to Fanny Brawne, Keats touches upon the fever-chill contrast in a passage that also touches upon the love-death equation, though here the chill figures in an untransfigured state:

> I fear that I am too prudent for a dying kind of Lover. Yet, there is a great difference between going off in warm blood like Romeo; and making one's exit like a frog in a frost.

from the fact that it is uttered at a time when the poem has taken us to a level where earthly contradictions do not operate. But we might also, in purely conceptual terms, attain a level where "poetry" and "science" cease to be at odds; namely: by translating the two terms into the "grammar" that lies behind them. That is: we could generalize the term "poetry" by widening it to the point where we could substitute for it the term "act." And we could widen "science" to the point where we could substitute "scene." Thus we have:

"beauty"   equals   "poetry"   equals   "act"
"truth"   equals   "science"   equals   "scene"

We would equate "beauty" with "act," because it is not merely a decorative thing, but an assertion, an affirmative, a creation, hence in the fullest sense an act. And we would equate "truth" or "science" with the "scenic" because science is a knowledge of *what is*—and *all that is* comprises the over-all universal *scene*. Our corresponding transcendence, then, got by "translation" into purely grammatical terms, would be: "Act is scene, scene act." We have got to this point by a kind of purely conceptual transformation that would correspond, I think, to the transformations of imagery leading to the oracle in the Ode.

"Act is scene, scene act." Unfortunately, I must break the symmetry a little. For poetry, as conceived in idealism (romanticism) could not quite be equated with *act,* but rather with *attitude.* For idealistic philosophies, with their stress upon the subjective, place primary stress upon the *agent* (the individual, the ego, the will, etc.). It was medieval scholasticism that placed primary stress upon the *act.* And in the Ode the Urn (which is the vessel or representative of poetry) is called an "attitude," which is not outright an act, but an incipient or arrested act, a *state of mind,* the property of an *agent.* Keats, in calling the Urn an attitude, is *personifying* it. Or we might use the italicizing resources of dialectic by saying that for Keats, beauty (poetry) was not so much "the *act* of an agent" as it was "the act of an *agent.*"

Perhaps we can re-enforce this interpretation by examining kindred strategies in Yeats, whose poetry similarly derives from idealistic, romantic sources. Indeed, as we have noted elsewhere,[5] Yeats's vision of immortality in his Byzantium poems but carries one step further the Keatsian identification with the Grecian Urn:

[5] "On Motivation in Yeats" (*The Southern Review,* Winter 1942).

> Once out of nature I shall never take
> My bodily form from any natural thing,
> But such a form as Grecian goldsmiths make
> Of hammered gold and gold enamelling . . .

Here certainly the poet envisions immortality as "esthetically" as Keats. For he will have immortality as a golden bird, a fabricated thing, a work of Grecian goldsmiths. Here we go in the same direction as the "overwrought" Urn, but farther along in that direction.

The ending of Yeats's poem, "Among School Children," helps us to make still clearer the idealistic stress upon agent:

> Labour is blossoming or dancing where
> The body is not bruised to pleasure soul,
> Nor beauty torn out of its own despair,
> Nor blear-eyed wisdom out of midnight oil.
> O chestnut tree, great rooted blossomer,
> Are you the leaf, the blossom or the bole?
> O body swayed to music, O brightening glance,
> How can we know the dancer from the dance?

Here the chestnut tree (as personified agent) is the ground of unity or continuity for all its scenic manifestations; and with the agent (dancer) is merged the act (dance). True, we seem to have here a commingling of act, scene, and agent, all three. Yet it is the *agent* that is "foremost among the equals." Both Yeats and Keats, of course, were much more "dramatistic" in their thinking than romantic poets generally, who usually center their efforts upon the translation of *scene* into terms of *agent* (as the materialistic science that was the dialectical counterpart of romantic idealism preferred conversely to translate *agent* into terms of *scene,* or in other words, to treat "consciousness" in terms of "matter," the "mental" in terms of the "physical," "people" in terms of "environment").

To review briefly: The poem begins with an ambiguous fever which in the course of the further development is "separated out," splitting into a bodily fever and a spiritual counterpart. The bodily passion is the malign aspect of the fever, the mental action its benign aspect. In the course of the development, the malign passion is transcended and the benign active partner, the intellectual exhilaration, takes over. At the beginning, where the two aspects were ambiguously one, the bodily passion would be the "scene" of the mental action (the "objective symptoms" of the body would be paralleled by the "subjective symptoms" of the mind, the bodily state thus being the other or ground of the mental state). But as the two become separated out, the mental action transcends the bodily passion. It becomes an act in its own right, making discoveries and assertions not grounded in the bodily passion. And this quality of action, in transcending the merely physical symptoms of the fever, would thus require a different ground or scene, one more suited in quality to the quality of the transcendent act.

The transcendent act is concretized, or "materialized," in the vision of the "immortal" scene, the reference in Stanza IV to the original scene of the Urn, the "heavenly" scene of a dead, or immortal, Greece (the scene in which the Urn was originally enacted and which is also fixed on its face). To indicate the internality of this vision, we referred to a passage in Yeats relating the "depths" of the sky without to the depths of the mind within; and we showed a similar pattern in Keats's account of the vision that followed his reading of Chapman's Homer. We suggested that the poet is here coming upon a new internal sky, through identification with the Urn as act, the same sky that he came upon through identification with the enactments of Chapman's translation.

This transcendent scene is the level at which the earthly laws of contradiction no longer prevail. Hence, in the terms of this scene, he can proclaim the unity of truth and beauty (of science and art), a proclamation which he needs to make precisely because here was the basic split responsible for the romantic agitation (in both poetic and philosophic idealism). That is, it was gratifying to have the oracle proclaim the unity of poetry and science because the values of technology and business were causing them to be at odds. And from the perspective of a "higher level" (the perspective of a dead or immortal scene transcending the world of temporal contradictions) the split could be proclaimed once more a unity.

At this point, at this stage of exaltation, the fever has been replaced by chill. But the bodily passion has completely dropped out of account. All is now mental action. Hence, the chill (as in the ecstatic exclamation, "Cold Pastoral!") is proclaimed only in its benign aspect.

We may contrast this discussion with explanations such as a mate-

rialist of the Kretschmer school might offer.   I refer to accounts of motivation that might treat disease as cause and poem as effect.   In such
accounts, the disease would not be "passive," but wholly active; and
what we have called the mental action would be wholly passive, hardly
more than an epiphenomenon, a mere symptom of the disease quite as
are the fever and the chill themselves.   Such accounts would give us
no conception of the essential matter here, the intense linguistic activity.

B

THE PROBLEM OF THE INTRINSIC

(as reflected in the Neo-Aristotelian School)

I

THERE is a *rhetorical* explanation for doctrines proclaiming the eternity of art. We can say that, esthetic standards being transitory, men try to compensate for this changefulness by denying its existence. Then we might fill out this explanation on the rhetorical level by sociological considerations, noting for instance that the doctrine would fit well with a collector's or antiquarian's attitude towards art, and thus with the business of selling art objects to customers in search of sound esthetic investments. And when art is approached from the antiquarian point of view, men may ask so little of it that it can easily meet the requirements. Thus a work that, in its original context, might have seemed "terrifying" or "divine," could at least remain eternally "interesting" or "odd," thereby possessing a kind of permanence as tested by dilettantish criteria. Much esthetic theory stressing the appreciation of "form" would doubtless fall under this head.

Or noting how much of art has been a secularized variant of religious processes, particularly since the rise of the romantic reaction against capitalism and technology, we may offer a *symbolical* interpretation. A doctrine proclaiming the eternity of art would, from the symbolic point of view, be the natural secular analogue of a belief in the eternity of God.

But we may discuss motives on three levels. Besides Rhetoric and Symbolic, there is Grammar. We are on the grammatical level when we begin with the "problem of the intrinsic," as reflected in the attempt to characterize the substance of a work. We are faced with *grammatical* problems when we would consider a given work of art "in itself," in what I believe the scholastics might have called its *aseitas,* or "by-itselfness." Considered "intrinsically," the work is said to embody

465

certain "principles." And these principles are said to reside in the division of the work into its parts, and in the relation of these parts to one another and to the whole.

Even though a work of art were to last but a few moments, being destroyed almost immediately after its production, during its brief physical duration you might deal with it *sub specie aeternitatis,* in terms of timelessness. This you could do by considering solely the relation of its parts to one another and to the whole. And you would thereby be thinking in terms of the "eternal" or "timeless" since the relations prevailing among the parts just are. Each part *is* in a certain relation to the others; and all the parts *are* in certain relations to the whole. You would thus be concerned with a work in terms of its *being*—and being is by definition an "eternal now." (Recall that the Aristotelian word for substance is *ousia,* being. Anything capable of consideration by itself, *kath auto,* would be a substance in this sense: as a man, a tree, a stone.) "Beings" may come and go; but insofar as you treat of something in terms of its *being* (in contrast, for instance, with treatment of it in terms of its genesis), by the sheer technicality of the treatment you are working in terms of the eternal—outside the category of time. (It may possess a kind of "internal time," in the sense that, if it is a work of literature or music, some of its parts may precede others. But such order can be discussed in terms of purely structural relationships. And time in this sense is not the kind of time we have in mind when we consider the work in terms of personality, or class, or epoch, etc.)

In sum, when you consider a thing just as it *is,* with the *being* of one part involved in the *being* of its other parts, and with all the parts derived from the being of the whole considered as a generating principle, there is nothing but a "present tense" involved here, or better, a "tenselessness," even though the thing thus dealt with arises in time and passes with time.

In Aristotle, such a concept of substance or being (*ousia*) was carried to its full metaphysical limits. For he abided by the logic of his terminology to the extent of concluding that the world itself was not created, but was eternal. Every vocabulary has its limits, imposed by the internal logic of its terms; and Aristotle, as a superior thinker, carried his own vocabulary to its limits. And though individual beings came and went, he held that their *genera* (their family identities that contain the principles of their being, as the principles of an equilateral triangle reside in the class of such triangles) had existed and would exist forever.

But, though in Aristotle every individual stone or tree or man, or any other thing capable of treatment as a separate entity, was a being, I think we should be wrong in saying that he treated beings simply in terms of their *individuality*. Rather, he located an individual thing's principle of being in its identity as a member of a *tribe* (his word *genos,* or genus, being originally a word of strong familistic connotations, with the same root as our words "generate" and "generation"). It was the types, or kinds, or classes, or families of natural beings that continued permanently. Hence, the intrinsic principles of a being were not unique, but were variations of principles common to the whole family, or genus, of such beings. The internal principle of motivation, the "entelechy" (or "that which contains its own aim") was the incentive of the thing to attain the kind of perfection proper to the kind of thing it was (a stone's kind of perfection thus being quite different from a tree's, or a man's).

Aquinas in his borrowing from Aristotle retained the Aristotelian stress upon being. But the Christian acceptance of Genesis made it impossible for Aquinas to retain the ultimate implications of this key term. For him, as a Christian, the most important fact about the nature of the world was that we might call a *genetic,* or "historical," or "temporal," fact: its derivation from a divine Creator. Thus the *substance* of things was determined not solely by their nature as beings in themselves; it also involved their place, or grounding, as *creatures* of God in a *creation* of God. And by giving the Aristotelian concept of the genus this "ancestral" emphasis, he engrafted an "extrinsic" principle of substance. Men's abilities and habits were said to be "intrinsic" principles of action —the "extrinsic" motives were God and the Devil.[1]

---

[1] You will note the beginning of an ambiguity here. For an ancestral God is not wholly "extrinsic." A creature who was descended from God and whose substance was grounded in the creative act of God would somehow bear this qualification "within." The logical completion of such thinking, however, would lead to pantheism, as the substance of God would be "within" his creation—and in Aquinas God is expressly classed as an "extrinsic" principle of motivation. From the sociological point of view, we may note that in proportion as the notion of an "extrinsic" God attained its institutional counterpart in the formal-istic externalization of religion, the Protestant pietistic stress upon God as a principle "from within" came by reaction to the fore. And at the time when this change was taking place, the meanings of two very strategic terms in philosophy

Spinoza, taking the Aristotelian notion that a being, or substance, is to be considered "in itself" (*id quod per se concipitur*), went on to observe that nothing less than the totality of all that exists can meet this requirement. For any single object in the universe must be "defined" (limited, determined, negated) by the things that surround it. Only when considering the universe as a whole, and in considering the principles of the relations of the universe's parts to this universal whole, would we really be dealing with an "intrinsic" motivation. And when dealing with such individual things as a tree, a man, a stone (which are merely *parts* of the universe), we should have to consider their nature as grounded in a wider context, rather than simply as individuals embodying principles of their own. As Locke was to point out later, though we use the word "substance" to designate properties within a thing, etymologically the word means that which supports or grounds a thing (in brief, not something *inside* it but something *outside* it). And when the most "intrinsic" statement we can make about a thing is a statement not about it in itself but about its place as part of the whole world, have we not just about reversed the meanings of the words "intrinsic" and "extrinsic"?

Paradoxically, the Spinozistic advice to see things *sub specie aeternitatis* was really a splendid introduction into philosophies that would see things in the terms of history. Spinoza, to be sure, considered the universe in terms of *being;* he proposed to treat of the parts in terms of this eternal whole; and when considering *historical* sequence, he proposed to consider it in terms of *logical* sequence (here using one of the profoundest puns in all thought, as one event in history is said to "follow" another the way the conclusion of a syllogism "follows" from the premises). But to treat individuals in terms of a much more inclusive whole is certainly not to consider them "eternally" in the Aristotelian sense, which required that they be treated "in themselves." As soon as you begin treating things in terms of a surrounding context (and a naturalistic context at that) you have laid the way for their treatment temporally, in terms of history. At every important point in Spinoza's doctrines, he had a compensation for such a movement. His history was equated with a timeless logic; his nature was equated with God.

changed places. The terms "subjective" and "objective" (bearing upon the "inner" and the "outer") reversed their meanings; medieval philosophers had called the "objective" what modern philosophers call "subjective" and vice versa.

But when you equate two terms, either can replace the other, which is to say that the equating of two terms prepares the way for eliminating one of them. Hence, Spinoza's equating of naturalistic history and pantheistic being could be developed into a doctrine of naturalistic history pure and simple by merely dropping the theological side of the equation. (Spinoza himself made seminal contributions to the study of religion from the *historicist* point of view.)

In proportion as theological geneticism developed into a purely secular historicism, the notion of a thing's intrinsic substance dissolved into the out-and-out extrinsic, until now many philosophers of science would formally abolish the category of substance. Aquinas had balanced intrinsic and extrinsic motivations by saying that, though God moved all beings, he moved each according to its nature. But modern science is *par excellence* the approach "from without" (the "scenic," "environmentalist," or "situational" approach). It is interested not in what men "are," for instance, "in themselves," but in what respects men are to be treated as animals, in what respects they are to be treated as vegetables, in what respects as minerals, as electro-physical impulses capable of conditioning by material manipulations, as creatures of food, or climate, or geography, etc. Thus, typically, the papers recently reported of a "gerontologist" who was making investigations designed to increase longevity by increasing the "intrinsic resistance" of the body to the processes that make for old age; and he proposed to do this by dosage of the body with various sorts of chemicals. We are not in a position to know what are his chances of success. But we may raise doubts about his terms. Could such extrinsic agencies as chemical dosage properly be expected to *increase* the body's intrinsic resistance? Insofar as it was effective, wouldn't it rather gain its effects by *decreasing* intrinsic resistance (somewhat as we keep warm "scientifically" not by methods that increase our intrinsic resistance to cold, but by improved modes of heating that decrease our resistance to cold).

Indeed, the question as to what a thing is "in itself" is not a scientific question at all (in the purely empiricist sense of the term science), but a philosophical or metaphysical one. Recently, for instance, there appeared a very intelligent book by a contemporary psychiatrist, Dr. Andras Angyal, entitled *Foundations for a Science of Personality*. But opening it, one finds the entire first half of this project for a "science" of personality constructed about the relationships between "organism" and "environment," two terms that in their very nature *dissolve* the concept of personality by *reducing* it to non-personal terms.   Strictly speaking, the expression "science of personality" is a contradiction in terms, a "perspective by incongruity."   For "personality" (derived from a word referring to a man's role) is a "dramatist" concept, and as such involves philosophical or metaphysical notions of human identity.   But a "science" of personality would be evolved by translating matters of personality into terms wholly outside the personal (as the biologistic terms "organism" and "environment" are outside the personal).   I do not say that there cannot be a "science" of the personality, for Dr. Angyal's valuable book goes a long way towards showing that there can be.   (Or at least it shows that there can be a "scientific terminology" of the personality.)   I am trying simply to suggest that such a science will be totally "extrinsic" in its approach, not aiming to consider the philosophic problem of what the personality is "in itself," but perfectly at home in a vocabulary that simply dissolves the person into a non-person.

II

One will quickly realize why we wanted to approach the three essays[2] thus circuitously as we turn now to Mr. Crane's "Prefatory Note," built about his opposition to the method he calls "Coleridgean."   In the Coleridgean method, Mr. Crane says, one begins by expounding some general philosophic or metaphysical or psychological frame.   Next one treats poetry in general as a representative aspect of this frame.   And finally one treats specific poems as individual instances of vessels of poetry.   The Coleridgean critic thus employs what we might call a process of narrowing-down.   For he begins with the terms that apply to much broader fields of reference than to poetry alone; these are paired with contrary terms (such as "subjective and objective," or "extension and intension"); then other terms, more specific in reference, are added (I think Mr. Ransom's "structure and texture" pair would be an example); and this process is repeated "until, by a series of descending

[2] This article was written as comment on three essays (by the "Neo-Aristotelians," R. S. Crane, Norman Maclean, and Elder Olson) originally published in *The University Review*.   Mr. Maclean's was constructed about the analysis of a sonnet by Wordsworth, Mr. Olson's about the analysis of one of the Yeats "Byzantium" poems; and Mr. Crane contributed a general statement on the theory and method exemplified by the two analyses.

proportions, a transition is effected between the universality of the 'principles' and the particularity of the texts."

The poem would thus not be explained in itself, but "as a kind of emblem or exemplar of principles broader in their relevance than poems or any given kind of poems." The conclusions of such inquiry could be related to the texts "only as universal forms or platonic ideas are related to the particulars in the world which are their more or less adequate reflection." There might even be no need to consider the poem as a whole, since representative passages or lines can be also treated as vessels of the abstract qualities which the critic would discover in the particular work. Hence, "Coleridgean" critics are given to talk about "poetry" rather than about "poems"—and they may like to cite passages that can serve as "touchstones" of the qualities they would select as "poetic."

Messrs. Maclean and Olson, on the other hand, "represent a radical departure" from this tradition:

> They are interested in lyrics not as exemplars but as objects; they insist on approaching them as poems of a distinctive kind rather than as receptacles of poetry. . . . The appreciation they wish to make possible is one of which the object is not a universal form or value reflected in the poem but the poem itself in its wholeness and particularly as a structure of mutually appropriate parts.

To attain this "theoretical grasp of the parts of lyrics and of the principles of their unification," Mr. Crane says, we must confine ourselves to "an inductive study of lyrics pursued apart from any a priori assumptions about the nature of poetry in general." And after many more such essays, on many more poems, we may begin to see "what an inductive poetics of the lyric is likely to be." It is a necessary part of Mr. Crane's position, taken in dialectical opposition to the "Coleridgean," that he adopt this excessive stress upon the *inductive*.

If you consider philosophic or critical terminologies as languages, however (languages from which we derive kinds of observation in accordance with the nature of the terms featured in the given philosophic idiom), you find reason to question his claims in advance. For the critic does not by any means begin his observations "from scratch," but has a more or less systematically organized set of terms by which to distinguish and characterize the elements of the poem he would observe.

In this sense, one's observations will not be purely "inductive," even though they derive important modifications from the observing of the given poem. They will also in part (and in particular as to their grammar, or form) be deduced or derived from the nature of the language or terminology which the critic employs. Such languages are developed prior to the individual observation (though one may adopt the well known philosophic subterfuge: "Let us begin simply by considering this object in front of us, just as it is").

If there were only some few "true" things to be said about a poem's structure, and if men of various sorts readily made these same observations independently of one another, one might be justified in considering these observations a matter of "induction." But since so many valid things are to be said, a given vocabulary coaches us to look for certain kinds of things rather than others—and this coaching of observations is a deductive process, insofar as one approaches the poem with a well-formed analytic terminology prior to the given analysis, and derives observations from the nature of this terminology. Hypothetically, one might be perceptive or imaginative enough to transcend any vocabulary, as one might hypothetically add enough "epicycles" and other qualifications to the Ptolemaic system of astronomy to make it do the work now done by the modern system of astro-physics. But under conditions of ordinary experience, such a transcending of vocabulary is decidedly limited. Ordinarily, we see somewhat beyond the limits of our favorite terms—but the bulk of our critical perceptions are but particular applications of these terms. The terms are like "principles," and the particular observations are like the judicial casuistry involved in the application of principles to cases that are always in some respects unique.

Some terminologies contain much richer modes of observation than others. And the "dramatist" nature of the Aristotelian vocabulary could be expected to provide the observer with very rich modes indeed. But one cannot be purely "inductive" in his observation of poems when making these observations through the instrumentality of so highly developed a philosophic language. One owes too much to the language. However, if Mr. Crane admitted that his "inductive" method also contained strongly "deductive" elements, he would have to relinquish the symmetry of his own dramatizing, got by pitting his position in dialectical opposition to the "Coleridgean" mode of derivation.

When considered in a linguistic, or terministic, perspective (the perspective in which we would consider "dramatism"), the apparent distinctness between "inductive" and "deductive" modes of observation and derivation here ceases to exist. Indeed, insofar as the writers do abide by their pretensions, and begin with each analysis anew, their interpretation of the principles by which a given poem is organized is mere "prophecy after the event," which is not a very exacting kind of "induction." Induction must also use generalizations which, in effect, prophesy *before* the event. It should not be merely a casuistry ready to rationalize any case after the case has occurred (a temptation to which Aristotelianism has been prone in the past). It must also risk statements as to *what to expect,* and *why.* Otherwise, such criticism becomes merely a disguised variant of impressionism, a kind of improvisation wherein the critic simply translates the unique imaginative sequence of the poem into a correspondingly unique conceptual equivalent.

III

As for the two long analytic essays by Messrs. Maclean and Olson, I should have to quote or paraphrase nearly every paragraph to convey how ably and discerningly they carry out their project. But as one cannot do justice to a poem in paraphrase, but must follow it from line to line, and from word to word, in its unique order, so these exegetes analyze their poems with a particularity that must be read in its particularity to be appreciated. However, in the course of their analysis, they make generalizations about their method and their conclusions—and we can consider these.

Mr. Maclean takes as his opponent specifically a critic who had based his discussion of a Wordsworth sonnet upon a theory about its reference to the poet's illegitimate daughter. Against this somewhat sorry position, Mr. Maclean says of his own:

> As the unity of a poem arises from the facts that it is divisible into parts and that these parts are harmoniously related, so the obligations resting upon this kind of criticism are twofold: to discover the parts of a poem and to render an account of their relationships.

He convincingly divides the sonnet into three parts, and considers their relation to the whole, in producing a "spiritual and religious trans-

lation of the evening." And he does well in making us realize the steps
by which this translation progresses, as in his remarks on "the completeness with which the beauty and serenity of the Nun have been transferred to the immensity of the evening." [3]

At this point I must introduce some reference to the line of thought
developed in my Grammar. In my analysis of the drama, I try to show
how the quality of the scene contains the quality of the act that is
enacted on that scene. (Most obvious example: the Shakespearean use
of storm or darkness as setting for a sinister bit of action. Hardy's use
of background as a source of motivation is an obvious instance of this
scene-act ratio in the novel.) This is a "grammatical" principle of
much wider application than the drama (hence, open to Mr. Crane's
charge of "Coleridgean"). For in the various mythological, theological, metaphysical, and scientific theories of motivation the character
we attribute to human action changes according to the character we
attribute to the universal scene in which human acts take place. (Contrast, for instance the quality of human acts when placed against a background of struggles among the gods, and the quality of human acts in a
behaviorist's background of mechanism and reflexes.) In considering
the lyric, where there is no action but where there may be reference to
persons (agents), we find that this same relationship may apply
between scene and agent. Indeed, it is this scene-agent identification
that makes it possible for the poet to convey states of mind (psychological processes) by the use of corresponding scenic imagery.
"Dramatistically," therefore, one is invited to observe that this particular

---

[3] I quote the sonnet herewith:

It is a beauteous evening, calm and free,
The holy time is quiet as a Nun
Breathless with adoration; the broad sun
Is sinking down in its tranquillity;
The gentleness of heaven broods o'er the Sea:
Listen! the mighty Being is awake,
And doth with his eternal motion make
A sound like thunder—everlastingly.
Dear Child! dear Girl! that walkest with me here,
If thou appear untouched by solemn thought,
Thy nature is not therefore less divine:
Thou liest in Abraham's bosom all the year;
And worshipp'st at the Temple's inner shrine,
God being with thee when we know it not.

sonnet is constructed quite neatly about this scene-agent ratio. The octave establishes the quality of the scene; then at the beginning of the sestet, we turn to the agent ("Dear Child! dear Girl!"); and we find the quality of the agent so imbued with the divine quality of the scene containing this agent, that she can possess this quality even without knowing it, by the simple fact of having it as her ground.

Also, I would hold that a "dramatistic" placement of the lyric is to be arrived at "deductively" in this sense: one approaches the lyric from the category of *action,* which Aristotle considers the primary element of the drama. And then by dialectic coaching one looks for a form that will have as its primary element the moment of *stasis,* or *rest.* We are admonished, however, to note that there are two concepts of "rest," often confused because we may apply the same word to both. There is rest as the sheer cessation of motion (in the sense that a rolling ball comes to rest); and there is rest as the end of action (end as finish or end as aim), the kind of rest that Aristotle conceived as the *primum mobile* of the world, the ground of motion and action both. It is proper for the physical sciences, we would grant, to treat experience nondramatically, in terms of motion, but things in the realm of the social or human require treatment in terms of action or drama. Or rather, though things in the realm of the human *may* be treated in terms of motion, the result will be statements not about the intrinsic, but about the extrinsic (as per our remarks on an "incongruous" science of the personality).

A treatment of the lyric in terms of action would not by any means require us merely to look for analogies from the drama. On the contrary, the *state of arrest* in which we would situate the essence of the lyric is not analogous to dramatic action at all, but is the dialectical counterpart of action. Consider as an illustration the fourteen Stations of the Cross: The concern with them in the totality of their progression would be dramatic. But the pause at any one of them, and the contemplation and deepening appreciation of its poignancy, in itself, would be lyric.

A typical Wordsworthian sonnet brings out this methodological aspect of the lyric (its special aptitude for conveying a *state* of mind, for erecting a moment into a universe) by selecting such themes as in themselves explicitly refer to the arrest, the pause, the hush. However, this lyric state is to be understood in terms of action, inasmuch as it is to be understood as a state that sums up an action in the form of an attitude.

Thus approached, an attitude is ambiguous in this sense: It may be either an incipient act or the substitute for an act. An attitude of sympathy is incipiently an act, for instance, in that it is the proper emotional preparation for a sympathetic act; or it may be the substitute for an act in that the sympathetic person can let the intent do service for the deed (precisely through doing nothing, one may feel more sympathetic than the person whose mood may be partially distracted by the conditions of action). In either case, an attitude is a state of emotion, or a moment of stasis, in which an act is arrested, summed up, made permanent and total, as with the Grecian Urn which in its summational quality Keats calls a "fair Attitude." [4]

We have here a cluster of closely related words: action, rest (designated in the sonnet by such synonyms as "calm," "quiet," "tranquillity," "gentleness"), motion, attitude or potential action. Mr. Maclean says something much to our purposes here, in his gloss on the word "free" in the first line: "It is a strange word when coupled with 'beauteous' and 'calm.' As endowing the evening with the power to act, it seems at variance with the beauty of tranquillity." The comment enables us to discern that in "free" we find obliquely a reference to potential action. However, our thoughts on the relation between action and the rest that is the end of action would lead us to hold that there is nothing "strange" about this usage. Who would be more "tranquil" than the wholly "free"? For his complete freedom would so thoroughly contain the potentialities of action that there would be no problem to disturb the state of rest.

Nearly every particular observation that Mr. Maclean makes about the sonnet, I could salute and zestfully, if he but gave it the pointedness that would derive from an explicit recognition of the "dramatistic" element in his vocabulary. Thus I would hold that an explicit concern with the scene-agent ratio provides a central statement about the grammatical principles involved in the structure of the poem. Or Mr. Maclean cites a passage from "Lines Composed Above Tintern Abbey":

> . . . that serene and blessed mood
> In which the affections gently lead us on,—

---

[4] Wordsworth's formula, "emotion recollected in tranquillity," could be translated into our terms as "a state of emotion conveyed as a moment of stasis."

Until, the breath of this corporeal frame
And even the motion of our human blood
Almost suspended, we are laid asleep
In body, and become a living soul:
While with an eye made quiet by the power
Of harmony, and the deep power of joy,
We see into the life of things.

And here by the use of an explicitly dramatist perspective we would distinguish between a level of bodily motion ("the motion of our human blood") and a level of mental or spiritual action ("a living soul"). The "power of harmony" here would be another synonym for the rest of "potential action." And the state of arrest is said to be attained when the level of mental action transcends the level of bodily motion. (The "Ode on a Grecian Urn" is constructed about a similar transcendence. Progressively through the stanzas we can watch the poet's fever split into two parts: a bodily passion and a mental action. But in the "Ode" it is a state of agitation that is arrested, to be transformed into its transcendent counterpart.)

IV

It is to be regretted that none of these three writers, in stressing the importance of an analysis which considers the relations of parts to whole, makes any mention of the fact that in Aristotle's treatment of tragedy, there are *two* versions of this relationship. In Chapter 6, Aristotle writes:

> There are six parts consequently of every tragedy, as a whole (that is) of such or such quality, *viz.* a Fable or Plot, Characters, Diction, Thought, Spectacle, and Melody.

But in Chapter 12, he writes:

> The parts of Tragedy to be treated as formative elements in the whole were mentioned in a previous Chapter. From the point of view, however, of its quantity, i. e., the separate sections into which it is divided, a tragedy has the following parts: Prologue, Episode, Exode, and a choral portion, distinguished into Parode and Stasimon.

In any event, it is notable that both these treatments of part-whole relationships apply not only to single tragedies but to tragedies as a *class*. Yet Mr. Maclean says, in conclusion to his article: "To explain the poem . . . in terms of its particular beginning is to explain as exactly as possible its uniqueness, and to distinguish it from other poems by Wordsworth that treat much the same 'theme.'" And likewise Mr. Olson will end his article on a similar remark to the effect that "great art . . . is always in the last analysis *sui generis*." There is, of course, a sense in which every work is unique, since its particular combination of details is never repeated. But is the emphasis upon this fact feasible if one would develop an "Aristotelian" poetics of the lyric, treating lyrics as a class? And a mere concern with one lyric, then another lyric, then another would not yield the kind of observations needed to treat of lyrics as a class. For to treat lyrics as a class, one must examine individual lyrics from the standpoint of their generic attributes. And to do this, one must have terminological prepossessions, prior to the analysis, even before one can select a poem that he considers representative of the lyric. At least, one must have negative or tentative touchstones that enable him roughly to differentiate lyrics as a class from such classes as epic, drama, epigram, etc.

One does not place a form in isolation. The placement of a given form involves the corresponding placement of other forms. Thus *a vocabulary wider in reference than the orbit of the given form is needed for the classifying of that form*. Though the authors would presumably get immunity from such objections by presenting their analyses as mere *preparations* for a poetics of the lyric, we would object that observations confined in their reference to the unique are not classificatory at all.[5]

---

[5] Mr. Crane reminds us of Coleridge's distinction between "poetry" and "poem," in the *Biographia Literaria*. But perhaps he and his colleagues have been victimized by the "Coleridgean" here: perhaps the distinction between "poetry" and "poem" is not enough. "Poetry" itself may have two different meanings. We may use it as one member of such dialectical pairs as "poetry and science," "poetry and mathematics," "poetry and anarchism," "poetry and politics," "poetry and morals," etc. Or we may use it as a term for poems in a *generic* sense (as Aristotle in his *Poetics* treats of part-whole relationships not by treating of tragedies one by one, in their uniqueness, but generically). So we may need three terms rather than two here: a term for "poetry" (as member of a dialectical pair), and a term for "poem" (this poem, that poem, the next poem),

The point is made still clearer by considering another citation from Mr. Olson:

> The scrutiny of particular poems would thus be the beginning of the critical enterprise; but the principles eventually reached, as disclosed by analysis, would not be rules governing the operations involved in the construction of any further poem, nor would the enumeration of poetic parts and poetic devices suffer extension beyond those objects to which analysis had been turned. . . . Poetic questions would be concerning the poetic structure of a particular work . . . [and] would terminate in a discovery of the parts of a work and of the interrelations through which the parts are parts of a whole.

Now, if the principles of a specific work were so defined that the definition would not apply to "any further poem," would not this also mean that the definition would not apply to any *other* poem? In brief, would not this conception of the relation between parts and whole be so particularized as to make statements about the lyric as a *genus* impossible? And could a critic, aiming at analyses that meet these particularized requirements, go beyond the merely statistical to the generic unless at the same time he happened to be taking some other kind of step not expressly signalized? Surely it is ironic to find Aristotle, who was so long admired and resented as the Prince of Deducers, now serving as Prince of Inducers.

As a matter of fact, there are many passages in Mr. Olson's essay where he profits by going beyond his principle of uniqueness. For he launches into generalizations about the lyric generically that are not at all confined to the particular poem he is analyzing (Yeats's "Sailing to Byzantium," of which by the way he makes what I think is a really superb analysis). These place the lyric as a class with relation to other classes. When he says, for instance, that tragedy, epic, and comedy are "dynamic, for they imitate change," whereas "the kind we have been scrutinizing is static," his concern here with stasis profits by dramatistic reference.

His discussion of the poem itself is thoroughly dramatistic in its choice of vocabulary, being built about distinctions between "action"

and a term for "poems" (as a class, with corresponding terms for classes and subclasses).

and "passion," explicitly recognizing the theme as a problem of "regeneration," and treating the whole series of transformations from stanza to stanza as a "dialectic" wherein character is determined "not by its share in an action, but by its role in a drama, not of action, but of thought." Yet, surprisingly, this highly developed vocabulary is employed quite as though it had been forced upon the critic purely by inspection of the given poem—and we are warned against an attempt to find in the lyric "some analogue of plot in the drama and epic." However, imagery, like attitude, has the quality of "incipient action"—and in noting how, in a given poem, it undergoes a series of developments from ambiguous potentiality to clear fulfilment, we should be considering it "dramatistically" without thereby treating it merely as the analogue of dramatic plot.

And let us cite two other statements that are thoroughly *generic,* and as such are derived not from mere observation of the single poem but from the nature of the "dramatist" vocabulary:

> There can be no plot because there can be no incidents; the "events" in a lyric poem are never incidents as such, connected by necessity or probability, but devices for making poetic statements. . . .
> Since there is no action, there is no agent, that is, *character,* in the sense in which there are differentiated agents in the drama; rather, the character in the sense in which character may be said to exist here is almost completely universalized. . . . [6]

[6] "Universalized" is a good word here. The poetic "I" that is the ground of a lyric fills the whole universe of discourse.

Mr. Olson's distinction between the dramatic "act" and the lyric "event" opens up interesting possibilities. In the *Philosophy of Literary Form* I had used a similar distinction, but with a quite different application. But by combining Mr. Olson's application with my own, I believe I come a bit closer to glimpsing why the lyric is a better fit with the scientific than the dramatic is. The steps are as follows (first quoting from my summary of the dramatistic perspective, *op. cit.*):

> We have the drama and the scene of the drama. The drama is enacted against a background. . . . The description of the scene is the role of the physical sciences; the description of the drama is the role of the social sciences. . . . The physical sciences are a calculus of events; the social sciences are a calculus of acts. And human affairs being dramatic, the discussion of human affairs becomes dramatic criticism, with more to be learned from study of tropes than from a study of tropisms. . . . The error of the social sciences has usually resided in the attempt to appropriate the scenic calculus for a charting of the act.

V

What, then, is the upshot of our fluctuancy between agreement and disagreement? It is not merely that we would have these authors ply

Now science, as we have observed in the present paper, is "scenic." And since it speaks in terms of motion rather than in terms of action, the typical scientific vocabulary is non-dramatic.

Recall next Yvor Winters' notion of "Pseudo-Reference," one kind of which is "reference to a non-existent plot." As an instance of "pseudo-reference," he cites from "Gerontion":

> To be eaten, to be divided, to be drunk
> Among whispers; by Mr. Silvero
> With caressing hands, at Limoges
> Who walked all night in the next room;
> By Hakagawa, bowing among the Titians;
> By Madame de Tornquist, in the dark room
> Shifting the candles; Fräulein von Kulp
> Who turned in the hall, one hand on the door.

On this Mr. Winters comments:

> Each of these persons is denoted in the performance of an act, and each act, save possibly that of Hakagawa, implies an anterior situation, is a link in a chain of action; even that of Hakagawa implies an anterior and unexplained personality. Yet we have no hint of the nature of the history implied. A feeling is claimed by the poet, the motivation, or meaning, of which is withheld, and of which in all likelihood he has no clearer notion than his readers can have.

In this form which Mr. Winters is considering, do we not see a "watershed moment," the very point at which dramatic "actions" are undergoing a transformation into lyric "events"? Indeed, this would be the way of translating the concept of pseudo-reference into our present terms.

By reason of correspondences between the "objective" and the "subjective" (or what we have called the scene-agent ratio) these "events" (which are more like "scenes" than "acts") convey attitudes, or states of mind, through the use of "objective imagery." The "events" here are "moody," quite as though they were such attitude-purveying imagery as storms, sunsets, or bird sounds. In their nature as imagery, as "scenic," they invite us to *feel* as the situation *is*.

From the standpoint of science, the content of a scene is "knowledge." And knowledge is a *state*. Hence, scientific events and lyric events are both received in the psychological form of *states*. A whole set of such relations would be: science is to the lyric as the impersonal is to the personal, as materialism is to idealism, as scene is to agent, as knowledge is to knower, as the epistemological is to the psychological. (In the "dramatistic" perspective, the primary category is not the epistemological-psychological one of *knowing*, but that of acting.)

their trade under the trade-name of "dramatism" rather than "Aristotle." Mr. Crane gives us a choice between the poem as "exemplar" and the poem as "object"—and as though these alternatives had exhausted the field, he discusses no other. But if we begin by explicitly recognizing the dramatistic nature of the vocabulary, then looking at our pentad (the terms Act, Scene, Agent, Agency, Purpose), we may ask ourselves: "What about the poem considered as an *act?*" Thus, when Mr. Crane says that the poem is to be considered "as a product of purposive activity on the part of its author," we would agree with him, only more intensely than he would want us to.

The treatment of the poem as act would not, by any means, require us to slight the nature of the poem as object. For a poem is a *constitutive* act—and after the act of its composition by a poet who had acted in a particular temporal scene, it survives as an objective structure, capable of being examined in itself, in temporal scenes quite different from the scene of its composition, and by agents quite different from the agent who originally enacted it. The enactment thus remaining as a constitution, we can inquire into the principles by which this constitution is organized.

The poem, as an object, is to be considered in terms of its nature as "finished." That is, it is to be considered in terms of "perfection," as per the stressing of part-whole relationships. These men have done criticism a great service in helping to reaffirm this aspect of criticism, particularly at a time when the state of the sciences has offered so many extrinsic approaches to poetry, which can be considered as the "exemplar" of political exigencies, neurosis, physique, diet, climate, cultural movements, economic classifications, etc. But consideration of it as an act surviving as a constitution would also enable one to consider its intrinsic relations.

The dramatistic perspective, if I may refer to my *Philosophy of Literary Form,* points equally towards a concern with "internal structure" and towards a concern with "act-scene relationships." "Words are aspects of a much wider communicative context, most of which is not verbal at all. Yet words also have a nature peculiarly their own. And when discussing them as modes of action, we must consider *both* this nature as words in themselves *and* the nature they get from the nonverbal scenes that support their acts." But while proposing to consider words "as acts upon a scene," I held that the approach to literature in terms of "linguistic, or symbolic, or literary action" could avoid the excesses of the purely environmental schools "which are usually so eager to trace the relationships between act and scene that they neglect to trace the structure of the act itself."

The explicit treatment of the poem as an act, however, would remind us that it is not enough to consider it solely in terms of its "perfection," or "finishedness," since this conventionalized restriction of our inquiry could not possibly tell us all the important things about its substance. This seems to be particularly the case with the study of lyrics—for often, to grasp the full import of the terms employed in one poem, we must see how these terms are qualified by their use in other poems. That is, the individual lyrics are not to be considered solely as isolated acts, but also as stages or stations of a more comprehensive act. And statements about this more comprehensive act are also statements about the *intrinsic* nature of the enactment in the single poem. I began by speaking of the three fields: Grammar, Rhetoric, and Symbolic. It is perhaps only in the third of these categories that modern criticism has something vitally new to offer the student of literature. And it would be a pity indeed if a dogmatic or formalistic preference for an earlier method interfered with the progress of such inquiry, which promises greatly to increase our knowledge of poetic substance in particular and of human motivation in general. (Nor would it be the first time that the great name of Aristotle had served to stifle fresh inquiry.)

The concern with Symbolic has already been developed to a point where we can see that, as regards the analysis of literary texts at least, it can be more empirical in its methods than is possible to most studies in the human realm. Yet in trying to abide by the neo-Aristotelian ideals for the compartmentalizing of inquiry, one would simply be taking on many encumbrances that interfered with the development of methods proper to the nature of the subject-matter.[7]

[7] To complete the placement of these critics, perhaps we should also have considered the part that the Scotist stress upon the "thisness" (*haeccëitas*) of a thing might have had in shaping their aims. They seem to be encountering in their way what Duns Scotus encountered in his, when he contended that the step from genus to species should be completed by a step from species to individual. And their concern to define the lyric as a *kind* while placing stress upon the unique generating principles of *particular* lyrics seems similarly on the road to nominalism. Or should we say rather that, having encountered the nominalist stress by way of modern empirical science, they would translate it back into scholastic terms?

And always on the look-out for secular analogues to theological doctrine, perhaps we should note that the stress upon the individual poem as *sui generis,* coupled with a search for the principle of the lyric as a *kind,* has somewhat the pattern of Aquinas' doctrine of angels, each of which in his view is both a genus
and an individual at the same time.   The search for the intrinsic, demanding in
its logical completion a complete divorce of relations with contextual impurities,
would seem to require in the end such a view of "pure" or "separate" forms subsisting without admixture of "matter."   That is, the subsistence of the poem
must be discussed without reference to any individuating principle drawn from
some extrinsic source, which would function as "matter" in being *scenic* to the
poem as act.

C

MOTIVES AND MOTIFS IN THE POETRY
OF MARIANNE MOORE

IN THIS essay we would characterize the substance of Miss Moore's work as a specific poetic strategy. And we would watch it for insights which the contemplation of it may give us into the ways of poetic and linguistic action generally. For this purpose we shall use both her recently published book, *What Are Years,* and her *Selected Poems,* published in 1935 with an introduction by T. S. Eliot (and including some work reprinted from an earlier volume, *Observations*).

On page 8 of the new book, Miss Moore writes:

> The power of the visible
> is the invisible;

and in keeping with the pattern, when recalling her former title, *Observations,* we might even have been justified in reading it as a deceptively technical synonym for "visions." One observes the visibles—but of the corresponding invisibles, one must be visionary. And while dealing much in things that can be empirically here, the poet reminds us that they may

> dramatize a
> meaning always missed
> by the externalist.

It is, then, a relation between external and internal, or visible and invisible, or background and personality, that her poems characteristically establish. Though her names for things are representative of attitudes, we could not say that the method is Symbolist. The objects exist too fully in their own right for us to treat them merely as objective words for subjects. T. S. Eliot says that her poetry "might be classified as 'descriptive' rather than 'lyrical' or 'dramatic.'" He cites an early poem that "suggests a slight influence of H. D., certainly of H. D.

rather than of any other 'Imagist.'" And though asserting that "Miss Moore has no immediate poetic derivations," he seems to locate her work in the general vicinity of imagism, as when he writes:

> The aim of 'imagism,' so far as I understand it, or so far as it had any, was to introduce a peculiar concentration upon something visual, and to set in motion an expanding succession of concentric feelings. Some of Miss Moore's poems—for instance with animal or bird subjects—have a very good spread of association.

I think of William Carlos Williams. For though Williams differs much from Miss Moore in temperament and method, there is an important quality common to their modes of perception. It is what Williams has chosen to call by the trade name of "objectivist."

Symbolism, imagism, and objectivism would obviously merge into one another, since they are recipes all having the same ingredients but in different proportions. In symbolism, the subject is much stronger than the object as an organizing motive. That is, it is *what the images are symbolic of* that shapes their treatment. In imagism, there would ideally be an equality of the two motives, the subjective and objective. But in objectivism, though an object may be chosen for treatment because of its symbolic or subjective reference, once it has been chosen it is to be studied in its own right.

A man might become an electrician, for instance, because of some deep response to electricity as a symbol of power. Yet, once he had become an electrician and thus had converted his response to this subject into an objective knowledge of its laws and properties, he would thereafter treat electricity as he did, not because each of his acts as an electrician would be symbolic like his original choice of occupation, but because such acts were required by the peculiar nature of electricity. Similarly, a poet writing in an "objectivist" idiom might select his subject because of some secret reference or personal significance it has had for him; yet having selected it, he would find that its corresponding object had qualities to be featured and appraised for themselves. And he might pay so much attention to such appraisal that the treatment of the object would in effect "transcend" the motive behind its original singling-out.

Thus, the poem "Four Quartz Crystal Clocks" (in *What Are Years*) begins:

> There are four vibrators, the world's exactest clocks;
>   and these quartz time-pieces that tell
> time intervals to other clocks,
>   these workless clocks work well;
> and all four, independently the
>   same, are there in the cool Bell
>   Laboratory time
>
> vault. Checked by a comparator with Arlington
>   they punctualize . . .   (Etc.)

I think there would be no use in looking for "symbolist" or "imagist" motives behind the reference to the fact that precisely *four* clocks are mentioned here. It is an "objectivist" observation. We read of four, not because the number corresponds, for instance, to the Horsemen of the Apocalypse, but simply because there actually are four of them in the time vault. Similarly, "cool Bell Laboratory time vault" might have outlying suggestions of something like the coolness of a tomb— but primarily one feels that the description is there for purposes of objective statement; and had the nature of the scene itself dictated it, we should be reading of a "hot Bell Laboratory time tower." Though not journalism, it is reporting.

Yet any reader of Miss Moore's verse will quickly acknowledge that this theme, which provides an "objective" opportunity for the insertion of transitions between such words as "exactest," "punctualize," "careful timing," "clear ice," "instruments of truth," and "accuracy," is quite representative of her (and thus "symbolic" in the proportions of imagism). And the secondary level of the theme (its quality as being not the theme of clocks that tell the time, but of clocks that tell the time to clocks that tell the time)—I should consider thoroughly symbolic, as signalizing a concern not merely for the withinness of motives, but for the withinness-of-withinness of motives, the motives behind motives.[1]

---

[1] In passing we might consider a whole series of literary ways from this point of view. Allegory would deal with correspondences on a purely dogmatic, or conceptual basis. In the article on "Vestments," for instance, in the *Encyclopædia Britannica*, we read of various "symbolical interpretations": "(1) the *moralizing school*, the oldest, by which—as in the case of St. Jerome's treatment of the Jewish vestments—the vestments are explained as typical of the virtues proper to those who wear them; (2) the *Christological school, i. e.* that which considered the minister as the representative of Christ and his garments as typical of some aspects of Christ's person or office—*e. g.* the stole is his obedience and servitude for our sakes; (3) the *allegorical school*, which treats the priest as a warrior or champion, who

We can call Miss Moore "objectivist," then, only by taking away the epithet in part. For though many details in her work seem to get there purely out of her attempt to report and judge of a thing's intrinsic qualities, to make us feel its properties as accurately as possible, the fact remains that, after you have read several of her poems, you begin to discern a strict principle of selection motivating her appraisals.

In *Selected Poems,* for instance, consider the poem, "People's Surroundings," that gives us a catalogue of correspondence between various kinds of agents and the scenes related to their roles. The poet is concerned to feature, in a background, the details that are an objective portrait of the person to whose kind of action this background belongs. "A setting must not have the air of being one"—a proscription one can ob-

---

puts on the amice as a helmet, the alb as a breastplate, and so on." A work constructed about the systematic use of any such theories of correspondence would, to our way of thinking, be allegorical. The symbolic would use an objective vocabulary for its suggestion of the subjective, with the subjective motive being organizationally more important than the objective one. The specific literary movement called Symbolism would exemplify this stress to a large extent, but would also gravitate towards Surrealism, which stresses the incongruous and contradictory nature of motives by the use of gargoyles as motifs. Imagism would be "personalistic," in the idealistic sense, in using scenic material as the reflection, or extension of human characters. The "objectivist," though rooted in symbolic and imagist concerns, would move into a plane where the object, originally selected by reason of its subjective reference, is studied in its own right. (The result will be "descriptive" poetry. And it will be "scientific" in the sense that, whereas poetry is a kind of act, the descriptiveness of science is rather the *preparation* for an act, the delayed action of a Hamletic reconnaissance in search of the accurate knowledge necessary for the act. And descriptive poetry falls across the two categories in that it acts by describing the scene preparatory to an act.) Naturalism has a greater stress upon the scenic from the polemic or depreciatory point of view (its quasi-scientific quality as delayed action, or preparation for action, often being revealed in that such literature generally either calls for action in the non-esthetic field or makes one very conscious of the fact that a "solution" is needed but is not being offered). True realism is difficult for us to conceive of, after so long a stretch of monetary idealism (accentuated as surrealism) and its counterpart, technological materialism (accentuated as behaviorism and operationalism), while pragmatic philosophies stress *making* and *doing* and *getting* in a localized way that obscures the realistic stress upon the *act*. The German term, *Realpolitik,* for instance, exemplifies a crude brand of pragmatism that completely misrepresents the realistic motive. The communicative nature of art gives all art a realistic ingredient, but the esthetic philosophies which the modern artist consciously or unconsciously absorbs continually serve to obscure this ingredient rather than to cultivate it.

serve if he makes the setting the extension of those in it.   Here are relationships among act, scene, and agent (I use the three terms central
to the philosophy of drama embodied in Henry James's prefaces).
And among these people who move "in their respective places," we
read of

> . . . the acacia-like lady shivering at the touch of a hand,
> lost in a small collision of orchids—
> dyed quicksilver let fall
> to disappear like an obedient chameleon in fifty shades of mauve
>   and amethyst.

Here, with person and ground merged as indistinguishably as in a
pontillist painting by Seurat, the items objectify a tentative mood we
encounter throughout Miss Moore's verses.   The lines are like a miniature impression of her work in its entirety.   And when, contemplating
a game of bowls, she writes, "I learn that we are precisians, not citizens
of Pompeii arrested in action / as a cross-section of one's correspondence would seem to imply," she here "learns" what she is forever learning, in her contemplation of animals and natural and fabricated things,
as she seeks to isolate, for her appreciation and our own, the "great
amount of poetry in unconscious fastidiousness."

I think appreciation is as strong a motive in her work as it was in the
work of Henry James.   "The thing is to lodge somewhere at the heart
of one's complexity an irrespressible *appreciation,*" he says in his preface.
to *The Spoils of Poynton.*   And: "To criticise is to appreciate, to appropriate, to take intellectual possession, to establish in fine a relation with
the criticised thing and make it one's own."   It is a kind of private
property available to everyone—and is perhaps the closest secular equivalent to the religious motive of glorification.   It is a form of gratitude.
And following out its possibilities, where one might otherwise be
querulous he can instead choose to be precise.   This redemption or
transformation of complaint is, I think, essential to the quality of perception in Miss Moore's verse.   (Rather, it is an anticipation of complaint: getting there first, it takes up all the room.)

In "Spenser's Ireland" (*What Are Years*), we may glimpse somewhat how this redemption can take place.   Beginning in a mood of appreciation almost studious, the poem ends

> The Irish say your trouble is their
> trouble and your
>   joy their joy?   I wish
> I could believe it;
> I am troubled, I'm dissat-
>   isfied, I'm Irish.

Since it is towards this end that the poem is directed, we may assume
that from this end it derives the logic of its progression.

Note the general tenor of the other observations: on family, on marriage, on independence and yielding, on the freedom of those "made
captive by supreme belief."   There is talk of enchantments, of transformations, of a coat "like Venus' mantle lined with stars . . . the
sleeves new from disuse," of such discriminations as we get

> when large dainty
> fingers tremblingly divide the wings
> of the fly.

And there are lines naming birds, and having a verbal music most
lovely in its flutter of internal rhymes:

> the guillemot
>   so neat and the hen
> of the heath and the
> linnet spinet-sweet.

All these details could be thought of as contextual to the poem's ending (for, if you single out one moment of a poem, all the other moments
automatically become its context).   If, then, we think of the final assertion as the act, we may think of the preceding contextual material as the
scene, or background, of this act (a background that somehow contains
the same quality as the act, saying implicitly what the act of the final
assertion says explicitly).   Viewed thus we see, as the underlying structure of this "description," a poem that, if treated as a lyric, would have
somewhat the following argument: "Surrounded with details appropriate to my present mood, with a background of such items as go with
matters to do with family, union, independence, I, an Irish girl (while
the birds are about—and sweetly) am dissatisfied."

I won't insist that I'm not wrong.   But in any case, that's the way
I read it.   And I would discern, behind her "objectivist" study and

editorializing, what are essentially the lineaments of a lyric. But where the lyrist might set about to write, "In the moonlight, by the river, on a night like this in Spain," I can think of Miss Moore's distributing these items (discreetly and discretely) among conversational observations about the quality of light in general and moonlight in particular, about rivers mighty and tiny, in mountains, across plains, and emptying into the desert or the sea, about the various qualifications that apply to the transformation from twilight to darkness, in suburbs, or over bays, etc.; and from travel books of Spain we might get some bits that, pieced together, gave us all those elements into which, in her opinion, the given night in Spain should be "broken down."

We might try from another angle by suggesting that Miss Moore makes "because" look like "and." That is, the orthodox lyrist might say, in effect, "I am sad *because* the birds are singing thus." A translation into Miss Moore's objectivist idiom would say in effect: "There are such and such birds—*and* birds sing thus and so—*and* I am sad." The scenic material would presumably be chosen because of its quality as objective replica of the subjective (as observed moments in the scene that correspond to observing moments in the agent). But even where they had been selected because of their bearing upon the plaint, her subsequent attention to them, with appreciation as a motive, would transform the result from a purely psychologistic rhetoric (the traditional romantic device of simply using scenic terms as a vocabulary for the sympathetic naming of personal moods). And the result would be, instead, an appraisal or judgment of many things in and for themselves. They would be encouraged to disclose their traits, not simply that they might exist through the vicarage of words, but that they might reveal their properties as workmanship (workmanship being a trait in which the ethical and the esthetic are one).

What are years? That is, if we were to assemble a thesaurus of all the important qualifications of the term "years" as Miss Moore uses it, what would these qualifications be? I suppose a title is always an assertion because it is a thing—and every thing is positive. Years, we learn by her opening poem of that title, are at least a quality of observation (vision), involving the obligation of courage, of commands laid upon the self to be strong, to see deep and be glad. And years possess the quality of one

> . . . who
>   accedes to mortality
>   and in his imprisonment, rises
>   upon himself as
>   the sea in a chasm . . .

Who does this, we are told, "sees deep and is glad."   Years are also, by
the nature of the case, steps from something to something.   And to indicate a curve of development from the earlier volume, we might recall
this same theme (of the rising water) as it was treated previously.   I
refer to a poem, "Sojourn in the Whale," which, beginning on the
theme, "Trying to open locked doors with a sword," had likewise
talked of Ireland.   It is addressed to "you," a "you" who has heard
men say: "she will become wise and will be forced to give / in.   Compelled by experience, she / will turn back; water seeks its own level."
Whereat

> . . . you
>   have smiled. 'Water in motion is far
>   from level.' You have seen it, when obstacles happened to bar
> the path, rise automatically.

In the earlier poem, the figure was used defensively, even oppositionally.   It is a tactic not common in Miss Moore's verse; as against
the dialectician's morality of eristic, she shows a more feminine preference for the sheer ostracizing of the enemy, refuting by silence—disagreement implying the respect of intimacy, as in her poem on "Marriage," wittily appraising the "fight to be affectionate," she quotes, "No
truth can be fully known until it has been tried by the tooth of disputation."

(When Miss Moore was editor of *The Dial,* her ideal number, as regards the reviews and articles of criticism, would I think have been one
in which all good books got long favorable reviews, all middling books
got short favorable reviews, and all books deserving of attack were
allowed to go without mention.   One can imagine how such a norm
could be reached either charitably, through stress upon appreciation as
motive, or not so charitably, by way of punishment, as when Miss
Moore observes in "Spenser's Ireland": "Denunciations do not affect
the culprit: nor blows, but it / is torture to him not to be spoken to."
We need not decide between these motives in all cases, since they can
comfortably work in unison.)

In contrast with the "oppositional" context qualifying the figure of the rising water in the earlier poem, "Sojourn in the Whale," its later variant has a context almost exaltedly positive. And repeating the same pattern (of affirmation in imprisonment) in another figure, the later poem widens the connotations of the years thus:

> . . . The very bird
> grown taller as he sings, steels
> his form straight up.   Though he is captive
> his mighty singing
> says satisfaction is a lowly
> thing, how pure a thing is joy.
> This is mortality,
> this is eternity.

The pattern appears more conversationally (*What Are Years,* p. 12) in the suggestion that it must have been a "humorous" workman who made

> this greenish Waterford
> glass weight with the summit curled down toward
> itself as the
> grass grew,

and in "The Monkey Puzzle" (*Selected Poems*) we read

> its tail superimposed upon itself in a complacent half spiral,
> incidentally so witty.

Still, then, trying to discover what are years (or rather, what all are years), we might also recall, in *Selected Poems,* the poem on "The Fish," where the one fish featured as representative of its tribe is observed "opening and shutting itself like / an / injured fan"—in quality not unlike "The Student" of *What Are Years* who

> . . . is too reclusive for
> some things to seem to touch
> him, not because he
> has no feeling but because he has so much.

As the poem of "The Fish" develops, we might say that the theme is transferred "from the organism to the environment"; for we next read

of a chasm through which the water has driven a wedge—and injury is
here too, since

>   All
>   external
>   marks of abuse are present on this
>   defiant edifice.—

And finally

>   Repeated
>   evidence has proved that it can live
>   on what cannot revive
>   its youth.   The sea grows old in it.

A chasm in the sea, then, becomes rather the sea in a chasm.   And
this notable reversal, that takes place in the areas of the "submerged,"
would also seem to be an aspect of "years."   Which would mean that
"years" subsume the synecdochic possibilities whereby those elements
that cluster together can represent one another: here the active can become passive, the environed can become the environment, the container can be interchangeable with the contained.   In possessing such
attributes, "years" are poetry.

We may at this point recall our beginning—the citation concerning
visible and invisible.   In "The Plumet Basilisk" (*Selected Poems*) we
read of this particular lizard that, "king with king,"

>   He leaps and meets his
>   likeness in the stream.

He is (in the poem it is a quotation)

>   'the ruler of Rivers, Lakes, and Seas,
>   invisible or visible'—

and as scene appropriate to the agent, this basilisk is said to live in a
basilica.   (Another lizard, in the same poem, is said to be "conferring
wings on what it grasps, as the airplant does"; and in "The Jerboa," we
are told of "this small desert rat" that it "honours the sand by assuming
its colour.")   Likewise

>   the plumet portrays
>   mythology's wish
>   to be interchangeably man and fish.

What I am trying to do, in reaching out for these various associations, is to get some comprehensive glimpse of the ways in which the one pervasive quality of motivation is modified and ramified. I am trying, in necessarily tenuous material, to indicate how the avowed relation between the visible and the invisible finds variants, or sophistications, in "objectivist" appreciation; how this appreciation, in an age of much querulousness, serves rather to transcend the querulous (*Selected Poems,* p. 34: "The staff, the bag, the feigned inconsequence / of manner, best bespeak that weapon, self-protectiveness"); and how this same pattern takes form in the theme of submergence, with its interchangeabilities, and so in the theme of water rising on itself. At another point the motive takes as its object the motif of the spinster ("You have been compelled by hags to spin / gold thread from straw," with incidental suggestions of esthetic alchemy, lines that appear in "Sojourn in the Whale," and so link with submergence, Ireland, and the theme of spirited feminine independence, thus relating to kindred subjects in the later poem, "Spenser's Ireland"). I have also suggested that a like quality of imagination is to be found in the intellectual ways of one who selects as his subject not clocks, but clocks for clocks. (To appreciate just what goes on here, one might contrast these contemplative clocks—serene in their role as the motives behind motives—with the ominous clock-faces of Verhaeren, or in the grotesque plays of Edmund Wilson, which no one seems to have read but me.) From these crystal clocks, I could then advance to another variant, as revealed in the treatment of ice and glass. These would, I think, be animated by the same spirit. See for instance (in *Selected Poems*) the study of the glacier as "an octopus of ice":

> this fossil flower concise without a shiver,
> intact when it is cut,
> damned for its sacrosanct remoteness.

"Relentless accuracy is the nature of this octopus / with its capacity for fact"—which would make it a glacier with an objectivist esthetic. And two levels of motive are figured in the splendid concluding vista of

> . . . the hard mountain 'planed by ice and polished by the wind'—
> the white volcano with no weather side;

the lightning flashing at its base,
rain falling in the valleys, and snow falling on the peak—.[2]

We might have managed more easily by simply demarcating several themes, like naming the different ingredients that go to make up a dish. Or as with the planks that are brought together, to make a campaign platform, regardless of their fit with one another. But the relation among the themes of a genuine poetry is not of this sort. It is *substantial*—which is to say that all the branches spread from a single trunk.

I am trying to suggest that, without this initial substantiality, "objectivism" would lead not to the "feigned inconsequence of manner" that Miss Moore has mastered, but to inconsequence pure and simple. But because of this substantiality, the surfaces are derived from depth; indeed, the strict lawfulness in their choice of surfaces is depth. And the objects treated have the property not simply of things, but of volitions. They derive their poignancy as motifs from their relation to the sources of motive. And the relation between observer and observed is not that of news and reporter, but of "conversities" (her word).

In the earlier volume there is a poem, "Black Earth," wherein surprisingly the poet establishes so close an identification with her theme

[2] This is cited from the poem that follows the one on "Marriage," and is in turn followed by "Sea Unicorns and Land Unicorns." The three could be taken together as a triptych that superbly illustrates three stages in the development of one idea. First, we have the subtly averse poem on marriage (done in a spirit of high comedy that portrays marital quarrelings as interrelated somewhat like the steps of a minuet). Then comes the precise yet exalted contemplation of the glacier. And finally a discussion of the unicorn, a legendary solitaire:

> Thus this strange animal with its miraculous elusiveness,
> has come to be unique,
> 'impossible to take alive',
> tamed only by a lady inoffensive like itself—
> as curiously wild and gentle.

And typically, she cites of it that, since lions and unicorns are arch enemies, and "where the one is the other cannot be missing," Sir John Hawkins deduced an abundance of lions in Florida from the presence of unicorns there.

The theme of the lightning that flashes at the base of the glacier is varied in the unicorn poem (in a reference to "the dogs / which are dismayed by the chain lightning / playing at them from its horn"). And it is varied also in a poem on the elephant (still to be discussed) that

> has looked at the electricity and at the earth-
> quake and is still
> here; . . .

as not merely to "observe" it with sympathy and appreciation, but to speak for it. This is one of her rare "I" poems—and in it the elephant sometimes speaks with the challenge and confidence of an Invictus. Beginning on the theme of emergence (coupled with delight in the thought of submergence at will), there is first a celebration of the sturdy skin; then talk of power ("my back is full of the history of power"); and then: "My soul shall never be cut into / by a wooden spear." Next comes mention of the trunk, and of poise. And interwoven with the vigor of assertion, the focal theme is there likewise:

> that tree-trunk without
> roots, accustomed to shout
>   its own thoughts to itself . . .

and:

> . . . The I of each is to
> the I of each
> a kind of fretful speech
>   which sets a limit on itself; the elephant is
>   black earth preceded by a tendril?

I think we can make a point by recalling this earlier poem when, in "Smooth Gnarled Crape Myrtle" (*What Are Years*), the theme of the elephant's trunk appears again, this time but in passing, contextual and "tangential" to the themes of birds, union, loneliness:

> . . . 'joined in
> friendship, crowned by love.'
> An aspect may deceive; as the
> elephant's columbine-tubed trunk
> held waveringly out—
> an at will heavy thing—is
> delicate.

Surely, "an at will heavy thing" is a remarkable find. But one does not make such observation by merely looking at an elephant's trunk. There must have been much to discard. In this instance, we can know something about the omissions, quite as though we had inspected earlier drafts of the poem with their record of revisions. For though a usage in any given poem is a finished thing, and thus brilliant with surface, it becomes in effect but "work in progress" when we align it with kindred usages (emergent, fully developed, or retrospectively condensed) in

other poems. And here, by referring to "Black Earth," we can find
what lies behind the reference to the elephant's trunk in "Smooth
Gnarled Crape Myrtle." We can know it for a fact what kind of connotations must, for the poet, have been implicit in the second, condensed usage. Hence we can appreciate the motives that enabled this
trunk to be seen not merely as a *thing,* but as an *act,* representative of
the assertion in "Black Earth." And by reviewing the earlier usage we
can know the kind of volitional material which, implicit in the later
usage, led beyond the perception of the trunk as a thing to this perception of it as an act. At such moments, I should say, out of our
idealistic trammels we get a glimpse of realism in its purity.

Or let us look at another instance. Sensitivity in the selection of
words resides in the ability, or necessity, to feel behind the given word a
history—not a past history, but a future one. Within the word, collapsed into its simultaneous oneness, there is implicit a sequence, a complexity of possible narratives that could be drawn from it. If you
would remember what words are in this respect, and how in the simultaneity of a word histories are implicit, recall the old pleasantry of asking someone, "What's an accordion," whereat invariably as he explains
he will start pumping a bellows.

Well, among Miss Moore's many poems enunciating aspects of her
esthetic credo, or commenting on literary doctrines and methods, there
is one, "To a Snail," beginning:

> If 'compression is the first grace of style,'
> you have it. Contractility is a virtue
> as modesty is a virtue.

And this equating of an esthetic value with a moral one is summed up
by locating the principle of style "in the curious phenomenon of your
occipital horn."

In her poem on the butterfly (*What Are Years,* p. 17), the mood of
tentativeness that had been compressed within the term "contractility"
reveals its significant narrative equivalents. As befits the tentative, or
contractile, it is a poem of jeopardy, tracing a tenuous relationship between a butterfly ("half deity half worm," "last of the elves") and a
nymph ("dressed in Wedgewood blue"), with light winds (even a
"zephyr") to figure the motives of passion. Were not the course of a

butterfly so intrinsically akin to the "inconsequential ease" and "drover-like tenacity" of Miss Moore's own versa-tilities, one might not have much hope for a poem built about this theme (reminiscent of many musical Papillons—perhaps more than a theme, perhaps a set idiom, almost a form). Here, with the minute accuracy of sheerly "objectivist" description, there is a subtle dialectic of giving and receiving, of fascinations and releases—an interchange of delicately shaded attitudes. In this realm, things reached for will evade, but will follow the hand as it recedes.

Through the tracery of flight, there are two striking moments of stasis, each the termination of a course: one when "the butterfly's tobacco-brown unglazed / china eyes and furry countenance confront / the nymph's large eyes"—and the second when, having broken contact with the nymph's "controlled agitated glance," the "fiery tiger-horse" (at rest, but poised against the wind, "chest arching / bravely out") is motivated purely by relation to the zephyr alone. The poem concludes by observing that this "talk" between the animal and the zephyr "was as strange as my grandmother's muff."

I have called it a poem of jeopardy. (When butterfly and nymph confront each other, "It is Goya's scene of the tame magpie faced / by crouching cats.") It is also a poem of coquetry (perhaps our last poem of coquetry, quite as this butterfly was the last of the elves—coquetry now usually being understood as something that comes down like a ton of brick).[3]

[3] In the earlier volume there is an epigram-like poem, "To a Steam Roller," that I have always thought very entertaining. It excoriates this sorry, ungainly mechanism as a bungling kind of fellow that, when confronting such discriminations as are the vital purpose of Miss Moore's lines, would "crush all the particles down / into close conformity, and then walk back and forth / on them." We also read there:

> As for butterflies, I can hardly conceive
>   of one's attending upon you, but to question
>   the congruence of the complement is vain, if it exists.

Heretofore I had been content to think of this reference to a butterfly simply as a device for suggesting weight by a contrasting image of lightness. But the role of butterfly as elf conversant to nymph might also suggest the presence of such overtones as contrasting types of masculinity. (This would give us a perfect instance of what Coleridge meant by fancy, which occurs when we discern behind the contrast an element that the contrasted images share in common.) As for the later poem, where the theme of the butterfly is fully developed, I

The tentativeness, contractility, acquires more purely the theme of jeopardy in "Bird-Witted" (*What Are Years*), reciting the incident of the "three large fledgling mocking-birds," awaiting "their no longer larger mother," while there approaches

the
intellectual cautious-
ly c r e e p ing cat.

If her animals are selected for their "fastidiousness," their fastidiousness itself is an aspect of contractility, of jeopardy. "The Pangolin" (*What Are Years*), a poem which takes us through odd nocturnal journeys to the joyous saluting of the dawn, begins: "Another armoured animal"—and of a sudden you realize that Miss Moore's recondite menagerie is almost a thesaurus of protectivenesses. Thus also, the poem

might now try to make more clearly the point I had in mind with reference to the two moments of stasis. In the opening words ("half deity half worm" and "We all, infant and adult, have / stopped to watch the butterfly") the poem clearly suggests the possibility that it will figure two levels of motivation, a deity being in a different realm of motives than a worm, and the child's quality of perception being critically distinct from the adult's. Examining the two moments of stasis, we find here too the indications of an important difference between them. At the first stasis, elf and nymph confront each other, while "all's a-quiver with significance." But at the final stasis, the conversity is between butterfly and west wind, a directer colloquy (its greater inwardness linking it, in my opinion, with the motive-behind-motive figuration in the theme of clocks-for-clocks). At this second stage, the butterfly is called "historic metamorphoser / and saintly animal"; hence we may take it that the "deity" level of motive prevails at this second stage. The quality of the image in the closing line ("their talk was as strange as my grandmother's muff") would suggest that the deified level is equated with the quality of perception as a child. (The grandmother theme also appears in "Spenser's Ireland," where we are told that "Hindered characters . . . in Irish stories . . . all have grandmothers." Another reason for believing that the second stage of the butterfly poem is also the "motives-behind-motives" stage is offered tenuously by this tie-up with the word "hindered," since the final poem in the book, as we shall know when we come to it, does well by this word in proclaiming a morality of art.)

Another poem, "Virginia Britannia" (*What Are Years*), that seems on the surface almost exclusively descriptive (though there is passing reference to a "fritillary" that "zig-zags") is found to be progressing through scenic details to a similar transcendence. At the last, against sunset, two levels are figured, while the intermediate trees "become with lost identity, part of the ground." The clouds, thus marked off, are then heralded in words suggestive of Wordworth's ode as "to the child an intimation of / what glory is."

in which occur the lines anent visible and invisible, has as its conclusion:

> unsolicitude having swallowed up
>   all giant birds but an
>   alert gargantuan
> little-winged, magnificently
> speedy running-bird. This one
>   remaining rebel
>   is the sparrow-camel.

The tentativeness also manifests itself at times in a cult of rarity, a
collector's or antiquarian interest in the present, a kind of stylistic tour-
ism.   And it may lead to a sheer word play, of graduated sort (a La-
forguian delight in showing how the pedantries can be reclaimed for
poetry):

> The lemur-student can see
> that the aye-aye is not
>
> an angwan-tíbo, potto, or loris.

Yet mention of the "aepyornis" may suggest the answer we might have
given, were we up on such matters, to one who, pencil in hand and with
the newspaper folded to make it firmer, had asked, "What's a gigantic
bird, found fossil in Madagascar in nine letters?"   As for her invention, "invis   ible," I can't see it.

Tonally, the "contractility" reveals itself in the great agility, even
restlessness, which Miss Moore imparts to her poetry by assonance, internal rhyme, and her many variants of the run-over line.   We should
also note those sudden nodules of sound which are scattered throughout her verses, such quick concentrations as "rude root cudgel," "the
raised device reversed," "trim trio on the tree-stem," "furled fringed
frill," or tonal episodes more sustained and complex, as the lines on the
birds in Ireland (already quoted), or the title, "Walking-Sticks and
Paper-Weights and Water-Marks," or

> . . . the redbird
> the red-coated musketeer,
>   the trumpet-flower, the cavalier,
> the parson, and the
>   wild parishioner. A deer-
>   track in a church-floor
> brick . . .

One noticeable difference between the later selection and the earlier one is omission of poems on method. In *Selected Poems* there were a great many such. I think for instance of: "Poetry," containing her ingenious conceit, "imaginary gardens with real toads in them"; "Critics and Connoisseurs"; "The Monkeys"; "In the Days of Prismatic Colour"; "Picking and Choosing"; "When I Buy Pictures"; "Novices" (on action in language, and developed in imagery of the sea); "The Past is the Present" ("ecstasy affords / the occasion and expediency determines the form"); and one which propounds a doctrine as its title: "In This Age of Hard Trying, Nonchalance is Good and."

But though methodological pronouncements of this sort have dropped away, in the closing poem on "The Paper Nautilus," the theme does reappear. Yet in an almost startlingly deepened transformation. Here, proclaiming the poet's attachment to the poem, there are likenesses to the maternal attachment to the young. And the themes of bondage and freedom (as with one "hindered to succeed") are fiercely and flashingly merged.

D

FOUR MASTER TROPES

I REFER to metaphor, metonymy, synecdoche, and irony. And my primary concern with them here will be not with their purely figurative usage, but with their rôle in the discovery and description of "the truth." It is an evanescent moment that we shall deal with—for not only does the dividing line between the figurative and literal usages shift, but also the four tropes shade into one another. Give a man but one of them, tell him to exploit its possibilities, and if he is thorough in doing so, he will come upon the other three.

The "literal" or "realistic" applications of the four tropes usually go by a different set of names. Thus:

For *metaphor* we could substitute *perspective;*
For *metonymy* we could substitute *reduction;*
For *synecdoche* we could substitute *representation;*
For *irony* we could substitute *dialectic.*[1]

We must subsequently try to make it clear in what respects we think these substitutions are justifiable. It should, however, be apparent at a glance that, regardless of whether our proposed substitutions are justifiable, considered in themselves they do shade into another, as we have said that the four tropes do. A dialectic, for instance, aims to give us a representation by the use of mutually related or interacting perspectives—and this resultant perspective of perspectives will necessarily be a reduction in the sense that a chart drawn to scale is a reduction of the area charted.

Metaphor is a device for seeing something *in terms of* something else. It brings out the thisness of a that, or the thatness of a this. If we employ the word "character" as a general term for whatever can be thought of as distinct (any thing, pattern, situation, structure, nature, person, object, act, rôle, process, event, etc.,) then we could say that metaphor tells us something about one character as considered from

---

[1] "Dialectic" is here used in the restricted sense. In a broader sense, all the transformations considered in this essay are dialectical.

the point of view of another character. And to consider A from the point of view of B is, of course, to use B as a *perspective* upon A.

It is customary to think that objective reality is dissolved by such relativity of terms as we get through the shifting of perspectives (the perception of one character in terms of many diverse characters). But on the contrary, it is by the approach through a variety of perspectives that we establish a character's reality. If we are in doubt as to what an object is, for instance, we deliberately try to consider it in as many different terms as its nature permits: lifting, smelling, tasting, tapping, holding in different lights, subjecting to different pressures, dividing, matching, contrasting, etc.

Indeed, in keeping with the older theory of realism (what we might call "poetic realism," in contrast with modern "scientific realism") we could say that characters possess *degrees of being* in proportion to the variety of perspectives from which they can with justice be perceived. Thus we could say that plants have "more being" than minerals, animals have more being than plants, and men have more being than animals, because each higher order admits and requires a new dimension of terms not literally relevant to the lower orders.

By deliberate coaching and criticism of the perspective process, characters can be considered tentatively, in terms of other characters, for experimental or heuristic purposes. Examples may be offered at random: for instance, human motivation may, with varying degrees of relevance and reward, be considered in terms of conditioned reflexes, or chemicals, or the class struggles, or the love of God, or neurosis, or pilgrimage, or power, or movements of the planets, or geography, or sun spots, etc. Various kinds of scientific specialists now carry out the implications of one or another of such perspectives with much more perseverance than that with which a 17th Century poet might in one poem pursue the exploitation of a "conceit."

In *Permanence and Change* I have developed at some length the relationship between metaphor and perspective. I there dealt with such perspectives as an "incongruity," because the seeing of something in terms of something else involves the "carrying-over" of a term from one realm into another, a process that necessarily involves varying degrees of incongruity in that the two realms are never identical. But besides the mere desire not to restate this earlier material, there is another reason why we can hurry on to our next pair (metonymy and reduction). For since the four pairs overlap upon one another, we shall be carrying the first pair with us as we proceed.

II

Science, concerned with processes and "processing," is not properly concerned with substance (that is, it is not concerned with "being," as "poetic realism" is). Hence, it need not be concerned with motivation. All it need know is correlation. The limits of science, *qua* science, do not go beyond the statement that, when certain conditions are met, certain new conditions may be expected to follow. It is true that, in the history of the actual development of science, the discovery of such correlations has been regularly guided by philosophies of causation ("substantial" philosophies that were subsequently "discredited" or were so radically redefined as to become in effect totally different philosophies). And it is equally true that the discovery of correlations has been guided by ideational forms developed through theology and governmental law. Such "impurities" will always be detectible *behind* science as the act of given scientists; but science *qua* science is abstracted from them.

Be the world "mind," or "matter," or "both," or "several," you will follow the same procedure in striking a match. It is in this sense that science, *qua* science, is concerned with operations rather than with substances, even though the many inventions to do with the chemistry of a match can be traced back to a source in very explicit beliefs about substances and motivations of nature—and even of the supernatural.

However, as soon as you move into the social realm, involving the relation of man to man, mere *correlation* is not enough. Human relationships must be *substantial,* related by the copulative, the "is" of "being." In contrast with "scientific realism," "poetic realism" is centered in this emphasis. It seeks (except insofar as it is affected by the norms of "scientific realism") to place the motives of action, as with the relation between the seminal (potential) and the growing (actualized). Again and again, there have been attempts to give us a "science of human relations" after the analogy of the natural sciences. But there is a strategic or crucial respect in which this is impossible; namely: there can be no "science" of substance, except insofar as one is willing to call philosophy, metaphysics, or theology "sciences" (and they are not sciences in the sense of the positive scientific departments).

Hence, any attempt to deal with human relationships after the analogy of naturalistic correlations becomes necessarily the *reduction* of some higher or more complex realm of being to the terms of a lower or less complex realm of being.   And, recalling that we propose to treat *metonymy* and *reduction* as substitutes for each other, one may realize why we thought it necessary thus to introduce the subject of metonymy.

The basic "strategy" in metonymy is this: to convey some incorporeal or intangible state in terms of the corporeal or tangible.   E.g., to speak of "the heart" rather than "the emotions."   If you trail language back far enough, of course, you will find that all our terms for "spiritual" states were metonymic in origin.   We think of "the emotions," for instance, as applying solely to the realm of consciousness, yet obviously the word is rooted in the most "materialistic" term of all, "motion" (a key strategy in Western materialism has been the reduction of "consciousness" to "motion").   In his *Principles of Literary Criticism,* Richards is being quite "metonymic" in proposing that we speak not of the "emotions" aroused in the reader by the work of art, but the "commotions."

Language develops by metaphorical extension, in borrowing words from the realm of the corporeal, visible, tangible and applying them by analogy to the realm of the incorporeal, invisible, intangible; then in the course of time, the original corporeal reference is forgotten, and only the incorporeal, metaphorical extension survives (often because the very conditions of living that reminded one of the corporeal reference have so altered that the cross reference no longer exists with near the same degree of apparentness in the "objective situation" itself); and finally, poets regain the original relation, in reverse, by a "metaphorical extension" back from the intangible into a tangible equivalent (the first "carrying-over" from the material to the spiritual being compensated by a second "carrying-over" from the spiritual back into the material); and this "archaicizing" device we call "metonymy."

"Metonymy" is a device of "poetic realism"—but its partner, "reduction," is a device of "scientific realism."   Here "poetry" and "behaviorism" meet.   For the poet spontaneously knows that "beauty *is* as beauty *does*" (that the "state" must be "embodied" in an actualization).   He knows that human relations require actions, which are *dramatizations,* and that the essential medium of drama is the posturing, tonalizing body placed in a material scene. He knows that "shame," for instance, is not merely a "state," but a movement of the eye, a color of the cheek, a certain quality of voice and set of the muscles; he knows this as "behavioristically" as the formal scientific behaviorist who would "reduce" the state itself to these corresponding bodily equivalents.

He also knows, however, that these bodily equivalents are but part of the *idiom of expression* involved in the act. They are "figures." They are hardly other than "symbolizations." Hence, for all his "archaicizing" usage here, he is not offering his metonymy as a *substantial* reduction. For in "poetic realism," states of mind as the motives of action are not reducible to materialistic terms. Thus, though there is a sense in which both the poetic behaviorist and the scientific behaviorist are exemplifying the strategy of metonymy (as the poet translates the spiritual into an idiom of material equivalents, and may even select for attention the same bodily responses that the scientist may later seek to measure), the first is using metonymy as a *terminological* reduction whereas the scientific behaviorist offers his reduction as a "real" reduction. (However, he does not do this *qua* scientist, but only by reason of the materialist metaphysics, with its assumptions about substance and motive, that is implicit in his system.)

III

Now, note that a reduction is a *representation*. If I reduce the contours of the United States, for instance, to the terms of a relief map, I have within these limits "represented" the United States. As a mental state is the "representation" of certain material conditions, so we could —reversing the process—say that the material conditions are "representative" of the mental state. That is, if there is some kind of correspondence between what we call the act of perception and what we call the thing perceived, then either of these equivalents can be taken as "representative" of the other. Thus, as reduction (metonymy) overlaps upon metaphor (perspective) so likewise it overlaps upon synecdoche (representation).

For this purpose we consider synecdoche in the usual range of dictionary sense, with such meanings as: part for the whole, whole for the part, container for the contained, sign for the thing signified, material for the thing made (which brings us nearer to metonymy), cause for effect, effect for cause, genus for species, species for genus, etc. All such conversions imply an integral relationship, a relationship of convertibility, between the two terms.

The "noblest synecdoche," the perfect paradigm or prototype for all lesser usages, is found in metaphysical doctrines proclaiming the identity of "microcosm" and "macrocosm." In such doctrines, where the individual is treated as a replica of the universe, and vice versa, we have the ideal synecdoche, since microcosm is related to macrocosm as part to whole, and either the whole can represent the part or the part can represent the whole. (For "represent" here we could substitute "be identified with.") One could thus look through the remotest astronomical distances to the "truth within," or could look within to learn the "truth in all the universe without." Leibniz's monadology is a good instance of the synecdochic on this grand scale. (And "representation" is his word for this synecdochic relationship.)

A similar synecdochic form is present in all theories of political representation, where some part of the social body (either traditionally established, or elected, or coming into authority by revolution) is held to be "representative" of the society as a whole. The pattern is essential to Rousseau's theory of the *volonté générale,* for instance. And though there are many disagreements within a society as to what part should represent the whole and how this representation should be accomplished, in a complex civilization any act of representation automatically implies a synecdochic relationship (insofar as the act is, or is held to be, "truly representative").

Sensory representation is, of course, synecdochic in that the senses abstract certain qualities from some bundle of electro-chemical activities we call, say, a tree, and these qualities (such as size, shape, color, texture, weight, etc.) can be said "truly to represent" a tree. Similarly, artistic representation is synecdochic, in that certain relations within the medium "stand for" corresponding relations outside it. There is also a sense in which the well-formed work of art is internally synecdochic, as the beginning of a drama contains its close or the close sums up the beginning, the parts all thus being consubstantially related. Indeed, one may think what he will of microcosm-macrocosm relationships as they are applied to "society" or "the universe," the fact remains that, as regards such a "universe" as we get in a well-organized work of art, at every point the paradoxes of the synecdochic present themselves to the critic for analysis. Similarly, the realm of psychology (and particularly the psychology of art) requires the use of the synecdochic reversals. Indeed, I would want deliberately to "coach" the concept of the synecdochic by extending it to cover such relations (and their reversals) as: before for after, implicit for explicit, temporal sequence for logical sequence, name for narrative, disease for cure, hero for villain, active for passive. At the opening of *The Ancient Mariner,* for instance, the Albatross is a *gerundive:* its nature when introduced is that of something *to be* murdered, and it implicitly contains the future that is to become explicit. In *Moby Dick,* Ahab as pursuer is pursued; his action is a passion.

Metonymy may be treated as a special application of synecdoche. If, for instance, after the analogy of a correlation between "mind and body" or "consciousness and matter (or motion)" we selected quality and quantity as a "synecdochically related pair," then we might propose to treat as synecdoche the substitution of either quantity for quality or quality for quantity (since either side could be considered as the sign, or symptom, of the other). But only *one* of these, the substitution of quantity for quality, would be a metonymy. We might say that representation (synecdoche) stresses a *relationship* or *connectedness* between two sides of an equation, a connectedness that, like a road, extends in either direction, from quantity to quality or from quality to quantity; but reduction follows along this road in only *one* direction, from quality to quantity.[2]

Now "poetic realism," in contrast with "scientific realism," cannot confine itself to representation in this metonymic, one-direction sense. True, every art, in its nature as a medium, reduces a state of consciousness to a "corresponding" sensory body (so material that it can be reproduced, bought and sold). But the aim of such *embodiment* is to produce in the observer a corresponding state of *consciousness* (that is,

---

[2] Unfortunately, we must modify this remark somewhat. Reduction, *as per scientific realism,* would be confined to but one direction. Reduction, that is, as the word is now generally used. But originally, "reduction" was used in ways that make it closer rather to the margin of its overlap upon "perspective," as anything considered in terms of anything else could be said to be "reduced"—or "brought back" ("referred")—to it, so that the consideration of art in terms of morality, politics, or religion could have been called "the reduction" of art to morality, or politics, or religion.

the artist proceeds from "mind" to "body" that his representative reduction may induce the audience to proceed from "body" to "mind"). But there is an important difference between representing the quality of an experience thus and reducing the quality to a quantity. One might even "represent" the human body in the latter, reductive sense, by reducing it to ashes and offering a formula for the resultant chemicals. Otto Neurath's "isotypes" (see his *Modern Man in the Making,* or our review of it, "Quantity and Quality," in the appendix of *The Philosophy of Literary Form*) are representations in the latter, reductive sense, in contrast with the kind of representation we get in realistic portrait-painting.

Our point in going over this old ground is to use it as a way of revealing a tactical error in the attempt to treat of *social* motivations. We refer to the widespread belief that the mathematico-quantitative ideal of the physical sciences can and should serve as the ideal of the "social sciences," a belief that has led, for instance, to the almost fabulous amassing of statistical surveys in the name of "sociology." Or, if one insisted upon the right to build "sciences" after this model (since no one could deny that statistics are often revealing) our claim would be that science in this restricted sense (that explains higher orders by reduction to lower orders, organic complexities by reduction to atomistic simplicities, being by reduction to motion, or quality by reduction to number, etc.) could not *take the place* of metaphysics or religion, but would have to return to the role of "handmaiden."

Let us get at the point thus: *A terminology of conceptual analysis, if it is not to lead to misrepresentation, must be constructed in conformity with a representative anecdote—whereas anecdotes "scientifically" selected for reductive purposes are not representative.* E.g., think of the scientist who, in seeking an entrance into the analysis of human motivations, selects as his "informative anecdote" for this purpose some laboratory experiment having to do with the responses of animals. Obviously, such an anecdote has its peculiarly simplificatory ("reductive") character, or genius—and the scientist who develops his analytic terminology about this anecdote as his informative case must be expected to have, as a result, a terminology whose character or genius is restricted by the character or genius of the model for the description of which it is formed. He next proceeds to transfer (to "metaphor") this terminology to the interpretation of a different order of cases, turning for instance from animals to infants and from infants to the acts of fully developed adults. And when he has made these steps, applying his terminology to a kind of anecdote so different from the kind about which it was formed, this misapplication of his terminology would not give him a representative interpretation at all, but a mere "debunking." Only insofar as the analyst had not lived up to his claims, only insofar as his terminology for the analysis of a higher order of cases was *not* restricted to the limits proper to the analysis of a lower order of cases, could he hope to discuss the higher order of cases in an adequate set of terms. Otherwise, the genius of his restricted terminology must "drag the interpretation down to their level."

This observation goes for any terminological approach to the analysis of human acts or relationships that is shaped in conformity with an unrepresentative case (or that selects as the "way in" to one's subject an "informative anecdote" belonging in some other order than the case to be considered). For instance, insofar as Alfred Korzybski really does form his terminology for the analysis of meaning in conformity with that contraption of string, plugs, and tin he calls the "Structural Differential," his analysis of meaning is "predestined" to misrepresentation, since the genius of the contraption itself is not a representative example of meaning. It is a "reduction" of meaning, a reduction in the restricted sense of the term, as Thurman Arnold's reduction of social relations into terms of the psychiatric metaphor is reductive.

What then, it may be asked, would be a "representative anecdote?" But that takes us into the fourth pair: irony and dialectic.

IV

A treatment of the irony-dialectic pair will be much easier to follow if we first delay long enough to consider the equatability of "dialectic" with "dramatic."

A human rôle (such as we get in drama) may be summed up in certain slogans, or formulae, or epigrams, or "ideas" that characterize the agent's situation or strategy. The rôle involves properties both intrinsic to the agent and developed with relation to the scene and to other agents. And the "summings-up" ("ideas") similarly possess properties derived both from the agent and from the various factors with which the agent is in relationship.   Where the ideas are in action, we have drama; where the agents are in ideation, we have dialectic.

Obviously, there are elements of "dramatic personality" in dialectic ideation, and elements of dialectic in the mutual influence of dramatic agents in contributing to one another's ideational development.   You might state all this another way by saying that you cannot have ideas without persons or persons without ideas.   Thus, one might speak of "Socratic irony" as "dramatic," and of "dramatic irony" as "Socratic."

Relativism is got by the fragmentation of either drama or dialectic. That is, if you isolate any one agent in a drama, or any one advocate in a dialogue, and see the whole in terms of his position alone, you have the purely relativistic.   And in relativism there is no irony.   (Indeed, as Cleanth Brooks might say, it is the very absence if irony in relativism that makes it so susceptible to irony.   For relativism sees everything in but one set of terms—and since there are endless other terms in which things could be seen, the irony of the monologue that makes everything in its image would be in this ratio: the greater the *absolutism* of the statements, the greater the *subjectivity* and *relativity* in the position of the agent making the statements.)

Irony arises when one tries, by the interaction of terms upon one another, to produce a *development* which uses all the terms.   Hence, from the standpoint of this total form (this "perspective of perspectives"), none of the participating "sub-perspectives" can be treated as either precisely right or precisely wrong.   They are all voices, or personalities, or positions, integrally affecting one another.   When the dialectic is properly formed, they are the number of characters needed to produce the total development.   Hence, reverting to our suggestion that we might extend the synecdochic pattern to include such reversible pairs as disease-cure, hero-villain, active-passive, we should "ironically" note the function of the disease in "perfecting" the cure, or the function of the cure in "perpetuating" the influences of the disease.   Or we should note that only through an internal and external experiencing of folly could we possess (in our intelligence or imagination) sufficient "characters" for some measure of development beyond folly.

People usually confuse the dialectic with the relativistic.   Noting that the dialectic (or dramatic) explicitly attempts to establish a distinct set of characters, all of which protest variously at odds or on the bias with one another, they think no further.   It is certainly relativistic, for instance, to state that any term (as per metaphor-perspective) can be seen from the point of view of any other term. But insofar as terms are thus encouraged to participate in an orderly parliamentary development, the dialectic of this participation produces (in the observer who considers the whole from the standpoint of the participation of all the terms rather than from the standpoint of any one participant) a "resultant certainty" of a different quality, necessarily ironic, since it requires that all the sub-certainties be considered as neither true nor false, but *contributory* (as were we to think of the resultant certainty or "perspective of perspectives" as a noun, and to think of all the contributory voices as necessary modifiers of that noun).

To be sure, relativism is the constant *temptation* of either dialectic or drama (consider how often, for instance, Shakespeare is called a relativist). And historians for the most part *are relativistic*. But where one considers different historical characters from the standpoint of a total development, one could encourage each character to comment upon the others without thereby sacrificing a perspective upon the lot. This could be got particularly, I think, if historical characters themselves (i.e., periods or cultures treated as "individual persons") were considered never to begin or end, but rather to change in intensity or poignancy. History, in this sense, would be a dialectic of characters in which, for instance, we should never expect to see "feudalism" overthrown by "capitalism" and "capitalism" succeeded by some manner of national or international or non-national or neo-national or postnational socialism—but rather should note elements of all such positions (or "voices") existing always, but attaining greater clarity of expression or imperiousness of proportion of one period than another.

Irony is never Pharisaic, but there is a Pharisaic temptation in irony. To illustrate the point, I should like to cite a passage from a poet and critic who knows a good deal about irony, and who is discussing a poet who knows a good deal about irony—but in this particular instance, I submit, he is wrong. I refer to a passage in which Allen Tate characterizes the seduction scene in *The Waste Land* as "ironic" and the poet's attitude as that of "humility." (I agree that "humility" is the proper partner of irony—but I question whether the passage is ironic enough to embody humility.)

Mr. Tate characterizes irony as "that arrangement of experience, either premeditated by art or accidentally appearing in the affairs of men, which permits to the spectator an insight superior to that of the actor." And he continues:

> The seduction scene is the picture of modern and dominating man. The arrogance and pride of conquest of the "small house agent's clerk" are the badge of science, bumptious practicality, over-weening secular faith. The very success of this conquest witnesses its aimless character; it succeeds as a wheel succeeds in turning; he can only conquer again.
>
> His own failure to understand his position is irony, and the poet's insight into it is humility. But for the grace of God, says the poet in effect, there go I. There is essentially the poetic attitude, an attitude that Eliot has been approaching with increasing purity.

We need not try to decide whether or not the poet was justified in feeling "superior" to the clerk. But we may ask how one could *possibly* exemplify an attitude of "humility" by feeling "superior"? There is, to be sure, a brand of irony, called "romantic irony," that might fit in with such a pattern—the kind of irony that did, as a matter of fact, arise as an aesthetic opposition to cultural philistinism, and in which the artist considered himself *outside of* and *superior to* the rôle he was rejecting. And though not "essentially *the* poetic attitude," it is essentially *a* poetic attitude, an attitude exemplified by much romantic art (a sort of pamphleteering, or external, attitude towards "the enemy").

True irony, however, irony that really does justify the attribute of "humility," is not "superior" to the enemy. (I might even here rephrase my discussion of Eliot in *Attitudes Toward History* by saying that Eliot's problem in religion has resided precisely in his attempt to convert romantic irony into classic irony, really to replace a state of "superiority" by a state of "humility"—and *Murder in the Cathedral* is a ritual aimed at precisely such purification of motives.) True irony, humble irony, is based upon a sense of fundamental kinship with the enemy, as one *needs* him, is *indebted* to him, is not merely outside him as an observer but contains him *within,* being consubstantial with him. This is the irony of Flaubert, when he recognizes that Madame Bovary is himself. One sees it in Thomas Mann—and in what he once called, when applying the term to another, "Judas psychology." And there was, if not the humility of strength, at least a humility of gentle surrender, in Anatole France.

In *The Waste Land,* the poet is not saying "there but for the grace of

God go I." On the contrary, he is, if not thanking God, at least congratulating himself, that he is not like other men, such other men as this petty clerk. If this was "humility," then the Pharisee is Humble Citizen No. 1. With Newton, on the other hand, there was no "superiority" in his exclamation as he observed the criminal. He did not mean that that man was a criminal but he, Newton, thank God, was not; he meant that *he too was a criminal, but that the other man was going to prison for him.* Here was true irony-and-humility, since Newton was simultaneously both outside the criminal and within him.

"Superiority" in the dialectic can arise only in the sense that one may feel the need of *more characters* than the particular foolish characters under consideration. But in one sense he can *never* be superior, for he must realize that he also *needs this particular foolish character as one of the necessary modifiers.* Dialectic irony (or humility) here, we might even say, provides us with a kind of "technical equivalent for the doctrine of original sin." Folly and villainy are integral motives, necessary to wisdom or virtue.[3]

[3] I would consider Falstaff a gloriously ironic conception because we are so at one with him in his vices, while he himself embodies his vices in a mode of identification or brotherhood that is all but religious. Falstaff would not simply rob a man, from without. He *identifies himself* with the victim of a theft; he *represents* the victim. He would not crudely steal a purse; rather, he *joins forces* with the owner of the purse—and it is only when the harsh realities of this imperfect world have imposed a brutally divisive clarity upon the situation, that Falstaff is left holding the purse. He produces a new quality, a state of synthesis or merger—and it so happens that, when this synthesis is finally dissociated again into its analytic components (the crudities of the realm of practical property relationships having reduced this state of qualitative merger to a state of quantitative division), the issue as so simplified sums up to the fact that the purse has changed hands. *He* converts "thine" into "ours"—and it is "circumstances over which he has no control" that go to convert this "ours" into a "mine." A mere thief would have directly converted "thine" into "mine." It is the addition of these intermediate steps that makes the vital difference between a mere thief and Falstaff; for it is precisely these intermediate steps that mark him with a conviviality, a sociality, essentially religious—and in this *sympathetic* distortion of religious values resides the irony of his conception.

We might bring out the point sharply by contrasting Falstaff with Tartuffe. Tartuffe, like Falstaff, exploits the coöperative values for competitive ends. He too would convert "thine" into "mine" by putting it through the social alembic of "ours." But the conception of Tartuffe is not ironic, since he is pure hypocrite. He uses the religious values simply as a swindler. Tartuffe's piety, which he uses to gain the confidence of his victims, is a mere deception. Whereas Tartuffe is all competition and merely *simulates* the sentiments of coöperation, Falstaff is

A third temptation of irony is its tendency towards the simplification of literalness. That is: although *all* the characters in a dramatic or dialectic development are necessary qualifiers of the definition, there is usually some one character that enjoys the rôle of *primus inter pares*. For whereas any of the characters may be viewed in terms of any other, this one character may be taken as the summarizing vessel, or synecdochic representative, of the development as a whole. This is the rôle of Socrates in the Platonic dialogue, for instance—and we could similarly call the proletariat the Socrates of the Marxist Symposium of History, as they are not merely equal participants along with the other characters, but also represent the *end* or *logic* of the development as a whole.

This "most representative" character thus has a dual function: one we might call "adjectival" and the other "substantial." The character is "adjectival," as embodying one of the qualifications necessary to the total definition, but is "substantial" as embodying the conclusions of the development as a whole. Irony is sacrificed to "the simplification of literalness" when this duality of rôle is neglected (as it may be neglected by either the reader, the writer, or both). In Marxism as a literally libertarian philosophy, for instance, slavery is "bad," and is so treated in the rhetoric of proletarian emancipation (e.g., "wage slavery"). Yet from the standpoint of the development as a whole, slavery must be treated ironically, as with Engel's formula: "Without the slavery of antiquity, no modern socialism." Utilization of the vanquished by enslavement, he notes, was a great cultural advance over the wasteful practice of slaying the vanquished.

V

Irony, as approached through either drama or dialectic, moves us into the area of "law" and "justice" (the "necessity" or "inevitability" of the *lex talionis*) that involves matters of form in art (as form affects anticipation and fulfilment) and matters of prophecy and prediction in history. There is a level of generalization at which predictions about "inevitable" developments in history are quite justified. We may state

genuinely coöperative, sympathetic, a synecdochic part of his victim—but along with such rich gifts of identification, what is to prevent a purse from changing hands?

with confidence, for instance, that what arose in time must fall in time (hence, that any given structure of society must "inevitably" perish). We may make such prophecy more precise, with the help of irony, in saying that the developments that led to the rise will, by the further course of their development, "inevitably" lead to the fall (true irony always, we hold, thus involving an "internal fatality," a principle operating from within, though its logic may also be grounded in the nature of the extrinsic scene, whose properties contribute to the same development).

The point at which different casuistries appear (for fitting these "general laws of inevitability" to the unique cases of history) is the point where one tries to decide exactly what new characters, born of a given prior character, will be the "inevitable" vessels of the prior character's deposition. As an over-all ironic formula here, and one that has the quality of "inevitability," we could lay it down that "what goes forth as A returns as non-A." This is the basic pattern that places the essence of drama and dialectic in the irony of the "peripety," the strategic moment of reversal.

A Rhetoric of Motives

TO W. C. BLUM

INTRODUCTION

THE ONLY difficult portion of this book happens, unfortunately, to be at the start. There, selecting texts that are usually treated as pure poetry, we try to show why rhetorical and dialectical considerations are also called for. Since these texts involve an imagery of killing (as a typical text for today should) we note how, behind the surface, lies a quite different realm that has little to do with such motives. An imagery of killing is but one of many terminologies by which writers can represent the process of change. And while recognizing the sinister implications of a preference for homicidal and suicidal terms, we indicate that the principles of development or transformation ("rebirth") which they stand for are not strictly of such a nature at all.

We emerge from the analysis with the key term, "Identification." Hence, readers who would prefer to begin with it, rather than to worry a text until it is gradually extricated, might go lightly through the opening pages, with the intention of not taking hold in earnest until they come to the general topic of *Identification,* on page 543.

Thereafter, with this term as instrument, we seek to mark off the areas of rhetoric, by showing how a rhetorical motive is often present where it is not usually recognized, or thought to belong. In part, we would but rediscover rhetorical elements that had become obscured when rhetoric as a term fell into disuse, and other specialized disciplines such as esthetics, anthropology, psychoanalysis, and sociology came to the fore (so that esthetics sought to outlaw rhetoric, while the other sciences we have mentioned took over, each in its own terms, the rich rhetorical elements that esthetics would ban).

But besides this job of reclamation, we also seek to develop our subject beyond the traditional bounds of rhetoric. There is an intermediate area of expression that is not wholly deliberate, yet not wholly unconscious. It lies midway between aimless utterance and speech directly purposive. For instance, a man who identifies his private ambitions with the good of the community may be partly justified, partly unjustified. He may be using a mere pretext to gain individual advantage at the public expense; yet he may be quite sincere, or even may willingly make sacrifices in behalf of such identification. Here is a rhetorical area not analyzable either as sheer design or as sheer simplicity. And we would treat of it here.

Traditionally, the key term for rhetoric is not "identification," but "persuasion." Hence, to make sure that we do not maneuver ourselves unnecessarily into a weak position, we review several classic texts which track down all the major implications of that term. Our treatment, in terms of identification, is decidedly not meant as a substitute for the sound traditional approach. Rather, as we try to show, it is but an accessory to the standard lore. And our book aims to make itself at home in both emphases.

Particularly when we come upon such aspects of persuasion as are found in "mystification," courtship, and the "magic" of class relationships, the reader will see why the classical notion of clear persuasive intent is not an accurate fit, for describing the ways in which the members of a group promote social cohesion by acting rhetorically upon themselves and one another. As W. C. Blum has stated the case deftly, "In identification lies the source of dedications and enslavements, in fact of cooperation."

All told, persuasion ranges from the bluntest quest of advantage, as in sales promotion or propaganda, through courtship, social etiquette, education, and the sermon, to a "pure" form that delights in the process of appeal for itself alone, without ulterior purpose. And identification ranges from the politician who, addressing an audience of farmers, says, "I was a farm boy myself," through the mysteries of social status, to the mystic's devout identification with the source of all being.

That the reader might find it gratifying to observe the many variations on our two interrelated themes, at every step we have sought to proceed by examples. Since we did not aim to write a compendium, we have not tried to cover the field in the way that a comprehensive historical survey might do—and another volume will be needed to deal adequately with the polemic kinds of rhetoric (such as the verbal tactics now called "cold war").

But we have tried to show what portions of other works should be selected as parts of a "course in rhetoric," and how they should be considered for our particular purposes. We have tried to show how rhetorical analysis throws light on literary texts and human relations generally. And while interested always in rhetorical devices, we have sought above all else to write a "philosophy of rhetoric."

We do not flatter ourselves that any one book can contribute much to counteract the torrents of ill will into which so many of our contemporaries have so avidly and sanctimoniously plunged. But the more strident our journalists, politicians, and alas! even many of our churchmen become, the more convinced we are that books should be written for tolerance and contemplation.

The fortunate arrangement whereby *A Grammar of Motives* and *A Rhetoric of Motives* are now being published in one volume calls for a few additional words with regard to the relation between the two.

In the *Rhetoric* the problems of definition and placement that were treated in the *Grammar* become transformed into a concern with the terministic marvels that have to do with the magic and rationality of Order, and its corresponding modes of Identification.

There has been some disagreement as to whether or to what extent my treatment of "identification" allows my work to be called a "New" Rhetoric. But in any case, my main hope is that it will soon become unquestionably an "Old" Rhetoric. May other analysts join me in the task of tracking down the ways in which the realm of sheerly worldly powers becomes endowed with the attributes of "secular divinity." Such appeals to imagination and authority can be revealed by the analysis of literary texts.

I have tried to show that Rhetoric, as so conceived, lends itself particularly well to those areas where sociological and literary speculations overlap.

PART ONE

THE RANGE OF RHETORIC

I

THE RANGE OF RHETORIC

The "Use" of Milton's Samson

An old poet, libertarian and regicide, blind, fallen on evil days, in sullen warlike verse celebrates Samson. On its face, his poem tells of Samson among the Philistines. A prisoner chained "eyeless in Gaza ... blind among enemies" because he could not keep "the secret of his strength" ... himself his "sepulchre" ... himself his own "dungeon" ... his sightlessness in captivity a "prison within prison" ... enraged with himself for having

> divulged
> The secret gift of God to a deceitful
> Woman,

for having given up his "fort of silence to a woman," he hugely laments his "corporal servitude." He talks of patience, and mouths threats of revenge in the name of God. And finally, when brought to the pagan temple, standing between "those two massy pillars, That to the arched roof gave main support, by his own hands," in "self-violence" ("O lastly over-strong against thyself! ... Among thy slain self-killed ..."), he sufferingly acts:

> As with the force of winds and waters pent
> When mountains tremble, those two massy pillars
> With horrible convulsion to and fro
> He tugged, he shook, till down they came, and drew
> The whole roof after them with burst of thunder
> Upon the heads of all who sat beneath,
> Lords, ladies, captains, counsellors, or priests,
> Their choice nobility and flower, not only
> Of this, but each Philistian city round,
> Met from all parts to solemnize this feast.
> Samson, with these immixed, inevitably
> Pulled down the same destruction on himself;
> The vulgar only scaped, who stood without.

And at this act, or sufferance, a notable transformation has taken place. We learn that the enemy, "drunk with adolatry, drunk with wine," had been led by the wrath of Samson's God to bring on "their own destruction." For they were "with blindness internal struck." But Samson had been "with inward eyes illuminated." They are the sightless, he is the seer, and

> . . . as an eagle
> His cloudless thunder bolted on their heads.

The vanquished enemy, by comparison, were but "tame villatic fowl."

More than twenty years before, in the *Areopagitica* ("A Speech for the Liberty of Unlicensed Printing, to the parliament of England"), his great verbal monument that gives dignity, resonance, and ultimate grounding to the doctrine of the free press, a related reference to the eagle appeared:

> Methinks I see in my mind's eye a noble and puissant nation rousing herself like a strong man after sleep, and shaking her invincible locks. Methinks I see her as an eagle mewing her mighty youth, and kindling her undazzled eyes at the full midday beam; purging and unscaling her long-abused sight at the fountain itself of heavenly radiance; while the whole noise of timorous and flocking birds, with those also that love the twilight, flutter about, amazed at what she means, and in their envious gabble would prognosticate a year of sects and schisms.

The prose reference is clearly rhetorical. It occurs in a work written with a definite audience in mind, and for a definite purpose. It was literature for *use*. Today, it would be called "propaganda."

But what of the poem? One can read it simply *in itself,* without even considering the fact that it was written by Milton. It can be studied and appreciated as a structure of internally related parts, without concern for the correspondence that almost inevitably suggests itself: the correspondence between Milton's blindness and Samson's, or between the poet's difficulties with his first wife and Delilah's betrayal of a divine "secret."

Besides this individual identification of the author with an aggressive, self-destructive hero who was in turn identified with God, there is also factional identification. Samson has said:

> All the contest is now
> 'Twixt God and Dagon. Dagon hath presumed,
> Me overthrown, to enter lists with God,
> His deity comparing and preferring
> Before the God of Abraham.

And this exalting of the issue, in terms of rival divinities at war, is allusive: the Philistines and Dagon implicitly standing for the Royalists, "drunk with wine," who have regained power in England, while the Israelites stand for the Puritan faction of Cromwell. The poem's righteous ferocity is no mere evidence of a virtuoso's craftsmanship; it is not sheer poetic exercise, as with a versatile playwright able to imagine whatever kind of role the exigencies of plot happened to require.

Rather, it is almost a kind of witchcraft, a wonder-working spell by a cantankerous old fighter-priest who would slay the enemy in effigy, and whose very translation of political controversy to high theologic terms helps, by such magnification, to sanction the ill-tempered obstinacy of his resistance. In saying, with fervor, that a blind Biblical hero *did* conquer, the poet is "substantially" saying that he in his blindness *will* conquer. This is moralistic prophecy, and is thus also a kind of "literature for use," use at one remove, though of a sort that the technologically-minded would consider the very opposite of use, since it is wholly in the order of ritual and magic.

Qualifying the Suicidal Motive

Note another result here: The recurring stress upon the *reflexive* nature of Samson's act (the element of self-destruction in his way of slaying the enemy) can be a roundabout device for sanctioning suicide; yet Milton's religion strongly forbade suicide. Compelled by his misfortunes to live with his rage, gnawed by resentments that he could no longer release fully in outward contest, Milton found in Samson a figure ambivalently fit to symbolize both aggressive and inturning trends. Here too, though still more remotely, would be "literature for use": the poetic reënactment of Samson's role could give pretexts for admitting a motive which, if not so clothed or complicated, if confronted in its simplicity, would have been inadmissible. By dramatic subterfuge Milton could include what he would have had to exclude, if reduced to a conceptually analytic statement.

The dramatic terms provide a rich context that greatly modifies whatever modicum of suicide may be present in the motivational formula as a whole. But all such important modifications, or qualifications, are dropped when we reduce the complexity to one essential strand, slant, or "gist," isolating this one reflexive element as the implicitly dominant motive, an all-pervasive generating principle. And these qualifications which the reduction would omit are strategic enough to make the motivations quite different from an out-and-out featuring of suicide as cause, in a poem stressing the theme directly, efficiently, without the modifiers of Milton's context. By comparison with such a poem, Milton's meaning would not be a recipe for suicide at all, having but a mere dash, or soupçon, of such an ingredient.

We do not mean to suggest that the figure of Samson in Milton's poem is to be interpreted purely as a "rationalization," in the psychoanalytic sense. We are taking the poem at its face value. If two statements, for instance, one humorous and the other humorless, are found to contain the same animus against someone, we are not thereby justified in treating them as the same in their motivational core. For the humorless statement may *foretell* homicide, and the humorous one may be the very thing that *forestalls* homicide. Thus *surrounded,* or modified by the total motivational context, the animus in one case may be as different from the other as yes from no. Indeed, the humorous motivation could lead to intentional homicide only insofar as it were reduced, with the qualifications of humor dropped from it. It could not, as *humor,* lead to this result, however "homicidal" might be the imagery in which it was expressed. For this imagery, *so long as it was humorous,* would contain a dimension which essentially qualified the animus. The imagery could "foretell" homicide only in the sense that it contained an ingredient which, if efficiently abstracted from its humorous modifiers, would in its new purity be homicidal. And such abstracting can take place, of course, whenever conditions place too much of a strain upon the capacity for humor.

Similarly, a motive introduced in one work, where the context greatly modifies it and keeps it from being drastically itself, may lack such important modifications in the context of another work. The *proportions* of these modifications themselves are essential in defining the total motivation, which cannot, without misinterpretation, be reduced merely to the one "gist," with all the rest viewed as mere concealment or "rationalization" of it. And in this sense, we would take the motivation of Milton's poem at face value, considering the aggressive and theocratic terms just as significant in the total recipe as the reflexive terms are. Whether there are gods or not, there is an *objective* difference in motivation between an act conceived in the name of God and an act conceived in the name of godless Nature.

Self-Immolation in Matthew Arnold

Contrast the imagery of self-immolation in Matthew Arnold's "Empedocles on Etna," for instance. Thinking of himself "as an orphan among prosperous boys"; complaining that "we feel, day and night,/ The burden of ourselves"; introspective ("Sink in thyself!"); renouncing ("thou hast no *right* to bliss,/No title from the gods to welfare and repose"); nonaggressively nostalgic ("Receive me, hide me, quench me, take me home!"); weary of both solitude and multitude ("thou fencest him from the multitude . . . Who will fence him from himself?"); yearning to descend "Down in our mother earth's miraculous womb . . ." Empedocles sees promise of freedom as he "plunges into the center," a self-immolation that unites him idealistically with mountain, sea, stars, and air, while the volcano, into which he had hurled himself, is also by legend the prison of a buried titan, a "self-helping son of earth" who had been "oppress'd" by the "well-counsell'd Zeus."

When matched with so clear an imagery of suicide, one could make out a good case for denying that Milton's identification with the "self-slain" Samson has any ingredient of suicide at all. Yet how do things look if we insert another step here? Though Arnold came to distrust his poem of Empedocles, and even suppressed its publication, much the same motives are discernible in his narrative of "Sohrab and Rustum," where the two warriors fight in single combat without knowing that they are father and son, and the son receives his death wound when paralyzed at the sound of his father's name, thus:

> When Rustum raised his head; his dreadful eyes
> Glared, and he shook on high his menacing spear,
> And shouted: *Rustum!*—Sohrab heard that shout,
> And shrank amazed; back he recoil'd one step,
> And scann'd with blinking eyes the advancing form;
> And then he stood bewilder'd; and he dropp'd
> His covering shield, and the spear pierced his side.
> He reel'd, and staggering back, sank to the ground,
> And then the gloom dispersed, and the wind fell,
> And the bright sun broke forth, and melted all
> The cloud; and the two armies saw the pair—
> Saw Rustum standing, safe upon his feet,
> And Sohrab, wounded, on the bloody sand.

Following the recognition, and the son's death, there is even the same cosmically unifying end as with Empedocles' self-immolating plunge into the crater. But here the action is transferred from the personae to sympathetic nature (from agents to similarly motivated scene, itself a new and transcendent order of action). As "Rustum and his son were left alone" by the river marge, "the majestic river floated on," a solemn course, charted by the poem through many lines,

> till at last
> The long'd for dash of waves is heard, and wide
> His luminous home of waters opens, bright
> And tranquil, from whose floor the new-bathed stars
> Emerge, and shine upon the Aral Sea.

Here, the son having been killed by the father, through the progress of the river to the sea he plunges by proxy into the universal home. And graced by the son's sacrifice, the armies are at peace.

Our knowledge of Matthew Arnold's relation to his father suggests an extra-literary "use" for the imagery of self-effacement in both these poems. Despite their many differences, both are acts of the same poetic agent, sharing the common substance of the one authorship. And both can be seen as aspects of the same attitude towards life. Indeed, when we put them together, we note this possibility: that Arnold could poetically identify himself with the figure of Empedocles because his pious deference to the authority of his father could be aptly expressed in such imagery of self-effacement as goes with Empedocles' cosmically motivated despair. And this self-abnegatory attitude, being in the same motivational cluster with his attitude towards his father, could find still more accurate expression in the imagery of a son "unconsciously" killed by his father, and *in the name of* his father.

Seen from this point of view, the "gist" of "Sohrab and Rustum" would be as "suicidal" as "Empedocles on Etna," where this theme is *explicitly* there. It would be "implicit" in "Sohrab and Rustum" because, for all the imagery of war surrounding the combat between father and son, it all "adds up" or "boils down" to a son's fatal admiration for his father. The poet, in both cases, imagines that the figure with whom he identifies himself is *being killed;* and in both cases the destruction terminates in imagery of a homecoming, a return to sources probably maternal.

Quality of Arnold's Imagery

Just what are we getting at here? We have tried to see how matters look if we put a transitional step between "Empedocles on Etna" and *Samson Agonistes*. Since Samson is self-killed in a warlike act that kills the enemy, we tried to match him against two figures by a later poet in the same "curve of history." The first figure (Empedocles) is killed by suicide; the second (Sohrab) is killed by war. But by putting Empedocles and Sohrab together, as variants of one attitude in the one poetic agent who had identified himself with both figures, we tried to establish the common character of both a suicide and a warlike death. Then, looking back at the poem by Milton, we find there, united in one poem, what Arnold has divided between two poems: the suicide and the warlike death are united in the same image.

See what our problem is. We seem to be going two ways at once. In some respects, we are trying to bring these poems together as instances of the *same* motivation; yet in other respects we are insisting that the unique context in which this motive appears in each poem makes the motive itself *different* in all three cases. Can we keep our line of thinking clear here for the reader? Milton's theocratic rage, for instance, is "warlike" in a much different way from the combats in "Sohrab and Rustum." Modifying this warrior, whose death was caused by the sound of his father's name, there are some significantly unwarlike images. Thus when Rustum, gazing in desolation at the wounded Sohrab,

> saw that Youth,
> Of age and looks to be his own dear son,
> Piteous and lovely, lying on the sand,
> Like some rich hyacinth which by the scythe
> Of an unskilful gardener has been cut,
> Mowing the garden grass-plots near its bed,
> And lies, a fragrant tower of purple bloom,
> On the mown, dying grass—so Sohrab lay,
> Lovely in death, upon the common sand.

And when Sohrab finally draws the spear, to ease "His wound's imperious anguish,"

> all down his cold, white side
> The crimson torrent ran, dim now and soil'd,
> Like the soil'd tissue of white violets

> Left, freshly gather'd, on the native bank,
> By children whom their nurses call with haste
> Indoors from the sun's eye . . .

Such unwarlike modifiers radically modify the motive of war here, quite as the motive of self-destruction which we saw clearly stated in "Empedocles on Etna" is modified by the dramatic irony whereby the son is sacrificed in the name of the father. And as contrasted with the righteous fury of Milton, we see how Arnold's attitudes were more closely akin, rather, to the *next* step in the curve of literary history; we see how they led into the estheticism of Pater, and thence to father-problems as transformed perversely in the estheticism of Oscar Wilde.

The Imaging of Transformation

By adding one more confusion, we may add the element that can bring clarity. This time, from the same "curve of history," from Coleridge's "Religious Musings":

> . . . in His vast family no Cain
> Injures uninjured (in her best-aimed blow
> Victorious Murder a blind Suicide).

This statement suggests a point at which murder and suicide can become convertible, each in its way an image for the same motive. The quotation is not quite analogous to the three other poems, since it is from a *doctrinal* poem (one of what Coleridge called his Conversation Pieces, "*sermoni propriora*"). But although it lacks the dramatic modifiers that complicate the motivation in the other poems, it avoids overefficient reduction to "gist," at least in the sense that it is dialectical, ironically making motives interchangeable which might usually be considered mutually exclusive. Indeed, the terms being equivalent, we might just as well read them backwards: "blind Suicide a Victorious Murder." Then we might think either of a poem which symbolized suicide by imagery of murder, or one which symbolized murder by imagery of suicide. And when you get to that point, you need one more step to complete your thinking: You need to look for a *motive that can serve as ground for both these choices,* a motive that, while not being exactly either one or the other, can ambiguously contain them both.

A term serving as ground for both these terms would, by the same token, "transcend" them. The battlefield, for instance, which permits rival contestants to join in battle, itself "transcends" their factionalism, being "superior" to it and "neutral" to their motives, though the conditions of the terrain may happen to favor one faction. The *principles* of war are not themselves warlike, and are ultimately reducible to universal principles of physics and dialectic. Similarly, a poet's identification with imagery of murder or suicide, either one or the other, is, from the "neutral" point of view, merely a concern with *terms for transformation in general.*

When we consider the resources of dialectic so broadly, of course, we necessarily disregard the animus of any particular image. This would be a very wrong thing to do, when some specific set of transformations is to be analyzed. But when considering transformation in general, we may stress the respects in which many different kinds of image can perform the same function. One may prefer imagery of the Upward Way and Downward Way, or of the Crossing and Return, or of Exile and Homecoming, or of a Winding-up and an Unwinding, or of Egressus and Regressus, or of a Movement Inward and a Movement Outward, or of seasonal developments, or of various antitheses, like Day and Night, Warmth and Frigidity, Yes and No, Losing and Finding, Loosing and Binding, etc., where the pairs are not merely to be placed statically against each other, but in given poetic contexts usually represent a development *from* one order of motives *to* another. Such terms, here selected at random, suggest different families of images in terms of which the processes of transformation in general might be localized, or particularized.

The Education of Henry Adams, for instance, exemplifies ritual transformation by a shift from personal images to impersonal ones. The student of life "in search of a father" (that is, looking for self-identification with a new motivating principle) would abandon his eighteenth-century identity as a member of the Adams family and adapt himself to the conditions of modern history, as he interprets them. Thus the ritual transformation is also, in its way, a kind of self-immolation. But instead of hurling himself, like Arnold's Empedocles, into the volcano as matrix, Adams contrives a methodic surrender to the sweep of history, which in turn is identified with impersonal force (his transformation by identification with it thus being a rite of depersonalization). That is, Adams' "law of the acceleration of history," considered from the symbolic point of view, is nothing other than the *imaging of a fall,* expressed roundabout in doctrinal or "educational" terms. Within the limitations imposed by the nature of the book, the final proclaiming of this "law," in strict analogy with the accelerated motion of falling bodies, in its way expresses but the same leap into the cosmic abyss that Matthew Arnold expresses through the suicide of Empedocles.

The range of images that can be used for concretizing the process of transformation is limited only by the imagination and ingenuity of poets. But the selective nature of existence favors some images above others—and high among them, naturally, is the imagery of Life and Death, with its variants of being born, being reborn, dying, killing, and being killed. Consider, now, the hypothetical case of a poet who would identify himself with some particular imagery of transformation selected from this order of terms, terms using the imagery of Life and Death. We can easily conceive of a poet who, wanting to symbolize the transformation of some evil trait within himself, writes a poem accordingly; and in this poem he might identify himself with a figure who, marked by this trait, takes his own life, thereby ritualistically transforming the trait. (That is, if the figure in the fiction possessed some outstanding vice, and slew himself as an act of judgment against this vice, such imagery of suicide could be a ritualistic means whereby the poet sought to purge his own self of this vice, or purified the vice by identifying it with the dignity of death.) Or another might symbolize this same transformation by imaginatively endowing some "outward enemy" with the trait, and then imaginatively slaying that enemy. Or a third poet might identify himself with a figure who possessed that trait, and then might imagine an enemy who slew his poetic counterpart. The trait, whatever its stylistic transformation (magnification, purification, martyrdom, etc.), may not even be "slain" by an "alien" principle at all, so far as the original poet was concerned; the contest may most likely symbolize the pitting of one motivational principle against another where *both* principles are strongly characteristic of the poet personally. (Think, for instance, of the "murderous" relation between the critical and poetic "selves" of T. S. Eliot, as symbolized in his *Murder in the Cathedral,* and previously discussed in our *Attitudes Toward History.*) Similarly, if a principle were located in the figure of mother, father, child, tyrant, or king, and were ritually transformed under these guises, we should have respectively: matricide, patricide, infanticide, tyrannicide, or regicide. The Nazis, locating the *transformandum* in the whole Jewish people as their chosen vessel, gave us a "scientific" variant: genocide. And the frequent psycho-analytic search for "unconscious" desires to kill some member of the family, either through rivalry or through love frustrated and expressed in reverse, puts the emphasis at the wrong place. For the so-called "desire to kill" a certain person is much more properly analyzable as a desire to *transform the principle* which that person *represents*.

Dramatic and Philosophic Terms for Essence

Since imagery built about the active, reflexive, and passive forms of death (killing, self-killing, and being killed) so obviously contributes to dramatic intensity, and since thoughts of death are so basic to human motivation, we usually look no farther to account for their use. But there is also an ultimate "Grammatical" incentive behind such imagery, since a history's *end* is a formal way of proclaiming its *essence* or *nature*, as with those who distinguish between a tragedy and a comedy by the outcome alone and who would transform "tragedy" into "comedy" merely by changing the last few moments of the last act.

Elsewhere (notably on "the temporizing of essence," *A Grammar of Motives*, pp. 430-440) we have discussed the puns of logical and temporal priority whereby the *logical* idea of a thing's essence can be translated into a temporal or narrative equivalent by statement in terms of the thing's source or beginnings (as feudal thinking characterized a person's individual identity in terms that identified him with his family, the paradoxical ultimate of such definition being perhaps the use of "bastard" as epithet to describe a man's *character*). But if there is this ultimate of *beginnings,* whereby theological or metaphysical systems may state the essence of mankind in terms of a divine parenthood or an originating natural ground, there is also an ultimate of *endings,* whereby the essence of a thing can be defined narratively in terms of its *fulfillment* or *fruition.* Thus, you state a man's timeless essence in temporal terms if, instead of calling him "by nature a criminal," you say, "he will end on the gallows."

Metaphysically, this formal principle gets its best-rounded expression in the Aristotelian *entelechy,* which classifies a thing by conceiving of its kind according to the perfection (that is, finishedness) of which that kind is capable. Man is a "rational animal," for instance, not in the sense that he is immune to irrational motives, but in the sense that the perfection of humankind is in the order of rationality (an order or finishedness which one would not apply to things incapable of Logos, the Word).

Such thinking was probably itself a translation of narrative terms into "timeless" ones (as the Homeric ways of essentializing in terms of act and image eventually became transformed into the high generalizations of philosophy). But once we have a mature set of such abstract fixities (which are "fixities" in the sense that the "laws" or "principles" of motion do not themselves move, if they are stated abstractly enough), we can turn the matter around; and thus, whereas the philosophic expressions were later translations of the earlier narrative ones, we may look upon narrative expressions as translations of philosophic ones. By such heuristic reversal, we note how the imagery of death could be a narrative equivalent of the Aristotelian entelechy. For the poet could define the essence of a motive narratively or dramatically (in terms of a *history*) by showing how that motive *ended:* the maturity or fulfillment of a motive, its "perfection" or "finishedness," if translated into the terms of tragic outcome, would entail the identifying of that motive with a narrative figure whose acts led to some fitting form of *death.* By its fruition, we should judge it. In this respect, the Christian injunction to lead the "dying life" is itself a formula that translates the Aristotelian entelechy into its tragic equivalent; for in both the speculative and the tragic expressions, there is the same underlying Grammatical principle, the defining of an essence in terms of the *end* (the *perfection* being by the same token *death,* quite as the attaining of a given end marks the death of such efforts as went with the attaining of that end). The relations among our words "define," "determine," "termination," suggest the same ambiguities and possibilities of conversion. Taking a hint from the English translation of Richard Strauss's tone poem, *Death and Transfiguration,* we might say that the tragic dignifying of a motive is got by identifying it with death *as* transfiguration.

In sum: When considering "the temporizing of essence" in the *Grammar,* we were both put on the trail and misled somewhat by the suggestions in the word "prior." Following its leads, we saw how the search for "logical" priority can, when translated into temporal, or narrative terms, be expressed in the imagery of "regression to child-hood," or in other imagery or ideas of things past. This concern with the statement of essence in terms of *origins* (ancestry) caused us to overlook the exactly opposite resource, the statement of essence in terms of *culminations* (where the narrative notion of "how it all ends up" does serve for the logically reductive notion of "what it all boils down to"). In either choice (the ancestral or the final) the narrative terminology provides for a *personalizing* of essence. Along similar lines we may note that the imagery of adult illness (*e.g.* Mann's use of the tuberculosis sanitarium in *Tristan* and *The Magic Mountain*) may serve particularly well as a narrative terminology of essence in that it combines both "regressive" and "culminative" principles of identifica-tion. For the adult patients, in being constantly nursed and cared for, are in a condition that harks back to the "priority" of childhood, and at the same time they are tragically under the culminative sign of death.

"Tragic" Terms for Personality Types

So universally felt is the Grammatical principle behind the defining of essence in terms of death, or tragic end, that in our pseudoscientific days, when the cult of questionnaires has developed its own peculiar unction, perhaps one might come closer to an accurate classifying of "personality types" if he worked out a system of "tragic" categories. Surely, for instance, the person who chooses to end his life by violence thereby distinguishes himself from those late Romans who preferred cutting their veins and bleeding to death in a warm bath. And the end of Milton's Samson differs from the end of Arnold's Empedocles quite as Milton differs from Arnold.

But perhaps to get the most generalized approach to such classifica-tion, while still keeping it in the *narrative* terminology of definition, our hypothetical neotragic categorist should greatly broaden the ques-tion of human endings. He should hire a batch of poets; and instead of putting them to work, as is usually the case now, on the avid imagin-ing of reasons why our citizenry should intensely yearn for all sorts of manufactured and "processed" things (a narrow but unending suc-cession of ends) he should commission them to fully realize, for the average middle-class audience, all the different ways in which, it is thought, the world itself might end.   Surely, it would not take much to distinguish between the character of a person who foresaw a world ending "not with a bang but a whimper," and one who feared some mighty holocaust, as were the planets ripped into smithereens by explosions from within.   Or contrast the medieval imagery of the mighty burning with many modern scientists' pale preference for the "heat death," according to the principle of inturning, or entropy, whereby the earlier potency of matter must finally dwindle into a universal, uniform impotence.   Those who thought of a lethal gas that, wandering through space, stealthily enveloped the earth would be quite different from those obsessed by thoughts of huge astral collisions, or from those who worried lest our sun suddenly burst forth as a Nova, so intense in its new activity that even Neptune and Pluto would be scorched.   People would here spontaneously classify themselves; for by reason of the "scene-agent ratio" [1] the individual can identify himself with the character of a surrounding situation, translating one into terms of the other; hence a shift to a grander order, the shift from thoughts of one's own individual end to thoughts of a universal end, would still contrive to portray the character of the individual, even while acquiring greater resonance and scope and enabling men to transcend too local a view of themselves.

Perhaps our plans here are too ambitious. We can at least claim, as remote members of our "neotragic" school of ethnic classification, certain modern biologists who propose to classify plant species according to differences in response to various kinds of mutilation (though such science perhaps has a trace of that purely *sadistic* motive which usually obscures our understanding of tragedy itself today).

Recapitulation

First, we noted Milton's identification with Samson, who was identified with God.   Then we noted the identification of Royalists with Philistines and Puritans with Israelites.   Next we noted the poet's opportunity to conquer ritualistically by writing a poem that used these identifications, whereas actually Milton as citizen was frustrate.

[1] See *A Grammar of Motives,* notably pages 7-9.

Next, while recognizing that the reflexive nature of Samson's act amounted to suicide, we noted how the dramatic identification of this motive contains other important strands. Such thoughts led us to consider the *proportions* of a motivational recipe: one cannot simply reduce the totality to the suicidal "gist" and feel that one has done justice to the motivation as a whole. The point was made clearer by contrasting *Samson Agonistes* with the imagery of self-immolation in Matthew Arnold. We noted modalities of holy war in Milton, as contrasted with modalities near to Pater and Wilde in Arnold.

Then, by quoting lines from Coleridge that make murder and suicide interchangeable, we went beyond imagery, to the subject of transformation in general. Thus we gave a list of other paired images, that might serve as well as Life and Death for localizing or dramatizing the principle of transformation. And we noted that killing, being killed, and the killing of the self might all localize the same principle of transformation.

However, there was one respect in which the imagery of killing was especially apt here. The depicting of a thing's *end* may be a dramatic way of identifying its *essence*. This Grammatical "Thanatopsis" would be a narrative equivalent of the identification in terms of a thing's "finishedness" we find in the Aristotelian "entelechy."

Then, in an aside, as an illustrative conceit, we proposed a project whereby personality types be defined in terms of the world's end, depending upon the type of such "eschatological" imagery with which a given person most readily identified himself.

All told, we would take care of two contrary purposes here. We would find ways of transcending the imagery of killing that pervades our opening anecdote. At the same time, we do not want to ignore the import of the imagery in its own right, first as needed for characterizing a given motivational recipe, and second for its rhetorical effect upon an audience.

Imagery at Face Value

Taken simply at its face value, imagery invites us to respond in accordance with its nature. Thus, an adolescent, eager to "grow up," is trained by our motion pictures to meditate much on the imagery of brutality and murder, as the most noteworthy signs of action in an ideal or imaginary adult world. By the time he is fifteen, he has "witnessed" more violence than most soldiers or gunmen experience in a lifetime. And he has "participated in" all this imagery, "empathically reënacting" it. Thus initiated, he might well think of "growing up" (that is, of "transformation") in such excessive terms. His awareness of himself as a developing person requires a vocabulary—and the images of brutality and violence provide such a vocabulary, with a simple recipe for the perfecting or empowering of the self by the punishing and slaying of troublesome motives as though they were wholly external. One can surely expect such imagery to have sinister effects, particularly in view of the fact that the excessive *naturalism* of modern photographic art presents the violence, as nearly as possible, without formal devices that bring out the purely *artistic* or *fictive* nature of such art. There is no difference, in photographic style, between the filming of a murder mystery and the filming of a "documentary." Nor should we forget the possible bad effect of the many devices whereby such brutality is made "virtuous," through dramatic pretexts that justify it in terms of retaliation and righteous indignation.

Our objections arise when certain kinds of speculation (often of psychoanalytic cast) unwittingly exemplify these same sinister trends. By itself stressing the primacy of vengeance and slaughter as motives (and looking upon friendly or ethical motives purely as a kind of benign fiction for harnessing these more nearly "essential" impulses), such thought is really more like the *forerunner* of modern militarism than its *critic*. And often the analysts will show such zeal, in behalf of "killing" as the essential motive, that they will seek many ingenious ways of showing that a work was motivated by the desire to slay some parental figure who suffered no such fate at all, in the imagery of the plot as interpreted on its face. They apparently assume that to show "unconscious" parricidal implications in a motive is by the same token to establish parricide as *the* motive. Where a play is explicitly about parricide, one might feel some justification in complaining if we would see behind it merely the choice of a parental symbol to represent some motivation not intrinsically parricidal at all, but using parental identifications as "imagined accidents" that personify it. But whatever may be the objections in such cases, they would not apply at all in cases where there is no explicit imagery of parricide, and one must by exegesis hunt out parricide as motive. Why, one may then ask, must an imagery of parricide be taken as essential, as primary, as the true designation of the ultimate motive? And we, of course, would similarly ask: why must *any* imagery of killing, even when explicit, be taken as ultimate, rather than as an "opportunistic" terminology for specifying or localizing a principle of motivation "prior" to *any imagery,* either scenic or personal?

That is, we can recognize that our anecdote is in the order of killing, of personal enmity, of factional strife, of invective, polemic, eristic, logomachy, all of them aspects of rhetoric that we are repeatedly and drastically encountering, since rhetoric is *par excellence* the region of the Scramble, of insult and injury, bickering, squabbling, malice and the lie, cloaked malice and the subsidized lie. Yet while admitting that the genius of our opening anecdote has malign inclinations, we can, without forcing, find benign elements there too. And we should find these; for rhetoric also includes resources of appeal ranging from sacrificial, evangelical love, through the kinds of persuasion figuring in sexual love, to sheer "neutral" *communication* (communication being the area where love has become so generalized, desexualized, "technologized," that only close critical or philosophic scrutiny can discern the vestiges of the original motive).

Identification

We considered, among those "uses" to which *Samson Agonistes* was put, the poet's identification with a blind giant who slew himself in slaying enemies of the Lord; and we saw identification between Puritans and Israelites, Royalists and Philistines, identification allowing for a ritualistic kind of historiography in which the poet could, by allusion to a Biblical story, "substantially" foretell the triumph of his vanquished faction. Then we came upon a more complicated kind of identification: here the poet presents a motive in an essentially magnified or perfected form, in some way tragically purified or transcended; the imagery of death reduces the motive to *ultimate* terms, dramatic equivalent for an "entelechial" pattern of thought whereby a thing's nature would be classed according to the fruition, maturing, or ideal fulfillment, proper to its kind.

As seen from this point of view, then, an imagery of slaying (slaying of either the self or another) is to be considered merely as a special case of identification in general. Or otherwise put: the imagery of slaying is a special case of transformation, and transformation involves the ideas and imagery of *identification*. That is: the *killing* of something is the *changing* of it, and the statement of the thing's nature before and after the change is an *identifying* of it.

Perhaps the quickest way to make clear what we are doing here is to show what difference it makes. Noting that tragic poets identify motives in terms of killing, one might deduce that "they are essentially killers." Or one might deduce that "they are essentially identifiers." Terms for identification in general are wider in scope than terms for killing. We are proposing that our rhetoric be reduced to this term of wider scope, with the term of narrower scope being treated as a species of it. We begin with an anecdote of killing, because invective, eristic, polemic, and logomachy are so pronounced an aspect of rhetoric. But we use a dialectical device (the shift to a higher level of generalization) that enables us to transcend the narrower implications of this imagery, even while keeping them clearly in view. We need never deny the presence of strife, enmity, faction as a characteristic motive of rhetorical expression. We need not close our eyes to their almost tyrannous ubiquity in human relations; we can be on the alert always to see how such temptations to strife are implicit in the institutions that condition human relationships; yet we can at the same time always look beyond this order, to the principle of identification in general, a terministic choice justified by the fact that the identifications in the order of love are also characteristic of rhetorical expression. We may as well be frank about it, since our frankness, if it doesn't convince, will at least serve another important purpose of this work: it will reveal a strategic resource of terminology. Being frank, then: Because of our choice, we can treat "war" as a *"special case of peace"* —not as a primary motive in itself, not as *essentially* real, but purely as a *derivative* condition, a *perversion*.

Identification and "Consubstantiality"

A is not identical with his colleague, B. But insofar as their interests are joined, A is *identified* with B. Or he may *identify himself* with B even when their interests are not joined, if he assumes that they are, or is persuaded to believe so.

Here are ambiguities of substance. In being identified with B, A is "substantially one" with a person other than himself. Yet at the same time he remains unique, an individual locus of motives. Thus he is both joined and separate, at once a distinct substance and consubstantial with another.

While consubstantial with its parents, with the "firsts" from which it is derived, the offspring is nonetheless apart from them. In this sense, there is nothing abstruse in the statement that the offspring both is and is not one with its parentage. Similarly, two persons may be identified in terms of some principle they share in common, an "identification" that does not deny their distinctness.

To identify A with B is to make A "consubstantial" with B. Accordingly, since our *Grammar of Motives* was constructed about "substance" as key term, the related rhetoric selects its nearest equivalent in the areas of persuasion and dissuasion, communication and polemic. And our third volume, *Symbolic of Motives,* should be built about *identity* as titular or ancestral term, the "first" to which all other terms could be reduced and from which they could then be derived or generated, as from a common spirit. The thing's *identity* would here be its uniqueness as an entity in itself and by itself, a demarcated unit having its own particular structure.

However, "substance" is an abstruse philosophic term, beset by a long history of quandaries and puzzlements. It names so paradoxical a function in men's systematic terminologies, that thinkers finally tried to abolish it altogether—and in recent years they have often persuaded themselves that they really did abolish it from their terminologies of motives. They abolished the *term,* but it is doubtful whether they can ever abolish the *function* of that term, or even whether they should *want* to. A doctrine of *consubstantiality,* either explicit or implicit, may be necessary to any way of life. For substance, in the old philosophies, was an *act;* and a way of life is an *acting-together;* and in acting together, men have common sensations, concepts, images, ideas, attitudes that make them *consubstantial*.

The *Grammar* dealt with the universal paradoxes of substance. It considered resources of placement and definition common to all thought. The *Symbolic* should deal with unique individuals, each its own peculiarly constructed act, or form. These unique "constitutions" being capable of treatment in isolation, the *Symbolic* should consider them primarily in their capacity as singulars, each a separate universe of discourse (though there are also respects in which they are consubstantial with others of their kind, since they can be classed with other unique individuals as joint participants in common principles, possessors of the same or similar properties).

The *Rhetoric* deals with the possibilities of classification in its *partisan* aspects; it considers the ways in which individuals are at odds with one another, or become identified with groups more or less at odds with one another.

Why "at odds," you may ask, when the titular term is "identification"? Because, to begin with "identification" is, by the same token, though roundabout, to confront the implications of *division*. And so, in the end, men are brought to that most tragically ironic of all divisions, or conflicts, wherein millions of cooperative acts go into the preparation for one single destructive act. We refer to that ultimate *disease* of cooperation: *war*. (You will understand war much better if you think of it, not simply as strife come to a head, but rather as a disease, or perversion of communion. Modern war characteristically requires a myriad of constructive acts for each destructive one; before each culminating blast there must be a vast network of interlocking operations, directed communally.)

Identification is affirmed with earnestness precisely because there is division. Identification is compensatory to division. If men were not apart from one another, there would be no need for the rhetorician to proclaim their unity. If men were wholly and truly of one substance, absolute communication would be of man's very essence. It would not be an ideal, as it now is, partly embodied in material conditions and partly frustrated by these same conditions; rather, it would be as natural, spontaneous, and total as with those ideal prototypes of communication, the theologian's angels, or "messengers."

The *Grammar* was at peace insofar as it contemplated the paradoxes common to all men, the universal resources of verbal placement. The *Symbolic* should be at peace, in that the individual substances, or entities, or constituted acts are there considered in their uniqueness, hence outside the realm of conflict. For individual universes, as such, do not compete. Each merely *is*, being its own self-sufficient realm of discourse. And the *Symbolic* thus considers each thing as a set of interrelated terms all conspiring to round out their identity as participants in a common substance of meaning. An individual does in actuality compete with other individuals. But within the rules of Symbolic, the individual is treated merely as a self-subsistent unit proclaiming its peculiar nature. It is "at peace," in that its terms *cooperate* in modifying one another. But insofar as the individual is involved in conflict with other individuals or groups, the study of this same individual would fall under the head of *Rhetoric*. Or considered rhetorically, the victim of a neurotic conflict is torn by parliamentary wrangling; he is heckled like Hitler within. (Hitler is said to have confronted a constant wrangle in his private deliberations, after having imposed upon his people a flat choice between conformity and silence.) Rhetorically, the neurotic's every attempt to legislate for his own conduct is disorganized by rival factions within his own dissociated self. Yet, considered Symbolically, the same victim is technically "at peace," in the sense that his identity is like a unified, mutually adjusted set of terms. For even antagonistic terms, confronting each other as parry and thrust, can be said to "cooperate" in the building of an over-all form.

The *Rhetoric* must lead us through the Scramble, the Wrangle of the Market Place, the flurries and flare-ups of the Human Barnyard, the Give and Take, the wavering line of pressure and counterpressure, the Logomachy, the onus of ownership, the Wars of Nerves, the War. It too has its peaceful moments: at times its endless competition can add up to the transcending of itself. In ways of its own, it can move from the factional to the universal. But its ideal culminations are more often beset by strife as the condition of their organized expression, or material embodiment. Their very universality becomes transformed into a partisan weapon. For one need not scrutinize the concept of "identification" very sharply to see, implied in it at every turn, its ironic counterpart: division. Rhetoric is concerned with the state of Babel after the Fall. Its contribution to a "sociology of knowledge" must often carry us far into the lugubrious regions of malice and the lie.

The Identifying Nature of Property

Metaphysically, a thing is identified by its *properties*. In the realm of Rhetoric, such identification is frequently by property in the most materialistic sense of the term, economic property, such property as Coleridge, in his "Religious Musings," calls a

> twy-streaming fount,
> Whence Vice and Virtue flow, honey and gall.

And later:

> From Avarice thus, from Luxury and War
> Sprang heavenly Science; and from Science, Freedom.

Coleridge, typically the literary idealist, goes one step further back, deriving "property" from the workings of "Imagination." But meditations upon the dual aspects of property as such are enough for our present purposes. In the surrounding of himself with properties that name his number or establish his identity, man is ethical. ("Avarice" is but the scenic word "property" translated into terms of an agent's attitude, or incipient act.) Man's moral growth is organized through properties, properties in goods, in services, in position or status, in citizenship, in reputation, in acquaintanceship and love. But however ethical such an array of identifications may be when considered in itself, its relation to other entities that are likewise forming their identity in terms of property can lead to turmoil and discord. Here is *par excellence* a topic to be considered in a rhetoric having "identification" as its key term. And we see why one should expect to get much insight from Marxism, as a study of capitalistic rhetoric. Veblen is also, from this point of view, to be considered a theorist of rhetoric. (And we know of no better way to quickly glimpse the range of rhetoric than to read, in succession, the articles on "Property" and "Propaganda" in *The Encyclopaedia of the Social Sciences*.)

Bentham's utilitarian analysis of language, treating of the ways in which men find "eulogistic coverings" for their "material interests," is thus seen to be essentially rhetorical, and to bear directly upon the motives of property as a rhetorical factor. Indeed, since it is so clearly a matter of rhetoric to persuade a man by identifying your cause with his interests, we note the ingredient of rhetoric in the animal experimenter's ways of conditioning, as animals that respond avidly at a food signal suggest, underlying even human motives, the inclination, like a house dog, to seek salvation in the Sign of the Scraped Plate. But the lessons of this "animal rhetoric" can mislead, as we learn from the United States' attempts to use food as an instrument of policy in Europe after the war. These efforts met with enough ill will to suggest that the careful "screening" of our representatives, to eliminate reformist tendencies as far as possible and to identify American aid only with conservative or even reactionary interests, practically *guaranteed* us a dismal rhetoric in our dealings with other nations. And when Henry Wallace, during a trip abroad, began earning for our country the genuine good will of Europe's common people and intellectual classes, the Genius of the Screening came into its own: our free press, as at one signal, began stoutly assuring the citizens of both the United States and Europe that Wallace did not truly represent us. What did represent us, presumably, was the policy of the Scraped Plate, which our officialdom now and then bestirred themselves to present publicly in terms of a dispirited "idealism," as heavy as a dead elephant. You see, we were not to be identified with very resonant things; our press assured our people that the outcome of the last election had been a "popular mandate" to this effect. (We leave this statement unrevised. For the conditions of Truman's reëlection, after a campaign in which he out-Wallaced Wallace, corroborated it "in principle.")

In pure identification there would be no strife. Likewise, there would be no strife in absolute separateness, since opponents can join battle only through a mediatory ground that makes their communication possible, thus providing the first condition necessary for their interchange of blows. But put identification and division ambiguously together, so that you cannot know for certain just where one ends and the other begins, and you have the characteristic invitation to rhetoric. Here is a major reason why rhetoric, according to Aristotle, "proves opposites." When two men collaborate in an enterprise to which they contribute different kinds of services and from which they derive different amounts and kinds of profit, who is to say, once and for all, just where "cooperation" ends and one partner's "exploitation" of the other begins? The wavering line between the two cannot be "scientifically" identified; rival rhetoricians can draw it at different places, and their persuasiveness varies with the resources each has at his command. (Where public issues are concerned, such resources are not confined to the intrinsic powers of the speaker and the speech, but depend also for their effectiveness upon the purely technical means of communication, which can either aid the utterance or hamper it. For a "good" rhetoric neglected by the press obviously cannot be so "communicative" as a poor rhetoric backed nation-wide by headlines. And often we must think of rhetoric not in terms of some one particular address, but as a general *body of identifications* that owe their convincingness much more to trivial repetition and dull daily reënforcement than to exceptional rhetorical skill.)

If you would praise God, and in terms that happen also to sanction one system of material property rather than another, you have forced Rhetorical considerations upon us. If you would praise science, however exaltedly, when that same science is at the service of imperialist-militarist expansion, here again you bring things within the orbit of Rhetoric. For just as God has been identified with a certain worldly structure of ownership, so science may be identified with the interests of certain groups or classes quite *unscientific* in their purposes. Hence, however "pure" one's motives may be actually, the impurities of identification lurking about the edges of such situations introduce a typical Rhetorical wrangle of the sort that can never be settled once and for all, but belongs in the field of moral controversy where men properly seek to "prove opposites."

Thus, when his friend, Preen, wrote of a meeting where like-minded colleagues would be present and would all be proclaiming their praise of science, Prone answered: "You fail to mention another colleague who is sure to be there too, unless you take care to rule him out. I mean John Q. Militarist-Imperialist." Whereat, Preen: "This John Q. Militarist-Imperialist must be quite venerable by now. I seem to have heard of him back in Biblical times, before Roger B. Science was born. Doesn't he get in everywhere, unless he is explicitly ruled out?" He does, thanks to the ways of identification, which are in accordance with the nature of property. And the rhetorician and the moralist become one at that point where the attempt is made to reveal the undetected presence of such an identification. Thus in the United States after the second World War, the temptations of such an identification became particularly strong because so much scientific research had fallen under the direction of the military. To speak merely in praise of science, without explicitly dissociating oneself from its reactionary implications, is to identify oneself with these reactionary implications by default. Many reputable educators could thus, in this roundabout way, *function* as "conspirators." In their zeal to get federal subsidies for the science department of their college or university, they could help to shape educational policies with the ideals of war as guiding principle.

Identification and the "Autonomous"

As regards "autonomous" activities, the principle of Rhetorical identification may be summed up thus: The fact that an activity is capable of reduction to intrinsic, autonomous principles does not argue that it is free from identification with other orders of motivation extrinsic to it. Such other orders are extrinsic to it, as considered from the standpoint of the specialized activity alone. But they are not extrinsic to the field of moral action as such, considered from the standpoint of human activity in general. The human agent, *qua* human agent, is not motivated solely by the principles of a specialized activity, however strongly this specialized power, in its suggestive role as imagery, may affect his character. Any specialized activity participates in a larger unit of action. "Identification" is a word for the autonomous activity's place in this wider context, a place with which the agent may be unconcerned. The shepherd, *qua* shepherd, acts for the good of the sheep, to protect them from discomfiture and harm. But he may be "identified" with a project that is raising the sheep for market.

Of course, the principles of the autonomous activity can be considered irrespective of such identifications. Indeed, two students, sitting side by side in a classroom where the principles of a specialized subject are being taught, can be expected to "identify" the subject differently, so far as its place in a total context is concerned. Many of the most important identifications for the specialty will not be established at all, until later in life, when the specialty has become integrally interwoven with the particulars of one's livelihood. The specialized activity itself becomes a different thing for one person, with whom it is a means of surrounding himself with family and amenities, than it would be for another who, unmarried, childless, loveless, might find in the specialty not so much a means to gratification as a substitute for lack of gratification.

Carried into unique cases, such concern with identifications leads to the sheer "identities" of Symbolic. That is, we are in pure Symbolic when we concentrate upon one particular integrated structure of motives. But we are clearly in the region of rhetoric when considering the identifications whereby a specialized activity makes one a participant in some social or economic class. "Belonging" in this sense is rhetorical. And, ironically, with much college education today in literature and the fine arts, the very stress upon the pure autonomy of such activities is a roundabout way of identification with a privileged class, as the doctrine may enroll the student stylistically under the banner of a privileged class, serving as a kind of social insignia promising preferment. (We are here obviously thinking along Veblenian lines.)

The stress upon the importance of autonomous principles does have its good aspects. In particular, as regards the teaching of literature, the insistence upon "autonomy" reflects a vigorous concern with the all-importance of the text that happens to be under scrutiny. This cult of patient textual analysis (though it has excesses of its own) is helpful as a reaction against the excesses of extreme historicism (a leftover of the nineteenth century) whereby a work became so subordinated to its background that the student's appreciation of first-rate texts was lost behind his involvement with the collateral documents of fifth-rate literary historians. Also, the stress upon the autonomy of fields is valuable methodologically; it has been justly praised because it gives clear insight into some particular set of principles; and such a way of thinking is particularly needed now, when pseudoscientific thinking has become "unprincipled" in its uncritical cult of "facts." But along with these sound reasons for a primary concern with the intrinsic, there are furtive temptations that can figure here too. For so much progressive and radical criticism in recent years has been concerned with the social implications of art, that affirmations of art's autonomy can often become, by antithesis, a roundabout way of identifying oneself with the interests of political conservatism. In accordance with the rhetorical principle of identification, whenever you find a doctrine of "nonpolitical" esthetics affirmed with fervor, look for its politics.

But the principle of autonomy does allow for historical shifts whereby the nature of an identification can change greatly. Thus in his book, *The Genesis of Plato's Thought,* David Winspear gives relevant insight into the aristocratic and conservative political trends with which Plato's philosophy was identified at the time of its inception. The Sophists, on the other hand, are shown to have been more closely allied with the rising business class, then relatively "progressive" from the Marxist point of view, though their position was fundamentally weakened by the fact that their enterprise was based on the acceptance of slavery. Yet at other periods in history the Platonist concern with an ideal state could itself be identified with wholly progressive trends.

During the second World War many good writers who had previously complained of the Marxist concern with propaganda in art, themselves wrote books in which they identified their esthetic with an anti-Fascist politics. At the very least such literature attributed to Hitlerite Germans and their collaborators the brutal and neurotic motives which in former years had been attributed to "Everyman." (Glenway Wescott's *Apartment in Athens,* for instance.) So the overgeneralized attempt to discredit *Marxist* Rhetoric by discrediting *all* Rhetoric was abandoned, at least by representative reviewers whose criticism was itself a rhetorical act designed to identify the public with anti-Fascist attitudes and help sell anti-Fascist books (as it later contributed to the forming of anti-Soviet attitudes and the sale of anti-Soviet books). In the light of such developments, many critics have become only too accommodating in their search for covert and overt identifications that link the "autonomous" field of the arts with political and economic orders of motivation. Head-on resistance to the questioning of "purity" in specialized activities usually comes now from another quarter: the liberal apologists of science.

The "Autonomy" of Science

Science, as mere instrument (agency), might be expected to take on the nature of the scenes, acts, agents, and purposes with which it is identified. And insofar as a faulty political structure perverts human relations, we might reasonably expect to find a correspondingly perverted science. Thus, even the apologists of the Church will grant that, in corrupt times, there is a corresponding corruption among churchmen; and it is relevant to recall those specialists whose technical training fitted them to become identified with mass killings and experimentally induced sufferings in the concentration camps of National Socialist Germany. Hence, insofar as there are similar temptations in our own society (as attested by the sinister imagery of its art), might we not expect similar motives to lurk about the edges of our sciences (though tempered in proportion as the sinister political motives themselves are tempered in our society, under our less exacting social and economic conditions)? But liberal apologetics indignantly resists any suggestion that sadistic motives may lurk behind unnecessary animal experiments that cause suffering. The same people who, with reference to the scientific horrors of Hitlerism, admonish against the ingredients of Hitlerite thinking in our own society, will be outraged if you follow out the implications of their own premises, and look for similar temptations among our specialists.

One can sympathize with this anxiety. The liberal is usually disinclined to consider such possibilities because applied science is for him not a mere set of instruments and methods, whatever he may assert; it is a *good* and *absolute,* and is thus circuitously endowed with the philosophic function of *God* as the grounding of values. His thinking thus vacillates indeterminately between his overt claims for science as sheer method, as sheer coefficient of power, and his covert claims for science as a substance which, like God, would be an intrinsically *good* power. Obviously, any purely secular power, such as the applications of technology, would not be simply "good," but could become identified with motives good, bad, or indifferent, depending upon the uses to which it was put, and upon the ethical attitudes that, as part of the context surrounding it, contributed to its meaning in the realm of motives and action.

The unavowed identification, whereby a theological *function* is smuggled into a term on its face wholly secular, can secretly reënforce the characteristically liberal principle of occupational autonomy, itself reënforced by the naïvely pragmatist notion that practical specialized work is a sufficient grounding of morality. If the technical expert, as such, is assigned the task of perfecting new powers of chemical, bacteriological, or atomic destruction, his morality *as technical expert* requires only that he apply himself to his task as effectively as possible. The question of what the new force might mean, as released into a social texture emotionally and intellectually unfit to control it, or as surrendered to men whose *specialty* is *professional killing*—well, that is simply "none of his business," as specialist, however great may be his misgivings as father of a family, or as citizen of his nation and of the world. The extreme division of labor under late capitalist liberalism having made dispersion the norm and having transformed the state of Babel into an ideal, the true liberal must view almost as an affront the Rhetorical concern with identifications whereby the principles of a specialty cannot be taken on their face, simply as the motives proper to that specialty. They *are* the motives proper to the specialty *as such,* but not to the specialty as *participant in a wider context of motives.*

In sum, as regards tests of "autonomy," the specialist need only consider, as a disciplinary factor, the objective resistances supplied by the materials with which he works. The liberal criterion was that propounded by Rousseau in *Émile:* the principle of constraint was to come from the nature of *things,* not from authorities and their precepts. Yet, willy nilly, a science takes on the moral qualities of the political or social movements with which it becomes identified. Hence, a new anguish, a crisis in the liberal theory of science. In his *Genealogy of Morals,* Nietzsche met the same problem keenly, but perversely, by praising "autonomy" as the *opposite* of the moral. Modern political authoritarianism, like the earlier theocratic kinds, would subordinate the autonomous specialty to over-all doctrinal considerations. The rhetorical concept of "identification" does not justify the excesses to which such doctrinaire tendencies can be carried. But it does make clear the fact that one's morality as a specialist cannot be allowed to do duty for one's morality as a citizen. Insofar as the two roles are at odds, a specialty at the service of sinister interests will itself become sinister.

"Redemption" in Post-Christian Science

With a culture formed about the idea of redemption by the sacrifice of a Crucified Christ, just what does happen in an era of post-Christian science, when the ways of socialization have been secularized? Does the need for the vicarage of this Sacrificial King merely dwindle away? Or must some other person or persons, individual or corporate, real or fictive, take over the redemptive role? Not all people, perhaps, seek out a Vessel to which will be ritualistically delegated a purgative function, in being symbolically laden with the burdens of individual and collective guilt. But we know, as a lesson of recent history, how anti-Semitism provided the secularized replica of the Divine Scapegoat in the post-Christian rationale of Hitler's National Socialist militarism; and we know how Jews and other minority groups are thus magically identified by many members of our society. And since we also know that there are at large in the modern world many militaristic and economic trends quite like those of Germany under the Hitlerite "science" of genocide, we should at least be admonished to expect, in some degree, similar cultural temptations. For the history of the Nazis has clearly shown that there are cultural situations in which scientists, whatever may be their claims to professional austerity, will contrive somehow to identify their specialty with modes of justification, or socialization, not discernible in the sheer motions of the material operations themselves. In its transcendence of natural living, its technical scruples, its special tests of purity, a clinic or laboratory can be a kind of secular temple, in which ritualistic devotions are taking place, however concealed by the terminology of the surface. Unless properly scrutinized for traces of witchcraft, these could furtively become devotions to a satanic order of motives. At least such was the case with the technological experts of Hitlerite Germany. The very scientific ideals of an "impersonal" terminology can contribute ironically to such disaster: for it is but a step from treating inanimate nature as mere "things" to treating animals, and then enemy peoples, as mere things. But they are not mere things, they are persons—and in the systematic denial of what one knows in his heart to be the truth, there is a perverse principle that can generate much anguish.

Dual Possibilities of Science

But one cannot be too careful here. Religion politics, and economics are notoriously touchy subjects, and with many persons today, the cult of applied science has the animus of all three rolled into one. We should take pains to make this clear: we are most decidedly *not* saying that science *must* take on such malign identifications as it presumably has, for some scientists, when fitted into the motives of a Fascist state. In the United States, for instance, the Federation of American Scientists has been urgently seeking to dissociate the idea of atomic war power from the idea of national security. Thus, the Federation proclaimed, in a statement issued September 1, 1947, on the second anniversary of V-J Day:

Many persons have justified the support of science for its war potential, implying that national security will result. We hear this justification in Congress. We hear it even from the atomic mission. We assert that national security cannot result from military preparedness or the support of science for its war potential.

When men are of good will, we can always expect many such efforts to break such sinister identifications, which their knowledge of their special field enables them to recognize as false.

Unfortunately, good will as thus circumscribed is not enough. The same statement goes on to say: "Our Government has advocated a sound policy in the United Nations concerning atomic energy." Yet there seems much justice in the complaint of the Soviet delegates that the measures we propose would guarantee the United States perpetual superiority in this field, unless other nations deliberately violated the proposed treaty by finding ways to continue their experiments in secret.

In a speech made before the United Nations Atomic Energy Commission (Sept. 10, 1947), the Soviet representative, Gromyko, came upon some paradoxes in this connection. He was attacking United States' proposals for giving "the right of ownership" to an *international* organ of control. He contended that this arrangement would contradict the principle of state sovereignty. Thus the *socialist* delegate was arguing for the *restriction* of ownership to national boundaries, while the world's greatest *capitalist* country argued for ownership by a *universal* body. *On its face,* the capitalist proposal seems much nearer to the ideal socialist solution than the position of the Soviet Union is.

However, the history of corporate management in the United States, and of political parties everywhere, gives ample evidence of all the devices whereby *actual control* of a property differs from *nominal ownership* of it. And obviously the interests in *actual control* of the agency that allocated the rights and resources of atomic development could have all the advantages of *real* ownership, however international might be the *fictions* of ownership. Where the *control* resides, there resides the *function* of ownership, whatever the *fictions* of ownership may be. It would certainly be no new thing to rhetoric if highly *discriminatory* claims were here being protected in the name of *universal* rights. And the Soviet delegate was at least justified in calling for measures that *unmistakably* avoid such a possibility, which was not considered in the scientists' statement as published in the press. There was a hint of "maneuvering" in our proposals, maneuvering to put the Russians in the position of seeming to delay an adequate international control over the atomic bomb, when there were strong doubts whether our own Congress would itself have agreed to any such control.

Lying outside the orbit of the scientists' specialty, there are psychological considerations which are nearly always slighted, since they involve identifications manifestly extrinsic to atomic physics in itself. Possibilities of deception arise particularly with those ironies whereby the scientists' truly splendid terminology for the expert smashing of lifeless things can so catch a man's fancy that he would transfer it to the realm of human relations likewise. It is not a great step from the purely professional poisoning of harmful insects to the purely professional blasting and poisoning of human beings, as viewed in similarly "impersonal" terms. And such inducements are particularly there, so long as factional division (of class, race, nationality, and the like) make for the ironic mixture of identification and dissociation that marks the function of the scapegoat. Indeed, the very "global" conditions which call for the greater identification of all men with one another have at the same time increased the range of human conflict, the incentives to division. It would require sustained rhetorical effort, backed by the imagery of a richly humane and spontaneous poetry, to make us fully sympathize with people in circumstances greatly different from our own. Add now the international rivalries that goad to the opposite kind of effort, and that make it easy for some vocalizers to make their style "forceful" by simply playing up these divisive trends, and you see how perverted the austere scientific ideal may become, as released into a social texture unprepared for it.

The good will of scientists is not enough, however genuine it may be. There is the joke of the father who put his little son on the table and, holding out his arms protectively, said, "Jump." The trusting child jumped; but instead of catching him, the father drew back, and let him fall to the floor. The child was hurt, both physically and in this violation of its confidence. Whereupon the father drove home the moral: "Let that be a lesson to you. Never trust anyone, not even your own father." Now, when the apologists of science teach their subject thus, instead of merely exalting it, we can salute them for truly admonishing us, in being as "scientific" about the criticism of science as in the past they have been about the criticism of religion.

To sum up:

(1) We know, as a matter of record, that science under Fascism became sinister. (2) We are repeatedly being admonished that there is a high percentage of Fascist motivation in our own society. (3) Why, then, should there not be, in our society, a correspondingly high incentive to sinister science? Particularly inasmuch as sinister motives already show in much of our art, both popular and recondite, while the conditions of secrecy imposed upon many experimental scientists today add a "conspiratorial" motive to such "autonomous" activity. In the past, the great *frankness* of science has been its noblest attribute, as judged from the purely humanistic point of view. But any tendency to place scientific development primarily under the heading of "war potential" must endanger this essential moralistic element in science, replacing the norms of *universal clarity* with the divisive demands for *conspiracy*. Insofar as such conditions prevail, science loses the one ingredient that can keep it wholesome: its enrollment under the forces of *light*. To this extent, the scientist must reject and resist in ways that mean the end of "autonomy," or if he accepts, he risks becoming the friend of fiends. Scientific discoveries have always, of course, been used for the purposes of war. But the demand that scientific advance *per se* be guided by military considerations *changes the proportions* of such motivation tremendously. Scientists of good will must then become uneasy, in that the morality of their specialty is no longer enough. The liberal ideal of autonomy is denied them, except insofar as they can contrive to conceal from themselves the true implications of their role.

Ingenuous and Cunning Identifications

The thought of self-deception brings up another range of possibilities here. For there is a wide range of ways whereby the rhetorical motive, through the resources of identification, can operate without conscious direction by any particular agent. Classical rhetoric stresses the element of explicit design in rhetorical enterprise. But one can systematically extend the range of rhetoric, if one studies the persuasiveness of false or inadequate terms which may not be directly imposed upon us from without by some skillful speaker, but which we impose upon ourselves, in varying degrees of deliberateness and unawareness, through motives indeterminately self-protective and/or suicidal.

We shall consider these matters more fully later, when we study the rhetoric of *hierarchy* (or as it is less revealingly named, *bureaucracy*). And our later pages on Marx and Veblen would apply here. But for the present we might merely recall the psychologist's concept of "malingering," to designate the ways of neurotic persons who, though not actually ill, persuade themselves that they are, and so can claim the attentions and privileges of the ill (their feigned illness itself becoming, at one remove, genuine). Similarly, if a social or occupational class is not too exacting in the scrutiny of identifications that flatter its interests, its very philosophy of life is a profitable malingering (profitable at least until its inaccuracies catch up with it)—and as such, it is open to either attack or analysis, Rhetoric comprising both the *use* of persuasive resources (*rhetorica utens,* as with the philippics of Demosthenes) and the *study* of them (*rhetorica docens,* as with Aristotle's treatise on the "art" of Rhetoric).

This aspect of identification, whereby one can protect an interest merely by using terms not incisive enough to criticize it properly, often brings rhetoric to the edge of cunning. A misanthropic politician who dealt in mankind-loving imagery could still think of himself as rhetorically honest, if he meant to do well by his constituents yet thought that he could get their votes only by such display. Whatever the falsity in overplaying a role, there may be honesty in the assuming of that role itself; and the overplaying may be but a translation into a different medium of communication, a way of amplifying a statement so that it carries better to a large or distant audience. Hence, the persuasive identifications of Rhetoric, in being so directly designed for *use,* involve us in a special problem of *consciousness,* as exemplified in the Rhetorician's particular *purpose* for a given statement.

The thought gives a glimpse into rhetorical motives behind many characters in drama and fiction. Shakespeare's Iago and Molière's Tartuffe are demons of Rhetoric. Every word and act is addressed, being designed to build up false identifications in the minds of their victims. Similarly, there is a notable ingredient of Rhetoric in Stendhal's Julien Sorel, who combines "heightened consciousness" with "freedom" by a perversely frank decision to perfect his own kind of hypocrisy as a means of triumphing over the hypocrisy of others. All his actions thus become rhetorical, framed for their effect; his life is a spellbinding and spellbound address to an audience.

Did you ever do a friend an injury by accident, in all poetic simplicity? Then conceive of this same injury as done by sly design, and you are forthwith within the orbit of Rhetoric. If you, like the Stendhals and Gides, conceive a character by such sophistication, Rhetoric as the speaker's attempt to identify himself favorably with his audience then becomes so transformed that the work may seem to have been written under an esthetic of pure "expression," without regard for communicative appeal. Or it may appeal perversely, to warped motives within the audience. Or it may be but an internalizing of the rhetorical motive, as the very actions of such a representative figure take on a rhetorical cast. Hence, having woven a rhetorical motive so integrally into the very essence of his conception, the writer can seem to have ignored rhetorical considerations; yet, in the sheer effrontery of his protagonist there is embedded, however disguised or transformed, an *anguish* of communication (communication being, as we have said, a generalized form of love).

As regards the rhetorical ways of Stendhal's hero, moving in the perverse freedom of duplicity: After the disclosure of his cunning, Julien abandons his complex rhetorical morality of hypocrisy-to-outhypocritize-the-hypocrites, and regains a new, suicidally poetic level of simplicity. *"Jamais cette tête n'avait été aussi poétique qu'au moment où elle allait tomber."* The whole structure of the book could be explained as the account of a hero who, by the disclosure of his Rhetoric, was jolted into a tragically direct poetic. Within the terms of the novel, "hypocrisy" was the word for "rhetoric," such being the quality of the rhetoric that marked the public life of France under the reign of *Napoléon le Petit*.

Rhetoric of "Address" (to the Individual Soul)

By our arrangement, the individual in his uniqueness falls under the head of Symbolic. But one should not thereby assume that what is known as "individual psychology" wholly meets the same test. Particularly in the Freudian concern with the neuroses of individual patients, there is a strongly rhetorical ingredient. Indeed, what could be more profoundly rhetorical than Freud's notion of a dream that attains expression by stylistic subterfuges designed to evade the inhibitions of a moralistic censor? What is this but the exact analogue of the rhetorical devices of literature under political or theocratic censorship? The *ego* with its *id* confronts the *super-ego* much as an orator would confront a somewhat alien audience, whose susceptibilities he must flatter as a necessary step towards persuasion. The Freudian psyche is quite a parliament, with conflicting interests expressed in ways variously designed to take the claims of rival factions into account.

The best evidence of a strongly rhetorical ingredient in Freud's view of the psyche is in his analysis of *Wit and Its Relation to the Unconscious.* In particular, we think of Freud's concern with the role of an audience, or "third person," with whom the speaker establishes rapport, in their common enterprise directed against the butt of tendentious witticisms. Here is the purest rhetorical pattern: speaker and hearer as partners in partisan jokes made at the expense of another. If you "internalize" such a variety of motives, so that the same person can participate somewhat in all three positions, you get a complex individual of many voices. And though these may be treated, under the heading of Symbolic, as a concerto of principles mutually modifying one another, they may likewise be seen, from the standpoint of Rhetoric, as a parliamentary wrangle which the individual has put together somewhat as he puts together his fears and hopes, friendships and enmities, health and disease, or those tiny rebirths whereby, in being born to some new condition, he may be dying to a past condition, his development being dialectical, a series of terms in perpetual transformation.

Thus by a roundabout route we come upon another aspect of Rhetoric: its nature as *addressed,* since persuasion implies an audience. A man can be his own audience, insofar as he, even in his secret thoughts, cultivates certain ideas or images for the effect he hopes they may have upon him; he is here what Mead would call "an 'I' addressing its 'me' "; and in this respect he is being rhetorical quite as though he were using pleasant imagery to influence an outside audience rather than one within. In traditional Rhetoric, the relation to an external audience is stressed. Aristotle's *Art of Rhetoric,* for instance, deals with the appeal to audiences in this primary sense: It lists typical beliefs, so that the speaker may choose among them the ones with which he would favorably identify his cause or unfavorably identify the cause of an opponent; and it lists the traits of character with which the speaker should seek to identify himself, as a way of disposing an audience favorably towards him. But a modern "post-Christian" rhetoric must also concern itself with the thought that, under the heading of appeal to audiences, would also be included any ideas or images privately addressed to the individual self for moralistic or incantatory purposes. For you become your own audience, in some respects a very lax one, in some respects very exacting, when you become involved in psychologically stylistic subterfuges for presenting your own case to yourself in sympathetic terms (and even terms that seem harsh can often be found on closer scrutiny to be flattering, as with neurotics who visit sufferings upon themselves in the name of very high-powered motives which, whatever their discomfiture, feed pride).

Such considerations make us alert to the ingredient of rhetoric in all *socialization,* considered as a *moralizing* process. The individual person, striving to form himself in accordance with the communicative norms that match the cooperative ways of his society, is by the same token concerned with the rhetoric of identification. To act upon himself persuasively, he must variously resort to images and ideas that are formative. Education ("indoctrination") exerts such pressure upon him from without; he completes the process from within. If he does not somehow act to tell himself (as his own audience) what the various brands of rhetorician have told him, his persuasion is not complete. Only those voices from without are effective which can speak in the language of a voice within.

Among the Tanala of Madagascar, it is said, most of those tribesmen susceptible to *tromba* ("neurotic seizure indicated by an extreme desire to dance") were found to be among the least favored members of the tribe. Such seizures are said to be a device that makes the possessed person "the center of all the attention." And afterwards, the richest and most powerful members of the sufferer's family foot the bill, so that "the individual's ego is well satisfied and he can get along quite well until the next tromba seizure occurs." In sum, "like most hysterical seizures, tromba requires an audience."

The citations are from A. Kardiner, *The Individual and His Society* (New York: Columbia University Press). They would suggest that, when asking what all would fall within the scope of our topic, we could also include a "rhetoric of hysteria." For here too are expressions which are *addressed*—and we confront an ultimate irony, in glimpsing how even a catatonic lapse into sheer automatism, beyond the reach of all normally linguistic communication, is in its origins communicative, addressed, though it be a paralogical appeal-that-ends-all-appeals.

Rhetoric and Primitive Magic

The Kardiner citations are taken from a paper by C. Kluckhohn on "Navaho Witchcraft," containing observations that would also bring witchcraft within the range of rhetoric. Indeed, where witchcraft is imputed as a motive behind the individual search for wealth, power, or vengeance, can we not view it as a primitive vocabulary of *individualism* emerging in a culture where *tribal* thinking had been uppermost, so that the individualist motive would be admitted and suspect? And any breach of identification with the tribal norms being sinister, do we not glimpse rhetorical motives behind the fact that Macbeth's private ambitions were figured in terms of witches?

At first glance we may seem to be straining the conception of rhetoric to the breaking point, when including even a treatise on primitive witchcraft within its range. But look again. Precisely at a time when the *term* "rhetoric" had fallen into greatest neglect and disrepute, writers in the "social sciences" were, under many guises, making good contributions to the New Rhetoric. As usual with modern thought, the insights gained from *comparative culture* could throw light upon the classic approach to this subject; and again, as usual with modern thought, this light was interpreted in terms that concealed its true relation to earlier work. And though the present writer was strongly influenced by anthropological inquiries into primitive magic, he did not clearly discern the exact relation between the anthropologist's concern with magic and the literary critic's concern with communication until he had systematically worked on this *Rhetoric* for some years. Prior to this discovery, though he persisted in anthropological hankerings, he did so with a bad conscience; and he was half willing to agree with literary opponents who considered such concerns alien to the study of literature proper.

Now, in noting methodically how the anthropologist's account of magic can belong in a rhetoric, we are better equipped to see exactly wherein the two fields of inquiry diverge. Anthropology is a gain to literary criticism only if one knows how to "discount" it from the standpoint of rhetoric. And, ironically, anthropology can be a source of disturbance, not only to literary criticism in particular, but to the study of human relations in general, if one does not so discount it, but allows *its* terms to creep into one's thinking at points where issues *should* be studied explicitly in terms of rhetoric.

We saw both the respects in which the anthropologists' study of magic overlaps upon rhetoric and the respects in which they are distinct when we were working on a review of Ernst Cassirer's *Myth of the State*. The general proposition that exercised us can be stated as follows:

We must begin by confronting the typically scientist view of the relation between science and magic. Since so many apologists of modern science, following a dialectic of simple antithesis, have looked upon magic merely as an early form of bad science, one seems to be left only with a distinction between bad science and good science. Scientific knowledge is thus presented as a terminology that gives an accurate and critically tested description of reality; and magic is presented as antithetical to such science. Hence magic is treated as an early uncritical attempt to do what science does, but under conditions where judgment and perception were impaired by the naïvely anthropomorphic belief that the impersonal forces of nature were motivated by personal designs. One thus confronts a flat choice between a civilized vocabulary of scientific description and a savage vocabulary of magical incantation.

In this scheme, "rhetoric" has no systematic location. We recall noting the word but once in Cassirer's *Myth of the State,* and then it is used only in a random way; yet the book is really about nothing more nor less than a most characteristic concern of rhetoric: the manipulation of men's beliefs for political ends.

Now, the basic function of rhetoric, the use of words by human agents to form attitudes or to induce actions in other human agents, is certainly not "magical." If you are in trouble, and call for help, you are no practitioner of primitive magic. You are using the primary resource of human speech in a thoroughly realistic way. Nor, on the other hand, is your utterance "science," in the strict meaning of science today, as a "semantic" or "descriptive" terminology for charting the conditions of nature from an "impersonal" point of view, regardless of one's wishes or preferences. A call for help is quite "prejudiced"; it is the most arrant kind of "wishful thinking"; it is not merely descriptive, it is *hortatory*. It is not just trying to tell how things are, in strictly "scenic" terms; it is trying to *move people*. A call for help might, of course, include purely scientific statements, or preparations for action, as a person in need might give information about particular dangers to guard against or advantages to exploit in bringing help. But the call, in itself, as such, is not scientific; it is *rhetorical*. Whereas poetic language is a kind of symbolic action, for itself and in itself, and whereas scientific action is a preparation for action, rhetorical language is inducement to action (or to attitude, attitude being an incipient act).

If you have only a choice between magic and science, you simply have no bin in which to accurately place such a form of expression. Hence, since "the future" is not the sort of thing one can put under a microscope, or even test by a knowledge of *exactly equivalent conditions* in the past, when you turn to political exhortation, you are involved in decisions that necessarily lie beyond the strictly scientific vocabularies of description. And since the effective politician is a "spellbinder," it seems to follow by elimination that the hortatory use of speech for political ends can be called "magic," in the discredited sense of that term.

As a result, much analysis of political exhortation comes to look simply like a survival of primitive magic, whereas it should be handled in its own terms, as an aspect of what it really is: rhetoric. The approach to rhetoric in terms of "word magic" gets the whole subject turned backwards. Originally, the magical use of symbolism to affect natural processes by rituals and incantations was a mistaken transference of a proper linguistic function to an area for which it was not fit. The realistic use of addressed language to *induce action in people* became the magical use of addressed language to *induce motion in things* (things by nature alien to purely linguistic orders of motivation). If we then begin by treating this *erroneous* and *derived* magical use as *primary,* we are invited to treat a *proper* use of language (for instance, political persuasion) simply as a vestige of benightedly prescientific magic.

To be sure, the rhetorician has the tricks of his trade. But they are not mere "bad science"; they are an "art." And any overly scientist approach to them (treating them in terms of flat dialectical opposition to modern technology) must make our world look much more "neo-primitive" than is really the case. At the very least, we should note that primitive magic prevailed most strongly under social conditions where the rationalization of social effort in terms of money was negligible; but the rhetoric of modern politics would establish social identifications atop a way of life highly diversified by money, with the extreme division of labor and status which money served to rationalize.

Realistic Function of Rhetoric

Gaining courage as we proceed, we might even contend that we are not so much proposing to import anthropology into rhetoric as proposing that anthropologists recognize the factor of rhetoric in their own field. That is, if you look at recent studies of primitive magic from the standpoint of this discussion, you might rather want to distinguish between magic as "bad science" and magic as "primitive rhetoric." You then discover that anthropology does clearly recognize the rhetorical *function* in magic; and far from dismissing the rhetorical aspect of magic merely as bad science, anthropology recognizes in it a pragmatic device that greatly assisted the survival of cultures by promoting social cohesion. (Malinowski did much work along these lines, and the Kluckhohn essay makes similar observations about witchcraft.) But now that we have confronted the term "magic" with the term "rhetoric," we'd say that one comes closer to the true state of affairs if one treats the socializing aspects of magic as a "primitive rhetoric" than if one sees modern rhetoric simply as a "survival of primitive magic."

For rhetoric as such is not rooted in any past condition of human society. It is rooted in an essential function of language itself, a function that is wholly realistic, and is continually born anew; the use of language as a symbolic means of inducing cooperation in beings that by nature respond to symbols. Though rhetorical considerations may carry us far afield, leading us to violate the principle of autonomy separating the various disciplines, there is an intrinsically rhetorical motive, situated in the persuasive use of language. And this persuasive use of language is not derived from "bad science," or "magic." On the contrary, "magic" was a faulty derivation from it, "word magic" being an attempt to produce linguistic responses in kinds of beings not accessible to the linguistic motive. However, once you introduce this emendation, you can see beyond the accidents of language. You can recognize how much of value has been contributed to the New Rhetoric by these investigators, though their observations are made in terms that never explicitly confront the rhetorical ingredient in their field of study. We can place in terms of rhetoric all those statements by anthropologists, ethnologists, individual and social psychologists, and the like, that bear upon the *persuasive* aspects of language, the function of language as *addressed,* as direct or roundabout appeal to real or ideal audiences, without or within.

Are we but haggling over a term? In one sense, yes. We are offering a rationale intended to show how far one might systematically extend the term "rhetoric." In this respect, we are haggling over a term; for we must persist in tracking down the *function* of that term. But to note the ingredient of rhetoric lurking in such anthropologist's terms as "magic" and "witchcraft" is not to ask that the anthropologist replace his words with ours. We are certainly not haggling over terms in that sense. The term "rhetoric" is no substitute for "magic," "witchcraft," "socialization," "communication," and so on. But the term rhetoric designates a *function* which is present in the areas variously covered by those other terms. And we are asking only that this *function* be recognized for what it is: a linguistic function by nature as *realistic* as a proverb, though it may be quite far from the kind of realism found in strictly "scientific realism." For it is essentially a realism of the *act:* moral, persuasive—and acts are not "true" and "false" in the sense that the propositions of "scientific realism" are. And however "false" the "propositions" of primitive magic may be, considered from the standpoint of scientific realism, it is different with the peculiarly *rhetorical* ingredient in magic, involving ways of identification that contribute variously to social cohesion (either for the advantage of the community as a whole, or for the advantage of special groups whose interests are a burden on the community, or for the advantage of special groups whose rights and duties are indeterminately both a benefit and a tax on the community, as with some business enterprise in our society).

The "pragmatic sanction" for this function of magic lies outside the realm of strictly true-or-false propositions; it falls in an area of deliberation that itself draws upon the resources of rhetoric; it is itself a subject matter belonging to an art that can "prove opposites."

To illustrate what we mean by "proving opposites" here: we read an article, let us say, obviously designed to dispose the reading public favorably towards the "aggressive and expanding" development of American commercial interests in Saudi Arabia. It speaks admiringly of the tremendous changes which our policies of commerce and investment will introduce into a vestigially feudal culture, and of the great speed at which the rationale of finance and technology will accomplish these changes. When considering the obvious rhetorical intent of these "facts," we suddenly, in a perverse *non sequitur,* remember a passage in the Kluckhohn essay, involving what we would now venture to call "the rhetoric of witchcraft":

> In a society like the Navaho which is competitive and capitalistic, on the one hand, and still familistic on the other, any ideology which has the effect of slowing down economic mobility is decidedly adaptive. One of the most basic strains in Navaho society arises out of the incompatibility between the demands of familism and the emulation of European patterns in the accumulating of capital.

And in conclusion we are told that the "survival of the society" is assisted by "any pattern, such as witchcraft, which tends to discourage the rapid accumulation of wealth" (witchcraft, as an "ideology," contributing to this end by identifying new wealth with malign witchery). Now, when you begin talking about the optimum rate of speed at which cultural changes should take place, or the optimum proportion between tribal and individualistic motives that should prevail under a particular set of economic conditions, you are talking about something very important indeed, but you will find yourself deep in matters of rhetoric: for nothing is more rhetorical in nature than a deliberation as to what is too much or too little, too early or too late; in such controversies, rhetoricians are forever "proving opposites."

Where are we now? We have considered two main aspects of rhetoric: its use of *identification* and its nature as *addressed.* Since identification implies division, we found rhetoric involving us in matters of socialization and faction. Here was a wavering line between peace and conflict, since identification is got by property, which is ambivalently a motive of both morality and strife. And inasmuch as the ultimate of conflict is war or murder, we considered how such imagery can figure as a terminology of reidentification ("transformation" or "rebirth"). For in considering the wavering line between identification and division, we shall always be coming upon manifestations of the logomachy, avowed as in invective, unavowed as in stylistic subterfuges for presenting real divisions in terms that deny division.

We found that this wavering line between identification and division was forever bringing rhetoric against the possibility of malice and the lie; for if an identification favorable to the speaker or his cause is made to seem favorable to the audience, there enters the possibility of such "heightened consciousness" as goes with deliberate cunning. Thus, roundabout, we confronted the nature of rhetoric as *addressed* to audiences of the first, second, or third person. Socialization itself was, in the widest sense, found to be addressed. And by reason of such simultaneous identification-with and division-from as mark the choice of a scapegoat, we found that rhetoric involves us in problems related to witchcraft, magic, spellbinding, ethical promptings, and the like. And in the course of discussing these subjects, we found ourselves running into another term: persuasion. Rhetoric is the art of persuasion, or a study of the means of persuasion available for any given situation. We have thus, deviously, come to the point at which Aristotle begins his treatise on rhetoric.

So we shall change our purpose somewhat. Up to now, we have been trying to indicate what kinds of subject matter not traditionally labeled "rhetoric" should, in our opinion, also fall under this head. We would now consider varying views of rhetoric that have already prevailed; and we would try to "generate" them from the same basic terms of our discussion.

As for the relation between "identification" and "persuasion": we might well keep it in mind that a speaker persuades an audience by the use of stylistic identifications; his act of persuasion may be for the purpose of causing the audience to identify itself with the speaker's interests; and the speaker draws on identification of interests to establish rapport between himself and his audience. So, there is no chance of our keeping apart the meanings of persuasion, identification ("consubstantiality") and communication (the nature of rhetoric as "addressed"). But, in given instances, one or another of these elements may serve best for extending a line of analysis in some particular direction.

And finally: The use of symbols, by one symbol-using entity to induce action in another (persuasion properly addressed) is in essence not magical but *realistic*. However, the resources of identification whereby a sense of consubstantiality is symbolically established between beings of unequal status may extend far into the realm of the *idealistic*. And as we shall see later, when on the subject of order, out of this idealistic element there may arise a kind of magic or mystery that sets its mark upon all human relations.

PART Two

TRADITIONAL PRINCIPLES
OF RHETORIC

TRADITIONAL PRINCIPLES OF RHETORIC

Persuasion

"SPEECH designed to persuade" (*dicere ad persuadendum accommodate*): this is the basic definition for rhetoric (and its synonym, "eloquence,") given in Cicero's dialogue *De Oratore*. Crassus, who is spokesman for Cicero himself, cites it as something taken for granted, as the first thing the student of rhetoric is taught. Three hundred years before him, Aristotle's *Art of Rhetoric* had similarly named "persuasion" as the essence and end of rhetoric, which he defined as "the faculty of discovering the persuasive means available in a given case." Likewise, in a lost treatise, Aristotle's great competitor, Isocrates, called rhetoric "the craftsman of persuasion" (*peithous demiourgos*). Thus, at this level of generalization, even rivals could agree, though as De Quincey has remarked, "persuasion" itself can be differently interpreted.

Somewhat more than a century after Cicero, Quintilian, in his *Institutio Oratoria* changed the stress, choosing to define rhetoric as the "science of speaking well" (*bene dicendi scientia*).* But his system is clearly directed towards one particular kind of persuasion: the education of the Roman gentleman. Thus, in a chapter where he cites about two dozen definitions (two-thirds of which refer to "persuasion" as the essence of rhetoric), though he finally chooses a definition of his own which omits reference to persuasion, he has kept the *function* of the term. For he equates the perfect orator with the good man, and says that the good man should be exceptional in both eloquence and moral attributes. Rhetoric, he says, is both "useful" and a "virtue." Hence his notion of "speaking well" implies the moralistically hortatory, not just pragmatic skill at the service of any cause.

Add now the first great Christian rhetoric, the fourth book of St.

---

* He used the word "science" loosely. This definition is in Book II, Chapter XV. At the beginning of Book III he says he has shown rhetoric to be an "art."

Augustine's *De Doctrina Christiana* (written near the beginning of the fifth century) and you have ample material, in these four great peaks stretched across 750 years, to observe the major principles derivable from the notion of rhetoric as persuasion, as inducement to action, *ad agendum,* in the phrase of Augustine, who elsewhere, in the same book, states that a man is persuaded if

> he likes what you promise, fears what you say is imminent, hates what you censure, embraces what you commend, regrets whatever you built up as regrettable, rejoices at what you say is cause for rejoicing, sympathizes with those whose wretchedness your words bring before his very eyes, shuns those whom you admonish him to shun . . . and in whatever other ways your high eloquence can affect the minds of your hearers, bringing them not merely to know what should be done, but to do what they know should be done.

Yet often we could with more accuracy speak of persuasion "to attitude," rather than persuasion to out-and-out action. Persuasion involves choice, will; it is directed to a man only insofar as he is *free*. This is good to remember, in these days of dictatorship and near-dictatorship. Only insofar as men are potentially free, must the spellbinder seek to persuade them. Insofar as they *must* do something, rhetoric is unnecessary, its work being done by the nature of things, though often these necessities are not of a natural origin, but come from necessities imposed by man-made conditions, as with the kind of *peithananke* (or "compulsion under the guise of persuasion") that sometimes flows from the nature of the "free market."

Insofar as a choice of *action* is restricted, rhetoric seeks rather to have a formative effect upon *attitude* (as a criminal condemned to death might by priestly rhetoric be brought to an attitude of repentance and resignation). Thus, in Cicero and Augustine there is a shift between the words "move" (*movere*) and "bend" (*flectere*) to name the ultimate function of rhetoric. This shift corresponds to a distinction between act and attitude (attitude being an incipient act, a leaning or inclination). Thus the notion of persuasion to *attitude* would permit the application of rhetorical terms to purely *poetic* structures; the study of lyrical devices might be classed under the head of rhetoric, when these devices are considered for their power to induce or communicate states of mind to readers, even though the kinds of assent evoked have no overt, practical outcome.

All told, traditionally there is the range of rhetoric from an "Art of

Cheating" (as systematically "perfected" by some of the Greek Sophists) to Quintilian's view of rhetoric as a power, art or science that identifies right doing with right speaking.   Similarly Isocrates in his *Antidosis* reminds the Athenians that they make annual sacrifices to the Goddess of Persuasion (Peitho), and he refers to speech as the source of most good things.   The desire to speak well, he says, makes for great moral improvement.   "True, just, and well-ordered discourse is the outward image (*eidolon*) of a good and faithful soul."

Or, since "rhetoric," "oratory," and "eloquence" all come from roots meaning "to speak," you can have the Aristotelian stress upon rhetoric as *sheer words*.   In this respect, by his scheme, it is the "counterpart" of dialectic (though "dialectic" itself, in such a usage, is to be distinguished from the modern "dialectic of Nature").   Some theorists may choose to look upon the rhetorician as a very narrow specialist.   On the other hand, since one can be "eloquent" about anything and everything, there are Quintilian's grounds for widening the scope of rhetoric to make it the center of an entire educational system.   He was here but extending an emphasis strong in Cicero, who equated the ideal orator with the ideal citizen, the man of universal aptitude, sympathies, and experience.   And though Aristotle rigorously divided knowledge into compartments whenever possible, his *Art of Rhetoric* includes much that falls under the separate headings of psychology, ethics, politics, poetics, logic, and history.   Indeed, according to him, the characteristically rhetorical statement involves "commonplaces" that lie outside any scientific specialty; and in proportion as the rhetorician deals with special subject matter, his proofs move away from the rhetorical and towards the scientific. (For instance, a typical rhetorical "commonplace," in the Aristotelian sense, would be Churchill's slogan, "Too little and too late," which could hardly be said to fall under any special science of quantity or time.)

As for "persuasion" itself: one can imagine including purely logical demonstration as a part of it; or one might distinguish between appeals to reason and appeals to emotion, sentiment, ignorance, prejudice, and the like, reserving the notion of "persuasion" for these less orderly kinds of "proof."   (Here again we encroach upon the term "dialectic."   Augustine seems to follow the Stoic usage, in treating dialectic as the logical groundwork underlying rhetoric; dialectic would thus treat of the ultimate scenic reality that sets the criteria for rhetorical persuasion.)

The Greek word, *peitho*, comes from the same root as the Latin word for "faith." Accordingly, Aristotle's term for rhetorical "proof" is the related word, *pistis*. In his vocabulary, it names an *inferior* kind of proof, as compared with scientific demonstration (*apodeixis*). (See *Institutio Oratoria,* Book V, Chapter X.) But it is, ironically, the word which, in Greek ecclesiastical literature, came to designate the *highest* order of Christian knowledge, "faith" or "belief" as contrasted with "reason." While the active form of *peitho* means "to persuade," its middle and passive forms mean "to obey."

But the corresponding Latin word, *suadere,* comes from the same roots as "suavity," "assuage," and "sweet." And following these leads, one may want to narrow the scope of persuasion to such meanings as "ingratiation" and "delight." Thus Augustine often uses the term in this very restricted sense, preferring words like "move" and "bend" (*movere, flectere*) when he has the ultimate purpose of rhetorical utterance in mind. (In Sidney's statement that the end of speech is "the uttering sweetly and properly the conceits of the minde," one can discern the lineaments of "persuasion" behind "sweet utterance" when one appreciates the relation between English "sweet" and Cicero's stress upon the *suavitas* of oratory.)

More often, however, the ability of rhetoric to ingratiate is considered secondary, as a mere device for gaining good will, holding the attention, or deflecting the attention in preparation for more urgent purposes. Since persuasion so often implies the presence or threat of an adversary, there is the "agonistic" or competitive stress. Thus Aristotle, who looks upon rhetoric as a medium that "proves opposites," gives what amounts to a handbook on a manly art of self-defense. He describes the holds and the counter-holds, the blows and the ways of blocking them, for every means of persuasion the corresponding means of dissuasion, for every proof the disproof, for every praise the vituperation that matches it. While *in general* the truer and better cause has the advantage, he observes, no cause can be adequately defended without skill in the tricks of the trade. So he studies these tricks from the purely technical point of view, without reference to any one fixed position such as marks Augustine's analysis of the Christian persuasion. Even as Aristotle is teaching one man how most effectively to make people say "yes," he is teaching an opponent how to make them say just as forceful a "no."

This "agonistic" emphasis is naturally strong in Cicero, much of whose treatise is written out of his experiences in the Senate and the law courts. It is weaker in Quintilian with his educational emphasis; yet his account of eloquence frequently relies on military and gladiatorial images. (Which reminds us that Cicero's dialogue *De Oratore,* is represented as taking place among several prominent public figures who *have left Rome* for the far suburbs *during the season of the Games*.)

Whatever his polemic zeal in other works, in the *De Doctrina Christiana* Augustine is concerned rather with the *cajoling* of an audience than with the routing of opponents. Despite the disrepute into which pagan rhetoric had fallen in Augustine's day, he recognized the persuasiveness implicit in its forms. And though some Christians looked upon rhetoric as by nature pagan, Augustine (himself trained in rhetoric before his conversion) held that every last embellishment should be brought to the service of God, for the glory and power of the new doctrine.

The notion of rhetoric as a means of "proving opposites" again brings us to the relation between rhetoric and dialectic. Perhaps, as a first rough approximate, we might think of the matter thus: Bring several *rhetoricians* together, let their speeches contribute to the maturing of one another by the give and take of question and answer, and you have the *dialectic* of a Platonic dialogue. But ideally the dialogue seeks to attain a higher order of truth, as the speakers, in competing with one another, cooperate towards an end transcending their individual positions. Here is the paradigm of the dialectical process for "reconciling opposites" in a "higher synthesis."

But note that, in the Platonic scheme, such dialectic enterprise starts from *opinion.* The Socratic "midwifery" (maieutic) was thus designed to discover truth, by beginning with opinion and subjecting it to systematic criticism. Also, the process was purely verbal; hence in Aristotle's view it would be an art, not a science, since each science has its own particular extraverbal subject matter. The Socratic method was better suited for such linguistic enterprises as the dialectical search for "ideas" of justice, truth, beauty, and so on, than for the accumulating of knowledge derived from empirical observation and laboratory experiment. Dialectic of this sort was concerned with "ideology" in the primary sense of the term: the study of ideas and of their relation to one another. But above all, note that, in its very search for "truth," it began with "opinion," and thus in a sense was *grounded* in opinion.

The point is worth remembering because the verbal "counterpart" of dialectic, rhetoric, was likewise said to deal with "opinion," though without the systematic attempt to transcend this level.

The competitive and public ingredient in persuasion makes it particularly urgent that the rhetoric work at the level of opinion. Thus, in a situation where an appeal to prejudice might be more effective than an appeal to reason, the rhetorician who would have his cause prevail may need to use such means, regardless of his preferences. Cicero says that one should answer argument with argument and emotional appeal by a stirring of the opposite emotions (goading to hate where the opponent had established good will, and countering compassion by incitement to envy). And Aristotle refers with approval to Gorgias' notion that one should counter an opponent's jest with earnest and his earnest with jest. To persuade under such conditions, truth is at best a secondary device. Hence, rhetoric is properly said to be grounded in opinion. But we think that the relation between "truth" and the kind of opinion with which rhetoric operates is often misunderstood. And the classical texts do not seem to bring out the point we have in mind, namely:

The kind of opinion with which rhetoric deals, in its role of inducement to action, is not opinion *as contrasted with truth*. There is the invitation to look at the matter thus antithetically, once we have put the two terms (opinion and truth) together as a dialectical pair. But actually, many of the "opinions" upon which persuasion relies fall outside the test of truth in the strictly scientific, T-F, yes-or-no sense. Thus, if a given audience has a strong opinion that a certain kind of conduct is admirable, the orator can commend a person by using signs that identify him with such conduct. "Opinion" in this ethical sense clearly falls on the bias across the matter of "truth" in the strictly scientific sense. Of course, a speaker may be true or false in identifying a person by some particular sign of virtuous conduct. You may say that a person so acted when the person did not so act—and if you succeed in making your audience believe you, you could be said to be trafficking in sheer opinion *as contrasted with* the truth. But we are here concerned with motives a step farther back than such mere deception. We are discussing the underlying ethical assumptions on which the entire tactics of persuasion are based. Here the important factor is opinion (opinion in the moral order of *action,* rather than in the "scenic" order of truth). The rhetorician, as such, need operate only on this principle. If, in the opinion of a given audience, a certain kind of conduct is admirable, then a speaker might persuade the audience by using ideas and images that identify his cause with that kind of conduct.

Identification

"It is not hard," says Aristotle, in his *Rhetoric,* quoting Socrates, "to praise Athenians among Athenians." He has been cataloguing those traits which an audience generally considers the components of virtue. They are justice, courage, self-control, poise or presence (magnificence, *megaloprepeia*), broad-mindedness, liberality, gentleness, prudence and wisdom. And he has been saying: For purposes of praise or blame, the rhetorician will assume that qualities closely resembling any of these qualities are identical with them. For instance, to arouse dislike for a cautious man, one should present him as cold and designing. Or to make a simpleton lovable, play up his good nature. Or speak of quarrelsomeness as frankness, or of arrogance as poise and dignity, or of foolhardiness as courage, and of squandering as generosity. Also, he says, we should consider the audience before whom we are thus passing judgment: for it's hard to praise Athenians when you are talking to Lacedaemonians.

Part of the quotation appears in Book I. It is quoted again, entire, in Book III, where he has been discussing the speaker's appeal to friendship or compassion. And he continues: When winding up a speech in praise of someone, we "must make the hearer believe that he shares in the praise, either personally, or through his family or profession, or somehow." When you are with Athenians, it's easy to praise Athenians, but not when you are with Lacedaemonians.

Here is perhaps the simplest case of persuasion. You persuade a man only insofar as you can talk his language by speech, gesture, tonality, order, image, attitude, idea, *identifying* your ways with his. Persuasion by flattery is but a special case of persuasion in general. But flattery can safely serve as our paradigm if we systematically widen its meaning, to see behind it the conditions of identification or consubstantiality in general. And you give the "signs" of such consubstantiality by deference to an audience's "opinions." For the orator, following Aristotle and Cicero, will seek to display the appropriate "signs" of character needed to earn the audience's good will. True, the rhetorician may have to change an audience's opinion in one respect; but he can succeed only insofar as he yields to that audience's opinions in other respects. Some of their opinions are needed to support the fulcrum by which he would move other opinions. (Preferably he shares the fixed opinions himself since, "all other things being equal," the identifying of himself with his audience will be more effective if it is genuine.)

The so-called "commonplaces" or "topics" in Aristotle's *Art of Rhetoric* (and the corresponding *loci communes* in Latin manuals) are a quick survey of "opinion" in this sense. Aristotle reviews the purposes, acts, things, conditions, states of mind, personal characteristics, and the like, which people consider promising or formidable, good or evil, useful or dangerous, admirable or loathsome, and so on. All these opinions or assumptions (perhaps today they would be treated under the head of "attitudes" or "values") are catalogued as available means of persuasion. But the important thing, for our purposes, is to note that such types are derived from the principle of persuasion, in that they are but a survey of the things that people generally consider persuasive, and of methods that have persuasive effects.

Thus, Aristotle lists the kind of opinions you should draw upon if you wanted to recommend a policy or to turn people against it; the kind of motives which in people's opinion lead to just or unjust actions; what personal traits people admire or dislike (opinions the speaker should exploit to present himself favorably and his adversary unfavorably); and what opinions can be used as means for stirring men to rage, friendliness, fear, compassion, shame, indignation, envy, rivalry, charity, and so on. Reasoning based on opinion he calls "enthymemes," which are the rhetorical equivalent of the syllogism. And arguments from example (which is the rhetorical equivalent for induction) are likewise to be framed in accordance with his various lists of opinions. (Incidentally, those who talk of "ethical relativity" must be impressed by the "permanence" of such "places" or topics, when stated at Aristotle's level of generalization. As *ideas*, they all seem no less compelling now than they ever were, though in our society a speaker might often have to individuate them in a different *image* than the Greeks would have chosen, if he would convey a maximum sense of actuality.)

Aristotle also considers another kind of "topic," got by the manipulation of tactical procedures, by following certain rules of thumb for inventing, developing, or transforming an expression, by pun-logic, even by specious and sophistical arguments. The materials of opinion will be embodied in such devices, but their characterization as "topics" is got by abstracting some formal or procedural element as their distinguishing mark. Aristotle here includes such "places" as: ways of turning an adversary's words against himself, and of transforming an argument by opposites ("if war did it, repair it by peace"). Some other terms of this sort are: recalling what an adversary advocated in one situation when recommending a policy for a new situation ("you wanted it then, you should want it now"); using definitions to advantage (Socrates using his previous mention of his *daimonion* as evidence that he was not an atheist); dividing up an assertion ("there were three motives for the offense; two were impossible, not even the accusers have asserted the third"); tendentious selection of results (since a cause may have both good and bad effects, one can play up whichever set favors his position); exaggeration (the accused can weaken the strength of the accusation against him by himself overstating it); the use of signs (arguing that the man is a thief because he is disreputable); and so on. Among these tactics, he calls particular attention to the use of a shift between public and private orders of motivation. In public, one praises the just and the beautiful; but in private one prefers the test of expediency; hence the orator can use whichever of these orders better suits his purposes. Here is the paradigm for the modern rhetorician's shuttling between "idealistic" and "materialistic" motives, as when one imputes "idealistic" motives to one's own faction and "materialistic" motives to the adversary; or the adversary can be accused of "idealistic" motives when they imply ineffectiveness and impracticability.

Though the translation of one's wishes into terms of an audience's opinions would clearly be an instance of identification, this last list of purely formal devices for rhetorical invention takes us farther afield. However, it seems to be a fact that, the more urgent the oratory, the greater the profusion and vitality of the formal devices. So they must be *functional,* and not mere "embellishments." And processes of "identification" would seem to figure here, as follows:

Longinus refers to that kind of elation wherein the audience feels as though it were not merely receiving, but were itself creatively participating in the poet's or speaker's assertion. Could we not say that, in such cases, the audience is exalted by the assertion because it has the feel of collaborating in the assertion?

At least, we know that many purely formal patterns can readily awaken an attitude of collaborative expectancy in us. For instance, imagine a passage built about a set of oppositions (*"we* do *this,* but *they* on the other hand do *that; we* stay *here,* but *they* go *there; we* look *up,* but *they* look *down,"* etc.). Once you grasp the trend of the form, it invites participation regardless of the subject matter. Formally, you will find yourself swinging along with the succession of antitheses, even though you may not agree with the proposition that is being presented in this form. Or it may even be an opponent's proposition which you resent—yet for the duration of the statement itself you might "help him out" to the extent of yielding to the formal development, surrendering to its symmetry as such. Of course, the more violent your original resistance to the proposition, the weaker will be your degree of "surrender" by "collaborating" with the form. But in cases where a decision is still to be reached, a yielding to the form prepares for assent to the matter identified with it. Thus, you are drawn to the form, not in your capacity as a partisan, but because of some "universal" appeal in it. And this attitude of assent may then be transferred to the matter which happens to be associated with the form.

Or think thus of another strongly formal device like climax (*gradatio*). The editor of Demetrius' *On Style,* in the Loeb edition, cites this example from *As You Like It,* where even the name of the figure appears in the figure:

> Your brother and my sister no sooner met but they looked, no sooner looked but they loved, no sooner loved but they sighed, no sooner sighed but they asked one another the reason, no sooner knew the reason but they sought the remedy; and in these *degrees* they have made a *pair of stairs* to marriage.

Here the form requires no assent to a moot issue. But recall a *gradatio* of political import, much in the news during the "Berlin crisis" of 1948: "Who controls Berlin, controls Germany; who controls Germany controls Europe; who controls Europe controls the world." As a proposition, it may or may not be true. And even if it is true, unless people are thoroughly imperialistic, they may not want to control the world.   But regardless of these doubts about it as a proposition, by the time you arrive at the second of its three stages, you feel how it is destined to develop—and on the level of purely formal assent you would collaborate to round out its symmetry by spontaneously willing its completion and perfection as an utterance.   Add, now, the psychosis of nationalism, and assent on the formal level invites assent to the proposition as doctrine.

Demetrius also cites an example from Aeschines: "Against yourself you call; against the laws you call; against the entire democracy you call."   (We have tinkered with the translation somewhat, to bring out the purely linguistic structure as greatly as possible, including an element that Demetrius does not discuss, the *swelling* effect at the third stage.   In the original the three stages comprise six, seven, and ten syllables respectively.)   To illustrate the effect, Demetrius gives the same *idea* without the cumulative form, thus: "Against yourself and the laws and the democracy you call."   In this version it lacks the three formal elements he is discussing: repetition of the same word at the beginning of each clause (epanaphora), sameness of sound at the close of each clause (homoeoteleuton), and absence of conjunctions (asyndeton). Hence there is no pronouncedly formal feature to which one might give assent.   (As a noncontroversial instance of cumulative form we recall a sentence cited approvingly in one of Flaubert's letters: "They proceeded some on foot, some on horse, some on the backs of elephants."   Here the gradation of the visual imagery reënforces the effect of the syllabic elongation.)

Of the many "tropes" and "figures" discussed in the eighth and ninth books of Quintilian's *Institutio Oratoria,* the invitation to purely formal assent (regardless of content) is much greater in some cases than others.   It is not our purpose here to analyze the lot in detail.   We need but say enough to establish the principle, and to indicate why the expressing of a proposition in one or another of these rhetorical forms would involve "identification," first by inducing the auditor to participate in the form, as a "universal" locus of appeal, and next by trying to include a partisan statement within this same pale of assent.

Other Variants of the Rhetorical Motive

When making his claims for the universality of rhetoric (in the first book of the *De Oratore*) Cicero begins at a somewhat mythic stage when right acting and right speaking were considered one (he cites Homer on the training of Achilles). Next he notes regretfully the sharp dissociating of action and speech whereby the Sophists would eventually confine rhetoric to the verbal in a sheerly ornamental sense. And following this, he notes further detractions from the dignity of rhetoric caused by the dissociating of rhetoric and philosophy. (Cicero blames Socrates for this division. Thus, ironically, the Socratic attempt to make systematic allowance for the gradual increase of cultural heterogeneity and scientific specialization was blamed for the very situation which had called it forth and which it was designed to handle.) Rhetoric suffers by the division, Cicero notes, because there arises a distinction between "wisdom" and "eloquence" which would justify the Sophists' reduction of rhetoric to sheer verbal blandishments.

Later, philosophy and wisdom could be grouped under "dialectic," dialectic treated *as distinct from* the ingratiations of rhetoric (a distinction which the Stoics transformed into a flat opposition between dialectic and rhetoric, choosing the first and rejecting the second). Or dialectic could be treated as the ground of rhetoric, hence as not merely verbal, but in the realm of things, the realm of the universal order, guiding the rhetorician in his choice of purposes (as we noted with respect to Augustine). Cicero himself stressed the notion that, since the rhetorician must also be adept in logic and worldly knowledge, such universal aptitude is *intrinsic* to his eloquence.

Also (continuing our review) there is rhetoric as an art of "proving opposites"; as appeal to emotions and prejudices; as "agonistic," shaped by a strongly competitive purpose.

On this last score, we might note that Isocrates, responding to the element of unfairness in the war of words, chose to spiritualize the notion of "advantage" (*pleonexia*). While recognizing the frequent rhetorical aim to take advantage of an opportunity or to gain advantage for oneself, he located the "true advantage" of the rhetorician in *moral* superiority. He was thinking of an ideal rhetoric, of course, rather than describing the struggle for advantage as it ordinarily does take place in human affairs. But he here adds a very important term to our list: Among the marks of rhetoric is its use to *gain advantage,* of one sort or another.

Indeed, all the sources of "happiness" listed in Aristotle's "eudaimonist" rhetoric, as topics to be exploited for persuasion and dissuasion, could be lumped under the one general heading of "advantage," as could the nineteenth-century Utilitarians' doctrine of "interest," or that batch of motives which La Rochefoucauld, in his 213th maxim, gave as "the causes of that valor so celebrated among men": love of glory with its corollaries (fear of disgrace and envy of others), desire for money (and its corollary, comfortable and agreeable living) (*l'amour de la gloire, la crainte de la honte, le dessein de faire fortune, le désir de rendre notre vie commode et agréable, et l'envie d'abaisser les autres*).

We think this term, "advantage," quite useful for rhetorical theory, in that it can also subsume, before we meet them, all posssible "drives" and "urges" for the existence of which various brands of psychology and sociology may claim to find empirical evidence (terminologies with rhetorical implications of their own, as you can readily see by contrasting them, for instance, with the rhetorical implications of the Marxist terminology). Surely all doctrines can at least begin by agreeing that human effort aims at "advantage" of one sort or another, though there is room for later disputes as to whether advantage in general, or particular advantages are to be conceived idealistically, materialistically, or even cynically. Advantage can be individual, or the aim of a partisan group, or even universal. And that men should seek advantage of some sort is reasonable and ethical enough—hence the term need not confine one's terminology of rhetorical design to purely individualist cunning or aggrandizement, as with the rhetorical implications lurking in those "scientific" terminologies that reduce human motives to a few primitive appetites, resistances, and modes of acquisition ("post-Christian" terminologies in the sense that you could arrive at motivational orders of this sort, as La Rochefoucauld in his *Maxims* on the operations of self-love is said to have done, by merely deducting from the orthodox Christian version of human motives, until human behavior is but *"celle de la lumière naturelle et de la raison sans grâce"*).

Perhaps we should make clear: We do not offer this list as a set of ingredients all or most of which must be present at once, as the test for the presence of the rhetorical motive. Rather, we are considering a wide range of meanings already associated with rhetoric, in ancient texts; and we are saying that one or another of these meanings may be uppermost in some particular usage. But though these meanings are often not consistent with one another, or are even flatly at odds, we do believe that they can all be derived from "persuasion" as the "Edenic" term from which they have all "Babylonically" split, while "persuasion" in turn involves communication by the signs of consubstantiality, the appeal of *identification*. Even *extrinsic* consideration can thus be derived in an orderly manner from persuasion as generating principle: for an act of persuasion is affected by the character of the scene in which it takes place and of the agents to whom it is addressed. The same rhetorical act could vary in its effectiveness, according to shifts in the situation or in the attitude of audiences. Hence, the rhetorician's exploiting of opinion leads into the analysis of non-verbal factors wholly extrinsic to the rhetorical expression considered purely as a verbal structure.

Thus, if the Aristotelian concern with topics were adapted to the conditions of modern journalism, we should perhaps need to catalogue a kind of *timely topic,* such as that of the satirical cartoon, which exploits commonplaces of a transitory nature. The transitoriness is due not to the fact that the expressions are wholly alien to people living under other conditions, but to the fact that they are *more persuasive* with people living under one particular set of circumstances. Thus, even an exceptionally good cartoon exploiting the subject of unemployment (as with satire on federal "leaf-raking" and "boondoggling" projects during the "made work" period of the Franklin Roosevelt administration) would have a hard time getting published during a period of maximum employment, when a timelier topic might be the shortage of workers in general and of domestic help in particular (and when an editor would consider even a poor cartoon on labor shortage preferable to an exceptional one on unemployment).

When reduced to the level of *ideas,* timely cartoons will be found to exploit much the same list of universal commonplaces that Aristotle assembles. But topical shifts make certain *images* more persuasive in one situation than another. Quintilian touches upon such a narrowing down of the commonplaces when he notes how a general topic is made specific not merely by being attached to some individual figure, but also by a coupling with other particularizing marks, as "we make our adulterer blind, our gambler poor, and our profligate old." And Cicero, when discussing the function of *memory* in the orator, refers to a lost contemporary work on the systematic associating of topics and images (*simulacra*). Thus, a statement about "timely topics" would seem to be, not an extension of the rhetorical motive to fields not traditionally considered part of it, but merely as the application of classical theory to a special cultural condition set by the modern press. We pass over it hastily here, as we plan to consider the two major aspects of it in later sections of this project (when we shall consider the new level of "reality" which journalistic timeliness establishes, and shall study the relation between transient and permanent factors of appeal by taking the cartoons in *The New Yorker* as test case).

Meanwhile, again, the thought of the timely topic reminds us that sociological works reviewing the rise and fall of slogans, clichés, stock figures of folk consciousness, and the like, impinge upon the rhetorical motive. Indeed, unless this is material for rhetoric, an aspect of *rhetorica docens,* a body of knowledge about audiences, pragmatically available for use when planning appeals to audiences, then such material lacks pragmatic sanction and must be justified on purely "liberal" grounds, in terms of literary or philosophic "appreciation," as knowledge assembled, classified, and contemplated not for use, but for its own sake. There is most decidedly no objection to such a motive, when it is recognized for what it is; but it is usually concealed by the fact that much "pure" science, cultivated without concern for utility, was later found to be of pragmatic value. The fact that anything *might* be of use has allowed for a new unction whereby an investigation can be justified, not for what it is, but for what it might possibly lead to. Nature is so "full of gods" (powers) that a systematic directing of the attention anywhere is quite likely to disclose a new one, some genius local to the particular subject matter. Hence, a cult of "fact-finding," with no order of facts considered too lowly for the collector. In itself, the attitude has much to recommend it. It is scientific humility in the best sense. But it should not be allowed to give specious justification for inquiries where the sheer *absence of intrinsic value* is assumed to imply the *presence of pragmatic value.*

Equivalent to the narrowing and intensifying of appeal by the featuring of timely topics, there is another aspect of address more characteristic of modern conditions, particularly the kind of canvassing shaped primarily by postal communication. Both Aristotle and Cicero laid stress upon the differences among audiences. Indeed, Aristotle's recipes that distinguish between the commonplaces as appealing to a young audience and those appealing to an old one could serve as a play-wright's formulas for the contrasted stock characters of "fiery youth" and timid age. For however strong Aristotle's bias towards science may have been, it was always modified by a highly dramatistic context. His rhetoric is thoroughly dramatist in its insights.

But Aristotle does not discuss varieties of audience with the systematic thoroughness which he brings to the classification of opinion in general. And both Aristotle and Cicero consider audiences purely as something *given*. The extreme heterogeneity of modern life, however, combined with the nature of modern postal agencies, brings up another kind of possibility: the systematic attempt to *carve out* an audience, as the commercial rhetorician looks not merely for persuasive devices in general, but for the topics that will appeal to the particular "income group" most likely to be interested in his product, or able to buy it. If immediacy or intensity of appeal is got by narrowing the topics and images to the group likely to be his best audience, he will seek to prod only these to action (if we could call it "active," rather than "passive," when a prospective customer is bent towards one brand of a commodity rather than another, though the brand he passes up may be a better buy than the one he purchases, a kind of conduct that may not be informed enough to be "rational" and "free," hence not rational and free enough to be truly an act, at least in the full philosophic sense of the term). In any case, here too would be a consideration of audiences; hence even by the tests of the classic tradition it would fall under the head of rhetoric, though it necessarily extended the range of the term to cover a situation essentially new.

Thus, all told, besides the *extension* of rhetoric through the concept of identification, we have noted these purely traditional evidences of the rhetorical motive: persuasion, exploitation of opinion (the "timely" topic is a variant), a work's nature as addressed, literature for use (applied art, inducing to an act beyond the area of verbal expression considered in and for itself), verbal deception (hence, rhetoric as instrument in the war of words), the "agonistic" generally, words used "sweetly" (eloquence, ingratiation, for its own sake), formal devices, the art of proving opposites (as "counterpart" of dialectic). We have also suggested that the "carving out" of audiences is new to the extent that there are new mediums of communication, but there is nothing here *essentially* outside the traditional concerns of rhetoric. As for the recognition of nonverbal, situational factors that can participate in a work's effectiveness, the neatest statement we know of, for establishing this principle, is by the late Bronislas Malinowski. We refer to his article on primitive languages (published as a supplement in Ogden and Richards' *The Meaning of Meaning*). His concept of "context of situation" establishes a principle which can, we believe, be applied in many ways for the New Rhetoric, most notably when considering the semiverbal, semiorganizational kinds of tactics one might classify as a "rhetoric of bureaucracy."

Formal Appeal

As for the purely formal kinds of appeal which we previously mentioned when trying to show how they involve the principle of identification, their universal nature makes it particularly easy to shift them from rhetoric to poetic. Thus, viewing even tendentious oratory from the standpoint of literary appreciation rather than in terms of its use, Longinus analyzes "sublimity" of effect in and for itself. Where Demosthenes would transport his auditors the better to persuade them, Longinus treats the state of transport as the aim. Hence he seeks to convey the quality of the excitement, and to disclose the means by which it is produced. Indeed, might not his key term, that is usually translated "sublime," come close to what we mean by "moving," not in the rhetorical sense, of moving an audience to a decision, but as when we say of a poem, "How moving!"

Admittedly, the cataloguing of rhetorical devices was carried to extreme lengths. You can't possibly make a statement without its falling into some sort of pattern. Its formality can then be abstracted and named, without reference to any particular subject matter, hence can be looked upon as capable of "reindividuation" in a great variety of subject matters. Given enough industry in observation, abstraction, and classification, you can reduce any expression (even inconsequential or incomplete ones) to some underlying skeletal structure. Teachers of Greek and Latin rhetoric had such industry; and they amassed so many such terms that they had a name for the formal design in practically any expression possible to words. Thus, if a statement proceeds by the repeating of a conjunction ("this *and* that *and* the other"), it will be a *polysyndeton*. Drop the connectives ("this, that, the other") and it becomes *asyndeton*. Build up, by expatiation or intensification, and you have amplification (*auxesis*); treat the more dignified in terms of the less dignified, and you have *meiosis;* amplify a build-up until you have it established as expectation, then break the symmetry of your series with a sudden let-down, and you have *bathos*. Allow a fleeting music of words with the same ending, and you have *homoioteleuton*. (Remember, incidentally, that the Greeks could not say "homoioteleuton"; they had to say, rather, "similarly ended.") Repeat the same word at the beginning of successive phrases, and you have *epanaphora*. And so on. Croce seems to have taken this terminology of piecemeal effects as the very essence of rhetoric. And though, in accordance with Croce's attitude, the modern replacing of logic, rhetoric, and poetic by "esthetics" relegated such forms to the class of "mere rhetoric," he could have quoted from Cicero and Quintilian passages that derived "artifice from eloquence, not eloquence from artifice."

The rhetorical devices can become obtrusive, sheer decadent decoration (as during the era of the "second sophistic" in Rome); but we have offered reasons for believing that even the most ostentatious of them arose out of great functional urgency. When pagan rhetoric grew weak, such verbal exercising could be sought for itself alone, for its appeal as a display of virtuosity. Thus, ironically, the splendidly enthusiastic analyses of Longinus ("enthusiasm" is one of his words) marked a step towards this very decay. But Augustine, who had been trained in pagan rhetoric prior to his conversion, reinfused many of the decaying forms with the zeal of the Christian persuasion.

A list of the more characteristic devices used by Augustine will be found in the volume, *S. Aureli Augusti De Doctrina Christiana Liber Quartus, A Commentary With a Revised Text, Introduction, and Translation,* by Sister Thérèse Sullivan. (For a quite comprehensive study of their vigorous use in English, see *Shakespeare's Use of the Arts of Language,* by Sister Miriam Joseph.) And the third book of Cicero's *De Oratore* gives a quick survey of such resources for varying an address "with the lights of thought and language" (*luminibus sententiarum atque verborum*). Here are selections from Cicero's list:

Dwelling on a subject, driving it home (*commemoratio*), bringing it before one's very eyes (*explanatio*), both of them devices valuable for stating a case, illustrating and amplifying it; review (*praecisio*);

disparagement (*extenuatio*), accompanied by raillery (*illusio*); digression (*digressio*), with neatly contrived return to the subject; statement of what one proposes to say; distinguishing it from what has already been said; return to a point already established; repetition, reduction to sharply syllogistic form (*apta conclusio*); overstatement and understatement; rhetorical question; irony, saying one thing and meaning another (*dissimulatio*), a device which, he says, is particularly effective with audiences if it is used in a conversational tone, not rantingly; stopping to ponder (*dubitatio*); dividing a subject into components (*distributio*), so that you can effectively dispose of them in one-two-three order; finding fault with a statement (*correctio*) which has been made by the opponent, or which one himself has said or is about to say; preparing the audience for what one is about to say (*praemunitio*); shifting of responsibility (*traiectio in alium*); taking the audience into partnership, having a kind of consultation with them (*communicatio*); imitation; impersonation (which he calls an especially weighty *lumen* of amplification); putting on the wrong scent; raising a laugh; forestalling (*anteoccupatio*); comparison (*similitudo*) and example (*exemplum*), "both of them most moving"; interruption (*interpellatio*); alignment of contrasting positions, antithesis (*contentio*); raising of the voice even to the point of frenzy, for purposes of amplificacation (*augendi causa*); anger; invective, imprecation, deprecation, ingratiation, entreaty, vowing "O would that . . ." (*optatio*)—and, yes, also, lapses into meaningful silence.

Regarding this last point, we recall a lecturer on music who interspersed his talk with songs accompanied on old instruments. Every now and then he paused, took a handkerchief from his breast pocket, carefully unfolded it, touched his hands with it ever so lightly, then slowly, painstakingly folded it again and replaced it in his pocket. In time the audience got to watching this silent ritual as attentively as though he were a magician about to do a trick.

We saw another speaker, a theologian, who periodically interrupted his sermonlike lecture while he gazed into space. The audience waited for a marvel—and slowly, as was made apparent by the changing expression on the speaker's face, there became manifest the signs of the next idea which he was about to fetch from these distant depths. Sometimes, when thus seeking to descry the next message, he turned his eyes intently upward, and to the right. At other times, he bent, and looked down, intently, to the left. Presumably he alternated these postures for the sake of variety; but we began to speculate: If, by looking upward, and to the right, he can bring forth ideas from heaven, then by the same token, when he has looked downward, and to the left, does he also have other things brought steaming hot from hell?

Cicero likens his lists of devices to weapons, which can be used for threat and attack, or can be brandished purely for show. He also mentions several kinds of repetition with variation (the highly inflected nature of Latin, with its corresponding freedom of word order, allows readily for many such effects which English can approximate only with difficulty). And he continues (we quote the *Loeb Classical Library* translation by H. Rackham, from which we adapted the previous citation):

> There is also advance step by step (*gradatio*), and inversion (transposition, metathesis, *conversio*), and harmonious interchange of words, and antithesis (*contrarium*), and omission of particles (*dissolutum*), and change of subject (*declinatio*), and self-correction (*reprehensio*), and exclamation (*exclamatio*), and abbreviation (*imminutio*), and the use of a noun in several cases [an English equivalent would be Mead's sloganlike formula, "An 'I' contemplating its 'me' "].

He goes on to mention such things as deliberate hesitation over the choice of a word, conceding of a point, surprise, continuity and discontinuity (*continuatum et interruptum*), the use of images (*imago*), metonymy (*immutatio*), "and distinguishing terms, and order, and reference back, and digression, and periphrasis" (*disiunctio et ordo et relatio et digressio et circumscriptio*), asking questions which one answers oneself.

Incidentally, when an issue is highly controversial, this last device can have disastrous results, unless one is an expert orator. Thus, shortly after the Allied armies had occupied Italy in the last war, the philosopher Croce was speaking in favor of monarchy. It was a good opportunity, since the gathering had been called to do him honor, as an old liberal. At one point, he asked himself, "Do we want the restoration of the King?" But before he had a chance to answer himself by saying, "We do," the audience shouted back a thunderous "No!" (Coleridge tells of an instance, on the other hand, where Demosthenes deliberately provoked an unruly answer from his audience. In his speech "On the Crown," when attacking his opponent Aeschines, he asked the audience: "Do you think Aeschines is Alexander's hireling, or his friend?" But he slightly mispronounced the word for "hireling," putting the accent on the wrong syllable. The audience, as connoisseurs of speech, shouted back at him the correct pronunciation for "hireling." Whereupon he concluded with an air of satisfaction: "You hear what they say.")

Of all rhetorical devices, the most thoroughgoing is amplification (Greek, *auxesis*). It seems to cover a wide range of meanings, since one can amplify by extension, by intensification, and by dignification. The last two kinds have an opposite: diminution (*meiosis*). But as extension, expatiation, the saying of something in various ways until it increases in persuasiveness by the sheer accumulation, amplification can come to name a purely poetic process of development, such systematic exploitation of a theme as we find in lyrics built about a refrain. In this sense, we could designate as "rhetorical" the characteristic method of a popular song, though the persuasive aspects of rhetoric in the sense of an ulterior purpose are wholly lacking. Perhaps a work efficiently exploiting the tactics of *meiosis* (the satire of *Gulliver's Travels*, for instance) could be treated paradoxically as an amplification of diminution.

Rhetorical Form in the Large

There is also persuasive form in the larger sense, formulated as a progression of steps that begins with an exordium designed to secure the good will of one's audience, next states one's own position, then points up the nature of the dispute, then builds up one's own case at length, then refutes the claims of the adversary, and in a final peroration expands and reinforces all points in one's favor, while seeking to discredit whatever had favored the adversary (vituperation, irony, and appeal to the emotions also being drawn upon here). The great concern with the classifying and analyzing of minute incidental effects has caused writers on ancient rhetoric to say that these larger principles of form were slighted. Yet they are recognized as set stages in the strucure of an oration, almost as formal as the movements of a symphony. (Aristotle's third book treats of them energetically, without running against the law of diminishing returns that does damage to

Quintilian. The steps listed above are a rough paraphrase of a passage in Cicero, where Crassus is briefly reviewing the standard education of an orator.)   But literary theory is traditionally weak in the analysis of structure in the larger sense, if only because isolated stylistic effects lend themselves readily to quotation, whereas the discussion of formal development in the large is unwieldy. (Even Coleridge, with his stress upon the *unifying* function of the imagination, does not analyze structural unity in the over-all sense, but becomes involved in a kind of methodological oxymoron, illustrating total unity by fragmentary examples.)

But there were ways in which the art of persuasion could be conveniently discussed in the large; this was by generalizations about kinds of rhetoric, kinds of style, and the functions or duties of the rhetorician (Cicero's *officia oratoris*).

Considered broadly, in terms of *address,* an audience can have three primary purposes in listening: to hear advice about the future, or to pass judgment on some action in the past, or merely for the sake of interest in a speech or subject as such.   Use these distinctions as a basis for classifying *kinds* of rhetoric, and you get the traditional three formulated in Aristotle's *Rhetoric:* (1) deliberative, directed towards the future, as with communication designed to sway an audience on matters of public policy; (2) forensic or judicial, involving the past, as with speeches designed to establish in a jury's mind the guilt or innocence of an accused person; and (3) demonstrative (epideictic, "display" oratory, sometimes also called panegyric). This third kind readily becomes a catch-all. Aristotle says that it aims at praise or blame. And he says that it is concerned primarily with the present. Even at the height of Greek rhetoric, its range included: funeral orations; tributes to some public character (or diatribes against such figures); patriotic addresses lauding one's city or one's countrymen; playful, often punning encomiums on animals and things (or playful invectives against them).

Perhaps the sturdiest modern variant of epideictic rhetoric is in "human interest" stories depicting the sacrificial life of war heroes in war times, or Soviet works (including propaganda motion pictures) that celebrate the accomplishments of individuals and groups who triumph over adversity in carrying out the government's plans for exploitation of the nation's resources. For Cicero says that epideictic (panegyric, *laudatio*) should deal especially in those virtues thought beneficial "not so much to their possessors as to mankind in general." Thus, the praise most welcome "is for deeds that seem to have been done without profit and reward." Toil and personal danger are good subjects, since the mark of an outstanding citizen is "virtue profitable to others" (*virtus . . . fructuosa aliis*).

Aristotle probably assigned this third kind to the present because, having defined the others with reference to the future (the deliberative concern with expedients) and the past (the forensic concern with the justice or injustice of things already done), by elimination he needed a kind aiming primarily at the present. Then he goes on to say that "epideictic" or demonstrative speakers, in their concern with praise and blame (the honorable and dishonorable) also frequently recall the past or look to the future—which would seem to take back all that had been given. But the selecting of the present as the most appropriate time for this kind is justified by another consideration. Often this third kind, as a rhetoric of "display," was aimed at praise, not as an attempt to win an audience's praise for the subject discussed, but as an attempt to win praise for the oratory itself. The appropriate time for such oratory could then be called the present in the sense that the appeal was directed to the very presence of the words and speaker themselves, not for some ulterior purpose, as with convincing a jury about a past act or moving an assembly to make a decision about the future, but purely because it aimed to give delight in the exercise of eloquence as such. We can see the appeal of subject matter merging with the appeal of diction in and for itself when Cicero selected toil and personal danger as good themes for panegyric on the ground that they get the readiest reception, since they offer "the richest opportunities for praise" and can be discussed "most ornately" (*ornatissime*).

Obviously, this third form would become uppermost in periods of rhetorical decay, as when the democratic functions of public debate were curtailed in Rome after the fall of the Republic. At such time, the sturdiest rhetoric with ulterior motive would be found, not in public utterance, but in the unrecorded cabals of courtiers. And public rhetoric, with only the forms of persuasion left, came eventually, as in school exercises, to deal with arbitrarily chosen subjects, which were then developed with all the resources of amplification, displayed for their own sake. But this was merely an extreme expression of a tendency present in epideictic at the start. For this kind contained the most essential motive of all: persuasion by words, rather than by force, on the part of those who loved eloquence for itself alone (those born verbalizers, so close to the very center of human motives, as distinct from the motives of other animals, those humane word-slingers who would rather fail in seeking to persuade by words than succeed in persuading by other means). Critics must have epideictic in mind who say that eloquence begins in the love of words for their own sake.

The "presentness" of epideictic, which brought it closest to appeal by sheer delight, also explains why it is, according to Aristotle, the kind that lends itself best to the written word. For its effects can be savored, hence may profit by a closer, more sustained scrutiny. Also, since pure display rhetoric comes closest to the appeal of poetic in and for itself, it readily permits the arbitrary selection of topics halfway between rhetoric and poetic. And here even methods originally forensic may be used as artifice. Thus, in the English tradition of love poems written in praise of one's mistress or as mock invective against love, etc., or where the lover pleads the "cause" of his mistress or brings indictments against her, the poet's tactics are not read as he would have them read unless the reader watches their playful adaptation of rhetorical forms to poetic purposes. (See Rosemond Tuve, *Elizabethan and Metaphysical Imagery,* for a good discussion of the rhetorical tradition implicit in such lyrical conceits.)

This application touches upon an aspect of rhetoric which, besides allowing for such playful or esthetic usages as we have been just considering, also figured in the rhetoric of ulterior purposes. Both Cicero and Quintilian make much of a traditional distinction between general theses (*quaestiones*) and particular cases (*causae*). The *quaestiones* were often of a sort wholly outside the scope of the flatly true-or-false (as were one to debate whether truth was greater than justice). The *causae* (as with debates whether such-and-such a man had been guilty of such-and-such an offense meriting such-and-such punishment) brought rhetoric within the orbit of *casuistry* (thereby suggesting that an extension of the rhetorical range to cover all cases in their *uniqueness* would be in order, Cicero saying that there are as many *causae* as there are people). The general and the particular directions of rhetoric overlap insofar as all unique cases will necessarily involve the application of the universal topics to the particular matter at hand, and insofar as even situations considered very broadly may possess uniqueness. (Since any one particular era in history, for instance, will be unlike any other in its exact combination of cultural factors, historiography seems naturally vowed to a measure of rhetorical casuistry, however scientific may be the pretensions of historians, economists, sociologists, etc., though the scientific pretensions themselves might be less effective rhetorically if such enterprise were formally recognized as involved in the rhetoric of casuistry.)

The forensic or judicial kind (as with speeches by prosecuting or defense attorneys in a law suit) seems clear enough. And so with deliberative, though by listing its main concerns, as stated in Aristotle, we might better realize how ubiquitous such "oratory" is today, particularly in written forms that often pass for sheer "information," "knowledge," "science." They are: ways and means, war and peace, national defense, imports and exports, legislation.

If we confine the third kind of rhetoric to praise and blame, just where, Quintilian asks, are we to place the rhetorical function of a speaker who would "complain, console, pacify, incite, frighten, encourage, instruct, interpret, narrate, plead for mercy, give thanks, congratulate, reproach, curse, describe, command, retract, state views and preferences," etc.? Such questions led to other ways of classification: by style and function (Cicero's three *officia oratoris*). In his *Orator,* an earlier work than the *De Oratore,* when defending his verbal opulence against a rising "Attic" school in Rome which called for simpler diction, Cicero distinguishes three styles (*genera dicendi, genera scribendi*): the grandiloquent, plain, and tempered. And he names as the three "offices" of the orator: (1) to teach, inform, instruct (*docere*); (2) to please (*delectare*); (3) to move or "bend" (*movere, flectere*).

He also refers to styles in a more personal or individual sense, when observing that orators are next of kin to poets, and that each poet has his own way of writing (and in a critical digression he gives a catalogue of formulas for succinctly characterizing and savoring the distinctive qualities in the personal style of various writers well known to antiquity). However, the three over-all styles of oratory are not thought of thus, as personal expression, but as a means for carrying out the three "offices." That is, the plain style is best for teaching, the tempered style for pleasing, and the ornate (grandiloquent) style for moving. Though human weakness makes an orator more able in one or another of these styles, the ideal orator should be master of all three, since an oration aims at all three functions. For though it aims ultimately to *move* the audience by a sweeping appeal to the emotions, it can do so only if it holds their interest (hence, using all the resources of verbal delight); and it can't either hold their interest or move them unless it has a groundwork of clarity. (Cicero says that the orator should call as much attention to his use of instruction as possible, but should thoroughly though unnoticeably infuse his speech with the other two functions.)

This way of dividing in terms of styles and offices cuts at an angle across the Aristotelian theory of kinds. But the tempered style, with its aim to delight, does closely parallel the motive of eloquence for its own sake that centers in epideictic (the *genus demonstrativum*). Cicero puts it to use; but it becomes the *end* of eloquence insofar as ulterior rhetorical purpose drops away.

Longinus' treatise *On the Sublime* is thought to have been written in the first century or the third, A.D. But with Aristotle's *Art of Rhetoric* dated at 330 B.C., Cicero's *De Oratore* at 55 B.C., Quintilian's *Institutio Oratoria* in the latter half of the first century A.D., and the fourth book of Augustine's *De Doctrina Christiana* in 426-7 A.D., it would make a very neat "curve" if Longinus could be placed as a transition between Quintilian and Augustine. For while its stress upon the sheer delight of literature (with even purposive oratory discussions from this "es-thetic" point of view) would assign it to a period of decadence, and Longinus himself regrets the triviality of the times, so far as new writing is concerned, the quality of the exaltation in his love of literature seems like a matching, in pagan terms, for the Augustinian fervor in Christian persuasion. Longinus' treatise would seem to qualify perfectly as an estheticizing of the Christian motive *before* its institutional triumph, quite as much modern love of literature is a *relique* of Christianity, the reduction of its persuasion and passion to a cult of purely esthetic "grace."

In any case, when we turn to Augustine, we find the Ciceronian stress upon ulterior purpose restored in all its vigor. Also, the rhetoric with which Augustine is exclusively concerned, a rhetoric for persuad-ing audiences to a Christian way of life, does not aim at systematic observations about the art of "proving opposites." His treatment is at once both narrowed and widened: narrowed in the sense that it is

concerned only with the use of words for one purpose, the teaching of
Christianity; widened in the sense that the persuasion it would establish was a doctrine of universal motivation. Thus, his discussion of
persuasion in general is built about a close analysis of Biblical texts,
which he selects and studies for their *craftsmanship*. His sense of
purely literary appreciation is as vigorous and acute as with Longinus,
but the appreciation is always subordinated to his ulterior purpose as
propagandist of the Faith. He is particularly convincing in his treatment of St. Paul, like him a master of apologetics, and like him one
of the twice-born whose sensitiveness to communicative problems was
sharpened by the memory of harsh conflict within, of inner voices at
one time opposing each other like rivals in debate.

Applying the three Ciceronian offices, he characteristically names
the plain style (that is, the style for teaching, *docere*), the "subdued"
(*genus submissum*), thereby spontaneously indicating perhaps, that
both as a Christian and as an individual, he *had to impose restraint
upon himself* in the use of a manner which many would practice
merely through having nothing to restrain. Next comes the "tempered" or moderated style. (He is obviously affected by the category
of the epideictic here, as he says that the temperate style is best suited
for criticism and praise, even the praise of God being named as a
fit subject for this style.) But one must speak grandly (*granditer*)
when there is something to be done and "minds are to be swayed"
(*ad flectendos animos*). Here again we see a replica of the Longinus
esthetic in terms of Christian persuasion: for just as the concern with
the "sublime" in Longinus culminates in ideas and images of the fearsome, so the ardor and vehemence of the grand style in Augustine is
said to be particularly fit for admonishing against the neglect of God.

But the *totality* of motivation propounded by Christian doctrine
provided a new poignancy to the relation between the rhetoric of
particular cases and the rhetoric of generalization For though each
of the three styles is appropriate for certain purposes, Augustine says
there is a sense in which all topics of Christian rhetoric deserve treatment in the grand style, since there is nothing in life that does not
somehow bear upon God. Thus, though money matters may be trivial
from an ordinary point of view, no sum, however small, can be trivial
to the true Christian. Wherefore St. Paul spoke of money in the grand
style, since justice, charity, and righteousness are involved, "and no

sane man can doubt that these are great, even in things exceptionally slight." The resonance of such a rhetoric is obvious. Since all was of God, for God, through God, the step from the lowly to the lofty was everywhere at hand. And just as, in the *Grammar of Motives,* we saw that "God" is the Term of Terms, the Title of Titles, the X of X's (Aristotle's definition of God as "thought of thought" can be the paradigm), so in the *Rhetoric of Motives* (using "commonplace" in the sense assigned it in classical theory) we see that "God" is the Commonplace of Commonplaces, the Topic of Topics, the universal *Quaestio* behind each local *Causa,* the Ultimate to which any particular matter of controversy might be grandly reduced.

Ironically, though Augustine was restoring the dignity of rhetoric, after the decay into which it had fallen during the pagan "second sophistic," he expressly denies the Ciceronian and Quintilian attempts to equate eloquence with moral excellence. Augustine was pleading for a "truth" greater than any purely human kind of moral grandeur. Hence, while saying that a good life on the part of the preacher was the most persuasive ingredient of all in commending Christian doctrine, he placed the power of this doctrine outside and beyond any merely human or natural vessels. A preacher might preach Christian doctrine purely for purposes of self-aggrandizement, or even as a lie, but if he preached it correctly his preaching could do good, because of its intrinsic worth, despite the viciousness of his motives.

This notion that the power of truth transcends the limitations of the personal agent who propounds it (or, as Augustine puts it, that the chair, *cathedra,* forces him to say what is good), finds its ironic counterpart in a situation today, when the "truth" of the Christian terminology has found its materialistic counterpart in the terminologies of science. For here again, the truth can transcend the vices of those who communicate it. Indeed, unfortunately, there is the risk that it can by the same token transcend their virtues also, as when earnest, hard-working men, whose efforts are guided by discipline and devotion, perfect powers which, in their pragmatic validity, can be used by men of different cast, in ways that threaten the very existence of mankind.

In the *De Oratore,* Cicero had said that "the faculty of speech flows from the deepest founts of wisdom" (*ex intimis sapientiae fontibus*). With the same distinctions in mind, Augustine refers to St. Paul as "a follower of wisdom, a leader of eloquence" (*comes sapientiae, dux eloquentiae*). But there is a notable difference: for Cicero is equating rhetoric with wisdom, whereas Augustine is relating them in a preferential order. In his scheme, wisdom (philosophy, "dialectic") is a "source of eloquence," not because it is one with eloquence (since the "truth" of Christian doctrine can be stated without eloquence), but because it is the *ground* of eloquence. Thus, whereas Aristotle grouped rhetoric with dialectic by reason of the fact that both were purely verbal instruments, in Augustine (as with the Stoics) dialectic is more than words: for when it is correct, it deals with the ultimate nature of *things,* hence has a kind of extraverbal reference to guide the use of ornament (eloquence, rhetoric). The end of rhetoric was "to persuade with words" (*persuadere dicendo*); but the principle of Logos behind such purely human language was "the Word" in another sense, a kind of Word that was *identical with* reality. Such seem to be the assumptions underlying Augustine's theories of rhetoric. And they seem to follow from the stress upon *teaching* as an "office" of rhetoric.

Cicero had made much of the distinction between words and things (*verba* and *res*). Aristotle was thinking along the same lines when he distinguished rhetoric, as an art of words, from the sciences, each having a special extraverbal subject matter. A passage in Aristotle's *Rhetoric* making a distinction between natural incentives, such as hunger, and those arising "through reason" (*para logou*) is often rendered in English as a distinction between "logical" and "illogical" motives; but *logos* means both "reason" and "word," hence we might assume that Aristotle was seeking to distinguish between nonverbal motives (*alogoi*—appetites that would arise even if there were no such thing as language) and "verbal" motives (*para logou*—appetitions depending upon language for their development, as with the "new needs" that go with the change of human purpose from mere "living" to "living well").

In any case, note that once you treat instruction as an aim of rhetoric you introduce a principle that can widen the scope of rhetoric beyond persuasion. It is on the way to include also works on the theory and practice of exposition, description, *communication* in general. Thus, finally, out of this principle, you can derive contemporary "semantics" as an aspect of rhetoric.

We thus see how each of the three "offices" comes to the end of a line, each in its way transcending the motive of persuasion (ulterior purpose) by becoming an end in itself. An ideal descriptive language *can be* aligned *in contrast with* hortatory languages. But one can also derive it *out of* the rhetorical. For one can get to this ideal by dwelling exclusively upon the first of the three rhetorical "offices." And, in so doing, one will be at the point where, in the Augustinian scheme, rhetoric overlaps upon dialectic, which in turn is taken to be one with the nature of *things* (the nonverbal ground of all verbalizing).

Imagination

Perhaps because theories of imagination, as a kind of *knowledge,* work best in those areas where poetic and scientist thought overlap, the concern with "imagination" as a suasive device does not reach full expression until the modern era. Also, such concern in the classical rhetorics was often treated in terms of "actualization" (*energeia,* the use of words that suggest purposive movement) and "vividness" (*enargeia*). And Aristotle's classing of "actualization" along with "antithesis" and "metaphor" as the three most effective devices of speech, would include much other matter which might in modern theory be treated from the standpoint of imagination.

According to Aristotle's scheme, and even in a philosopher so on the edge of modern scientific naturalism as Spinoza, "imagination" is quite low in the scale of mental functions, being next to brute sensation, and the highest faculty of which brutes were thought capable. In human beings, according to this hierarchy, it stood midway between sensation and intellect.*

But whereas, in this terminology, sensation requires the actual presence of the thing sensed, imagination does not require the presence of the thing imagined. Hence, though the imagination's necessary use of images testifies to its beginnings in sense, it can deal in images independently of sense (as in both dreams and willed imaginings). This consideration opens another set of possibilities whereby imagina-

---

* It so appears in the *Ethics*. In the *Tractatus Theologico–Politicus* it is treated as a medium of prophetic vision for communicating the revelations of religion. Here is the kind of imagination which could later be secularized in romantic theories of artistic vision.

tion can be thought of as reordering the objects of sense, or taking them apart and imagining them in new combinations (such as centaurs) that do not themselves derive from sensory experience. It can thus become "creative," and even visionary of things forever closed to sense, as with the language of the mystic, who would express his intuitions in images meant to transcend imagery. Coleridge's "desynonymizing" of "fancy" and "imagination" was in part an attempt to dissociate these two meanings, leaving for "fancy" (from the Greek *phantasia*) the purely "mechanical" recombinations of sensory experience, and giving to "imagination" (from the Latin *imaginatio* that had been usually used to translate the Greek word) creative and supersensory meanings.

Longinus tells us that in his day, imagination (*phantasia,* which contributes to *enargeia*) had "come to be used of passages where, inspired by enthusiasm and passion, you seem to see what you describe and bring it vividly before the eyes of your audience." After citing examples in *poetry* which "show a strongly mythic exaggeration, far beyond the limits of literal belief," he says that the "best use of imagination" in *rhetoric* is to convince the audience of the "reality and truth" of the speaker's assertions. He also cites passages from Demosthenes where, according to him, imagination persuades by going beyond mere argument. ("When combined with argument, it not only convinces the audience, it positively masters them.") And he ends by equating imagination with genius (*megalophrosyne,* high-mindedness) and with imitation.

This is probably the highest tribute to "imagination" in all Greek and Roman literature (significantly, it appeared in a work not known to have been mentioned by any writer in antiquity, a work which did not come into its own until the currents of modern romanticism were well under way). But though he considers the aim of poetry "to strike with astonishment," and introduces talk of "ecstasy" into literary criticism, he attributes a different role to imagination in rhetoric, where it presumably serves to make the real seem doubly real rather than to make us, within the conditions of a fiction, believe in the "reality" of things which we may not otherwise believe at all. (Rosemond Tuve cites a relevant formula in Mazzoni: "The credible as credible is the subject of rhetoric, and the credible as marvelous is the subject of poetry.")

See Pico della Mirandola's *On the Imagination* (the Latin text, with an introduction, an English translation, and notes; by Harry Caplan: footnote, p. 36) for references showing that medieval writers had often distinguished between productive and reproductive kinds of imagination, thus anticipating Coleridge's systematic dissociation, though not with his emphases. But Pico did not share this "desynonymizing" (in his tract written at the end of the fifteenth century). Aristotle had said, in the third book of his *Psychology:* "To the mind, images serve as if they were contents of perception. If it judges them to be good, it pursues them. If it judges them to be bad, it avoids them. That is why the mind never thinks without an image." According to his scheme, both imagination and reason can originate movement, the movements originated by imagination being dangerous except insofar as they are controlled by reason (which should in turn be guided by religion). Similarly Pico, when objecting to Avicenna's distinction between the phantastic and the imaginative, wrote: Man is moved to action (*ad operandum*) for the sake of either real or apparent good; but desire depends on perception: perception in turn depends on the senses (which require images). Hence, since even one who reasons and understands must observe images, "we must admit that our actions depend greatly on the nature of this power" (*actiones nostras de eius potestatis ingenio plurimum dependere*).

But while, in Pico's scheme, man shares imagination with the lower animals, human imagination extends farther, and includes motives of decoration, ambition, and honor to which animals are but slightly susceptible. Children are mostly motivated by the brutish kind of imagination. Hence, and because of their weak intellects, one best guides them in the ways of virtue by bringing them to imagine in detail the tortures of hell and the delights of Paradise.

The rhetorical implications of such thinking are brought out clearly by Francis Bacon's formula, in *The Advancement of Learning:* "The duty and office of Rhetoric is to apply Reason to Imagination for the better moving of the Will." According to Bacon, Rhetoric should "fill the imagination, to second Reason, and not to oppress it." And "it is the office of Rhetoric to make pictures of virtue and goodness, so that they may be seen." Or, in a fuller statement: "Rhetoric is subservient to the imagination, as logic is to the understanding; and the duty and office of rhetoric . . . is no other than to apply and recommend the dictates of reason to imagination, in order to excite the appetite and will."

Will itself, according to Bacon, is altered by religion, opinion, and apprehension—and obviously imagination could be brought to the reënforcement of all three. And in the remarks we have cited, he is considering the good uses of a power which will deserve distrust, once you stress rather the negative possibilities that imagination may reënforce prejudiced opinion, false apprehensions, and lapses from religion. Like Augustine, he here considers rhetorical inducement to action from the standpoint of sermonizing, and he judges imagination as a means of persuasion to this end.

Aristotle had said that, particularly in the arousing of pity, the rhetorician is most effective if he can bring before the audience the actual evidence of hardship and injustice suffered. Thus, in proportion as "imagination" went up in the scale of motivational values, one might come to speak of an appeal to the *imagination* in many instances which classical theory might have treated as persuasion by the appeals of *pathos* and *ethos* (appeals to "emotion" and by "character" or personality). In literary theories of romanticism, poetic appeal to the imagination could even be considered the very antithesis of logical appeals to reason, quite as appeal to passion and emotion had often been. There was also an opportunity here to think of imagination dualistically, advocating its use, as higher than reason, in the esthetic realm, while calling for vocabularies that completely outlawed it (in its emotional aspects) from the realm of practical administration (a dualism whereby the same person can now subscribe to both poetic estheticism and scientific positivism).

In sum, today any representation of passions, emotions, actions, and even mood and personality, is likely to be treated as falling under the heading of "images," which in turn explicitly or implicitly involve "imagination." Often "imagination" seems to sum up the "lyric motive," as distinct from the "dramatic motive" (whereupon it may also take unto itself the area of overlap between the two terms). It is a miscellany ranging all the way from the visible, tangible, here-and-now to the mystically transcendent, from the purely sensory and empirical, even the scientifically exact observation, to the dramatically empathic and sympathetic, from the literal to the fantastic, including all shades of sentiment and refinements of taste and judgment. It may also be taken to include the "unconscious," as the critic "unconsciously" feels that his term subsumes a batch of other terms variously at odds with one another; and often by the "imagination" today, as by the "unconscious," we mean simply the awareness of distinctions and discriminations not yet reduced to the systematic order of a filing system.

A good place to look, if you would see how imagination can come to take over areas once occupied by a more directly dramatist vocabulary of action, is George Santayana's *Realms of Being*. For Santayana's work is particularly designed to merge the realistic Latin stress upon the dramatic with the subjective-epistemological-psychological-scientist-lyrist stress of German transcendental idealism. Most notably one should examine his alignments in what he calls the "realm of Spirit," since "the only possible way for spirit to create is to imagine." (*Realms of Being,* p. 575.)   Here we are told that spirit endures all passions (715), transmutes sympathy and pity into charity (783), and is liberated through suffering and death (761).   Again:

> The potential sympathy that spirit has with all life is not purely perceptive but dramatic. . . .   In the act of surveying and understanding action, spirit raises that action into an image; and the imagination, though likewise a living process, moves at another level (715).

Here the philosopher is considering the point at which imagery can cease to be a sensory representation of things in the practical realm, and can through imagination come to transcend that realm.   But though holding that spirit naturally loves knowledge, he disagrees with Bacon's pragmatist equating of such knowledge with power (725).   Rather, he says, spirit's love of knowledge is a "love of imagination"—and imagination relies on real knowledge, rather than confining itself to sheer fantasy, only because "it needs to be fed by contact with external things and by widening vital rhythms."

Also, when considering contemporary theory (which often, under the auspices of Blake and Coleridge, would make imagination and poetry identical, so that the study of poetry becomes the study of images), it is good to remember that in its beginnings, the term belongs in *psychology*.   Then, in Western thought, it next seems to have been treated in rhetoric (because of the persuasive effect that a speaker's images may have upon the audience's acts and attitudes).   And only much later, when critics were thinking less of expressions that move to responses beyond words and more of expressions that were "moving" in themselves, it began to take on the almost exclusively esthetic meaning so often imputed to it by some literary schools today. One may legitimately remember that the word is not "essentially poetic," as it now seems to be, but was originally a term applied to the general psychology of mankind, and even to animals; and except perhaps for the prophetic references in Longinus, it was not wholly poetized until the philosophic and literary theories that flowered in nineteenth-century romanticism. The fact is worth recalling when a critic resents the use of new psychological terms, objecting on the grounds that they introduce principles alien to poetry as such. There may be valid objections to such terms. But whatever the objections may be, the merely categorical one that the terms are, by their very nature, extraliterary, seems dubious, unless one is willing at the same time to surrender the term "imagination," as being overly psychologistic and extraliterary in its origins.

Even so "literary" a writer as William Hazlitt could treat of "imagination" more from the ethical than the esthetic point of view. In his *Essays on the Principles of Human Action,* he writes:

> The direct or primary motive, or impulse which determines the mind to the volition of anything must . . . in all cases depend on the idea of that thing as conceived by the imagination, and on the idea solely.

He also explains in terms of imagination both "the motives by which I am impelled to the pursuit of my own good, and those by which I am impelled to pursue the good of others." But whereas Pico and Bacon would subordinate imagination to the control of reason, Hazlitt prepares the way for its modern emancipation from reason when he says that imagination itself "must be the immediate spring and guide of action." He assumes that imagination can control "the blind impulses of associated mechanical feelings . . . making them subservient to the accomplishment of some particular purpose." While deriving from imagination both our ideas of self-interest and our sympathy for others, he uses relative ease of *identification* to account for instances where the motive of self-interest is the stronger:

> The only reason for my preferring my future interest to that of others must arise from my anticipating it with greater warmth of present imagination. It is this greater liveliness and force with

which I can enter into my future feelings, that in a manner identifies them with my present being: and this notion of identity being once formed, the mind makes use of it to strengthen its habitual propensity, by giving to personal motives a reality and absolute truth which they can never have. Hence it has been inferred that my real substantial interest in anything must be derived from the impression of the object itself, as if that could have any sort of communication with my present feelings, or excite any interest in my mind, but by means of the imagination, which is naturally affected in a certain manner by the prospect of future good or evil.

Image and Idea

The stress upon image involves a corresponding counterstress upon idea. Edmund Burke would doubtless have wanted to treat idea and image simply as reënforcements of each other, since by his prescription every important statement should have a thought, an image, and a sentiment. William Hazlitt bridged the distinction at one stroke by referring to "ideas of the imagination."

In Kant, "ideas" belonged to *reason;* and thus they were "dialectical," in the realm of "principle," as contrasted with empirical or positive experiences comprising intuitions of sensibility and concepts of the understanding. By "house," for instance, we refer to a vast manifold of sensations which we bring together, in one meaning, insofar as we can sum up the whole batch of sensations by the concept, "house."

Obviously, if we looked at such a house, the "image" that we saw would not correspond with the images of modern poetic theory. Rather, "image" in Kant's sense would be quite close to Aristotle's kind: it would be perceived through the senses, and remembered or anticipated in the imagination. The "poetic" image, on the other hand, can *stand for* things that never were or never will be. Hazlitt's usage is well worth considering here. The "poetic" image of a house is also an "idea" of a house, insofar as it has purely dialectical significance, allowing for verbal manipulations that transcend the empirical or positive. You can't *point to* the house that appears in a poem; even if the poet may have had a particular house in mind. For his word "house" will also *stand for* relationships alien to the *concept* of house as such. The *conceptual* house is a dwelling of such-and-such structure, material, dimensions, etc. The *poetic* house is built of *identifications*. (Thus it may equal sufferings in childhood, or sense of great security in childhood; a retreat from combat, or a place from which one sallies forth to combat; a "maternal" house as contrasted with some alternative location "paternal" in motive, etc.).

If these other, invisible meanings surrounding the poetic image are not exactly "ideas" in the purely intellectualistic sense of the term, they are certainly not empirical in the purely positivistic sense. And such connotations or overtones of the poetic image are at least "confused ideas," both in the sense that critical analysis can often discern some of them with sufficient clarity to name their "ideational" equivalents, and in the sense that such "imaginary" meanings are *fused together* in the image (as it functions in the poem).

The old rhetoricians used to be much concerned about a distinction between "infinite" (or "general") and "definite" (or "specific") questions. (Or, from the Greek, "theses" and "hypotheses.") Thus, to quote from Thomas Wilson's *Art of Rhetoric*, where he is practically paraphrasing a passage in Quintilian:

> Those questions are called infinite which generally are propounded, without the comprehension of time, place, and person, or any such like: that is to say, when no certain thing is named, but only words are generally spoken. As thus, whether it be best to marry, or to live single. Which is better, a courtier's life, or a scholar's life.
>
> Those questions are called definite, which set forth a matter, with the appointment and naming of place, time, and person. As thus, Whether it now be best here in England for a Priest to marry, or to live single. Whether it were mete for the King's Majesty that now is, to marry with a stranger, or to marry with one of his own Subjects. Now the definite question (as the which concerneth some one person) is most agreeing to the purpose of an Orator, considering particular matters in the law ... etc.

The more we puzzle over the relation between idea and image, the more we come to feel that it should be considered in accordance with the pattern of the old distinction between "infinite" and "definite" questions. One may write of "security" in general ("infinitely," without reference to conditions), while having about the edges of his consciousness the image of some particular place or condition that means security to him. Or one's writing may assemble the imagery of some particular place or condition which represents for him the "idea" of security, an organizing principle that may guide his selection and treatment of images, even though he never "consciously" refers to the general topic of security at all.

That is, behind productive *poetic* imagery, as contrasted with the reproductive imagery of raw sensation, there are *organizational principles*. And given acute enough means and terms of analysis, such organizational principles can be named in terms that express their equivalent in the vocabulary of *ideas*. This is the realm of reason (the "dialectical" realm of "principles" and "ideas"). And it is shared by poetic imagination (hence the justice of Coleridge's equations, which assign to "imagination" in the poetic sphere the place corresponding with that assigned to "reason" in the sphere of philosophy and ethics).

In sum: Insofar as a poet's images are organically related, there is a formal principle behind them. The images could be said to *body forth* this principle. The principle itself could, by a properly discerning critic, be named in terms of *ideas* (or one basic idea with modifiers). Thus, the imagery could be said to convey an invisible, intangible idea in terms of visible, tangible things. In this respect, the *pattern* of Platonism would seem to provide an accurate technical description of poetic structure.

In keeping with the genius of Hazlitt's expression, "ideas of the imagination," we began thinking that there should be a term for ideas and images both. "Titles" (or "epithets") seemed to meet the requirement. For the rhetorician uses "titles" (either imaginal or ideological) to identify a person or a cause with whatever kinds of things will, in his judgment, call forth the desired response. He will select such "titles" in accordance with the bias of his intention and the opinions of his audience. But what are such "titles" (or "entitlings," or "identifications") but another term for the Aristotelian "topics," which shift so easily and imperceptibly between ideas and images that you wonder how the two realms could ever come to be at odds?

Yet there is a difference between an abstract term naming the "idea" of, say, security, and a concrete image designed to stand for this idea, and to "place it before our very eyes." For one thing, if the image employs the full resources of imagination, it will not represent merely one idea, but will contain a whole bundle of principles, even ones that would be mutually contradictory if reduced to their purely ideational equivalents. Ideationally, a speaker might have to go through much reasoning if he wanted to equate a certain measure with public security. But if he could translate it imaginally into terms of, say, the mother, he might profit not only from this one identification, but from many kindred principles or ideas which, when approached in this spirit, are associated with the mother-image (or mother principle, or idea of the mother). Yet, whereas these further meanings might serve as implicit "arguments" if the speaker's thesis were translated into an *image,* they would not figure in the explicit *ideological* statement at all. Assume, for instance, that there are five major principles of appeal in a mother-image (security, affection, tradition, "naturalness," communion). Then assume an ideological argument identifying a cause in terms of security, but not explicitly pleading for it in terms of these four other principles. Now, if the speaker, in winding up his argument for his cause as an aid to security, translates it into a mother-image, might he not thereby get the "unearned increment" from the other four principles vibrant in this same image? (It would be "unearned," that is, from the standpoint of the purely ideological argument.)

Also, like the Leibnizian *petites perceptions,* images may anticipate clear ideas in history, or in a man's personal development, as he may *imagine* some character or act before clearly diagnosing the motivational *ideas* which it stands for. Or he may imagine dramatic or narrative figures or events which stand for *combinations of motives* not ideationally named. (Hobbes and Spinoza, for instance, give recipes for the complexity of motives underlying the various passions and emotions already named in their culture; but dramatic poets can offer imaginal equivalents for these, or for other combinations of motives not thus reduced to abstract philosophic formulation.)

Once you have a distinction so clear as that between image and idea at their extremes, you can expect to find some vocabularies treating them as almost diametrical opposites. Hence, the distinction could be taken as grounds for the feeling that, despite Aristotle's remarks about the close kinship between poetry and philosophy, and Cicero's remarks about the close kinship between poetry and rhetoric, there has arisen, along with the stress upon imagination as the very essence of poetry, a tendency to treat of ideas as though they were antithetical to poetry, until finally we come to the proportion: imagination is to poetry as ideology is to rhetoric. By this alignment, insofar as the rhetorician gains effects by the use of imagery, he would be said to have a "poetic strain" in him. In line with such thinking as it figures in much modern esthetics, you often find imagination and logic treated as *essentially antithetical* (though a more pliant attitude would, at the very least, call for a terminology which treated them as consistent in some respects and at variance in others).

The sensationalist position also fits well with the widespread resistance to "didactic" poetry, a resistance which reaches its fullest expression in the esthetic of Symbolism, Imagism, and Surrealism (though medieval thinkers who looked upon the "enigma" as natural to poetry would probably have found plenty of didactic, or even moralistic, motives in the work of such modern schools). Even an extremely imagistic poem is organized only insofar as it abides by integrating principles; and because they are principles, if criticism were discerning enough it could detect their counterparts in the realm of ideas; thus the sensory images could be said to embody ideas that transcend the sensory. In any case, the tendency to view image and idea as antithetical has given us today a frequent distinction between imagery (a cluster of interrelated images) and ideology (a structure of interrelated ideas). And though "ideology" originally meant but the study of ideas in themselves (as with Socrates' systematic concern with the problems involved in defining the idea of justice), it usually refers now to a system of political or social ideas, framed and propounded for an ulterior purpose. In this new usage, "ideology" is obviously but a kind of rhetoric (since the ideas are so related that they have in them, either explicitly or implicitly, inducements to some social and political choices rather than others). Yet, though rhetorical ideology thus comes to be contrasted with poetic imagery, Jeremy Bentham warned us to look for the images that, overtly or covertly, serve as models for ideas.

Where are we now? We have been saying that, since ideas and images are capable of being distinguished at least in their extremes, it follows that, from certain points of view, they may be treated as opposites. But we have also been considering how images are so related to ideas that an idea can be treated as the *principle* behind the systematic development of an image.

Another way of stating this would be by taking as a paradigm the relation between spirit and matter proclaimed in idealistic metaphysics. (See our remarks on Hegel's *Philosophy of History,* for instance, in the *Grammar.*) Since in such schemes, the principle of unification or relationship binding a cluster of related natural phenomena can be looked upon as an invisible, intangible spirit represented by the imagery, so a cluster of images organized in accordance with some principle of artistic order would correspond to the temporal or historical conditions by which the Universal Idea makes itself manifest at a given time and place. Whatever you may think of this pattern, as a *metaphysics of history,* such a view of nature as the representative embodiment of Universal Purpose is a good way in which to consider the relationship between some *limited artistic purpose* and its embodiment, or representation, in the imagery of nature and experience. The imagery is thus treated as the "natural incarnation" of the idea or organizing principle that guided the choice and development of it. (We should here have a secular esthetic equivalent of the Pauline formula for the word made flesh.)

As the imagery would be a translation of the idea into sensory terms, criticism might conversely propose to retranslate this sensory version back into purely dialectical or ideological terms, abstractions transcending sheer sensory experience. And it would look upon an image, not as the merely "positive" thing our senses take it to be, but as "negative," in the sense that the image existed by *exclusion,* by differentiation from other images, each of which would, in its way, be one particular, unique embodiment of the over-all principle organizing or generating the lot. This is like Hegel's doctrine of the "concrete universal," according to which any one "moment," any one thing, in its particularity or divisiveness, is not "positive" but "negative," when considered from the standpoint of the general principles represented by its thinghood.

Metaphysically this may be dubious. But the esthetic equivalent amounts to little more than the statement that, where a shifting body of imagery is considered in a unified work of art, the "spirit" of each individual image is to be found, not in itself, but in the artistic purpose behind the whole body of imagery. Of course, even if critics agreed on this statement of the case, there would still be room for much haggling as to just what may be behind a given artistic structure, and inspiriting it. We should also note that the distinction between "positive" and "negative" again allows an opening for those who would treat image and idea as in opposition, rather than in apposition. But that tendency can be "pantheistically" reversed by applying the thought of a correspondence between symbol and symbolized, as with Carlyle's formula, in *Sartor Resartus:* "Matter [i.e., image], being the manifestation of Spirit [i.e., idea], is Spirit."

But the point is: Seen from this angle, the antithetical relation between image and idea is replaced by a partial stress upon the bond of kinship between them. Add the fact that all abstractions themselves are necessarily expressed in terms of weakened and confused images, a consideration which doubtless explains why Aristotle said that we cannot think without images. It also figures in Jeremy Bentham's "theory of fictions," a method for disclosing the *imagery* that lurks behind purely *ideological* expressions.

Rhetorical Analysis in Bentham

Bentham's great contributions to the study of persuasion were made almost in spite of himself. In trying to promote ways of discussion that could truly transcend the suggestiveness of imagery, he revealed how thoroughly imaginal our thinking is. Scrutinizing the most abstract of legalistic terms, asking himself just what it meant to plead and pass judgment in terms of "legal fictions," he proposed a methodic search for "archetypes." By "archetypes" he meant the images that underly the use of abstractions. (To quote one of his favorite examples: Consider the irrelevant but suggestive and provocative images of *binding* that lurk in the term, "obligation.")

Bentham here discovered a kind of poetry concealed beneath legal jargon usually considered the very opposite of poetry. It was *applied poetry,* or rhetoric, since it was the use of poetic resources to affect judgments, decisions, hence attitudes and actions. As we noted when discussing Richards and Mead in the *Grammar,* the notion of an attitude or incipient act is ambiguous; an attitude of sympathy, for instance, may either lead into an overt act of kindness, or it may serve "liberally" as the *substitute* for an act of kindness. And since Richards stresses in the "imaginal" action of poetry its role as an alternative to the overt act, we can see how he "repoetized" Bentham's essentially rhetorical concerns. For when one thinks of poetry as the exercise of imaginal suggestiveness in areas that transcend the practical, one has again made the step from Cicero to Longinus: one admires an expression, not for its power to move a hearer towards this or that decision, but for its use of images that are "moving" in and for themselves. Once you think of the imaginal, not as inducement to action, but as the sensitive suspension of action, invitations that you might *fear* in rhetoric can be *enjoyed* in poetry.

In keeping with his search for "archetypes," or latent images, Bentham was also resentful of the linguistic device whereby, when the king is meant, we say instead the Crown or the Throne; instead of a churchman, the Church or Altar; instead of lawyers, the Law; instead of a judge, the Court; instead of rich men, Property. As he puts it, in his typically crabbed style:

> Of this device, the object and effect is, that any unpleasant idea that in the mind of the hearer or reader might happen to stand associated with the idea of the person or the class, is disengaged from it: and in the stead of the more or less obnoxious individual or individuals, the object present is a creature of the fancy, by the idea of which, as in poetry, the imagination is tickled—a phantom which, by means of the power with which the individual or class is clothed is constituted an object of respect and veneration.

He was here attacking from one angle an idealistic resource of language which Coleridge uses to great rhetorical advantage in his tract on *The Constitution of Church and State, According to the Idea of Each*. For by treating of institutions and social classes "according to the *idea* of each," Coleridge could, as it were, discover a perfect archetypal design lying behind the imperfections of his contemporary society, hence could lay more weight upon such perfect spirit than upon actual conditions. Bentham also calls such kinds of amplification "allegorical idols," and diagnoses them as appeal *ad imaginationem*.

Bentham's work has long been out of print. But his main concerns with "archetypation" have been reprinted in C. K. Ogden's *Bentham's Theory of Fictions*. Two other important contributions of Bentham's to rhetoric were his *Table of the Springs of Action* and his *Book of Fallacies* (the *Fallacies* as incisive as Schopenhauer's *Art of Controversy*, the *Table* probably the source of modern efforts to develop a vocabulary of purely descriptive, or "neutral" terms for the treatment of human relations).

The discussion of "question-begging appellatives" in the *Book of*

Fallacies states the principle of the triplicate vocabulary developed at length in the *Springs of Action*. Since the point he is considering is unquestionably the primary weapon in the war of words, we should dwell on it here. The "question-begging appellative," he says, is a "fallacy of confusion" that is used "for the designation of objects belonging to the field of moral science." If we include the "political" in his term "moral," we have here a name for a basic rhetorical device of modern journalism.

> Begging the question is one of the fallacies enumerated by Aristotle; but Aristotle has not pointed out (what it will be the object of this chapter to expose) the mode of using the fallacy with the greatest effect, and least risk of detection—namely, by the employment of a single appellative.

Thus, whereas we might speak of desire, labor, disposition, character, or habit (all of which, in his scheme, would be "neutral" terms), we might on the other hand use either laudatory ("eulogistic") words like industry, honor, generosity, gratitude, or vituperative ("dyslogistic") words like lust, avarice, luxury, covetousness, prodigality. Bentham believes that originally all words for "pains, pleasures, desires, emotions, motives, affections, propensities, dispositions, and other moral entities" were "neutral." But "by degrees they acquired, some of them an eulogistic, some a dyslogistic, cast. This change extended itself, as the *moral sense* (if so loose and delusive a term may on this occasion be employed) advanced in growth."

The project of a "neutral" vocabulary midway between the two "censorious" extremes of "eulogistic" and "dyslogistic" terms presents a notable contrast with the analysis of the virtues in Aristotle's *Ethics*. In Aristotle, a virtue is the happy medium between two extremes (which are vices). Thus, "courage" is a virtue midway between the vicious extremes, cowardice and rashness; liberality midway between squandering and meanness; good temper midway between irascibility and sluggishness; friendliness midway between obsequiousness and churlishness; truthfulness, midway between boastfulness and false modesty, etc. Here the middle terms are themselves "eulogistic," striking a balance between extremes that would be "dyslogistic." There are no "neutral" terms in the Benthamite sense.

The Benthamite project, as outlined in the Table, is constructed by a different principle. Thus: for the "pecuniary interest," there would be such "neutral" expressions as "desire of subsistence, plenty, profit, acquisition." And its two "censorial" counterparts would be: "economy, frugality, thrift" (eulogistic) and "parsimony, niggardliness, cupidity, avarice, venality, lust for gain" (dyslogistic). Or such "neutral" appellatives as "curiosity, inquisitiveness, desire of information" would have, as their rhetorically weighted counterparts: "love of knowledge, passion for literature, science," etc. (eulogistic) or "pryingness, impertinence, meddlesomeness," etc. (dyslogistic). The (neutral) expressions to name the desire of obtaining public good will, or the fear of ill-repute, would be matched eulogistically by honor, conscience, principle, probity, and dyslogistically by vanity, ostentation, pride, vainglory, arrogance. Fear of God or hope from God could be eulogized as piety, devotion, holiness, sanctity; dyslogized as superstition, bigotry, fanaticism, sanctimoniousness, hypocrisy. And so on, through fourteen different "interests" in all.

Aristotle does discuss a similar device. (See his *Art of Rhetoric*, I, IX, 28-29.) But Bentham analyzes it in much greater detail. Whereupon we realize that Nietzsche's entire work on *The Genealogy of Morals* is a picturesque interpretation of all Christian virtues as a rhetoric of this sort. Thus, in section 14, "how *ideals* are *manufactured* in this world," he lists substitutions whereby impotence is called goodness, cravenness is called meekness, a cowardly waiting, hat in hand, is called patience, submission to hated authority is called obedience to God, inability to avenge oneself is called forgiveness, and hope for revenge eventually is called the triumph of righteousness. A bit later, to make his perverse translations more plausible, he quotes from the Angelic Doctor: "The blessed in the heavenly kingdom shall look upon the tortures of the damned, that their blessedness please them the more."

Usage has already so changed that the Benthamite list has somewhat lost its symmetry. Thus, he is hard put to name a eulogistic expression for the "self-regarding interest" for which the subsequent spread of his own utilitarian thinking has since given us "enlightened self-interest." And he can find no eulogistic appellatives for sexual desire, which seems an austere limitation even for the England of those days. (Elsewhere at least he observes that "gallantry" can be used as a flattering word for "adultery.") But the list is much more valuable "in principle" than for its particulars. And as he says in his *Book of*

Fallacies, when considering the choice of censorial terms that reflect "interest-begotten prejudice":

> It neither requires nor so much as admits of being taught: a man falls into it but too naturally of himself; and the more naturally and freely, the less he finds himself under the constraint of any such sense as that of shame. The great difficulty is to unlearn it: in the case of this, as of so many other fallacies, by teaching it, the humble endeavour here is, to unteach it.

The persuasive function of this most spontaneous and ubiquitous rhetorical practice (this use of weighted words that makes all men rhetoricians because they are all poets) is analyzed thus:

> Having, without the *form,* the *force* of an assumption,—and having for its object, and but too commonly for its effect, a like assumption on the part of the hearer or reader,—the sort of allegation in question, how ill-grounded soever, is, when thus masked, apt to be more persuasive than when expressed simply and in its own proper form: especially where, to the character of a *censorial* adding the quality and tendency of an *impassioned* allegation, it tends to propagate, as it were by contagion, the passion by which it was suggested. On this occasion, it seeks and finds support in that *general* opinion, of the existence of which the eulogistic or dyslogistic sense, which thus, as it were by adhesion, has connected itself with the import of the appellative, operates as proof.

This is an unlovely paragraph, and not very viable. But it is well worth dwelling on. And dwelling on it, we find that it is the analysis of the appeal to "imagination" in terms of a *logical* fallacy (or deception), the *petitio principii.* Here, we might say, by the use of tonalities, one begins by positing the very thing that is to be proved. That is what Bentham means by saying that the censorial term has the *force* of an assumption, without its *form.* It would have the *form* of an assumption only if the speaker said explicitly, "I am here assuming the judgment which is to be proved." Obviously, in such a form, the suggestiveness of the censorial tonality would be lost. But by basing one's statement on a censorial assumption without labeling it as such, the speaker has an opportunity to *establish this very assumption* in the mind of his hearer.

Of course, where the interests of an audience are strongly bound to the contrary assumption, too obvious a use of such *tonality* (we inject a term not used by Bentham) would cause the audience rather to recoil. Thus, in *Julius Caesar,* Mark Antony cautiously begins his speech to the mob by using the expression "honourable men" as a "eulogistic appellative" for the murderers of Caesar. And only gradually, by the ambiguities of irony to bridge the transition, does he dare convert it into the dyslogistic. Had he begun by using dyslogistic tonalities, he would have turned the mob fatally against himself.

Would we be excessive in glimpsing, beneath the Benthamite project, an almost mystical way of thinking? For the dialectic of mysticism aims at a systematic withdrawal from the world of appearances, a crossing into a realm that transcends everyday judgments—after which there may be a return: the Upward Way is matched by a Downward Way; or the period of exile, withdrawal, and negation terminates in a new vision, whereupon the visionary can once again resume his commerce with the world, which he now sees in a new light, in terms of the vision earned during his stage of exile. But in his homecoming to the world of appearances, he sees things quite differently, so that what he had formerly contemned he seeks, and what he had formerly sought, he contemns. Eulogistic and dyslogistic have changed places, with a *neutral period of transition* between them.

We thus seem to see lurking behind the Benthamite triplicate vocabulary, a kind of attenuated and secularized dialectic of the *via negativa*. And we believe that we can similarly see, in the peripety scene of Shakespeare's play, a playwright's equivalent, as Antony employs the devices of irony to replace the realm of pure neutrality (ironic ambiguity being the dramatic equivalent of a dialectic movement towards neutrality which, in its purity, would be the transcending of drama).

But perhaps we are here taking on more burdens than we need to. In any case, we should also note that, whatever his contribution to the ideal of a scientifically neutral vocabulary, Bentham did not by any means attempt to deny himself weighted terms. Indeed, insofar as a motive met his standard (in contributing to what he considered "the greatest good of the greatest number"), he was quite frank in applying a eulogistic appellative to it. He would doubtless have explained that he was not merely exploiting an assumption, since he was always willing to show why, in his opinion, a given act should be named eulogistically or dyslogistically. That is, though a given appellative might, considered *in itself,* have the force without the form of an assumption, in its *context* he justified it by explicit argument. Thus, on reasoned assumptions that monarchy is a power inimical to the greatest good of the greatest number, he unhesitatingly asserts that we should not say "the influence of the crown" (an expression either neutral or eulogistic) but "the corruption of the crown." And the term "innovation" being generally used in his day as a "dyslogistic appellative" for legislative change, the measures which he favored in the name of the greatest good of the greatest number were named by him, not neutrally but eulogistically: "improvements."

Where inducement to action is concerned, a genuinely neutral vocabulary would defeat its own ends: for there would be no act in it. It would give full instructions for conditioning—but it could not say to what one should condition. But since purposes indigenous to the monetary rationale are so thoroughly built into the productive and distributive system as in ours, a relatively high proportion of interest in purely "neutral" terminologies of motives can be consistent with equally intense ambition. For however "neutral" a terminology may be, it can function as rhetorical inducement to action insofar as it can in any way be used for monetary advantage.

In fact, "neutralization" may often serve but to eliminate, as far as is humanly possible, the various censorial weightings that go with the many different philosophic, religious, social, political, and personal outlooks extrinsic to the monetary motive. Thus, the terminology of investment is "neutral," but the mortgagee, personally, may want to employ a heavily weighted term as "appellative" for the mortgagor who would foreclose. And if the mortgagor could foreclose at a profit, but is deterred by other scruples, then he abides by censorial weightings alien to the pure "neutrality" of the financial logic alone.

We do not mean that the Benthamite concern with a neutral terminology was "nothing but" a reflex of the monetary motive. Obviously, the utilitarian principle of "the greatest good of the greatest number" itself surpassed purely individualistic theories of profit. But just as orthodox capitalism could be said to have institutionalized, in one particular set of historical conditions, a competitive-cooperative process true of dialectic in general, so the tests of strictly monetary utility could be considered as a reduction of Bentham's broader utilitarian formula. Despite Bentham's distrust of idealizations, his principle of social utility could serve as a rhetorical cloak for purely monetary utility. The close connection between them (in that the profits were earned by business men aiming eventually at mass markets) made it possible for the two orders of motives to become interwoven. Hence any proposals to neutralize nonutilitarian motives would be influenced by the extent to which the monetary motive had already transcended other motivational weightings.

While such neutralization of vocabulary is not confined to monetary incentives, it could fit well with the monetary rationale precisely because the original insight *did* owe much to the "emancipatory" workings of money. For the strengthening of the monetary rationale of action had favored motives alien to more primitive ethical vocabularies, thereby making it easier for men to adopt a relativistic attitude towards the censorial appellatives rooted in other motives.

True, as we have noted, there can also be purely dialectical ways (akin to the mystical search for the *via negativa*) whereby the censorial weightings of rhetoric can be transcended. Though, in a money economy, we can expect such purely dialectical processes to be *institutionalized* in terms of monetary organization, the mystical process of transcendence is traditionally stated in nonmonetary terms, and the dialectic underlying it has nothing to do with money. Yet, if an *organized priestly technique* for the mystical neutralization and transcending of opinion has ever arisen outside a monetary economy, we should have to conclude that a wide diversity of social classes can arise without money to mediate among the corresponding diversity of occupations. And we strongly doubt such a possibility. However, a little money might go a long way in providing the insight of a money-grounded diversity: the illumination would not require such full development as with modern finance. A society would need only enough monetary development to support a priestly class which, in meditating by profession, and in mediating between classes, could "get the idea" of a neutral stage alien to any single class.

Of all fables, surely the best for characterizing the discomfitures of rhetoric is the one of the father and son leading an ass to market. Whether the father walks and the son rides, or the son walks and the father rides, or they both walk, or they both ride, there is someone to find fault. Eventually, in their eagerness to meet all possible objections, they try to carry the ass—and that is no solution either. As Aristotle showed systematically, there are objections to any position. You can even attack a thing on the grounds that it is exactly what it claims to be, as were you to "refute" a philosophy by saying, "The trouble with this is, it is a philosophy."

Such is particularly the case because the rhetorical striving for advantage is usually conducted in a very piecemeal way, with refutations of a purely opportunistic and catch-as-catch-can sort. "It's smart to be shifty in a new country"—and the equivalent in an old country would be the rhetorical smartness that shifts with the news. Given the world as it is, with its jangling variety of imputed motives, most often one merely assumes that there is a well-rounded philosophic, scientific, or theological rationale to justify the censorial weighting of his terms.

You meet a new person, and the *first* sentence he utters on some controversial subject is spoken in such tonalities as though he were speaking *in conclusion*. To be sure, his tonalities are not in the stentorian accents of a Demosthenes, topping off his arguments by an appeal to the emotions. Rather they are a barely detectable inflection, which you must strain to catch, but which unmistakably implies, "This is the slant you have too, if you have the proper slant." It is a device used especially by teachers: as the adolescent, uneasy and puzzled at best, keeps watching furtively for leads into the "right things," conditions are favorable for the teacher, by subtle tonalities, to *suggest* a set of judgments which establish and protect his position; but if he explicitly mustered the arguments for that position, he would risk *freeing* the students of his limitations, by enabling them to become critically aware of those limitations.

It is by such tonalities, more than by reasoned arguments, that our newspapers persuade. The arguments are on the editorial page, which relatively few readers ever see. The tonalities are in the headlines, which no reader can possibly avoid. These headlines are the "single appellatives," which we call "tonalities" because they imply a certain tone of voice, and this is the tone of voice proper to a certain kind of conclusion. We might as justly call them "gestures," "postures," "attitudes." Subtly, they act by the principle of empathy (for, as Cicero reminds us, in the mere representation of emotion there is something which invites the beholder to participate in it). And they are "question-begging" terms in that they are *suggestive* ("suggestiveness" being perhaps one word for Bentham's formula: "having, without the *form*, the *force* of an assumption"—or as we might put it, *beginning* with the tonality that would suit the desired *conclusion*).

Hence, the importance of the Benthamite principles, not only for analyzing rhetoric, but also for use by rhetoricians. Bentham but offers systematic terms for linguistic procedures that are spontaneous, even inevitable. Thus he may induce us to ask ourselves in each instance just what resource should be exploited. (This is not, we grant, exactly the purpose Bentham had in mind. Hence his linguistic analysis can be a kind of rhetoric-in-spite-of-itself.)

Subsequently, in the use of rhetoric to attack rhetoric, there has been much talk of "unmasking," as rival ideologies are said to compete by "unmasking" one another. The groundwork of this approach is laid in Bentham, with his methodical search for *tegumen* and *res tegenda,* the *tegumen* being a linguistic covering for an interest that itself lies outside the linguistic. (For though his mode of analysis was centered upon the linguistic, he likewise sought to characterize the extralinguistic elements in rhetorical situations.) In the *Table,* he explains that there are usually several motives involved in any particular act. But where there is such "conjunct action of motives," the speaker may represent the lot by selecting one motive as significant and neglecting the others. Such a procedure is inevitable, since any decision usually sums up a complexity of motives. Rhetorically, this fact invites to censorial appellatives since, if the speaker is identifying an act of his own, or of an ally, he can gain an easy advantage by picking out the most favorable motive and presenting it as either predominant or exclusive (or as the one that sets the tone for the lot). And conversely, he can select the least favorable to name the essence of an enemy's motives. But sometimes "no such sufficiently respected motive can be found"—and then, Bentham observes, instead of the actual motive, a speaker may select some other which "shall, by the nearness of its connexion with the actual one, have been rendered most difficultly distinguishable from it." He calls such changes "substituted" or "covering" motives. Or, as he explains:

> In political contention, no line of conduct can be pursued by either of two parties, but what, by persons of the *same* party, is ascribed to *good* motives; by persons of the *opposite* party, to *bad* motives:—and so in every case of *competition,* which (as most cases have) has anything in it of enmity. On any such occasion, the motive which, though but one out of several actual and cooperating motives, or though it be but . . . a *substituted* motive; is thus put forward, may be designated by the appellation of the *covering motive* being em-

ployed to serve as a covering, to whatever actually operating motives would not have been so well adapted as itself to the purpose in view.

Thus, he notes that the "desire corresponding to the *pleasures of the palate*" can have, as "eulogistic covering," the motive of "sympathy," stressing the elements of sociability and companionship that may go with eating and drinking. Or "sexual desire" can have *love* as its eulogistic covering. The desire for gain can be eulogistically covered by *industry; love of power* can be eulogized as *love of country; fear of punishment* or *of bad reputation* can be called *love* or *sense of duty;* desire to get the good offices of friends can have *sympathy* or *gratitude* as coverings; and *antipathy* or *ill will* can be eulogistically covered in the name of *public spirit* or *love of justice.* Since such desires and motives, in their unadorned form, "may be considered as *the unseemly parts of the human mind,"* he has here offered specimens "of the fig-leaves, commonly employed for the covering of them."

Similarly, in the *Book of Fallacies* Bentham calls attention to ways whereby "Vague Generalities" can also be used as covering devices. Thus, since "order" is a more inclusive word than the term for any particular order, it may include both good order and bad, whereby a call for order can cloak a call for *tyranny,* tyranny also being a species of order. (Perhaps we could class, as a contemporary variant of such devices, De Gaulle's Rally of the French People, a project for *political* unification presented in the name of *no politics.*) In Bentham's case, since men were, to his way of thinking, using the British Constitution in ways that gave them many antisocial advantages, they could leave the advantages unmentioned, while becoming edified in their zeal for the Constitution itself, the "matchless Constitution." Thus, at the peak of his attack upon "Vague Generalities," he writes:

> Rally round the constitution: that is, rally round waste, rally round depredation, rally round oppression, rally round corruption, rally round imposture—imposture in the hustings, imposture in the Honourable House, imposture in every judicatory.

At the end of his *Book of Fallacies,* this great methodologist of debunking (the Greeks might have called him *Rhetoromastix,* The Scourge of Spellbinders) permits himself a vision. Having analyzed the various standard devices whereby men are induced to fight their battles at the wrong place, so that, while they aim and fire to the left, the enemy advances undetected and unharmed from the right, Bentham foresees the day when it would be risky indeed if anyone were "so far off his guard, as through craft or simplicity to let drop any of these irrelevant, or at one time deceptious arguments." But if any speaker does speak thus, in an unguarded moment, "instead of Order! Order! a voice shall be heard, followed, if need be, by voices in scores, crying aloud, 'Stale! Stale! Fallacy of authority! Fallacy of Distrust!' Etc., etc."

But that, he says, "will form an epoch in the history of civilization." So much for his vision, at once simple and sophisticate.

Marx on "Mystification"

Discussing rhetorical theory in the early middle ages (*Speculum*, January, 1942), Richard McKeon writes: "According to Cassiodorus, 'The art of rhetoric is, as the masters of secular letters teach, the science of speaking well in civil questions,' and that definition is repeated in almost the same words by Isidore, Alcuin, and Rhabanus Maurus." Both Bentham's and Marx's contributions to the analysis of rhetoric would fall under this same head, except that their polemic emphasis might rather have led them to define rhetoric (or those aspects of it upon which they centered their attention) as: the knack of speaking ill in civil matters.

Whatever may be the claims of Marxism as a "science," its terminology is not a neutral "preparation for action" but "inducement to action." In this sense, it is unsleepingly rhetorical, though much of its persuasiveness has derived from insistence that it is purely a science, with "rhetoric" confined to the deliberate or unconscious deceptions of non-Marxist apologetics. Thus, we once saw a Marxist (he has since left the Communist Party) get soundly rebuked by his comrades for the suggestion that leftist critics collaborate in a study of "Red Rhetoric." Despite their constant efforts to find the slogans, catchwords, and formulas that will most effectively influence action in given situations, and their friendliness to "propaganda" or "social significance" in art, they would not allow talk of a "Red Rhetoric." For them, "Rhetoric" applied solely to the persuasiveness of capitalist, fascist, and other non-Marxist terminologies (or "ideologies").

Yet in actual practice their position seems (*mutatis mutandis!*) to be pretty much that of Augustine. That is: the Marxists have a rhetoric, a persuasion, which in turn is grounded in a dialectic. The rhetoric is words; the dialectic, being concerned with the non-verbal order of motives, could be equated with "science." And an art in keeping would be grounded in "science" (or "dialectic") insofar as it took its start from the experiences of natural reality, while being rhetorical in proportion as its persuasiveness helped form judgments, choices, attitudes deemed favorable to Communist purposes. All this seems obvious enough; but rhetoric having become identified with non-Marxist rhetoric, the Marxist persuasion is usually advanced in the name of no-rhetoric.

In his *Book of Fallacies,* Bentham had recognized both factional and universal interests. Factionally, he treated parliamentary wrangles in terms of the ins vs. the outs. And since, "whatsoever the *ins* have in possession, the *outs* have in expectancy," to this extent he saw no difference in their "sinister interests," nor in the fallacies by which they sought to protect or further these interests. But in addition to such factional splits, he observed, "these rivals have their share in the universal interest which belongs to them in their quality of members of the community at large. In this quality, they are sometimes occupied in such measures as in their eyes are necessary for the maintenance of the universal interest."

For a comprehensive statement of human motives, this distinction of Bentham's seems very necessary. An ideal of cooperation, for instance, can certainly be applied for sinister *factional* advantage, as when conspirators cooperate against a common victim. Yet cooperation is also an ideal serving the interest of *mankind in general*.

It might be said that the Marxist analysis of rhetoric is primarily designed to throw new light on Bentham's "Fallacy of Vague Generalities." Otherwise put: As a critique of capitalist rhetoric, it is designed to disclose (unmask) sinister *factional* interests concealed in the bourgeois terms for benign *universal* interests. Though Marx twitted Bentham for his stress upon "interests," Marxism gives grand lineaments to the Benthamite notion of "interest-begotten prejudice." In its analysis of property, it puts an almost architecturally firm foundation beneath Bentham's somewhat flimsy distinction between ins and outs (indeed, as Bentham himself would probably have agreed, Marxism shows that often the shifts between ins and outs is but the most trivial of palace revolutions, where an apparently cleansing change of agents has left the morbidities of the scene itself substantially unchanged). And where Bentham had looked into extraverbal, situational factors behind rhetorical expressions, recognizing "the influence of time and place in matters of legislation," and holding that a law good for one situation was not thereby to be considered categorically good, Marx imposingly formalized such "conditional" thinking by linking it with his revisions of the Hegelian dialectic. All told, Marx thus forged a formidable machine; and he could apply it to shatter, as deceptive "ideology," traditions which had been the pride of mankind, but which in being upheld by economic and social classes that got special advantage from them, and in being put forward as universally valid, thus protected factional interests in the wider, more general name of universal interests.

To expose the workings of such "ideologies," it was necessary to give an exhaustive analysis of the "objective situation" in which they figured. Insofar as the terms describing this extraverbal situation were correct, they would apparently be a "dialectic" (in the sense that equates "dialectic" with "science"—i.e., with a subject matter of nonverbal things and relationships). They could be called a rhetoric, however, in several important senses: (1) The account of extralinguistic factors in a rhetorical expression (as when disclosing how economic interests influence modes of expression that, considered "in themselves," seem wholly to transcend the economic) is itself an aspect of *rhetorica docens,* though perhaps on the outer edges; (2) insofar as the Marxist vocabulary itself is partial, or partisan, it is rhetorical, and we could not have a dialectic in the fullest sense unless we gave equally sympathetic expression to competing principles (though we shall later see that this objection must be modified); (3) it is concerned with advantage, not only in analyzing the hidden advantage in other terminologies (or "ideologies"), but also in itself inducing to advantages of a special sort. (Here it becomes a kind of *rhetorica utens.*)

The main principles of Marxism, as a theory of rhetoric, are most directly stated, perhaps, in an early work by Marx and Engels, *The German Ideology.* But though Marxist writings probably contributed much to the current prestige of the word, "ideology," it is seldom used in exactly the sense that Marx gave it. So we might begin by noting the several meanings it now seems to have, meanings which, while not necessarily antagonistic to one another, are quite different in insight and emphasis:

1. The study, development, criticism of ideas, considered in themselves. (As in a Socratic dialogue.)

2. A system of ideas, aiming at social or political action. (Pareto's sociology, or Hitler's *Mein Kampf.*)

3. Any set of interrelated terms, having practical civic consequences, directly or indirectly. (A business men's code of fair practices might be a good instance.)

4. "Myth" designed for purposes of governmental control. ("Ideology" would here be an exact synonym for "myth of the state.")

5. A partial, hence to a degree deceptive, view of reality, particularly when the limitations can be attributed to "interest-begotten prejudice." (For instance, a white Southern intellectual's "ironic resignation" to a *status quo* built on "white supremacy.")

6. Purposefully manipulated overemphasis or underemphasis in the discussion of controversial political and social issues. (For instance, the kind of verbalizing done by a statesman, home from a discordant conference with foreign diplomats. In a "confidential" radio talk he gives the people a "frank and simple report of the facts." But the report is scrupulously designed to allow them no inkling of how the matter looks from the other side.)

7. An inverted genealogy of culture, that makes for "illusion" and "mystification" by treating ideas as *primary* where they should have been treated as *derivative.*

This last meaning is the most difficult. But because Marxism is a materialist revision of Hegel's idealism, not only do the authors of *The German Ideology* take their start from this seventh definition, they continually circle back to it. If we understand this special usage, we can see why a Marxist might legitimately object when, after he has attacked his political opponents as "ideologists," they retort by calling Marxism an "ideology" too. In the special sense of the word, as used in *The German Ideology,* it is quite true that the schools and movements there selected for attack are "ideologies," while Marxism is not.

Of course, in the War of Words, there is nothing to prevent contestants from hitting one another with anything they can lay hands

on. So you could be sure that, once the Marxists had given the word
a strong dyslogistic weighting, they too would be resoundingly
dyslogized by it (as, having zealously helped make "fascism" a dyslogistic word, they end by being called "Red Fascists"). But for our
present purposes, we should try to see the word exactly as Marx used
it. For only by trying to get the matter straight can we understand
the Marxist contribution to rhetoric, and thereby isolate a principle
which can even be applied beyond the purposes of Marxism.

We consider it a sign of flimsy thinking, indeed, to let anti-Com-
munist hysteria bulldoze one into neglect of Marx. (We say "bulldoze," but we are aware that the typical pedagogue today is not
"bulldozed" into such speculative crudity; he welcomes it, and even
feels positively edified by it. If he cannot grace his country with any
bright thoughts of his own, he can at least persuade himself that he
is being a patriot in closing his mind to the bright thoughts of his
opponents. No wonder the tendency is so widespread. It is a negative
kind of accomplishment for which many can qualify.)

With the division of labor, Marx says, and the corresponding cleavage of society into different social and economic classes, there arises a
ruling class; likewise, from the distinction between manual and intellectual work, there arise specialists in words (or "ideas"), such as
priests, philosophers, theoreticians, jurists, in general, "ideologists,"
who see things too exclusively in terms of their specialty, and thereby
misinterpret the role played by "consciousness," "spirit," "idea," in
human history. The whole relationship between "matter" and "spirit"
thus seems to be exactly the reverse of what it really is. Property and
the division of labor give rise to a ruling class with its peculiar set
of ideas; each economic change calls forth a corresponding change
in the nature of the ruling class (or at moments of revolutionary
crisis a new ruling class takes over)—and each such alteration in the
conditions of the ruling class is reflected as a corresponding change
of "ideas."

The "ideologists" of the ruling class, in keeping with the nature of
their specialty, perfect and systematize the ideas of the ruling class.
And, since the ruling class controls the main channels of expression,
the ideas of the ruling class become the "ruling ideas."

But, such is the nature of documents, after the economic basis of
society has changed, and the class structure has changed accordingly,

the ideas that had prevailed seem to remain unchanged. That is, once the verbal or esthetic expressions are recorded, they retain substantially the form that they had when they arose.

Imagine, now, an "ideologist" who, with the documents of many centuries to work from, inspects a whole developmental series of such successive "ruling" ideas, and who, considering these ideas "in themselves," attempts to work out an explanation for their development. If he proceeds in accordance with the Hegelian dialectic, he will get the kind of reversed genealogy which Marxism is attacking. He can treat these particular sets of ideas in terms of some over-all title, a word for ideas in general, such as Spirit, or Consciousness, or *die Idee.* Hence he can look upon the succession of "ruling" ideas (like "honor," "loyalty," "liberty") as though each were an expression of the one Universal Idea (his title for the lot, which he uses not just as a summarizing word, but as a "sub-ject" in the strict philosophic sense, that is, an underlying basis, a sub-stance, of which any step along the entire series can be considered as a property, or expression). He can next assign some direction to the entire series, such as the gradual increase of freedom or self-consciousness. Then he can treat this ultimate direction as the essence of the whole series, the end towards which the entire series strives, whereby it can be considered latent in even the first step of the series. Then this Purpose, or Universal Idea, can be viewed as the creative principle operating within the entire series. Each step along the way would be a limited expression of this universal principle; its nature would be determined by its particular place in the series; yet within the limitations of its nature, each stage would represent the principle of the total development (as bud, flower, and seed could each, at different stages in a plant's growth, be called successive momentary expressions of a single biologic continuity).

"The Idea" thus becomes a universal self-developing organism. Its successive stages make a dialectical series, as shifts in the nature of property, production, and rule make for shifts in the ruling ideas; but these ruling ideas are considered "purely" (as manifestations, not of particular ruling classes, but of the "Absolute Idea"). The Absolute Idea thus becomes the creator of nature and history, which are but concrete expressions of it. Hence, all the *material* relations in history are interpreted as the products of this Universal Spirit, manifesting itself in the empirical world. The study of this empirical world, of course, would include such matters as conflicts over property. But instead of considering ideas as weapons shaped by their use in such conflicts, the kind of "ideologist" Marx is attacking would treat the conflicts as themselves but "moments" in the expression of the Universal Idea underlying all historical development.

In this strictly Hegelian form, Marx may here seem to be attacking a doctrine to which few practical-minded persons would subscribe. Quite true, yet once you begin to follow the logic of Marx's critique, you see that most people differ from Hegel, not in being immune to such thinking, but in being immune to its *thoroughness*. Marx shows how this position generates a whole *set* of beliefs. And what you usually encounter, in the piecemeal thinking of the non-philosophic mind, is a view comprising various detached fragments of such "ideology." Since these fragments prevail on important issues, such as our views of nationalism, a rhetorical critique of such patterns, as they lurk in our thinking, is of tremendous importance.

The authors list three telltale tricks of such "theodicy," whereby the "hegemony" or "hierarchy" of spirit in history is "proved": (1) The thinker separates the ruling ideas from the ruling class, and by thus dealing with the ideas in their "pure" form, concludes that the ruling force of history is "ideas" or "illusions"; (2) the ideas are arranged in a developmental series, with a "mystical" connection among them (this is done by treating the successive ideas as though they were "acts of self-determination" on the part of the divine, absolute, or pure Idea); (3) the "mystical appearance" can be removed by putting progressively increasing "self-consciousness" in place of "the self-determining concept"; or it can be made to *look* thoroughly materialistic (despite its underlying principle of "mystification") if it is transformed into a developmental series of persons, thinkers, philosophers, "ideologists," who are said to be the historical representatives of the "concept."

From the standpoint of rhetoric, the picture that emerges from *The German Ideology* looks somewhat like this:

Private property and the division of labor are identical. This is an important *situational* fact, since it leads to "illusions" or "mystifications" in the realm of ideas. The ideologist's inclination to consider ideas in their "purity" makes for an approach to human relations in terms of such over-all god-terms as "consciousness" or "the human essence," whereas the typical conflicts of society are rooted in *property*. If, when there is a quarrel over property, instead of confronting it squarely you begin considering abstruse problems of universal consciousness or looking for remote kinds of metaphysical or theological anguish and alienation embedded in the very essence of humanity, you are blinded by a principle of "mystification." At every significant point where there is an economic factor to be faced, your "ideology" introduces an "illusion," a purely spiritual "appearance." Where empires are striving for *world markets,* you are "ideologically" inclined to ponder the ways of "universal spirit." Where classes within a nation are struggling for dominance, you are likely to confuse the issue by ideals that give a semblance of national unity.

The same newspapers that are run for money, that get their income by advertising goods sold for money, that are read by people on their way to and from the place where they work for money, and that distribute accounts of political, economic, and social events bearing upon money (high among them, news of the crimes against property)— these same papers, in their more edified moments, will talk rather of "liberty," "dignity of the individual," "Western man," "Christian civilization," "democracy," and the like, as the motives impelling at least *our* people and *our* government, and to a lesser extent the "nations" that "we" want as allies, but not the small ruling class, or clique, that dominates countries with which "we" are at odds.

It takes abstruse metaphysics to use such "ideological mystifications" (or what Bentham would have called "eulogistic coverings"). An uncriticized idea of "the nation" is as thoroughly an ideology, in the specifically Marxist sense, as any Hegelian talk of the Absolute. A nationalist "we" is at least as dubious as an editorial "we," which generously includes writers, readers, and owners under the same term (*up to a certain point,* at which point readers and writers will be *excluded*).

Dialectically, the Marxist analysis would apparently begin with a principle of division where idealism begins with a principle of merger. And, as regards the purposes of rhetoric, it admonishes us to look for "mystification" at any point where the social divisiveness caused by property and the division of labor is obscured by unitary terms (as with terms whereby a state, designed to protect a certain structure of ownership, is made to seem equally representative of both propertied and propertyless classes). Indeed, we find the stress upon private property as a rhetorical motive so convincing, that we question whether communism is possible under the conditions of extreme specialization (division of labor) required by modern industry. *The German Ideology* explicitly pictures man under communism, shifting from job to job like a Jack-of-all-trades, as the mood strikes him (hunting in the morning, fishing in the afternoon, rearing cattle in the evening, and criticizing after dinner, "without ever becoming hunter, fisherman, shepherd, or critic"). Given the highly specialized nature of modern technology, which requires of its operators an almost Puritanic severity of application, if so dilettantelike a way of life as Marx describes is the sign of a true communist society, then every step in the evolution of Soviet Russian industry would seem likely to take it farther from a world free of the cleavage that arises with the division of labor (and with the separation of property that goes with it, and the disparate states of consciousness that go with that).

But we do not have to believe the Marxist promises to apply the Marxist diagnosis for rhetorical purposes. We might question whether, by Marx's own theory, private property could possibly be abolished in a technological society marked by extreme division of labor; we might expect no more than changes which produce a structure of ownership better suited to the conditions of modern industrial production. With the means of production "owned" by the state, private property might arise secondarily, through the diversity of ways in which different individuals and classes of workers participated in the economic process and derived rewards from it. But such ownership, or structure of private expectancies and rights, might not look at all like private property as tested by the criteria of orthodox capitalism. Maybe yes, maybe no. That's not what we have to settle for our present purposes. It is enough for our purposes to note the value of the admonition that private property makes for a rhetoric of mystification, as the "ideological" approach to social relations sets up a fog of merger-terms where the clarity of division-terms is needed.

We do not pretend to have given here a complete summary of *The German Ideology*. For our present purposes we are concerned only with the ways in which its analysis of "ideology" becomes a contribution to rhetoric. Formally, we might say that, whereas one can talk of generic, specific, or individual human motives, the treatment of "ideas" in terms of class conflicts would place the stress upon specific motives. That is, instead of some generally human motive, such as "the essence of mankind," Marx stresses the specifically *class* nature of ideologies. And the imputing of universal or generic motives is then analyzed as a concealment of the specific motives (hence, as "mystification"). Then, according to Marx, only by the abolition of property relationships that make for such specific, or class motives, might we hope to get truly universal motivation. And such universal or generic motivation would, by the same token, mean the freeing of the individual. Hence, dialectically, all three levels of motivation are involved (generic, specific, and individual). One may argue that social classification is inevitable in a state of high occupational diversity, even under communism. But we need not settle that argument here. We need only note that the materialist critique of Spirit is the analysis of it as a rhetorical device, and that the dialectical symmetry behind the Marxist terms of analysis seems to involve the approach to generic and individual motives through the specific.

All told, "ideology" is equatable with illusion, mystification, discussion of human relations in terms like absolute consciousness, honor, loyalty, justice, freedom, substance, essence of man—in short, that "inversion" whereby material history is derived from "spirit" (in contrast with the method of dialectical materialism whereby the changing nature of consciousness would be derived from changes in material conditions).

Terministic Reservations (in View of Cromwell's Motives)

Might the Marxist critique of ideology be partly misled by the fact that only the "ideas" survive in the literary or esthetic reliques of the past? Any over-all term for motivation, such as honor, loyalty, liberty, equality, fraternity, is a *summing up* of many motivational strands. And though *on its face* it reduces a whole complexity of terms to one apparently simple term, the people who used it may have been quite aware of many other meanings subsumed in it, but not explicitly proclaimed.

Thus, if a tangle of relationships (including a clear recognition of the material privileges and deprivations that went with a given social structure) was epitomized in the god-term *honor,* but if all that survived for us was the "spirituality" of the term, then it might be the materialist who was duped. For he might accuse the term of much more reticence and deception than it actually possessed, for persons who once summed up their *material* conditions in its name.

In the *Grammar* we noted: If a tribe is living by a river, and has adapted its entire way of life to the conditions of that river, it might sum up its motives in the name of what we would call a "river god." Yet such a title would not be a mere animistic superstition; there would be much realistic and materialistic justification for it (to say nothing of its purely dialectical advantages, as a term for summing up the tribe's ways and recognizing the material conditions mainly responsible for these ways). "Animism" is too much the mark of a nineteenth-century idealistic philosopher trying to be a materialistic anthropologist (at least as regards somebody else's gods, or summarized terms for motives).

In brief, a summarizing term like "honor" might be much more "illusory" and "mystifying" to us, in the abstract and "spiritual" form it has for us, than it was for those who used it as a counter in their everyday life, and so found plenty of cause to discount it. The very term, which looks absolute and unconditional to us, was but the *title for all the conditions*. In this sense, even the most theological of terms can be implicitly modified by very accurate nontheological meanings which, though they may not show through the expression itself, were clearly felt by the persons using it.

A meaning can be omitted from an expression either because those who used it were unaware of the meaning, or because they were aware of it but wanted to conceal it, or because it was so obvious to them that it did not need mention. If the expressions surviving from a given past era were sufficiently ample, we could eventually extract from these themselves all the meanings that were known but concealed, and the meanings that were too obvious to be mentioned. (Even the wholly unperceived meanings might be detected by studying what-goes-with-what and what-follows-what in the images and ideas overtly expressed.) But the expression of past eras survives in fragments, and often without explicit reference to the situations in which it arose (but of which people were wholly conscious at the time). So the "mystifications" are in part merely a by-product of the written record, and in this sense mystify us as they did not mystify their contemporaries. Marx seems quite correct in his discovery that idealistic history built a whole life's work out of such misinterpreted abstractions. But the same error would affect us too, if we assumed that the people who used such god-terms as counters in their daily lives had been equally mystified by them. Insofar as a "context of situation" had participated, for them, as a part of the term's meaning, the documentary survival of the term after the death of its historical context might make it seem to have been much more "spiritual" than it actually was. In the books, it is but a spirit; yet those who used it when it flourished may have recognized it rather by its body.

For instance, consider Cromwell's speech, delivered before the House of Commons, January 22, 1655. He here looks upon the Revolution as "God manifesting Himself"; he justifies it on the grounds that its success is *per se* the evidence of God's will; he sees in it the "necessity" imposed by Providence. Judged by Marxist criteria, such expressions would be a perfect instance of the "mystifying."

Now, he might conceivably have stopped at such statements. But he is addressing a legislative body; there is business to be done. So he himself provides the qualifications which might have been missing:

> Religion was not the thing at first contested for "at all": but God brought it to that issue at last; and gave it unto us by way of redundancy; and at last it proved to be that which was most dear to us.

Not an opponent, but Cromwell himself, says that the conflict did not begin with religious motives. He is saying what his contemporaries knew, but what a *later* mystification might deny (as Carlyle actually did, when asserting that, although Cromwell's remark was "true in form," it was not true "in essence").

Again, after asserting that "they do vilify and lessen the works of God" who accuse him of "having, in these great Revolutions, 'made Necessities,'" he says:

> There is another Necessity, which you have put upon us, and we have not sought. I appeal to God, Angels and Men,—if I shall now raise money according to the Article in the Government, whether I am not compelled to do it!

Indeed, if you would inspect this speech as a theory of revolutionary motives, but a slight emendation is necessary to make it a perfect fit for Marxist thinking. You need but think of "God" or "Providence" in a "neutral" or "technical" sense, merely as a term for the universal scene, for the sum total of conditions (scholastic theology itself having provided the bridge, in defining God as "the ground of all possibility").

Thus Cromwell ridicules the charge that the Revolution depended upon his special skill as a conspirator:

> "It was," say some, "the cunning of the Lord Protector,"—I take it to myself,—"it was the craft of such a man, and his plot, that hath brought it about!" And, as they say in other countries, "There are five or six cunning men in England that have skill; they do all these things." Oh, what blasphemy is this! Because men that are without God in the world, and walk not with Him, know not what it is to pray or believe, and to receive returns from God.

This reference to "five or six cunning men in England" may have been the source of Churchill's remark about the "handful of very able men who now hold 180 million Soviet citizens in their grasp." But in any case, the reference to "God in the world" gives us our hint as to how this statement would be translated into Marxism. The reference to "blasphemy" would become a reference to "enemy propaganda." Instead of the partnership with God (as word for universal ground) there would be a knowledge of dialectical materialism (as word for universal ground). Praying and believing in God would become planning according to belief in the materialist interpretation of history. The "returns from God" would have, as their analogue, the success that comes of acting in accordance with the nature of the "objective situation." Both would agree that the situation cannot be forced, that one cannot rule in violation of "necessity." If the régime in Russia is but the work of a handful of cunning men, then it cannot succeed, as the most devout Stalinist would assure you. The course of history must be behind it. Or, in Cromwell's terms:

> If this be of human structure and invention, and if it be an old Plotting and Contriving to bring things to this Issue, and that they are not the Births of Providence,—then they will tumble.

We are not trying to deny the obvious differences in motivation between the English protectorate and the Russian dictatorship. We are trying to indicate that, even the most "mystifying" of terms may subsume much materialistic relevancy. And, conversely, there is a very close parallel between both Cromwellian and Marxist appeal to "necessity"; for any ultimate terms of motivation must, by their very nature as "high abstractions," omit important ingredients of motivation. The *general* statement of historical motives in terms of dialectical material-

ism is as "mystifying" as any such statement in terms of "Providence"—
for in both, all reference to minute administrative situations is omitted.
In either language, the bureaucratic, administrative details are "spiritualized."   As regards the pragmatic operations of production and
government, the treatment of conditions in terms of "necessity" is as
"mystifying" when the necessity is identified with the inevitable laws
of history as when it is identified with the will of Providence manifesting itself through such laws.   Yet on the other hand, neither statement may be as "mystifying" or "general" as it seems, since it is used
by people in specific social contexts, and in various unspecified ways
derives meaning from such material conditions.

Indeed, even where people choose to present their motives in terms
of a "eulogistic covering," La Rochefoucauld has suggested reasons for
treating such usage, not as self-deception, but as roundabout evidence
of self-criticism.   For when people are talking of their own conduct,
he says, the self-love that usually blinds them gives them so accurate
a view that they suppress or disguise the slightest unfavorable details.
And he takes such tactics as evidence that they know their faults better
than you'd think:

> Ce qui fait voir que les hommes connaissent mieux leurs fautes
> qu'on ne pense, c'est qu'ils n'ont jamais tort quand on les entend
> parler de leur conduite; le même amour-propre qui les aveugle
> d'ordinaire les éclaire alors et leur donne des vues si justes qu'il leur
> fait supprimer ou déguiser les moindres choses qui peuvent être
> condamnées.

Where a class, or company, prefers words that similarly disguise (La
Rochefoucauld's remark would suggest), there is not so much "illusion"
as *conspiracy*.   But he is considering only individual cases, his concern
being *amour-propre* as manifested by the individuals of his class.   And
perhaps when disguise has attained the proportions of a social conspiracy, it really is on the way to becoming an out-and-out illusion.

Carlyle on "Mystery"

Marx's insight into the mystification of class can get corroboration
from an unexpected quarter, an equally urgent nineteenth-century
writer, but one who, treating "mystery" as a eulogistic term, would
have looked upon the rejection of it as an atheistic abomination.   We
refer to Carlyle and his "philosophy of clothes" in *Sartor Resartus*.

Carlyle says in terms of stomach trouble what the Promethean Marx says in terms of a gnawed liver.

Reading *The German Ideology* and *Sartor Resartus* together, with the perhaps somewhat perverse pleasure of seeing how they can be brought to share the light that each throws upon the other, we might begin with the proposition that mystery arises at that point where different *kinds* of beings are in communication. In mystery there must be *strangeness;* but the estranged must also be thought of as in some way capable of communion. There is mystery in an animal's eyes at those moments when a man feels that he and the animal understand each other in some inexpressible fashion.

While the mystery of sex relations, which leads to the rhetoric of courtship, is grounded in the communication of beings *biologically* estranged, it is greatly accentuated by the purely *social* differentiations which, under the division of human labor, can come to distinguish the "typically masculine" from the "typically feminine."

Similarly, the conditions for "mystery" are set by *any* pronounced social distinctions, as between nobility and commoners, courtiers and king, leader and people, rich and poor, judge and prisoner at the bar, "superior race" and underprivileged "races" or minorities. Thus even the story of relations between the petty clerk and the office manager, however realistically told, draws upon the wells of mystery for its appeal, since the social distinction between clerk and manager makes them subtly mysterious to each other, not merely two different people, but representing two different *classes* (or "kinds") of people. The clerk and the manager are identified with and by different social *principles*.

And all such "mystery" calls for a corresponding rhetoric, in form quite analogous to sexual expression: for the relations between classes are like the ways of courtship, rape, seduction, jilting, prostitution, promiscuity, with variants of sadistic torture or masochistic invitation to mistreatment. Similarly, there are strong homosexual analogies in "courtly" relations between persons of the same sex but of contrasting social status. This tendency is a marked attribute of youth at college age when, with sexual experience still vague and tentative, adolescents related to each other as bully and toady can carry their mutual fascination quite to the borders of the mystical, particularly if they come of different social classes, or if a sense of social discrimination so pervades the school that it puts its mark even on the relation between persons of the same class (as each is afraid of appearing outclassed in the other's eyes).

The consummate literary expression of social courtship translated into homosexual terms is found in the sonnets of Shakespeare. There seems little point in trying to decide whether the poet "really was homosexual." For our purposes, whether he was or wasn't, in his role as a literary expert looking for the kind of imagery that would best convey his courtly theme he could be expected to find that the situation where a man of lower class addresses flattering appeals to a man of higher class can be readily dramatized by the use of terms homosexual in their implications. And the imagery that marked the precious and perverse author of *The Soul of Man Under Socialism* would disclose but a fraction of its meaning, if we saw in it only Wilde's sexual quandaries, while we overlooked its relations to his motives as a social climber. By the same token, the strong intermixture of mysticism and homosexuality among some of our best contemporary English writers (at one time or another, they have shown Leftist leanings) might well be examined, not so much for signs of "unconscious" fixations upon the parents, as for "unconscious" fixations on *substitutes* which might represent, in parental imagery, the principle of a "superior" class. Hence, the suggestions of awe, guilt, incest, parricide, and the like, might derive most from the pudencies of intercourse between social classes.

But in mentioning the pudencies of social intercourse, we are reminded that, in making a tentative analysis of the key words in some works by the snob-conscious Henry James, we noted his special fondness for the ambiguities of that word, "intercourse." In the case of so conscious a writer, we hesitated to assume that he completely overlooked the sexual connotations of the word. Yet we hesitated also to assume that so subtle and scrupulous a writer was aiming merely to exploit its mildly pornographic suggestions. But our thoughts on the sexual and homosexual analogies in courtship between classes seem to provide the missing qualification.

In particular they would seem to indicate the full significance of the word in *The Turn of the Screw,* where the vaguely and morbidly sexual implications of the plot involve an ambiguous relation between the master's children and the servants (a governess and her sinister predecessors), who are struggling for the possession of the children. The struggle is "preternaturally" (his word) infused with malign attributes (the conventions of the ghost story enabling the author to deal with *unnatural* attachments in terms of the "preternatural," though the word "unnatural" is also used). The governess' struggle with the ghosts of her predecessors for the possession of the children is not sexual, as judged by literal tests of sexual appetite. But it is ambiguously sexual, a sexuality surrounded at every point by *mystification*—and we believe that this mystification can be largely explained if seen in terms of one class struggling to possess the soul of another class. The fact that the other class is symbolized in terms of children may, of course, indicate still other possible orders, neither precisely social nor sexual, but rather personal or familial, as were the prototypes of this story, in the author's own life, to derive from the "mysteries" of childhood. (For there is also, at the roots of everyone's experience, a sense of classification solely by age: parents and offspring, generalized as the sense of a qualitative distinction between adults and children—a classification "prior" to sex, and leading into the mysteries of ancestor worship, and thence into the strong feeling for social differentiation that goes with ancestor worship.)

Sexual analogies are clearly enough revealed in the white man's fantasies or apprehensions that regularly accompany the doctrine of "white supremacy." And we find them expressed, from the Negro's side, in the interweaving of social and sexual tension that runs through the plot of Richard Wright's *Native Son* (where the wealthy white girl, though she had befriended the Negro, is killed in a context of imagery connoting coitus, and becomes the vicarious bearer of Bigger's heavy social load).

Dostoevski, writing in Czarist Russia at a time when the distinction between nobles and peasants was so pronounced that the physical beating of peasants by the upper class or their representatives was the norm, gives us a mysticism of many strands, but among these strands are such ambiguous associations as we are now considering. The cult of abjectness, the strangely mystical dream (in *Crime and Punishment*) of the horse being beaten to death, by a peasant who afflicts upon this still more abject creature the signs of his own socially abject status, the masochistic cult of suffering—there is an endless labyrinth of possibilities here, which we can never exhaust: social, sexual, and personal or familial. The familial order of motives (grounded in the relation between elders and children as "classe"), presumably impinges upon the reverence for the "Little Father" on the side of social distinctions, while its sexual implications are revealed in the theme of paedophilia that runs throughout Dostoevski's works. The mystic reverence for the saintly prostitute seems to symbolize the very essence of the hierarchic order. This figure combines both maternal and erotic woman (she is in essence virginal, but in the accidents of her social status a whore); in this duality she is as exalted as Christ the King and as abject as Christ the Crucified. (There is a Bengalese proverb: "He who gives blows is a master, he who gives none is a dog.")

Kafka's novels are fanciful delving into the mystery of bureaucracy and the rhetoric that goes with it. Indeed, if we were to propose, for readers of Kafka, a work that matches him in the same perversely illuminating way that Carlyle matches Marx, we would select the writings of Dionysius the Areopagite, on the Celestial Hierarchy and the Ecclesiastical Hierarchy. "Hierarchy" is the old, eulogistic word for "bureaucracy," with each stage employing a rhetoric of obeisance to the stage above it, and a rhetoric of charitable condescension to the stage beneath it, in sum, a rhetoric of courtship, while all the stages are infused with the spirit of the Ultimate Stage, which sums up the essence implicit in the hierarchic mode of thought itself, and can thus be "ideologically" interpreted as its "cause." In Kafka this same mystery of class distinctions is all-pervasive, while the Ultimate Bureaucrat, ever Above and Beyond and Behind, is a vaguely dyslogistic but always mysterious mixture of God and Mr. Big.

But let us return to Carlyle, and his particular way of handling the element of "mystification" in the social order: "Is it not to Clothes that most men do reverence?" Carlyle asks, or rather the ironically conceived representative of himself, Teufelsdröckh, asks in his chapter on "Old Clothes." And in this same chapter he says, "Trust not the heart of 'that man for whom old Clothes are not venerable." But Carlyle is not writing a book on the clothing industry. He is writing a book about symbols, which demand reverence because, in the last analysis, the images of nature are the Symbols of God. He uses Clothes as a surrogate for the symbolic in general. Examining his book to see what they are symbolic of, you find how Carlyle resembles Marx: Both are talking about the kind of hierarchy that arose in the world with the division of labor. Marx says that the modern division of labor began in earnest with the manufacture of Cloth. Carlyle approaches the same subject in his figurative way by saying that Tools are Clothes.

In his chapter on "The World in Clothes," where he proposes to write on "The Spirit of Clothes" as Montesquieu had written on the Spirit of Laws, Carlyle says: "The first purpose of clothes . . . was not warmth or decency, but ornament." For "the first spiritual want of a barbarous man is Decoration." Next, you find him talking about Money, how Money transformed Barter into Sale; whereupon, now

> whoso has sixpence is Sovereign (to the length of sixpence) over all men; commands Cooks to feed him, Philosophers to teach him, Kings to mount guard over him,—to the length of sixpence.—Clothes too, which began in foolishest love of Ornament, what have they not become! Increased Security, and pleasurable Heat soon followed: but what of these? Shame, divine Shame (Schaam, Modesty), as yet a stranger to the Anthropophagous bosom, arose there mysteriously under Clothes; a mystic grove-encircled shrine for the Holy in man. Clothes gave us *individuality, distinctions, social polity;* Clothes have made Men of us; they are threatening to make Clothes-screens of us. [The four italicized words in the last sentence are our emphasis.]

Then he turns abruptly to say that man is a "Tool-using animal," and concludes: "of which truth Clothes are but one example." The chapter ends by mentioning ultimate instances of the division of labor: modern transportation ("Steam-carriages" at that time), and political representation ("the British House of Commons," whose members "toil for us, bleed for us, hunger, and sorrow, and sin for us"). Elsewhere he refers to "the moral, political, and even religious Influences of Clothes," since "Man's earthly interests are all hooked and buttoned together, and held up, by Clothes," and "Society is founded upon Cloth . . . sails through the Infinitude on Cloth." Much to our purposes is his remark on the propriety of saying that men are "clothed with Authority." Without clothes, not "the smallest Politeness, Polity, or even Police, could exist." And "how, without Clothes, could we possess the master-organ, soul's seat, and true pineal gland of the Body Social: I mean, a Purse?"

There are two other primary steps in Carlyle's thinking. First, there is his application of the Pauline doctrine, proclaiming the body to be

as Clothes of the Mind, all Nature as the visible garment of invisible Spirit, and any "imagined" thing as but "a Clothing of the higher, celestial Invisible, 'unimaginable, formless dark with excess of bright,'" since Nature is a "Flesh-Garment" which Imagination wove with "Metaphors as her stuff," and Fantasy (that is, Imagination) is "the organ of the Godlike."

This doctrine brings him to the ultimate mystery, the Symbol as Enigma, as both clarification and obfuscation, speech and silence, publicity and secrecy. For it simultaneously expresses and conceals the thing symbolized:

> Of kin to the so incalculable influences of Concealment, and connected with still greater things, is the wondrous agency of *Symbols*. In a symbol there is concealment yet revelation: here, therefore, by Silence and by Speech acting together, comes a doubled significance.

Hence, while attacking "Thought without Reverence," "profess'd Enemies to Wonder," and those who would "have no Mystery and Mysticism," he is after a profounder vision that permits him to say of purely social reverence:

> Happy he who can look through the Clothes of a Man . . . into the Man himself; and discern, it may be, in this or the other Dread Potentate, a more or less incompetent Digestive-apparatus; yet also an inscrutable venerable Mystery, in the meanest Tinker that sees with eyes!

For round a man's "mysterious ME,"

> there lies, under all those wool rags, a Garment of Flesh (or of Senses), contextured in the Loom of Heaven; whereby he is revealed to his like, and dwells with them in UNION and DIVISION.

But though he would thus seem to complete his journey by arriving at a "mother-idea, Society in a state of Nakedness," we must never overlook the spontaneous judgment in such an expression as, "Clothes, from the King's mantle downwards, are Emblematic." True, he admonishes:

> Perhaps not once in a lifetime does it occur to your ordinary biped, of any country or generation, be he gold-mantled Prince or russet-jerkined Peasant, that his Vestments and his Self are not one and indivisible; that *he* is naked, without vestments, till he buy or steal such . . .

But his doctrines of reverence for the mysterious ground that unifies all men come to a head, so far as history is concerned, in the worship of heroes who represent the principle of divinity in the world. (This is the "identification" principle.) Thus, in *Heroes and Hero-Worship*, he tells us that the king "may be reckoned the most important of great men." For

> He is practically the summary for us of *all* the various figures of heroism; priest, teacher, whatsoever of earthly or of spiritual dignity we can fancy to reside in a man, embodies itself here, to *command* over us, to furnish us with constant practical teaching, to tell us for the day and hour what we are to *do*.

Perhaps the whole matter is summed up in his chapter on "Adamitism," where he sees through the "clothes" of class distinction to the naked universal man beneath, but restores with one hand the very hierarchic reverence he would take away with the other. Carlyle has just brought together the Judge "in fine Red" and the shuddering prisoner, "in coarse threadbare Blue," whom the judge has sentenced to be hanged. Carlyle meditates:

> How is this; or what make ye of your *Nothing can act but where it is?* Red has no physical hold of Blue, no *clutch* of him, is nowise in *contact* with him: neither are those ministerial Sheriffs and Lord Lieutenants and Hangmen and Tipstaves so related to commanding Red, that he can tug them hither and thither; but each stands distinct within his own skin. Nevertheless, as it is spoken, so it is done: the articulated Word sets all hands in Action; and Rope and Improved-drop perform their work.
>
>   Thinking reader, the reason seems to me twofold: First, that *Man is a Spirit,* and bound by invisible bonds to *All Men:* Secondly, that *he wears Clothes,* which are the visible emblems of that fact. Has not your Red hanging-individual a horsehair wig, squirrel-skins, and a plush gown; whereby all mortals know that he is a JUDGE?—Society, which the more I think of it astonishes me the more, is founded upon Cloth.

Carlyle then goes on to say how, when reading of "pompous ceremonials," Coronations, Levees, Couchees, and the talk is of Dukes, Archdukes, Colonels, Bishops, Admirals, and "miscellaneous Functionaries," all "advancing to the Anointed Presence," in his "atrabiliar moods" he imagines that the clothes "fly off the whole dramatic corps." It is a good reduction. *But in its very fantasy of irreverence, it but once more reveals that in clothes, as thus symbolic of distinguished office, there is mystery.*

In sum, the stages of his doctrine are these:

1. Clothes symbolize a social order that, while it elicits men's reverence, does not represent man's true nature.

2. There should be reverence, but it should be more deeply directed. Seeing behind the pageantry of social distinctions ("Clothes"), we find that all nature and history are symbolic of a profounder reality. Here is the Mystery at once revealed and concealed by "Clothes" (the "garments" of the visible world). To this our reverence is due.

3. But because the world's "Clothes" symbolize this profounder, divine order, we must reverence them too, insofar as they are representative of it. In ultimate reality, all men are united—and it is by reason of this ultimate union that the different classes of men can communicate with one another. Hence, at stage 3 we can restore with a difference the reverence for "Clothes" (i.e., the "garments" of nature and the social order both) that we had withdrawn at stage 2. In particular, we can restore reverence for that major class distinction, between ruler and ruled (a pattern of thinking which could then, presumably, be reproduced in miniature, where lesser hierarchic differences were concerned). We should revere a true king ("hero") because he really does rule by divine right.

If the course of the argument still escapes you, we might make another try. In fact, perhaps our point can be made most clearly by deliberately letting the argument escape us, and noting merely what it "all adds up to," from the standpoint of "identifications." As thus telescoped, what you get is this: Over and above all the qualifications, *mystery* is equated with *class distinctions*.

We have not been trying to abolish, or debunk, or refute, or even to "approve with reservations." Above all, we are not trying to decide whether mystery should be considered dyslogistically, as with Marx, or eulogistically, as with Carlyle. For we need not decide here whether there should or should not be reverence and mystery (hence "mystification").

Perhaps there would be no mystery, of any appreciable resonance, if distinctions of class were abolished (as they do not seem to have been abolished in Soviet Russia, with regard to the courtly, Carlylean relations between the dictator and the people). Or perhaps there would be a truer kind of mystery, now hidden behind the fog of social inequality. Maybe, if there were no hierarchy of privilege, the imagination would not be led to conceive of divine dignity in such trivial forms, as with the feudal imaging of Man and God in terms of liege and lord, or servitude (like a theologically-minded dog conceiving of God in terms of his pudgy and puffy master). Perhaps reality would not look mysterious at all to our literary mystics, if it did not also include the reverence due their professional careerism; perhaps without such impunities, it would disclose a more urgent wonder.

Maybe there would be no mystery. Maybe there should be none. For present purposes, it does not matter. As regards rhetoric, our point is: Marx and Carlyle, taken together, indicate the presence of a "mystifying condition" in social inequality; and this condition can elicit "God-fearing" attitudes towards agents and agencies that are not "divine." The two doctrines, taken together, can put us on the lookout for expressions that both reveal and conceal such an aspect of "consciousness," as is the way with symbols (for the dictionaries tell us that "mystery" is related to *muein* which, accented on the second syllable, means "to initiate into the mysteries," and, accented on the first syllable, means "to shut the eyes"). But we believe that, if you will read *Sartor Resartus* with *The German Ideology* in mind, and without a blinding prejudice for or against either, Carlyle's enigmatic symbol may contribute as much as Marx towards indicating a relation between mystification and class relationships. This is a very important consideration for rhetoric, since it puts rhetorical analysis on the track of much courtship that might otherwise remain undetected. And courtship, however roundabout, is a form of persuasion.

Empson on "Pastoral" Identification

We previously spoke of "courtship, however roundabout." William Empson's ingenious work, *English Pastoral Poetry* (English edition entitled: *Some Versions of Pastoral*), can for our purposes be treated as an investigation into this recondite rhetoric. His book, which is his rare response to a vogue for "proletarian" literature, is profoundly concerned with the rhetoric of courtship between contrasted social classes. For pastoral, as a literary *genre,* was, in its essence, "felt to imply a beautiful relation between rich and poor."

True, whereas the "proletarian" critic's emphasis upon "class consciousness" would bring out the elements of class *conflict,* Empson is concerned with a kind of expression which, while thoroughly conscious of class differences, aims rather at a stylistic transcending of conflict. We might say that he examines typical social-stylistic devices whereby spokesmen for different classes aim at an over-all dialectic designed to see beyond the limitations of status. To this extent, the orthodox Marxist might want to accuse him of contributing to the "mystifications" of class, since the ruling class presumably profits more than any other by the maintenance of the *status quo.* And certainly an orthodox critic writing in Russia today would object because the approach to "proletarian" literature in terms of "pastoral" makes the relation between the common people of Russia and their representatives in the Kremlin seem much like the "pastoral" relation between nobleman and shepherd.

But the important consideration, for our purposes, is the concern with a politeness, or humility, stemming simultaneously from the conventions of love poetry and the mimetics of social inferiority. Empson analyzes variants of literary simplicity, irony, and mock-simplicity, as developed out of social pudencies (Carlyle's *"Schaam,* Modesty"). That is, the "mystery" is still present in such expression, but it is transformed into subtle embarrassments that cover a range extending from outright flattery to ironically veiled challenge. Or we might say that the "reverence" of social privilege has been attenuated into respect, the respect itself sometimes being qualified until it has moved as far in the direction of disrespect as one might go without unmistakably showing his hand. In the literary strategies Empson is examining, ideas and images under the sign of cajolery, however strained, are never abandoned for ideas and images under the sign of outright insult and injury. And we are led to feel that the impulse behind such compromises is not merely an underling's fear of a superior, but rather the magic of the hierarchic order itself, which imposes itself upon superior and inferior both, and leads them both to aim at a dialectic transcending their discordancy of status. Looking at matters thus, you find that many attitudes quite different from outright approval can serve such ends. Relations between classes, even where the aim is to make both sides feel themselves part of a larger unity, may be treated "as well by mockery as admiration."

Perhaps the clearest instance of Empson's book, considered as a contribution to the rhetorical analysis of "mystification," is with his comments on four lines from Gray's *Elegy:*

> Full many a gem of purest ray serene
> The dark, unfathomed caves of ocean bear;
> Full many a flower is born to blush unseen
> And waste its sweetness on the desert air.

While granting that it would be hard to say just how much "bourgeois ideology" there is in these lines, he analyzes them for their "latent political ideas." And his observations might be summed up under four heads:

1. The lines allude to society's neglect of such scholarly talents as this poet's.

2. Such neglected talents are presented in terms of virginal modesty (as of the blushing but unplucked flower).

3. The note of melancholy suggests that, while understanding "the conditions opposed to aristocracy," the poet will not protest, but will resign himself.

4. The churchyard setting, the universality and impersonality of the reflections, "claim as if by comparison that we ought to accept the injustice of society as we do the inevitability of death."

Perhaps we might add a fifth step here, when considering the "poetic" lines rhetorically, as a *social* strategy. For we have the feeling that the poem is not wholly resigned. Isn't there a possibility that the virginal flower might be plucked after all? Can't the bowed posture of ingredients 3 and 4 be an unassuming appeal (of a nature that befits ingredient 2) for someone to correct the condition of ingredient 1? For here is a kind of resignation that might also, in "mystifying" terms, serve as a bid for preferment. The sentiments expressed are thus a character reference, describing a person doubly reliable, since he doesn't protest even when neglected. In an imaginative way the poem answers such questions as a personnel director would record in his files, if interviews and questionnaires were capable of such subtle disclosures, rather than supplying merely such entries as would fit a punch card.

As we have seen, when considering Carlyle, the "mystery" of social relations can become identified with the mystery of first and last things. But as attenuated, in the forms of social embarrassment, it can perhaps be reduced to this: Where there is wealth and poverty, there is awkwardness in any one of these four situations:

> a rich man speaking in praise of wealth
> a rich man speaking in praise of poverty
> a poor man speaking in praise of wealth
> a poor man speaking in praise of poverty

Attenuate this in turn, and you get, as a rhetorical situation, the proposition that in any social inequality there is awkwardness, making for the kinds of squeamishness which Empson is studying in their most imaginative manifestations.

Among these pudencies, for instance, is what Empson calls "comic primness." Comic primness, or "prim irony," is an attitude characterizing a member of a privileged class who somewhat questions the state of affairs whereby he enjoys his privileges; but after all, he does enjoy them, and so in the last analysis he resigns himself to the dubious conditions, in a state of ironic complexity that is apologetic, but not abnegatory.

The analysis of such attitudes, as expressed in literary tactics, we would class under the head of rhetorical identification. Hence we would assign Empson's book an important place in the New Rhetoric. Above all, we can derive from his account of pastoral and its variants good hints as to the way in which irony may simultaneously reflect and transcend class motives. Such considerations have important bearing on the cult of irony among our Southern intellectuals, a commingling of irony and irrationality which, whatever its "cosmic" pretensions, is also qualified by its relation to the conditions of "white supremacy."

The literary criticism in Empson's *Seven Types of Ambiguity* is rhetorical in that it analyzes obscure savors having to do with poetic effects as such. It is a study of "eloquence." But perhaps we should recall that De Quincey *distinguished between* rhetoric and eloquence. Under rhetoric he classed all effects having to do with purely literary ingenuity (love of rhetorical tactics for their own sake: the "epideictic" interest, that gravitates towards sheer technical display). And he assigned to eloquence all urgencies of emotion and passion. (Thus Ovid's playful ostentation is his ideal instance of rhetoric, whereas Demosthenes is disqualified by the high degree of eloquence in his orations.) The book on "pastoral" is rhetorical in a different sense: in its bearing upon matters of advantage.

Having matched Marx and Carlyle, Kafka and the pseudo-Dionysius, we suggested that the concerns in Empson's book might serve as a bridge between the two kinds. But we might propose a match for it too: Veblen's *Theory of the Leisure Class*. Though its strongly sociological stress places it rather in our earlier chapter, where we tried to disclose the rhetorical motive in works not usually so considered, Veblen's book applies to rhetoric in the strictly literary sense because it centers upon the purely *symbolic expression* of advantage. All told, we might say that where Empson deals with the courtship of classes, Carlyle with their marriage, and Marx with their divorce, Veblen deals with one class and its fascinated appeal to itself.

The "Invidious" as Imitation, in Veblen

We consider Thorstein Veblen's *Theory of the Leisure Class* better "in principle" than in the particular. Where Empson is fine to the point of evanescence, Veblen treads cumbrously. And his terminology of motives is far too limited in scope; hence, at every step in his explanation, important modifiers would be needed, before we could have a version of human motives equal to the depths at which the ways of persuasion (appeal, communication, "justification") must really operate. His primary distinction (between the "invidious" or "pecuniary" motive and the "instinct of workmanship") is neither comprehensive nor pliant enough. For instance, when discussing "honorific" and "humilific" words like noble, base, higher, lower, he says that "they are in substance an expression of sportsmanship—of the predatory and animistic habit of mind." Or again: "The canons of pecuniary decency are reducible for the present purposes to the principles of waste, futility, and ferocity." But we would question whether any motive ample enough to rationalize wide areas of human relationship can be so reduced without misrepresentation. Allow, if you will, that there may be a high percentage of such ingredients in it. Yet there is nothing essentially "predatory" in the symbolic nature of money. Its nature is in its *dialectical* or *linguistic* function as a "spiritual" entity, a purely symbolic thing, a mode of abstraction that "transcends" the materially real.

Veblen's psychology is not so much dramatistic, as dramatized. Consider his choice of the "invidious" as the term in which to treat of the "competitive," "sportsmanlike," and "pecuniary." (For in

Veblen these four terms are equated with one another.) Presumably in keeping with the genius of Bentham's search for scientifically neutral "appellatives," he writes:

> In making use of the term "invidious," it may perhaps be unnecessary to remark, there is no intention to extol or depreciate, or to commend or deplore any of the phenomena which the word is used to characterize. The term is used in a technical sense as describing a comparison of persons with a view to rating and grading them in respect of relative worth or value—in an aesthetic or moral sense—and so awarding and defining the relative degrees of complacency with which they may legitimately be contemplated by themselves and by others. An invidious comparison is a process of valuation of persons in respect of worth.

Similarly, having identified the "invidious" with a cult of "conspicuous waste," he writes:

> The use of the term "waste" is in one respect an unfortunate one. As used in the speech of everyday life the word carries an undertone of deprecation. It is here used for want of a better term that will adequately describe the same range of motives and of phenomena, and it is not to be taken in an odious sense, as implying an illegitimate expenditure of human products or of human life. In the view of economic theory the expenditure in question is no more and no less legitimate than any other expenditure. It is here called "waste" because this expenditure does not serve human life or human well-being on the whole, not because it is waste or misdirection of effort or expenditure as viewed from the standpoint of the individual consumer who chooses it.

To use key terms as censorially charged as "invidious" and "waste," while at the same time assuring one's reader that one is being merely technical, and does not want the reader to read any unfavorable implications into them—well, it is a good stylistic device, and may be enjoyed for its blandness (rhetorically dramatizing in the name of the non-dramatic). Yet it reminds us of the wag who, having called his enemy a son of a bitch, went on to explain: "I want it understood that I employ the expression, not as an oath, but in the strictly scientific sense."

We have elsewhere complained that anthropological terminologies of motives often mislead, when applied to the contemporary world, because they slight the role of money in human relations. This objection seems particularly important, as regards the contemporary rhetoric of advantage, since the divisive aspects of money pervade the modern rhetorical situation with an especially urgent need for "mystifying" terms that proclaim the ideal unity of people thus set apart. Accordingly, one might think that Veblen's overwhelming stress upon the "pecuniary" motive would be just what we are asking for. However, his approach to money as motive is in terms of a "predatory instinct" which is even more "primitive" than the behavior studied by anthropologists, and which at best analyzes modern society in terms of a dyslogistically simplified version of the motives for ostentation in savages and the medieval nobility. Modern life itself becomes a kind of epideictic oratory, wherein social display itself, rather than the malaise behind it, is taken as a basic motive.

The "pecuniary" motive, we contend, should be analyzed as a special case of the linguistic motive. And the linguistic motive eventually involves kinds of persuasion guided not by appeal to any one local audience, but by the *logic of appeal in general* (treated in secular terms as "socialization," in theology as "justification"). The reductive, abstractive, metaphorical, analytic, and synthesizing powers of all language find their correspondences in the monetary idiom. Whatever fantastic appetites may finally arise under the goading of the pecuniary motive (particularly when it is not functioning adequately), Veblen's reductions are misleading unless they are enjoyed as a kind of deadpan satire. As so read and discounted, they are extremely illuminating. When taken at their face value, their very revelation of a superficial rhetoric in human relations but conceals a profounder rhetoric that Veblen leaves unanalyzed.

The book is valuable as an illustration of the ways in which identification (and a primary function of it, the vicarious) can operate. The notion of "vicarious leisure" whereby a man may work himself to death earning the money to help his wife be useless for the both of them, is good irony, good satiric reduction. At its best his book is a systematic exploiting of this solemn absurdity, until we see the reflections of it throughout society's assumptions about the good, the true, and the beautiful (respectability, the "higher learning," the esthetic).

When discussing "The American Way" we shall indicate why we think that this economist is not economist enough, in his account of the motives for "conspicuous consumption" and "vicarious consumption." The forms of ostentation which he eruditely ridicules may be treated as ways of "bearing witness"—a low order of such persuasion, perhaps, but with an ingredient of genuine piety, however ironically perverted its manifestations may be.

"The motive that lies at the root of ownership," Veblen writes, "is emulation; and the same motive of emulation continues active in the further development of the institution to which it has given rise." But wherein reside the "roots of ownership"? Do they not reside in the *individual centrality of the nervous system,* in the *divisiveness* of the individual human organism, from birth to death? What the body eats and drinks becomes its special private property; the body's pleasures and pains are exclusively its own pleasures and pains. True, there is the vicarious sharing by empathy, by sympathy, the "imaginative" identification with one another's states of mind. And there is the mutuality of cooperation and language whereby human society becomes, not an aggregate of isolated individuals, but a superentity, involving principles of interdependence that have in the past gone by such names as rationality, consciousness, conscience, and "God." Bring together a number of individual nervous systems, each with its own unique centrality, and from this indeterminate mixture of cooperation and division there emerge the conditions for the "basic rhetorical situation": an underlying biological incentive towards private property, plus the fact that the high development of production and language owes so much to its public or communal nature. And once a high development of public property has accumulated, private property is rather a function of that accumulation than an expression of the original biologic goading that is located in the divisive centrality of the nervous system. The cult of property comes to reflect public norms, norms identified with social classes which are differentiated by property. And emulation seems to derive from the imitation of class ways considered in some respect superior.

We previously spoke of Isocrates' device for "spiritualizing" the idea of "advantage." Similarly, "emulation" can be spiritualized (as in the Plutarchian theory of biography, where emulation means the ethical desire to pattern one's life after "noble" models). Veblen would warn us to be wary of such "nobility," or to see in it symbolic claims to more exclusive kinds of preferment. But when we get so far, we ask ourselves: Emulation being but a special case of imitation, what of imitation itself as motive?

We recall but one place in Veblen's book where the "competitive," "predatory," "pecuniary," "invidious" nature of emulation shows signs of giving way to this wider notion, of imitation in general. Thus, he writes:

> A still more characteristic and more pervasive alien element in the motives which have gone to formally uphold the scheme of the devout life is that non-reverent sense of aesthetic congruity with the environment, which is left as a residue of the latter-day act of worship after elimination of its anthropomorphic content. . . . This sense or impulse of aesthetic congruity is not primarily of an economic character, but it has considerable indirect effect in shaping the habit of mind of the individual for economic purposes in the later stages of industrial development.

Is not "non-reverent sense of aesthetic congruity with the environment" but a special case of imitation? But perhaps before pressing for an answer to this question, we should make clear just what we are after.

In considering the whole subject of competition, as the term is used either in capitalist apologetics or in critiques of capitalism, we began to see that competition itself is but a special case of imitation. For when you discuss competition as it has actually operated in our society, you discover that the so-called ways of competition have been almost fanatically zealous ways of *conformity*. And considering how men in their businesses, and how the families of business men in their social relations attempt to amass and display all the insignia felt proper to their status, we conclude: From the standpoint of "identification" what we call "competition" is better described as men's attempt to *out-imitate* one another.

Imitation is an essentially dramatistic concept. It makes for consubstantiality by community of ways ("identification"), since men can either crudely imitate one another's actions as revealed on the surface, or subtly imitate the *underlying principles* of such actions. (And in calling the motive "dramatistic" rather than "anthropomorphic," we can avoid the false promises too often lurking in the discarded word, which suggests that people can be "human" in some other way than by being "anthropomorphic.")

With imitation as the most generalized term, competition would be treated as a special case of it. The "invidious" would be at one further remove. We might characterize in another way the rhetorical blandness of Veblen's satire-masked-as-science by saying: He substitutes a censorially partisan word for a more generalized word, then asks us to discount the partisan connotations.

Emulation, as used by earlier writers, would be the word for imitation in the moral vocabulary, though its ethical pretensions might well be quizzically examined for traces of more mundane ambitions, and even for "magical" attempts to coerce material reality by ritual means. (Consider, for instance, the lurking hope that moral goodness will draw rewards from nature, as in *Comus,* where chastity is a protection against wild beasts.) However, whereas such ways may be latently "magical" where some of man's relations with nonverbal nature are concerned, they may be correctly rhetorical as regards human relations. Thus, as the rhetorically minded moralist, Rochefoucauld, put it: To establish yourself in the world, you do all you can to look established (*"Pour s'établir dans le monde, on fait tout ce que l'on peut pour y paraître établi"*). Another variant would be "admiration," as used in the dramatic theory of Corneille, where it is a special term linking esthetic criteria with the pageantry of privilege.

In sum, when Veblen reduces to the "invidious," we believe that this expression in turn should be reduced to imitation (except of course insofar as the purpose of his tract is not literally scientific, but satirical). If his statement of motives were reduced to a term of this scope, he might next consider the special "invidious" stress which certain conditions favor. In showing how this "invidious" stress, in conjunction with identification and the vicarious, makes for roundabout manifestations, he would give us the valuable insights into rhetoric which he now gives. But such modified procedure would of itself provide the correctives which otherwise must be introduced from without. The same remark applies, in varying degrees, to any discussion of imitation exclusively in terms of competition, where one has to stumble upon factors which he should have explicitly begun with, or where one leaves them in the offing, but pressing for acknowledgment.

Priority of the "Idea"

The "rhetoric of class" involves kinds of identification distinguishable somewhat like Coleridge's fancy, "primary" imagination and "secondary" imagination.

There are mechanical associations of the sort that Pavlov studied in his experiments with the "conditioned reflex." Thus, the mere associating of an idea with an image, or of a cause with a topic, could be called "mechanical." There is such association in the act of a child who, by the mere *noise* of hammering, imitates a carpenter driving nails.

A more organic kind would arise when the principles of one order are transferred to another order. We here have in mind the Marxist statement that the ideologist's view of history is derived from his nature as a specialist in ideas. And Bacon had said much the same, though in an almost reverse application, to account for the imaginings he called "Idols of the Cave." As he put it: When the scientific specialist takes "to philosophy and contemplations of a general character," he is likely to "distort and color them in obedience to" his "former fancies." Thus:

> The race of chemists . . . out of a few experiments of the furnace have built up a fantastic philosophy, framed with reference to a few things; and Gilbert also, after he had employed himself most laboriously in the study and observation of the lodestone, proceeded at once to construct an entire system in accordance with his favorite subject.

John Dewey has favored the term "occupational psychosis" to designate the same "imaginative" transference of principles from one field to another.

There is a most engaging example of such reversal in George Bernard Shaw's preface for his *Back to Methuselah*. He comes upon the principles of dialectic, which he discovers by speculating about the principles of his profession as playwright. Then, looking at nature, he conceives the dialectic of nature after the analogy of his dialectic as playwright. That is: He rejects Darwinian evolution for a view of "creative" evolution which he has developed after the analogy of his experiences as a playwright. Then he claims to derive his views of the playwright's art from this version of nature. Nature having been interpreted dramatistically, he can "deduce" drama from it. The "firsts" or principles of drama have thus been stated twice, once in their own terms and once in terms of a mythic ground or "past," an ideological "prehistory" that looks scientific in its pretense to be a discussion of natural evolution. Then, whereas his terms for nature are derived from his calling as dramatist, he can appear to be proceeding the other way round, and deriving drama from nature.

But how would Veblen's *Theory of the Leisure Class* fit into such a distinction? Sometimes the identifications he reveals seem of the first, more accidental sort. People seem to be bent on doing and acquiring certain things simply because these things happen to have become the signs of an admired status. And one can imagine these same people doing exactly the opposite, if the opposite happened to be the sign of the same status.

At other times the identification seems to be more deeply imaginative. Bacon had said that the Idols of the Cave "take their rise in the peculiar constitution, mental or bodily, of each individual; and also in education, habit, and accident." And the "predatory" instinct which Veblen imputed as the basic motive of the "leisure class" would seem to be such an idol, grounded in the natural constitution, but inured through "education, habit, and accident." "Accident," of course, would refer to linkages of the first sort, the almost automatic response to signs, as to the stop-and-go of traffic lights. But the notion of a natural trait, selected, developed, and trained by the conditions of living, implies rather a central core or principle from which all sorts of expressions could radiate. A "predatory" art, for instance, would not be formed merely by imitation of "predatory" business; rather, art would be "predatory" in ways proper to art while business would be "predatory" in ways proper to business, etc. The "predatory principle" would be generic; but the expression of it would be shaped by the principles specific to each kind of cultural activity.

In trying thus to decide wherein different fields seem to borrow from one another, and wherein they seem to be but different specialized radiations from a common center, you would find yourself involved in issues that would soon carry you far from Veblen. But now we see at least the possibility of three orders here: (1) There is the realm of accident, mechanical association, response to signs as signs, "magical" in the sense that it begins in infancy; it is related to Carlyle's pageantry of "Clothes," as the child gets a "mysterious" sense of class distinction through such appearances long before understanding their occupational logic. (2) There are *analogizing* associations, where terms are transferred from one order to another. Thus, a business culture may become much exercised over a work's "value" as an estheticized equivalent of "price." Or the classic criterion of fitness (decorum, *to pre-pon*), while referring to a purely technical adaptation of *artistic* means to *artistic* end, can be invoked against a work which violates dominant criteria of *social* propriety. That is, though the adaptation of means to end may be quite adequate, the fitness of the end itself may be questioned under the guise of questioning the means, a canon of artistic expression thereby acting as a canon of social suppression. (3) There are distinct, specialized expressions, *all derived from the same generating principle, hence all embodying it, without the need of direct "interactive" borrowing* (the sort of cultural essences that Spengler was always seeking to codify).

The third kind might bring us again, by another route, to the "ideological." For, given sufficient discernment and expressiveness on the part of the critic, such a unitary principle should lend itself to statement in terms of an *idea*. And it would be "prior" to the economic in the sense that it would be more general, so that the economic behavior, like all other modes of expression, would in its peculiar way manifest this same character.

Consider the bourgeois-Bohemian antithesis (the treatment of the esthetic as directly opposed to the practical, backed by the tendency to equate artistic imagination with unreason, since reason itself is conceived strictly in terms of financial or technological utility). The first step in this direction is probably taken at the beginning of inter-tribal trade, which breaks art from primitive magic. By the time the monetary rationale has emancipated men from a belief in any spiritual power but money itself and its psychoses, art is viewed not directly, but as refracted through the medium of money.

However, money itself is symbolic of general dialectical processes themselves not monetary. It is an aspect of reductive, abstractive, and substitutive resources inborn to symbolism. There is its nature as an imagery interwoven with other images (Freud, for instance, notes how the miser can be "anally" motivated, Gide in *The Counterfeiters* parallels monetary and personal relations, and we have frequently considered money as a burlesque of "spirit"). But beyond its relation to imagery, there lie its roots in dialectic, so that its origins are as mysterious as the word, with which it is identical, and as the Word, with which it is often identified. Ultimately, like moral striving and scientific or philosophic ordering, it is under the sign of the Ladder, hence its rhetorical convertibility with the patterns of "celestial hierarchy."

The typical nineteenth-century doctrines of esthetics seem to have been monetary in all three of the senses we have here tried to distinguish. Thus, in part, the cult of beauty can be analyzed merely as a symbolic claim to social distinction, in Veblen's term an "invidious" motive. In part, as where "aesthetic values" are a "spiritualized" equivalent of "monetary price," beauty was conceived analogously to money. (This would seem to fit our second category.) The third level seems to manifest itself in writers as different as Shelley and Freud. Shelley's anarchistic idealism is the "perfection" of monetary freedom, transcending it, but *from within*. Similarly, the Marxist critique of capitalism is intrinsic to capitalism, and could only be evolved by a man conversant with the very essence of capitalist motives. And both the Shelleyan and the Marxist departures from the orthodoxy of capitalist motives lead into a wider area of dialectic, where money is but a limiting image. Man, *qua* man, is a symbol user. In this respect, every aspect of his "reality" is likely to be seen through a fog of symbols. And not even the hard reality of basic economic facts is sufficient to pierce this symbolic veil (which is intrinsic to the human mind). One man may seek to organize a set of images, another may strive for order among his ideas, a third may feel goaded to make himself head of some political or commercial empire, but however different the situations resulting from these various modes of action, there are purely symbolic motives behind them all, for in all of them there is "overproduction."

Would it then be possible to make a distinction that allowed for "ideology" within limits? That is, could we consider the Marxist critique as usefully limiting the application of the ideological, but not as wholly discrediting it? For the human mind, as the organ of a symbol-using animal, is "prior" to any *particular* property structure— and in this sense the laws of symbols are prior to economic laws. Out of his symbols, man has developed all his inventions. Hence, why should not their symbolic origin remain concealed in them? Why should they not be not just *things,* but *images* of "ideas"?

So why could we not allow for a certain cooperation between "ideology" (in the sense distrusted by Marx) and the Marxist reversal of it ("in all ideology men and their circumstances appear upside down as in a *camera obscura*")? We are not merely trying to strike a compromise between irreconcilable opponents, or treating the two positions as ideal opposites, with the truth somewhere in between. Rather, we are assigning a definite function to each of the positions—and we are saying that, insofar as each performs its function, they are no more at odds than the stomach and liver of a healthy organism.

Given an economic situation, there are ways of thinking that arise in response to it. But these ways of living and thinking, in complex relationship with both specific and generic motives, can go deep, to the level of *principles*. For a way of living and thinking is reducible to terms of an "idea"—and that "idea" will be "creative" in the sense that anyone who grasps it will embody it or represent it in any mode of action he may choose. The idea, or underlying principle, must be approached by him through the sensory images of his cultural scene. But until he intuitively grasps the principle of such an imaginal clutter, he cannot be profoundly creative, so far as the genius of that "idea" is concerned. For to be profoundly representative of a culture, he will imitate not its mere insignia, but the principle behind the *ordering* of those insignia.

A Metaphorical View of Hierarchy

Let us try again. (A direct hit is not likely here. The best one can do is to try different approaches towards the same center, whenever the opportunity offers.)

Imagine a myth of this sort, built around the hierarchic principle of "higher" and "lower" beings, a principle found in both the Darwinian doctrine of natural evolution and the Marxist doctrine of social evolution. According to this myth, since all living kinds came out of the sea, the sea is their natural home. And they are, let us say, nostalgic for the sea. Physiologically, this state of longing manifests itself as "undernourishment." That is, only foods in and of the sea can wholly nourish forms of life descended from the sea. Hence, in birds and land animals, particularly those living far inland, there can never be complete "biological satiety." Accordingly there is a sect which holds that we should live as much as possible on raw sea food; should bathe often in the sea, for the pores of the body to absorb the sea environment; and as partial compensation for the fact that land organisms have lost the more radical mode of assimilating sea air through gills, we should try always to breathe spindrift, should experiment with the injection of natural sea water into the blood stream, and should try to heal wounds with emulsions and salves made from sea creatures.

Our myth is doubly "regressive." According to it, the offspring's yearning for a return to the womb is but a replica of a prior motive, the womb's yearning for a return to the sea. Though the womb can make a kind of internal sea environment for the foetus, it cannot enjoy this same relation in reverse. It must make a sea, without itself having a sea. Here again is frustration, a biological interference with the body's attempt to "live on the level of principle." For the hierarchic principle is complete only insofar as it works both ways at once. It is not merely the relation of higher to lower, or lower to higher, or before to after, or after to before. The hierarchic principle is not complete in the social realm, for instance, in the mere arrangement whereby each rank is overlord to its underlings and underling to its overlords. It is complete only when each rank accepts the *principle of gradation itself,* and in thus "universalizing" the principle, makes a spiritual *reversal* of the ranks just as meaningful as their actual material arrangement.

The Christian doctrine that the first shall be last and the last shall be first is often interpreted as a pattern of social revolution couched in theological terms. But looking at it from the present standpoint, we should interpret its rhetorical appeal as a dialectic more roundabout, thus: The state of first and last things, the heavenly state, is the realm of *principle.* In this state (a mythical term for the *logically prior*) the reversal of social status makes as much sense as its actual mundane order. For on this level, all that counts is the principle of hierarchy, or levels, or developments, or unfoldings, *per se* (the dialectic principle in general, which is "prior" to any particular kind of development, a kind of priority that can be stated mythically either in terms of a heavenly society before the world began, or one after the world has ended, or one outside of time). The reduction of such reversibility to the world of property can add up to political or social revolution, as the "Edenic" world of universal principle is ironically broken down into the divisions of property, confronting one with a choice between the frozen order of the *status quo* and the reversal of that order, through its "liquidation." We are then in the state of the "fall," the communicative disorder that goes with the building of the technological Tower of Babel.

So, out of the sea came the womb, out of the womb came the child, out of the child came the enlightened division of labor, out of the division of labor came the hierarchy, and out of the hierarchy came the new goadings of social property. And out of this came the variety of attitudes: first, ideally, love, charity, the attempt of the divided beings to overcome division; then, when the tension increased, the various departures from love, beginning with the slight ironic embarrassments, the modified tributes of courtship (as regards the relations between either social or sexual classes); then the tragic attempt to transform hate into love "on a higher level"; and finally, the organization of hate and war, the farthest stage of division, though out of it in turn arises a new compensatory union, the *conspiratorial* unity of faction, where "spies" go by the name of "intelligence." (There is a satanic caricature of the Trinity here. God being the source of power, the Son the bringer of light, the Holy Ghost the Gift of Love, in the conspiratorial unity of faction the war machine is power, espionage is the bringer of light, and the breathing-together of the warrior-conspirators is love.)

But would not our myth have started in the middle of things? Is not the sea itself a jungle of divisiveness? And were not its first denizens already marked by "original sin," as participants in the sea's division from a sea-behind-the-sea? And in the pride of their singularity, when they chose to risk nostalgia by living on the land, did they not do so because their sea-home had already become a wrangle, and the new hunger that would arise in time with their departure and evolution from the sea seemed at that stage more like a promise? How could they know that, in moving from the sea-jungle towards enlightenment, they had but begun a progress towards the speed-up of a Detroit factory, and thence towards atomic and bacteriological war? They had not yet encountered the "rhetorical situation," wherein division may be idealistically buried beneath a terminology of love, or ironically revealed in combination with varying grades of compensatory deference, or where the continuity is snapped, and there is war, hate, conspiracy, with a new terminology of "love" to mask the divisions among the conspirators.

So, the myth of society's return to the child, or the child's return to the womb, or the womb's return to the sea, can all but point towards a myth still farther back, the myth of a power prior to all parturition. Then divided things were not yet proud in the private property of their divisiveness. Division was still but "enlightenment."

The notion of the Son as bringer of light seems in its essence to suggest that the division of the part from the whole is enlightening, a principle that might be stated dialectically thus: Partition provides *terms;* thereby it allows the parts to comment upon one another. But this "loving" relation allows also for the "fall" into terms antagonistic in their partiality, until dialectically resolved by reduction to "higher" terms. (The reversibility possible when hierarchic or opposed orders are reduced to their common ground usually makes at best for a slovenly kind of dispute where the opponents switch sides, as each is tricked into taking over the other's arguments in the attempt to buttress his own.)

Where are we, then? Are we proposing that men cannot resolve their local fights over property until they have undergone the most radical revolution of all, a return to their source? Are we saying that because the warlike divisiveness of property is inherent in our very nature, such mythic design justifies the *status quo* or can properly serve as an argument for the "inevitability" of some particular war? We are not—but we do take our myth seriously to this extent: It reminds us how far back the unrest of *Homo Dialecticus* really goes, and suggests how thorough our shrewdness about property and hierarchy must be, before we could build a whole human society about the critique of ambition.

From the standpoint of pattern, for instance, the Marxist view of social evolution is no less hierarchic than the Areopagite's version of the heavenly and earthly orders. And as the principle of *any* hierarchy involves the possibility of reversing highest and lowest, so the moralizing of status makes for a revolutionary kind of expression, the scapegoat. The scapegoat is dialectically appealing, since it combines in one figure contrary principles of identification and alienation. And by splitting the hierarchic principle into factions, it becomes ritually gratifying; for each faction can then use the other as *katharma*, the unclean vessel upon which can be loaded the dyslogistic burdens of vocabulary (a procedure made all the more zealous by the secret awareness that, if not thus morally "protected," each faction might "court" the other). When this state of affairs prevails, it is not merely men's differences that drive them apart, it is also the *elements they share*, "vices" and "virtues" alike, since the same motives are capable of both eulogistic and dyslogistic naming.

The hierarchic principle itself is inevitable in systematic thought. It is embodied in the mere process of growth, which is synonymous with the class divisions of youth and age, stronger and weaker, male and female, or the stages of learning, from apprentice to journeyman to master. But this last hierarchy is as good an indication as any of the way in which the "naturalness" of grades rhetorically reënforces the protection of privilege. Though in its essence purely developmental, the series is readily transformed into rigid social classifications, and these interfere with the very process of development that was its reason for being.

To say that hierarchy is inevitable is not to say that any particular hierarchy is inevitable; the crumbling of hierarchies is as true a fact about them as their formation. But to say that the hierarchic principle is indigenous to all well-rounded human thinking, is to state a very important fact about the rhetorical appeal of dialectical symmetry. And it reminds us, on hearing talk of equality, to ask ourselves, without so much as questioning the possibility that things might be otherwise: "Just how does the hierarchic principle work in this particular scheme of equality?"

Though *hierarchy* is exclusive, the *principle* of hierarchy is not; all ranks can "share in it alike." But: It includes also the entelechial tendency, the treatment of the "top" or "culminating" stage as the "image" that best represents the entire "idea." This leads to "mystifications" that cloak the state of division, since the "universal" principle of the hierarchy also happens to be the principle by which the most distinguished rank in the hierarchy enjoys, in the realm of worldly property, its special privileges. Hence, the turn from courtship to ill will, with ironic intermediate grades. At the stage of blunt antithesis, each class would deny, suppress, exorcise the elements it shares with other classes. This attempt leads to the scapegoat (the use of dyslogistic terms for one's own traits as manifested in an "alien" class).

Diderot on "Pantomime"

Let us go back and examine, from the standpoint of our myth, the "enigmatic" quality of Diderot's almost hysterically brilliant dialogue between "Moi" and "Lui" in his *Neveu de Rameau*. Do not the reasons for its puzzling and picturesque perversity forthwith become clear? In his role as a social philosopher, Diderot would not be content to stop at the antitheses of political polemics. While favoring the movement from royalism towards bourgeois liberty, he would be thorough enough to desire such systematic rounding out of a philosophy as the principle of feudal hierarchy in its heyday had provided. Yet he was too enlightened to consider the actual court a fitting exemplar of such a form. Hence, in the deepest sense he would be frustrated. Insofar as the king represented the symmetrical *crowning* of a terminology, Diderot in turning against the king was turning somewhat against *himself*.

There were also complications, of course, in the purely practical realm. He wrote under the threat of imprisonment. In this sense, the mere choice of the dialogue form can be rhetorically motivated. In dividing his thoughts between a "Him" and a "Me," the author could let "Him" voice brightly certain dangerous opinions or attitudes which could be somewhat ploddingly and not too convincingly disapproved by "Me." But there is a profounder working-at-cross-purposes here than can be explained by the mere pragmatic need to outwit a censor. There is the *conflict within,* leading the author at times to say things so perverse and antinomian that they could not possibly serve as alignments for the next phase.

The divisiveness of the dialogue is both implicit and explicit. It is implicit in the sense that the author himself is split into the roles of Lui and Moi, confronting each other in an ambiguously courtly relationship at once frank and estranged, but showing their kinship despite their differences of "position." Next there is the divisiveness within Lui himself, a condition that is carried to the extreme by the picturesque amplifying of his showmanship, as his wide emotional swings are always histrionically exaggerated (the book is further interwoven with a contemporary quarrel over rival theories of opera that, roundabout, had revolutionary implications). The divisiveness is further amplified, as with Lui's account of a certain Bouret, who, having changed his office, made a corresponding change of costume. His dog followed him loyally in his habit as a *fermier général,* but was terrified at the sight of him as *garde des sceaux* (presumably dogs too can sense the "mystery" of class). And the work comes to a rousing finale in an ironic replica of the Carlylean vision. But it uses the *positions of pantomime,* instead of clothes, as the symbol of class.

In his essay on style, De Quincey refers to the pageantry of comedy that enlivened the earlier periods of English society, when all occupational types were very clearly demarcated by their dress. The passage would serve well as a bridge from Carlyle's "Clothes" to Diderot's "positions of pantomime." But though there are signs of the "mystery" everywhere, Diderot manifests them rather like laughter in church. By "pantomime" he means little more than obsequiousness. But the very choice of so gracious a word, however ironic, is in itself a vestige of "courtly" tactics.

The discussion of pantomime comes near the end of the dialogue. Lui has been talking of sensual appetite in general, and of hunger in particular. Next he refers to the postures of indigence; then he talks of viewing from a distance "the different pantomimes of the human race." He launches into one of his brilliant, half-hysterical improvisations, concluding: *"Voilà ma pantomime, à peu près la même que celle des flatteurs, des courtisans, des valets et des gueux."* The author, himself taking over at this point, says: "I see Pantalon in a prelate, a satyr in a president, a pig in a cénobite, an ostrich in a minister, a goose in his chief clerk." (The passage makes an interesting comparison with the one in Rimbaud's *Season in Hell,* where he is describing how his "reasoned derangement of the senses" enables him to translate the literal into the visionary. In Rimbaud the distortion seems more arbitrary, more purely "esthetic." The social reference is far in the background. But in Diderot the social bearing of the "mystery" is systematically obvious.)

Lui says: "In all the realm there is but one man who walks upright. That is the sovereign. The rest take positions." But Moi answers:

> Whoever has need of another is indigent and takes a position. The
> King takes a position before his mistress and before God; he does

his bit of pantomime. The minister does the steps of the courtier, the flatterer, the valet and the knave before his King. The crowd of the ambitious dances your positions, in a hundred manners each more loathsome than the next, before the minister. . . .

And so on; concluding: *"Ma foi, ce que vous appelez la pantomime des gueux est le grand branle de la terre."*

As Moi talks, Lui dances the part of each type mentioned. There follow some remarks by Moi, on the subject of philosophers like Diogenes, who have dispensed with pantomime. But not so Lui, "who has danced, and will continue to dance, vile pantomime." Lui admits it and turns to tearful memories of his lost wife, who had presumably been his refuge from the world of pantomime, had seemed to him apart from it, *"une espèce de philosophe"* and *"ah! Dieu, quelle croupe!"*

Roundabout, this aspect of Diderot called Lui could even be said to represent the king. For Lui represents the disorder of the hierarchic principle, and so does the king. Perhaps we might even dare to glimpse behind his name a pun on "Louis." In any case, there are Lui's tributes to the gold *louis,* after which Moi starts to speak of being "profoundly penetrated by the value of the *louis,*" but Lui interrupts him: "I understand. We must close our eyes to that."

Lui must also represent a disorder within Diderot himself, since his desire for pyramidal symmetry could not have been gratified unless he had been critically impervious to the conditions about him. Then, however bad things were in actuality, like Coleridge in later life, he could have viewed them idealistically, interpreting Church and State "according to the idea of each." He might have worked out a gladsome vision of the perfect form behind the imperfect image. Such a contrivance would have been Diderot's particular *pas de pantomime,* danced before the king, or the cardinal, or the king's minister, or the king's minister's chief clerk. In doing so, under those conditions, he would have been demoralized in one way. But in refusing to do so, he was demoralized in another, since the refusal required him to frustrate his architectonic imagination as a social philosopher (though his work on the encyclopedia could probably serve as a good substitute for all but such wayward moments as this dialogue).

In sum, the character of Lui was a point of convergence that represented both the "royal" *cause* of the disorder and its demoralizing *effects.* Lui is demoralized, but imaginatively so, and above all, *aristocratically.*

He can represent both a masterly *dévergondage d'intelligence* (according to one editor—a "spilling over" of spirit?) and the wretchedness and even downright physical hunger of an ailing society headed in the king. The confusion attains symbolic unity in an esthetic of crime which is infused, however perversely, with the "mystery" of aristocracy. *"S'il importe d'être sublime en quelque genre,"* Lui says, *"c'est surtout en mal."* Here is talk of the grand crime. And we see the bearing upon class when we recall that, in a monarchic society, the nobility corresponds in the social realm to the sublime in the esthetic. Though Lui represents a side of Diderot, he does not represent bourgeois, antiroyalist "virtue." He represents aristocratic vice, crime that has the appeal of *style*. (Recall Nietzsche on ways in which *class* distinctions become *moral* distinctions.) Variants of the same expression are found in Stendhal's Julien Sorel. But when we turn from Lui and Julien to the esthetic criminals of André Gide, the social reference has retreated behind "pure" demoralization (the change being much like the change we noted, when contrasting the passage in Diderot with the passage in Rimbaud).

Generic, Specific, and Individual Motives in Rochefoucauld

It may be argued that there are other ingredients in the "idea" of one culture than in another. Or it may be argued that all the elements are there always, but in different proportions. Thus, the principles of a society run by barter could be said to overlap upon those of a society run by money, not only because objects of barter are themselves incipient money, or because monetarily rationalized exchange is a roundabout kind of barter, but also because either mode of transaction involves principles prior to both (as numbers are indifferent to trade of any sort, and property, or "mine-own-ness," is grounded not socially, but biologically).

But whatever the ingredients of a culture might be, whatever the exact combination of local and universal motives went to compose it, and however greatly it is determined by relations to the "productive forces," the feeling for the particular combination as a unity would be an idea, or intuition, in its own right, a "new thing." And an artist who exemplified the gist of the entire cultural combination would embody an idea not reducible to certain of the factors, since the "idea" would be the grasp of that precise combination of factors, in precisely that proportion.

Ideology cannot be deduced from economic considerations alone. It also derives from man's nature as a "symbol-using animal." And since the "original economic plant" is the human body, with the divisive centrality of its particular nervous system, the theologian's concerns with Eden and the "fall" come close to the heart of the rhetorical problem. For, behind the theology, there is the perception of generic divisiveness which, being common to all men, is a universal fact about them, prior to any divisiveness caused by social classes. Here is the basis of rhetoric. Out of this emerge the motives for linguistic persuasion. Then, *secondarily,* we get the motives peculiar to particular economic situations.

In parturition begins the centrality of the nervous system. The different nervous systems, through language and the ways of production, erect various communities of interests and insights, social communities varying in nature and scope. And out of the division and the community arises the "universal" rhetorical situation.

Look at La Rochefoucauld's maxims, with this thought in mind. Note his concern with what he calls *intérêt, orgueil, amour-propre.* And with the many kinds of persuasion, frank, amicable, ironic, roundabout, diplomatic, and downright hypocritical, he derives from this divisive source. For his conception is strikingly rhetorical, a "pantomimic" morality ever on the alert for the minutiae of advantage.

Thus La Rochefoucauld speaks of humility as a ruse, a false submissiveness designed to make others submissive, a self-abasement used for self-exaltation, the "first stratagem" of pride. He scrutinizes the rhetoric of weeping, when women grieve over the death of their lovers "not through having loved them, but to show themselves more worthy of being loved." Or he discerns an invidious ingredient in good will, when people publicly deplore the misfortunes of an enemy, not from the goodness of their heart, but because, by giving signs of compassion, they let it be seen that they are superior to the enemy. Or he remarks that people blame themselves only to elicit praise. Or he notes that they confess minor faults in order to persuade (his word) that they have no big ones. Or he derives from *amour-propre* "the absurd persuasions that we have of ourselves." Or he comments variously on the use to which the *appearance* of moral attributes is put, as when he says that "the true mortifications are those which are not known; vanity makes the others easy." And above all, there is the strongly rhetorical ingredient in

La Rochefoucauld's lore on the relations between the sexes, which are discussed almost entirely in terms of coquetry and gallantry, which is to say persuasion and advantage.

Note particularly his statement that our devotion to princes is a second self-love (*la dévotion qu'on donne aux princes est un second amour-propre*).

Here is an aspect of such reversal as Marx sees in "ideology." For if the ways which Rochefoucauld has been describing are strongly affected by the motives of the courtier, then the "self-love" would derive much of its nature from the "devotion paid to princes." That is, the social motive would be "prior" to the individual one, insofar as the court itself is a social institution. But La Rochefoucauld, beginning with self-love as his primary term for the motives of man in society, and scrutinizing it closely enough to discern the element of courtship responsible for its formation, then states the matter the other way round. He says not that the self-love is derived from the courting of princes, but that the courting of princes is a second self-love.

However, we may appear to be contradicting ourselves here. For though we located the rhetorical situation in an individual divisiveness prior to all class cohesion, we are now saying that La Rochefoucauld gets things backwards in deriving a social motive (the honoring of princes) from an individualistic one (self-love). But the self-love La Rochefoucauld describes is not to be confused with man's original biological divisiveness (the "centrality of the nervous system"). Rather, La Rochefoucauld is describing a *courtly* morality—and the "self-love" he is discussing is the individual consciousness that is epitomized in the honoring of princes. Thus, following a Marxist kind of analysis, we would contend that La Rochefoucauld has the two motives "ideologically" reversed. But at the same time, we would interpret the individualist term as justified by an individual divisiveness prior to the social. The irony is that "self-love" is a *social* term for this divisiveness. La Rochefoucauld's maxims are a courtly rhetoric, with the individual defined by his place in an institution.

Perhaps we could break down the process into six distinct moments, thus:

(1) There are the incentives to individual advantage (and its corresponding rhetoric) indigenous to the "centrality of the nervous system," and to the ambiguously divisive and unitary conditions that go with it.

(2) There is implanted in individuals the thinking local to their social class (their place in a community restricted by traditions of property which emerged with the division of labor).   (3) Such local thinking is reducible to a principle or idea.   In this case it is the idea of courting. It is summed up in the image or topic of "the devotion paid to princes." (4) Then one's own individual identity is conceived in terms of this same principle.   (Incidentally, note the pun on "prince" and "principle." It is more than a mere accident.   Here again is an instance of what we have called the "entelechial" mode of thought, the feeling that the principle of a genus is represented by its "highest" potentialities.   When such a mode of thought is translated into terms of social rank, it makes the prince, or highest rung of the social ladder, represent the general principle of such hierarchic order.)   Then, if one conceives his own motives in terms of the devotion paid to princes, it follows that one conceives of oneself rhetorically, in terms of *courting and being courted*.   Telescope the two, as the ultimate principle should, and you get self-love. (5) At this point, La Rochefoucauld begins his book.   He has reduced the motives of man in society to "self-love" (which equals "pride" and "interest").   And he proceeds to view all passions, sentiments, pretenses and self-deceptions in the light of this term.   (6) In the course of scrutinizing his key term, he comes upon the princely principle that lies behind it.   But since he has already chosen a "first" term, self-love, he calls this genus of his terminology a "second."   Had Rochefoucauld stated this discovery in terms of an Hegelian ideologist, he would probably have given the second self-love some such title as *Ur-Höflichkeit,* to designate an innate, "pre-historic" tendency towards courtship, an "idea" which, in its evolution towards self-consciousness, at one stage of its historical unfolding manifested itself both as a devotion to princes and as *amour-propre*.

But "self" and "king" do not quite round out the design.   Where is God, and the ultimate scene, the ground of all possibility?   By our interpretation, the term for God should apply to the conditions at the *first* of the six moments into which we divided La Rochefoucauld's maxim. It should deal with the rhetorical motive indigenous to all men, not local to their social position, but characteristic of the human situation universally.   Stated theologically, the divisive condition in which all men share is called "original sin."   And approaching the problem of God (or ultimate community) in such terms, La Rochefoucauld says that self-love sets up another god, a god that torments, in aggravating the state of division. Thus:

Dieu a permis, pour punir l'homme du péché originel, qu'il se fît un dieu de son amour-propre, pour en être tourmenté dans toutes les actions de sa vie.

This rounds out the pattern. It comes upon the ultimate division, prior to the community of status (the unity got by common interests, by participation in properties that bring some men together in one estate or class by setting them at odds with other estates or classes).

Pride, interest, self-love, are aristocratically dyslogistic words for motives that the bourgeois vocabulary may transform into such eulogistic forms as "ambition," "private enterprise," perhaps even "dignity of the individual" and "respect for the person." "Honor" was its eulogistic equivalent in the aristocratic scheme. We think of three different routes by which to approach the rhetoric of the judgment contained in the idea of pride:

1. You can think of the term being used as a deterrent to possible encroachments by inferior classes. (There are connotations of the upstart here.) Then this factional use could become universalized, so that the admonition is applied also by members of the nobility to overbearing members of their own class.

2. Or you can think of the term being used as a summing up of age's admonition to youth. And this usage in the universal class war of the generations could then be applied specifically by a ruling class, in praising traits that would perpetuate the *status quo*.

3. Or we could ground the fear of pride in a universal dramatic principle of irony, the purely formal resource of the dramatist, who knows that he gets his best effect by peripety (building up for a let-down, strengthening the confidence, or expectations of a character just prior to the development that will overwhelm him). This formal, ironic grounding, as revealed in the proverb that "pride goes before a fall," would be universally prior to any use for class domination of either social or biological sorts.

De Gourmont on "Dissociation"

Perhaps the most picturesquely radical approach to the subject of identification and division, as they affect the nature of persuasion, is in an essay by Remy de Gourmont, *"La Dissociation des Idées."* (There is an English translation in a volume entitled *Decadence, and Other Essays on the Culture of Ideas*.) De Gourmont, as a literary critic who did much to introduce the French Symbolists, was surely one of the most graceful "ideologists" who ever specialized in that fluctuant realm midway between ideas and images.

Here the great stress is upon *division*. De Gourmont looks upon disassociation as the distinctive mark of his favorite virtue, intelligence. "Divorce," he says, "is the permanent rule in the world of idea, which is the world of free love."

You can accept old associations of ideas, he says, or form new ones— or, if you are rare and expert in the kind of intellectuality he advocates, you can make "original dissociations" (or disassociations). But looking more closely at his essay, we see that its great emphasis upon *division* really serves to sharpen our understanding of *identification*. Indeed, if we were allowed but one text to illustrate how identification operates in language, we would select this essay, which is almost sadistically concerned with the breaking of identifications.

Observing that an idea "is but a worn-out image," he describes the rhetorical commonplaces as associations which resist dissociation because of the part that special interests play in human thinking. Ordinarily, he says, such "truths" are composed of "a fact and an abstraction." He is here using "truth" in the sense of "opinion," associations which people accept without question. If we assume that business enterprise is naturally good, for instance, we automatically combine the "fact" of business institutions with the abstraction, goodness. The goodness would be a "pure" idea; and the commonplace linking it with some conditional matter, some time, place, persons, operations, and the like, would be such a "truth" (in our usage, opinion) as men ordinarily live by.

But the pure cult of ideas is not concerned with pragmatic necessities. It has responsibilities only to the perfection of its craft. Though the world of practical life could not abide by its rules, this problem need not concern the specialist in free inquiry. Maybe the outcome of such inquiry, if carried to its logical conclusion, would mean the end of mankind? That's not the concern of a fine and free intelligence, dissociating ideas for love of the art, and admitting whatever intellectual exercise limbers the mind and fits it for its proper state of "disdainful nobility" (*noblesse dédaigneuse*). His own method of dissociation provided him with a striking stylistic device, a kind of mild schizophrenia, whereby he could talk of dire things blithely. And so he carried the logic of specialization to its ultimate conclusion, in acknowledging only a responsibility to the principles of his profession. Had he been a physicist, and commissioned to make an infernal engine of destruction, he would have striven to make it as efficiently infernal as possible. In the course of his experiments, his "morality of production" would have been Puritanically rigid. He thus gave a sort of operatic gesture to liberal professionalism, as he skeptically and nihilistically broke "truths" apart, to show that their factual side has no logically necessary connection with their abstract, ideal side.

In the course of his essay, he proceeds to "liberate" various commonplaces that men have lived by. That is, he methodically questions the assumption that the conditions in which an abstract ideal is materialized are inherently identified with that abstract ideal. Thus, purely as a specialist in the analysis of ideas, he perfects the critique of idealism. In effect, he discovers that the pattern of the god incarnate lurks in every single commonplace, which links some particular image, or set of worldly conditions, with some abstract principle or idea. (The abstraction is the "purity" or "divinity" that is embodied in whatever empirical condition the given commonplace, or topic, identifies with it. For instance, if the topic identifies a particular kind of economic structure with "freedom," then "freedom" is the god-term, the pure abstraction; and the particular kind of economic structure is the "fact" to which it is topically tied, quite as though it were a pure divinity that came down to earth and took this particular economic structure as its bodily form—for though De Gourmont does not use this theologic analogy, it is what his analysis amounts to.)

Once he has sharpened our perception in such matters, we see that a counter-essay could be written, to show how many "new associations" De Gourmont spontaneously built up, while ostensibly aiming to do nothing but "liberate" old ones. (We have already noted that, as a free thinker, he identified the ideal intellectual enterprise with divorce.) "Freely" improvising cleavage, he smuggles in new linkage. But he himself encourages the kind of scrutiny that enables us to qualify his statements.

As an instance of his method, consider his approach to the idea of justice. Beginning with what Bentham would have called "archetypation," he discerns in the idea of justice the image of scales, of equilibrium. Then, in a free improvisation, he "liberates" the traditional associations linking justice with punishment, tentatively asking whether one might, with much more justice, punish not the swindler but the fool who let himself be swindled. Next, responsible only to his essay, he equates existence with disequilibrium, injustice, on the grounds that each thing exists by robbing other things of their existence. (Is he not here but universalizing the Proudhon proposition that property is theft?) Somewhat in the spirit of La Rochefoucauld, he next points out how the idea of justice is often contaminated with motives of hatred and envy. Bentham at the same place might have said that "justice" can be the "eulogistic covering" for a combination of motives, many of them not socially presentable. Veblen might have called attention to the "invidious" aspects of justice. Marx might have agreed with all of De Gourmont's playful, professional asceticism, provided only it were taken as applying to the conditions of capitalist justice, and De Gourmont's own intellectual nihilism were interpreted as the expression of an acute, late-capitalist stage in culture. And he might have similarly taken De Gourmont's definition of freedom as "an emphatic corruption of the idea of privilege."

Methodologically, we should also note that when De Gourmont treats the *idea* of justice in terms of justice as an *image* (scales in equilibrium), he lays himself open to an error of his own. He is here using his special kind of "archetypation" to disclose how imagery operates unnoticed in our legal and ethical "fictions." Yet even the exposing of an undeclared image can itself be too imagistic, if it is allowed to carry too much weight in the analysis. Such abstract ideas as "justice" will often disclose their meaning more fully if we treat them realistically as *verbs* than if we interpret them nominalistically as *weakened images*.

Realistically inspecting abstractions for their verbal element, we find that "heroism" stands for the way of being a hero, "greenness" for a way of being green, and "justice" for a just way of life. Thus, in the *Grammar,* we pointed out how the Greek word for "justice" does in fact come from a word for "way." And referring to the discussion in *The Republic,* we noted how there were different "justices" in the sense that different social classes had different living conditions, with judgments to match. Methodologically, linguistic realism would correct De Gourmont's overimagistic emphasis. It would call for kinds of analy-

sis more nearly Marxist. For whereas the De Gourmont kind of archetypation might lead one to be content with shuttling between idea and
image, a realistic approach to abstraction would lead one to consider it
in terms of acts, by agents, in scenes. True, in images there is an attitudinal content. Hence, if you follow them through far enough, you
come upon their verbal nature. But this is true only insofar as nominalism is already yielding to realism.

In any case, one should keep in mind the sense in which operational
words, like go, run, see, put, bring, etc., are the really "abstract" ones.
A thing is here or there, large or small, round or square, etc., but what
of a "running" or a "putting"? Or a "may," a "must," a "will," an
"ought"? Here are the true universals, capable of representation only
by admixture with some incomplete example, such as a particular animal running, etc. Indeed, as regards the archetypal form or idea of
"houseness" which Plato would treat as prior to its material embodiment in various particular houses, is he not here seeking for the *verb*,
"to-be-a-house," as the universal in which every particular "being-a-
house" would participate?

But whatever our reservations on the scope of De Gourmont's analysis,
from the standpoint of rhetoric, it is good to make oneself adept at the
kind of mental gymnastics in which De Gourmont was so agile. We
need not accept the doctrine wholly as stated in his essay. We need not
try to persuade ourselves that dissociation is the ultimate in intellectual
prowess, since that very argument for dissociation is an association. But
we can make out a strong case for it as a method for helping the initiate
experimentally to break free of all topical assumptions, and thereby to
cease being the victim of his own naïve rhetoric.

De Gourmont here seems to contain the same near-mystical ingredient
we saw in Bentham. Accordingly, we should want to place dissociation
in a series of stages, as a cleansing transition from old associations that
were automatically formed and may enslave by "infancy," to new associations, rationally adopted after "withdrawal" during the period of experimental liberation. Particularly where an association is seen to be
moving the world towards a universal calamity, we should try the experiment of dissociating it, not just for love of the art, as De Gourmont
might have advised, but for the vision that may come of such ideological
manipulations.

Thus there is always the need for the experimental dissociating of

patriotism and militarism. (Or, as regards recent conditions, the dissociating of patriotism from a cult of "cold war," since old men are given
to talk of a cold war, which younger men are potently prone to translate
into talk of a "shooting war.") Return to this suicidal association (or
"identification") if you must. But at least put it to the dissociative test,
to make sure that your choice has been made after free inquiry, and is
not imposed upon you by a dismal rhetoric of warmongering. It is a fallacy to make personal freedom identical with the liberating of all ideas;
there is freedom also in associations, if they are the right ones; but no
one in the world is free so long as large sections of our population, however inattentively, are being bound by the identifying of patriotism with
military boastfulness.

Pascal on "Directing the Intention"

The Pascalian principle of rhetoric is succinctly stated in his seventh
Provincial Letter, devoted to the analysis, itself vigorously rhetorical, of
a corrupt theological rhetoric. We might have used it as a way into our
pages on Bentham; but there is also something to be gained by considering it after we have gone from Bentham to Marx and De Gourmont.

Pascal is attacking the casuistry of the Jesuits. Not because it is casuistry, for the application of general principles to particular cases is a
necessary act of judgment in law of any sort. But because the Jesuit
rhetoric attacked by Pascal was a perversion of casuistry. And though
the theological nature of the controversy may lead some to assume that
Pascal's analysis has only a historical interest, the linguistic processes he
is analyzing are perennial with language, with its shifts between "spiritual" and "material" terms, or between "abstractions" (which are technically "divinities") and words for the "facts" or "material conditions"
in which the abstractions are embodied like gods incarnate.

This "Pauline" element at the roots of language (hence at the roots
of rhetoric) can be confronted most directly in theological controversy.
And where it is perceived with finesse and disclosed with polemic clarity,
as in Pascal's seventh letter, you have a device applicable to wholly different linguistic situations. For you can then trace the vestiges of such
theology in expressions on their face secular. And whatever the rhetorical powers in theology itself, there is a set of further powers in theology

undetected. Marx's attacks upon "ideology" were, of course, aimed at precisely such vestiges, as were Bentham's observations on "eulogistic coverings." But their own concerns were far too secular to disclose the theological principle of language most directly. For that we go to Pascal's piety and De Gourmont's impiety (each in its way concerned with "pure" ideas).

We have said that, casuistry being the application of abstract principles to particular conditions, the relation is essentially like that of mind and body, spirit and matter, God and God's descent into Nature. Or the abstract principle could be considered as the purpose or end, and the material conditions could be considered as the means for embodying the end. But means are necessarily "impure," from the standpoint of any *one* purpose, since they have a nature of their own. This nature allows them to be used for many purposes; but they are "impure" as means to the extent that their intrinsic nature is not wholly formed for any one such purpose. Such "impurity" is not necessarily "bad." It can be a merely technical impurity, due to the fact that its intrinsic nature contains elements irrelevant to the purpose.

But some means are relatively purer than others. Their nature makes them better able than other means to serve the given purpose. Thus, even a blow with a fist might be considered closer to the nature of peace than a blast from a shotgun. (In general, though not in all cases.) A tongue-lashing might be closer to peace than a blow; an argument closer than a tongue-lashing; a plea closer than an argument; a compliment closer than a plea, etc. This being the case, a scrupulous man will never abandon a purpose which he considers absolutely good. But he will choose the purest means available in the given situation. As with the ideal rhetoric in Aristotle, he will consider the entire range of means, and then choose the best that this particular set of circumstances permits.

Here, you will note, the moral question involves the selection of *means*. But such a casuistry readily permits of two caricatures. First, we can choose inferior means, and quiet the conscience by assuring ourselves that they were the best means available. By this device, the doctrine that "the end justifies the means" becomes a mockery (as it always is when not corrected by a methodical concern with a *hierarchy* of means, and an exacting effort to choose the very best means possible to the given situation). For it can be made to justify *any* means, hence can become a mere "eulogistic covering" for means so alien to the nature of the avowed end, and so far below other means actually available, that it amounts to nothing but a blunt perverting of that end.

But this resource prepares the way for another, whereby we can do whatever we like (in accordance with the enlightened Rabelaisian principle, *fais ce que vouldras,* but without the good will by which Rabelais spontaneously limited such liberties). Then having done what we wanted to do, we can *assign* a purpose to our act, selecting some intention socially approved. And we can ask that the act be considered as a means for carrying out this avowed intention.

Pascal's seventh letter is a brilliant attack upon the Jesuits for their use of this rhetorical convenience. True, the Jesuits had faced a bothersome situation. The quality of devotion among great numbers of the faithful had deteriorated alarmingly. The most devout at that time were either turning to Protestant pietism; or, like Pascal, though they remained in the Church, they favored austerities which exposed them to the suspicion of Protestant hankerings. In contrast, there was a large body of easygoing people, people who would not be religiously zealous even in a time of great religious zeal, but whom the Jesuits wanted to retain for the Church, or to reclaim for the Church. They had strayed far from the exacting kind of Christianity preached by St. Paul. In fact, not only did they violate Christian principles (as in the code of dueling, for instance); they didn't even pretend to abide by Christian principles. And the Jesuits, as a propaganda order formed to regain for the Church the ground lost since the Protestant Reformation, had to solve a purely organizational problem: How could they keep these backsliders nominally within the fold? Since these people were living un-Christian lives, yet were not minded to change their ways, how might theology adapt itself to such an embarrassing condition?

In *A Portrait of the Artist as a Young Man,* Joyce's hero ponders how the Jesuits "had earned the name of worldlings at the hands not of the unworldly only but of the worldly also for having pleaded, during all their history, at the bar of God's justice for the souls of the lax and the lukewarm and the prudent." Pascal was ardent. And his letter is a satirical rhetoric pitted against the hypocritical or opportunist rhetoric by which the Jesuits proposed to solve their problem in his day. Their slogan was: "Direct the intention"—so Pascal satirizes *la grande méthode de diriger l'intention.* Since people would not change their ways, and since any severe attempt to make them do so might but lose them for the Church entirely, then let them go on doing exactly the un-Christian things they had been doing. But teach them how to change the intention, by attributing a Christian motive to these same un-Christian acts.

Pascal uses the most effective of all satiric devices, in adopting the role of a somewhat stupid and gullible questioner who is very eager to learn. He consults the Jesuit masters, with plodding earnestness. He struggles hard to understand the depths of their reasoning. He is patient, and very hopeful—and of a sudden he breaks into loud rejoicings, when their formulae have finally enlightened him. These are always the moments, of course, when he is reducing them to absurdity.

As Pascal puts it, supposedly reporting the words of his Jesuit monitor: "If we cannot prevent the act, we at least purify the intention; and thus we correct the viciousness of the means through the purity of the end." (*Quand nous ne pouvons empêcher l'action, nous purifions au moins l'intention; et ainsi nous corrigeons le vice du moyen par la pureté de la fin.*) Or, as Pascal says, in the blunt overzealousness of his delight at this invention for the worldly rescue of the Church: If one is going to a duel, since dueling is forbidden one must instead so "direct the intention" that one is merely going for a walk at the place where the duel is to be held; and when the duel takes place, one directs his intention towards the need of protecting oneself against an enemy who is threatening one's life.

The chapter is hilarious and devastating. But we will say this in favor of the Jesuits: Pascal's most telling blows are struck, not by satirically making up cases which reduce the Jesuit doctrine to absurdity, but by *citation* from Jesuit sources. In carrying out their principle of the directed intention, they had speculated zealously upon all kinds of cases. Hence the Jesuit theorists had thought up the most extreme and embarrassing kinds of cases, to test and illustrate their handy principle with maximum thoroughness. Their professional enterprise gave Pascal his most telling examples. In this respect their role as corruptors of religion compares favorably with many modern spokesmen for the Church, who are content merely to envelop materialist ambitions in an idealistic fog, translating each worldly interest into a spiritual equivalent, thereby doing again the Jesuit trick, but without the theoretical precision which the Jesuits contributed to their own exposure.

In the sphere of international relations, the politicians of one nation may seek to build and subsidize a mighty economic and military alliance against another nation, while "directing the intention" towards peace.

"Administrative" Rhetoric in Machiavelli

Machiavelli's *The Prince* can be treated as a rhetoric insofar as it deals with the *producing of effects upon an audience*. Sometimes the prince's subjects are his audience, sometimes the rulers or inhabitants of foreign states are the audience, sometimes particular factions within the State. If you have a political public in mind, Machiavelli says in effect, here is the sort of thing you must do to move them for your purposes. And he considers such principles of persuasion as these: either treat well or crush; defend weak neighbors and weaken the strong; where you foresee trouble, provoke war; don't make others powerful; be like the prince who appointed a harsh governor to establish order (after this governor had become an object of public hatred in carrying out the prince's wishes, the prince got popular acclaim by putting him to death for his cruelties); do necessary evils at one stroke, pay out benefits little by little; sometimes assure the citizens that the evil days will soon be over, at other times goad them to fear the cruelties of the enemy; be sparing of your own and your subjects' wealth, but be liberal with the wealth of others; be a combination of strength and stealth (lion and fox); *appear* merciful, dependable, humane, devout, upright, but be the opposite in actuality, whenever the circumstances require it; yet always do lip-service to the virtues, since most people judge by appearances; provoke resistance, to make an impression by crushing it; use religion as a pretext for conquest, since it permits of "pious cruelty"; leave "affairs of reproach" to the management of others, but keep those "of grace" in your own hands; be the patron of all talent, proclaim festivals, give spectacles, show deference to local organizations; but always retain the distance of your rank (he could have called this the "mystery" of rule); in order that you may get the advantage of good advice without losing people's respect, give experts permission to speak frankly, but only when asked to speak; have a few intimates who are encouraged to be completely frank, and who are well plied with rewards.

Correspondingly, there are accounts of the human susceptibilities one can play upon, and the resistances one must expect. Thus: new benefits won't make great personages forget old injuries; it is easy to persuade people, but you need force to keep them persuaded; acquisitiveness being natural, those who acquire will be praised, not blamed; the nobles would oppress the people, the people would avoid oppression by the nobles; one can satisfy the people, but not the nobles, by fair dealing; men are bound to you as much by the benefits they give as by the benefits they receive; mercenaries are to be feared for their dastardy, auxiliaries for their valor; the unarmed are despised; often what we call virtue would ruin the State, and what we call vice can save it; cruelty may reconcile and unify; men in general are *ungrateful, fickle, false, cowardly, greedy;* since all men are evil, the prince can always find a good pretext for breaking faith; it is safer to be feared than loved, since people are more likely to offend those they love than those they fear; yet though the prince should be feared, he should not be hated; the worst offense is an offense against property, for a man more quickly forgets the death of his father than the loss of his patrimony; people want to be deceived; if the prince leaves his subjects' property and women untouched, he "has only to contend with the ambitions of a few"; a ruler's best fortress is not to be hated by his own people; any faction within the State can always expect to find allies abroad.

The difference between the two lists is mainly grammatical. For instance, if we use a gerundive, "valor in auxiliaries is to be feared," the statement belongs in the second set. But we can transfer it to the first merely by changing the expression to an imperative: "Fear valor in auxiliaries." Both lists are reducible to "topics" in the Aristotelian sense.

We think of another "Machiavellian" work, written many centuries earlier. It is in praise of "eloquence," the eloquence, it says, that serves in the conquest of the public, of the senate, and of women. But it would concentrate on the third use, for it is Ovid's *Ars Amatoria.* It deals not with political power, but with another order of potency; and where Machiavelli is presumably telling how to get and hold a principality, Ovid is telling how to get and hold a woman.

Grounded in figures of soldiery, of gladiators, of the hunt, of animals enraged or ruttish, it is in form a manual of instructions, like *The Prince.* But it is really a poetic display, an epideictic exercise, the sort of literary ostentation that De Quincey had in mind when selecting Ovid as prime example of rhetoric. For one does not usually read it as he would read instructions for opening a package (though a yearning adolescent might); one reads it rather for the delight he may take in the imagery and ideas themselves, the topics or "places" of love.

But to consider some of the poet's picturesque advice is to see how close it is to the thinking of Machiavelli, except of course for the tonalities, since the Italian is solemn, the Latin playful. Having begun scenically, with a survey of locations where the hunting is good, he proceeds thus:

On deceiving in the name of friendship; feigning just enough drunkenness to be winsome; of feigned passion that may become genuine; on astute use of praise and promises; inducement value of belief in the gods; deceiving deceivers; the utility of tears; the need to guard against the risk that entreaties may merely feed the woman's vanity; inducement value of pallor, which is the proper color of love; advisability of shift in methods, as she who resisted the well-bred may yield to the crude; ways to subdue by yielding; how to be her servant, but as a freeman; risks that gain favor; on operating with the help of the servants; need for caution in gifts; get your slaves to ask her to ask you to be kind to them; the controlled use of compliments; become a habit with her; enjoy others too, but in stealth, and deny if you are found out; rekindle her love by jealousy; make her grieve over you, but not too much, lest she muster enough strength to become angry (as she might, since she always wants to be shut of you); if she has deceived you, let her think you don't know it; give each of her faults the name of the good quality most like it.

And to women he offers advice on dress, cosmetics, the use of pretty faults in speech, gait, poetry, dance, posture, cadence, games, on being seen in public (you may find a husband at the funeral of your husband), deceit to match deceit, on being late at banquets, on table manners, on drinking to excess but only as much as can be deftly controlled.

Machiavelli says of war: "This is the sole art proper to rulers." And similarly Ovid's epideictic manual of love-making is founded on the principle that "love is a kind of war" (*militiae species amor est*). "I can love only when hurt," the poet confesses (*non nisi laesus amo*). And Machiavelli rounds out his politics by saying that it is better to be adventurous than cautious with Fortune, since Fortune is a woman, "and if you wish to keep her subdued, you must beat her and ill-use her."

True, though both books are concerned with the rhetoric of advantage, principles of amative persuasion rely rather on fraud than force. But the point to note for our purposes is that in both cases the rhetoric includes a strongly "administrative" ingredient. The persuasion cannot be confined to the strictly verbal; it is a mixture of symbolism and definite empirical operations. The basic conception in Stendhal's book on love, for instance, is not rhetorical at all. For the rhetoric of love in Stendhal, we should go rather to his *The Red and the Black*. There, as in Ovid, the work is developed on the principle that love is a species of war. But the basic principle underlying Stendhal's *De l'Amour* is that of "crystallization," a concept so purely "internal," so little "addressed," that it belongs completely under the heading of "symbolic" in these volumes, naming but a kind of accretion (both unconscious and consciously sentimental) that grows about the idea of the beloved, and for all its contagiousness is rather a flowering within the mind of the lover than a ruse shaped for persuasive purposes.

We might put it thus: the nonverbal, or nonsymbolic conditions with which both lover and ruler must operate can themselves be viewed as a kind of symbolism having persuasive effects. For instance, military force can persuade by its sheer "meaning" as well as by its use in actual combat. In this sense, nonverbal acts and material instruments themselves have a symbolic ingredient. The point is particularly necessary when we turn to the rhetoric of bureaucracy, as when a political party bids for favor by passing measures popular with large blocs of voters. In such a case, administrative acts themselves are not merely "scientific" or "operational," but are designed also with an eye for their *appeal*. Popular jokes that refer to policemen's clubs and sex organs as "persuaders" operate on the same principle. For nonverbal conditions or objects can be considered as signs by reason of persuasive ingredients inherent in the "meaning" they have for the audience to which they are "addressed."

It is usual now to treat Machiavelli as a founder of modern political "science," particularly because he uses so naturalistic a terminology of motives, in contrast with notions of justification that go with supernaturalism. But this simple antithesis can prevent accurate placement of *The Prince*. For one thing, as in the case of La Rochefoucauld, you need but adopt the theological device of saying that Machiavelli is dealing with the motives typical of man after the "fall," and there is nothing about his naturalism to put it out of line with supernaturalism. But most of all, the approach to *The Prince* in terms of naturalism *vs.* supernaturalism prevents one from discerning the rhetorical elements that are of its very essence. Here again we come upon the fact that our contemporary views of science are dislocated by the failure to consider it methodically with relation to rhetoric (a failure that leads to a blunt opposing of science to either religion or "magic"). For if the rhetorical motive is not scientific, neither is it in its everyday application religious or magical. The use of symbols to induce action in beings that normally communicate by symbols is essentially realistic in the most practical and pragmatic sense of the term. It is neither "magical" nor "scientific" (neither ritualistic nor informational) for one person to ask help of another. Hence, in approaching the question through a flat antithesis between magic and science, one automatically vows himself to a faulty statement of the case.

Above all, we believe that an approach to the book in terms of rhetoric is necessary if one would give an adequate account of its *form* (and the ability to treat of form is always the major test of a critical method). Thus, though the late Ernst Cassirer gives a very good account of Machiavelli in his *Myth of the State,* his oversimplified treatment in terms of science alone, without the modifications and insights supplied by the principles of rhetoric, completely baffles an attempt to account for the book's structure. Not only does he end by treating the last chapter as a misfit; having likened the earlier chapters to Galileo's writings on the laws of motion, and thereby having offered a description that could not possibly apply to the last chapter, he concludes that the burden of proof rests with those who would consider the last chapter as a fit with the rest. By the rhetorical approach, you can meet his challenge, thus:

The first twenty-four chapters discuss typical situations that have to do with the seizing and wielding of political power. They are analytic accounts of such situations, and of the strategies best suited to the conditions. Thus they are all variants of what, in the *Grammar,* we called the scene-act ratio; and they say, in effect: "Here is the kind of act proper to such-and-such a scene" (the ruler's desire for political mastery being taken as the unchanging purpose that prevails throughout all changes of scene).

However, in the next-to-the-last chapter, Machiavelli modifies his thesis. Whereas he has been pointing out what act of the ruler would, in his opinion, have the most persuasive effect upon the ruled in a given situation, he now observes that people do not always act in accordance with the requirements set them by the scenic conditions. People also act in accordance with their own natures, or temperaments. Thus, a man may act cautiously, not because the scene calls for caution, but merely because he is by nature a cautious man. Conversely, if a man is adventurous by nature, he may act with adventurous boldness, characteristically, even though the situation itself may call for caution. In the *Grammar* we listed such motivations under the heading of the agent-act ratio, since they say, in effect: "Here is the kind of act proper to such-and-such a person."

But there may be fortunate moments in history when both kinds of motives work together, Machiavelli is saying. The scenic conditions require a certain kind of act; and the ruler may happen to have exactly the kind of temperament and character that leads him into this same kind of act. Given such a lucky coincidence, the perfect manifestation of the scene-act ratio is one with the perfect manifestation of the agent-act ratio.

Far from there being any formal break in the book, this concern in the next-to-the-last chapter forms a perfect transition to the final "Exhortation to Liberate Italy from the Barbarians." For this chapter rounds things out in a "Now is the time . . ." manner, by calling for the agent to arise whose acts will simultaneously be in tune with the times and with himself. This man will be the ruler able to redeem Italy from its captivity. And given such a combination, there will be grounds too for the ultimate *identification* of ruler and ruled, since all will benefit, each in his way, by the liberation of their country.

True, in the last chapter there is a certain prayerlike lift not present in the others. Whereas the earlier chapters are a kind of *rhetorica docens,* the peroration becomes a kind of *rhetorica utens.* But that is a standard aspect of rhetorical form, traditional to the wind-up. Far from being added on bluntly, it is very deftly *led into* by the motivational shift in the preceding chapter.

When the ruler happens to be of such a nature that the act characteristic of his nature would also be the act best suited to the situation, we could attribute the happy combination to chance, or fortune. Here again the stress upon science *vs.* magic can somewhat mislead. True, references to a fatal confluence of factors will almost inevitably bring up connotations of "design." Hence, the "fortune" that makes the ruler temperamentally a fit for his times may take on fatelike connota-

tions alien to science. One may find such metaphors of cosmic purpose flitting through Machiavelli's discussion. But they are not the
central matter. The central matter is this fortuitous congruity of temperament and external conditions, whereas an "unlucky" combination
can prevent the ruler from adopting the proper mode of action (somewhat as Cicero said that the ideal orator should be accomplished in all
styles, but human limitations would restrict his range in actuality).

Machiavelli's concern is brought out clearly by La Rochefoucauld, in
his comments *Des Modèles de la Nature et de la Fortune.* "It seems,"
he says, "that Fortune, changing and capricious as she is, renounces
change and caprice to act in concert with nature, and that the two
concur at times to produce singular and unusual men who become
models for posterity. Nature serves to furnish the qualities; Fortune
serves to put them into operation." By "nature" he is obviously referring to human nature, capacities of human agents; "fortune" is his
word for scenic conditions, which impose themselves independently
of human will. He calls the congruence of agent and scene an *"accord
de la nature et de la fortune."*

Concerns with the "lucky" or "unlucky" accident that may make a
man temperamentally fit or unfit to employ the strategy best suited to
the situation may eventually involve one in assumptions about fatal
cosmic design along the lines of Carlyle's "mystifications" about heroes
in history. And too great a concern with science as antithetical to
magic may get one to thinking that the important point lies there. But
by treating the book as a manual of "administrative rhetoric," we can
place the stress where it belongs: on the problem of the orator's ability
to choose the act best suited to the situation, rather than choosing the
act best suited to the expression of his own nature.

Likewise, the proper approach to Machiavelli's *choice of vocabulary*
is not exclusively in terms of science, but through considerations of
rhetoric. (We have in mind his paradoxical distinctions between the
virtues of princes and the virtues of private citizens, or his proposal to
base political action on the assumption that all men are "ungrateful,
fickle, false, cowardly, and greedy.") Is not Machiavelli here but giving a new application to a topic in Aristotle's *Rhetoric?* Aristotle had
said in effect that privately we admit to acquisitive motives, but publicly we account for the same act in sacrificial terms. In the Christian
terminology that had intervened between Aristotle and Machiavelli,

however, the public, sacrificial motives were attributed to the state of *grace,* and the private, acquisitive motives were due to the state of *original sin* after the fall. In the Christian persuasion, the rhetorical distinction noted by Aristotle had thus become written dialectically into the very nature of things. And insofar as a man was genuinely imbued with Christian motives, his *private* virtues would be the traits of character which, if cultivated in the individual, would be most beneficial to mankind *as a whole*.

But Machiavelli is concerned with a different kind of universality. He starts from the principle that men are *universally at odds with one another*. For this is what his stress upon predatory or warlike motives amounts to. He is concerned with motives which will protect *special* interests. *The Prince* is leading towards the period when the interests of a feudal ruler will be *nationalistically* identified, thought to represent one state *as opposed to* other states.

Now, national motives can be placed in a hierarchy of motives, graded from personal and familial, to regional, to national, to international and universal. As so arranged, they might conceivably, in their different orders, complement or perfect one another rather than being in conflict. But where the princes, or the national states identified with them, are conceived antithetically to the interests of other princes and states, or antithetically to factions within the realm, the "virtues" of the ruler could not be the "virtues" which are thought most beneficial to mankind as a whole (in an ideal state of universal cooperation). Similarly, if we carry the Machiavelli pattern down from political to personal relations, the individual may become related to other individuals as ruler to ruled (or at least as would-be ruler to would-not-be ruled)—for here again the divisive motives treated by Machiavelli apply.

Once a national identity is built up, it can be treated as an individual; hence like an individual its condition can be presented in sacrificial terms. Thus, in the case of *The Prince,* the early chapters are stated in acquisitive terms. They have to do with the ways of getting and keeping political power. But the last chapter, looking towards the redemption of Italy as a nation, is presented in sacrificial tonalities; the "virtue of an Italian spirit" is oppressed, enslaved, and scattered, "without head, without order, beaten, despoiled, torn, overrun," and enduring "every kind of desolation." So Italy "entreats God to send some

one who shall deliver her from these wrongs and barbarous inso-
lencies." And "she is ready and willing to follow a banner if only
some one will raise it." This is the shift in tone that led Ernst Cassirer to treat the last chapter as incongruous with the earlier portions.

In this last chapter, the universal, sacrificial motives are adapted to
a competitive end. The Christian vision of mankind's oneness in the
suffering Christ becomes the vision of Italians' oneness in the suffering
Italy. Since Italy actually is invaded, the analogy is not forced as it is
in the vocabulary of imperialist unction. (Contrast it, for instance,
with the building of empire under slogans like "the acceptance of
grave world responsibility," or "the solemn fulfillment of international commitments," when the support of reactionary regimes was
meant.) But whether the nationalist exaltation be for conquest or for
uprising against conquerors, in either case there is the possibility of
identification between ruler and ruled. Hence the new prince, in
bringing about the new order, "would do honor to himself and good
to the people of his country." And by such identification of ruler and
ruled, Machiavelli offers the ruler precisely the rhetorical opportunity
to present privately acquisitive motives publicly in sacrificial terms.

Machiavelli is concerned with political cooperation under conditions
which make such cooperation in part a union of conspirators. Where
conspiracy is the fact, universality must often be the fiction. The ambiguity in Machiavelli is thus the ambiguity of nationalism itself, which
to some extent does fit with the ends of universal cooperation, and to
some extent is conspiratorial. The proportions vary, with the Hitlerite
State probably containing as high a percentage of the conspiratorial
as will be attained in our time, though the conspiratorial motive is now
unusually strong in all international dealings. Sovereignty itself is
conspiracy. And the pattern is carried into every political or social
body, however small. Each office, each fraternal order, each college
faculty has its tiny conspiratorial clique. Conspiracy is as natural as
breathing. And since the struggles for advantage nearly always have
a rhetorical strain, we believe that the systematic contemplation of them
forces itself upon the student of rhetoric. Indeed, of all the motives in
Machiavelli, is not the most usable for us his attempt to transcend the
disorders of his times, not by either total acquiescence or total avoidance, but by seeking to scrutinize them as accurately and calmly as
he could?

Dante's De Vulgari Eloquentia

At the point where the rhetoric of "identification" merges with the "unconscious," we might consider Dante's *De Vulgari Eloquentia* for its bearing on this subject. As with Longinus' *On the Sublime,* though the emphasis is upon poetry, the essay operates in the realm where poetic and rhetoric cross. Dante wants a language that will be "illustrious, cardinal, courtly (*aulicum*), and curial." Honor, power, dignity, glory—such are the terms that surround his formula to guide his search for the perfect poetic medium. The "cardinal" we might translate as "central" (like a hinge), while also noting its ecclesiastical connotations. The "illustrious" are those who, themselves illuminated by power (*potestate illuminati*) illuminate others by their justice and charity (*alios et iustitia et caritate illuminant*). Dante is perhaps here following the Ciceronian concern with styles and offices, though he is looking for the important elements that should be combined in one style. But above all we should note, for our purposes, how the four ingredients for the ideal language of poetry all have strongly hierarchic connotations.

Distinguishing between a secondary speech, which is taught, and an earlier kind "which we acquire, without rule, by imitating a nurse (*quam sine omni regula nutricem imitantes accipimus*)," he says that of these two, the popular is the more noble (*"harum quoque duarum nobilior est vulgaris"*). Is that not almost a conceit, equating the "noble" with the "common"? (A conceit with a future.) In any case, just as Longinus was asking what made for tension (the heightened or moving) in language, Dante carried the problem a step farther, in recognizing that such an effect could be got best by using speech that seemed "natural" (his word), through having emerged out of infancy.

As for "infancy" itself, there are, you might say, several "infancies": for besides the speechlessness of the infant, there is the speechlessness of the nonverbal (as the quality of a sensory experience is beyond language, requiring immediate experience); and there is the speechlessness of the "unconscious," as regards complexities vaguely intuited but not yet made verbally explicit (in sum, the symbolically "enigmatic"). Thus, Dante's concern with the "nobility" of the speech learned in infancy would seem to be, within the limits of his terminology, the adumbration of a concern with the motives of the "unconscious" and its kinds of "identification."

In a mixture of positivism and myth, Dante attributes the rise of different languages to the occupational diversity required for building the Tower of Babel. The members of each trade or profession had their own language, the division of labor thus making for the diversity of tongues. And perhaps with theological Latin in mind, he says that the higher the intellectual quality of the specialty, the more barbarous the language.

Dante's search for a "nobler" language learned in childhood, and his discovery of it in the "vulgar" idiom, finds a picturesque parallel (or should we say a caricature?) in the principles of linguistic selection which D. H. Lawrence embodied in *Lady Chatterley's Lover*. For was not Lawrence, too, trying to reclaim, beneath the layers of education, a more primitive, childhood speech? It would have the "nobility" of the "unconscious" (somewhat as Nietzsche's "artistocratic" blonde beast was a markedly "regressive" image, the mythically heroicized replica of a spontaneous child).

True, in both Lawrence and Nietzsche, the search was for a kind of nature's gentleman rather than for the illustrious, cardinal, courtly, and curial. Dante combined the norms of infant-unconscious with the norms of hierarchic splendor (though purely as an ideal; he admitted that he was looking only for such language as would be spoken in Italy's political and legal institutions if they were not in disarray). Lawrence's hierarchy, though essentially "rightist" along Carlylean lines, was identified with no dialectic of vast architectural symmetry. And the cult of sunlight had turned into a cult of darkness.

Yet, matching his project with Dante's, as regards the attempt to re-furbish language by drawing upon the appeal of words learned in childhood and outside the areas of *grammatica,* do we not see in Lawrence's "dirty" words for love-making, not a pornographic motive, but a much more pious one? At all intimate moments, Mellors used dialect. As against the "grammatical," learned language of "society," dialect was for Lawrence the truly spontaneous speech of his child-hood. It was in this sense "more noble" than the pretentious speech of the culturally decadent, represented by all that Chatterley stood for. And the use of the "dirty" words was an extension of the same principle that he embodied in his use of dialect. The "dirty" words for making love were thus a kind of "baby-talk."

The use of such words as a vocabulary of endearment between the lovers thus drew upon the appeal to the "infancy" of both childhood and the unconscious (the "unconscious" presumably being gratified to the extent that its resistance to taboos could be broken down). There is also the likelihood that the unconscious appeal of "cloacal" ambiguities could figure here too, in the choice of "dirty" words. The privacy of the sexual would thus be regressively linked with the privacy of the fecal, as Freud says the two are mingled in the experiences of the child, in whose fantasies all the private bodily functions and parts may be confused with one another. Lawrence thus aimed at a variant of "vulgarity" that would be more "noble," since it would be more moving as regards the "natural" gratifications of the unconscious.

Rhetoric in the Middle Ages

We do not pretend that our foregoing pages have been a comprehensive survey of works on rhetoric. We have attempted to consider only those writers who, by one device or another, could be brought to "cooperate" in building this particular "philosophy of rhetoric," and whose presence might prevent it from becoming too "idiosyncratic." We want to contemplate the basic principles of the subject, for their bearing both on literary criticism in particular and on human relations in general. But though we have no desire to write a compendium, we should have touched upon all major directions which rhetoric can take. And we should have indicated how they can all be placed with reference to persuasion and/or identification as generating principles. However, since we have mentioned no work appearing in the centuries between Augustine and Pico della Mirandola, to round things out we might refer the reader to two scholarly and authoritative articles by Richard McKeon covering the long stretch which we have perforce neglected.

In his essay on "Rhetoric in the Middle Ages" (published in *Speculum,* January, 1942) McKeon subdivides the era into an earlier period, when rhetoric was treated as "the science of speaking well in civil matters," and a second period with three major strands: (1) rhetoric as a part of logic; (2) as an art of stating truths certified by theology; (3) as an art of words. He also indicates how all these emphases continued to be developed in the Renaissance, despite pretensions to a break with the medieval tradition. And he notes that inquiries so apparently restricted as the study of words led into consideration of the nonverbal things to which words referred, by this route contributing to developments in science and scientific method. ("Symbolic logic, though unconcerned with its past, still repeats the elements of this heritage.")

To give the whole range of rhetoric through the entire era, McKeon sums up thus:

> Rhetoric is at most an unusually clear example among the arts and sciences of a tendency which is possible in the history of rhetoric only because it is universal in intellectual disciplines. In application, the art of rhetoric contributed during the period from the fourth to the fourteenth century not only to the methods of speaking and writing well, of composing letters and petitions, sermons and prayers, legal documents and briefs, poetry and prose, but to the canons of interpreting laws and scripture, to the dialectical devices of discovery and proof, to the establishment of the scholastic method which was to come into universal use in philosophy and theology, and finally to the formulation of scientific inquiry which was to separate philosophy from theology. In manner of application, the art of rhetoric was the source both of doctrines which have long since become the property of other sciences (such as the passions, which were considered in handbooks of rhetoric until Descartes proposed a "scientific" treatment of them different only in details) and of particular devices which have been applied to a variety of subjects (such as to the "common-places," which were sometimes techniques for inventing arguments, sometimes means for dilating statements, sometimes methods for discovering things, or to "definition" or "order" which may be determined entirely by consideration of the verbal conditions of expression, the psychological requirements of persuasion, or the circumstantial probabilities of fact). In theory of application, the art of rhetoric was now identified with, now distinguished from, the whole or part not only of grammar, logic, and dialectic (which were in turn distinguished from or identified with each other), but also of sophistic and science, of "civil philosophy," psychology, law, and literature, and finally of philosophy as such. Yet if rhetoric is defined in terms of a single subject matter—such as style, or literature, or discourse—it has no history during the Middle Ages; the many innovations which are recorded during that period in the arts with which it is related suggest that their histories might profitably be

considered without unique attachment to the field in which their advances are celebrated.

McKeon mentions another aspect of rhetoric, half in the nonsymbolic realm as with the "administrative" devices of Ovid and Machiavelli:

> The crossing lines of rhetoric and medicine are apparent in Eunapius' *Lives of the Philosophers;* cf. particularly his accounts of Zeno of Cyprus, Magnus, Cribasius, and Ionicus. . . . Magnus made a happy combination of rhetoric and medicine by persuading the patients of other doctors that they had not been cured and then restoring them to health, apparently also by talk and questions; Ionicus was master of philosophy and medicine as well as the arts of rhetoric and poetry. Cf. P. H. and E. A. De Lacy, Philodemus: *On Methods of Inference,* . . . where the relations between medicine and rhetoric are discussed in terms of an "empirical" or "conjectural" method.

Applying this statement to our purposes, we could observe that even the medical equipment of a doctor's office is not to be judged purely for its diagnostic usefulness, but also has a function in the *rhetoric* of medicine. Whatever it is as apparatus, it also appeals as imagery; and if a man has been treated to a fulsome series of tappings, scrutinizings, and listenings, with the aid of various scopes, meters, and gauges, he may feel content to have participated as a patient in such histrionic action, though absolutely no material thing has been done for him, whereas he might count himself cheated if he were given a real cure, but without the pageantry. (What McKeon calls "the crossing lines of rhetoric and medicine" would, in our terms, be: "extending the range of rhetoric into medicine." A related *popular* term is "bedside manner," which Aristotle might have classed under topics that appeal by *ethos.*)

A friend said:

"When I was a boy, a companion of mine showed me a device 'for detecting heart trouble.' It was a glass tube with a bulb at each end, and partly filled with a red fluid. He explained: If a person had anything wrong with his heart, when you pressed one of these bulbs against his chest the fluid in the tube would begin to bubble. First he tried the experiment on himself; the fluid remained calm. But when he put one of the bulbs against my heart, I was terrified to see the fluid begin boiling convulsively. As for *enargeia,* the rhetorical appeal to the imagination by the use of images that 'bring a situation before one's very eyes,' that visible, tangible 'medical instrument' certainly did it. I could literally *see* my heart trouble—and from that day to this, I have been 'heart-conscious.'

"Rhetorically amplifying, the boy then handed the contrivance to me. Though it had been quiet while he held it, the moment I took hold of it, it again boiled violently. He even tried pressing one bulb against my shoe—and my heart ailment was shown to be so acute that the fluid boiled even at that remote contact.

"Then, praise God, having got enough delight from my terror, he explained. This device was an instrument used in that most rhetorical of businesses, medical quackery. The fluid in the glass tube was so susceptible to slight changes in temperature, that the warmth of your hand made it boil if you firmly grasped one of the bulbs. But if you wanted the liquid to remain inert, you held the device between two fingers pressed loosely against the tube. In my fright I had not noticed that he held it differently when using it on himself than when using it on me—and when handing it to me, he had held out one of the bulbs, so that I naturally grasped it in a way to make it boil.

"A quack had used it to persuade the ignorant that they had heart trouble. But he assured them that he could guarantee a cure. So, after he had given them a series of 'treatments,' charging all the traffic would bear, he pronounced them well, and sent them on their way rejoicing, filled with an evangelical zeal that brought the quack new customers."

We cite the story to indicate the extra margin of rhetoric in medical apparatus, over and above its purely technical, operative value. Such instruments present diagnosis in terms of the senses, and can thus be so consoling that, even when the apparatus can't restore a man's health, it can help him die well.

Considering together Ovid, Machiavelli, and the rhetorical ingredient in medicine, we could sum up by the proposition that, in all such partly verbal, partly nonverbal kinds of rhetorical devices, the nonverbal element also persuades by reason of its symbolic character. Paper need not *know the meaning* of fire in order to burn. But in the "idea" of fire there is a persuasive ingredient. By this route something of the rhetorical motive comes to lurk in every "meaning," however purely "scientific" its pretensions. Wherever there is persuasion, there is rhetoric. And wherever there is "meaning," there is "persuasion."

Food, eaten and digested, is not rhetorical. But in the *meaning* of food there is much rhetoric, the meaning being persuasive enough for the idea of food to be used, like the ideas of religion, as a rhetorical device of statesmen.

But we were referring to an essay on medieval rhetoric, by Richard McKeon. And we should note that he continues the subject in another, "Poetry and Philosophy in the Twelfth Century, the Renaissance of Rhetoric" (*Modern Philology,* May, 1946). It is particularly notable because the poets and critics of the period did not share the modern tendency to treat didacticism as anthetical to poetry. In their more ample view,

> Moral problems are made poetic by obscuring suggestions of resolution; and poetry may be didactic if its lessons are vague, or metaphysical if it is without commitment to a philosophy, or religious if religion furnishes a restraint to sentiment in the construction of figures.

However, such a latitudinarian view of the didactic might sometimes be closer to modern criteria than the word itself would indicate. For often those today who would exile the "didactic" from poetry could subscribe wholly to the twelfth century position as here formulated. Similarly, they could probably concede the importance of logic in modern art, once they saw that an effect got by *direct violation* of a logical canon belongs as fully under the head of logic as an effect got by obedience to it.

This same latitudinarian usage seems to have prevailed fruitfully in the twelfth century's attitude towards obscurity in art. Recalling Bentham's reference to *tegumen* and *res tegenda* in his remarks on the use of "eulogistic coverings" as *rhetorical* concealments of motives, we may compare it with these comments, scattered through McKeon's essay, on the *poetics* of obscurity: According to Bernard, Virgil "describes under concealment [*sub integumento*] what the human spirit does and suffers, situated temporarily in the human body. . . . Concealment, moreover, is a genus of demonstration which enfolds the understanding of truth under a fabled narration, and therefore it is also called envelopment [*involucrum*]." In Alan of Lille's *De Planctu Naturae,* Alan asks "concerning the nature of Cupid, which various authors have depicted under the concealing envelopment of enigmas (*sub integumentali involucro aenigmatum*)." Hildebert of Lavardin says of wisdom, *"We heard of it in Ephrata,* that is, in a mirror or in a watch-tower, that is, hidden in an image, that is, in the manifestation of the New Testament and the obscurity of the Old Testament." Bernard reproaches Abailard "for trying to see all things face to face and for making no use in his philosophy of the device, familiar to poets, of seeing truth in a mirror and enigma."

Here we confront a period when even the image in the mirror could be thought of, not as "clear," but as a kind of "concealment" (*which was in turn a kind of demonstration*). Theological doctrines proclaiming the mysteriousness of God, with history and nature as vague signatures of the divine intention, presumably made critics more willing to accept the puzzles of art. Or rather, the acceptance of obscurity in an artist's symbols was *consistent with* the Pauline view that all images are obscure. With this view we would agree. However, from the standpoint of rhetorical persuasion and identification, we would place the stress upon the *social* implications of the enigmatic, in keeping with Marx on "ideology," Carlyle on "Clothes," and Empson on "Pastoral."

"Infancy," Mystery, and Persuasion

Rhetorically considered, the acceptance of the "enigma" as an element in a symbol's persuasiveness has led us to note the place of "magic" or "mystery" both as a passive reflection of class culture and as an active way of maintaining cultural cohesion. We shall further consider the dialectics of such persuasion in our next section on Order.

The "secret" sometimes concerns privy parts of a strictly economic nature (consider the dislike of having one's income or one's bank account a matter of common knowledge). Yet such secretiveness (possibly involving furtive identifications between monetary and genital treasure) impinges upon many still uncharted realms of "infancy," comprising a "speechlessness" or "unspeakableness" derived at the very least from the technical fact that in all expression there is a convergence of unexpressed elements.

If one feels as an "act," for instance, the generating principle of the logarithmic curve in the spiral of a seashell, to the extent that he cannot reduce it to a mathematical formula he is in a state of "infancy," working with a kind of "intuition" that overlaps upon the realm of the "unconscious" in dreams. On the other hand, if the accurate reduction of the spiral to a mathematical formula implies, however remotely, ideas of the convolvulus that would require, for their expression, imagery of an "enigmatic," poetic nature (of roses, sheaths, fleshy receivings, and the like), then the mathematical expression, however explicit and rigorous, would in its abstractness have its own kind of "infancy." Hence, even in the unformulated appreciation of the purely linguistic principles underlying imagery, there is the mystery of infancy. "Infancy" figures all the more in theories of correspondence whereby empirical objects are treated as symbols of a generating principle itself invisible. And such a theological scheme could have its social equivalent in a "fetishistic" world where all the objects were imbued with "magical" properties by reason of their covert or overt identification as insignia of privilege or signs of deprivation.

Underlying any such social mysteries, there are the natural mysteries, reducible ultimately to the infancy of intuitions (as with the "unspeakable" ingredient in the intuitions of senses and seasons). There is room for argument as to what a poet's image of springtime stands for (what equivalents we would substitute for the medieval concern with allegorical, tropological, and anagogic meanings). But in any case the image derives its resonance from its ability to stand for more than spring as a positivist's "fact."

An "intuition" of spring is not a mere passive perception, a datum of sensory (or even supersensory) *knowledge*. It is an *acting-with,* as our "intuitions" of a phoebe's song in spring are not merely the sensory perception of the air in vibration, nor even a sheerly physical response to the return of spring which the song may signalize, but an acting-with a wider orbit of meanings, some of them not intrinsically "spring-like" at all. The "mystery" here centers in the fact that the articulate tonal *image* stands for a partly inarticulate *act*. The principles of such a contemplative act we may seek to formulate as idea, since in idea there is action, drama. It would thus seem more correct to say that, when intuitively acting-with the bird's song, we respond to the *idea* of spring. And this idea, in its completeness, will probably comprise personal, sexual, social, and universal promises.

Empirically, what theologians discuss as the ultimate Oneness of God is equivalent to the ultimate oneness of the linguistic principle. Rhetoric is thus made from fragments of dialectic. For expression,

as persuasion, seeks to escape from infancy by breaking down the oneness of an intuition into several terms, or voices. It defines by partisanship, by de-termination. These terms may bring clarifications that are
themselves confusions on another level. For the conversion of dialectical principles into the persuasive topics of rhetoric is somewhat as
though one were to call the principle of composition "Loyalty" and
the principle of division "Rebellion," and were thereafter to treat of
addition and multiplication in arithmetic as "Pure Loyalty," or of subtraction and division as "Absolute Rebellion." (Pythagorean speculations on numbers apparently did something like that. And "Eden"
and "the fall" are mythic terms for composition and division. Such
terms are *concealments,* so far as their ultimate dialectical reduction
is concerned. But they are enigmas of a *revealing* sort, too, insofar as
they sum up, or stand for, a complexity of personal, sexual, social, and
universal motives. In any case, when their surrounding and modifying imagery is ample, we can begin to see them as a kind of *demonstration,* revealing a complexity of motives that would be *concealed* if
reduced to such terms as "composition" and "division" alone.)

All told, may we not glimpse the possibility that "ideological mystification" can be but a "dyslogistic appellative" for an intrinsic property
of persuasion itself? Where language is concerned, "spirit" comes before "body" in the sense that the capacity for language must precede
its use. In a symbol-using animal, there must be a feeling for the principles of language. The tribe that could spontaneously manipulate a
Greek verb was implicitly a tribe of "grammarians." And since the
ability to use the grammar of one language argues the ability to use
the grammar of other languages, we could say that the feeling for
grammar in general is prior to the feeling for this or that particular
grammar (quite as the ability to walk is prior to the ability to walk in
one particular place, though one learns to walk in general by learning
to walk in particular places). And the feeling for dialectic is "spiritual" at least in the sense that the acts of expression and interpretation
are not "objects."

Here are steps that might indicate how the "ideological priority of
spirit" (and of the "mystifications" derived from it) would be implicit
in persuasion itself:

(1) Persuasion is a kind of communication. (2) Communication is
between different things. (3) But difference is not felt merely as be-

tween *this* entity and *that* entity. Rather, it is felt realistically, as between *this kind* of entity and *that kind* of entity. (That is, communication between entities becomes communication between *classes* of entities.) (4) A persuasive communication between kinds (that is, persuasion by identification) is the abstract paradigm of *courtship*. Such appeal, or address, would be the technical equivalent of love. (5) But courtship, love, is "mystery." For love is a communion of estranged entities, and strangeness is a condition of mystery. (6) When courtship attains its equivalent in the realm of *group* relations, differences between the sexes has its analogue in the difference between *social* classes. (7) In the respect, reverence, embarrassment, and ironies that go with intercourse between classes, there is the "mystification" of Carlyle's "Clothes," of Diderot's "pantomime," of *genres* like pastoral as treated by Empson, or of such tentative attitudes as Empson calls "comic primness." (Out-and-out hatred is a snapping of the continuity, but it can be socially organized only by the building of a countercontinuity; hence the mystery of persuasion is not categorically abolished, it is transformed.)

(8) Persuasion is "spiritual," in contrast with the producing of change by purely material agencies. For if it is "bodily" to move a man from here to there by pushing him, then by antithesis it is "spiritual" to produce the same movement in pleading, "Come hither." (9) But such "spiritual" communication is abstract. Hence, in it there is the possibility of a *completely* abstract communication (or "courtship") between kinds, or classes. In the *Phaedrus* (as we noted in the *Grammar*) Socrates shows us what the completion of abstract courtship would be. It would be the insemination of *doctrine;* that is to say, it would be *education,* the bringing of the *message.* (10) But there is no message without *science.* And so, out of persuasion, we can even derive pure *information,* which is usually *contrasted* with persuasion.

The tie-ups and cross-references here are endless. But they all start in the proposition that, with a symbol-using animal, the logic of symbols must be "prior" to the effects of any "productive forces" in the socioeconomic meaning of that expression. And one should not forget that the productive forces themselves owe much of their development to linguistic agencies, not merely in the sense that vocabulary is needed for guiding the production of complex instruments and for maintaining the tradition of their use, but also in a more radical sense.

For the distinctive insight in human invention is not the use of tools, since animals use tools; it is in the use of tools for making tools. And this insight-at-one-remove, this reflexive pattern, is much like the insight of language itself, which is not merely speech about things (a dog's barking at a prowler could be called that), but speech about speech. This secondary stage, allowing for "thought of thought," is so integrally connected with the human power to invent tools for making tools, that we might call such power linguistic in essence (as Carlyle did).

Of course, there is always the possibility of "mystification," in the sense that language can be used to deceive. And at least as a kind of rough preparation for finer scrutiny, rhetorical analysis should always be ready to expose mystifications of this simple but ubiquitous sort (mystifications broadly reducible either to "unitary" devices whereby a special group gains unjust advantage from the services of other groups, or to "scapegoat" devices whereby an "enemy abroad" is wholly blamed for untoward conditions due mainly to domestic faults). But we are here asking whether there may be a profounder kind of mystification as well, implicit in the very act of persuasion itself.

As the mystery of courtship is in the act of persuasion intrinsically, so also there is implicit in it the invitation to the mystification of class. We note such motives also in the ambiguously classlike relationships that figure in science, as the material of education involves *classes* of learners hierarchically arranged among themselves. Or there is the class of students as against the class of teachers. And there are classes of teachers, among themselves "invidiously" ranked. Persuasion, thus roundabout, brings a mystery into science, into the very disciplines that are usually taken to be the opposite of mystification.

But also, implicit in persuasion, there is *theology,* since theology is the ultimate reach of communication between *different classes* of beings. The steps here would seem to be: (1) In the courtship of persuasion there are the rudiments of love, respectful pleading. (2) The *ultimate* of this attitude is reverent beseechment, prayer. (3) Prayer has its own invitation to the universalizing of class distinction, the pleader being by nature inferior to the pled-with. (4) The relation attains its utmost thoroughness in the contrast between the mightiest sovereign and the lowliest of his subjects. (We can next note that the pattern may be *brought to earth* in an attenuated form, as social hierarchy.) (5) But in its "pure" form, there is need to find a discussable content, or object. One cannot without an almost suicidal degree of perfection merely pray. One must pray *to something*. (6) Hence, the plunge direct to the *principle* of persuasion, as reduced to its most universal form, leads to the theologian's attempt to establish an *object* of such prayer; namely: God (largely applying to this end terms set by the *social* hierarchy). In sum, we are suggesting: The "theology" that Marx detected in "ideological mystification" is the *last reach of the persuasive principle itself*. And quite as in the social counterpart of such theology, there is likewise a hierarchy implicit in the route from persuasion to science.

If our approach is just, such mystifications cannot be cleared away by a mere debunker's reduction. The high development of magic as a persuasion that promotes cooperation in primitive tribes, and the many reversions to "mystique" in modern policies of right, center, and left, seem to indicate a profounder element here. These manifestations seem to indicate that people are more thorough than they think, and that the *superficial* uses of persuasion (as a mere call that induces action) do have in them the *ultimates* of persuasion, however these may be concealed.

If this were so, if the *ultimate reaches* in the principle of persuasion are implicit in even the *trivial* uses of persuasion, people could not escape the ultimates of language merely by using language trivially (as with some mothers who seem to think that they can make their children "wholesome" merely by keeping them stupid). The choices between war and peace are ultimate choices. Men must make themselves over profoundly, when cooperatively engaged in following such inescapable purposes. And as the acts of persuasion add up in a social texture, they amount to one or the other of those routes—and they are radical, no matter however trivial the errors by which war is permitted to emerge out of peace.

There would then seem to be two kinds of mystification, a special kind and a general kind. You may have no great difficulty in spotting the first kind, though it may be hard to spread the glad tidings of your discovery, since there is usually powerful social organization behind the errors you would clear away, the errors making for the misunderstandings that goad to war. But as for the possibility of a second kind, mystification as the "logical conclusion" of the persuasive principle:

Even if we finally discover that such a development is not *inevitable* to persuasion, there are many reasons to believe that it is a constant *threat,* a constant *tendency* or *temptation* in those who are thorough enough to build a way of thinking in accordance with the implications of persuasion as courtship.

At least, beyond the purely fallacious devices by which our editorial writers build up the notion that the ways of the "Russian East" are "mysterious," surely Stalin in the Kremlin is more "mysterious" as a leader than Truman in the White House, to his own people as well as to ours. Marxism teaches us not to forget the mysteries of class; and Empson shows how they may figure "pastorally" in even a socialist society. And there are also the mysteries of courtship in subtler ways, as we have tried to indicate.

There are also sources of mystery beyond rhetoric. These can be rooted in the secrecy of plans during gestation. Or they are found in fears that arise from the sense of limits (so that one says in effect: "Another perhaps can go beyond that point, but not I"—or "Maybe I can go beyond that point after preparation, but not now"). Or there is mystery in the infancy of the "unconscious," nonverbal, postverbal, and superverbal. By nonverbal we mean the visceral; by postverbal the unutterable complexities to which the implications of words themselves give rise. (Maybe the word should be "coverbal.") And if we go through the verbal to the outer limits of the verbal, the superverbal would comprise whatever might be the jumping-off place. It would be not nature minus speech, but nature as the ground of speech, *hence nature as itself containing the principle of speech.* Such an inclusive nature would be more-than-verbal rather than less-than-verbal.

PART THREE

ORDER

III

ORDER

Positive, Dialectical, and Ultimate Terms

F IRST, we take it, there are the *positive* terms. They name par excellence the things of experience, the *hic et nunc,* and they are defined *per genus et differentiam,* as with the vocabulary of biological classification. Here are the words for what Bentham called "real entities," in contrast with the "fictitious entities" of the law. ("Tree" is a positive term, but "rights" or "obligations" are legal fictions.) In Kant's alignment, the thing named by a positive term would be a manifold of sensations unified by a concept. Thus, the "sensibility" receives a bundle of "intuitions," intimations of size, shape, texture, color, and the like; and as the "understanding" clamps a unifying term, a "concept," upon the lot, we can say, "This is a house."

The imagery of poetry is positive to the extent that it names things having a visible, tangible existence. We have already observed that there is an important difference between a house as a practically existing object and the image "house" as it appears in a poem. But we are now considering only the respect in which the poetic image, house, can also be defined *per genus et differentiam:* that is, the respect in which, when a poet uses the term, "house," we could get his meaning by consulting Webster's, where we are told that a house is "a structure intended or used as a habitation or shelter for animals of any kind; but especially, a building or edifice for the habitation of man; a dwelling place."

A positive term is most unambiguously itself when it names a visible and tangible thing which can be located in time and place. Hence, the positive ideal is a "physicalist" vocabulary that reduces reference to terms of *motion.* Since the modern mathematics of submicroscopic motion is far indeed from the visible and tangible, the sensory aspect of positive experience can become quite tenuous. But since such manifestations must, in the last analysis, reveal themselves on dials, in

707

measurements and meter readings of one sort or another, the hypothetical entities of electronics can be considered as "positive," insofar as they are capable of empirical recording. A skeptic might offer reasons to believe that such science is less positive than its apologists take it to be. Particularly one might ask himself whether the terms for *relationships* among things are as positive as are the names for the things themselves. But we need not attempt to decide that question here; we need only note that there is a basic terminology of perception grounded on sensation, memory, and "imagination" (in the general, psychological, nonpoetic meaning of the word). And whatever else it may be in its ultimate reaches, such a terminology of perception is "positive" in its everyday, empirical availability. There is nothing "transcendent" about it, for instance.

Bentham's reference to "fictitious entities" of the law indicates another order, comprising terms which we would call "dialectical." These have no such strict location as can be assigned to the objects named in words of the first order. Even insofar as the positive terminology acquires theoretical champions who proclaim the "principles of positivism," we are in the realm of the purely dialectical. "Positivism" itself is not a positive term. For though you may locate the positive referent for the expression "house," you will have a hard time trying to locate a similarly positive referent for the expression, "principles of positivism." Here are words that belong, not in the order of *motion and perception,* but rather in the order of *action and idea.* Here are words for *principles* and *essence* (as we might ask, "Just what is the *essence* of the positivist doctrine?").

Here are "titular" words. Titles like "Elizabethanism" or "capitalism" can have no positive referent, for instance. And though they sum up a vast complexity of conditions which might conceivably be reduced to a near-infinity of positive details, if you succeeded in such a description you would find that your recipe contained many ingredients not peculiar to "Elizabethanism" or "capitalism" at all. In fact, you would find that "Elizabethanism" itself looked different, if matched against, say, "medievalism," than if matched against "Victorianism." And "capitalism" would look different if compared and contrasted with "feudalism" than if dialectically paired with "socialism." Hence terms of this sort are often called "polar."

Bentham said that fictitious entities could not be adequately defined

per genus et differentiam. He said that they required, rather, definition by *paraphrase,* hence his method of "phraseoplerosis" and "archetypation" for discovering just what people really meant when they used
legal fictions. We equate his "fictitious entities" with "dialectical
terms" because they refer to *ideas* rather than to *things.* Hence they
are more concerned with *action* and *attitude* than with *perception* (they
fall under the head of *ethics* and *form* rather than *knowledge* and *information*). You define them by asking how they *behave;* and part
of an expression's behavior, as Bentham pointed out, will be revealed by
the discovery of the secret modifiers implicit in the expression itself;
hence Bentham's project for filling out the expression (phraseoplerosis)
and discounting its images (archetypation).

If an expession were complete, such paraphrase would not be necessary. One could then derive all the modifiers explicitly by citation
from the expression itself. But particularly in the strife of rhetoric,
the expression is left fragmentary. If a poet says, "I love" when he
really hates, he will scrupulously proceed, however enigmatically, to
round out his statement with the expressions that introduce the necessary modifiers. But when Preen says to Prone, "I want to help you,"
his statement is incomplete, and may even require interpretation on a
purely behavioristic basis. If this "help," as tested behavioristically,
amounts to nothing more than what folk rhetoric calls the "run
around," then the ultimate test of his meaning is extralinguistic. And
much rhetorical statement requires such circumstantial interpretation.

Hypothetically, if our discrimination were keen enough, we could
know by the tonalities of Preen's statement, or by the flicker of his eye,
just what he meant when he said, "I want to help you." In brief, the
expression itself would contain its future implications. But our discrimination is not always keen enough; and besides, the record is
usually but a fragment of the expression (as the written word omits
all telltale record of gesture and tonality; and not only may our "literacy" keep us from missing the omissions, it may blunt us to the appreciation of tone and gesture, so that even when we witness the full
expression, we note only those aspects of it that can be written down).

In public relations, most expressions are as though wigwagged from
a great distance, or as uttered behind masks, or as transmitted by hearsay. Hence, one must go to the first frank level of analysis, the extra-
verbally behavioristic. Next, there are sloganlike utterances by which

all men are partially fooled, the orator and his public alike. For this we have Bentham's concern with "archetypation," the images that *improperly* affect our ideas. But here we meet the need for another kind of "filling out," half behavioristic, half imaginal, an ambiguity due to the fact that so much pragmatic behavior itself has symbolic elements.

If, for instance, the church spire actually has been an image of aspirations "towards heaven," and if churchmen pay verbal tribute to the power of the supernatural, and if then on church property they erect business structures soaring far above their church, does not this combination of behavioristic and imaginal tests require us to conclude that their true expression is not in their words, but in the conditions of steel and stone which are weightily there, to dwarf you as the church spire never dwarfed you, and to put you at the bottom of a deep, windswept gulch? Regardless of what they may say in their statements telegraphed world-wide by the news agencies, without gesture, without tonality, have they not, in their mixture of behavior and image, *really* proclaimed that they live by a "post-Christian" order of motives?

If church spires mean anything, they must overtop the buildings that surround them. However, the opposition might point out: There are the catacombs of religion, too. True, there is the *underground*.

In any case, we have again come upon an area where nonverbal things, in their capacity as "meanings," also take on the nature of words, and thus require the extension of dialectic into the realm of the physical. Or, otherwise put, we come to the place where the dialectical realm of ideas is seen to permeate the positive realm of concepts. For if a church spire is a symbolic thing, then the business structure that overtowers it must participate in the same symbolic, however antithetically, as representing an alternate choice of action. Thus the ethical-dramatic-dialectical vocabulary so infuses the empirical-positive world of things that each scientific object becomes available for poetry.

But the distinction between positive and dialectical terms, with the interrelation of the two realms, can deflect attention from a third aspect of vocabulary, which might be called "ultimate." We had thought of calling it "mystical," but that designation too quickly makes readers take sides for or against us. So let us call it "ultimate," and approach this third element of vocabulary thus:

Dialectic in itself may remain on the level of parliamentary conflict, leading to compromise. It being the realm of ideas or principles, if you organize a conflict among spokesmen for competing ideas or principles, you may produce a situation wherein there is no one clear choice. Each of the spokesmen, whose ideas are an extension of special interests, must remain somewhat unconvinced by any solution which does not mean the complete triumph of his partisan interests. Yet he may have to compromise, putting through some portion of his program by making concessions to allies whom, if he could get his wishes absolutely, he would repudiate. Here are standard parliamentary tactics. "Compromise" is perhaps the neutral term, though on the edge of the dyslogistic. "Horse-trading" is clearly a dyslogistic term for the same thing. And a resoundingly dyslogistic term would be "demoralization," justifiable insofar as all "interests" can be translated into terms of "principles," and when they have thus been stylistically ennobled, any yielding on interests becomes a yielding on principles (a stylistic embarrassment upon which our State Department under General Marshall based the rigidity of its dealings with Soviet Russia).

Now, the difference between a merely "dialectical" confronting of parliamentary conflict and an "ultimate" treatment of it would reside in this: The "dialectical" order would leave the competing voices in a jangling relation with one another (a conflict solved *faute de mieux* by "horse-trading"); but the "ultimate" order would place these competing voices themselves in a *hierarchy,* or *sequence,* or *evaluative series,* so that, in some way, we went by a fixed and reasoned progression from one of these to another, the members of the entire group being arranged *developmentally* with relation to one another. The "ultimate" order of terms would thus differ essentially from the "dialectical" (as we use the term *in this particular connection*) in that there would be a "guiding idea" or "unitary principle" behind the diversity of voices. The voices would not confront one another as somewhat disrelated competitors that can work together only by the "mild demoralization" of sheer compromise; rather, they would be like successive positions or moments in a single process.

Thus, confronting the sort of "dialectical" procedure required when "interests" have been translated into a corresponding terminology of "principles," with parliamentary spokesmen aiming to further their interests somewhat by compromising with their principles—we can get a glimpse into a possible alternative, whereby a somewhat formless parliamentary wrangle can, by an "ultimate" vocabulary, be creatively endowed with design. And even though the members of the parliament, being "horse-traders" by nature, may not accept this design, it can have a contemplative effect; it can organize one's attitude towards the struggles of politics, and may suggest reasons why one kind of compromise is, in the long run, to be rated as superior to another.

Consider, for instance, how Plato treats the four kinds of "imperfect government" in *The Republic* (Book VIII and beginning of Book IX). They are presented not merely as one might draw up a list, but *developmentally*. The steps from his ideal government to "timocracy," and thence successively to "oligarchy," "democracy," and "tyranny" are interpreted as the unfolding of a single process. Here, as repeatedly in Platonic dialogues, the interrelationship among the terms for the kinds of government is "ultimate." Indeed, when Socrates celebrates dialectic as the highest kind of knowledge, rising above the separate sciences and mediating among them, he means by dialectic not merely the step from sensory terms to ideas, but also a hierarchic ordering of steps.

"Governments vary as the dispositions of men," Socrates says; and "there must be as many of one as of the other." Whereupon he seeks to define the human dispositions brought to the fore by each of the different political structures. His resulting remarks on the "timocratic man," and on the "oligarchic," "democratic," and "tyrannical man" amount to recipes for what today might be called four different "ideologies." Each of these has its own peculiar idea or summarizing term: "honor" for timocracy, "wealth" for oligarchy, "freedom" for democracy, "protection" for tyranny. And the human dispositions which he describes under these heads could be treated as four different motivational clusters which one must appeal to, when trying to win adherents in an audience typical of each such political state. "As the government, so the citizen," Plato says. Yet he is not content merely to give us four "personality types" (four corresponding types of government, each with its appropriate ideology or kind of consciousness). He is seeking to grade them with reference to their relative distance from a single norm. We are not here arguing for the justice of his grading; we are merely pointing to the principle involved. We are saying that to leave the four kinds merely confronting one another in their diversity would have been "dialectical" in the sense of the parliamentary jangle, but that this attempt to arrange them hierarchically transforms the dialectical into an "ultimate" order.

In an ultimate dialectic, the terms so lead into one another that the completion of each order leads to the next. Thus, a body of positive terms must be brought to a head in a titular term which represents the principle or idea behind the positive terminology as a whole. This summarizing term is in a different order of vocabulary. And if such titles, having been brought into dialectical commerce with one another, are given an order among themselves, there must be a principle of principles involved in such a design—and the step from principles to a principle of principles is likewise both the fulfillment of the previous order and the transcending of it.

We thought of calling the ultimate order "mystical" because the mystic invariably aims to encompass conflicting orders of motivation, not by outlawing any order, however "inferior," but by finding a place for it in a developmental series. Thus at moments when a mystic vocabulary is most accurate, we should not expect to find a flat antithesis between "body" and "spirit." Rather, we should expect "body" (in even its "lowliest" forms) to be treated as a *way into* "spirit." Since antithesis is so strong a verbal instrument in both rhetoric and dialectic, we may often find "short cuts" where the extremes of a developmental series are presented as harshly antithetical. But we should not judge by this alone. Rather, look into the writings of any mystic who has left a record of his methods, and you will find that the entry to ultimate communion is made *through* body, nature, image, systematically treated as a necessary disciplinary step. Indeed, so thoroughly is this the case, that for the most ultimate of his experiences, the mystic will again employ the terms of body, nature, image (on the assumption that, if one has gone through the proper series of steps, one knows how to discount the inadequacies of such language, while the clash of images by oxymoron comes closest to expressing the experience for someone who has not been through it).

Ultimate Elements in the Marxist Persuasion

Once you have placed your terms in a developmental series, you have an arrangement whereby each can be said to participate, within the limitations of its nature, in the ultimate perfection ("finishedness") of the series. Each stage, at its appropriate "moment," represents the movement, the ultimate direction or principle, of the entire series. In this sense, Hegel's "concrete universal" would be "mystical," in that it represents not only itself, in its nature *hic et hunc,* but the universal essence of the development in its entirety (quite as bud, preceding blossom, represents not only its own concrete bud-nature, and its nature as incipient blossom, but also the fruit, the seed, and decline, and the futurity beyond that decline). And since any moment, here and now, would thus represent a developmental principle transcending the concrete particularity of any one moment in the series, here would be a kind of mystical unity, a oneness that both is and is not, as with the paradox of substance discussed in the *Grammar.*

Marx wrote good satire on Hegel's "concrete universal." And in keeping with the same line of thought, he notes in *The German Ideology* how, by the use of an ultimate design for interpreting moments along the path of history, later history can be made to look like the goal of earlier history (as were we to say that America was discovered in order to bring about the French Revolution). Thereby, he says, "history receives its own special aims and becomes 'a person ranking with other persons' (to wit: 'self-consciousness, criticism, the Unique,' etc.), while what is designated with the words 'destiny,' 'goal,' 'germ,' or 'idea' of earlier history is nothing more than an abstraction formed from later history, from the active influence which earlier history exercises on later history."

But can a mode of thought so strongly built upon Hegelian patterns avoid the "mystical" merely by "turning Hegel upside down"? In any case, much of the *rhetorical* strength in the Marxist dialectic comes from the fact that it is "ultimate" in its order. The various classes do not confront one another merely as parliamentary voices that represent conflicting interests. They are arranged hierarchically, each with the disposition, or "consciousness," that matches its peculiar set of circumstances, while the steps from feudal to bourgeois to proletarian are grounded in the very nature of the universe.

Precisely by reason of this ultimate order, a spokesman for the proletariat can think of himself as representing not only the interests of that class alone, but the grand design of the entire historical sequence, its final outcome for all mankind. When gauging the historical situation correctly, when knowing the nature of the moment as part of a universal movement, he finds in the "revolutionary situation" precisely the double nature that permits it to be simultaneously the concrete thing it is, in its own unique combination of conditions, and a participant in the perfection of the total sequence. (To see both the "science" and the "intuition," see Lenin's letters when he had become convinced that the time was ripe in Russia.)

In general, the ultimate hierarchic order of the terminology rises materialistically from the fundamental, unknown particles of the universe, to atoms, to crystals and planetary formations, to the emergence of life, to the evolution of biological forms, to the evolution and revolution of social forms. We cite from the report of a lecture on dialectical materialism by the English physicist, J. D. Bernal, referring to this "natural hierarchy of development in the universe." But from the standpoint of rhetoric, the implanting of an ultimate hierarchy upon social forms is the important thing. Here the hierarchic ordering of the subsocial realms could be considered as an "ideological reflex" or extension of the persuasive principle experienced in the social realm. That is, rhetorically considered, the Marxist hierarchy may go not from a science of nature to a science of society, but from an ultimate dialectic of social development to a corresponding dialectic of natural development. For though there may be a "Marxist physics," Marxism is primarily a *sociology*.

In accord with such thinking as regards current positivist doctrines, one may take a stand that, while neither flatly for nor flatly against, need not be reduced merely to the lame and formless admission that "there is something to be said for both sides." Not only is the positive order of vocabulary "allowable"; we should be reluctant to leave this order. Every question should be reduced to such terms, insofar as the nature of its subject-matter permits. The positivist ideal of language is athletic and exacting. And we should object to it only when dramatic elements are present which cannot legitimately be treated in the positive order alone. The improper migration of positive terms to areas of investigation and contemplation for which they are unfit calls for a flatly antipositivist position, as regards any such cases of terministic impropriety. But from the standpoint of terminology in general, we are not thereby vowed to a doctrine of out-and-out anti-positivism, since we can and should accept the positivist order of terms as the proper first stage in a hierarchy of terms.

The same admonition should be introduced with regard to our reservations on technologism, as it is manifested in the cult of manu-factured commodities (the doctrine that might be summed up: "It's culture if it's something you can buy"). Man is essentially a "rational" (that is, symbol-using) animal (as stated in the opening words of St. John, *In the beginning* was the Word," the prior in substance being here expressed as the prior in time). And when we use symbols for things, such symbols are not merely reflections of the things sym-bolized, or signs for them; they are to a degree a *transcending* of the things symbolized. So, to say that man is a symbol-using animal is by the same token to say that he is a "transcending animal." Thus, there is in language itself a motive force calling man to transcend the "state of nature" (that is, the order of motives that would prevail in a world without language, Logos, "reason"). And in this sense, we can recognize even the cult of commodities (which is an outgrowth of language-guided invention), as a *mode of transcendence.* So we need not be placed in the position of flatly "rejecting" it, a particularly un-comfortable position in view of the fact that the cult of commodities seems able to recruit just about as many devotees as can afford to bear witness (testifying to the sincerity of their faith by money-offerings).

An out-and-out antithetical vocabulary would require you either to live by the cult of commodities, in effect adoring them as household gods, or to reject such a cult quite as a devout believer in the One God would reject idolatry. But by using a graded vocabulary, you can in-stead recognize the cult of commodities as a mode of transcendence that is genuine, but inferior.

Employing the same hierarchic principle, we note that even a Hitler-ite political philosophy, or any such "collusion," would require treat-ment, not as flatly "antisocial," but rather as a low order of sociality. Such an approach becomes particularly necessary where an inferior order actually prevails, and one is so placed that a flat rejection of the doctrine would be suicidally ineffectual, whereas a grudging minimum acceptance of it might put one in a position to work towards its gradual improvement. But unfortunately, while this way of reasoning is just, it readily lends itself to use unjustly.

Any improvement in social status is a kind of transcendence. And where one is a member of an extremely underprivileged class, as with the Negro in America, an individual attempt at the transcending of inferior status gets increased poignancy from the fact that, atop all the intensity of such effort in itself, there is a working at cross-purposes. The Negro intellectual, Ralph Ellison, says that Booker T. Washington "described the Negro community as a basket of crabs, wherein should one attempt to climb out, the others immediately pull him back." Is there not also an internal compulsion of the same sort, as the individual Negro visits this same judgment upon himself? For he may also take the position of what Mead would call the "generalized other": he may visit upon himself the antagonistic attitude of the whites; or he may feel as "conscience" the judgment of his own class, since he would in a sense be "disloyal" to his class, in transcending the limitations traditionally imposed upon him as a member of that class. Striving for freedom as a human being generically, he must do so as a Negro specifically. But to do so as a Negro is, by the same token, to prevent oneself from doing so in the generic sense; for a Negro could not be free generically except in a situation where the color of the skin had no more social meaning than the color of the eyes.

Recall the lines in *The Merchant of Venice,* where Shakespeare is considering an analogous conflict, as Shylock says:

> I am a Jew. Hath not a Jew eyes? hath not a Jew hands, organs, dimensions, senses, affections, passions? fed with the same food, hurt with the same weapons, subject to the same diseases, healed by the same means, warmed and cooled by the same winter and summer, as a Christian is? If you prick us, do we not bleed? if you tickle us, do we not laugh? if you poison us, do we not die?

Then, following this statement of his identity as a member of mankind generically, Shylock turns to the theme of his specific identity as a Jew in Christian Venice:

> and if you wrong us, shall we not revenge? If we are like you in the rest, we shall resemble you in that. If a Jew wrong a Christian, what is his humility? Revenge. If a Christian wrong a Jew, what should his sufferance be by Christian example? Why, revenge. The villainy you teach me I will execute, and it shall go hard but I will better the instruction.

Note the paradoxical way in which the words "humility" and "sufferance" are used. Revenge as a kind of humble, Christian duty. One might call the notion Shylock's failure to understand Christian doctrine. Or, more justly, one might call it Shylock's very accurate gauging of the way in which Christians themselves characteristically distort Christian sufferance to serve the rhetoric of property. In any case, we see that Shylock would here use the advantages of vengeance itself as a kind of transcendence, a "static" way of lifting himself above his disadvantages as a Jew while in the very same act he reaffirms his status.

Such conflicts are clearly "dialectical." We are beyond the purely positive level of vocabulary; we are in the realm, not of knowledge, but of ideas and action. Hence, unless the terminology becomes ultimate, there is an unresolved, parliamentary jangle, a discordancy of conflicting voices which at best could attain an uneasy compromise, and at worst arrive at the equating of vengeance with humility (which means, in sum, accepting the judgment of the opponent, and merely turning the tables against him). Shylock's "vengeance" is but the most highly generalized statement of such a solution, which in each particular case calls for a joining in a conspiracy against the oppressor, in the hopes that eventually the roles can be reversed. In Richard Wright's *Native Son,* Bigger's criminal protest *as a Negro* is another particularization of the same response. The "humility" of such vengeance is in the acceptance of the opponent's judgment, in finally agreeing to let him set the rules, and then aiming at advantage within the restrictions he has imposed. Purely "racialist" or "nationalist" doctrines of emancipation are a more benign transformation of such "counterconspiracy" (or exclusive league of the excluded). And they may even seem like an ultimate solution, until there develop the wrangles within nationalism, and among rival nationalisms.

Clearly, the rhetorical appeal of the Marxist terminology in such situations is that it can allow for an ultimate order. You may question whether it is the "ultimate-ultimate." You may fear that, as it operates in social textures, it ceases to be the conspiracy-to-end-conspiracy that it claims to be, instead becoming but the condition of a new conspiracy. Maybe yes, maybe no. That is not for us to decide at the moment. It is enough for us to note, as students of rhetoric, that the Marxist terminology is "ultimate" enough to meet at least the primary requirements of this sort. It permits the member of a minority to place his problem in a graded series that keeps transcendence of individual status from seeming like disloyalty to one's group status, and keeps the sufferance of one's group status from assuming some form of mere "vengeance." It allows the member of an underprivileged minority, for instance, to confront the world at once specifically and generically. The Negro does not become equal to the white by a kind of intellectual "passing." He can explicitly recognize that his particular act must be adapted to the nature of his historical situation in which he happens to be placed; yet at the same time, he can view this situation universally (thereby attaining the kind of transcendence at which all men aim, and at which the Negro spiritual had aimed, though there the aim was at the spiritual transcending of a predestined material slavery, whereas the Marxist ultimates allow for a material transcending of inferior status).

True, there is much that no vocabulary can do in these matters. Where there are so many intense conflicts of an extraverbal sort, no merely verbal manipulations can remove them. But verbal manipulations may offer a more orderly approach to them, permitting them to be contemplated with less agitation. And where this is the case, verbal manipulations are the very opposite of the "evasive."

Marxism, considered as an ultimate vocabulary, also owes much of its persuasiveness to the way in which its theory of action fits its theory of order. For if any point, or "moment," in a hierarchic series can be said to represent, in its limited way, the principle or "perfection" of the ultimate design, then each tiny act shares in the absolute meaning of the total act. Thus, the "truth" is not grasped and tested by merely "perceiving" the logic of the entire series. Perception must be grounded in enactment, by participation in some local role, so that the understanding of the total order is reached through this partial involvement. There is perception from without, made possible through nonparticipation. Or there is local participation, which may become so involved in particulars that one never sees beyond them. But there is a third way, the fullest kind of understanding, wherein one gets the immediacy of participation in a local act, yet sees in and through this act an over-all design, sees and *feels* the local act itself as but the partial expression of the the total development. The Marxist persuasion is in the name of this third way. Consider Lenin's *What Is to Be Done?* for instance:

We might first note in the very title a contribution to our previous concern with the relation between rhetoric and opinion. For in his *Book of Fallacies,* Bentham had distinguished between matters of fact (what was done, *quid factum*) and matters of opinion (what is to be done, *quid faciendum*). The future can only be a matter of opinion. Until it has actually come to pass, it must lie outside the orbit of empirically verifiable "scientific fact." So Lenin's question, *What Is to Be Done?* is by such tests clearly in the realm of opinion, and to this extent in the realm of rhetoric. (It is "deliberative.")

The crucial point, as we quoted it in the *Grammar,* revolves about the distinction between trade union activity and the worker's *consciousness* of his role as member of a revolutionary proletariat. Lenin would distinguish between the "spontaneous" response to a situation and the kind of *new act* that arises under a deliberately Marxist interpretation of that situation. And we would interpret the design of Lenin's thinking in this wise: The trade unionist, as such, has no consciousness of the workers' "historical role" in the revolutionary change from capitalism to socialism. Hence, in the mere spontaneity and localism of his responses, he does not transcend the limitations of his class. He acts, and to this extent he has a profounder kind of participation than the purely outside observer. But his act is beclouded by the particulars of his situation, the day-to-day contingencies of earning a livelihood. Now add the Marxist doctrine of universal historical necessity, defining the worker's place in an *ultimate* development. The worker whose understanding becomes infused with this doctrine then sees himself not merely as an individual joining with other individuals to improve his bargaining position with his employer: he sees himself as *member of a class,* the proletariat, which is destined to play *a crucial role in the unfolding of history as a whole.* Thus, while participating with maximum activity in the particular organizational and propagandist problems that mark his local situation, he transcends the limitations of these local conditions and of his "spontaneous" nature as member of the working class. For he sees his role in terms of an *absolute,* an ultimate. In participating *locally,* he is participating in the total dialectic, communicating directly with its universal logic, or ultimate direction. Indeed, we could even say that he now sees himself in *formal* or *ritual* terms, not just as Mr. So-and-so working under such-and-such conditions, but as *"the* Proletarian," with a generic personality calling creatively to ways of action that transcend his limited nature as Mr. So-and-so, and derive their logic from motives of universal scope.

Call it fallacious if you want. That need not concern us here. We are discussing the rhetorical advantages of an ultimate vocabulary as contrasted with a vocabulary left on the level of parliamentary conflict. We are but pointing to a notable formal advantage, got by the union of drama and reason, a wholesome rhetorical procedure in itself, at a time when typical "parliamentary" works like Thurman Arnold's *The Folklore of Capitalism* would ask us rather to unite drama with unreason.

Perhaps the "ultimate" order comes most natural to narrative forms (hence its ease of adaptation to the Hegelian and Marxist "stories" of history). Usually, in narrative, it is so implicit that we may not even discern it. For instance, if the fate of our hero is developed through a succession of encounters, each of these encounters may represent a different "principle," and each of these principles or stages may so lead into the next that the culmination of one lays the ground for the next. In fact, if the work is properly constructed, it will necessarily have such a form. If one breaks down a "dramatic idea" into acts of variously related agents, the successive steps of the plot could be reduced to corresponding developments of the idea; and the agent or scene under the aegis of which a given step was enacted could be said to represent personally the motivational principle of that step. The plot is unnoticeably ultimate, as the reader need not "choose between" different phases of its unfolding, but by going through each becomes prepared for the next. Ultimate vocabularies of motivation aim at the philosophic equivalent of such narrative forms, with a series of steps that need not precede one another in time, but only "in principle," though the formal appeal in the Marxist dialectic of history seems to reside in the fact that, as with narrative, the series in time is also a series "in principle."

"Sociology of Knowledge" vs. *Platonic "Myth"*

Karl Mannheim's project for a "sociology of knowledge," as discussed in his *Ideology and Utopia,* might be described as a methodology that aims at the neutralizing and liberalizing of the Marxist rhetoric. When viewed from the standpoint of the distinction between positive, dialectical, and ultimate terminologies, it seems to go beyond the purely parliamentary kind of dialectic, yet to fall somewhat short of an ultimate order. We might improvise a term, and call it "pro-ultimate." For it would move towards a gradual increase of precision, got by an exact study of the relationship between the positive and dialectical orders.

At least, that is how we would interpret Mannheim's distinction between "relativism" and "relationism." "Relativism" would merely recognize the great variety of ideological perspectives, would describe them in their diversity, and at best would look for workable compromises among them. But "relationism" should be able to build up an exact body of knowledge about ideologies by studying the connection between these ideologies and their ground.

To this end, Mannheim generalizes the Marxist exposure of "mystification" to the point where it becomes the "unmasking" of *any* doctrinal bias. That is, a human terminology of motives is necessarily partial; accordingly, whatever its claims to universal validity, its "principles" favor the interests of some group more than others; and one may look to opposing theorists for discoveries that "unmask" the partisan limitations lurking in speciously "universal" principles.

Any such "unmasking" of an ideology's limitations is itself made from a limited point of view. But each such limited perspective can throw light upon the relation between the universal principles of an ideology and the special interests which they are consciously or unconsciously made to serve. Each point of view could thus reveal something about the relation between an ideology (we might call it a systematized verbal act) and its nonverbal conditions (the scene of that act).

One might thus use rhetorical partisanship for dialectical operations that led towards a body of exact knowledge about the relation between all ideologies and the conditions of living out of which they arise. And by this method, the specialist in such analysis should also be able to discount the partiality of his own position somewhat (a transcending of partiality to which competing specialists might contribute, by unmasking the undetected partiality of their colleagues, thereby making it possible to work steadily towards an increase in the exactitude of ways for discounting bias in views that had seemed to be universally valid). The lore gradually accumulated by such procedures would constitute a "sociology of knowledge."

Only if all the returns were in, could one lay claim to an ultimate order here. But the project for thus systematically utilizing both rhetorical and dialectical elements in the search for an ever closer approximate to absolute knowledge about the nature of "ideologies," would clearly be much nearer to an "ultimate" order than a mere relativistic study of opinions and their background would be. "Relativism" would be hardly more than the first preparatory positivistic research needed to provide the material for the dialectical discipline of "relationism."

In such a project, of course, Marxism would be but one voice among many. And the edges are so knocked off the Marxist definition of ideology that Marxism too becomes analyzable as an ideology. That is, whatever its pretensions to an ultimate vocabulary, as seen from the standpoint of a "sociology of knowledge" it becomes but one step, however important, in the development from the overemphasis and underemphasis of partiality towards a perfectly balanced vocabulary which the systematic use of rhetorical and dialectical operations has wholly discounted for partisanship.

In one sense, "Utopias" are but a special case of ideologies. Specifically, the Utopian bias is progressive, futuristic, whereas the ideological bias is conservative or reactionary, designed to maintain a *status quo* or to reinstate an earlier social order. But Mannheim also seems to employ the term "ideology" in a more general sense, to include both kinds. This shifting of usage is made all the more necessary by the fact that changing historical conditions can change the function of a perspective, so that terms once progressive in their implications can become conservative. However, we would want to add our contention that, if you could analyze a structure of terms fully and closely enough, you should be able to discover by purely internal analysis when such a change in quality occurred, and you would not have to rely simply upon knowledge of the different uses to which the terms had been put in the two different eras.

But there may be another element hidden in the idea of Utopia, as it figures in Mannheim's book. There are good reasons to believe that this "sociology of knowledge" owes some of its appeal, above the general run of sociological works, to a wholly unsociological cause.

It grounds its analysis in the study of chiliastic doctrines, and for all
its unwieldiness it never quite loses the resonance of this mythic anecdote. We thus have more the *feel* of an ultimate order than would be
the case if the approach were strictly sociological. One can even discern
here the elements, broken and reassembled, of a Platonic dialogue.

As written by Plato, the work would probably have proceeded thus:
First, the setting up of several voices, each representing a different
"ideology," and each aiming rhetorically to unmask the opponents;
next, Socrates' dialectical attempt to build a set of generalizations that
transcended the bias of the competing rhetorical partisans; next, his
vision of the ideal end in such a project; and finally, his rounding
out the purely intellectual abstractions by a myth, in this case the
chiliastic vision. The myth would be a reduction of the "pure idea"
to terms of image and fable. By the nature of the case, it would be
very limited in its range and above all, if judged literally, it would be
"scientifically" questionable.*

But insofar as the Platonic dialogue lived up to its pretensions, the
bias of this concluding myth would be quite different from the bias of
the rhetorical partisans with which the discussion began. For the
myth should not have emerged until such rhetorical or ideological
bias had been dialectically transcended in terms of pure ideas. However, if you disregarded the steps by which the myth had been arrived
at, you might find implicit in it much the same partiality and partisanship as was explicitly present in the opening statements of opposing
"ideologies." The "myth" might then be said to represent a forward-
looking partisanship, in contrast with the backward-looking partisan-
ships of the "ideologies." And you could next scramble the elements
of the dialogue, seeking to get a new dialectic by a method that transcended the partiality of both the ideologies and the myth.

There would be this difference lurking at the basis of one's dialectic:
In the Platonic dialogue, the step from pure abstract ideas to imaginal
myth had been simultaneously a step down and a step up. It was a
step down, because it descended from the purity of abstractions to
the impurity of images   It was a step up, because it here introduced a
new level of motivation, motivation *beyond* the ideas, not present in
the dialectical reduction to pure ideas.

* In this chapter we are adapting for our purposes the account of Platonist
transcendence given in *The Myths of Plato,* by J. A. Stewart.

However, a motivational problem arises, if you treat the mythic motive as on a par with the ideological motives. For you find that, if your method for eliminating all such bias were successful, it would deprive society of its primary motive power. For though bias is false promise, it is promise. Hence, if you eliminate bias (illusion) from men's social motives, where do you find an equally urgent social motive? Such appears to be the nostalgic problem which Mannheim, in the thoroughness of his scrambled "Platonic dialogue," finally confronts. For he explicitly asks himself where the zeal of human effort would come from, if it were not for the false promises of our Utopias. And he asks this, even as he aims by scrupulous method to destroy the zeal of such false promises, or mythic Utopian illusions.

His attempt is all the more justified by the fact that myths are not usually approached through the initiatory discipline of a Platonic dialogue. And insofar as they are taken literally, they do function as ideologies, hence require the kind of discounting provided by a "sociology of knowledge." But if you apply the same sociological methods to eliminate the bias from both ideologies and myth, the success of your method would necessarily transcend a sociological motivation. The mythic motive would differ from the ideological motives only insofar as it could survive the elimination of false ideological motives. But by the method of discounting prescribed for the "sociology of knowledge," it could not survive.

This is not to say that we would find fault with a method of sociological discounting as such. There is a fallacy here only if sociology is expected to provide the ultimate ground of motivation. Thus, the "pro-ultimate" nature of the sociological vocabulary should be interpreted as indigenous to the nature of sociology itself, which cannot figure ultimate motives, and but brings us to the edge of them. At that point, myth may become necessary for figuring motives not sociological at all, hence not grounded in either sociological error or sociological knowledge. And whereas such myths should always be discounted for their biased application, in a formal dialectic their nature as biased translations can be formally recognized at the start.

To review, the steps were, in sum:

1. Mutual exposure of imperfect ideas (ideas bound to the sensory image).

2. Socratic transcending of this partiality.

3. Socratic summarizing vision of the pure idea.

4. Translation of the pure idea into terms of the mythic image.

5. Whereupon enters Mannheim, who proposes to develop a "sociology of knowledge" by treating the first and last steps as though they were of the same nature. Hence, he would perfect a method for discounting the limitations of both ("unmasking" their bias).

6. But:

The step from 3 to 4 had not merely been a translation downward (an incarnation of the "pure idea" into the conditions of the mythic image). For the arrival at the level of pure ideas had been in itself but a *preparation*. It had prepared the understanding to confront a motive which, being *beyond* ideas, would not lend itself to statement in ideas. Only by going from *sensory* images to ideas, then through ideas to the end of ideas, is one free to come upon the *mythic* image. True, such an ultimate motive would not be correctly stated in terms of image. But men have only idea and image to choose from. And the *disciplined arrival at the mythic image through the dialectical transcending of sensory images and the dialectical critique of ideas,* should be a protection against a merely literal interpretation of such a mythic image (as contrasted with the purely empirical or conceptual image that forms the positive ground of dialectical operations).

But though the mythic image had thus figured a motive beyond ideas of reason, in treating the ultimate mythic image as though it were in the same order with the competing ideologies you would find no further motivational element in it than you had found in the ideologies.

Or rather, the original qualitative distinction would now look at most like a distinction between forward-looking (Utopian) and backward-looking ideologies. Hence, insofar as you correct the bias of both ideology and myth (Utopia), you rob yourself of a motive. But of course, if the myth had been interpreted as *figuring a motive beyond the reach of ideology,* the motive of the myth would be felt to *lie beyond the motivational order treated in the competing ideologies.* Its motive would be "ultimate," as the motives of the ideologies were not. True: the fact is that the myths in their heyday *are* taken literally, without the preparatory discipline of Socratic criticism—and to this extent they do lend themselves to admonitory analysis as ideologies. But only a "philosophy of the myth" (and the Platonist dialectic might be called that) could reveal their true nature, in figuring a motive beyond sociological knowledge, a movement from and towards a real and ultimate universal ground.

"Mythic" Ground and "Context of Situation"

You may hold that there is no essential difference between sensory image and mythic image. And both may be treated merely as rhetorical reënforcements of ideas. Hence, all three would be "ideological," in the sense that, where they gain social currency in formal expression, they can be shown to represent the particular perspective of some more or less limited group, to sanction special interests in terms of universal validity. And Mannheim's treatment does seem to proceed on this basis.

However, if you take the Platonic form at face value, analyzing it simply in terms of dialectical structure, you find there an ultimate order whereby ideas would transcend sensory images, and mythic images would in turn transcend ideas. The final stage would be reached through a moral and intellectual development, through processes of discipline and initiation. Such formal preparation would enhance the persuasiveness of the doctrine; hence it requires our attention as a rhetorical device even where we distrust its claims.

In the sense that discursive reason is dialectical, the mythic image may be treated as figuring a motive that transcends reason. It may also make claims to be "religious," since it presumably represents man's relationships to an ultimate ground of motives not available for empirical inspection.

Various possibilities thus present themselves. We can get esthetic myths (in the Hart Crane manner), idealistic and autoerotic. And inasmuch as any "unconscious" motive can be equated with the divine (if only because both are beyond the realm of discursive reason), the "esthetic" myth can become a substitute for the "religious" myth.

We need not try to decide here the extent to which this confusion may be justified. Suffice it to note that, in accordance with many puns about weapons, a "mythic" figure of the "religious gunman" might stand for many ambiguous or "unconscious" sexual motives. Also, a recondite style could itself be simultaneously an "enigmatic" confession of guilt and a symbolic claim of preferment. This preferment would be "spiritual," as compared with hopes for strictly material advantage. And since public acceptance of the stylized and enigmatic confession would be a roundabout exoneration of the poet, there would be ethically motivated courtship here too. It is easy to see why any images thus rich in implications would be felt as transcendentally "mythical" rather than as nakedly sensory.

Thus, often now, with the esthetic myth, image may be taken to so transcend idea that the mere intrusion of idea is resented. Consider how many readers, for instance, have objected to the doctrine of beauty in the last stanza of Keats's "Ode on a Grecian Urn." Or recall the similar disgruntlement with the "moral" that terminates "The Rime of the Ancient Mariner." The resistance is probably due in large part to the fact that idea, rather than mythic image, becomes the final stage in the unfoldment. And other kinds of analysis are needed, to make such an "ultimate" acceptable.

As regards Keats's line, we have an uneasy hunch that it contains an "enigmatic" meaning. And this meaning, if we are right, could best be got by "joycing," that is, by experimentally modifying both "beauty" and "truth" punwise until one found some tonal cognates that made sense, preferably obscene sense, insofar as the divine service to beauty may, with a poet who has profoundly transformed the Christian passion into the romantic passion, be held in an *ecclesia super cloacam*. A combination of pudency and prudence has long prevented us from disclosing how we would translate this Orphic utterance. (However, to give an illustration of the method, we would say that *one* of the meanings we quickly discern in "beauty" is "body," while "truth" could be joyced meaningfully by a metathesis of two letters and the substitution of a cognate for one of the consonantal sounds.)

As for Coleridge's "moral": In his romantic surrender, complicated as it was by identification with his drug, there was a point at which he rescued himself repeatedly, by a purely moralistic effort, or perhaps we should say, more accurately, by a *moralizing* effort. While this was acutely true of him, we trust that it is somewhat true of everyone, though the esthetic conventions of romanticism have usually demanded that the rational recovery from an obsessive imagery must not itself be represented in the work, but must be left to take care of itself outside the work.

But obviously, no matter how "mythic" a reference to the "ultimate" ground may be, it itself arose out of a temporal ground, available to sociological description. In this sense, it may represent such local interests as are disclosed by the Marxist analysis of "ideological mystification." Or we can use the attenuated, neutralized variant of such an approach in Mannheim's perspectivism. Or for a still more generalized form of analysis, on the positive level, we can use the concept of "context of situation," as explained and developed in Bronislaw Malinowski's essay on "The Problem of Meaning in Primitive Languages" (published as a supplement in Ogden and Richards' *Meaning of Meaning*).

Here the relation between the verbal act and its nonverbal scene is stated in a still more generalized form than in the Mannheim book, because Malinowski's anthropological approach lays a greater stress upon the elements of tribal homogeneity as they affect language, whereas Mannheim is concerned rather with a sophisticated technique for transcending strong elements of discord within society. The beginnings of social diversification are visible enough in the tribal culture Malinowski is studying; and its modes of livelihood already have sufficient division of labor, with corresponding social distinctions, to call for the use of magic (mystification) as a rhetorical device for maintaining unity of action in diversity of role. But the stress here is upon the analysis of language in its wholly collective aspect, rather than from the standpoint of the parliamentary agon.

Malinowski is describing a problem he encountered when attempting an English translation of some texts assembled in the course of his research among Polynesian tribes of New Guinea: "magical formulae, items of folk-lore, narratives, fragments of conversation, and statements of my informants." He found that there was no direct dictionary equivalent for much of this material. Hence, instead of translating by "inserting an English word for a native one," he found it necessary to describe the customs, social psychology, and tribal organization that were implicit in a given utterance.

To generalize this requirement, he proposed the expression, "context of situation" which, he says, indicates

> on the one hand that the conception of *context* had to be broadened
> and on the other that the *situation* in which words are uttered can
> never be passed over as irrelevant to the linguistic expression.

Malinowski applies the term to living, primitive, spoken languages, in contrast with the written documents of dead classical languages, where the records are "naturally isolated from any context of situation." For he holds that such documents are written "for the express purpose of being self-contained and self-explanatory." But we have already considered both Benthamite and Marxist concerns with such situational elements, even in sophisticated recorded utterance. And in a previously mentioned essay on "Rhetoric in the Middle Ages," Richard McKeon writes:

> When Peter Abailard assembled apparently contradictory texts in his *Sic et Non,* the rules for interpreting them which he set forth in the Prologue are developments of the rules elaborated by a long line of canon lawyers . . . and involve such directions as careful consideration of context, comparison of texts, specification of time, place, and person, determination of original cause of statement, differentiation of general measures from particular. Although this method led to a further step in the dialectical resolution of the contradictions, the method at this stage is rhetorical rather than dialectical.

Such canons of rhetorical discounting are obviously also concerned with extraverbal circumstances, as they figure in even formal and recorded utterance. They are the equivalent in scholastic terms for what Malinowski considers in anthropological terms; and they indicate wherein the principle of "context of situation" may apply to all linguistic expression.

Malinowski's anthropological (or ethnological) treatment of the matter is valuable as a kind of "scientific anecdote" for illustrating in the most general way the relation between verbal act and nonverbal scene. And since he is studying language as used pragmatically in primitive speech "to produce an action and not to describe one," his discussion is particularly useful for pedagogical purposes, to illustrate generally the rhetorical element in speech (as the Ogden and Richards chapter on "The Power of Words" does likewise).

All such rhetorical concerns with the extraverbal circumstances of a verbal act, treated as an aspect of its meaning, are in the positive order of vocabulary, and have their grounding in the conditions of sensory experience (the realm of sensory images and concepts). But they also deal with relations and situations—and since these often require highly rationalized interpretations, we here move towards the dialectical order. The various systematized theories as to just what important relationships and situations there are, particularly in the social and political realm, confront one another as competing orators, hence requiring either dialectical compromise or dialectical resolution by reduction to an ultimate order.

Also, it is worth noting that there is a technical sense in which any ground, not only the mythically ultimate, but even the positivistically sociological, could be treated as "transcending" the verbal act itself. For it is other-than-words—hence even a positivistic reduction of it must contain "mythic" elements to the extent that all verbal accounts are but "suggestive." Add now to this mystery of the unspeakable, the mystery symbolically engendered (when nature is perceived, for instance, through the hierarchic psychosis of the prevailing social order, which causes the things of nature to become emblematic of promises and deprivations not intrinsic to nature but derived secondarily from the relationships of property).

But though such considerations are needed when we begin to ask ourselves in what respects even the most purely pragmatic aspects of technology may be "mythic," we cannot be so exacting for ordinary purposes. Roughly, we could say that the Mannheim project for a sociology of knowledge seems representative of the ways in which modern liberal science would aim at the transcending of "ideology." And for purposes of illustrating the nature of rhetoric, without "invidious" attempt to decide which is better, we can contrast it with the method in a Platonic dialogue (taken as representative of the dialectical progress from rhetorical partisanship to resolution in an ultimate order). A "science" of social relations, to approach positive truth, would note the correlation between ideologies and positive terms designating the non-verbal conditions which the ideologies serve. It would strive thus to advance from opinion (rhetoric) to knowledge (considered as antithetical to rhetoric). And one might afterwards introduce a kind of rhetoric in the sense that vivid, appealing exposition (Cicero's *docere*) could be called rhetorical.

The dialectical method would also be rhetorical in this sense. But we may note its use of other rhetorical elements likewise: First, there is the rhetoric of the dramatic agon, the clash of the partisan rivals, each of whom seeks to overthrow the others; next, there is the rhetorical appeal of the dialectical resolution, the formal satisfaction that comes of transcending such conflicts by systematic means; and finally, there is the rhetoric of *enargeia,* as the New Vision, which transcended imagery, is reduced to terms that "bring it before our very eyes" (though clarity in this sense is not quite the same as the clarity of scientific exposition, since it would involve the use of a "mythic" image for figuring a motive beyond the realm of the empirical, whereas scientific exposition would use imagery but to make empirical knowledge itself more vivid).

For purposes of rhetorical analysis, we need not choose between these methods. We need only note just wherein the difference between them would lie, just how the rhetorical and dialectical ingredients operate in each. Furthermore, one cannot always expect to find the two thus so strictly opposed; any rounded statement of motives will probably have something of both, as we tried to indicate when considering the possible rhetorical function of the chiliastic anecdote in Mannheim's book.

Courtship

By the "principle of courtship" in rhetoric we mean the use of suasive devices for the transcending of social estrangement. There is the "mystery" of courtship when "different kinds of beings" communicate with each other. Thus we look upon any embarrassment or self-imposed constraint as the sign of such "mystery." Quite as Sappho's poem on the acute physical symptoms of love is about the *magic* of love (the beloved is "like a god"), so we interpret any variants, however twisted or attenuated, of embarrassment in social intercourse as sign of a corresponding mystery in communication.

If a woman of higher social standing ("a woman of refinement") were to seek communion by profligate abandonment among the "dregs of society," such yielding in sexual degradation could become in imagination almost mystical (a thought that suggests, from another approach, the strong presence of the Czarist hierarchy in Dostoevski's mysticism of the people). And a writer who gave particularized descriptions of sexual yielding under such conditions might fascinate in a way that mere "pornography" could not. The work might be prosecuted as pornography; but it would really embody (roundabout and in disguise) much the same rhetorical element as shapes the appeal of Shakespeare's *Venus and Adonis* (which treats of a hot-and-cold relation between persons of different classes, here figured as divine and mortal, while the real subject is not primarily sexual lewdness at all, but "social lewdness" mythically expressed in sexual terms).

The thought makes one glimpse the possibility of hierarchic motives lurking behind forms of censorship that would supposedly prohibit only *sexual* indecency while permitting the free expression of *political* attitudes. And recalling the Puritan attitude towards the licentious manners of Restoration drama, we can question whether any revolutionary *political* cause can possibly get its full expression unless corresponding variants of it in *sexual* terms are likewise developed.

Ironically, since censorship, if given time enough, invariably defeats its ends, the damming of a revolutionary expression sexually may greatly contribute to the sturdiness of its expression politically. In this respect, for instance, consider Wilhelm Reich's gradual turn from Communist sympathies to ideas of "sexual revolution" that led him to renounce Marxist politics as reactionary. His comparative immunity as a "scientist" permitted him to avoid the laws here as Henry Miller's engaging "pornography" could not, though Miller got the same immunity by publishing in English in France. Both men might be taken as evidence of the ways in which concentration upon "sexual revolution" can weaken the fervor of political revolution. But the political implications of sexual imagery would not stop at this point. For, in a subtler sense, all such terminologies may contribute ultimately to the same broad social and political changes.

But returning to the factor of embarrassment, we could say that any kind of "stage fright" is evidence of social mystery. Thus the coy relations between performer and audience show endless variants of mystification. Consider Thomas Mann's "Death in Venice" or "Mario and the Magician," for instance. And the paradigm perhaps would be the courtship of the *Arabian Nights* sort, where the narrator and author, across their social gulf, have a kind of fascination for each other. (Was there ever a culture where the powers of magic were more clearly associated with social hierarchy than the Arabian?) In "Death in Venice" the artist-audience relation is subtly interwoven with courtship between youth and age as classes; in "Mario and the Magician" the social mystery has strongly political connotations.

A ruler who would put people at their ease would do so at his cost, unless he could still somehow manage to glow in the light of his office, being at once both a "good fellow" and "standoffish." (Falstaff's relations to Prince Henry derive piquancy from the subtle intermingling of these two principles.) And we know of teachers who, assigned to interview students, have not been above exploiting the "mystery" (of the class distinction between teacher and taught) by maintaining an awesome silence, except for brief oracular questions that seem to be probing into the very depths of things, until the disconcerted student strives uneasily to fill every gap in the conversation, and comes away thinking this has been an audience with the Buddha. If one has little to say, by this device he can give the impression of leaving whole volumes unsaid.

"Glamour" is now a term, in the world of publicity, for mystery. And recalling the rigid mysteries of caste that seem essential for infusing free people with rigidly militaristic motives, we glimpsed the scope of the term in one political dopester's assertion that, with General Eisenhower's refusal to run for the presidency, the campaign had lost much of its "glamour." *

On the subject of post-hypnotic suggestion, it is said that people can be hypnotically induced to commit minor offenses after they have awakened (as were the hypnotist to suggest that the hypnotized, after coming out of the hypnotic spell, slap a certain person's face when the phone rings, an injunction that the patient might carry out in obedience to the suggestion, possibly even offering some attempt at a rational explanation for his behavior). But the patient's resistance to such suggestions increases with the gravity of the offense, so that the suggestion to commit highly reprehensible things, such as murder, would not be followed. Now, army discipline must be strong enough in its suggestiveness to produce a kind of "post-hypnotic spell" wherein people will do even the vilest of things, if they have been so commanded. Of course, the sanction of conspiracy helps in this task somewhat. But the conspiracy itself

---

* It is worth dwelling on the meanings of this term, for they clearly indicate an instinctive popular recognition of a hierarchic motive that affects the very nature of perception, endowing objects with a radiance due to their place in the social order. According to Webster's, the word may be a corruption of "gramarye," which means necromancy, magic. (The relation between grammar and magic doubtless goes back to the days when the knowledge of reading and writing was in itself a strong mark of status, because of the cleric's role in civil and religious administration.) The word is also thought to be connected with an Icelandic word for weakness of sight, while Icelandic *glamr* is a name for the moon, and of a ghost. Four meanings for "glamour" are given: a charm affecting the eye, making objects appear different from what they are; witchcraft, magic, a spell; a kind of haze in the air, causing things to appear different from what they really are; any artificial interest in, or association with, an object, through which it appears delusively magnified or glorified.

cannot attain its full magic unless strongly reënforced by the mystery of caste, particularly in the case of a regular army, where the lower ranks have no strong political cause to motivate their actions, but are guided primarily by the *esprit de corps* as manifested in the commands of their superiors.

Thus we doubt whether there is anything but deception in the idealistic hope of having a "democratic" army that would dispense with the offensiveness of military caste. Caste *is* the motive of military discipline as such. Without caste, one might fight for a good cause. But such would not be the motive of the army man as such. The true army man fights when he is told. It is the "glamour" of caste alone that makes him ready to subordinate his will to the will of an institution. Thus, army men will constantly sabotage attempts to "democratize" the army; for an army is in essence not democratic, but Prussian, and they instinctively know it. (We should also recognize the morality of the many purely technical operations here, as with the occupational hierarchy needed for flying a large plane. But though these modes of activity are not essentially military at all, they require a kind of organization that makes them a distressingly perfect fit with the military pattern.)

The Mannheim book we have reviewed seems to pass over the rhetoric of courtship. But can we think of the hierarchic (bureaucratic) structure necessary for teaching scientific method and managing a scientific society, without finding there the conditions for a "rhetorical situation" that requires some "bourgeois," "socialist," or "technocratic" variant of courtliness? Mannheim thinks of intellectuals as a special class whose intellect is their capital. And having ignored the peculiarly Marxist analysis of mystification, Mannheim was not led to ask whether the division of labor, in making for occupational classes, might by the same token create the need for a rhetoric of courtly intercourse between these classes. Mannheim was as eager to overlook such possibilities as Marx was to deny them.

Mannheim seems to assume that a gradually perfected sociology of knowledge would *pari passu* eliminate the mystery of Teufelsdröckh's "Clothes." (We are improvising, since the subject is not discussed.) But at least insofar as the sociological discounting of partisan ideologies fell short of perfection, we assume that there would still be a need for the traditional function of rhetoric. Rhetoric remains the mode of appeal essential for bridging the conditions of estrangement "natural" to society as we know it (be it primitive, feudal, bourgeois, or socialist), with its reliance upon the devices of magic, pantomime, clothes, or pastoral.

Here again, in case you are abolitionist-minded, you can choose to maintain that such rhetoric would end if the "reign of natural science" were fully established. We cannot agree with you, particularly in view of the scientific mystery fiction that is vigorously on the rise. But agreement about the future is not necessary for the analysis of rhetoric as such. It is sufficient for our purposes to note the presence of mystery in works actually written, on the assumption at the very least that there would be a "strong tendency" for such modes of social intercourse to creep undetected into even the ideal "mystery-less" scientific society, unless men exercised a constant antirhetorical vigilance that would likewise call for exactly the same kind of inquiry as we are here undertaking. Believe, if you will, that social classes will be "abolished." Even so, at least grant that there will be a constant "temptation" for them to again arise. And insofar as there are such temptations, there are corresponding "temptations" to the rhetoric of "courtly intercourse" between classes.

"Socioanagogic" Interpretation of Venus and Adonis

For considering characteristic expressions of the courtly motive in literary works, Shakespeare's narrative poem, *Venus and Adonis,* is a good item to examine; for certain oddities in it, as a story of *sexual* courtship, make its implicit *social* identifications more available to our scrutiny.

What are the main elements to which we should reduce this poem of courtship? First, a sexually mature goddess ardently courts a sexually immature human male. He resists, saying that he is interested only in the hunt. However, the alternatives are not so great as they might at first seem. For he says, "I know not love . . . nor will not know it, unless it be a boar, and then I chase it"—and the boar's fatal attack upon him is described in imagery of love, thus:

> He ran upon the boar with his sharp spear,
> Who did not whet this teeth at him again,
> But by a kiss thought to persuade him there;
> And nuzzling in his flank, the loving swine
> Sheath'd unaware the tusk in his soft groin.

If, following the poet's leads, we treat the hunt and its hazards as a form of courting too, we find three major characters in this dramatic narrative, each of them at a different qualitative stage in the hierarchy of motives: a goddess ("sick-thoughted Venus"), a human ("rose-cheek'd Adonis" ... "the tender boy"), and an animal ("this foul, grim, and urchin-snouted boar"). Would it then be excessive to say that each of these major figures in the action is of a different "class"?

There are two subsidiary characters, the "breeding jenny" and Adonis' "trampling courser." At the very least they serve a vital rhetorical function: they amplify the theme of courtship, repeating it by analogy, as Venus' ardor is duplicated in the stallion's. They also provide a dramatic comment, since their relationship contrasts Adonis' real coldness with the mare's coy eagerness (which is described in terms of human coquetry, as "outward strangeness" that only "seems unkind"). Perhaps we already have enough to account for the episode of the "palfrey's" courtship, particularly if we add a matter of mere business, that the loss of his horse makes it more explainable why Adonis, despite his disgruntlement, does not leave while Venus is wearying him with her attentions.

However, there may be more here. For Adonis and his horse may be considered parts of one motivational cluster; and Venus, as the principle of love, must be acting upon the mare, and through the mare, even though her suit of Adonis is frustrate. This amorous horse is an "unback'd breeder"—and a horse's power is not under completely rational control if it has escaped from its human master, and in erotic ardor will not obey him. At the very least we might say that the narrative here acts out a metaphor, is a figure for unbridled passion. Or, assuming still more accuracy in the poem's symbols, we might ask whether Adonis' horse, as proxy for Adonis, can be so zestful precisely because he has escaped from his master (the important clue here being in the stanza where he "breaketh his rein"). Then the moral could be: In the total cluster of motives comprising both Adonis and his horse, there is a heterosexual ardor that is lacking to Adonis alone. And this ardor is present only when the animal appetites alone are active, having escaped from such influences as would characterize the motives of the horse's human ("rational") master.

What, then, might be the motives that deterred Adonis with regard to the goddess, in contrast with the horse's eagerness to join with a mare?

At the sounds indicating that the hunt has begun, Venus in her fear for Adonis' safety runs through the bushes

> Like a milch doe, whose swelling dugs do ache,
> Hasting to feed her fawn hid in some brake.

And previously Venus had said to him,

> I'll be a park, and thou shalt be my deer;
> Feed where thou wilt, on mountain or in dale:
> Graze on my lips, and if those hills be dry,
> Stray lower, where the pleasant fountains lie.

Similarly, elsewhere he yields to her caresses "like the froward infant still'd with dandling."

The maternal connotations of these figures, along with the many establishing Adonis as "unripe," give one cause to believe that, so far as concerns the male motives *underlying* the conception of this poem, Venus is to Adonis as mother is to child. Hence, the boy's appetites are centered upon a kind of venery better suited to the "incest tabu." And he acts in accordance with the traditional shifts between the courting of women and the hunting of game. (Consider, for instance, the heart-hart pun near the opening of *Twelfth Night;* or we might note a doctrinal equivalent for this conceit in Rousseau's tract on education, where he advises that Emile's early sexual stirrings be quieted and deflected by the hunt; and in *Sir Gawain and the Green Knight,* to the quest of game and of woman the appetite for food is added, so that, though courtship is spiritualized beyond possibility of sensual fulfillment, there is compensation in the avid pursuit of quarry and the gorgeous banqueting.)

A failure to make the dissociation between the two "kinds" of woman (maternal and erotic) could account for the vaguely homosexual terms that define Adonis' relation to the boar. (The terms are not unmistakably homosexual; for they occur in outcries of Venus, who might properly be expected to take a feminine view of the male's erotic motives.) We have already quoted the most explicit passage of this sort, which might even allow for orgastic connotations of dying (the *Liebestod* ambiguity), as Adonis' groin fatally becomes a sheath for the boar's tusk. If this interpretation is correct, Adonis' death would include, in the one symbol, a guilty yielding and the tragic retribution (such merging of opposites as makes for the most effective kind of symbol), while the death would further serve as tragic dignification of the guilty "cause." Also, we could explain why Adonis' horse, as proxy for Adonis, by lacking some of Adonis' rational or heady motives could be completely heterosexual in his appetites, whereas Adonis was not. The homosexual motive and the problem of the mother would be part of a single moral complex in Adonis; but this complex would not bind the appetites when they have only their riderless, or headless simplicity, as in the horse.

However, our major concern is to discuss the poem in terms of *hierarchy*—and we have considered the mother-son implications merely to get them recognized and cleared away, lest their unformulated presence keep the reader from following another line of explanation. We want now to develop from the observation that goddess, boy, and boar represent three different motivational *classes*.

Recall again Spinoza's seminal formula, *Deus sive Natura*. Here, by a grammatical function, the conjunction "or," Spinoza provides a bridge between two realms of motives. Similarly Carlyle used an image for such a function, his figure of "Clothes," which served to make a communicative bridge between reverence for the divine and reverence for secular highness. Considering the two realms, with or without pontification, we can note these various terminological possibilities: terms in the celestial order alone; terms in the social order alone; terms that avowedly bridge the two realms; terms explicitly celestial but implicitly social; terms explicitly social but implicitly celestial; terms speciously social but actually celestial; terms speciously celestial but actually social. The last five could all be treated as variants of the bridging principle (which is, under another guise, the principle of *identification*).

The "celestial" here need not be a very high order of godhead. Any term for supernatural motivation (be it justified or not) would meet the requirements. Thus we could include under this head even the "preternatural" figures, Peter Quint and Miss Jessel, that symbolize the "spirit" of the motivation in Henry James's ghost story, "The Turn of the Screw." And especially, in accordance with our previous consideration of "mystery" and "mystification," we should be on the lookout for occasions when expressions for motives on their face "divine" are better explained as stylizations of motives belonging to the social hierarchy.

And would not the Venus of Shakespeare's *Venus and Adonis* be better explainable in social terms than theologically? Though she is nominally a goddess courting a mortal, no one would think seriously of reading the poem as he might read a mystic nun's account of courtly intercourse between her and the Celestial Bridegroom, nor as theologians interpret the Canticles. Venus is not a "goddess" in any devout sense. She is a distinguished person compelled to demean herself by begging favors of an inferior. Viewing the poem from this standpoint, judging by its courtly style, and getting stray hints through its imagery, we would take the underlying proportion to be: goddess is to mortal as noblewoman is to commoner. The "divine" attributes here are but those of social preferment. This would be a "fustian" goddess, though she stands somewhat "enigmatically" for an aspect of noble status in general rather than for any particular noblewoman.

We do not intend to plead for a set of perfect correspondences, based on this substitution of social superiority for "divinity." If hard pressed, one could work out such an interpretation. Venus would stand for the upper class, Adonis for the middle class, the boar for the lower classes (as seen through middle-class eyes using courtly spectacles). The horses might represent the potent aspect of the middle class, though ambiguously noble (like all love-making, because of its "divine" elation). The figure of the boar could, roundabout, identify the lower classes with the dregs, with moral evil. In this particular poem the boar (hence the lower classes) could be the evil embodiment of the homosexual offense that seems involved in Adonis' unresponsiveness. Or it could stand for offensiveness generally; and in accordance with the usual workings of the scapegoat mechanism, offensiveness which is situate within is hunted without, so that there is odd intercourse between hunter and hunted. We say so much, to show how a "socioanagogic" interpretation might be filled out, if one were hard pressed.

But we would settle for much less. We would merely contend that one should view this poem in terms of the hierarchic motive, or more specifically, in terms of the *social order,* as befits any inquiry into the rhetoric of *courtship.* Whereupon we should lay much stress upon the notable inversion whereby a superior is depicted begging favors of an inferior. And we would not let the brilliance of the erotic imagery blind us to the underlying pattern here, a pattern in which the erotic enigmatically figures, but which "in principle" is not erotic at all, at least in the narrowly sexual sense of the term. (Our stand would be different if you widened the term to include dialectical motives in general, a realm of ultimate principle, as with the Socratic erotic.)

Looking at the poem "socioanagogically," we would now lay stress upon lines that might otherwise be lost beneath the imagery of ardent wooing. Thus, we note that Adonis is "forc'd to content, but never to obey." Or Venus says,

> What bargains may I make, still to be sealing?
> To sell myself I can be well contented,
> So thou wilt buy and pay and use good dealing.

Or when she forebodingly sees the hounds bleeding from their encounter with the boar,

> Look, how the world's poor people are amaz'd
> At apparitions, signs, and prodigies,
> Whereon with fearful eyes they long have gaz'd,
> Infusing them with dreadful prophecies;
>> So she at these sad sighs draws up her breath,
>> And, sighing it again, exclaims on Death.

Venus is here belittled astronomically, a "goddess" looking at premonitions of Adonis' death like "the world's poor people" staring at the heavens. The passage continues a theme of apotheosis (with Adonis meteorologically exalted) that was introduced at the moment when Adonis finally abandoned her. Coleridge made much of the passage, Richards reminds us, as an instance of "imagination":

> Look, how a bright star shooteth from the sky,
> So glides he in the night from Venus's eye.

Here is signalized a New Order, in which not Venus but Adonis is celestial. The passive superiority he had possessed, in his indifference to her, here blazes into an act. His cult of acquisition (as huntsman) is raised to the very heavens.

To see such developments as dominantly sexual is indeed to be sex-ridden. Rather, one should scrutinize them for certain *principles* of courtship, a *social* manifestation, which by the same token figures a *hierarchic* motive. The vocabularies of social and sexual courtship are so readily interchangeable, not because one is a mere "substitute" for the other, but because sexual courtship is intrinsically fused with the motives of social hierarchy.

Thus, when this poem is viewed "socioanagogically," it will be seen to disclose, in enigmatically roundabout form, a variant of revolutionary challenge. By proxy it demeans the old order, saying remotely, in sexual imagery, what no courtly poet could have wanted to say, or even have thought of saying, in social or political terms. Yet as evidence that the poet had such qualified reversals on his mind, note how the work ends, on Venus' prophecy of a topsy-turvy world where love (among its other turbulent conditions)

. . . shall be sparing and too full of riot,
Teaching decrepit age to tread the measures;
The staring ruffian shall it keep in quiet,
Pluck down the rich, enrich the poor with treasures;
 It shall be raging mad and silly mild,
 Make the young old, the old become a child.

It shall be cause of war and dire events,
And set dissension 'twixt the son and sire;
Subject and servile to all discontents,
As dry combustious matter is to fire. . . .

Granted: We here come upon paradoxes that lead back into ultimate problems of motives, rooted in situations beyond or prior to social hierarchy. The indeterminately dialectical and natural grounds whereby certain motives readily become convertible (as with relations between love and the hunt, or between sexual appetite and food) seem to be epitomized in the transformations of Venus, as with the antinomian yet intimate relation between love and war. (In the poem the principles are sexualized, as a marriage between Venus and Mars, a love match that is itself a kind of war, as Venus says that Mars was "servile" to her "coy disdain.") We grant that the motivation behind the reversals on which the poem ends could not be exhaustively discussed in terms of social order alone. Yet the ultimate motives, whatever they may be, get poignancy and direction from the social order (that is, from the social hierarchy), so far as the medium of their formal artistic expression is concerned. And we may fittingly note that the poem does not arrive at this prophecy of upheaval until Adonis has died for his affront (an affront which, while involving a principle of social reversal, was stated in terms suited to a pre-Reichian kind of "sexual revolution").

In his *De Vulgari Eloquentia,* Dante selects love, valor, and welfare (*Venus, Virtus, Salus*) as the three themes worthy of heroic verse. Clearly this poem, though somewhat perversely, meets Dante's requirements. Perhaps all three could be reduced to some one recondite ultimate term. But as regards social motives, note that the poem hinges about a question of pride. The jenney (in this poem the paradigm of a woman wooed normally, as judged by courtly standards of those times) is "proud, as females are, to see him woo her." The palfrey, having broken loose, was "proud" in his freedom from the master's constraint. Such pride obviously reflects fluctuant relations of inferiority and superiority (con-

cerns the hierarchic motive, quite as in the myths of the celestial revolt).
Thus, subtly, if you grant that her "divinity" is more social than celestial,
Venus has been unsexed, that is, outclassed. The class she represents
has given up its austere status. Its courtly devices have become suspect.
Adonis says to her, "I hate not love, but your device in love."

We do not assume that the poem's concealment of a social allegory in
a sexual enigma was consciously contrived. True, scholars who favor
the "fustian" theory are tirelessly examining pure poetry for evidence of
disguised allusions to prominent contemporary personages. But even
where such allusions were deliberately inserted by poets and discerned
by readers, such tactics would not argue deliberateness in the sort of expression we are here studying. These identifications can be implicit, and
"unconscious."

To get at the sort of thing we are here considering, one must first reject
all speculations in keeping with the typical empiricist question: "What
do I see when I look at this object?" A poetic observation involves no
naked relation between an observed object and the observer's eye. The
topics that the poet uses are "charismatic." They glow. You may argue
that the medievalist was wrong when he anagogically interpreted the
poet's image as a concealment that enigmatically figured the mysteries
of the celestial hierarchy. But by combining Marx and Carlyle, with
hints from Empson, we should at least see how right the medievalist
was in his conviction that the poet's symbols *are* enigmatic, that they
stand for a *hidden* realm, a *mystery* (though its "divinity," like that of
the Roman Emperor or "Pontifex Maximus" of a secular realm, may be
derived from a social hierarchy).

Even the world of natural objects, as they figure in poetry, must have
secret "identification" with the judgments of status. (Thus, music and
leisure by the sea are profoundly mood-laden, bringing as they do the
culminations of social order to confront the abyss of an ultimate order.)
The veil of Maya is woven of the strands of hierarchy—and the poet's
topics glow through that mist. By "socioanagogic" interpretation we
mean the search for such implicit identifications. Though admitting
that one can go far wrong in the particular here, we would insist that
such analysis is demanded "in principle." The poet's symbol *is* enigmatic, and its enigma *does* derive from its bearing upon "mystery," which
in turn is a hierarchic experience, as thinkers in the strongly hierarchized
middle ages clearly understood. Marxists today, when under a cloud,

call their criticism "sociological," thus fusing it with a modern liberalist science.   But what of the relations to an earlier medieval pattern of thought, polemically rediscovered in Marx's theory of "mystification"? "Socioanagogic" interpretation would seem to be the name for the Marxist insight, if one sought a "neutral" approach midway between Marx's rage against "mystification" and Carlyle's adulation of "mystery."

The four medieval kinds of interpretation are defined in the first question, articles eight and nine, of Aquinas' *Summa Theologica,* where Aquinas distinguishes three "spiritual" meanings in addition to the literal meaning. The literal meaning of Scripture is not in the figure, but in that which is figured. For instance, with a metaphor like "God's arm," the literal sense would be "God's operative power." Of the three spiritual senses: Insofar as the Old Law is said by Christians to figure the New Law, the interpretation of the Old Testament becomes "allegorical"; insofar as the acts of Biblical persons are said to provide a model of conduct for all men, the sense is "moral" or "tropological"; and the sense is anagogical insofar as the things of Scripture "signify what relates to eternal glory."

Since we are looking for elements of "social mystery" rather than of "celestial" mystery, hence our term, "socioanagogic." The new equivalent of "moral" or "tropological" criticism would probably be found in a concern with the poem as a ritual that does things for the writer and reader: re-forming, stabilizing, heartening, purifying, socializing, and the like. Any sense in which one order is interpreted as the sign of another would probably be the modern equivalent of the "allegorical." For instance, our psychoanalytic interpretation of Venus as mother; or a flat equating of Venus, Adonis, and the boar with three different social classes. Allegorical and moral senses lead into the socioanagogic insofar as the emphasis is placed upon the hierarchic mystery (the principle of secular divinity, with its range of embarrassment, courtship, modified insult, standoffishness, its possible meteorological dignifications, its scenic embodiment in the worldly equivalent of temples, ritual vestments, rare charismatic vessels, and the like). In brief, the socioanagogic sense notes how the things of books and of the book of Nature "signify what relates to worldly glory."

The scholastics had this jingle for distinguishing the four senses:

> *Littera gesta docet; quid credas allegoria;*
> *Moralis quid agas; quo tendas anagogia.*

The notion of trend, tendency, direction as the distinctive element of the anagogic in itself suggests how the concept of anagoge could be secularized.

The Paradigm of Courtship: Castiglione

Perhaps the best text for our purposes is *The Book of the Courtier*, by Baldassare Castiglione, a contemporary of Machiavelli, and like him concerned with the principles of the Prince. By its gradations, it builds a ladder of courtship dialectically, into a grand design that, in its ultimate stage, would transcend the social mystery, ending Platonically on a mystic, mythic vision of celestial mystery. The work is usually studied as a handbook of manners, or book of etiquette, which had a strong influence on the courtly style of Elizabethan poets. But we would stress rather its nature as a series of formal operations for the dialectical purifying of a rhetorical motive. When viewed thus formally, it is seen to contain a range of persuasiveness usually found but in fragments. And by observing its various kinds of persuasion thus brought together in a unity, we can better detect their significance where they are found only in fragments.

The book tells of four dialogues that supposedly took place on four successive evenings at the Court of the Duke of Urbino, in 1507. The duke being absent, the conversations are held in the presence of the duchess. A dozen members of the court participate in the dialogue. At first they talk of discussing, as a "pastime," the "sweet disdains" that the lover suffers "in the person beloved"; but it is finally decided "to shape in words a good courtier, specifying all such conditions and particular qualities, as of necessity must be in him that deserveth this name."

The first book lists the major endowments which the perfect courtier must have. Here are such items as noble birth, good fortune, skill at arms, good horsemanship, gracefulness, ability to "laugh, dally, jest, and dance," to speak and write well, to play musical instruments (particularly since at court the women's "tender and soft breasts are soon pierced with melody, and filled with sweetness"); the courtier should also be accomplished in drawing and painting (one speaker remarks that in Greece painting had been "received in the first degree of liberal arts, afterwards openly enacted not to be taught to servants and bondmen").

Objections are raised to some of these points. For instance, one speaker having said that the courtier should consider arms the most important thing of all, with "the other good qualities for an ornament thereof," Cardinal Peter Bembo replies that arms and all other gifts should be considered "an ornament of letters," letters being "in dignity so much above arms, as the mind is above the body." Cardinal Bembo's position will come into its own at the end of Book IV. Meanwhile, we need note only that the courtier's endowments are preëminently those of *appeal* (to this extent being rhetorical in essence); and, in keeping, his prime motive is to be "glory," a strongly addressed motive, that seeks to live in the good opinion of others.

The first dialogue closes with "every man taking his leave reverently" of the duchess.

In the second book, the rhetorical motive becomes still more obvious. This chapter deals with the tactics of address, the art of appearing to best advantage. Thus, when the courtier is "at skirmish, or assault, or battle upon the land, or in such other places of enterprise," he should "work the matter wisely in separating himself from the multitude" Whatever "notable and bold feats" he does, he should undertake them "with as little company as he can, and in the sight of noble men that be of most estimation in the camp, and especially in the presence and (if it were possible) before the very eyes of his king or great personage he is in service withal; for indeed it is meet to set forth to the show things well done."

Note that in this way of bearing witness, the courtier's relation to his social superior is as martyr to God, as writer to public, as actor to audience. Much that now goes under the name of "exhibitionism" might thus be placed as a species of the rhetorical motive. We recall a related maxim in La Rochefoucauld: *"Les véritables mortifications sont celles qui ne sont point connues; la vanité rend les autres faciles."* La Rochefoucauld is explicitly contrasting the pure rhetoric of religious appeal with the mere appeal to vanity. Mortifications *must* be witnessed; they are évidence, presented to an invisible divine audience. Martyrdom (bearing witness) is so essentially rhetorical, it even gets its name from the law courts. However, it is vanity when addressed not to the Absolute Witness, but to human onlookers. Martyrdom would be but a severe kind of "epideictic oratory," were it not for the supernatural witness which it postulates (the Christian persuasion being so essentially a rhetoric, that Cicero's thoroughness in rhetoric made him seem essentially Christian).

La Rochefoucauld was discussing a rhetorical situation where the testimony supposedly addressed to a supermundane principle was in actuality addressed to the *haut monde*. But *The Book of the Courtier* is discussing testimony explicitly addressed to a worldly principle. (With regard to the way in which the two realms rhetorically impinge upon each other, making social and religious reverence interchangable, we might recall an editor's reference to an early English book on manners instructing the youth to kneel on one knee before their worldly sovereign, on both knees to God. And when Edmund Burke said that European civilization depended "upon two principles—the spirit of a gentleman and the spirit of religion," his statement suggests the possibility that these "two principles" can be one principle named in two different orders of vocabulary. It is the magical confusion that allows spontaneously for the rhetorical use of religion as an instrument of politics, in keeping with the frank paganism of the old feudal expression, "your Worship.")

We thus confront three kinds of address: bearing witness to God, bearing witness to the sovereign, bearing witness to one's peers under the guise of bearing witness to God. If you bring them all together, and think of "glory" as both heavenly and courtly motive, do you not see the rhetorical ingredient in "conscience" itself, exacting a kind of conduct addressed to the ideal spirit of the community?

Conformism and hypocrisy would also be species of persuasion, but addressed to an audience not conceived in terms sufficiently universalized. And where the criminal seems "unconsciously" willing to be caught, need we assume that a motive of self-punishment, obedience to a self-imposed criterion of justice, leads him to place himself in jeopardy? Such a motive may be present. But can there not also be a more general motive, hence one "logically prior"? For he could be moved mainly by the rhetorical motive *per se,* the desire to bear witness, to address an audience, so that his transgression is an act of "martyrdom," and as such must be seen.

In the crime mysteries of Hollywood, the hierarchic motive (the magic of class relations) is concealed behind the images of private property in general. The cult of property as such (exemplified in reverse by infractions against the code) sometimes obscures the particular nature of property as class insignia. But the shift, by means of money, from low dives to expensive apartments and night clubs, is the basic pattern, along with quarrels over the ownership of "classy dames," while there is much display of the sort Veblen noted, as in the "distinction" of being served obsequiously. Display is felt as action only because it is felt as "mystery."

Under technology the division of labor requires a society of specialists serving one another. The garage man is the dishwasher's servant, and the dishwasher is the garage man's servant, an "invidious" relation made "democratic" by money and by the constant reversal of roles. Recalling the festival of the Roman Saturnalia, where master and servant changed places, we could describe our democracy as a kind of permanent but minute Saturnalia, with constant reversal in the relation between up and down. This is a strongly "irreverent" situation, as regards the mysteries of caste, except in the most generalized sense, as with quantitative, monetary tests of "quality." And the Hollywood crime mystery seems to be an answer to these conditions, giving full expression to the "free" or wayward impulses that go with so fluctuant a hierarchy, while at the same time profoundly reënforcing the hierarchic code at its most essentially capitalist point, the mystery of money as insignia of class distinction.

(We have wandered far from *The Book of the Courtier*. But we introduced Castiglione's work as a paradigm precisely for that purpose. So we should take any opportunity to depart from it. We want to draw the lines of inference from a clear textual example into areas where the same elements, though present, are transformed in keeping with changed conditions. Hence, we look to see what might be the equivalents of the courtly, or hierarchic relation in other modes of expression not usually considered in such terms. We can thus discern the presence of the same rhetorical, courtly motive in many varied transformations that on their face may seem disrelated; yet we need not say that they are all the same, since the very act of bringing them together helps make us aware of their specific differences.)

Returning to the dialogue itself, we should note that at this stage, in Book II, it is concerned mainly with courtly ways of appearing to good advantage. Thus, one speaker questions the propriety of wrestling with men of low social status, for if the man of noble rank wins, his gain is small, "and his loss in being overcome very great." There are warnings against too incessant a display of one's talent, as with those who, if they are good at music, speak as though they were on the verge of breaking into song, or as when you meet a fencer in the market place and he greets you with "a gesture as though he would play at fence." A useful ironic device is suggested for a courtier wearing a mask. Let him disguise himself as someone of inferior rank, such as an uncouth shepherd; then, if he performs superbly on horseback, the show will be doubly effective, since the horseman so greatly outstrips the expectations of the onlookers. The courtier is exhorted "to love and (as it were) to reverence the prince he serveth above all other things, and in his will, manners and fashions, to be altogether pliable to please him." (The transference of this principle from the courtier-sovereign relation to the relation between the courtier and world's judgment generally, is seen in the injunction "to use continually, and especially abroad, the reverence and respect that becometh the servant toward the master.")

The courtier is warned against asking favors for himself directly, lest they either be denied or, what is worse, granted with displeasure. And one eager "to purchase favor at great men's hands" should not "press into the chamber or other secret places where his Lord is withdrawn"; for when great men are alone, they often "love a certain liberty to speak and do what they please," and may resent being surprised. And if the courtier, engaged in important matters for his lord, happens to be "secretly in chamber with him," the courtier "ought to change his coat, and to defer grave matters till an other time and place," watching "that he be not cumbrous to him." The courtier should rather "look to have favor and promotion offered him, than crave it so openly in the face of the world, as many do." He should not be like those who, "if they happen to enter into favor, then passing a mean, they are so drunken on it, that they know not what to do for joy," and "are ready to call company to behold them, and to rejoice with them, as a matter they have not been accustomed withal." * For though a courtier should "esteem favor and promotion," he should not give the impression that he could not live without it, nor "show himself new or strange in it." On the other hand, he should not refuse it "as some, that for very ignorance receive it not, and so make men believe that they acknowledge themselves unworthy of it." The courtier should thus be neither too forward not too retiring but should always:

---

* We are quoting throughout from Sir Thomas Hoby's translation, but have modernized the spelling.

humble himself somewhat under his degree, and not receive favor and promotions so easily as they be offered him, but refuse them modestly, showing he much esteemeth them, and after such a sort, that he may give him an occasion that offereth them, to offer them with a great deal more instance.

The courtier should remember that favors and promotions, when received with modesty, seem to be more deserved—whereupon the speaker gives a Biblical parallel strong in hierarchic thought: "When thou art bid to a marriage, go and sit thee down in the lowest room, that when he cometh that bid thee, he may say, Friend come hither, and so it shall be an honor for thee in the sight of the guests." But we have cited enough to illustrate the "addressed" quality (hence the rhetorical element) in the courtier's ways, as they are treated in this opening section of Book II.

After a series of transitions, warning among other things against both rowdyism and the tendency to tell jokes at one's own expense, the chapter turns to another kind of address, making an almost systematic study of the things "which make men laugh," comic devices valued for their effect upon audiences (though no formal theater was needed since, in the pageantry of their self-absorbed society, the courtiers were audience for one another).

The cult of laughter is suited to the "courtly psychosis" on many counts: first, it is "liberal," befitting a class of freemen (the Rabelaisian motive); it is "humane," since only humans laugh (hence it is probably a function of "rationality," which confronts reality by the roundabout route of symbols). Impropriety can provoke laughter only because at one remove it reaffirms the very propriety it violates; and the explosive laughter of surprise is made possible by the sudden violation of expectancies—hence the "merry jest" could in a free way reaffirm the courtier's code. In displaying his sense of the "right" things to laugh at, the courtier thereby displayed the marks of his class. And in proving himself equal to the tests of merriment, he gave evidence that he was not being outclassed. While superiority to fools and boors draws strongly upon the hierarchic principle, it can readily couple such superiority with a sense of personal misgivings, through subterfuges whereby the laugher subtly identifies himself with the very victim to whom he is superior; for in laughter there can be a transcending of the distinction between laughing-at and laughing-with. Comedy is much more pronouncedly

addressed than tragedy, as is evident from the ease with which the come-
dian on the stage can take the audience into his confidence without
breaking the frame of the fiction, whereas in tragedy even an aside expressly inserted for the audience's benefit must be spoken rather as though
the actor were talking to himself.

The "invidious" element in laughter could deflect into less serious
channels all competition for the sovereign's favors. It could thus allow
for a kind of solidarity among the courtiers as a professional class. It
was like a fraternal meeting of business competitors, a commodity made
all the stronger when members of a lower class were chosen as butt of
the joke.

The discussion ends on the subject of the "merry prank," which we
are told relies on the same "places" as the jest for its effect. Boccaccio's
tales being cited as an example, we can thus glimpse behind them an
appeal not just as stories, but as a mark of rank. And once the hierarchic
relation is firmly established, the mystery can become so subtilized that,
as the duchess says, smiling:

> It is not against good manner sometime to use merry pranks with
> great men also. And I have heard of many that have been played
> to Duke Frederick, to King Alphonsus of Aragon, to Queen Isabel
> of Spain, and to many other great Princes, and not only they took
> it not in ill part, but rewarded very largely them that played them
> those parts.

Where the irreverence of laughter is thus directed against the very Principle of Courtly Favor itself, it must be so carefully qualified that it
signalizes reverence too—whereat the "sacrificial king" need not grow
wrathful to restore his dignity, but is grand in exercising with good
humor his powers of munificence.

The primary thing to note about *The Book of the Courtier,* from the
standpoint of dialectic, is the great change in the quality of motivation that occurs as one turns from the third book to the last. The third
book has some inklings of the final transcendence, since it deals with
the code of courtly intercourse between men and women. It thus introduces the theme of sexual love which Cardinal Bembo will platonically transform at the ecstatic, sermonlike close of the work. But
though there are occasional signs of a new stirring, in general men and
women here confront each other as classes, considering questions of
advantage, in a war of the sexes reduced to dance steps.

Book III begins with a recipe of traits deemed appealing in women, discusses such related matters as comparative prowess in feats of continence on the part of the two sexes; pathetic sorrow at loss of maidenhood due to forcing; situations that follow from the code of honor, one speaker saying, "in a thousand years I could not repeat all the crafts that men use to frame women to their wills"; and another, who has been complaining that women are cruel to him, is accused of using such complaints "as a certain kind of discretion," to "cloak the favors, contentations and pleasures" he had "received in love," and to assure other women that, if they reward him he will keep the secret. Among other things, the woman's code at court requires that, when invited to dance or play, like the courtier receiving favors, "she ought to be brought to it with suffering her self somewhat to be prayed"— and in innuendo, she should seem to miss the point.

In general, the chapter might have for its device this statement by Lord Cesar Gonzaga:

> Like as no Court, how great soever it be, can have any sightliness or brightness in it, or mirth without women, nor any Courtier can be gracious, pleasant or hardy, nor at any time take any gallant enterprise of Chivalry, unless he be stirred with the conversation and with the love and contentation of women, even so in like case, the Courtier's talk is most unperfect evermore, if the entercourse of women given them not a part of the grace wherewithall they make perfect and deck out their playing the Courtier.

And for the equating of love and war, we are told that "Who so could gather an army of lovers that should fight in the presence of the Ladies they love, should subdue the whole world, unless against it on the contrary part there were an other army likewise in love."

Through these first three books, though the quest of advantage has taken several forms, the motive of "reverence" has been kept within the realm of manners, as related to the sovereign and to the object of courtly sexual love. It has been manifested roundabout, through the perversities of the jest and the merry prank. And much has been said about the properties that make men and women appealing in courtly situations. We now turn to higher orders of persuasion. This fourth book is not less rhetorical than the other three. But the advantages to which it would persuade transcend those of the preceding chapters. Fittingly, the change in the quality of motives is signalized at the start of the last book by a deathy note. Though the talks were supposedly held on four successive nights, as the author prepares to write out the record of the fourth discourse a "bitter thought" causes him to remember "that not long after these reasonings were had, cruel death bereaved our house of three most rare gentlemen, when in their prosperous age and forwardness of honor they most flourished."

The device is perhaps borrowed from Cicero, who uses it similarly to make the final section of his *De Oratore* more solemn. The justification for it seems greater in this case (in accordance with the puns whereby finality can mean either purpose or demise), since this concluding book is to deal with "the end . . . of a perfect Courtier." It is to discuss the ultimate purpose of courtship. So, in introducing it with thoughts of great courtiers who have died, the author reënforces one kind of finality by topics belonging to the other kind (leads into the discussion of end in the philosophic sense through mention of end in the biologic sense). And we might even glimpse a subtler propriety in this opening talk of courtiers' deaths: henceforth the many variants of acquisitive advantage are to be abandoned for efforts more sacrificial.

Above the transitional matter, two themes stand out. The first concerns a rhetoric of *education,* considering the powers of the courtier as *informant* to the prince. In this context the courtier would be winsome for the advancement not of himself personally, but of human relations in general. He would seek ways whereby he can impart even unpalatable truths to his sovereign, "to dissuade him from every ill purpose, and to set him in the way of virtue," in contrast with those who, "to curry favor and to purchase good will," tell their lord only what he would most like to hear ("because among many vices that we see now a days in many of our Princes, the greatest are ignorance and self-liking," yet "there is no treasure that doth so universally hurt, as an ill Prince"). In sum: As the training in "pleasant fashions" is "the flower of Courtliness," so the fruit of it is in "the training and helping forward of the Prince to goodness, and the fearing him from evil."

For our purposes it is not necessary to consider the details of the argument, or even the theory of psychology that goes with it, beyond noting the customary identification of reason with authority: As reason rules over the affections of the body, so it "is chiefly requisite in Princes." The important consideration for our purposes is that this treatise on education grows out of the theories on courtship. Though, according to the hierarchic order in its perfection, the prince would rather be the exemplar for the courtiers, the unsettled nature of the times brought to the fore many princes new to the courtly tradition. Hence, the courtiers, as a special professional class, might find themselves in the role of educators to the prince, initiating him into the mysteries of their code. The situation is not unlike that of scientists today, who are hired to serve the interests of local financial or industrial sovereigns. As hirelings, they should be interested in the tactics of advancement; but as a class of scientific specialists, they represent, with varying degrees of honesty and obsequiousness, a purely professional interest in truth, not identical with the preferences of the "sovereign."

But there is a profounder connection here between courtship and education than derives from the accident of the times. It is an element inborn to the dialectic method itself, as we saw in the *Grammar* when considering the Socratic erotic, "loving" truth, beauty, and goodness pedagogically (a cult that had its variants of courtship, as with Socrates' gallantry when cajoling and enticing young men into the dialectical path of the Absolute).

The imagery of courtship in the Socratic education is to be interpreted mythically. Its primary motives are not positive, but dialectical. And education dialectically approached could not be reduced to sexual terms in the positivist sense. Nor, by the same token, could education dialectically approached be properly reduced to positivist terms of a mere job. It would have a mythic glow, as it would be a form of "pure persuasion," the rhetorical motive dialectically made ultimate. But it would gravitate about the imagery of courtship, since it would be a kind of courtship, as we can see in the *Phaedrus*. And variants of the same motive are seen in Castiglione's fourth book, where we are told that "to become the instructor of a Prince, were the end of a Courtier," quite as Aristotle and Plato "practiced the deeds of Courtiership, and gave themselves to this end, the one with the great Alexander, the other with the kings of Sicilia."

After the pages on the courtier as educator of the prince, by appropriate transitions the work rises to its exhilarating close, the oration by Cardinal Bembo, on Beauty as "an influence of the heavenly bountifulness." By the time the cardinal is finished, we have gone from the image of beauty to the pure idea of beauty (from sense to intellect);

we have united ideal beauty with truth, utility, and goodness; we have heard objections that "the possessing of this beauty which he praiseth so much, without the body, is a dream"; there has been talk of a transcendent insemination (putting the seeds of virtue into a mind, "the right engendering and imprinting of beauty in beauty," though the opposition claims that this should be done by "the engendering of a beautiful child in a beautiful woman"); a penetrating has been advised, but through eye and ear (the least sensual senses), and by the union of mouths, a bond called the "opening of an entry to the souls" (since an ecclesiastical orator is speaking, we may think of the oral as figuring not only the primary gratification of feeding, but also the vocation of prayer); imagination has been praised for its power to fashion "that beauty much more fair than it is in deed," to use perception of one beauty as a stair for climbing to a "universal conceit" for "meddling all beauty together"; then "by reason of the agreement that the fancies have with the body," even this stage must be transcended, until beauty is "seen only with the eyes of the mind," and the soul is turned "to the beholding of her own substance," which is angelic; whereupon the soul is kindled by the desire to partake of the heavenly nature, so that with images of burning, and mounting, and coupling, we end on a prayer to "the father of true pleasures, of grace, peace, lowliness, and good will," and on talk of hopes to "smell those spiritual savors," and of ultimate arrival through bodily death—whereat the cardinal pauses, "ravished and beside himself," having given to the others "a certain sparkle of that godly love that pricked him." It is discovered that the company has talked until dawn. And in contrast with our thoughts of journeys to the end of night, and our tracts foretelling a universal heat-death, "they saw already in the East a fair morning like unto the color of roses, and all stars voided, saving only the sweet Governess of heaven, Venus which keepeth the bounds of the night and day, from which appeared to blow a sweet blast, that filling the air with a biting cold, began to quicken the tunable notes of the pretty birds, among the hushing woods of the hills."

Is it not obvious why we could use this work as a paradigm, when looking for respects in which the rhetoric of persuasion leads dialectically to an ultimate of pure persuasion? The hierarchic principle of courtship sets a pattern of communication between "lower" and "higher" classes (or kinds). This can be universalized in terms of a climbing from body to soul, from senses through reason to understanding, from worldly to the angelic to God, from woman to beauty in general to transcendent desire for Absolute union. Or the communication may be between merely "different" kinds, where the relative grading is not established by general agreement. And, of course, when one analyzes a given case of such "courtship," one can also expect to find ambiguities whereby, even if a set scale is recognized, the roles become reversed, the superior in one respect becomes the inferior in another, or the superior must court the underling.

In making "beauty" both courtly and religious, *The Book of the Courtier* makes religion courtly, thereby "mystically" fusing social and religious "reverence." "Even as in the firmament the sun and the moon and the other stars show to the world (as it were) in a glass, a certain likeness of God: So upon the earth a much more liker image of God are those good Princes that love and worship him, and show unto the people the clear light of his justice." And by being so explicit in its way of advancing from a worldly to a celestial hierarchy, it gives us insight into situations where the "mystery of divinity" inspirits relations that, on their face, call for purely mundane motives.

Such an identification may be present in the man who cannot become a social rebel without becoming an atheist. And conversely, with some the cult of religion can be so grounded in class courtship that explicit instruction in the terms of theological hierarchy implicitly coaches obedience to one particular social hierarchy. Where such motives are formally denied (as with the pragmatic terminologies of technology, finance, and political administration), we are at least admonished to look for persuasive vestiges of them, or perhaps for their emergence in new guises.

For if man, as symbol-using animal, is *homo dialecticus,* and if the use of symbols is a kind of *transcendence,* then such a rounded instance of dialectical transcendence as we find in *The Book of the Courtier* may contain the overt expression of elements that elsewhere exist covertly, and in fragments. The work might thus make precise our understanding of the purely dialectical motives (ultimate verbal motives) behind the rhetorical convertibility between terms for social hierarchy and terms for theologic hierarchy. Here is a source of "mystery" grounded in the very perfection of formal thinking, with worldly and transcendent "reverence" each drawing sustenance from the other (and with all the variants of these, even to the rebel snapping of the continuity).

The Caricature of Courtship: Kafka (The Castle)

With the dialectical symmetry of *The Book of the Courtier* in mind, consider Franz Kafka's grotesque novel, *The Castle*. Thomas Mann calls Kafka "a religious humorist." A good formula, so good that it deserves a fuller explanation than the one its originator gives for it. Mann sees in Kafka the shift between love of the commonplace and desire "to be near to God, to live in God, to live aright and after God's will." And as in Mann's *Tonio Kröger* an unresolved conflict between artistic and bourgeois motives leads to sentiment and humor, so Mann says that the motives responsible for *The Castle* "corresponded in the religious sphere to Tonio Kröger's isolation."

But even in *Tonio Kröger,* as viewed from the standpoint of our concern with the magic of courtship, we should note that there is a pronounced concern with *caste.* Tonio's shy reverence for the bourgeois Ingeborg is but a localization, in sexual terms, of a nostalgic attitude towards the bourgeoisie as a class. True, as the returns have kept coming in, we have begun to see that the artistic "break-away," the bourgeois-turned-Bohemian, was not so antithetical to the motives of his class as he usually felt himself to be. The young Bohemian's wandering is but the first stage of the old Bohemian's homecoming. The Bohemian is "substantially" back before he leaves; but as with the Boyg's instructions to Peer Gynt, he must get there roundabout. Still, however indistinguishable the father and the prodigal son may be as regards their underlying community of motives, they can feel themselves as opposite extremes, as different in *kind*—and Mann's story got much poignancy from the distinction between the practical-bourgeois and the esthetic-bourgeois, treated as alien *classes,* with Tonio vacillating between them, and the two women, Ingeborg and Lizaveta, being courted not merely for themselves alone, but for the contrasting orders of social motives which they represented. They were mysterious vessels, for they were sexual embodiments of two nonsexual principles, two different castes. And the ambiguous courting of them was a roundabout intercourse between the castes.

If you substitute the religious motive for the esthetic motive, you see that Mann is quite correct in noting a motivational analogy between *The Castle* and *Tonio Kröger*. But for our purposes, the significant element of the analogy was omitted from Mann's account of his own story. Add this element, and if you then look at Kafka's novel with the dialectic of *The Courtier* in mind, you will see exactly why and how Mann's formula fits. Kafka is, if you will, "religious" in his concern with the ultimate mystery, the universal ground of human motives. But his account of the religious motive is "humorous" because he never forgets how the terms of the social order incongruously shape our idea of God, inviting men to conceive of communication with God after the analogy of their worldly embarrassments.

The principle of courtship is manifested in Expressionistically grotesque fragments. It is there, because the theme is bureaucracy, communication between higher and lower orders, involving the mysteries of "reverence." And since the ultimate of such courtship would be communion between lowly beings and "the highest," Kafka goes to the very essence of his subject, seeing through social mystery to divine mystery. But he never forgets, or lets us forget, the disproportion between social mystery and divine mystery. Thus, though the social mystery provides an imagery for figuring the divine mystery, this imagery is absurdly incommensurate with the hierarchic principle in its ultimate reaches.

In Kafka's personal case, of course, the social mystery was experienced, and suffered, in the form of anti-Semitism. The Jew in liberal, pre-Hitlerite Austria was never quite blackballed, never quite admitted. Where much liberalism prevailed even while the movement towards Nazism was taking form, the Jew's social status was unsettled. And this extraliterary situation had its analogue in the plot of *The Castle*, notably the uncertainty whether his principal character, "K.," would strengthen or lose his contacts with the Castle. (Similarly, in *The Trial*, there was uncertainty whether K. would be pronounced innocent or guilty by a mysterious court that was nowhere and everywhere; indeed, he could not even learn what the charge against him was.)

To an extent, the condition was like being blackballed, flatly excluded from participation in the mysteries of status. Yet to an extent it was like being hazed. For though hazing is a trial, the "guilty" defendant may hope for eventual admission into the inner sanctum, the holy of holies. The candidate who is being hazed can hope to become an *insider,* even while he undergoes ritual punishments that impress upon him his nature as a partial *outsider.* Or rather, the situation is like that of "exclusive" schools where the upper classmen impose menial duties upon the newcomers; or it is like hierarchic codes for imparting mystery to fraternities and secret orders. No, there is one important difference: usually, where such rituals prevail, they are recognized formally, so that, even while the discomfitures build up as much "reverence" as the dingy institution can command, the candidate knows where he is, knows what acts will finally permit him to become one with the mystic substance. But where there are no such formal fixities, the situation is not recognized for what it is. Though the candidate is being hazed, neither he nor his persecutors recognize what is going on. Hence, nobody is quite sure what the defendant's "guilt" is, or what kind of "trial" he must face, or for what purpose.

Thus, a friend said: "After the financial crash of 1929, you will re-member, there was a great rush of liberal intellectuals to join the cause of political radicalism. Of a sudden, radical literary organizations which had been struggling along for years were overwhelmed with new converts. Whereas the old-timers in these organizations had been laboriously attempting to increase the membership, the situation now became reversed. Instead of a welcome for the new men, there was a tendency to prove that they were poor material. And this tendency went so far that often, rather than being propagandists who delighted in the growth of their cause, the old-timers acted like residents of an exclusive neighborhood who resented a new real-estate development near-by.

"Years after, I understood what was wrong. It was not just that the old-timers feared for the loss of their former influence in the organiza-tion. It was the careless trampling on the mystery that disturbed them. The new men came in like a troop of boys entering a restaurant. There were no stages, there were no punishments, there was no hazing. At one moment, they weren't there, and at the next moment of a sudden they were. And lacking any formal ritual designed for this situation, the old-timers unbeknownst to themselves worked out a kind of informal hazing process, or tried to, in seeking to freeze out the very persons whom formerly they would have worked like demons to recruit." *

For the Jew Kafka, the hazing that would reaffirm the mystery was not formalized. Indeed, there was not even the assurance that he was being considered. As the novelist says of one ostracized character in *The Castle,* his superiors couldn't forgive him, because they hadn't accused him; and "before he could be forgiven he had to prove his guilt." Still further, there was no clear hint as to where the mystery was, or what it was. The nearest visible, formal signs of it were in the structure of bureaucracy. Giving it maximum resonance, one got to the connotations of "God," hence one was "religious"; but realizing how

---

* When an individual is being received into an alien social group, he may himself feel the need to be "hazed," just as the established members of the group may feel the need to haze him. The conditions of mystery may lead to apprehensions more or less clearly expressed, as the insiders feel that they are being silently judged, or that the newcomer threatens their ways, while he himself has the sense of protruding among the company like what Marcus Aurelius might have called an "abscess." But the embarrassments here go a step farther back, deriving in part from the fact that only a few of the rites necessary to such initiation are formally recognized; and insofar as the rites are uncertain, or are improvised, or are uncompleted, a magic propriety has been violated (the violation being felt on both sides, like an unpaid debt). Then the initiative ceremony is worked out piecemeal, in ways that are unacknowledged, or even unrecognized, except for vague embarrassments, subtle affronts, half-intentional oversights, and the like.

Looking back at Mark Twain's *Pudd'nhead Wilson* in the light of these speculations, we wonder whether some such "savage" or "mystical" level of motives might be found operating there. True, the good people of the community are at first most effusive in their welcome of the two foreigners, Angelo and Luigi ("lovely names; and so grand and foreign"). But it doesn't take a very skilled reader to suspect very early in the story that the author is building up for a letdown. The subsequent harsh treatment of the twins results from misunderstandings caused by the villainous Tom, who puts the foreigners in a bad light in order to conceal his own guilt. But if you drop the explanations, what do you get? The plot then boils down to this: Two foreigners enter a community; despite their exceptional strangeness, they are heartily welcomed; but immediately after, there is a long period when they are subjected to the most severe coolness and suspicion, and undergo painful trials, before they are finally exonerated and admitted. Leaving out the roundabout rationalization, which attributes the villagers' standoffishness to the machinations of a villain, one finds that the newcomers went through a long period of what amounts to informal, improvised hazing. Split the neighbors into two groups, and although both groups treat the strangers badly, the dissociation rationalizes the bad treatment by attributing it to the evil persons alone, thereby concealing its *collective* nature. But omit the rationalization of intent, merely looking at the over-all result, and you find that

inadequate it was as a figuring of the divine, one treated it with grotesque "humor." Thus, the mysterious official whose substance comes not from his intrinsic personality but solely from the dignity of his office here takes on a new dimension. He is a nonentity in the sense that he manifests no *intrinsic properties* fitting him to represent the religious motive; yet the mysteries of rank endow him with "reverence" anyhow. Indeed, his very unfitness as a vicar perversely suggests the dignifying effect of the office itself. (Thus a student wholly impressed with his college as a mystery would manifest this essence not through learning, but through a "college spirit" that would forgo learning. Or a man of means who distributed insults along with his funds, purchasing services solely through his money, beating his dogs with a bone, might more forcefully illustrate the power of money in its "purity" than if he also had appealing traits of character that engaged people's loyalties.) So in *The Castle* the very dinginess of the officialdom as *persons* absurdly suggests the omnipresence of the mystery that infuses their *office*.

Since, according to our view, *The Castle* is a fragmentary caricature of such an order, let us see to what extent the formal elements in Castiglione's dialogue have their grotesque counterpart in Kafka's novel.

The first concern of *The Courtier* is with the qualifications that make one presentable at court, and with the hopes of favor and advancement

---

the citizens, with one notable exception who was himself unjustly in bad repute with the community, had subjected the foreigners to harsh treatment.

Our notion is that, in accordance with the usual workings of the "scapegoat mechanism" as a dramatic device, Twain could break down the motive of hazing into two principles, a "good" and a "bad"—and as a result, the hazing need not be seen as such, even by the author. But its "mystic" or "magical" element, operating beyond or beneath the "rational" explanation (in terms of a dissociation between innocent and villainous neighbors) could be felt by both author and reader, without being explicitly defined.

The thought suggests that we might profitably approach all of Mark Twain's major books in such terms. For instance, we should look for magical and ritualistic motives (strongly infused with the principle of hierarchy), while he uses the figures of children (or of rogues like the king and the duke) to depict such motives realistically. Children and rogues may or not be as thoroughly formalists as he makes them out to be. But even if they aren't, readers can readily accept the novelistic convention that says they are. Hence the element of social "divinity" in the life about us can be lightly and ingratiatingly symbolized, without the reader ever becoming quite aware that his interest is being held by such a motive.

at the hands of the sovereign. This is also the primary concern of the land-surveyor, K. But whereas the courtier is concerned with the procuring of advantage *within* the court, K. is wholly an outsider, with a vast officialdom (the grotesque bureaucratic equivalent of the courtiers) vaguely interposed between him and the mysterious sovereign. K. is at several removes from the source of favor. He is a stranger among the villagers. Though the villagers belong to the castle, there is a gulf between them and the castle. There are messengers (the grotesque counterpart of angels) who live in the village but have access to outer offices in the castle. And there are the officials themselves, who represent the castle in the village, but are so imbued with the mystic standoffishness of hierarchy that throughout the entire novel K. exhausts himself in unsuccessful attempts to get preparatory interviews with them. Where the courtier can consider how one should conduct oneself in the lord's secret chamber, K. must worry how to get beyond the outer vestibule.

Frieda and Amalia are the main translations of the grotesque courtliness into terms of woman. Of Frieda, we are told: "It was her nearness to Klamm" (she had been his mistress before coming to live with K.) "that had made her so irrationally seductive" to K.—and Klamm was the official from the castle whom K. is constantly striving to meet in behalf of his nightmarishly indeterminate cause. Amalia is the girl whose life was ruined when she resented a letter from an official making filthy proposals to her (a letter couched in the language of courtship incongruously reversed). One character quotes a local saying, "Official decisions are as shy as young girls"; the novelist here ingeniously mixes the sexual and bureaucratic orders. And when Kafka is contrasting "the power, merely formal until now, which Klamm exercised over K.'s services" with "the very real power which Klamm possessed in K.'s bedroom," he says: "Never yet had K. seen vocation and life so interlaced as here. . . . One might think that they had exchanged places."

If we recall what we previously said on the relation between mystery and class, this remark seems unusually resonant. Status and division of labor being but two aspects of the same thing, the reference to "vocation" can be read as a roundabout reference to *class*. Indeed, in areas manifesting the cultural tone set by Protestantism, the substantiality of status that arose with the division of labor is likely to be expressed pragmatically, in terms of work. But Protestantism's doctrine of the divinity in secular toil had fused secular and supernatural "mystery" quite as Catholicism's divine sanction for status had done. Hence, in either scheme, there was the convertibility between the two kinds of "reverence," the social and the religious. Consider, thus, Kafka's reference to the interchangeability of "vocation" and "life." He is talking of the way in which Klamm (who represents the mystery of the courtly principle) pervades K.'s sexual relations with Frieda. And he is saying in effect that here the social motives of status ("vocation") become so interwoven with universal motives ("life") that they can exchange places. Recalling the nature of the book, in which the castle fluctuantly represents both the superiority of social caste and the superiority of the godly, do we not see in this passing remark a grotesque way of fusing both kinds of "reverence" (the social and the "divine") in terms of sexual relations?

Since the religious motivation in Kafka is explicitly recognized by both such authorities as Thomas Mann and Kafka's friend, Max Brod, we shall not pause here to establish it. But perhaps the single sentence that most quickly conveys this quality is in the second paragraph of the eighth chapter:

> When K. looked at the Castle, often it seemed to him as if he were observing someone who sat there quietly gazing in front of him, not lost in thought and so oblivious of everything, but free and untroubled, as if he were alone with nobody to observe him, and yet must notice that he was observed, and all the same remained with his calm not even slightly disturbed; and really—one did not know whether it was cause or effect—the gaze of the observer could not remain concentrated there, but slid away.

And in Chapter IX, the discussion of things done "in the name of Klamm," of things "filled by his spirit," or of a person who is but "an instrument in the hand of Klamm," adds a transcendent dimension to the purely bureaucratic mystery. Images of storm and eagle figure here too. Indeed, there is no trouble isolating the traditional theological motive in this work. The problem, rather, as both the Mann and Brod statements in the English translation indicate, is to keep one reminded of the important role played here by the motives of social class.

What of the other two major themes of *The Courtier*: Laughter and education (the themes gorgeously, almost hysterically, brought to-

gether in the Rabelaisian rhetoric)? In *The Castle,* the social rhetoric
of laughter and education (two forms of "pure persuasion" this side of
the religious) is not a subject of discussion, but is rather the essence
of the work itself. The laughter, in its grotesque modification, is embedded in the very conception and method of the book, the oddly "humorous" treatment of reverence. The social bid in such expression is
perhaps best revealed today in the mixture of grotesqueness and humor
that distinguishes the "smartness" of the *New Yorker* sort (the "hierarchic" appeal of which is indicated in turn by the commercial advertisements that accompany it, advertisements obviously addressed to
suburban, middle-class "elegance").

At one point, K. is told that the messenger Barnabas had cried
when receiving his first commission. As a comment on the mystery,
this incident is exceptionally telling. For Barnabas' first commission
had been to communicate with K. And previously we had seen the
mystery of Barnabas, as he looked to K. This sudden glimpse around
the corner, with A mysterious to B and B mysterious to A, all because
of their different participation in the mystery of C, does not merely
dispel the illusion. For everyone goes on acting *as though* there were
a mystery; and since acts are images, the mystery continues to be strong
in our imagination. Indeed, once you learn the rules, once you are at
home in its grotesque laughter, the very lack of motives for the mystery adds to the sense of mystery.

In a broken, grotesque version of courtship, we are not required to
find counterparts for each of the elements in the symmetrical, classical
version. Yet there do happen to be analogies for the educational principle. Judged as imagery, K.'s very role as land-surveyor, or rather, his
attempt to get himself formally accredited in this role, involves the
principle of education. For interpreted symbolically, a land-surveyor
is surely one who would specify positions and elevations. And since
this half-admitted, half-rejected K. so clearly represents the author,
whose account of K.'s quandaries in confronting social hierarchy is
itself a precise novelization of the hierarchic motive, it would hardly
be exorbitant to say that Kafka here writes as a Jewish "intellectual."
(He is "in" to the extent that an intellectual spontaneously considers
himself superior to manual workers, as with K.'s attitude towards the
peasants and workers of the village; he is "out" to the extent that an
unnamed and even unnamable curse is upon him, a curse that keeps

him permanently "guilty.") Kafka was "in" insofar as the intellectual spontaneously considers his status superior to that of the laboring classes, though he may "pastorally" court them, a social relation which a Leftist wag (he has since broken with the Party) formulated with suggestive gallantry, thus: "The intelligentsia must penetrate the proletariat." Kafka was "out" insofar as the intellectual class itself is somewhat suspect (though we will say for the Church, Aquinas' angels were pure intellectuals), and because in addition Kafka was Jewish in what was then preparing itself to become a part of Hitler's *Reich*.

Also, there is at least the image of education in the fact that, during much of his uncertainty, K. lives with Frieda in a school where he is supposed to be janitor, and where expressionistically the classroom he uses as living quarters is overrun by the schoolchildren. But the interweaving of education with the theme of childhood involves factors that belong rather under "grammar" and "symbolic." We have elsewhere noted the Grammatical resources that permit logical priority to be stated narratively in terms of temporal priority. By such convertibility, the essence of the hierarchic principle (the castle) can be identified with the conditions of childhood, since an essence is a logical "first," and childhood is a narrative first. Thus, near the beginning of the story, we are told that, at the first sight of the castle, "K. had a fleeting recollection" of the town in which he was born. The peasants are described as children, likewise the childish element in his assistants is commented on several times. When K. tries to phone the castle, the receiver gave out a buzz that "was like the hum of countless children's voices—but yet not a hum, the echo rather of voices singing at an infinite distance." In the schoolroom where he lives with Frieda, their constant invasion of his privacy sets the mark of childhood upon the entire situation.

Again, the German word for castle, *Schloss,* has connotations of internality not present in the English equivalent. For it clearly suggests the idea of enclosure, being related to the verb for closing or locking, *schliessen. Klamm,* as an adjective, means tight or close, related to another word for the act of enclosing, *klemmen.* We might recall the *hortus conclusus* of medieval thought, the ideal "closed garden" that duplicated the protectiveness of the walled town. And in the offing are the words for "advertising" and "calamity," *Reklam, Kalamität.*

So much for the Grammar of "regression." From the standpoint of

"Symbolic" note also that the imagery of childish sexuality is well suited to express the mystery of social courtship in one important respect: since social intercourse is not essentially sexual at all, such courtship is more nearly analogous to the "polymorphous-perverse" nature of infantile sexuality than to mature sexual mating. (See Shirley Jackson's novel, *The Road Through the Wall,* for a subtle and sensitive representation of the ways whereby the unspeakable mysteries of social discrimination become interwoven, in childhood, with the unspeakable mysteries of the sexually unclean.) Since K.'s union with Frieda is but a roundabout approach to Klamm (who represents the mystery of the order headed in the castle), there is a grotesque appropriateness in the fact that K. and Frieda are under the observation of others, even in the most intimate moments of love-making. Here are perhaps the strongest suggestions of the infantile, since children's experiments with sex lack intimacy, privacy, and purpose, quite as with the casual and almost absent-minded sexuality of Frieda and K.

The two major themes that complicate the analysis of *The Castle* in terms of grotesque courtliness are Kafka's illness and his personal conflicts with his father. Recalling Freud's suggestion that children are often figured in dreams as insects, we should probably find the clearest representation of the mysterious, troubled communication between father and son as different "kinds of being" expressed most directly in the story, *Metamorphosis,* about a son who was a monster cockroach. Rhetorically, we may note that, in this very disgrace of the offspring, there is a desperate vengeance against the parent from which it was descended.

Though the references to weariness in *The Castle* show signs of the author's personal illness, it is perhaps figured most clearly in the story of the *Hunger-Artist,* where the wastage of consumption has its analogue in the fantastic account of the performer who starved by profession. Anyone with a feeling for the grotesque might have hit upon the plot of this story as a conceit; but unless a writer were almost prodigiously imaginative, only by actually experiencing tuberculosis could he have developed this fictive counterpart of it with such gruesome thoroughness.

The disease here is also esthetically redeemed, as with much of Mann's work (*Tristan,* for instance) in becoming interwoven with the theme of art. (For a discussion of the story from this point of view, see

R. W. Stallman's essay, "Kafka's Cage," in the Winter 1948 *Accent*.)
There are rhetorical implications here, since the problem of being socially received is again considered, with much poignancy. And the
rhetorical element that can arise even out of purely physical discomfitures is discernible in the identifications surrounding disease itself, as
when Kafka writes: "Illness and weariness give even peasants a look
of refinement." Thus such obsessiveness as comes of the castle fits
well with the imagery of disease, both physical and mental (or with
such literary attenuations of mental disease as reside in the grotesque).
For grammatically, disease is "passion," and as such can be a romantic
and social analogue of the religious passion.

Kafka's study of law leads directly into rhetorical motives. The
paper work, and the strongly hierarchic nature of legal administration
could provide much material for the imagery of officialdom that is the
basis of the courtlinesss. And behind positive law there always loom
the questions of theologic law, as the castle looms above the village.

In his remarks on Kafka, Max Brod writes:

> The connection between the "Castle"—that is Divine Guidance—
> and the women, this connection half-discovered and half-suspected
> by K., may appear obscure, and even inexplicable, in the Sortini epi-
> sode where the official (Heaven) requires the girl to do something
> obviously immoral and obscene; and here a reference to Kierke-
> gaard's *Fear and Trembling* may be of value—a work which Kafka
> loved much, read often, and profoundly commented on in many let-
> ters. The Sortini episode is literally a parallel to Kierkegaard's
> book, which starts from the fact that God required of Abraham
> what was really a crime, the sacrifice of his child; and which uses
> this paradox to establish triumphantly the conclusion that the cate-
> gories of morality and religion are by no means identical. The in-
> commensurability of earthly and religious aims; this takes one right
> into the heart of Kafka's novel.

We might distinguish two important elements in this statement: the
problem of the sacrifice (involving the interpretation of a story in
Genesis 22) and the problem of the absurd (involving a doctrine of
"incommensurability" between religious and social motives). They are
so closely interwoven that we cannot discuss one intelligibly without
implicating the other. Yet they might be separated for systematic
purposes, since a cult of irrationality, or "the absurd," can be derived
from many other sources than this chapter in Genesis, and a theory of

sacrifice need not lay such stress upon the "kill" as marks Kierkegaard's interpretation of the Biblical story.

A "Dialectical Lyric" (Kierkegaard's Fear and Trembling)

In the department stores of some decades ago, there were little carriages running in tracks between the cashier and the individual sales booths. (You still see them occasionally, but they have mostly been replaced by pneumatic tubes.) They would spurt forth, making quick jerks (like Kierkegaardian leaps) at each right-angled turn—darting in zigzags across the ceiling, and then suddenly disappearing on the way up to some unseen chamber where they would be received, checked, and after appropriate operations would be sent racing back to the counter from which they had come. Their forthright rectangular urgency fascinated—and a pious child, watching them, could feel that they were like messengers bearing communications to Heaven, and returning with prompt answers. Somewhat the same idea crosses the mind now, when we see the capsules being put into pneumatic tubes, or hear them come plumping out again—except that now the communications seem rather to be with a counting house in hell.

Anyhow, we are reminded of those little messengers, communicating between a central terminus and a peripheral terminus, when we think of the Kierkegaardian dialectic, for changing finite species into the currency of the infinite. For the dialectician sends up one thing, something is abstracted from it, and it returns as another thing. However, the change that comes back is not merely something subtracted, or abstracted from the original sum: a notable element has been added as well. This sort of change is a rebirth, a transformation.

What, then, went up, and what came back, as per the "movements" treated in Kierkegaard's "dialectical lyric," Fear and Trembling? At first, reducing to sheerly behavioristic terms, we know that Kierkegaard had jilted a girl. When he announced that he had given up his intention of marrying her, she grew importunate. Then (we quote Mr. Walter Lowrie's introduction to the English translation): "In order to liberate Regina from her attachment and to 'set her afloat,' S. K. felt obliged to be cruel enough to make her believe he was a scoundrel who had merely been trifling with her affections." Onlookers might get the same impression. And Kierkegaard seems to have been threatened with doubts himself, at least to the extent that he spent the rest of his highly productive life protesting his innocence in some of the most ingenious dialectical operations known to Protestantism.

Reading *Fear and Trembling,* we see that the species he sent up to be changed comprised this jilting, with his picture of himself as a "scoundrel." After the change, it returned, properly abstracted, as the "knight of infinite resignation." Or was that but an *ad interim* notice that the message was being processed? In any case, after further communications, the jilting was wholly remade, and in its place was the knight of faith, who adores his princess in perpetual repetition. This is the currency of the infinite, but brought down to earth like a god incarnate, a spirit that henceforth infuses all things with its essence, bathes all things in its unitary light, subordinating the disparate facts of the world of contingencies to one transcendent, unitary principle, ironically called the Absurd. This transformation is also called a "leap" across the "incommensurable."

Behind it all should lie the standard Neo-Platonist pattern. That is, we could begin with the world of everyday contingencies (in which there had been a jilting, under slightly suspect conditions). We start this on its Upward Way until it reaches the realm of Oneness in Infinite Being. After it has been thus purified, we start it on its Downward Way, back to the world of business and gossip. When it has thus returned, we find that in its purified form it now requires a totally different vocabulary to chart its motivations. As contrasted with its earlier condition, there has been a momentous "leap." Something "incommensurable" has intervened. And this new step calls forth a new set of dialectical operations so radical, and so spirited, that they apply not only to itself, but can be extended to all things, natural, human, and divine. At the very least, this vocabulary had to be sufficiently transcendent to redeem the relations between Kierkegaard and Regina. But in the course of making it transcendent enough for those purposes, Kierkegaard came upon a principle that could be applied to all finite things; by the natural dialectics of the case it was a principle of "infinity." For once you get a generalization as broad as the "finite," its only proper dialectical partner or counter-term is the "infinite."

So much for the over-all dialectics. There are also fables and images that give the abstract processes body. First, there is the key analogy: Kierkegaard jilting Regina is as Abraham making ready to kill Isaac.

But this story, as told in the Bible, does not quite serve the purpose. For there is nothing in it to parallel the very important point about Kierkegaard's acting "like a scoundrel." The Bible does not say that Abraham lied to Isaac for Isaac's good. However: Kierkegaard, writing in a highly psychologistic century, improvises a "psychology" for Abraham. And *this improvised psychology, not the Biblical story,* is the element that helps him solve the most crucial problem in the redeeming of his conduct. For it is the part that parallels, in Biblical ennoblement, Kierkegaard's depicting of himself as a scoundrel who had trifled with Regina's affections.

Perhaps we should make a distinction here between the "amplifying" and the "psychologizing" of a Biblical story. One would amplify the story if one merely tried to make the reader feel more urgently each principle that the story itself exemplified. Thus, to jog the imagination of the sluggish, one might expatiate on Abraham's love for his son, going to such lengths that nobody could fail to realize this point. A principle already there would thus be rhetorically amplified, but no new principle would be added. In "psychologizing" the narrative, however, Kierkegaard added a new principle of his own—and precisely that is the one he needed to supply transcendent motives for his apparent conduct as a "scoundrel."

We refer, of course, to the ingenious Gidean conceit, which you will certainly not find in the Biblical story:

> He climbed Mount Moriah, but Isaac understood him not. Then for an instant he turned away from him, and when Isaac again saw Abraham's face it was changed, his glance was wild, his form was horror. He seized Isaac by the throat, threw him to the ground, and said, "Stupid boy, dost thou then suppose that I am thy father? I am an idolater. Dost thou suppose that this is God's bidding? No, it is my desire." Then Isaac trembled and cried out in his terror, "O God in Heaven, have compassion upon me. God of Abraham, have compassion upon me. If I have no father upon earth, be Thou my father!" But Abraham in a low voice said to himself, "O Lord in Heaven, I thank Thee. After all it is better for him to believe that I am a monster, rather than that he should lose faith in Thee."

If this addition to the Bible story teaches us anything tropologically, the moral seems to be that religion would sanction lying, even as regards first and last things. But we can pass that up. It is sufficient

for us to note that Kierkegaard is here making a purely personal addition to the sacred text. He is not just amplifying principles already
there; he is adding a new principle. And if that principle had not
been added, the Biblical story would have fallen short of his requirements.

Kierkegaard says in effect: "Here is a Biblical anecdote on which I
am basing my theological dialectic." But as regards his actual procedure, what he should have said is: "I would like to present my theological dialectic, in as persuasive a way as possible. Hence, to strike
the imagination, I have a picturesque introduction, a privately conceived anecdote, a personal invention of my own. To give it authority,
I shall call it Biblical. Then I shall proceed to transform its favorable
implications into explications, as an after-dinner speaker might begin
his talk with a witty story that illustrates his theme and disposes the
audience favorably towards his conclusions."

However, though there is questionableness here on one level, there
is extremely revealing honesty on another. For Kierkegaard follows
his Biblical psychologizing by a kind of parable. It is meant to re-
enforce the story, to say the same thing. But might it go deeper into
his underlying motives than the official example (Abraham's sacrifice
of Isaac)?

> When the child must be weaned, the mother blackens her breast;
> it would indeed be a shame that the breast should look delicious
> when the child must not have it. So the child believes that the
> breast has changed, but the mother is the same, her glance is as
> loving and tender as ever. Happy the person who had no need of
> more dreadful expedients for weaning the child!

Though the theme of weaning is repeated several times, the reference to the blackening (which would correspond to the "scoundrelly"
ingredient in his act of jilting) drops away. Only such motives as
maternal love and sorrow at separation are mentioned. In other words,
the very element that the story was supposedly introduced to supply
drops out. Yet without it, the act he is accounting for is left unex-
plained.

These other references, where mention of the blackened breast is
omitted, are of this sort: "When the child has grown big and must be
weaned, the mother virginally hides her breast, so the child has no
more a mother. . . . When the child must be weaned, the mother too

is not without sorrow at the thought that she and the child are separated more and more, that the child which first lay at her heart and
later reposed upon her breast will be so near to her no more. . . .
When the child must be weaned, the mother has stronger food in
readiness, lest the child should perish. Happy the person who has
stronger food in readiness!" In a subtle way, a "leap" has taken place
even here; we begin with explanation for a questionable way of jilting,
and we end on mention of a transcendent sustenance, with the apologetic feature having dropped out, while in its place there is an edified
and edifying promise.

Is it not possible that with this humble secondary example we can
come closer to the motives for Kierkegaard's relations to Regina than
with the one he features? The story of Abraham and Isaac (plus its
all-important psychologistic improvisations) sets up the case formally.
The figure of the weaned child discusses it informally, even confiden-
tially. And since the book is essentially autobiography, written by a
genius of introspection, we may assume that the example is not chosen
haphazardly, but is an essential and articulate figuring of his motives.
At least, in another reference which the editor quotes from the *Journal*,
Kierkegaard says: "He who has explained this riddle has explained
my life." Here he interweaves the two themes even more thoroughly
than in the book itself, concluding

> When the child has to be weaned the mother blackens her breast,
> but her eyes rest just as lovingly upon the child. The child believes
> it is the breast that has changed, but that the mother is unchanged.
> And why does she blacken her breast? Because, she says, it would
> be a shame that it should seem delicious when the child must not
> get it.— This collision is easily resolved, for the breast is only a part
> of the mother herself. Happy is he who has not experienced more
> dreadful collisions, who did not need to blacken *himself*, who did
> not need to go to hell in order to see what the devil looks like,
> so that he might paint himself accordingly and in that way if pos-
> sible save another person in that person's God-relationship at least.
> This would be Abraham's collision.

There is nothing unusual in the thought of acting towards others as
one has himself been acted upon. Hence, if Kierkegaard *had* experienced great disturbance during the weaning period of infancy, there
would be no difficulty in accounting for the reversal whereby the experience of being weaned is reversed in the figure, as he likens himself

to the one who did the weaning rather than to the one who suffered it.

You need only make the asumption that, Kierkegaard being a wholly essential and articulate writer, this anecdote is just as central to his thinking as he says it is. And then you need but look to see what there is in it, assuming that he selected an image of weaning rather than some other image, because this image of weaning came closer to summing up the nature of his basic motives than a different image might have done. And we assume that it came closer because the experience of weaning itself had been of similar outstanding importance.

However, we do not propose to derive the pattern of Kierkegaard's mind from an experience of weaning. A psychologist could point to many relevant connections here. Since the mouth is used for both taking in food and putting forth words, nutrient distress might conceivably be transformed, by a Kierkegaardian leap, into orational zeal. Such a reversal is not hard to think of. But one could with as much justice apply the opposite causal sequence here, noting that many are weaned but few are Kierkegaards. Hence, the child may have already possessed the susceptibilities that would make weaning a matter of such moment. If he were a born word-slinger, he might thereby be even more "mouth-conscious" than most children, at the time of weaning. And he could later connect this problem of dissociation with the problem of distinguishing, at adolescence, between maternal and erotic woman. (At least, his reference to the mother's breast as "virginal" is in the same cluster of motives with his "knightly" view of Regina as a "princess." The same kind of fond aloofness is implied in both.)

But we need only note how the verbal motive as such would be enough to account for his conduct towards Regina. For if this "knight of faith" would court in terms of the infinite, it follows that he would court eternally, in perpetual repetition. Here would be the motive of the dialectician, of Socratic erotic (as considered in the *Grammar,* when on the subject of Plato's *Phaedrus*). But if one would court forever, whereas the object of one's courtship is not only willing to yield, but even becomes importunate in yielding, then the goodly dialectician must supply resistances of his own, from within himself, out of his own "inner check," and by setting up a situation, both emotional and practical, that would restore the necessary distance. First, in somewhat of a panic, he would even act like a "scoundrel" if necessary. For he would do anything to retain the purity of his motives, being an individualist of integrity. If his woman wouldn't refuse him, if she was willing to accept him even when he was but lukewarm, then he would have to become frigid. When, affectionately importunate, she made an affront necessary, he affronted her. He became a "scoundrel."

However, once he had got away from her, and she had become married to another, since they were both highly proper he had again the objective situation necessary to his nature: he could now court her in terms of eternity, that is, in perpetual repetition. The dilemma was solved. On firm moral and legalistic grounds, their union was now impossible. Hence, he could safely become her knight again. To gallantly make amends for his affront, he could psychologistically amend the Bible. Everything was now in order—and with her marriage as the "objective correlative" that matched his own subjective "inner check" (this was the great century of the Schellingesque "identification of subject and object"), he could now court her in terms of the infinite, the incommensurable, the absurd, the faith that will somehow bring about the impossible. Kierkegaard had good grounds for his faith in the impossible—for it was the real impossibility of their marriage that again allowed this "knight of faith" to court his "princess." No wonder "Johannes de Silentio" could then say of the knightly "swain" who loves the "princess" as a distance: "He feels a blissful rapture in letting love tingle through every nerve and yet his soul is as solemn as that of the man who has drained the poisoned goblet and feels how the juices permeate every drop of blood—for this instant is life and death."

For the present we want to discuss the results of the false emphasis that came of Kierkegaard's turn from the amplifying of a Biblical text to the psychologizing of it. Here, we submit, was the true Kierkegaardian leap, so far as dialectic is concerned. For it is a dialectical fact that you cannot get more out of a term than you put into it. This is the reason why theologians insist upon Biblical "revelation" as the ground of faith. Technically, by grounding an argument in Biblical texts as "revelation," the dialectician can put in terms having "universal" authority, while his personal or individual function is exclusively that of translating the implications into explications. We need not here decide whether the authority is real. For as we have said, Kierkegaard does not start by merely putting in a Biblical text from which he will draw forth the implications. Rather, he starts by putting in a *strategic addition* to a Biblical text. Needing the story to motivate the leap, *he himself puts the leap into the story,* when he turns from mere amplification of the text to a psychologizing of the text; and thereby he gets a generating principle that is very much like an ingenious Gidean perversion (almost an early statement, in theological terms, of such transvaluations as Nietzsche was later to treat crisply, in his wholly secular paradoxes).

Or you could put the matter thus: If it is true that, having faith in God, one absurdly gets what one renounces, why should not Abraham have been sure that somehow, by virtue of the Existentialist Absurd, God would take care of any apparent breach between religion and morality? Or why couldn't he have faith in God's ability to so bring it about that the father could simultaneously meet the test and keep his son, as was indeed the case? If the anecdote, as amended by Kierkegaard, justifies such expectations on Kierkegaard's part with relation to Regina, why shouldn't it justify similar confidence on Abraham's part, with relation to Isaac? Or do we have another leap now, from the Old Law, to the New Law, to the Absurd Law (not revealed until the flourishing of nineteenth-century individualist psychologism)?

You can't have it both ways: If Kierkegaard is right in knowing that, by virtue of faith in the Absurd, he will regain Regina in the finite (though infused with the infinite), then by the same token, Abraham would know that he would regain his son in the very act of preparing to slay him, on condition that he genuinely intended to make the sacrifice. In this case, Abraham's confidence would remove the apparent discrepancy between morality and religion. If, on the other hand, Abraham's regaining of Isaac came wholly as a surprise to him, then Abraham's willingness to sacrifice Isaac doesn't indicate as powerful a faith as Kierkegaard's willingness to jilt Regina in accordance with his exalted paradox, "By faith I shall get her in virtue of the absurd." And that would seem to be a kind of absurdity that lies outside the Existentialist Absurd.

The only way out of these difficulties seems to be through our dialectical explanation of his dialectic as a metarhetoric (since by perpetual courtship he is forever getting her while forever not getting her, renunciation and advance being fused in the one attitude). Technically, this could be saluted as the presence of the infinite in the finite —for opposites have been reconciled, and that state of affairs is absurd, being "higher than human reason."

We believe, then, that Kierkegaard was essentially correct in saying that both his jilting of Regina and his subsequent lifelong courting of her involved motives in the realm of the "infinite." For "pure persuasion" is an absolute, logically prior to any one persuasive act. It is of the essence of language. And just as the over-all Title of Titles is a "god-term," so persuasion in all purity would transform courtship into prayer, not prayer for an end, but prayer for its own sake, prayer as Adoration, or as the Absolute Compliment. You can account for such motives by a thoroughly secular dialectic, as we have tried to do here. But even so, as regards the Platonist dialectic at least, they would be, technically, on the side of the "divine," since they would be abstract and universalized.

The Kill and the Absurd

With regard to the sacrifice: the statement quoted from Max Brod indicates how readers are led by Kierkegaard to interpret the Biblical story as saying that God required of Abraham the sacrifice of Isaac. Yet according to the Bible, just as Abraham "took the knife to slay his son," an angel stayed his hand, saying: "Lay not thine hand upon the lad, neither do thou any thing unto him; for now I know that thou fearest God, seeing thou hast not withheld thy son, thine only son from me."

In building a theology about a Biblical anecdote, why play down so important a part of it? The story in its entirety is brief. Yet when using it as a base on which to erect his theological doctrines, Kierkegaard here makes it even briefer. Isn't the assurance that the angel stayed Isaac's hand as important a part of the story as Abraham's willingness to sacrifice Isaac? At least, Isaac must have thought so.

As we see it, this chapter tells not of a father who sacrificed his son, but of a father who was *allowed to substitute a purely vicarious victim*. "Abraham lifted up his eyes, and looked, and beheld behind him a ram caught in a thicket by his horns: and Abraham went and took the ram, and offered him up for a burnt offering in the stead of his son."

Is this a story about a God who demands the killing of Isaac, or is it about a God who demands Abraham's *willingness to sacrifice*? The story itself is quite explicit on this point. It says that what God wanted was not a kill, but a sign; and when he got the sign, he ordered the son to be spared. The "categories of morality and religion" here seem to work quite well together. Religion demands of the devout the willingness to sacrifice even the most precious thing. And *in strictest accordance with the tribal morality,* Abraham's only son is chosen, as test case. For according to the tribal morality, the only son is a most precious thing. God's way here was in perfect keeping with the theory of "topics" in Aristotle's *Rhetoric.* He chose the very place which, in the realm of "opinion" then current, would stand most persuasively for the principle of supreme sacrifice. We need not bring in any "teleological suspension of the ethical."

Among the components of happiness, Aristotle lists the parent's delight in his children. And God, not absurdly, but like a good Aristotelian, was working this topic for all it was worth. As a result, so far as the story is concerned, it gets its effect by *ethos,* in employing exactly such a topic of invention as Aristotle would advocate for building up the character of Abraham.

The Kierkegaardian Existentialism, with typical overparticularization at this point, would not sufficiently generalize the anecdote. Hence, it lays too much stress upon the difference between the image, infanticide (which *in itself* would be morally criminal), whereas it should lay more stress upon the idea, supreme sacrifice (which is religiously pious). Also, there seems some perversity in the fact that no attempt is made to discuss all the important motivating elements. The psychologistic distortion is aggravated by at least one major omission: God's own statement of His motives. The product thus got by a combination of distortion and overparticularization is then generalized, with the perversely exciting literary result that the cult of the kill takes on a theological resonance. A story about Abraham's willingness to sacrifice is then cherished by the literati as though it were about the killing of Isaac.

Often the attempt to obey one moral injunction may oblige us to violate another. There is nothing essentially absurd in such a conflict. But it is true that, unless we are to remain undecided, the solution will require a new act of us, a "leap." To take this step, we may have to go from a principle to a principle of principles (from the dialectical order to an ultimate order of terms)—and such "incommensurability" may be called a "leap" from morality to religion.

In Kierkegaard's case, his personal relations to the "princess" who represented for him the hierarchic principle as translated into sexual terms required ultimate dialectical operations (as distinct from the restricted kind we find in parliamentary clashes). And so far as the appeal to the imagination goes, since he picturesquely reduced his dialectic to an anecdote featuring the mythic imagery of the kill, this image may come to stand for the spirit of his dialectic. Hence readers, in their awareness that man's way is through conflict, are invited to think that the cult of the kill is not a lower morality, but a higher one, even a religious one. Ironically, if the image is stressed more than the dialectic, such doctrine leads *towards* the Holocaust rather than *away from* it. For where personal conflict is solved by the kill, what do you have ultimately but the man who is at peace with himself only on the battlefield, in the midst of slaughter?

In another notable respect the Kierkegaardian alignment needs discounting. We refer to the fact that he summed up his dialectic by entitling it the Absurd.

Admittedly, dialectical operations do involve us in contradictions that might be dramatically called "absurd." Yet we would point out that the operations themselves are quite "rational," when approached methodically. Hence the slogan of the Absurd can easily transform a truth into a half-truth. It is somewhat like the pleasantries of those who remark that a man begins dying the day he is born. So he does, since in every change there is a dying; but in every change there is likewise a being-born—and we can safely use the partial statement only insofar as we know how to discount it. In sum, if one begins with "dialectic," one can come upon the Absurd. But if one begins with the Absurd, one is not likely to get a clear look at the dialectic, even though it is so inescapably in the offing that one is continually coming upon it. By approaching it in the Kierkegaardian manner, under a curse, one is in danger of subtly perverting it at every point; and each time he finds a new aspect of that quite "rational" of instruments (the processes of verbal composition and division) he is invited to think instead that he is coming upon new areas of the Absurd.

Consider the Existentialist movement in France, for instance. Rhetorically, it could serve well during the period of Nazi occupation. Where the French intellectual was under constraint, the Existentialist reworking of Kierkegaard allowed for a kind of "pure" freedom. Existentialism could confront the censor as a literary movement indeterminately midway between Resistance and Collaboration. It offered dialectical devices whereby Frenchmen could be "substantially" free while being subject politically. This was the freedom of "suicide," with the motives of attack being turned back upon the self, such purely private and recondite authority being eulogized as godlike. The movement had relevance, as the translation of a political predicament into "cosmological" terms.

But after the fall of the Nazis, the particular social conditions of the occupation no longer prevailed. The proponents of Existentialism then broadened their movement, developing the study of dialectical operations in general and applying them to "universal" drama. In accordance with the Kierkegaardian twist, however, dialectic may then be reduced to suicide, whereas suicide should be treated as a special case of dialectic (in accordance with the opening pages of this volume).

The ultimate sacrifice does involve a dying. And a dying may involve a killing, by another or by the self. Whereupon, one may come to displace the emphasis, until the element of sacrifice retreats behind the element of murder (or its recent Existentialist variant, suicide). By that time, things have become quite reversed; and whereas sacrifice is the very essence of peace, it becomes instead the essence of war, with men piously persuading themselves that they are never so comforted as when contemplating a blood-bath. Admittedly, there are absurdities here. But a cult of the Absurd in effect sanctions them, whereas an attempt to derive them by rational steps, "dialectically" implies the hope of mitigating their rawness.

When men believe in polytheism, there is no problem in accounting for such sacrifices as God the Father's surrender of Christ the Son. If the "one God" is at war with other gods (or, as in Manicheism, with an equally powerful principle of Evil) for the mastery of the universe, then it is quite "rational" that such a God might have to sacrifice his son to the Prince of Evil as ransom for the human race. However, once polytheism has been transformed into monotheism by quite understandable dialectical procedures that sum up all things in an ultimate Term of Terms, new problems arise in trying to account for the sacrifice. If you start here, you will confront a logical "mystery." For, under monotheism, the cosmologizing of sacrifice is far more difficult to rationalize than under polytheism, though any perversion of Christian sacrifice, as with literary cults of the hunt or with the varieties of fascism, simplify the whole problem in purely militarist terms, until "pure" slaying, for sheer love of the art, becomes a kind of spiritual devotion.

Dialectically, one can spin out the various solutions, and the various subsequent embarrassments proper to each solution. There is no essential "irrationality" here. For reason (Logos) is, at the very least, words—and dialectic is the study of verbal resources. And when we consider such resources formally, we can observe how verbal solutions arise, and how these in turn give rise to verbal difficulties.

Another respect in which the paradoxes of the Absurd can be derived dialectically involves the grammatical resource whereby the sacred and the obscene become interchangeable, since each is a kind of "untouchability." The ritual uncleanness of the lowest Hindu class was but the counterpart of the "absolute dignity" possessed by superior classes. And looking too hastily, we may tend to see a mere evidence of "irrationality" in the "ambivalence" whereby the Latins could apply to criminals their word for "sacred" (a relation also involved in the outlaw's right of sanctuary at the altar). When K. asks a schoolteacher about the castle, the teacher in embarrassment calls attention to the fact that there are children present, speaking to him in French (as the language of "social distinction" in which one can also speak of subjects socially forbidden). The incident foreshadows in quality the letter in which the official Sortini makes filthy proposals to Amalia. Such "irrational ambivalence" need not be derived from a source essentially absurd. It can be explained grammatically as the dramatic expression of a normal relation between species and genus. For if both the holy and the obscene are *set apart* from other classes of things or persons, this *exceptional* quality is something they share in common, *generically,* though each manifests its own *specific* variants of this common element.

The forbidden (of either holy or obscene sorts) can become identified with the magic experiences of infancy, the tabus of the excremental, which are established along with the first steps in language, and fade into the prelinguistic stage of experience. Thus, ironically, the very "seat of highest dignity" can become furtively one with the connotations of the human posterior, in a rhetorical identification between high and low, since both can represent the principle of the tabu. A friend said:

"When I was young, I thought that a king's 'royal highness' was his behind, and that his subjects were required to show it great deference. I could not have told you what the principle of hierarchy is, but in this error I showed that I had got to the very foundations of it."

Gulliver's Travels has many episodes which, in Swift's morbidly playful way, exemplify the symbolic connection between the "sacred" tabus of royalty and the "obscene" tabus of the fecal. Most notably the identification figures roundabout, in satiric denial, near the beginning of Chapter VI, in the "Voyage to Brobdingnag." Here Gulliver recounts:

> I desired the Queen's woman to save for me the combings of her Majesty's hair, whereof in time I got a good quantity, and consulting with my friend the cabinet-maker, who had received general orders to do little jobs for me, I directed him to make two chair frames, no larger than those I had in my box, and then to bore little holes with a fine awl round those parts where I designed the backs and seats; through these holes I wove the strongest hairs I could pick out, just after the manner of cane chairs in England. When they were finished, I made a present of them to her Majesty, who kept them in her cabinet, and used to show them for curiosities, as indeed they were the wonder of every one that beheld them. The Queen would have me sit upon one of these chairs, but I absolutely refused to obey her, protesting I would rather die a thousand deaths than place a dishonorable part of my body on those precious hairs that once adorned her Majesty's head.

Immediately after, there is another identification, though of a nature that could be detected only by internal analysis of Swift's vocabulary. Gulliver speaks of his "mechanical genius." And for the overtones of the word "mechanical" in Swiftian satire, the reader is referred to the grotesquely gnarled adumbrations of psychoanalysis in Swift's essay on "The Mechanical Operation of the Spirit," where he attacks idealistic enthusiasm by deriving it from sources connected with the privy parts.

In *The German Ideology,* Marx touches upon similar identifications when, discussing idealistic systems that lead up to "one sacred head," he says:

This "cranium system" is as old as the Egyptian pyramids, with which it has many similarities, and as new as the Prussian monarchy, in the capital of which it has recently been resurrected, as young as ever. The idealistic Dalai Lamas have this much in common with their real counterpart: they would like to persuade themselves that the world from which they derive their subsistence could not continue without their holy excrement. As soon as this idealistic folly is put into practice, its malevolent nature is apparent: its charlatanry, its pietistic hypocrisy, its unctuous deceit. Miracles are the asses' bridge leading from the kingdom of the idea to practice.

The last sentence suggests another route whereby the same connotations can arise: in the idealist doctrine whereby the material manifestation of spirit is like the externalizing of the internal.

In sum: Either elegant or filthy language can represent the hierarchic principle, just as both "up" or "down" represent the "principle of height." (The point is quite relevant to *Lady Chatterley's Lover*.) In this way, extremes can meet. To call a man very moral or to call him very immoral is at least "the same" in the sense that, in both cases, one is saying, "This man is to be considered exceptional from the standpoint of moral considerations"—and that is one of the purely "grammatical" factors behind "ambivalence" that might otherwise seem merely "irrational."

In a somewhat decadent bourgeois society, perverse and grotesque expressions of the hierarchic principle (variants of "Thersitism"?) would be more suitable than in a court where, for a stretch of years, much amenity had prevailed. In Kafka's case, there was added incentive to burlesque the "reverence," since he personally encountered such "transcendence" in a very low form, anti-Semitism. But though, as an enlightened intellectual, he could doubly contemn it, pragmatically it retained its "magic" nonetheless; as a going concern it actually did set the conditions of preferment.

Also, the greater shiftiness of status in bourgeois society is an invitation to blaspheme. The "shopkeeper" is absurd, from the "magical" point of view, because his store of riches is on display, not "awesomely," but *obsequiously,* in "aiming to please" the customer who is "always right" (though the ultra-fashionable shop contrives to restore the illusion by suggesting that merchant and client are united in a conspiracy to exclude "inferior" customers). The same problem, in a more exalted way, besets wealthy industrialists who have made their fortunes by the sale of products deemed ludicrous. Masefield's sonnet bathetically contrasting ancient poetic cargoes with modern prosaic ones derives its appeal from an "aristocratic" judgment of the bourgeoisie. For this he deserved to be knighted.

A friend said: "When at high school, mooning and moody with love, I was under an unusual puzzlement and constraint several times daily. For the father of the girl whom I revered in distant awe was a manufacturer of water closets. This sound citizen was proud enough of his commodity to have his name glazed in the enamel of the bowl. And since we had one of his excellent products in our bathroom, I had to confront the name of the beloved in ways that compelled its desecration. I fervently wished that the vessel had been given an impersonal trade name, such as Monarch, or Superior, or Little Gem."

Another incentive to the expression of hierarchy *via* the Absurd is found in the fact that the monetary test of "quality" impairs the magic so far as "racial superiority" goes. For some members of the "inferior" race may be financially better off than many of the "superior" race. In a society where monetary norms are as basic to the rationale of motives as they are in capitalism, a "racist" magic would be intact only if all the "superior" race were rich and all the "inferior" races were poor. Similarly the magic of "white supremacy" is impaired in the South, insofar as Negroes show earning capacity equal to the whites'. This is presumably the "rhetorical" motive for upholding the double standard of wages and jobs. (See Richard Wright's autobiography, *Black Boy,* for accounts of the sullenness and thoroughness with which this "order" can be imposed.) The South for magical reasons strives to hold down its wage scale, thereby as a region getting a smaller proportion of the national income, even while complaining of "Northern exploitation." In keeping the Negroes' wages low, it sets a competing lower standard for wages generally, except insofar as "outside union organizers from the North" can exert pressure for higher rates. A deliberate cult of the irrational, the Absurd, would obscure the perception of such conditions, even suggesting that there is a certain bad taste or literary crudeness in the mere mention of them; but a "dialectical" way of deriving these same absurdities can be "rational."

Again, insofar as an economy is beset by "crises," ("judgments") as the capitalist economy is periodically, the rational enlightenment which shows these to be man-made ills rather than "acts of God" redounds to the discredit of the ruling class, so that there are more incentives to "blaspheme" against the order than to treat it "reverently." But "blasphemy" soon invites to "irrational" excesses.

Again, to the extent that dignity is attested by monetary advantage, there seems to be a "magical" need for the higher officials in the typical business corporation to receive an income "awesomely" greater than that of any ordinary worker. It comes to seem dubious whether "authority" could be preserved by any other means. The "pursuit of happiness" is thus transformed into the search for "more magic," a condition of endless persecution besetting the successes and the failures, and the underlings who do not figure greatly in the race, but are prodded by its goading. The motive is not "greed." We could almost wish that it were, for greed might be sated, appeased, or grow weary. But the striving for "more reverence" in the social realm, this unconscious caricature of the quest for the divine, this illusion made "normal," can have no end. To seek for God in godly ways might be striving enough; all the more must the striving be endless, when men are "seeking for God" in terms of a social illusion, a "reverence" that attains its sympathetic, doctrinal counterpart in a cult of the "Absurd."

Order, the Secret, and the Kill

It is hard today to keep theological-esthetic cults of the Absurd and the Kill distinct from psychological-esthetic ones. Psychologically, for instance, one might begin by asking not, "What did God want of Abraham?" but, "Why did Abraham think that he 'ought to' kill his son?" Thus, with the "war of the generations" in mind (father and son as rival classes), one might interpret the religious motivation psychoanalytically as Abraham's mere "rationalization" of his "suppressed desire" to be rid of Isaac. Or giving the psychology an anthropological twist, one might ask, "What permanent antagonism between father and son is expressed in this story of a father who entertained thoughts of killing his son?" God's "command" would thus be interpreted as the disguised expression of a repugnant infanticidal impulse which Abraham, and all the "pious fathers" he stands for, translates into socially acceptable terms.

But here again, we would object to the stress upon the *killing* as primary. It would be another instance of our claim, stated earlier, that psychoanalysis too often reënforces the cult of the hunt, by transforming the by-product of sacrifice into its purpose, thus making a "devotion" of murder, quite as in fascist genocide and the "liberal" murder mystery. But, approached grammatically, through the "paradox of substance," the motivation acquires the other dimensions needed to present it in its true complexity. "Grammatically," we note that insofar as father and son are *consubstantial*, a father's fantasy of "scrupulously" slaying a beloved and only son would contain two elements: by thus "killing himself" vicariously, the father could simultaneously be destroyed and be saved. Thus, a friend said:

"On one occasion I took my son to the tower of a high building in New York, to show him the city below. When looking from a height, I had always had the fantasy of jumping. Many people have it. Even while knowing that they will not jump, they keep thinking, 'What if I jumped?'—and the imagining can sometimes be strong enough even to nauseate them. I often had this same feeling, though not to an alarming degree.

"But as I stood holding my son so that he could see over the parapet, a variant of this fantasy came over me intensely. I was seized with the thought, 'What if I threw him over?' And whereas, when I had had this fantasy with regard to my own descent, it was moderate, in this form it was brutally extreme. I was humiliated, and puzzled. For I thought I greatly loved this child; I thought he meant to me the very logic of my life. Yet here, even as he snuggled trustfully in my arms, I had thoughts of killing him. I took him to the street, in some haste, worried, and ashamed.

"For weeks I puzzled over this loathsome infanticidal motive, which seemed so contrary to the feelings that I consciously felt for my son. I remembered how, as a child, I had been told of the father rabbits eating the heads of the young, unless the mother was able to protect them. 'Am I no better than that?' I wondered. But I finally figured it out thus:

"With this child I identified myself as closely as I could possibly identify myself with someone other than myself. If, then, I threw him from the height, I could have had, simultaneously, both the jumping and the not-jumping. At least, without jumping, by the vicarious sacrifice of my son in my place, I could have had much more intensely the sense of jumping than when the fantasy involved me alone. Hence, the sudden almost overwhelming return of the old fantasy in this new, criminal form."

Of course, in the realm of fantasy, even mere velleities can take the form of killing (as revealed in the expression, "I could have killed him," to describe minor provocations). In this sense, fantasies of killing may at times be no more than a dramatic way of saying, "I wish I were, at the moment, free of this particular person." (André Gide's scrupulous villains transmogrify such irritability to demoniac proportions.) Under such conditions, fantasies of shooting a man dead might not be essentially different from fantasies of kicking him, or biting him in Stavrogin fashion.

Bunyan apparently felt great remorse for the many "protestant" obsessions of this sort that plagued him (the debtor, the victim of social hierarchy, who sought piously to impose upon himself the judgments of the socially superior, and thus was beset by tiny involuntary rebellions like the promptings of devils, until the problems of social reverence could attain their transcendence in terms of Christian's eventual religious preferment, with the hierarchy of the rich and poor transformed into the hierarchy of the saved and the damned, and the very last step into heaven being signalized by one last dispatching of the damned into hell).

Under some conditions, fantasies of killing can be as "unmoral" as the word "kill" itself, which is not even a "dirty" word as thus generalized, but is loathsome only in particular applications. And there is thus always the possibility that fantasy can approach the act of killing thus "impersonally," even when applied to personal cases conscientiously forbidden. This would be not so much an "eruption" of the "unconscious" as the operation of wholly "rational" faculties. For insofar as conscience itself is the *universalizing* of an act (considering it from the most general point of view), the universalizing of a personal element would be by the same token a kind of depersonalization. (This development may explain in part why a theater audience which would readily accept the sacrifice of a divine *dramatis persona* resents it when an "unhappy ending" befalls an ordinary likable character they have come to know.)

Is it not notable that, whereas the "four-letter words" for a few humble bodily functions are "indecent" and "obscene," the four-letter word for the taking of a human life is quite "neutral," though this act is forbid-

den us by Eternal commandment? God only knows what may be
the motives of a peace-loving wretch who, if left to himself, would harm
no one in all his life, and would be squeamishly humanitarian in his
attitude towards animals, but is drafted by his nation for service as a
professional killer. God only knows just what his confusions may be,
and by what strange furies they are later to be manifested. But where
the killing is "devotional," as in the Hemingway tradition, the relation
between the proscriptions against bodily uncleanness and the proscriptions against killing may give us some clue to the motives. For symbolically, killing may be a kind of "anal act" that is "pure," transcending
the tabus of the privy parts. (Anal-offal would be deathy, in contrast
with life-giving oral-edible.) "Devotional" killing may thus resolve a
psychic problem acquired when the infant is being taught control of
excretory functions.

The thought incidentally suggests that, if our militarists finally succeed
in establishing compulsory military training, they could not hope to
transform our citizens into really devoted soldiers unless they strenuously insisted on early and strenuous punishment in the training of children, to instill in them an almost mystic horror of befouling themselves.
By the use of excessive punishment to establish such tabus firmly in the
stage of infancy, they might get an army of Roman Stoics who would
be willing, with profoundest conscientiousness, to fight devoutly, whenever ordered, so that empire-builders could effectively "accept the solemn
responsibility" of an "American Century."

The thought may also suggest why so many of our religionists seem
so much more zealous today in helping out the movement towards
bigger armies than in trying to promote international amity. Symbolically, there may be a "purer" devotion, as regards transcending of the
"privy" tabus, in a cult of military discipline than in the more "unclean"
ways of peace. For genuine peace today could be got only by such a
dialectic as risked "contamination" by the enemy. Or rather, by such
a dialectic as sought deliberately to give full expression to the voice of
the enemy, not excluding it, but seeking to assign it an active place in
an ultimate order. But when confronting the need for "dyings" and new
"births" thus dialectically encouraged, men seem to prefer the simple
suicide and homicide of militarist devotion, having persuaded themselves
that the further dialectical growth of doctrine would be immoral.

Considering the Cult of the Kill from Veblen's angle of vision, we can also get glimpses of its earlier relation to social hierarchy. Only the upper classes could hunt. The lower classes could but poach. Hunting was thus not merely the insignia of privilege; it did reverence to the principle of *order*. (For though we tend to think of "law and order" as a pleonasm, like "house and home" or "day and time," the second word refers not merely to regulation, but to *hierarchy*. A genuine "new order" is a new *social ladder*.)

The "forest king" may have had his origins in a purely "universal" magic. One might get such an interpretation from the *Golden Bough*, at least to the extent that "primitive" psychology in general is being studied there, rather than "primitive class psychology," even though the signs of priestcraft are, on their face, signs of a "higher" class. In any case, even if one would hold that the "forest king" was not related to social privilege in his very origins, at the very least one would concede that the Robin Hood legends show how such reverence of early magic becomes interwoven with the principle of social hierarchy. For Robin Hood was the magical forest deity, Robert des Boix, *politicalized* (a "universal" myth transformed for "invidious" purposes). This benevolent poacher was the legendary hero of Saxon resistance to the Norman invader, resistance to a *ruling* class by a *subject* class.

In sum: On every hand, we find men, in their quarrels over property, preparing themselves for the slaughter, even to the extent of manipulating the profoundest grammatical, rhetorical, and symbolic resources of human thought to this end. Hence, insofar as one can do so without closing his eyes to the realities, it is relevant to attempt analyzing the tricky ways of thought that now work to complete the devotion of killing. Though churchmen may feel much genuine concern for human betterment in general, even the most scrupulous of them are susceptible to two major kinds of deception as regards religious motives: there can be the obscene mistaking of social reverence for religious reverence; and this obscenity is mingled with another, the furtive intermingling of the divine mystery with the "mystery" of the "demonic trinity," the excretory functions of the body.

The first of these is the more easily recognizable. It is unmistakably present insofar as any congregation is "exclusive." To say as much is to realize its ubiquity. The second is more difficult to detect, but attains its ultimate manifestation in "scrupulous" preference for militaristic solutions over peaceful solutions. The two probably merge in the "mystery" of private property, where many kinds of secrecy seem to converge: the secrecy of the holy, of plans in the stage of gestation, of conspiracy, of infancy and dream, of the privy parts and their functions, and of financial treasure. The study of human relations must attempt to make these interrelationships apparent, either in glimpses or when possible by organized critical method.

So we must keep trying anything and everything, improvising, borrowing from others, developing from others, dialectically using one text as comment upon another, schematizing; using the incentive to new wanderings, returning from these excursions to schematize again, being oversubtle where the straining seems to promise some further glimpse, and making amends by reduction to very simple anecdotes.

Order, the Secret, and the Kill. To study the nature of rhetoric, the relation between rhetoric and dialectic, and the application of both to human relations in general, is to circulate about these three motives. The appeal of Kierkegaard, for those who can follow him, may derive from the fact that his Cult of the Absurd (his word for the Secret) so profoundly involves the other two, Order and the Kill. Starting from any one of them, you find a vast network of dialectical possibilities in the offing, whereupon you may tend to see the whole of the dialectic itself in terms of this starting point, thereby being conservatively slavish to Order, morbidly fascinated by the Secret, militantly envenomed for the Kill. We must consider how the fullness of dialectic ("reality") is continually being concealed behind the mists of one or another of these rhetorical overemphases. Here would be the outer reaches of a Rhetoric of Motives.

We have given much thought to the hierarchic (Order, the ladder, cosmologized by the middle ages in what Lovejoy calls "the Great Chain of Being"). We have tried to show how it involves the Secret (though insofar as the "conspiratorical" secret merges into the private secret, it leads to themes that belong under Symbolic). At the moment we are centering our attention upon the Kill. And we are trying to show the important difference between an approach to the Kill through dialectic, and an approach to dialectic through the Kill.

With the evidence of the Crucifixion before us, we cannot deny that consubstantiality *is* established by common involvement in a killing. But one must not isolate the killing itself as the essence of the exaltation. Rather, one can account for the consubstantiality as arising from common participation in a notable, or solemn experience. Thus, we once saw the history of a human society in miniature, grounded in a rhetoric of primitive magic. Some boys, about ten years of age, had been playing in a vacant lot. They stirred up a rattlesnake, which the father of one boy killed with a hoe. Then they had their pictures taken, dangling the dead snake. Immediately after, they organized the Rattle-snake Club. Their members were made consubstantial by the sacrifice of this victim, representing dangers and triumphs they had shared in common. The snake was a sacred offering; by its death it provided the spirit for this magically united band. (We said that the incident was a human society in miniature. We had in mind the fact that there was also an electing of officers and the collecting of dues. The matter of offices and dues promptly gave rise to quarrels and cliques—thus quickly was the solemnizing spirit of the snake god sacrificed a second time, as there emerged the rhetoric of the Scramble, the discordancies of Babel.)

All told, there is the *self-abnegation* of "sacrifice." And sacrifice is the essence of religion. Symbolically, it is a kind of *suicide,* a willed variant of *dying,* dying to this or that particular thing ("mortification"), not because of those things in themselves, but because the yielding of them represents the principle of sacrifice in the absolute. So, the religious injunctions against suicide in the literal sense are matched by the many religious disciplines for attaining transcendence by dying "dialectically." And where there must thus be simultaneously a dying and a not-dying, what is more plausible than for the paradox of substance to figure here, in providing symbolic devices whereby a man can "substantially" slay himself through the sacrifice of another who is consubstantial with him? Indeed, among the psychological appeals of the Christian sacrifice, wherein the ultimate father sacrifices the ultimate son, may be the fact that in this myth there is the perfect paradigm for such simultaneous losing-and-having, since the two persons of father and son are consubstantial, and the ultimate father sacrifices the ultimate son for the sake of human betterment (as the principle of individual sacrifice itself is ultimately motivated by such social objectives, a sacrificial restraining of individual divisiveness in accordance with "virtues" designed for the advantage of mankind in general).

And when our friend, standing with his son in that high place, felt "infanticidal" impulses, perhaps he was but manifesting roundabout the fact that he felt exalted, as though he and his son shared the attributes of the Ultimate Father and the Ultimate Son in heaven. Even though he may not have got to such feelings by true religious reverence, he could have got to them by the temptations of social reverence. For here was the principle of hierarchy materialized, as he stood atop a high building, while that building itself represented nothing less than the straining social hierarchy of the great modern Babylon. "And upon her forehead was a name written, MYSTERY, BABYLON THE GREAT, THE MOTHER OF HARLOTS AND ABOMINATIONS OF THE EARTH." (Revelation 17:5.)

Pure Persuasion

Apparently the farthest one can go, in matters of rhetoric, is to the question of "pure persuasion." But since that would bring us to the borders of metaphysics, or perhaps better "meta-rhetoric," we should try as much as possible to keep particular examples in mind.

Thus, looking back at *Alice in Wonderland* "meta-rhetorically," let us consider how it looks, when judged as "pure persuasion." Psychoanalysis suggests the nature of its "impurity," its ambiguous gallantry as the courting of a girl child not yet nubile by a man advanced in years. The situation provides such obvious material for psychoanalysis that Empson's superb chapter on Alice is continually being deflected from its own best insight. Yet here is a perfect instance where the courtship is not primarily sexual at all, but a communication between classes, the subtle variants of appeal being strongly mixed with the telltale variants of "standoffishness."

Dodgson is not much concerned with the principle of abstract womanhood (as it might be variously represented in virgin-worship, prostitution, promiscuity, or a cult of seduction). But he never forgets the idea of social courtship. The fantasy represents this principle grotesquely, in reverse, by stories about the characters' comical rudeness and crudeness, as contrasted with Alice's mild priggishness.

In engaging the child's attention by puzzles that tease as well as entertain, the book gets its standoffish element. It says in effect: "I am at your mercy. I don't dare to bore you. But let us not forget that I also have a stance of my own. You are for me magic, music, and mystery. But I can magically, musically mystify you, too." Psychoanalysis makes us see too clearly the perverted sexual lover. He is unquestionably there.

But his presence should not conceal the rhetorical exercise, the artistic persuasion, emboding motives not of sexual but of social intercourse.

Perhaps "social" is not quite accurate. For youth and age, as contrasted communicating "kinds," could not be classed exactly as either sexual or social. They are biological, as with the hierarchal relation between weak and strong. However, both age-youth and weak-strong, with their complications and reversibilities, readily become identified with social elements, particularly as regards familial and political symbols of authority.

It would not be exorbitant to put *Alice in Wonderland* in the same bin not only with *The Castle,* but also with D. H. Lawrence's *Lady Chatterley's Lover.* Each in its way represents social reverence, grotesquely, perversely. Each in its way would repay analysis as observed from the standpoint of *The Book of the Courtier.* Each, in its way, is not merely a work that implicitly embodies the principle of courtship: in all three the principle of courtship is explicitly the subject matter.

We hesitate to say this because Lawrence's work is itself so strongly psychoanalytic in perspective, and so "sexual," that we seem to be impairing our own case. Yet we would have the reader see the entire situation the other way round, noting the intense factor of social hierarchy that characterizes relations among Lawrence's characters, and scrutinizing his view of "the unconscious" itself for connotations of upsurge from coal pits (though the translation of such revolt into psychoanalytic terms transcends the political implications, and thereby negates them). The "filthy" words for sex are but the obverse of the hierarchic reverence present in his psychoanalytically romantic ones. And if you had to make a flat choice between a social and a physical origin for the sexuality in his books, you would be much nearer to the truth if you took the social one (even its relation to the excitability of his disease being social insofar as it involves antitheses of weakness and strength, sensitiveness and bluntness, that fall primarily in the category of the "socially invidious").

With talk of "pure persuasion," the factor of degree can readily confuse us. Thus, we may think of social or literary courtship as pure persuasion, when we contrast it with a direct bid for sexual favors, or with commercial advertising. Similarly, education in contrast with debating might be called pure persuasion. And scientific or religious insemination may seem "pure" when compared with the injection of the doctrinal seed through political ideologies. But all these modes of expression are "impure," and seek advantage, as compared with the absolute, and therefore nonexistent, limit we here speak of. Yet, though what we mean by pure persuasion in the absolute sense exists nowhere, it can be present as a motivational ingredient in any rhetoric, no matter how intensely advantage-seeking such rhetoric may be. The point should become clearer as we proceed. At this stage we need only note that the indication of pure persuasion in any activity is in an element of "standoffishness," or perhaps better, *self-interference,* as judged by the tests of acquisition. Thus, while not essentially sacrificial, it *looks* sacrificial when matched against the acquisitive.

Pure persuasion involves the saying of something, not for an extra-verbal advantage to be got by the saying, but because of a satisfaction intrinsic to the saying. It summons because it likes the feel of a summons. It would be nonplused if the summons were answered. It attacks because it revels in the sheer syllables of vituperation. It would be horrified if, each time it finds a way of saying, "Be damned," it really did send a soul to rot in hell. It intuitively says, "This is so," purely and simply because this is so.

Or, since it is formal, it can arise out of expressions quite differently motivated, as when a book, having been developed so far, sets up demands of its own, demands conditioned by the parts already written, so that the book becomes to an extent something not foreseen by its author, and requires him to interfere with his original intentions. We here confront an "ultimate" motive (as distinct from an "ulterior" one). Or if you insist that there is only the "illusion" of such a motive, even so, that "illusion" can be strong enough to act as a motive in its own right. It would then be an "illusion of pure persuasion," after the analogy of De Gourmont's formula for the "illusion of liberty."

In such a realm of the absolute, of course, it is not hard to get quickly from "self-interference" to "freedom." We but exemplify in reverse Kant's discovery that the "free" legislating of a universal law would impose restrictions upon the legislator, a dialectical miracle which we again encounter, partially burlesqued, in the Existentialist notion (like the doctrine of the nihilist in Dostoevski's *The Possessed*) that one is "free," hence a god, in suicide. (Since the idea of self-interference would get its ultimate expression in images of suicide, a kind of religious exhilaration could accompany the Existentialist rationale of suicide whereby real loss is transformed into ideal gain.)

What the anthropologist Malinowski called "phatic communion" might seem close to "pure persuasion." He referred to talk at random, purely for the satisfaction of talking together, the use of speech as such for the establishing of a social bond between speaker and spoken-to. Yet "pure persuasion" should be much more intensely purposive than that, though it would be a "pure" purpose, a kind of purpose which, as judged by the rhetoric of advantage, is no purpose at all, or which might often look like sheer frustration of purpose. For its purpose is like that of solving a puzzle, where the puzzle-solver deliberately takes on a burden in order to throw it off, but if he succeeds, so far as the tests of material profit are concerned he is no further ahead than before he began, since he has advanced not relatively, but "in the absolute."

Yet the "self-interference" of "pure" persuasion can derive from many "impure" sources, or become compromised by "entangling alliances." Its utterances may become the vehicle for all sorts of private ambitions, guilts, and vengeances, or the instrument of other men so motivated. Persons who cannot solve their problems by victory in the Scramble can certainly "compensate for frustration" by solving arbitrary puzzles. Even elements of magic (in the sense of bad science) may come to figure here, as the puzzle-solver may furtively promise himself that, by the solving of arbitrarily chosen puzzles, he will "homoeopathically" solve puzzles imposed upon him by conditions beyond his control.

The devout man's relations to his God have a kind of standoffishness. For his sin is rebellion, and he never lets it be forgot that he is always sinning somewhat. Here are the rudiments for a grim kind of coyness.

Perhaps as near an instance of "pure persuasion" as one could find is in the actor's relation to his audience. Yet you could readily see how it might become homosexual in its implications, hardly other than a roundabout way of recruiting lovers who share the same "persuasion," particularly if the actor's talent was originally developed as an appeal to socially "superior" persons of the same sex. An audience, technically a sexless function, can stand furtively for a kind of *alter ego* that is the narcissistic, socially idealized version of the beloved self.

In Dodgson's case, the "meta-rhetorical" motive was unquestionably interwoven with odd sexual quandaries. Yet we may question whether these themselves were the truly "prior" motives, since they could be developed as a response to the awareness of "hierarchy in general." And while such order would be more social than sexual, it is "prior" even to the social, deriving ultimately from the nature of communication *per se*.

In its essence communication involves the use of verbal symbols for purposes of appeal. Thus, it splits formally into the three elements of speaker, speech, and spoken-to, with the speaker so shaping his speech as to "commune with" the spoken-to. This purely technical pattern is the precondition of *all* appeal. And "standoffishness" is necessary to the form, because without it the appeal could not be maintained. For if union is complete, what incentive can there be for appeal? Rhetorically, there can be courtship only insofar as there is division. Hence, only through interference could one court continually, thereby perpetuating genuine "freedom of rhetoric."

We are not offering this concept of "pure" rhetoric as the highest ideal of human conduct. We are simply trying to show how such a rhetorical motive can of itself supply a principle of interference which, whatever its origin, often has a high ethical value, as with the late Irving Babbitt's concept of the "inner check."

Put it this way. Suppose that there were no motives of incest awe to produce sexual tabus. Suppose that there were no higher and lower social classes, to instill "reverence" for the real, personal, or sentimental properties that came to be the insignia of privilege. Suppose there were no boasting, no goad to display superior prowess. Would there still be a source from which might be derived an athleticism of self-denial, as for instance in priestly or courtly cults of chastity, or in vows of poverty?

We are suggesting that there would be, that such an incentive is implicit in the "transcendent" nature of symbolism itself. And out of this could arise a *symbolically grounded* distrust of acquisitiveness, a feeling that one should not just "take things," but should court them, show gratitude for them, or apologize for killing them (as with the "natural courtesy" that some savages show to the game they have caught, a practice rationalistically explained as the savage's way of thanking the victim for participating so handsomely in the success of the hunt, but basically the incentive of courtliness). Another variant is perhaps discernible in the neurotic artist, suffering wretchedly from his neurosis, yet so slavish in his devotion to symbols that he is hesitant to be cured, lest he impair the persuasiveness of his art.

The "enlightened" absence of this motive (in the modern pragmatism of natural science, where the only acknowledged resistances to the acquisition of power must come from the nature of the physical conditions themselves) could make for more crudeness than it does, if it really prevailed as much as the "enlightened" think it does.

True, even if you granted that such a motive exists, derivable directly from the nature of language rather than indirectly from the social structure, there would be no reason why, in a complex society, with its many hierarchally ordered institutions and their corresponding properties and proprieties, such a motive should not often show rather as its opposite: in a tough cult of acquisition, born of impatience with such exactions. This should be particularly the case when, given the conditions of the Scramble, if one did not first grab, he would not have much chance not to grab. The "emancipated" would like nothing better than a society so burdened with "self-interference" that it could be scooped up easily, in one big fish net.

At the very least, even without intense competitive pressure, any sheer cult of self-denial would be enough, in its austerity, to build up resistances which the body and the mind found gratification in breaking down again. Hence, just as self-denial could come of persuasion, so an acquisitive "negating of the negation" could come from the same source. And for our part, rather than treating the fantastic acquisitiveness of imperialists as a mere "mental replica" of biological desires, we would explain it thus roundabout, as *the dialectical transformation of self-denial into its opposite*.

The mere fact that a withholding, or an interposing of distance, is worked into a system (as it is in the athleticism of the ascetic), makes for an intellectual fullness which may then be transformed into an instrument having new possibilities of gain. Such is apparently the way in which priestcraft comes to the aid of political and economic advantage (particularly when the priests are literate, since clericalism serves so well for tax-gathering, and in general for expansion of a ruler's realm, while also of course helping to ally the ruler with the "divine"). And if you look closely enough at capitalist motives, as the secularization of priestly symbolism, you can glimpse a similar roundabout development (signalized in the doctrine that profit on capital investment is justified as a reward for "postponed consumption"). It is the difference between the finance capitalist's amassing of monetary *symbols* and the earlier stage of "primitive accumulation" (though even in most "primitive accumulation," wealth is not sought for itself alone, but for its "transcendent" value as insignia).

Once we saw a performance by the Chinese ritual dancer, Mei Lan-fang. We were vastly impressed by his ceremony of reaching: the slow movements of hand, wrist, and arm whereby he first gradually worked back the long sleeve that covered his fingers—and then, after this patient preparation, the tentative approaching of the freed hand to the object, and finally, the cautious grasping and lifting. The next day we happened to attend an American movie. At one point in the story the phone rang—and the heroine swung around abruptly, to snatch up the receiver like a tigress leaping on a lamb. Ordinarily the incident would have been unnoticeable. This time we jumped.

Let's not deceive ourselves. There's a thoroughly "class" motive that goes far towards explaining such ritual. Where acquisition is assured to a class by the nature of the property structure itself, the class need not snatch. Accordingly, the esthetic spokesmen that represent its values need not snatch. We might also note how, by rites that teach others not to snatch, it might help to perpetuate its privileges. (We recall that, along with such pudency of acquisition, there was a sword dance in which symbolic heads were severed with dispatch.)

Yet note another element here: the ritual. This was a symbolic getting, not a real one. Hence, it could exist only by prolonging or delaying the act, or in the case of the sword dance, by "pure purpose" (Kant's purposiveness without purpose). This element is so intrinsic to the ritual act that, even without the class motive, you could derive it. All purely ritual getting is also a not-getting. After our many remarks on "mystification," we would be the last to deny the importance of the class motive. We only plead to recognize that there can be a factor even prior to that, in that a ritual acquisition is no acquisition, hence is intrinsically an interference with the ways of acquisition (though we would not deny that such rituals of the nonacquisitive might themselves, in bringing the performer prestige and other rewards, serve to his advantage in the most directly acquisitive sense).

We are not making a moralistic statement here. We are not saying that there "should be" pure persuasion, or more of it. Or that "human frailty" is forever making persuasion "impure." We are saying that, as the ultimate of all persuasion, its form or archetype, there *is* pure persuasion. If you want, we are even willing, for the sake of the argument, to take the opposite moralistic position, and say that there "should not be" pure persuasion, or that there "should be less of it." The important consideration is that, in any device, the ultimate form (paradigm or idea) of that device is present, and is acting. And this form would be the "purity."

Since the ultimate form of persuasion is composed of three elements (speaker, speech, and spoken-to), as regards the act of persuasion alone obviously you could not maintain this form except insofar as the plea remained unanswered. When the plea is answered, you have gone from persuasion to something else. Where you had previously been trying to get in, you may now have to try getting out, as we saw in the case of Kierkegaard. This is what we mean by the technical or formal need of "self-interference" as a motive in persuasion. This is why we say that the ultimate cult of persuasion would transcend the use of persuasion for local advantage, as the fourth book of *The Courtier* transcended the preceding three. If you were winsomely persuasive, you could keep on persuading only by yourself supplying the interferences which you over-come in your audiences, like lovers who "quarrel to make up," or as with "virtuous" women who develop a Carlylean cult of Clothes "in all its nakedness," as a mode of "pure persuasion" that ambiguously com-bines the pudencies of property with the pruriencies of propriety (a "rhetorical" motive that now forms the basis of a major industry).

Where an anthropologist or sociologist might derive sexual tabus from institutional sources, we would not deny his evidence. We would only say that, over and above all such derivations, there is, *implicit in language itself,* the act of persuasion; and *implicit in the perpetuating of persua-sion* (in persuasion made universal, pure, hence paradigmatic or formal) *there is the need of "interference."* For a persuasion that succeeds, dies. To go on eternally (as a form does) it could not be directed merely towards attainable advantages. And insofar as the advantages are ob-tainable, *that* particular object of persuasion could be maintained as such only by interference. Here, we are suggesting, would be the ultimate rhetorical grounds for the tabus of courtship, the conditions of "stand-offishness."

The frenzied human cult of advantage, the quest of many things that cannot bring real advantage yet are obtainable, would likewise seem ultimately to require such a "meta-rhetorical" explanation. (At least, this would account for its *origins*. Institutional factors would account for its *intensity*.) Insofar as a society rejects interference "from within" as a device for perpetuating the persuasive act, men can still get the same

result by a cult of "new needs" (with the continual shifting of objectives to which men are goaded by the nature of our economic system).
By such temporizings, the form of persuasion is permanently maintained.
For in proportion as men, threatened with the loss of persuasion through
attaining its object, turn to court other objects, such constant shifting of
purposes in effect supplies (as it seems, "from without") the principle of
self-interference which the perpetuating of the persuasive act demands.
To make the attaining of A but the condition for the need of B, and the
attaining of B but the condition for the need of C, etc., adds up to the
same "form" as if one merely went on forever courting A at a distance.
A single need, forever courted, as on Keats's Grecian Urn, would be
made possible by self-interference. Drop self-interference, plunge "extra-
vertedly" into the "rat race" of new needs forever changing, and you get
the equivalent. (The permanent form would be got in one case by excessive fixity of attention, in the other by excessive distraction; but the
distraction can have its kind of continuity too, insofar as all the "new
needs" are rationalized by the "unitary" symbolism of money.)

We are not moralistic about our thoughts on pure persuasion, because
we cannot see it as either "good" or "bad" in the moralistic, political,
institutional sense. We can only surmise that it comes quite close to
the origins of the Human Comedy, which gets its costumes from the
changing conditions of history, but the form of which, like laughter,
derives from the nature of language itself, the "rationality" of *homo
dialecticus,* of man as a symbol-using animal whose symbols simultaneously reflect and transcend the "reality" of the nonsymbolic.

Biologically, it is of the essence of man to desire. But by the same
token, biologically it is of the essence of man to be sated. Only the
motives of "mystery" (making for development towards ever "higher"
degrees of ordination) are infinite in their range, as a child learns for
himself when he first thinks of counting "to the highest number."

The dialectical transcending of reality through symbols is at the roots
of this mystery, at least so far as naturalistic motives are concerned. It
culminates in pure persuasion, absolute communication, beseechment
for itself alone, praise and blame so universalized as to have no assignable physical object (hence it is led to postulate the Principles of Goodness and Evil in general, as the only "audience" possible for an address
so generalized).

Here reverence, God, hierarchy are found to be the ultimates of the dialectical process. Call them the "basic errors" of the dialectic if you want. That need not concern us. We are here talking about ultimate dialectical tendencies, having "god," or a "god-term," as the completion of the linguistic process. If you want to conclude, "so much the worse for the linguistic process," that is your affair. We have enough areas of agreement for our study of rhetoric if you but concede that, language being essentially a means of transcending brute objects, there is implicit in it the "temptation" to come upon an idea of "God" as the *ultimate* transcendence.

Primitive peoples may have deities that are explainable wholly as "nature gods." We doubt it, but we are willing for argument's sake to give an opponent the benefit of the doubt. What we are saying is that, even if there are gods conceived wholly as replicas of natural powers, you would miss the whole point of "mystification" unless at the very least you allowed also for a "dialectic god" ("logos") which could perhaps merge with the "nature god" (somewhat as the God of the New Testament merged with the God of the Old). This title of titles would be the ultimate of what Kant would call the "transcendental dialectic," the all-summarizing Idea.

Our point is: Here, in this conclusion of dialectic, one should look for the ultimate rhetorical motive of *homo dialecticus*. Human effort would thus be grounded not in the search for "advantage," and in the mere "sublimating" of that search by "rationalizations" and "moralizations." Rather, it would be grounded in a *form,* in the persuasiveness of the hierarchic order itself. And considered dialectically, prayer, as pure beseechment, would be addressed not to an *object* (which might "answer" the prayer by providing booty) but to the *hierarchic principle itself,* where the answer is implicit in the address. There is a fallacy of over-formal interpretation, which so stresses "pure" motives that the factor of advantage is slighted. But there is also the fallacy of overly materialist interpretations which would slight dialectic as a factor. The fact that tabus get their character from the conditions of a particular property structure does not eliminate their further grounding in tendencies inborn to *oratio.*

We are not discovering "God" here, in the theologian's sense. God, in the theologian's sense, must be much more than an "Idea" dialectically arrived at. Judged from the standpoint of orthodox doctrine, we believe that a pure "dialectic god" would be as unsatisfactory in one way as a mere "nature god" would be in another. But going by the verbal route, from words for positive things to titles, thence to an order among titles, and finally to the title of titles, we come as far as rhetoric-and-dialectic can take us, which is as far as this book contracts to take us.

Yet, perhaps we here overstate the case. A god unites generalization with personification. And whereas a "dialectic god" might seem to lack the second of these elements, it clearly possesses the first. In this sense, "pure persuasion" could qualify as one member of a pantheon. It would be an equivalent for the "Goddess Peitho" at that point where Greek religion and Greek science overlapped (since the Greek equated science with *generalized* knowledge). Yet the principle of personality would be there too, though indirectly. For ideas are personal.

They are personal because only persons can have them. They are an aspect of something so essentially personal as symbol-using ("human rationality"). An idea can seem impersonal because many men, or all men, may share in its personality (or partake of its substance, quite like communicants ritualistically eating the blood and body of their god).

Indeed, once you linger on this question of personality, you find it bristling with dialectical paradoxes whereby the personal and the impersonal subtly change places (paradoxes that furtively invest humans with "divine" attributes, hence adding to the "mystifications" so important in rhetorical prodding). When a figure becomes the personification of some impersonal motive, the result is a *depersonalization*. The person becomes the charismatic vessel of some "absolute" substance. And when thus magically endowed, the person transcends his nature as an individual, becoming instead the image of the idea he stands for. He is then the representative not of himself but of the family or class substance with which he is identified. In this respect he becomes "divine" (and his distinctive marks, such as his clothing, embody the same spirit).

Thus, when the principle of social reverence attains its summing up in the person of a beloved, she is loved not merely "for herself," but for what she "represents," as charismatic vessel of a social motive which the lover, or communicant, would court roundabout. Indeed, marriage as a sacrament so binds social and religious reverence together that you could not tell where "careerism" ends and "God" begins.

Whether the beloved be thought of as "superior," "inferior," or "equal" in social status, she can represent the hierarchic principle, and is to this extent a mystery, a purchasable miracle. She is "ordained" with the properties of an absolute order. Her glow, an almost visible aura, is rhetorical. But the persuasiveness of this rhetoric derives from the perfection or thoroughness of the lover's dialectical enterprise. He loves her for the ordination that she stands for. He can then dream fondly even of her death. For in her ordination she is divine, in her divinity she is immortal, and the idea of immortality must be approached humanly through the imagery of dying, while furthermore, in their dying together, jointly godlike, there would also be symbolically a coitus (all told, a dialectic alchemy whereby acquisition is readily transformed into relinquishment—and the dialectic being verbal, "intellectual," we glimpse a purely dialectical reason why Aquinas' angels, or messengers, should be "intellectuals," as also with the kind of courtship permissible to ordination in priestly celibacy).

But we have digressed, since we saw an opportunity to approach rhetorical "mystery" from another angle. We were telling how we arrived at a "dialectic god" of "pure persuasion." Next we should reverse our direction. Going from "pure hierarchy" of the dialectical form down to its embodiment in particular kinds of effort, we note first such manifestations as in the "reverent" tributes to the earthly hierarchy. We note the equivalents of this, either in a "pastoral" rapport between high and low, or (when the bond is snapped) in such "mystic" hatred as spokesmen for the "toiling masses" sometimes feel for the very idea of the "ruling class," or as spokesmen for the ruling class feel for the leaders of revolt, or even of reform. So, we look for all the attenuations of mystery. For as students of rhetoric, we concede the great persuasive power of mystery (indeed, even to the extent of wondering whether those journalistic apologists of capitalism may be most ironically defeating their own purposes when they attempt to build up the notion that the motives of the Kremlin are "enigmatic," and "inscrutable," that the ancient mysteries of the "East" are threatening to sweep across the enlightened "West"—for the current cult of the mystery story seems indication enough that the people are more than ready to be raped by a mystery).

However, when we hold that there is a hierarchic incentive (with its "mystery") embedded in the very nature of language, when we insist that one would deceive himself who derived "mystery" purely from institutional sources, we are not arguing for or against any particular set of institutions. The relative value of institutions depends pragmatically, Darwinistically, on their fitness to cope with the problems of production, distribution, and consumption that go with conditions peculiar to time and place. Thus, one particular order (or property structure), with its brands of "mystery," may be better suited than another for the prevailing circumstances. Hence, to say that hierarchy is inevitable is not to argue categorically against a new order on the grounds that it would but replace under one label what had been removed under another. It is merely to say that, in any order, there will be the mysteries of hierarchy, since such a principle is grounded in the very nature of language, and reënforced by the resultant diversity of occupational classes. That claim is the important thing, as regards the ultimate reaches of rhetoric. The intensities, morbidities, or particularities of mystery come from institutional sources, but the *aptitude* comes from the nature of man, generically, as a *symbol-using animal*.

Similarly, noting how the Prussian officer had his cultural counterpart in the academic drillmaster whose teaching was like an imperial threat, we might want to deduce all scholastic discrimination from social discrimination. But such a view would slight the principle of ordination essential to the educational process, which inevitably requires a ladder of grading and instruction. The purely "dialectical" motive is real enough here, though forever being burlesqued in the academic "positions of pantomime."

As exclusively institutional explanations mislead us in one respect, so exclusively psychoanalytic explanations can mislead in another. First a dialectical motive implicit in the nature of language is treated psychoanalytically as a mere derivative of psychological motives. Hence, the principle of "self-interference" would be explained wholly as a "sublimation" of psychological drives, whereas these themselves are strongly affected by a purely "formal" situation, the fact that language makes for transcendence, and transcendence imposes distance (a generally dialectical consideration, rather than an exclusively psychological one). Second, psychoanalysis too often conceals the nature of social relations behind the terms for sexual relations. On the first point, what we have said about the way in which institutional explanations ignore the "priority" of the formal element could be applied *mutatis mutandis* to psychoanalytic theories. So let us turn now to the second point, noting how psychoanalysis, unless properly discounted, can lead us even farther afield, by concealing the nature of exclusive social relations behind inclusive terms for sexual relations.

The sheer dialectics of "justice" strongly invites this error. For justice is the *universalization* of a standard. Hence, if one is made neurotic by *social* discriminations (by the hierarchy of class), translation of the disorders into terms of the universally sexual and the universally familial may, by such speciously universal terms, appeal by speaking in the accents of "truth" and "justice." Instead of saying, "*My class* is the victim of a *social* problem," one can say, in terms of the universalizing required by justice, "We are *all* victims of a *sexual* problem." Since the social problem will have its counterpart in sexual disorders, much "evidence" will be found for such deflection. And the deflected universalization has a "charity" that would be lacking in the social version.

The error is not rectified by a stress upon individualistic aggression, compensation, inferiority, and the like. For individualism acts as strongly as universalism to conceal the "mysteries" of class. Similarly, while a theory of "psychological types" in a sense restores a stress upon class, such classes so fall on the bias across the motives of social hierarchy that they are little more than concealments of it. All such interpretation of hierarchic motives in terms of sexual motives seems to continue, under a new guise, the earlier functions of idealistic mystification.

Or we may at once express and conceal the social origins of a neurosis by attributing it to a "birth trauma." The *exclusive* traumatic accident of being born into the quandaries of a particular social situation is thus seen as the *inclusive* misfortune of having been born at all. A malaise which gets its neurotic intensity from the social structure is thus thought to be explainable obstetrically. The specific, *familial* connotations of *class* are interpreted as the generic, *universally physiological* fact of *birth*.

Thus, in literature, a cryptic style, developed by a person with a social "shame" or "secret" of some sort, might be used as a badge of distinction, yet might also symbolize the "guilt," as were the writer to have suffered or feared some form of social discrimination or judgment, an obsession that would manifest itself furtively in the hermetic confession that was simultaneously a boast. But though this bid for distinction arose from a sense of social stigma, and so requires a rhetorical explanation, the fact that it involves ideas of one's "substance" as member of a questioned "family" or "kind" might then lead the analyst instead to look for purely *medical* explanations, as were he to derive it from the shock of birth.

There *is* a "universal" lesson here. But it is in the fact that we confront a "hierarchic psychosis," prevailing in all nations, but particularly sinister in nations which are largely ruled by the "dead hand" of institutions developed from past situations and unsuited to the present. In one form or another, it affects every rung of the social ladder, however imperceptible or roundabout its workings may be. "Psychogenic illness" is now perhaps the usual symptom of such "social diseases"—and here again we confront the difficulty in a "universal" term that conceals its genesis. It is no accident that psychoanalysis grew under the shadow of the ailing Hapsburg bureaucracy.

An adolescent, let us say, goes to an exclusive secondary school. It is beyond his parents' financial reach. They strain every resource to send him there. For they have their son's good at heart. And what is their son's "good"? They are thinking, doubtless, of "connections." What they are not thinking of is the fact that, at a time when he is "normally" beset by sexual quandaries, they expose him to a further bewildering set of social quandaries. There are the morbidities of his questionable status, with its pretensions and guilt, that make him oversensitive, either too obsequious or too aggressive, and secretly in doubt where he really "belongs." So they send him to a psychologist, who discovers that all the misgivings derive from infantile relations to his family. Now, unquestionably, such factors are involved, along with the time he got chicken pox, and the time he got caught stealing fruit from a neighbor's garden, and the time some relative in some way startled or disappointed him. In being "born into" a new hierarchy, with all its unutterable magic, in attempting to acquire the suggestive insignia that will make him a new self, he is affected in every particle of his past. But the greater the stress upon such "universal" or "individual" elements, the greater the deflection from the main source of the mystery. You can take it as an axiom: Where the mystery is, there is the neurosis. Indeed, the entire stress upon early childhood experiences, valuable as it is in itself, can deflect by leading one to place in terms of *familial* substance motives that require placement more broadly in terms of *social* substance.

Popular reference to the "inferiority complex" is another instance where a motive which is really of a *class* nature has the deceptive appearances of individuality (and its dialectical counterpart, universality).

An "inferiority complex" is a sense that one's *kind of* being is inferior to another *kind of* being (or is endangered by that other *kind*). It is not merely an implied comparison between the self and another; it is a comparison between what I think I stand for and what I think the other stands for, in the terms of some *social* judgment. No individual could give another individual an "inferiority complex." Without the notion of an audience, an outside observer, to judge of the relation, the most one would feel would be the awareness of a literal inferiority. But there is a wide discrepancy between inferiority and an "inferiority complex." The first is merely a "fact" (a fact about everybody, by one test or another); the second is an *accusation,* in which one passes a social judgment upon oneself, condemning oneself from the standpoint of some real or imagined court of conscience (another variant of the "courtship" theme).

For this reason, persons who have broken away from their class or "race" (as Negro intellectuals, liberal Jews, or Gentiles who have notably altered their social position for better or worse) have more of an "inferiority complex" than persons who remain wholly within the traditions of their community. Those who remain unchanged feel the reënforcement that comes of being one with their kind, in the quite realistic sense, rather than suffering from a partial sense of isolation, through being, in their nature as the "break-away type," somewhat in a kind all by themselves, *sui generis,* except insofar as they meet cronies who, being similarly derived, are somewhat like fellow conspirators. (Recall the many variants in the Bohemian-expatriate literary movement, with the social mystery often taking the rhetorical form of the hermetic, its nature indicated in the formula, *épater le bourgeois,* a perverse way of courtship not fundamentally different from Dodgson's devices for puzzling little Alices.)

The psychoanalytic emphasis seems to be groping for an important distinction which it is not able to make. We have said that man, as a symbol-using animal, experiences a difference between *this* being and *that* being as a difference between *this kind of* being and *that kind of* being. Here is a *purely dialectical* factor at the very center of realism. Here, implicit in our attitudes toward things, is a principle of *classification*. And classification in this linguistic, or formal sense is all-inclusive, "prior" to classification in the exclusively social sense. The "invidious" aspects of class arise from the nature of man not as a "class animal," but as a "classifying animal."

We recall, for instance, a parlor game in which people were classified according to two antithetical groups of nonsense syllables. Say, for instance, they were distinguished not as "progressive and conservative," "extravert and introvert," or "bourgeois and Bohemian," but as "Vizzles and Vozzles," or "Sliffs and Smooves." Then various members of the party took turns in making up lists of the traits that characterized each such "class." Finally you would get confirmed Vizzelites who were fanatically set against Vozzlians, and Sliffists that were almost exalted in their detestation of Smoovies.

Unquestionably, even while burlesquing the "hierarchic psychosis" to which people are prone, the game was one more indication of "rage for order." That is, even the playful use of nonsense syllables derived piquancy from the animus of "invidious" social situations that really did form the background of the game. But the initial workability of mere nonsense syllables indicates a purely *formal* ground, implicit in the rationality of *homo dialecticus,* a generic aptitude for classification wherein social classification would be a special case.

When psychologists seek to derive human institutions from the nature of man, rather than deriving the nature of man from his institutions, they are apparently moved by the feeling that, as with the instance of the nonsense game, the pressure of institutions alone could not account for the entire expression. But when they looked for "priority," they sought it in the "unconscious-irrational," a psychological source, rather than in the *dialectical,* a formal source. And their rich contribution to the study of symbolism can thus mislead, if it causes us to treat formal logic as merely derivative from psycho-logic.

In our projected *Symbolic of Motives,* we hope to show, by analysis of Freud's work, how many logical and dialectical principles are, by his own account, involved in the operations of the dream. These elements are "prior" to dream life insofar as they are the basis of all "rational" thinking as well. But while psychologistic accounts of human motives seem, in their important stress upon symbolism, closer to the origins of *homo dialecticus* than institutionalist explanations are, we must discount Freud's own vocabulary somewhat; otherwise we cannot appreciate his great prowess as a dialectician, or note how well his analysis of the child's early experiences within the family reveal the operations of the hierarchic motive.

Go through the fantastic list of erotic aberrations in Krafft-Ebing's *Psychopathia Sexualis*. Examine his case histories of those many perverse sufferers with whom (as the translator and editor, Victor Robinson, puts it) "the ability to enjoy or perform the sexual act, in the normal manner, appeared to be the most difficult of the arts." Look there for evidence of the hierarchic motive. And does it not show immediately, in that vast thesaurus of dominance and submission, with the many intermediate variants? Note the odd identifications whereby one seeks to get, roundabout and at a distance, what he would not take simply and directly. Note the recondite "nobility" in the cult of vile things. Consider how abandonment to forms of sexual expression that society deems degrading could be at once a rebellion and a self-accusation, a morbidly tense acceptance of the very judgments by which one refuses to be bound. Consider the twisted beseechments, as with "stuff-fetichists dominated by a shoe or a handkerchief," or "lovers of fur and velvet," or "pageists," entranced by "the idea of being a page to a beautiful girl." Stories of lynchings make clear to us the hierarchic motive in fantasies and acts of sexual violence—and could we not see the same in "sadists who hurt their partners, masochists who thrilled at the sight of a whip," or in *"frotteurs* and *voyeurs, renifleurs* and *stercoraires,"* while a gloomy groveling, as were one to tell oneself meaner things about oneself than an enemy could think of, would surely beset the "slaves of scatology, defilers of statues, despoilers of women and children." Necrophiliacs, paedophiliacs, gerontophiliacs, satyromaniacs, nymphomaniacs—for whatever degree of physical eros there may be in the motives of such, must there not be very many degrees of the hierarchal? Here one finds all sorts of unnatural things, being sought in unnatural ways. Why, then, should they be treated as deriving primarily from natural appetite?

All these are such antics as Diderot would call "positions of pantomime." They are grotesque forms of social courtship. And you'd come closer to the truth if you called them remote variants of pure persuasion (like virgin-worship, or like poems proclaiming the frigidity, cruelty, aloofness, or infidelity of mistresses) than if you confined your explanation to a purely sexual source.

Both psychoanalytic and institutional accounts indicate important sources of pressure for the *animus* behind a given expression. Resources of classification, of abstraction, of comparison and contrast, of merger and division, of derivation, and the like, may characterize the thinking of man *generically,* over and above the nature of his social or personal problems. But his social and personal problems provide the incentive for the particular emphases of his expressions. You are not finished when you have analyzed the formal or dialectical devices implicit, say, in a doctrine of "white supremacy." The "pure persuasion" of the form is frail indeed, as compared with its localized rhetorical application. Psychoanalytic and institutional criticism is needed, to reveal the doctrine's nature as a "scapegoat mechanism" for flattering a sick psyche by proclaiming the categorical superiority of one's "kind," and by organizing modes of injustice that are morbidly considered advantageous to the conspirators as a class.

Our point is, however, that the urgency of such explanations must not be allowed to conceal the full scope of the motivational recipe. Otherwise, rather than being the analysis of rhetorical partisanship, the explanation itself is rhetorical (whereas in its completeness it would be dialectical). But by systematically retreating to the realm of "pure persuasion," we attain a degree of generalization which permits us to include as elements of rhetoric both psychological and institutional motivations (that is, motives in agent and scene respectively). And insofar as "God" is the Term of Terms in dialectic, one also thereby has easy access to the use of theological motives in rhetorical utterance (including the rhetorical use of naturalistic words for the ultimate scene).

For this very reason, you can expect "pure persuasion" always to be on the verge of being lost, even as it is on the verge of being found. And so, to talk about it by citing particular examples of rhetoric is always to find it embodied in the "impurities" of advantage-seeking. For even though the ultimate form is but that of speech relating speaker and spoken-to, this persuasive relation is in essence "courtly," hence involves communication between hierarchally related orders. True, the relation between the two orders need not remain fixed. Thus, as regards monetary tests, the artist who relies upon smartness as a mark of "urbanity" may be "socially inferior" to the "ideal public" he is courting. Yet he is "professionally superior," and courts as an "ideal public" many persons whom he would unquestionably despise in the particular. Yet again, as soon as you thus set him up, you must recall (as with the Arabian Nights relation) that the artist-entertainer is the servant of the very despot-audience he seeks to fascinate (as the spellbinder can tyrannize over his audience only by letting the audience tyrannize over him, in rigidly circumscribing the range and nature of his remarks).

Our mention of an "ideal audience" itself indicates how the simultaneous gain and loss of pure persuasion complicates a Rhetoric of Motives. Symbolically, the "pure exercise" of art for art's sake can become furtively and suicidally allied with motives ranging anywhere from castration to impotence, masturbation perhaps being the golden mean between them. An artist's courting is not just an address to others. His communicative act is subtly infused with motives of ordination that need not arise from without. A particular audience may be but a pretext, itself the symbol of a transcendence within himself (or, more accurately, a transcendence deriving from the nature of symbols as such). Even the artist who "writes down" for big money is thus motivated "ideally," in that the money represents for him the principle of ordination. It has often been said that a large amount of leisure is necessary for the high development of a culture. The statement is usually interpreted in a quantitative sense; for obviously, the society's ability to produce necessities must be great enough to permit a high expenditure of "man hours" on other than biologically or economically necessary work. Yet the analysis of "mystery" as a motive in ambition suggests that the element of "quality" has been a greater incentive. The quantity of extra productivity provides the physical conditions that allow for much concentration on economically unnecessary work. But whatever might be the incentives to "pure" creation in a truly equalitarian society (or rather, in a truly equal society, for equalitarianism is but an idealistic denial of actual inequality), the goad to ambition emanating from the idea of leisure as a privileged, "godlike" attribute has in the past come from the hierarchic structure of society (leisure being the condition antithetical to slavery).

Often artists are called childlike, "regressive." But there is also something childlike in the role of audience as tyrant—and a child-audience is perhaps the most tyrannical of all. (Thus, a teacher of children once told us of a recurring nightmare: She dreamed that, while she was talking to her class, they rose in a body and left the room.) In Dodgson's case ("the child as swain," according to Empson's formula), the entertainer could playfully punish the tyrannic child-audience in the very act of amusing her: his provoking social "mysteries" could serve this double purpose. As courtship, his communication was too essentially "standoffish" to be sexual; that element derived in part from its nature as social (intercourse between youth and age seen in terms of intercourse between "quality" and the vulgar, though this in turn was expressed grotesquely in reverse, the politeness being implied in the rudeness). But the *purely* rhetorical motive was in appeal for appeal's sake, in the "absolute summons" that would not know what to do with an audience who responded to the summons on any but the symbolic level.

Transferring the child-audience-tyrant relation to the realm of practical relations, we can see how the liberal child cult can work in connection with a sense of "substantial" inequality (through whatever form of discrimination, actual or feared, it may arise). The relation between the parents (as members of the "lower" or "subject" class) and their child (as "free") makes the child simultaneously one with them, yet a vessel of the major attribute identified with the "superior" class. The parents' courtship of the child, in allowing the child to be a "tyrant" in the home, is thus roundabout an ideal manifestation of the very hierarchic principle under which the parents suffer. The child, in being at once theirs and courted, simultaneously represents both ends of the hierarchic ladder.

The magic of virtue may also lurk about the edges of such public order made intimate. (By the magic of virtue we have in mind such motives as are expressed in Milton's "Comus," in the passages on the power of chastity to subdue wild beasts, a power that may be metaphorically true at least in one sense: If wildness in beasts stands for tempestuous erotic zeal in men, and if chastity in women stands for sexual frigidity, then truly "chastity" might dampen the ardor of "wildness.") The implied magical equivalent lurking beneath the "liberal" treatment of the child would derive from the fact that the parents, in establishing a pattern of mild courtship, "deserved" the same for themselves (though the sheer *imitation* of a way, the observing of it through sheer "esthetic consistency," is "prior" to its magical "use"). In any case, one has "ambivalence": the child, as their flesh and blood, represents their "inferiority," while at the same time it gets the deference they must show to their "superiors."

Recall Carlyle's equating of tools and symbols. He had much more than a metaphor to justify him. The high development of invented instruments was impossible without a corresponding development of language. And more formally, the kind of thinking that uses tools to make tools depends upon a peculiarly human "rationality" two removes from the nonsymbolic. This is the capacity for words about words ("thought of thought"), the "reflexive" function that modern idealists treat as the critical step from "consciousness" to "self-consciousness."

One might with some justice consider an animal's sounds and postures as "words about things," or about situations. One might say that such mimesis has the elements of grammar, rhetoric, and symbolic. They would be symbolic in their expressiveness as statements of attitude, rhetorical in their nature as threats and calls. And as for grammar, they "substantially" translate their past and future tenses into the behavioristic present, like a dancer. Thus, the dog dances "I will eat" by salivating now, and "I have eaten" by curling around three times now and settling himself to sleep. But (and we are obviously boasting) the dog cannot discourse about his discourse, cannot talk about his grammar, rhetoric, and symbolic. Similarly, all animals use tools in the primary sense. But only humans are tool-using in the secondary sense (as when external agencies are used to produce other external agencies). Thus, technology depends upon kinds of intuition and tradition that are impossible without the dialectic of "rationality."

Word-using is prior to tool-using even in the obscenely punning sense (and that too is always something to be considered, when discussing human motives). The emergence from infancy into word-using precedes by many years the emergence into sexual potency (hence the "polymorphous perverse" nature of infantile sexuality becomes interwoven with the power of symbols long before clear and direct sexual purpose has developed; and when it does develop, it must accommodate itself not to the "glandular situation" alone, but to the many years of symbolic practice that preceded it).

So, all told, though there are respects in which words and mechanical inventions may be classed together, as instruments ("weapons"), there are also important respects in which they must be distinguished. Attempts to divide people into "artisans" and "priests" have their ground in this distinction. It is at the basis of the distinction between the practical and the esthetic (bourgeois and Bohemian). Thus, *homo faber* (tool-using) would seem to come from different sources than *homo dialecticus* (word-using). But by the time you get to complex civilized conduct, the distinction becomes quite obscured. Priestcraft is often a very practical business, as also its secular variants in politics, journalism, and finance. Conversely, there is always a wide range of symbolic elements motivating conduct on its face practical.

And these considerations allow for a distinction between verbal productive forces (the nature of "rationality" or "human consciousness") and the "forces of production" in the economic sense (tools invented by operations of the human brain and transmitted with the help of vocabulary).

"Man" arises out of an extrahuman ground. His source is, as you prefer, "natural," or "divine," or (with Spinoza) both. In any case, the scene out of which he emerges is *ultimate*. And in this respect it must be "super-personal," quite as it must be "super-verbal." For it contains the principle of personality, quite as it contains the principle of verbalizing. The distinction between personal and impersonal, like that between verbal and nonverbal, is scientific, pragmatic, and thus is justified when our concerns are pragmatic. But from the standpoint of ultimate speculation, there must be an *order* here: First, there is "nature" in the less-than-personal sense; next, there is the "personal" distinguished from such "impersonal" nature as an idea of something is distinguished from the thing. But ultimately there must be nature in the "over-all" sense; and nature in this sense must be "superpersonal," since it embraces both "personality" and "impersonality."

Now, though invention of instruments is impossible unless the laws of nature in the less-than-personal sense are obeyed, it is likewise impossible, if attributed to scenic conditions alone, in the restricted meaning of scene (the "less than human," or the kind of nature that exists when the human, or personal, is deducted from it). The element of personality or humanity (agent and his acts) is the new secondary condition that necessarily interposes itself between the natural scene and the invented agency. No one expects our machines to go on inventing themselves after the human race is extinct, even though in the meantime they are doing much (as a mode of transcendence) to remake us, for better or worse. This necessary interposition of the human agent between scene and agency is what we have in mind when we say that "words" are prior to "tools," that *homo dialecticus* is more fundamental than *homo faber,* though the inventions of *homo faber* provide so overwhelmingly the distinctions of property and class that give animus to man's dialectical operations.

A Grammar of Substance was needed, at the very basis of human thinking, to shape traditions of living and thinking whereby a man can be induced to identify himself with the cause of some figure whom he has experienced only by hearsay, through the daily word-slinging of the news. But when thus "grammatically" and "symbolically" considering himself consubstantial with such a figure (a figure that is for him but a purely verbal creation but supposedly represents his interests) he gets the zeal of such identification from conditions of property and social status that were shaped by the economic forces of production. This more recondite development (from words, to tools, to words for social "substance" arising out of tools as property) is responsible for the animus in the logomachy ("cold war," an expression commending itself to the frigidity of old men, but unfortunately, with younger men, suggesting ideas of "warm" and "hot" war, and then finally, in accordance with the intermingling of Mars and Venus, a "shooting" war).

If you insist, we'll abandon, for argument's sake, the notion that nature is "super-personal." The argument is based on the assumption that there is such a thing as "personality" in the human realm. And when you get through dissolving personality into the stream of consciousness, or into dissociated subpersonalities, or into "conditioned reflexes," or into appearances of substance that derive purely from such extrinsic factors as status and role, there may not seem to be any intrinsic core left. So we'll retreat to our more easily defendable position: that nature must be more-than-verbal. For in its totality it encompasses verbal and nonverbal both; and its "nonverbal" ground must have contained the "potentiality" of the verbal, otherwise the verbal could not have emerged from it.

Arguments about nature as "more than personal" could then be protectively reframed and still claim enough for our purposes: We could say simply that, since such a view of nature as "super-personal" is a "natural conclusion" of dialectic, then it is an important ultimate trend of thought which must figure as a "lure" in rhetoric. An ultimate "error" is as important in rhetorical appeal as an ultimate "truth." So in either case we should consider the "dialectical proof of a super-personal ground of all action," because of the relation between rhetoric and dialectic. For no expression can be more profoundly appealing than a rhetoric which follows in the direction of a perfect dialectical symmetry. Suasion is thus "freest," most "edifying," when it embodies "the symmetrical necessity for the existence of God," though some lovers of such symmetry may insist that their god be named Atheos.

However, though our discussion of "pure persuasion" has brought us to the rhetoric of theology, we must again emphasize that "pure persuasion" in itself is not to be equated with "religious" persuasion. Pure persuasion is disembodied and wraithlike; but the benedictions and anathemata of religious persuasion are tremendously sanguine, even bloody. Consider the urgency of the Apocalypse. No bull fight was ever more gory, no Inquisition more eager to terrorize. "In righteousness he doth judge and make war." And punishments are heaped upon punishments for those serving the whore of Babylon, who "glorified herself" and "lived deliciously," until the "merchants of the earth" had "waxed rich through the abundance of her delicacies."

Does not the whole of Revelation swing about the resonant eighteenth chapter, where the voice cries, "Babylon the great is fallen"? And is there not a lovely tone of lamentation here, commingled with the gloating of vengeance? "Alas, alas, that great city Babylon, that mighty city!" Read it carefully, the eighteenth chapter. The prophet is condemning to the "second death" a city that looks surprisingly much like New York at its best. If there were less stench and more fragrance, less noise and more music, you'd have not New York but Babylon the Mysterious, as described in this chapter commemorating its destruction.

Surely the saint is visiting these horrors upon persons no more loathsome, say, than a would-be poet, or ex-poet, now working for an advertising agency, or for some publisher of commercial magazines. (All that is left of his early literary promise is a collection of first and rare editions. Preferably they are books with uncut pages. For here would be a remote variant of virgin-worship, a few secular traces of adolescent religiosity. We should also note, however, a mild renewal of religious interest in him, both for esthetic reasons and as a matter of good business, a neat combining of the "sacrificial" with the "acquisitive," as the collecting of firsts had been too, since he piously got for himself the vessels of the forbidden-virginal.)

Apparently the sin of Babylon was but in being a typical great metropolis. It was moved by the pleasant spirit of parties in a penthouse, drinks served expensively in a high place, to the accompaniment of dance music over the radio, with a girl arranging unobtrusively to spend the night after the guests had departed, for the delight of a man deemed potent in office. The mystery was reduced to sexual terms, there being perhaps more dramatic incentives for such translation in those days of sacred prostitution than now, when men are given uneasily to love-among-the-machines. Then "fornication" had much richer connotations, being recognized as not merely the satisfying of a sexual appetite, but as pious devotion to a rival god. The theme had been introduced early, in the references to "that woman Jezebel" who had cajoled members of the church in Thyatira "to commit fornication, and to eat things sacrificed unto idols." Thus, devotion to Babylon as a whore was devotion to Babylon as a god, an ultimate step in a rival order of motives. It was "reverence" expressed in sexual terms, and reverence among peoples who habitually made social reverence and religious reverence identical, in calling their emperors divine.

Yet as the recital of torments for the damned accumulates, we begin to wonder. The sinner we have spoken of, the well-to-do advertising man, the flower of metropolitan clericalism, would devoutly repent at the first faint rumble of the divine thunder. But the evildoers of the Apocalypse are almost magnificent in their refusal of heaven. Despite the mounting series of horrors and terrors to which they are subjected, one by one, with skilled husbandry on the part of the avenger, and with superb dramatic spacing on the part of the visionary (note, for instance, how, having established our expectation of seven calamities at the breaking of the seven seals, and having quickly run through six, the author interposes a whole chapter of delay between the breaking of the sixth seal and the breaking of the seventh), despite their total inability, in their human frailness, to strike back against the awesome tortures which an all-powerful Lord of All Creation is visiting upon them, they persist in their blasphemies.

Rhetorically, their perverseness offers some justification for continuing the torture. Had they begged to be forgiven, we with our
limited understanding of cosmic justice might have been tempted to
wish that the Lord would make peace with them. But by continuing
to blaspheme even as they cook, they seem more to deserve the cookery.
Symbolically, the saint also reads into them his own powers of resistance. He knows what sufferings he would undergo, as testimony to
his God; and with unconscious generosity he imparts to the enemy a
similar magnificence of motive, assuming that the ad-writer or news-
caster of Babylon would testify by actions and passions of the same
ferocious zeal.

Yet there is another point to note here. In these eschatological questions of reward and punishment, and of praise to a God of Wrath (the
most O.T. spot in the N.T.) we realize that the representatives of
Babylon are members of an alien and menacing order. Chapter 18
makes us see that, however frail they might be, as compared with the
God of heavenly reverence, their claim upon men's social reverence
had been as great as that of all our industrialists and financiers combined. Hence, the city was a menace, not by reason of the individuals
in it, but through its *ordination*. And in seeing the mild Babylonian
enterprisers as members of that rival ordination, the earnest saint
thought of them as persisting to the last in their blasphemies. For in
a sense they would persist, vowed to their order until Babylon had
fallen, and the New Jerusalem had risen in its place.

We have talked of the hierarchic principle being represented in
terms of the head. But particularly in a myth revealing the nature of
first and last things, it can also be represented "pastorally" by the least.
Or the most efficient reduction of all would be an image containing
both ideas: the sacrificial king who is, in one figure, the bleeding, victimized lamb and the victor to whom all do obeisance. Here, the same
ordination is represented by bringing the highest and lowest rungs
together.

Looking at examples of religious expression, you unquestionably
find the lineaments of "pure persuasion" there, as with St. Augustine's
use of the epideictic virtuosity cultivated during the "second sophistic"
of pagan decadence. Or, considered as an object of pure persuasion,
Dante's Beatrice would be not woman idealized, but rather the absolute audience realized. And likewise a prayer might be pure court-

ship, homage in general, the ultimate idea of an audience, without thought of advantage, but sheerly through love of the exercise.

Yet no material world could be run on such a motive, not even a world genuinely supernatural in its theory of motives. "Pure persuasion" is as biologically unfeasible as that moment when the irresistible force meets the immovable body. It is what Eliot might call the "dead center" of motives. It is the condition of Santayana's transcendental skepticism, where the pendulum is at rest, not hanging, but poised exactly above the fulcrum. It is the change of direction, from systole to diastole, made permanent. Psychologically it is related to a conflict of opposite impulses. Philosophically, it suggests the plight of Buridan's extremely rational ass, starving to death because placed between two exactly equidistant bales of hay. It is the moment of motionlessness, when the axe has been raised to its full height and is just about to fall. It is uncomfortably like suspended animation.

Theologically or politically, it would be the state of intolerable indecision just preceding conversion to a new doctrine. Less exactingly, for our purposes, it is the pause at the window, before descending into the street.*

Rhetorical Radiance of the "Divine"

I. HENRY JAMES ON THE DEITY OF "THINGS"

IN HIS preface to *The Spoils of Poynton* Henry James tells how, one Christmas Eve, before a "table that glowed safe and fair through the brown London night," he heard a remark which he promptly recognized as the "germ" of his plot. It involved a quarrel between a mother and son "over the ownership of the valuable furniture of a fine old house just accruing to the young man by his father's death." He saw this as a "row . . . over their household gods." And he valued the situation, he says, because of

> the sharp light it might project on that most modern of our current passions, the fierce appetite for the upholsterer's and joiner's and brazier's work, the chairs and tables, the cabinets and presses, the material odds and ends, of the more labouring ages. A lively mark

---

* The closing sentences were originally intended as transition into our section on The War of Words. But that must await publication in a separate volume.

of our manners indeed, the diffusion of this curiosity and this avidity, and full of suggestion, clearly, as to their possible influence on
other passions and other relations.   On the face of it the "things"
themselves would form the very centre of such a crisis; these
grouped objects, all conscious of their eminence and their price,
would enjoy, in any picture of a conflict, the heroic importance.

Later he resumes:

The real centre, as I say, the citadel of the interest, with the fight
waged round it, would have been the felt beauty and value of the
prize of battle, the Things, always the splendid Things, placed in
the middle light, figured and constituted, with each identity made
vivid, each character discriminated, and their common consciousness
of their great dramatic part established.

We dwell on these passages because we consider them a key not
only to this particular book, but to James's motivation as a whole.
Glancing over some of the tenser expressions scattered through his
preface, we find:

Vital particle . . . grain of gold . . . subtle secrets . . . madness
. . . zeal . . . mysteries . . . tiny nugget . . . the table that glowed
safe and fair . . . the *whole* of the virus . . . in a flash . . . glimmered
. . . builds and piles high . . . blocks quarried in the deeps of his
imagination . . . household gods . . . eminence . . . heroic . . .
great array . . . exquisite protection . . . the felt beauty and value
of the prize of battle . . . placed in the middle light, figured and
constituted . . . their great dramatic part . . . the general glittering
presence . . . the gleam of brazen idols and precious metals and
inserted gems in the tempered light of some arching place of
worship . . . romancingly . . . wondrous . . . in fine . . .

We should have the aura of these terms in mind as we read later:

Yes, it is a story of cabinets and chairs and tables; they formed the
bone of contention, but what would merely "become" of them,
magnificently passive, seemed to represent a comparatively vulgar
issue.   The passions, the faculties, the forces their beauty would,
like that of antique Helen of Troy, set in motion, was what, as a
painter, one had really wanted of them, was the power in them that
one had from the first appreciated.

This word, "appreciated," leads into his next development.   Thus,
on discussing how he might introduce human characters into this
drama of Things, he comes upon a typical Jamesian solution, his
recipe for the character of Fleda Vetch.   One must "lodge somewhere
at the heart of one's complexity an irrepressible appreciation," he

says, and "from beginning to end . . . appreciation, even to that of the very whole, lives in Fleda. . . . The 'things' are radiant, shedding afar, with a merciless monotony, all their light, exerting their ravage without remorse; and Fleda almost demonically both sees and feels, while the others but feel without seeing." She is likewise said to be endowed with "the free spirit," which is "always much tormented," and by no means always triumphant, and is "heroic, ironic, pathetic."

We could not say that his references to "mysteries," "household gods," "place of worship," and the like are merely opportunistic and negligible. Nor should we, on the other hand, treat the material "Things" as though he meant them to be endowed with true divinity, like sacred objects on the altar of an Almighty God. The second interpretation would seem by inference to accuse James of blasphemy. The first would make of us esthetic blasphemers, in failing to give the novelist credit for his artistic scruples. Yet clearly these household Things are also Spirits; or they are charismatic vessels of some sort. And Fleda is a rare character who can feel the magic of their presence. The quarrel over heirlooms, desired as a testimony of status, attains a higher dimension, as James finds in the objects a glow that can place them in some realm or order transcending the quarrel as such. Hence, though the preface does not tell us just what mysterious, radiant power they do possess, can we not "socioanagogically" see here an "enigmatic" signature of the hierarchic motive?

2. "SOCIAL RATINGS" OF IMAGES IN JAMES

In James's preface to *The Spoils of Poynton* we find the ground for the statement of policy regarding "socioanagogic" criticism in general. Yet we still do not have an exact procedure for disclosing the hierarchic value of particulars.

We can show how this further step might be contrived, by examining and reapplying some passages from Austin Warren's exceptional essay on Henry James in his book, *Rage for Order*. The entire book, by the way, is much to our purposes, since it is predominantly concerned with hierarchy, both religious and secular. On nearly every page Mr. Warren makes some observation which we could profitably borrow here. His remarks on the theme of bureaucracy in Kafka, for instance; or his suggestion that the appeal of astrology for Yeats "lay

in the honorific connection astrology establishes between man and
nature and in its imprecise determinism of the individual and the
state"; or his analysis of Pope's writings on society as a "wonder"; or
his reference to "the characterology (or perhaps hagiography) of
James's youth."

The discussion of James's late novels leads to exactly the kind of
pontificating device we require. And to make our point, we shall
combine portions from several passages:

> The Jamesian equivalent of myth lies . . . in the metaphors which
> . . . reach their high richness in *The Bowl* and *The Ivory Tower*. . . .
> Recollected images become metaphor. For years James had traveled
> diligently in France and Italy, written conscientious commentaries
> on cathedrals, chateaux, and galleries. Now people remind him
> of art, his heroines, almost without exception, are thus translated.
> . . . Some embarrassment prevents similar translation of the heroes
> into paintings or statutes; but the Prince (who is bought, after all,
> as a work of art and appraised by his father-in-law with the same
> taste which appraised a Luini) can scarcely be described except out
> of art history: by way of representing the superior utility and weight
> of the male, James renders him in architecture. . . . The obvious
> errand of these analogies is honorific; they belong to the high and
> hallowed world of "culture. . . ." Unlike his Prince, who "never
> saw . . . below a certain social plane," James had looked observantly,
> in his days of "notation," at zoos and aquariums and circuses; and
> he remembered the crowded perceptions of "A Small Boy" in a
> remote America. . . . Mrs. Newsome is massive because she has no
> imagination. She rests, sits, *is*—a fact without resilience. Others,
> the imaginative, must adjust, accommodate. . . . If Philistines are
> to be "imaged" as inflexibly massive, metallic (unimaginative), the
> children of light owe their erect posture, their equilibrium, to their
> flexibility. They summon up recollection of ballet dancers, show
> people, brave ritualists who perform, upon exhibition, feats of per-
> sistence and agility. . . . In *The Sense of the Past,* the most
> "imaged" relation is between Ralph Pendrel, American introspec-
> tive, and the blunt, massive, extraverted Perry Midmore, his con-
> trary. . . . Perry has the advantage of not being "cultured": he
> trusts, animal-like, to his instincts, scents the presence of the clever
> and alien "as some creature of the woods might scent the bait of the
> trapper," etc.

Through many pages, Mr. Warren refers to the particular images
by which James places each of his characters for the reader. Then,
looking through this list, we see that, for our purposes, *we need but*

reverse the direction. Where James has used an image to build up a character whose social and moral status is clearly defined in the book, turning things around we can interpret this known status as a hierarchal placement of the image. We thus have the bridging device (or "pontification") that will unite moral and social hierarchies with the natural and artificial objects that James treats as their equivalents. Hence we can unambiguously and methodically disclose the hierarchal judgment implicit for James in a given image.

We might thus perfect a method for disclosing the "hierarchic content" of objects, showing the difference between their perception in art (with the peculiar vibrancy that accompanies it) and the purely empiricist or psychological kinds of perception.

3. RHETORICAL NAMES FOR GOD

But what of those persons who believe that, under some conditions, men may establish a truly mystical communication with an ultimate ground of existence, behind or beyond the beautifying mists of social status? Would there still be room for a belief that natural objects are signatures of a celestial hierarchy too, infused with its motives and deriving their glow from it?

It is conceivable that, through the "infancy" (or speechlessness) of body and mind, there might be communication with elements that are, directly or indirectly, communicant with the ultimate speechless ground of things. Yet even if we grant the possibility of such mystic "revelations," we should ask ourselves how much of "divinity" can be explained neurologically, how much linguistically, and how much "socioanagogically." We should account for as much as possible by these three routes. Then God, genuinely transcendent, would be sought in the direction of whatever was still unaccounted for. The enigma of creation; the immensity of infinite and infinitesimal; love, patience, delight—here could be sufficient signs, perhaps, for most of us. But they are not enough for mystics who are content with nothing less than the conviction that they are God, that they have actually been one with God.

However, even if we grant them their claim, it still remains a fact that we should seek to account for as much of the mystical experience as possible in naturalistic terms. For the mystics have bodies; and other bodies, housing tenants who have not been officially recognized as *bona fide* mystical persons, manifest some natural symptoms like those of the "true" mystics. The area of overlap, then, is presumably not the area of the true revelation. Hence, even one who believed in the true revelation should be willing to look for as many naturalistic explanations as possible, since these would be the basis for a proper *distinction* between natural and supernatural motives.

But there is a consideration still more relevant to our purposes. Even if you grant the distinction between natural and supernatural motives, there is still the drastic fact that the power of rhetoric may arise rather from the *confusion* between the two orders. In his *Art of Rhetoric,* Aristotle noted how we may build up a character by imputing to him the virtues that most nearly resemble his vices, as when we call the foolhardy courageous and the cowardly cautious. And the rhetorical use of religion as an instrument of politics depends upon this very ambiguity. For the priest identifies some questionable secular faction or cause with a transcendent order held to be beyond question. Or consider the radio hack who, in a journalistic idiom that would be an insult even to the devil, praises the most bluntly imperialist of our ambitions as "spiritual," and presents world-wide expansion for bigger profits in terms of a holy war between the valiant armies of God and the vile hordes of Evil. The vulgarity of every word he says proves him to be about as spiritual as the machine out of which his voice is being projected. He is but a function of that machine, and he does the job he is hired for. Those to whom religion means mainly hate are not very exacting as regards the provocations to which they will respond.

But, because of the many "god-terms" that dot men's thinking constantly, most of such rhetoric is profoundly genuine. Dionysius the Areopagite wrote *On the Divine Names.* And a companion treatise, *in usum rhetoricae,* might consider the many declared and undeclared synonyms for God, or rather, for the extension of "God" into the area of "god-terms," generally. Thus, somewhat at random, we offer this list:

GOD: The ground of all possibility; substance; nature; history; society; necessity; mind; consciousness; self-consciousness; truth; *genius loci;* efficient cause. Title of titles; over-all motivation (hence, ultimate generalization, reduction, abstraction); principle of language or dialectic (logos); idea; center, circumference, apex, base (preferably all at once); unclassified, unfiled, miscellaneous, "All." Principle of hierarchy; any person, thing, or situation infused with the hierarchic motive (hence monarch, nobility, or people, as variously summing up or standing for the hierarchic order); hence, authority or resistance to authority; reason; object or source of reverence ("Your Worship"), fear, love, desire, justice; principle of property, privilege, status, Parent or principle of parenthood; principle of familial or social cohesion ("consubstantiality" and "communication"); authority; counterauthority; nation; "race supremacy"; the city. Vocation; calling; hence, science, art, technology, business; hence, laboratory, studio, real estate, counting house, money, the expedient. (The Protestant stress upon the religious motive in secular work is a notable bridging of the two orders.) Principle of action; hence "personality" (grounded in a "super-person"); ideal, plan, purpose; final cause; soul; freedom (hence, free market); conscience; duty; ought; good; grounds for doing what one wants to do; the opposite of what one wants to do; fulfillment (hence, "wish-fulfillment," hence wish, hence striving, hence absence of fulfillment, hence compensatory name for frustration); rest, end of action; beauty; the universal gerundive (maximum generalization of the to-be-done, a meaning closely related to role, hence to hierarchy). Death (in such good words as salvation and immortality); an act's "perfection" would be its "dying," its "finishedness," hence death relates to action insofar as a thing's end is its perfection. (See Pico on *teleutein,* as finish, die.) Unconscious; sleep; the implicit; the unexpressed; the to-be-expressed; the inarticulate; infancy; intuition; "imagination"; beyond-the-rational; insanity; neurotic compulsion experienced as mystic devotion (piety either in yielding or in inability to yield); natural motives (the nonverbal, hence "irrational," nutrient, sexual, excremental, seminal); any natural forms (including states of mind to match), as fire, thunder, power, calamities, mountains, plains, sea. A function of prayer (object of appeal of last resort); generalized principle of the audience; pure persuasion. Principle of rebirth; hence, principle of change or of substratum beneath change. "Evil" in disguise. An honorific name for oneself. A slogan of the Extreme Right. "Nothing" (with this reservation: Symbolically, "nothing" will equal something, though the referent may be dialectical rather than positive). Clash of opposites; resolution of opposites; synthesis of various motives felt but not clearly differentiated (Christ as divine pontification, as god-man, allows for range whereby God can be identified both with victim and victor).

The Romans knew that you could get a god merely by taking an adjective and transforming it into an abstract noun. (One should add, perhaps, that the noun would have in it the implications of an iterative verb.) And particularly, they would detach some attribute from another god, and set it up as a separate divine abstraction. Fides, Libertas, Victoria, Virtus, Felicitas are "instances of close connexion of abstract deities and adjectival cognomina." (*Encyclopaedia of Religion and Ethics.* Article on "Personification.") Thales: "The world is full of gods." Kafka, *The Castle:* "Does not the least degree of authority contain the whole?"

A poet's images, then, might be "enigmatically" infused with the spirit of either hierarchy. Or like the god-man of the Christian myth, or Carlyle's Clothes, or Keats's Grecian Urn, they could be "pontifications," for bridging the two orders.

4. THE "RANGE OF MOUNTINGS"

Aquinas says that the object of faith can be considered in two ways (*dupliciter*): (1) from the side of the thing believed (*ex parte ipsius rei creditae*); here the object of faith is simple (*aliquid incomplexum*); (2) from the side of the believer (*ex parte credentis*); here the object of faith is complex (*aliquid complexum*). Applying this pattern of thought to the symbols of poetry, we note that the symbol, while in itself "uncomplex" (the simple symbol), may readily be broken into various motivational strands, if approached *ex parte critici*.

The many ramifications of this subject could be studied better under the head of Symbolic than here. But because of our special stress upon the "hierarchic motive" in rhetorical identification, we might here consider a possible thesaurus of meanings in the symbol of mounting, either the act, or its corresponding image (for a mountain would be a kind of static mounting, the act congealed into a set design).

First, there is the purely "kinesthetic" appeal: the meaning of height (and depth) as experienced by a kind of being to whom climbing is both an effort and an exhilaration. Here too would be "em-

pathic" responses as Coleridge noted (*Anima Poetae*), in considering
how the eye was contented by running along the lines of a ridge:

> One travels along with the lines of a mountain. Years ago I
> wanted to make Wordsworth sensible of this. How fine is Keswick
> vale! Would I repose, my soul lies and is quiet upon the broad
> level vale. Would it act? it darts up into the mountain-top like
> a kite, and like a chamois-goat runs along the ridge—or like a boy
> that makes a sport on the road of running along a wall or narrow
> fence!

This is a jotting of the same Coleridge who wrote:

> The sot, rolling on his sofa, stretching and yawning, exclaimed,
> *"Utinam hoc esset laborare."*

"Would that this were work!" Putting the two passages together,
do we not glimpse precisely the elation in the purely imaginary act
he is noting? By the paradox of substance, such ideal identification
with the mountainous mass gives us in one "moment" both an
imaginary idea of huge effort and the effortlessness of sheer indolence.
Coleridge's cult of the "impulse," as aggravated by his yielding to
the euphoria of opiates, would make him particularly susceptible to
such an appeal, where there is no physical strain, but the massiveness
and weightiness of the scene envisioned are like a great burden borne
with infinite ease.

Close to this purely kinesthetic appeal, yet obviously involving other
motives as well, is the climbing of the Alpinist. We here have to
do with "Faustian" kinds of fascination. While involving physical
dangers and exertions, they seem to contain symbolic ingredients that
themselves require "anagogic" or "socioanagogic" explanation. We
have read descriptions of mountain-climbing which seem almost mystical, perhaps because the act itself sums up, in a physical operation and
its corresponding states of mind, the various orders we are here listing
as ingredients in a hypothetically full symbol of mounting, as it might
figure in a "compleat poem." Mountain-climbing, as a symbolic act,
is done in answer to a call. While carrying out an "attitude" in the
most literal way possible (as were you to "do a poem" on murder by
actually murdering someone), its motives are wholly "esthetic" (the
opposite of the utilitarian or practical) as with a Gidean criminal.

Psychoanalysis, and popular speech, remind us that there is also a sexual mounting. Its most monumental form is perhaps in the notion of the Venusberg. (Translated literally into Latin, "Venusberg" would be *"mons* Veneris.") Since dreams of rising and flight frequently signalize the climactic approach to the sexual orgasm, by the same token in "The Love Song of J. Alfred Prufrock" we find the timid courtier *hesitating* on the stairs. And the theme returns in "Portrait of a Lady," wryly:

> Except for a slight sensation of being ill at ease
> I mount the stairs and turn the handle of the door
> And feel as if I had mounted on my hands and knees.

Even where a fuller range of motivations is involved, traces of the sexual order seem present. Thus, as Virgil explains to Dante in the fourth canto of the *Purgatorio,* the Mount of Purgatory is such that the higher one rises, the easier becomes the ascent, until it is like going downstream in a boat (*come a seconda giuso andar per nave*). The figure incidentally suggests where we might place those magically dream-driven boats of Shelley's (as in "Alastor"), that seem to stand for the poet's state of mind, and idealistically *begin* with starry-eyed motivations that Dante led into realistically, through a long ladder of asperities.

In the English edition of *Fear and Trembling,* Walter Lowrie quotes a related passage from Kierkegaard's *Journal,* describing his condition while at work on his "dialectical lyric." He had been "indolently" pumping up a shower-bath, he says, and "now I have pulled the cord, and the ideas stream down upon me" (though the full value of the figure is lost, in our era of "modern conveniences" when it never occurs to us that a shower-bath should be earned by prior effort, and we take it for granted that one should begin, not with the pumping up, but with the pouring down). "Indolently" does not seem quite the proper word here, except insofar as it suggests a lack of engrossment which does not come until the stage of fullness and release.

Disturbingly interwoven with the motives of erotic mounting, there is the theme of the maternal mountain: the mountain as the parental source, quite as with Mother Earth. Hawthorne's "Great Stone Face" suggests that it may also take on paternal aspects of parenthood. The image could arise from a child's early experience of being carried by adults.

Baudelaire's sonnet, "La Géante," is the grandest instance of incestuous ambiguities in the mountain symbol. The conceit that the poet is living with a "giantess" makes him both lover and child. Looking up at her "like a voluptuous cat at the feet of a queen," peering "into the damp fogs of her eyes" to see if her heart is somberly aflame, he runs "at leisure along her magnificent curves." And as she lies lassitudinously stretched across the countryside, he crawls on the slope of her enormous knees, and sleeps in the shadow of her breasts, "like a peaceful hamlet at the foot of a mountain."

The thought suggests that the Venusberg is likely to contain the same ambiguities, as would certainly be the case were it identified with the Venus we saw in Shakespeare's poem.

Popular usage also suggests connotations of material advantage, or social betterment, as with the term, "climber." Here are the cruel popular distinctions between those "on the way up" and those "on the skids." Or recall how, during the administration of F. D. Roosevelt, an ingenious variant became popular, as officials were said to be "kicked upstairs" when, though dismissed from their active functions, they were rewarded for their loyalty to the Chief by being given some nominally higher job with good pay but no authority.

Jimmy Durante once rang a good variation on the theme of the social climb, thus: He was in the role of an unsuccessful actor waiting in the outer office of a casting bureau; a successful actor, whom he knew, passed him with some disdain; whereupon Durante told him: "You'd better be nice to those you pass on the way up; for you might pass them again on the way down."

We can glimpse how the motive takes on richness when we consider the many-faceted careerism of Stendhal's Julien Sorel (in *The Red and the Black*). Despising his own father, taking Napoleon as alternative ideal father, he seduces the woman who befriends him as a mother. Here he acts "conscientiously," in line of duty, like a soldier (for he conceives of command in sexual and social matters after the analogy of military power). All the hypocrisy in his scheming for position and wealth seems to him a kind of higher honesty, loyalty to a purpose that transcends mere utilitarian profit. And to this extent his attitude is justified: Behind his rhetoric of advantage lies a poetic of incestuous guilt, with relation to women generally. And in response to this motive (presumably implicit in Sorel because it was basic to his creator) the hero and the author share the disdainful conviction that Julien's careerism is essentially different from the ordinary varieties all about him.

Veblen's *Theory of the Leisure Class* indicates how standards of goodness, truth, and beauty might be infused with hierarchal promises of the sort that go with the social climb. Racine's prefaces to his tragedies well reveal the motives of social pageantry in the esthetic of dignity, aloofness, and stylistic exclusion motivating his art. And even in one's choice of questions, there can be a social claim. For among the wide range of questions which men may seek to answer, in philosophy, science, and criticism, the intrinsic value of these questions does not correspond with their rating in a given hierarchy. And though the emphasis is usually placed on the quest for *answers*, "socioanagogic" considerations suggest that much of the urgency comes rather from the hierarchic rating implicit in the *questions*. Questions are infused with social magic quite as are James's "household gods" or natural objects ("the world's body"). And thus, with different schools of literary criticism (which in turn imply different political and social alignments) an answer can seem wholly radiant only with those for whom the question itself has radiance.

Even in naturalism or imagism, regardless of what the writer thinks he is getting, he is really recording the fullness of a world hierarchally endowed. The motive comes clearer to recognition in symbolism and surrealism, though their aims are usually stated in terms of technique or psychology.

In sum: Insofar as things and situations are identified with various stages of social privilege, both "practical" and "esthetic" objects are infused with the spirit of government and business, taxes and price, through identification with the bureaucratic judgments that go with such order.

In his essay on "The Dissociation of Ideas," De Gourmont makes an observation that gives us a further insight into the "magical" view, as regards persons who are charismatic vessels of the hierarchic principle. He is discussing the savage's idea of death, noting that the savage looks upon death, not as accidental or necessary, but as caused by the design of occult forces. (He is here dealing with the attitude that the sociologist Levy-Bruhl labeled "mystic participation.") As evidence that the same attitude still survives, he notes how the death of a prominent personage nearly always starts rumors of foul play. He also mentions Stendhal's preference for explanations that attribute the death of historical figures to poisoning or similar undisclosed plots.

Is it not the principle of social "divinity" that leads the people, or a hierarchy-minded writer like Stendhal, to thus account for these deaths "mysteriously"? The thought suggests that many apparently "factual" statements about the mysterious assassination of kings and emperors might have arisen purely in response to the principle of "mystification" implicit in hierarchy.

Similarly, at the time when the demagogue Huey Long was killed, despite the clear public evidence as to the identity of the slayer a rumor spread among the people that he had been shot by bullets from a different gun the bearer of which was not known. In his death he was thus translated to the "divine" regions of "mystery," as befitted his quasi-imperial role.

Describing how he felt when put in control of the government's policies, Churchill writes:

> At last I had the authority to give directions over the whole scene. I felt as if I were walking with Destiny, and all my past life had been a preparation for this hour and this trial.

"Destiny" here is a word of maximum generalization. Thus, in the technical sense, as an over-all word for human motives, it is a "god-term."

So much for it as regards its place at the apex of a dialectical pyramid. What of it, as regards "context of situation"? The Tory statesman is here discussing his state of mind on being made the head of a social hierarchy. He is in a position to act, but the acts typical of his role will use the entire social structure as their instrument. Primitive action related to the "centrality of the nervous system" will be at a minimum. The characteristic acts of his office will be indirect, hierarchic.

Even the very word "hierarchy," with its original meaning of "priest-rule" (while in English one also hears "higher") has connotations of celestial mystery. And, as we have said, where the principle of hierarchy is involved, the "mystery" need not be confined to any one position in the scheme. A ruler, seeing himself "from within," might be expected to know that he is not "divine"; yet he may feel the motives of "reverence" as strongly as a lowly peasant witnessing, at a respectful distance, a royal pageant. For inasmuch as his typical acts of rule depend upon his place in the dialectical pyramid of the social structure, they are "his" acts only insofar as he identifies himself with the very *principle of order* to which he owes his power. Their sensory reference is just about nil—they are all "spirit."

The result is a "mystic participation." The feeling that one is "walking with Destiny" would then be the "celestialized" or idealistic counterpart to the quite realistic experience of "walking with hierarchy."

However, though ethical, esthetic, philosophic, and scientific norms are greatly affected by the norms of social advantage, there is also a purely moral motive here too, an ethical ascent, a morality of production, a motive of betterment so "autonomous" that it may often be sacrificial in quality, as when a craftsman who works for money refuses to stultify his work for more.

Dante's *Purgatorio* is a sustained symbolization of ethical mounting. The Mount of Purgatory is under the guardianship of Cato, the type of the moral virtues; and the immediate aim is to regain the Earthly Paradise. As the editor of the *Temple* edition puts it: "Physically and spiritually, man must climb back to the 'uplifted garden.' "

The attempt to make oneself generally appealing should, within the terms of this book, be treated as an *ethical* variant of pure persuasion. But our current success literature more often reverses the order of motives here, looking upon the cultivation of a glad and winsome personality purely as an instrument in the quest for advantage.

The doctrine of technological progress (the "higher standard of living") inextricably merges the ethical ascent with the narrower advantage-seeking of the "climber." Sometimes it even seems to be the direct descendant of earlier religious doctrines that looked upon the human body as vile and depraved. For when cherishing as a categorical improvement each new mechanical device that removes men a step further from the natural ways of life, it reaffirms the same mind-body dualism, with the equivalent of "mind" now being the corpus of mechanical inventions (born of intellect).

When discussing the "dialectics of pure practical reason," Kant writes:

Morality is not properly the doctrine how we should *make* ourselves happy, but how we should become *worthy* of happiness. It is
only when religion is added that there also comes in the hope of
participating some day in happiness in proportions as we have
endeavoured to be not unworthy of it.

Note that an attempt to make oneself "not unworthy of happiness"
can become transformed into a symbolic act designed really to *bring
about* the happiness. Insofar as "virtue" is used to coerce events (as
with the belief that virtue can command the elements), we move
towards the areas of magic (in the sense of bad science: the attempt
ritually to influence the natural order, or "acts of God"). And exhilaration can sometimes come, unquestionably, from the conviction
that somehow an operation of this sort is succeeding. In his *Ethics*
Spinoza proposes a doctrine whereby the spiritual goods, of which
one would make oneself worthy by virtue, could be said to have been
attained already in the beatitude of the virtuous state itself.

The ethical mounting (*"Excelsior! Excelsior!"*) takes so many forms
that, in a "Dramatist" analysis of motives, some fragment of it must appear on every page, since ethics is the field of action and drama is the
imitation of an action. So we can slight the category here, and turn
to the other two not yet considered.

Sometimes the design of the mountain may have fecal meanings.
Thus, the Egyptians, who held the dung-beetle sacred, might be said
to have buried their kings in pyramidal tombs that were mighty
stylized replicas of the dung-pile (the lowly connotations being, in
the enigmatic symbol, simultaneously expressed and concealed, affirmed and transcended). Economically, the motivation may have
received impetus from the fact that the fields were each year fertilized
by the deposits of the Nile, an alluvial soil easily equated with manure.
But once the culture had developed its intricate hierarchic structure,
then the priestly transcending of corruption, as with mummification
and all the magic lore that went with it, could in its own right perfect
a kind of "fecal idealism" to express eulogistically the motives that
Marx and Swift, in references previously quoted, characterized dyslogistically. Here scatology and eschatology overlap.

Where an expression is thorough, radical, "fundamental," one might
well expect the motive of "catharsis" to figure. And the question is:

Just how literally should we interpret this term of Aristotle's, particularly in view of the fact that Aristotelians praise his vocabulary for its "literalness," in contrast with Platonist "analogizing." It is our conviction that a transcendence is not complete until the fecal motive has in some way been expressed and "redeemed." Psychologists have pointed out that the feces are the child's first production. Hence such moral motives as duty and work can have fecal connotations. And esthetic production is often conceived of in fecal terms, either jocularly or in roundabout disguise.

We consider the golden bird of Yeats's Byzantium poem such a disguise, "immortality" itself being here conceived in terms of esthetic output, the ambiguities being more clearly revealed in Brancusi's sculpture of the Golden Bird. And we believe that there is a similar enigma in Hopkins' lines:

> I am soft sift
> In an hourglass—at the wall
> Fast, but mined with a motion, a drift
> And it crowds and it combs to the fall.

A gracious example that has been brought to our attention is in the second *cancion* of the *Cantico Espiritual,* by St. John of the Cross:

> Pastores, los que fuéredes
> allá por las majadas al otero,
> si por ventura viéredes
> aquel que yo más quiero
> decidle que adolezco, peno y muero,

which has been translated thus:

> Shepherds, who go
> up by the sheepcotes to the top of the hill,
> if you should happen to see
> the one I most desire,
> tell him I sicken, suffer and die.

The word *majadas* means "sheepcote, sheepfold" or "dung." It is related to *majadal* (good pasture ground for sheep; land improved by the manure of a flock), and to *majadear* (to take shelter in the night, said of sheep; to manure).

According to St. John, the desires, loves, and sighs are called "shepherds," since they instruct (the word also means "graze") the soul in spiritual goods. And the sheepcotes stand for "the hierarchies and choirs of the angels, through whom, from choir to choir, our signs and prayers go to God, who is here called hill, as he is the ultimate height, and because in him, as on the hill, you see all things, sheepcotes both high and low."

We might also glimpse the dim outlines of a pun here, that would introduce maternal connotations. The word for hill, *otero,* is very close to the word for womb, *utero.* And the Spanish words which are here translated "on the hill" are literally "in the hill." However, the similarity is greatly lessened by the fact that *utero* is accented on the first syllable, *otero* on the second.

Sometimes the transcendence may be got by purely tonal transformations. Notably by umlaut, ablaut, augmentation, diminution metathesis, substitution of cognate consonants, and by portmanteau formations. For instance, if "soteme" were a fecal word, and "seeteme" and "siteme" were words of neutral or honorific meaning, the first might be lurking in a usage of these other two. (Such concealments would involve umlaut and ablaut respectively.) A structure like "stome" would be a diminution; "sozeteme" would be an augmentation. "Metos" would be metathesis. "Sodebe" would be a substitution of cognates, *d* for *t* and *b* for *m*. Portmanteau words would be likely to occur only in dreams, or perhaps in some arbitrarily assigned proper name (except of course in writing like Joyce's). There could also be disguised expressions combining two or more of these resources, as "stobe" would be a diminution plus a replacing of *m* by its cognate *b*. If all these arbitrary syllables are assumed to be meaningful in some one language system, then it is our notion that they could perform this added poetic function, along with their strictly lexicological role, as defined in a dictionary. Thus we knew a man who had kidney trouble, and who jocularly signed his letters "yourn," without meaning to suggest the pun, "urine"—while a serious use of "urn" may, on some occasions, encompass the same ambiguity. Such usages would reduce, sometimes to a single letter or syllable, the process of catharsis, or ritual purging, that is developed at length in tragedy, with its elaborate rites of purification got through the offering of a victim hierarchally infused.*

---

* We have proposed as a term for critical method the verb "to joyce." By "joycing" we mean the deliberate and systematic coaching of such transformations for heuristic purposes. They can't often prove anything, but they may lead to critical hunches (or help one to discount hunches that one may himself have

In the quotation we previously made from Marx, likening the "cranium system" of German idealism to the fecal motivations of the Egyptian and Tibetan priesthoods, there are suggestions that the entire hierarchic pyramid of dialectical symmetry may be infused with such a spirit. But the form is, of course, likewise derivable from the nature of the symbolic medium in itself, the possibility of terms arranged in ever-mounting orders of generalization, until they reach their culmination in a title of titles which, in its absolute "being," has as its dialectical ground only an equally absolute "nothing."

Here are the resources of the Upward Way, by the *via negativa,* with the possible reversal of direction, a returning to the flatlands in a Downward Way. (On the return the system will contain a principle of transcendent unity which was reached at the culmination of the way up, and henceforth pervades all the world's disparate particulars, causing them to partake of a common universal substance.) This ultimate dialectical resource, while itself aiming beyond all imagery or local conditions, may lead to identification with some local figure, institution, or the like, or with the corresponding imagery. Hence, though it be but the pure form of the principle of hierarchy in general (the suasive principle of ultimate dialectical symmetry), it makes for a susceptibility to particular hierarchic embodiments. Thus it can be consciously used for speculative liberation from a given social order— or both consciously and unconsciously, it can be used for fixing men's loyalty to a given social order.

This would perhaps be an aspect of climactic form in general, the building up of an intensity and its subsidence, as in drama. Usually however, the pyramidal form is implicit, rather than being explicitly figured in terms of higher stages. Likewise, here, we might include those moments of transcendence when a work takes on a new dimension of insight, as with the speech of Shylock which does not merely exploit Christian prejudices against the Jew but suddenly lifts the

---

wrongly developed from such unconscious punning). However, the use of such a device extends far beyond the disclosing of "forbidden" words lurking behind socially acceptable disguises. A critic of twenty years ago, for instance, who had experimentally "joyced" Eliot's "Prufrock," to see what motives might be implicit there, would not have gone far amiss had he discerned, as enigmatic symbolizing of its future, "prove-rock" and "pure-frock." This matter requires further discussion in the *Symbolic.* It has also been treated somewhat in *The Philosophy of Literary Form,* notably pages 51-66, 258-271, 369-378.

situation to terms of universal mankind. (Is it not true that, with the comparing of the body politic to the physical body in *Coriolanus,* the playwright is aiming to establish such a moment of transcendence *at the very outset,* to lift the play but a few lines after it has begun, proclaiming the hierarchic principle as the very essence of its motivation, a motive that Coriolanus proclaimed to be not only his, but everyone's?)

An interesting variant of the ultimate dialectical mounting, where a questionable kind of exaltation is involved, is mentioned in an article by Eric Kahler, "The Secularization of the Devil," reviewing Thomas Mann's *Doctor Faustus* (*Commentary,* April, 1949). Mr. Kahler here speaks of modern "Faustian" man as being "in a diabolical plight, in the state of alienation, of the Fall—the Fall by rising, by ironic transcendence."

As most obvious indication of the way in which dialectical mounting makes for transcendence, imagine this hypothetical instance of "justice":

Imagine a moral code, decreed by yourself, and so narrow in its notion of advantage that every injunction was framed purely for your particular convenience. Thus, if each entry were exactly phrased it would have this form: *"Thou* shalt not do evil to *me."* Even so, you need but generalize this code completely, and the "thou" applies likewise to the propounder of the code, while the "me" stands for "everyman." Whereupon, by carrying out the dialectical process to its ultimate conclusion, you have transcended the original limitations of the code. However narrow its original quest of advantage, by sheer universalization it has moved into the areas of the sacrificial.

Or otherwise put: We need but universalize the idea of a right or privilege, and we have advanced from the acquisitive to the ethical. On the other hand, motives such as doctrines of race supremacy, that do not permit us to think of justice in universal terms, are essentially frustrating. The frustration is not of the sort that the term now usually suggests: the inability to procure some desired convenience or preferment. Rather, it derives from the inability to allow oneself the "expansive" hope for the maximum generalizing of "justice."

As we saw when considering Empson, such self-frustrations on the part of a "superior" class are frequently expressed in a cult of irony, which would thus in itself signalize the class status. Though such an ironist may, if he is a man of imagination, also extend the ironic principle in ways that transcend its local motivation, Marx might question universalizing of this sort as ideological mystification. For as regards its counterpart in the social texture, the more richly universal such irony becomes, the more thoroughly may it be in effect the "universalizing of inequity" (a subtle variant of the original injustice, with those who propound "race supremacy" as a "universal" doctrine).

However, though there is also this dubious transcendence, which allows for a certain range of ironic exaltation, the dialectical form in itself strains ever towards the universalization of justice, even as its counterpart in human institutions makes for hierarchic stratification. And the release through dialectical mounting seems to prevail in proportion as, truly or falsely, we can feel ourselves to be motivated by the universal principle infusing all stages of a hierarchy rather than by aims local to one stage. The two contrary motives are brought into unity by doctrines that proclaim the universal good to be derived from factional strife. Marxism, Adam Smith, and orthodox religions all have their variants of this pattern.

Might we look upon this entire "range of mountings" as a kind of ideal paradigm? Might we conclude that a writer's work would have the maximum vibrancy if all of these ascensions were somehow contained by the same symbol, in exhilarating harmony? And as the early philosophers used to say that maxims and proverbs were fragmentary survivals of an ancient wisdom originally as ample and architectonic as a great cathedral, so might we examine individual expressions for evidence that some portions of a "total mounting" are working within them? Thus whereas the mystic exaltation is in itself ineffable, might its analogue in language reside precisely in the happy simultaneity of all such motives? Similarly, might the mystic accidie set in precisely at the moment when the happy combination is somehow broken, and the motives that were thus being transcended are left like ashes after a bright fire?

5. ELATION AND ACCIDIE IN HOPKINS

Considering the poetry of Gerard Manley Hopkins, we might note these steps:

1. A precocious gift for almost lushly sensuous imagery. Consider the prize poem he wrote at college, for instance, almost an orgy of sensations, in his descriptions of light, flowers, gems, colors. "Spikes of light / Spear'd open lustrous gashes, crimson-white" . . . "an orb'd rose . . . by hot pantings blown / Apart" . . . "With coral, shells, thick-pearlèd cords, whate'er / The abysmal Ocean hoards of strange and rare" . . . "the dainty onyx-coronals deflowers, / A glorious wanton" . . . "the scarce troubled sea / Gurgled where they had sunk, melodiously" . . . "Slumber'd at last in one sweet, deep, heart-broken close."

2. When he joined the Jesuit order, he renounced his verse. He treated it as antithetical to his calling. He here made a choice the opposite to Stephen's in *The Portrait of the Artist as a Young Man.* And the turn from so sensory a medium would seem to be a fitting act of priestly mortification.

3. But a new motive entered when a superior suggested that a poem should be written in commemoration of the nuns who had lost their lives in the wreck of the *Deutschland.* Here, of a sudden, was a way whereby he could welcome the very gift he had rejected.

As regards mystical exaltation, and its analogue in poetry, we believe that this third step is the important one. A motive, when genuinely transcended, is not dropped, but transformed. It is redeemed not by subtraction, but by inclusion in a new fellowship. It is thus *not repressed,* but *expressed,* yet expressed with a difference: for its "nature" has been "graced."

Hopkins could now fill his notebooks with minute observations of natural objects. For if he saw in them, or thought he saw in them, an essence derivable from God, the more accurate his study in the empirical and positivist sense, the more devotional he could be in his conviction that these objects were signatures of the divine presence. Nature could serve as a kind of Christly pontification between the observer and God. If he, in a Schellingesque identification of subject and object, could identify himself as agent with particulars of the natural scene, and if (in his somewhat idealistic interpretation of Scotist *haecceitas*) he could identify the particularity of natural objects with the divine, when all was going well he would have a happy communion of self, nature, and God.

Thus by the same token, the whole range of sensuous imagery was again open to him, and he used it fervently. For what he had previously denied himself, as a way of mortification, he could now use with profusion, *ad majorem Dei gloriam*.

Very complex possibilities present themselves with such a change of motives. Thus, in writing of the shipwreck in which the five nuns perished, he could include passages that refer ambiguously to another kind of shipwreck, his own moral lapses. Then, as the poem shifts to the literal wreck, itself treated as a harvesting for God, there is the implication that roundabout his guilt has been ennobled. That is, there are three kinds of shipwreck here: the literal one, his own depravity, and the gathering of the heroic nuns to God. And in the general exaltation, he has confessed, but the oblique account of his carnal passions has been merged into the glorification of the nuns' religious passion.

Perhaps "The Windhover" is the poem where the exaltation is purest. There are signs of the burdensome motives (notably the reference to "sheer plod" of "plough down sillion," and to "blue-bleak embers" that are said to "fall, gall themselves, and gash gold-vermilion"). But the elation is so great that its spirit saturates the whole, and the down-turning moments are rather like something dropped in an elevator going up. Similarly, in terms like "dappled" and "pied beauty," he seems to have hit upon a signature that brings white and black motives together, not in dualistic conflict, but in a happy merger that redeems the black ones. The theme even flashes through the ecstatic account of the windhover's flight, since the bird, though likened to Christ, is called a "dappled-dawn-drawn Falcon."

Universalize the idea of purpose (as when the mark of God is seen in each creature). Then identify the individual with this universal design. The result is invigorating. But let anything go wrong with the identification, and all that is left is a sorely protruding ego, a very self-sick self. Hence, though the sense of mounting is kept vibrant while things are going well, when the witherings of accidie set in, the exalted identification of the self with a nature itself identified with God is disrupted, and there is left the self alone: "I am gall, I am heartburn" ... "God's most deep decree / Bitter would have me taste; my taste was me" ... "Selfyeast of spirit a dull dough sours" ... "self, self ... poor Jackself."*

* I am here giving the gist of an unpublished thesis, "Nature of the Transcendence in the Poetry of Gerard Manley Hopkins," by Judith Bailey, who did

"So will I turn her virtues into pitch," Iago says. What are we to make of the fact that Hopkins, who gave great thought to the overtones of words, uses this very word, "pitch," to name the concrete distinctness of a thing, its selfhood? He can also use it as a verb: man's self was said to be "more highly pitched" than that of other creatures. And in one of the last poems, written in the time of despair, we find: "pitched past pitch of grief." Clearly, the word had ambiguous markings from the start. It lurkingly signified the discomfitures of selfhood at those times when the moment of exaltation would vanish.

6. YEATS: "BYZANTIUM" AND THE LAST POEMS

"Mirror on mirror mirrored is all the show," Yeats wrote in the grim period of his own Last Poems. Or having asked himself out of what "masterful images" his earlier work had grown "in pure mind," he answered in terms of offal, thus:

> A mound of refuse or the sweepings of the street,
> Old kettles, old bottles, and a broken can,
> Old iron, old bones, old rags, that raving slut
> Who keeps the till. Now that my ladder's gone,
> I must lie down where all the ladders start,
> In the foul rag-and-bone shop of the heart.

The "ladder," in the happy days, had been the ascent of the "tower," the "winding stair." But here, indeed, Yeats is talking very explicitly of these hierarchic matters, and of what motives, in the unredeemed fecal order, threaten to proclaim themselves when several of the peaks in the "range of mountings" have ceased to figure, and the "mound of refuse" predominates in its starkness.

Earlier, he had written about the eggs of Leda, from one of which Helen had been born, from the other Castor and Pollux. He had written ecstatically on Leda and the Swan: the heroic history of the Iliad was prophesied as having been conceived at the moment of their union. Helen for love, Castor and Pollux for war; the two heroic themes of ancient Greece. But now, after the descent down the ladder, he finds their equivalence in states without radiance: he writes of "lust and rage."

---

work on Hopkins in conferences with me some years ago. The thesis, an exceptionally competent performance for an undergraduate student, is on file at the Bennington College Library.

In the two Byzantium poems, he had confronted death tragically, but with the full glow. Both poems are under the sign of gold, itself an ambiguous symbol, as psychoanalysts remind us—for in its more dismal fascination, as with the motives of the miser, it is said to have fecal connotations. When he here thinks of himself as gathered "into the artifice of eternity" (a kind of immortality, like that of Keats's Urn,* conceived in esthetic terms, and so possibly having the ambiguities of such output), the gold is transcendent, transformed into an ecstasy of gold, as the word springs forth in nervous, resonant repetition:

> Once out of nature I shall never take
> My bodily form from any natural thing,
> But such a form as Grecian goldsmiths make
> Of hammered gold and gold enamelling
> To keep a drowsy Emperor awake;
> Or set up a golden bough to sing
> To lords and ladies of Byzantium
> Of what is past, or passing, or to come.

Here the corruption of death is translated into its euphemistic equivalent: immortality. In English, too, "gold" has the added resonance of "God" in the offing. And similarly, at the close of the other Byzantium poem, when the poet writes of "that dolphin-torn, that gong-tormented sea," heuristically joycing here, dare we detect in these sounds a strange heresy, poetically disguised, by the enigma of the pun? Might we hear instead: "that devil-torn, that God-tormented sea"?

We would not consider the work of either Hopkins or Yeats prime instances of mystical poetry. But at least there is a trace of mysticism here, in the particular elated moments we have been considering. And in both cases, the indications are that "nature" becomes tyrannously burdensome, once the poet, having made himself at home in "grace," finds that it has been withdrawn.

---

* Since death, disease, the passions, or bodily "corruption" generally (as with religious horror of the body) may be variants of the fecal, their transcending may involve a corresponding translation of the fecal. See (in the *Grammar of Motives*) our analysis of the Keats Ode, as an indication of such transcendence, by the splitting of a distraught state into active and passive, so that the evil element (the suffering) can be abstracted and eliminated, while only purified spiritual activity remains.

7. ELIOT: EARLY POEMS AND "QUARTETS"

In the case of Eliot, we might note a reverse direction, not to any great extent, but enough to be observed and discussed. That is, the poet later uses with fuller connotations images that were at first used somewhat sparsely, as regards the "range of mountings" that seems to be contained in them. To illustrate, let us begin with a formula for the early poems, such as "The Love Song of J. Alfred Prufrock" and "Portrait of a Lady":

A down-turning mood. A subdued, and even smart kind of lamentation (a gesture first developed in Jules Laforgue, who had this way of being genuinely sad and desolate, in accents of literary elegance). Contrast such cautiousness with the full-throated outpourings of Biblical lamentation. The modern style involves social etiquette and literary tact. Here is fragility.

A crabbedness is suggested. Thus, when Prufrock says, "I should have been a pair of ragged claws / Scuttling across the floors of silent seas," he is in dramatic language defining an essential motivation within himself. Later, in the fluently moody "Rhapsody on a Windy Night," the theme is varied ingeniously: "And a crab one afternoon in a pool, / An old crab with barnacles on his back, / Gripped the end of a stick which I held him," the act itself thus standing for a kind of crabbed communication.

One should note also a strongly spectator attitude, a view of the city's dramas impersonally, almost statistically, as in the second Prelude: "One thinks of all the hands / That are raising dingy shades / In a thousand furnished rooms." This is city poetry, not nature poetry. The point is worth noting, for it has bearing upon the more sophisticatedly dialectical nature of the transcendence with which the poet will later be concerned.

A contemplative poet in a great metropolis must necessarily have a somewhat impersonal attitude towards most of the citizenry. This may be expressed through hail-fellow-well-met, idealistic gestures of the Whitman sort, embracing mankind generically, as a broad statement of policy. Or at the other extreme it may involve a kind of tight-lipped aloofness. But no poet is tight-lipped—so the distrust of superficial fraternization leads instead to a modified aloofness, the "statistical" attitude as in turn modified by the mood of fragile lamentation. And there is a strong suggestion of unfulfilled possibilities, even in cases where people do meet as personal acquaintances, in standoffish intimacy, in relations of vaguely frustrate courtship. Hence such elegiac references as

> . . . time yet for a hundred indecisions,
> And for a hundred visions and revisions,
> Before the taking of a toast and tea,

then, after an interruption

> And indeed there will be time
> To wonder, "Do I dare?" and, "Do I dare?"
> Time to turn back and descend the stair, . . .

With relation to this tentative mood, there arise two notable antitheses: One, the theme of Apeneck Sweeney, a crudely potent male so unrefined that he could shave while a woman on a bed near-by has an epileptic seizure; Sweeney who, in the bath, "shifts from ham to ham." There is a set of such gruff, low organisms, acting directly in response to animal appetites.

The other kind of antithesis is figured in images of faint distant music, or of submerged music, or of faint distant submerged music sung by mermaids, images that seem to match the tentative, unfulfilled possibilities by suggestions of an alternative actuality, with sweetly sexual connotations.

The down-turning mood reaches proportions close to accidie, or mystic drought, in "The Waste Land." Fertility here is under dismal auspices indeed, as in the third section, ironically called The Fire Sermon, where "Tiresias, throbbing between two lives," "old man with wrinkled female breasts," witnesses a crude love affair between "the typist home at tea-time" and the "small house agent's clerk." In this, and other episodes, witnessed from a distance, with deep disgruntlement, we have the poet's documents of social drought. Another kind of antithesis enters here, as mean expressions from contemporary scenes are contrasted with lines cited from contexts that went with earlier, gracious ways.

In the last episode, What the Thunder Said, the themes of social drought are finally summed up in a purely natural imagery of drought. This call for the fertilizing waters is followed by a stanza that prompts us to risk a somewhat foolhardy venture. For the poet gives one explanation of it in his notes. Everyone will agree that he ought to know. Yet we would offer another (our excuse being that this explanation does not contradict his, but supplements it).

The stanza is:

> Who is the third who walks always beside you?
> When I count, there are only you and I together
> But when I look ahead up the white road
> There is always another one walking beside you
> Gliding wrapt in a brown mantle, hooded
> I do not know whether a man or a woman
> —But who is that on the other side of you?

The notes comment thus: "The following lines were stimulated by the account of one of the Antarctic expeditions (I forget which, but I think one of Shackleton's): it was related that the party of explorers, at the extremity of their strength, had the constant delusion that there was *one more member* than could actually be counted."

Our gloss upon this gloss would be based on considerations of this sort: A friend once told us of a time when, after a notable change in his life, he found himself with a group of people whom he had known intimately before his change, but whom he had not, for a considerable time, seen thus together in one company. Despite all that had intervened, on this occasion something of the old relationship was reëstablished—except that a mild fantasy kept recurring. He found himself, again and again, counting the number of those present. No matter how many were in the room, he repeatedly caught himself thinking there must be one more. Afterwards, he explained the fantasy to himself thus: There *was* an extra person in the room. For he himself was of a divided mind, combining in one legal person both an earlier identity and a later one, so far as his attitudes toward these people were concerned. There were two of him, and in his fantasy he had kept saying so.

Is that not relevant to our present case? Here is the transitional poem *par excellence*. Here is the parched call for a new motive. The new motive is figured somewhat intellectualistically at the end of the poem; it is more of a resolve than an actual attainment; but it is present incipiently. And why, precisely, where the new motive is emerging, should it not show as a division within the poet himself? And why should not this division be symbolized in fantasies suggesting that this inward feeling had an outward counterpart (what Eliot the critic might have called an "objective correlative")?

The explanation is not essential to our case, however. For our purposes, one need grant only that the poem is transitional, midway between the early manner and the *Quartets*. The "peace" that it attains at the end is purely formal, like a conventional valediction. Though we are told that "shantih" means "the peace which passeth understanding," the expression as inserted here is several removes from a welling-forth in release. As regards the tests of mystic beatitude, it is little better than a slogan.

Since, even with the soundest of newly acquired positions, one might expect some backsliding, we need not be surprised that, three years later, with "The Hollow Men," the imagery of drought and impotence is even more extreme. However, the borrowing from the Upanishads is now replaced by stuttering, fragmentary abstractions from the Lord's Prayer. (The talk of the world's end, we take it, is a statement of *essential* motivation, hence also roundabout a figuring of the poet's motives.)

"Ash Wednesday" represents the new climb: "at the first turning of the second stair . . . at the second turning of the second stair . . . at the first turning of the third stair . . ." finally

> Fading, fading; strength beyond hope and despair
> Climbing the third stair.

Manifestly, there are still problems here. These stairs are arduous, lowly. In Dante, we are told that the higher one mounts, the easier becomes the climb. Saint Teresa, talking of a similar development, uses her figure of the watered garden, to name the mounting stages of prayer in the progress to mystic communion: first, the way that cannot be done without much labor, as with drawing water out of a well; next, by using a wheel with buckets; third, by letting a small stream run through the garden; and fourth, "By a good shower of rain falling; for then our Lord himself waters the garden, without any labor on our part; and this is by far the best method of all." In each stage, the procuring of the benefit is easier until in the fourth the downpour comes unbidden, somewhat as with the spontaneous rush Hopkins describes in his metaphor of the fruit bursting in the mouth:

> How a lush-kept plush-capped sloe
> Will, mouthed to flesh-burst,
> Gush!—flush the man, the being with it, sour or sweet,
> Brim, in a flash, full!

Admittedly, we here come upon ambiguities of the sort the psychoanalyst would make much of, when evaluating the mystic experience. We leave them unsettled. For our purposes, it is enough to note that, in mystic poetry, such ambiguities will be there, however you choose to interpret them (whether in terms of "nature," or of "grace").

Assuming that a wholly edifying symbol of the mount would contain all the elements we listed, and looking now for portions of the totality, we should first note that, in the Eliot poem, the mounting of the stairs remains arduous. There is no easing. Hence, on this score the imagery would not fully meet the requirements. But there is one notable transformation. For the image *has* taken on a much richer ethical content than it had in the passage we quoted from "Prufrock"; and it similarly transcends the wry reference to diffident courtship in "Portrait of a Lady":

> Except for a slight sensation of being ill at ease
> I mount the stairs and turn the handle of the door
> And feel as if I had mounted on my hands and knees.

In the *Quartets*, we find many such transformations. The rock of the parched desert in "The Waste Land" can become the rock of religious fortitude. The early laments about unfulfilled possibilities as regards one man's indecisions can give way to universal ponderings on human tentativeness. Talk of a rose garden can now stand ambiguously for: (1) purely secular delights; (2) vague adumbrations of exalted delights; (3) the final mystic unfolding and enfoldment. Fire can be of so double a nature that paradoxes are in order:

> The only hope, or else despair
> Lies in the choice of pyre or pyre
> To be redeemed from fire by fire.

Many related kinds of dialectical manipulation can be used. Since reduction to terms of highest generalization allows for permanent or "timeless" principles, and since "eternity" as so couched equals pure being (which in its transcending of conditions is indistinguishable from nothing) there are now even the possibilities of a good meaning for drought, as presented in terms of mortification and the *via negativa*:

> Internal darkness, deprivation
> And destitution of all property,
> Desiccation of the world of sense,
> Evacuation of the world of fancy,
> Inoperancy of the world of spirit.

The objectives of a movement are motionless. If you travel north, the direction itself does not move. And the structure of music just *is*, whether the music is heard or not. Dialectically, "everything moves but the ab-

straction of motion" (Marx). There are these opportunities for paradoxes.

A world of contingencies can now be placed antithetically to the unconditioned realm. The motivations here would be purely temporal,
the unilluminated domain of the Apeneck Sweeneys, its time-minded-
ness viewed statistically, the early aloofness now having become contemplation *sub specie aeternitatis*.

Also, there can be the temporal as infused with the eternal. This is
a variant of the Downward Way after the purifications of the Upward
Way.

A moment in history being needed to make the mortal's glimpse of
eternity possible, this moment can then become formative even of one's
past, which is now envisaged transcendently, in the light of the indeterminate moment when consciousness as an eternal possibility and consciousness as a passing occasion in history come together (or, dialectically,
where a term for the individual agent is taken as bridging the gap
between terms for particulars and terms for universals). Here are
the purely technical resources that allow for transformations whereby the
earlier unfulfilled possibilities can become "footfalls" that "echo in the
memory." And because they are now fused with the spirit of the formative moment, they have a double nature. The early, humbler possibilities
can now be seen as vague adumbrations of the later, higher possibilities.
The rose of the early rose garden (a choice not taken, but felt as beckon-
ing) can imply the ultimate mystic rose (celebrated at the close of the
fourth Quartet):

> When the tongues of flame are in-folded
> Into the crowned knot of fire
> And the fire and the rose are one.

In sum, we feel that, to approach the *Quartets* in terms of symbolic
action, we should first ask ourselves what primary dialectical resources
there are here, for exploitation. For, so far as verbal method is concerned, it is apparently the pyramid of dialectical mounting (the resources
of Heraclitus) that this poet relies upon mainly, as the means that can
endow the earlier down-turning images with new motives, by placing
them in the upward-turning configuration that dialectical reduction readily makes possible. There are the terms for change and the terms for
the universal, the unchanging; and the agent's mind or consciousness
can be the term that mediates between the two orders—and thereby the

poet can take us from a down-turning proposition to an up-turning one. Thus, the opening words of "East Coker" are: "In my beginning is my end"—and the last are: "In my end is my beginning." The first can sum up the world of contingent particulars, each leading by mechanical necessity to the next; the reversal of the proposition sums up the possibility of a shift to the realm of universal terms.

All told, the kinds of dialectical resources likely to be encountered here would be these:

> terms for the eternal;
> terms for the temporal;
> terms for the point of intersection between these two realms;
> terms for the temporal as infused with the eternal;
> terms that, in summing up the temporal, transcend it somewhat;
> terms that paradoxically glimpse the eternal in the momentary.

We might expect to find such resources embodied in varying kinds of imagery—and we might "call the plays" at any given point in the text by noting which of such resources is being utilized, and in what sort of images it is embodied.

8. PRINCIPLE OF THE OXYMORON

There is a ground, in both agent and scene, beyond the verbal. Yet as students of literature we should seek to disclose what purely verbal resources are being drawn upon, when the poet is talking of first and last things, or is using images that do not appeal merely to the senses, but derive radiance and vibrancy from their "anagogic" and/or "socio-anagogic" nature. And since the mystic communicates ultimately in terms of the oxymoron (the figure that combines contradictory elements within a single expression), we would see in the packing of an image or idea with divergent motives a more or less remote instance of "literary mysticism."

In a sense, of course, literary mysticism is a contradiction in terms. For as James points out, the mystic's experience is "ineffable." But poetry being expressive, mystic poetry would thus have to "express the ineffable" —and to do that it would have to be what Kant might have called a *Seiendes Unding*.

For practical purposes, however, no such embarrassments need beset us. We might experimentally acknowledge the existence of "mysticism proper" (as the term is applied to mystics like Saint John of the Cross and Saint Teresa, whom the Church has officially recognized). Next, noting the distinctive quality of their writings, we might, in the purely technical sense, apply the term mystical to other writers whose work possesses all or some of these same distinctive qualities. In some cases the likeness would be great; in other cases there would be but fragmentary resemblances. Even a trivial oxymoron might thus be related to the great mystic oxymorons. *But here one would be careful to note that he was dealing with a mere fragment of the mystical motive,* too tiny to be taken as an instance of "revelation," and at best indicating in "natural" terms a remote desire for the saint's "gracious" experience. (We would get such an analogue in turning from the theologian's "sanctifying grace" to its poetic counterparts in secular felicities of style.)

Thus Coleridge, looking at sea, sky, and mountain in a mood of entrancement, calling the scene "an awful omneity in unity," goes on to discuss it as a "perfect union of the sublime with ..ie beautiful, so that they should be felt, that is, at the same minute, though by different faculties, and yet each faculty be predisposed, by itself, to receive the specific modifications from the other." (We are again citing from *Anima Poetae.*) By "beauty" he meant the appeal to the eye, "in shape and color." By the "sublime" he meant appeal "to the mind," through the scene's "immensity."

The passage well illustrates an explicit concern with what we might call the meeting of the empirically esthetic and the hierarchal. For although, in Coleridge's distinction, the beautiful would concern the purely sensory modes of appeal, his idea of the sublime would seem to involve the principle of hierarchy. The sublime resides in moral and intellectual "immensities." And even when the sublimities are represented by physical objects, like plains, sea, sky, and mountains, they are "moral" because the contrast between us and their might and proportion is forcefully hierarchic. Next, insofar as sensory order and social order affect each other, awed and delighted identification with physical power can call forth a transcendent feeling of personal *freedom.* That is, by the paradox of substance, one can imaginatively identify oneself with the mountain's massive assertiveness while at the same time thinking of one's own comparative futility. The identification thus gives a sense of freedom, since it transcends our limitations (though the effect is made possible only by our awareness of these limitations). The logical contradition (of being simultaneously oppressed *and* free) is felt quasi-temporally, as a kind of fixed progression, or congealed sequence (as a change *from* oppression *to* freedom). The experience is thus "uplifting."* The hierarchic judgments that infuse tragic sublimity are exemplified in reverse by the devices of the ridiculous.

Identification in itself is a kind of transcendence. For instance, since the individual is to some extent distinct from his group, an identifying of him with the group is by the same token a transcending of his distinctness. Hence, just as persuasion terminates in the "meta-rhetoric" of pure persuasion, so identification attains its ultimate expression in mysticism, the identification of the infinitesimally frail with the infinitely powerful. Modes of identification with the "sublime" in nature would then be analyzable as large "fragments" of the mystical motive. And we could then discern faint traces in identifications and oxymorons still farther removed from the perfect paradigm.

Thus a novelist, ending on the death of his heroine, might picture the hero walking silently in the rain. No weeping here. Rather stark "understatement." Or look again, and do you not find that the very heavens are weeping in his behalf? As recall how Lear's brain-storm gets amplification, or Wagnerian scenic duplication, in the raging of the elements. (Act III, Scene IV, the thesaurus of madness: the fool, Edgar, Lear, and the storm, with Lear rounding out the pattern by his reference to "the tempest in my mind.") Or recall Verlaine's similar meteorological attitudinizing: "*Il pleure dans mon coeur comme il pleut sur la ville.*"

Rain, then, as a symbol of weeping. There is even a certain covert apotheosis of the emotion here, making it "heavenly" thus roundabout. But note that rain may also be a symbol of fertility. It may figure the vernally emergent. To water with one's tears can thus also ambiguously be to prepare for the next phase. Thus, the idea of weeping can be translated into its imaginal equivalent, as rain. But the image of rain

---

* Do we not here follow much the same course as guided our ideas on "pure persuasion"? There we noted how, in the absolute, the three elements of persuasion (speaker, speech, and spoken-to) coexist in triune simultaneity, as a "timeless" form; and how some kind of interference becomes necessary if the pattern of persuasion is to be perpetuated in temporal terms. Here we see an exaltation or "uplift" got by identification with an eminence. And such a "tendency" is also a *fixity*, an attitudinal incipience, as of a person who retains the expectancy of setting out on a journey by continuing to stay just where he is.

in its own right contains also the idea of rebirth. (The sociologist Thomas D. Elliot has noted what he calls a "ritual of riddance," whereby the very rites that serve to honor the departed also serve as a device for cutting the bonds between the mourner and the deceased.)

We speak of this plot as hypothetical. But might not the recipe apply to the ending of Hemingway's *A Farewell to Arms?* Add the fact that the hero is there returning in the rain to his hotel. Does not such a destination stand for the potentiality of new intimacies?

Or again: If fire can stand for the burnings of carnal appetite, or for transcendent radiance (as with the flames of the *Paradiso*), or for the avenging tortures of hell, or for purification (as with the cleansing fire of the *Purgatorio*), it would not need to stand for these various motives one at a time, but might combine them in a single moment.

Thus we recall a dismal story, conceived by a sex-hungry adolescent, of a man trapped in a burning building with a woman. She had fainted in terror—and as his last act on earth he was about to violate her, when the floor collapsed, so that the two bodies were hurled together into the flames. Here the very situation which first introduced the intent of transgression and then forestalled it, finally made it possible on a "transcendent" level, in the image of the couple's fall into flames that consumed them jointly.

Attention has frequently been called to the scene in Dante's *Inferno*, acting out the metaphor that is in such expressions as "the winds of passion" or "gusts of passion." Since in this canto carnal sinners are pictured as being perpetually blown about by turbulent winds in hell, the image of their passions on earth becomes the image of their suffering (another kind of *pati*) in hell. But is there not a further ambiguity here? After listing several damned lovers, such as Semiramis, Cleopatra, Helen, Achilles, Paris, Tristan, each of whom is alone, Dante tells of Paolo and Francesca, who are being swirled about together. When he would talk with them, they come "as doves called by desire." And after Francesca has told sadly of the occasion when she and her lover had fallen into sin, Dante says: "I fainted with pity, as if I had been dying; and fell, as a dead body falls."

When we recall that Dante proclaimed himself born under the sign of Venus, might we not see in his fall an imagistic counterpart of the same transgression, though his identification with the sinning lovers is here translated into a form moralistically correct? At the very least, the fainting indicates his special susceptibility here. (After all, he is still in hell, and his progress through the three realms also figures a moral and intellectual growth for him personally.) But we would go a step further, asserting that in the particular sympathetic form which the expression of susceptibility takes, the image can also "transcendently" represent the same "fall."

In the mystery of Christ as sacrificial king, the principle of the oxymoron is obvious, in Christ's double role as victimized and victorious. And identification with the tragic scapegoat ranges from the remotely fragmentary to the immediate and total. When criminals were sentenced to death in Athens, instead of being executed at the time, they might be kept imprisoned for some occasion when the gods had to be honored or propitiated by a public sacrifice. Such a prisoner was called a *katharma*, a name for the ritually unclean, and of the same root as the word for purgation, in both its medical meanings and its application by Aristotle to the cathartic effects of tragedy. The ambiguities whereby the object of such a public offering is at once sacred and loathsome are paralleled most startlingly in Luther's radical conception of Christ as the bearer of the world's sinfulness. "All the prophets saw," he says in his comments on the Epistle to the Galatians, "that Christ would be the greatest brigand of all, the greatest adulterer, thief, profaner of temples, blasphemer, and so on, that there would never be a greater in all the world." Again: "God sent his only begotten Son into the world, and laid all sins upon him, saying: 'You are to be Peter the denier, Paul the persecutor, blasphemer, and wild beast, David the adulterer, you are to be the sinner who ate the apple in the Garden of Eden, you are to be the crucified thief, you are to be the person who commits all the sins in the world." (We translate the citations from *Kierkegaard et la philosophie existentielle*, by Léon Chestov.) With drastic logicality, Luther here deduced that the God-man must become immeasurably the worst criminal of all, in taking upon himself the full guilt of humankind. And you begin to wonder whether he threw his inkwell at the Devil, or at this scrupulously morbid vision of Christ as universal *katharma*.

9. ULTIMATE IDENTIFICATION

In his *Varieties of Religious Experience*, in the chapter on Mysticism, William James quotes many excerpts from a wide range of witnesses who testified that they had been mystically exalted at certain rare moments, and who attempted to describe the mystic state. For our closing text, let us make excerpts from these excerpts, and assemble the cullings into one consecutive, dithyrambic but rambling account, which should give a composite portrait of the experience, mystic state, though it does justice to no single person's testimony:

Feeling as if one were "grasped and held by a superior power" ... "prophetic speech, automatic writing, or the mediumistic trance" ... as if one were "born anew," as if one "had the door of paradise thrown wide open" ... "a mighty fascination" ... "transport" ... "the strangely moving power" ... "eternal inner message" ... the sense of having "been there before" ... a state wherein individuality seems "to dissolve and fade away into boundless being" ... a state where "death was an almost laughable impossibility" ... "an innate feeling that everything I see has a meaning" ... "indescribable awe" ... "a gradual but swiftly progressive obliteration of space, time, sensation, and the multitudinous factors of experience" ... insight as to how "the present is pushed on by the past, and sucked forward by the vacuity of the future" ... "the 'now' keeps exfoliating out of itself" ... " 'You could kiss your own lips, and have all the fun to yourself,' it says, if you only knew the trick" ... "the Anaesthetic Revelation is the Initiation of Man into the Immemorial Mystery of the Open Secret of Being, revealed as the Inevitable Vortex of Continuity" ... "I know—as having known—the meaning of Existence: the sane centre of the universe—at once the wonder and assurance of the soul—for which the speech of reason has as yet no name but the Anaesthetic Revelation" ... the sense of having felt "the undemonstrable but irrefragable certainty of God" ... "oneness with this Infinite Power, and this Spirit of Infinite Peace" ..."the disappearance, in these rapturous experiences, of the motor adjustments which habitually intermediate between the constant background of consciousness (which is the Self) and the object in the foreground" ... "grand and spacious, immortal, cosmogonic reveries ... moments divine, ecstatic hours; in which our thought flies from world to world, pierces the great enigma, breathes with a respiration broad, tranquil, and deep as the respiration of the ocean, serene and limitless as the blue firmament" ... "instants of irresistible intuition" ... "such a transparent summer evening. Swiftly arose and spread around me the peace and knowledge that pass all the argument of the earth" ... "a soul-sight of that divine clue and unseen thread which holds the whole congeries of things, all history and time, and all events, however trivial, however momentous, like a leashed dog in the hand of the hunter" . . . "an inward state of peace and joy and assurance indescribably intense, accompanied with a sense of being bathed in a warm glow of light" . . . "a feeling of having passed beyond the body, though the scene around me stood out more clearly and as if nearer to me than before, by reason of the illumination in the midst of which I seemed to be placed" . . . "immersed in the infinite ocean of God" . . . "I knew that the fire was within myself" . . . "a sense of exultation, of immense joyousness accompanied or immediately followed by an intellectual illumination impossible to describe" . . . "experimental union of the individual with the divine" . . . "illumined by the light which proceeds from the prophetic source" . . . "total absorption in God" . . . "as if placed in a vast and profound solitude, to which no created thing has access, in an immense and boundless desert, desert the more delicious the more solitary it is. There, in this abyss of wisdom, the soul grows by what it drinks in from the well-springs of the comprehension of love" . . . "*raptus* or ravishment" . . . "stupefaction" . . . "the habit of ecstasy" . . . the soul is "adorned with virtues and adorned with supernatural gifts" . . . "intoxicating consolations" . . . "Invested with an invincible courage, filled with an impassioned desire to suffer for its God, the soul then is seized with a strange torment—that of not being allowed to suffer enough" . . . "this sublime summit" . . . "as from a smallness into a vastness . . . as from an unrest to a rest" . . . James on Dionysius: "It is *super*-lucent, *super*-splendent, *super*-essential, *super*-sublime, *super everything* than can be named" . . .

Even if you attributed the mystic state to supernatural sources, you could properly expect it to have its bodily counterpart. Thus, we are told that, under ordinary conditions, the nervous system in action is somewhat like a bureaucratic structure where the carrying-out of one master aim requires great subordination of functions. The expressing of some impulses is contrived by the repression of others, as a child learns to walk by controlling, among various possibilities, its impulse to kick. If this is so (as neurologists like Sherrington tell us it is), then even on the bodily level there is an "infringement of freedom" within us, a sheerly physiological state of "inner contradiction." Discord would have become the norm. However if, going beyond it, the nervous system could fall into a state of radical passivity whereby all nervous impulses "attitudinally glowed" at once (remaining in a halfway stage of incipience, the *status nascendi* of the pursuit figured on Keats's Grecian Urn) there could be total "activation" without the overt acts that require repressive processes. Hence "contradictory" moments could exist simultaneously.

Since our ordinary knowledge reaches us through the senses, any such unusual sensory condition would likewise be felt as knowledge. The mystic would thus have a strong conviction that his experience was "noetic," telling him of a "truth" beyond the realm of logical contradictions, and accordingly best expressed in terms of the oxymoron. And indeed, why would it not be "knowledge"? For if the taste of a new fruit is knowledge, then certainly the experiencing of a rare and felicitous physical condition would be knowledge too, a report of something from outside the mind, communication with an ultimate, unitary ground.

When considering mysticism and its "fragments," we should attempt to account for as much as possible in purely naturalistic terms. These would seem to involve neurological, linguistic, and "socioanagogic" explanations. Even if convinced that some mystics have established genuine union not merely with a pantheistic ground but with an eminent super-natural, super-personal Creator, we should be willing to look for as many sheerly natural elements here as speculation and method can indicate. For if "sanctifying grace" works through "nature," as the theologians say it does, then the more exactly one discriminates in his locating of the purely natural motives, the sounder should be his arguments for the further element of "divine revelation." And in particular, when considering the mystic motive in literary works, we should make every effort to discount for language, the nervous system, and the "eminences" of social hierarchy.

However, recalling James's list, even if you believe in the validity of certain mystic revelations, you must agree that, besides mysticism and its "fragments," there are substitutes for mysticism, *Ersatzmystiken*, as with drugs, insanity, crime, and the many fantastic appetites by which men are goaded, as by demons.

Technically, in fact, the votaries of these cults *are* in communication with demons. For when means become ends, and are sought to the exclusion of all else, then the man for whom they are thus transformed does indeed identify himself with a universal purpose, an over-all unitary design, quite as with mystical communion. He has a god, and he can lose himself in its godhead. He is engrossed, enrapt, entranced.

And the test of such substitute mysticisms, we have said, is the transforming of means into ends. Thus, the votary of speed will seek speed for itself alone, for the sheer ecstatic agony of speed, as with Lawrence of Arabia when, home from the wars, he raced along country roads on his motorcycle—and in the attempt to avoid killing a pedestrian, he killed himself. His entrancement would be a mysticism of speed. And whatever frustrations and contradictions were riding him, he in the moments of his free expression was riding them, or riding with them.

There are many such *Ersatzmystiken*. There is a mysticism of sex, a cult wherein sex is sought as one's overwhelming aim, about which all other motives subordinately cluster. There are mysticisms of money, crime, drugs—and many other such goadings that transform some instrumentality of living into a demonic purpose.

Thus, too, there is the mysticism of war. There are those for whom war is a vocation, to whom the thought of the universal holocaust is soothing, who are torn by internal strife unless, in their profession as killers, they can commune with carnage. The imagery of slaughter is for them the way of mortification. As leaders, they are not mere "careerists," looking for a chance to let their friends in on government contracts at a high figure. They are mystic soldiers, devout—and killing is their calling. What of them?

They find solace in the thought of the great holocaust; and they love the sheer hierarchal pageantry, the Stoicism of the disciplinary drill, the sense of unity in the communal act of all the different military orders marching in step, or the pious contemplation of the parade made static and "eternal," in the design of a military burial grounds, with its motionlessly advancing rank and file of graves.

What of *these* votaries, when their motives are hierarchally amplified, and empowered, with the great new weapons? And what of the fragments of such dedication, among the petty officials and journalistic hacks who know nothing of this quiet, deep-lying terror, but would do their lowly bit towards its unleashing, in daily pronouncements and bureaucratic finaglings that add steadily to the general ill will throughout the world?

Mysticism is no rare thing. True, the attaining of it in its pure state is rare. And its secular analogues, in grand or gracious symbolism, are rare. But the need for it, the itch, is everywhere. And by hierarchy it is intensified.

In hierarchy it can exist under many guises. Nature, society, language, and the division of labor—out of all or any of these the hierarchic motive inevitably develops. Anagogically, if you will, but at least "socio-anagogically," in hierarchy reside the conditions of the "divine," the goadings of "mystery."

But since, for better or worse, the mystery of the hierarchic is forever with us, let us, as students of rhetoric, scrutinize its range of entrancements, both with dismay and in delight. And finally let us observe, all about us, forever goading us, though it be in fragments, the motive that attains its ultimate identification in the thought, not of the universal holocaust, but of the universal order—as with the rhetorical and dialectic symmetry of the Aristotelian metaphysics, whereby all classes of beings are hierarchally arranged in a chain or ladder or pyramid of mounting worth, each kind striving towards the *perfection* of its kind, and so towards the kind next above it, while the strivings of the entire series head in God as the beloved cynosure and sinecure, the end of all desire.

INDEX

For both books

Abailard, Peter, 698, 730

Abraham, 769-72, 775, 776; Kierkegaard's psychology for, 770-1; willingness to sacrifice, 776-7

Absolute, paradox of the, 35-8

Abstracting, 241-2

Absurd, the, 778-80, 789; cult of, 779, 283-4; paradox of, 780

Act, 14-15; and potency, 252-62; as locus of motives, 64-9; defined, 227; philosophic schools, 227-74; relation between scene and, 3; synonyms for, 14-15

Act-agent ratio, 15-16; differentiated from scene-act ratio, 17

Action, 136-7; Korzybski's concept of, 241-2; overt, 236, 238; psychology of, 262-74

Action-passion, 418-20

Act of Creation, 61, 62-4

Act-purpose ratio, 15

Adams, Henry, 120-1, 535

Advancement of Learning, The, 604

Advantage, 584-5; cult of, 798-9

Aeneid, 124

Aeschines, 583, 593

Aeschylus, 20

Agency, 228; symbolic of, 283-6

Agency-purpose ratio, 15

Agent, 12; idealization, philosophic schools, 172-5; in general, philosophic schools, 171-226; synonyms for, 20; unification, philosophic schools, 175-6

Agent-agency ratio, 15

Agent-purpose ratio, 15

Agnostic stress, 576-7

Agrippa, Menenius, 132

Alan of Lille, 697

Alcuin, 625

Alice in Wonderland, 791-2

Ambrose, Saint, 316

Anarchism, 268, 345

Anarcho-syndicalism, 345-6; constitution, 346-9

"Ancient Mariner, The," 369, 370, 509

Anecdote: informative, 60-1; representative, 59-61, 323-5; terminal as, 326-7

Angyal, Andras, 31, 469-70

Anima Poetae, 826, 849

Animism, 14, 118-19

Antidosis, 575

Anti-Semitism, 407, 408, 782; as social mystery, 758-61

Apartment in Athens, 552

Appearances, 193, 194

Appetite, 134, 135

A priori, 183, 189

Aquinas, Thomas, 71, 102, 227-32, 254, 281, 468, 744, 765, 802

Areopagitica, 528

Aristotle, 118, 242-3, 252-4, 275-6, 340, 427-8, 549, 560, 573, 575, 576, 586, 601, 688, 754, 777, 823; and Aquinas, 227-32; appeal to audiences, 562; basic principles of nature, 273; definition of man, 410; elementalism of, 57; entelechy of, 538; idea of God, 35, 68, 245, 254, 428; kinds of rhetoric, 594-5; Neo-Aristotelian School, 465-84; on a dramatic plot, 308; on audiences, 587-8; on business utility and science, 215; on drama and the epic, 409; on freedom, 267; on geometry, 261; on imagination, 602, 604, 605; on nature, 76; on opinion, 580-1; on rhetorical form, 592-3; on substance, 25; on the physician, 407; on virtue, 579, 616; purpose in, 292-3

Arnold, Matthew, 167, 536, 539, 541; imagery of, 533-4; self-immolation in poetry of, 531-4

Arnold, Thurman, 413, 721

Ars Amatoria, 683-4

Art for art's sake, 284, 289-90

"Art of Cheating," 575

Art of Controversy, The, 615

Art of Rhetoric, The (Aristotle), 562, 573, 575, 580, 598, 617, 823

Art of Rhetoric, The (Wilson), 339

As You Like It, 582

Aspects of Scientific Rationalism in the Nineteenth Century, 131, 429

"Ash Wednesday," 845

Atomic scheme, 159-60

Atomistic reduction, 97-8

Attitudes Toward History, 298, 350, 514, 536

Auden, W. H., 407

Augustine, Saint, 142-4

Aurelius, Marcus, 161, 165, 166-9, 760

Autonomous principles, importance of, 552-3

Aversion, 134, 135

Avicebron, 220

Avicenna, 334

Babbitt, Irving, 369

Babylon, 815-17

Back to Methuselah, 657

Bacon, Francis, 604, 606, 607, 657, 658

Bailey, Judith, 839

"Basic Laws of Development of Socialist Economy," 213

Baudelaire, 286, 828
Beauty, 754-6
Becker, Carl, 12
Behaviorism, 78-9, 272-3
Being, 34-5, 73
Bell, Eric T., 405
Bembo, Cardinal, 746, 751, 754
Bentham, Jeremy, 162, 183, 284-5, 612, 622-3, 632, 675, 677, 678, 697, 720; on entities, 707-9; on archetypes, 615; recognition of interests, 626; rhetorical analysis in, 614-19
Bentham's Theory of Fictions, 615
Bergson, Henri, 152, 295-6, 412
Berkeley, George, 40, 97, 108, 177-81
Bernal, J. D., 715
Bernard, Claude, 31, 697, 698
Biddle, Francis, 18
Biographia Literaria, 105, 192, 325
Black, Hugo L., 13
Black Boy, 783
Blake, William, 606
Boccaccio, 751
Bohr, Niels, 415
Bonaventura, 30, 97
Book of Fallacies, 615-16, 618, 624, 626
Book of the Courtier, 745-57, 758, 761, 763, 792
Brand, 433
Bréhier, Émile, 71, 102, 122, 261
Breughel, 122
Bridgman, P. W., 80, 279-80, 284
British constitution, 340, 342-3, 345
Brod, Max, 763, 767, 776
Brothers Karamazov, The, 84-5
Bunyan, John, 786
Burke, Edmund, 359, 608, 747
Burlington Magazine, 51
Byron, Robert, 51

Caldwell, Erskine, 274
Cantico Espiritual, 833
Capital, 206
Capitalism, 45, 92, 113, 116, 119; and sacrifice, 397; terms between freedom and, 350-4
Carlyle, Thomas, 7, 190, 614, 667, 688, 739, 743, 812; doctrine of clothes, 646; on mystery, 638-51
Carroll, Lewis, *see* Dodgson, C. L.
Cartesian dualism, 146-7, 149, 234
Cassiodorus, 625
Cassirer, Ernst, 565, 686, 670
Castiglione, Baldassare, 745
Castle, The, 757-68
Cause, 228; and effect, Hume on, 182-3; Aristotle's classification of, 276
Chaplin, Charles, 18
Character, 230-1
Chateau d'Argol, 36
Chestov, Léon, 852
Christ, 19-20, 333, 336, 345; as sacrifice, 852
Christianity, 271-2, 311, 343, 369-70; acceptance of Genesis, 467; and martyrdom, 265; theology of, 79
Churchill, Winston, 575, 637, 830

Cicero, 577, 586, 587, 588, 594, 600-1, 622, 731, 746, 753; list of devices, 590-1, 592; on epideictic, 594-5; on persuasion, 573-5; on universality of rhetoric, 583-4; styles of rhetoric, 596-8
Class concept of Marxism, 215
Class-consciousness, 212-13
Class struggle, 204-5
Climb, social, 828-9
Clothes, 643-6, 739
Coleridge, Samuel Taylor, 14, 34, 192, 233, 299, 408, 411, 470, 471, 534, 541, 592, 594, 602, 604, 606, 615, 668, 740; as dialectician, 400; criticism of, 470-1; cult of the impulse, 826; dialectic of, 325; moral of, 728; on beauty and the sublime, 849; on Edmund Burke, 359-60; on flowers and insects, 411-12; on negation, 296; on poetry, 68, 105, 174, 224, 338; pantisocracy project of, 368-71
Commodities, 277-8; cult of, 716
Communication, 700-1
Communism, 116, 204, 337, 345
Communist Manifesto, 202, 204-9, 211, 215
"Composed upon Westminster Bridge," 82
"Comus," 656, 811
Concealment, 697-8
Constitution, 175; addressed by agents to agents, 360-2; and admonitory, 330-2; and the opponent, 357-60; behind the constitution, 362-3; Coleridge's pantisocracy project, 368-71; dialectic of, 323-401; limits and powers of, 367-8; makes extra-constitutionality mandatory, 376-8; meanings of, 341-4; new, for laissez-faire, 349-50; partially representative, 371-3
Constitution of the Church and State, According to the Idea of Each, 615
Constitutional unity and political diversity, 388-91
Controlled cases, 78-9
Copernicus, 327
Coriolanus, 132
Corneille, 656
Counterfeiters, The, 115, 659
Courtier, perfect, 745-6, 748-50, 753
Courtship, 732-6; abstract, 701; caricature of, 757; imagery of, 754; paradigm of, 745-7; principle of, 732, 758; rhetoric of, 638; social, 791-2
Covering, eulogistic, 624, 633
Crane, Hart, 727
Crane, R. S., 470ff.
Creative Evolution, 295, 412
Creator, agent as, 174
Crime, 307-8
Crime and Punishment, 307, 641
Criminal as scapegoat, 406-7
Critique of Pure Reason, 188, 196, 197, 404
Croce, Benedetto, 590, 592
Cromwell, Oliver, 636-7
Crucifixion, 789-90

Dante, 742, 817, 827, 831, 851-2; on languages, 691-2

Darwin, Charles, 152-8, 291, 431, 432
De Anima, 118
De Doctrina Christiana, 574, 577, 590, 598
De Gaulle, Charles, 624
De Lacy, E. A., 695
De Lacy, P. H., 695
De l'Amour, 685
De Oratore, 573, 577, 583, 590, 592, 598, 600, 753
De Planctu Naturae, 697
De Quincey, 573, 650, 667
De Rerum Natura, 162
De Vulgari Eloquentia, 691-3, 743
Death and Transfiguration, 538
Death in Venice, 427, 733
Decadence, and Other Essays on the Culture of Ideas, 674
Declaration of Independence, 343, 345, 363, 372
"Defense of Poetry," 225
Democracy, 17-18, 398
Democritus, 27, 132
Demosthenes, 560, 589, 592, 650
Demetrius, 582, 583
Des Modèles de la Nature et de la Fortune, 688
Descartes, 55, 177, 225, 311
Deus ex machina, 184
Deus sive Natura, 739
Devices, of speech, 602; rhetorical, 589-91
Dewey, John, 276, 279, 657; instrumentalism, 275; on naturalism, 50
Dialectic, 239, 240, 503, 584; in general, 402-43; of constitutions, 323-401; of the scapegoat, 406-8
Dialectical materialism, 200-2
Dialogue, Platonic, 724-5
Dictionary of Philosophy and Psychology, 131
Diderot, 666ff., 808
Die Wahlverwandtschaften, 60
Dionysius the Areopagite, 642, 823
Diplomacy, 52-3
Directional substance, 31-3
Discourse on Method, 311
Discourses, 11
Dissociation des Idées, La, 674, 829
Divine Comedy, The, 86
Division, 569-70; de Gourmont on, 674; merger and, 403-6; terms for, 700; variants of, 410-20
Doctor Faustus, 836
Dodgson, C. L., 791
Dostoevsky, 307, 433, 641-2, 732, 793
Drama, 245; dissolution of, 440-1
Dramatism, five key terms of, Introduction, xvii-xxv
Dreiser, Theodore, 29
Drives, 49, 79, 104
Dry Salvages, The, 263
Duchamp, Marcel, 327
Dunciad, The, 91
Durante, Jimmy, 306, 828
Dynamo, virgin and, 120-1

"East Coker," 848

Eater of Darkness, 31
Education, rhetoric of, 753; in Kafka, 764-5
Education of Henry Adams, The, 87, 120, 535
Eisenhower, Dwight David, 734
Elation, 836-40
Elections, 381-2
Elegy in a Country Churchyard, 648
Eliot, T. S., 263, 265, 298, 302, 485, 514, 536, 818, 836, 842-8; down-turning mood in poetry, 842-3
Elizabethan and Metaphysical Imagery, 596
Elliott, Thomas D., 851
Ellison, Ralph, 717
Emerson, Ralph Waldo, 176, 263, 283; idealism of, 277-9
Emile, 152, 285, 303, 555
Emotions, definitions of, Spinoza, 149
"Empedocles on Etna," 531, 532
Empirical, transcended by transcendental, 194
Empiricism, logical, 358
Empson, William, 18, 165, 647, 648, 650, 701, 743, 836
Encyclopedia of Religion and Ethics, 825
Encyclopedia of the Social Sciences, 548
Enemy of the People, An, 3-5, 433
Engels, Friedrich, 168, 201, 345, 516
English Pastoral Poetry, 647
Entelechy, Aristotelian, 261-2, 538
Entities, 707-9
Environment, 12, 158
Epictetus, 163, 166
Epicureanism, 159, 163, 164
Epideictic, 594-6
Essay Concerning Human Understanding, An, 22-3, 177
Essays on the Principles of Human Action, 607-8
Esse est percipi, 178, 181
Essence, 249; existence and, 219-20; Santayana's, 216; temporizing of, 430-40; terms for, 537-8
Ethics (Aristotle), 616
Ethics (Spinoza), 137, 147, 311, 832
Ethics of Competition, The, 256
Eunapius, 695
Every Man in His Humour, 266
Every Man out of His Humour, 266
Evolution, 63; Darwinian, 657; myth of, 661-4
Existence, and essence, 219-20
Existentialism, 793; in France, 778-9; Kierkegaardian, 777-8
Experience, 192-3; Hume on, 182-3

Facts, 282, 284
Faraday, Michael, 429
Farewell to Arms, A, 851
Fascism, 34, 116, 117
Fear and Trembling, 767-76, 827
Feuer, Lewis S., 358
Fichte, Johann, 177, 198, 199, 281
Finite species, 768-9
Flaubert, Gustave, 514, 583
Flowers and insects, 411-12
Focillon, Henri, 224

Folklore of Capitalism, 721
Fons Vitae, 220
Fools, wisdom of, 18
Foundations for a Science of Personality, 31, 469
Foundations of the Social Scientists, 431
France, Anatole, 514
Freedom, 74-5, 106, 203, 267, 268; choice of circumference for, 354-5; personal, 849-50; terms between capitalism and, 350-4
Free market, 351, 352-3
Freud, Sigmund, 305, 313, 431, 432, 562, 659, 660, 766

Galileo, 38, 81, 107, 686
"Géante, La," 828
Genealogy of Morals, 555, 617
Genesis of Plato's Thought, 552
Genocide, 537, 555
Geometric definition, 26
Geometric substance, 29
German Ideology, The, 627, 628, 631, 633, 634, 639, 714
Gide, André, 115, 561, 659, 669, 786
Gilson, Etienne, 227
Gnostics, 124
God, 43-4, 416-17; acts of, 160-1; and Nature, 138-46; Aristotle's, 230; Berkeley's idea of, 180-1; concepts of, 275-6; human person derived from, 35; money as substitute for, 108-13; personal, 90; rhetorical names for, 298-301; search for, 260
God and Philosophy, 227
Goethe, 60
Golden Bough, 788
Golden Bowl, The, 821
Golden Rule, 366
Gourmont, Remy de, 674-8, 793, 829-30
Gracq, Julien, 36
Grammar of Motives, The, 627, 628, 545, 546, 600, 613, 676, 686, 714, 720, 841
Gray, Thomas, 648
Great Chain of Being, The, 142, 789
"Great Stone Face, The," 828
Gregory, Horace, 225
Group Psychology and the Analysis of the Ego, 431
Gulliver's Travels, 8, 593, 781

Haeccëitas, 409
Hamlet, 6, 247, 304
Handmaiden of the Sciences, The, 405
Hardy, Thomas, 6
Hawthorne, Nathaniel, 827
Hazing, an affirmation of mystery, 758-60
Hazlitt, William, 607-8
Heavenly City of the Eighteenth-Century Philosophers, The, 12
Hegel, 35, 39, 177, 199, 202-4, 267, 281, 312, 613, 628, 631; concrete universal, 714; Hegelian *Insofern,* 415; idealism of, 12, 56; on development of spirit, 200-1; on material properties, 46-7; reversal of, by Marx, 281-2
Heisenberg principle, 260

Hemingway, Ernest, 274, 787, 851
Heraclitus, 329, 847
Hero, 42
Heroes and Hero-Worship, 7-8, 645
Hierarchy: metaphorical view of, 661-5; mystery of, 830
Hildebert of Lavardin, 697
Historic inevitability, 258-9
History, Hegel's philosophy of, 202-4
Hitler, Adolf, 373, 547; attacks on democracy, 398; 25-point program of, 390
Hobbes, Thomas, 131, 132-7, 611
Hoby, Thomas, 749
Holism, 411
"Hollow Men, The," 845
Homosexuality, 427, 639-40, 738
Hopkins, Gerard Manley, 302, 833, 837-40, 845; steps in the poetry of, 838
Humanism, 55, 80, 351-2; change in, 112-13; cult of "pure" personality, 80
Human person, derivation of, 35
Human relations, 323, 325, 335
Hume, David, 177, 181-4, 186, 415
Hunger-Artist, The, 766
Huxley, Aldous, 309
Hylozoism, 119

Ibn-Sina, theory of, 229
Ibsen, Henrik, 3, 433-9
Idea, 608-10; priority of 657-61; ruling, 629-30; universal, 630-1
Idealism, 128; after Kant, 185, 198-200; and written contract, 174; Berkeleian, 181; defined, 171; money and, 175-6; mysticism and, 299-300; of Spinoza, 150
Idealistic materialism, 200
Idealization, agent, philosophic schools, 172-5
Idealizing vocabularies, 100
Ideas, 12; Berkeley on, 178-81; Hume's, 182
Identification, 543-51, 549, 551-5, 569-70, 579-83; cunning, 559-61; of autonomous activities, 551-3; pastoral, 647-50; ultimate, 559-61
Ideology, as rhetoric, 627; definition of, 612; meanings of, 628
Ideology and Utopia, 721-3
Idols of the Cave, 657-8
Il Penseroso, 12
Iliad, 124
I'll Take My Stand, 24
Imagery: at face value, 541-3; effects of, 541-2; of Matthew Arnold, 633-4
Images: and the demonic trinity, 300-3; kinds of, 534; range of, 536; social rating of, 820-2
Imagination, 133, 134, 223-6, 602-8; Spinoza on, 150
Imagism, 612
Imitation, 655-6
Imitation of Christ, 311
Indebtedness, 114-15
Individual, relation of, to public medium, 114-15
Individual and His Society, The, 563
Industrialism, 45, 351, 353-4

Inevitability, 258-9
Infancy, 691-2, 698-9
Inferiority complex, 806
Inferno, 851
Informative anecdote, 60-1
Inquiry, socioanagogic, 743-4
Inquiry Concerning Human Understanding, 182
Insects and flowers, 411-12
Instincts, 49, 79, 104, 152
Institutio Oratoria, 573, 576, 583, 598
Intention, direction of, 678-82
Interpretation, medieval kinds of, 744
Intuition, 216; Kant's, 188; Spinoza's, 150-2
Irony, 503, 513-17
Isidore, 625
Isocrates, 573, 575
Ivory Tower, The, 821

Jackson, Shirley, 766
James, Henry, 171-2, 489, 640, 739; on the deity of things, 818-22
James, William, 69, 287, 288, 298, 300, 852-5; cash values of ideas, 286; "circumference," 77; on act as locus of motives, 64-6; on pragmatism, 275, 277; on the way of creation, 62-4, 69, 72-4; two principles of truth in, 282-3
Jean-Jacques Rousseau, 285
Jefferson, Thomas, 380
Jehovah, 63, 413, 414
Jesuits, 678, 680-1
Johnson, Edgar, 266
Jonson, Ben, 266
Joseph, Sister Miriam, 590
Josephson, Matthew, 285
Jowett, Benjamin, 421-3
Joyce, James, 670, 834
Judo, 36-7
Julius Caesar, 245, 618-19
Jung, Carl Gustav, 265
Justice, 15, 124, 675-6, 804; for the Sophists, 173; Plato's, 173

Kandinsky, 35-6
Kant, 70, 136, 137, 177, 182, 200, 219, 223, 281, 282, 300, 402, 410, 415; idealism after, 198-200; moral transcendence in, 192-7; on merger, 404-5; philosophy of, 185-97; pragmatism of, 275
Keats, John, 246, 447-63
Kierkegaard, 767-76, 789, 799, 827; existentialism of, 777-9; faith in the Absurd, 775; psychology of, 770-1; theme of weaning, 771-3
Kierkegaard et la philosophie existentielle, 852
Kill, cult of the, 784-91
Killing, fantasies of, 786-7; motives in terms of, 543-4
Kingship, 42-3
Kluckhohn, C., 564, 567, 569
Knight, Frank Hyneman, 256-7
Knight, G. Wilson, 450
Knowledge, 195-6; forms of, Spinoza, 150-2,

love and authority, 117-24; sociology of, 722-7
Korzybski, Alfred, 57, 173, 238-41, 247, 251, 293, 317, 440, 511
Krafft-Ebing, 808
Krock, Arthur, 381
"Kubla Khan," 299

La Philosophie du Moyen Âge, 71, 102
La Rochefoucauld, 97, 100, 585, 638, 688, 746; motives in, 669-73
Lady Chatterley's Lover, 692, 782, 792
Laforgue, Jules, 842
Laissez-faire, 351; new constitution for, 349-50
L'Allegro, 12
Language, 471-2; persuasive use of, 567-8; vocal gesture, 236-7, 238
Laughter: cult of, 750-1; in *The Castle,* 764
Law, 427, 428; constitutionality in, 378-80; positive, theories of, 174-5
Law of the acceleration of history, 535-6
Lawrence, D. H., 692-3, 792
Lawrence, T. E., 856
Leibniz, 35, 147, 177, 311-12, 400, 611; monads, 255; on knowledge of God, 225; philosophy of, 184-5
Lenin, V. I., 13, 174, 200, 201, 205, 207, 208, 715, 719, 720
Lenzen, Victor F., 415, 417
Leviathan, 132
Levy-Bruhl, 829
Lewin, Kurt, 240
Lindeman, Eduard C., 18
Little Gidding, 299
Lives of the Philosophers, 695
Locke, John, 23, 177, 468
Loeb, Harold, 289
Logic, 296
Logical empiricism, 358
Logic of Modern Physics, 279
Lombroso, Cesare, 255-6
Lonely Debate, The, 245
Long, Huey, 830
Longinus, 581-2, 589, 590, 598, 599, 607; on imagination, 603
Love: Greek, 426; knowledge, and authority, 117-24; Platonic, 425
"Love Song of J. Alfred Prufrock, The," 827, 835, 842-3
Lovejoy, Arthur, 142-3, 404, 789
Love's Comedy, 433
Lowrie, Walter, 768, 827
Lucretius, 159, 160, 162, 164
Luther, Martin, 852
Lyric poem, 243-4
Lyric ratio, 233

Machiavelli, 11-12, 682-90, 695, 745
McKeon, Richard, 625, 693, 695, 697, 730
Maclean, Norman, 470ff.
Magic, primitive, 564-6, 568
Magic Mountain, The, 539
Maitland, 340
Malinowski, Bronislas, 567, 589, 793; context of situation, 729-30

Man to Remember, A, 371
Mann, Thomas, 427, 514, 539, 733, 763, 766; on Kafka, 757-8
Mannheim, Karl, 721-2, 724-6, 729, 731, 735
Marcus Aurelius, *see* Aurelius, Marcus
"Mario and the Magician," 733
Mark Twain, 760
Marlowe, Christopher, 408-9
Marshall, Chief Justice, 385-8
Marshall, George, 711
Marshall, James, 87, 89
Marvell, Andrew, 36
Marx, Karl, 13, 15, 45, 47, 170, 216, 223, 560, 642, 647, 660, 661, 735, 743, 832, 835, 837; class action of, 218; on freedom, 356; on Hegel, 714; on mystification, 625-9, 744; preconstitution of Engels and, 345; Puritanism of, 168; reversal of Hegel by, 281-2; theory of a ruling class, 629
Marxism, 116, 117, 200-2, 209, 210, 215, 258, 337, 359, 378, 516, 548, 627-8; analysis of rhetoric, 626-8; as a vocabulary, 719-21; as an ideology, 627-8, 723; dramatist grammar for, 209-14; persuasion in, 713-21; terminology of, 625, 718-19
Marxism: An Autopsy, 344
Masefield, John, 783
Materialism, 19, 128; and mysticism, 291; defined, 131; dialectical, 200-3
Materialism and Empirio-Criticism, 200
Materialistic reduction, 100-1
Maternal, 283-6
Matter, 46-7
Mayakovsky, Vladimir, 347
Mead, George Herbert, 236-8, 379, 614, 717
Meaning of Meaning, The, 589, 729
Means: and ends, of Grammar, 317-20; mysticism of, 309-11; philosophy of, 275-81; selection of, 679
"Mechanical Operation of the Spirit, The," 781
Mein Kampf, 628
Melville, Herman, 36, 297
Mendel, 156
Merchant of Venice, The, 717-18
Metamorphosis, 766
Metaphysics, 227, 232, 242
Metonymy, 503, 506-7
Miles, Josephine, 233, 234
Mill, John Stuart, 106
Miller, Henry, 733
Milton, John, 12, 527-30, 534, 539, 541, 811
Mind, Self, and Society, 236
Moby Dick, 36, 509
Modern Man in the Making, 510
Moira, 172
Molière, 560
Monads, 184-5, 193, 255
Money: and idealism, 175-6; as God term, 355-6; as substitute for God, 108-13; motive, 93
Monopolies, 372-3
Montesquieu, 643
Moore, Marianne, 246, 485-502
Mosaic code, 343, 361

Motion, 135-7, 242; universal, 255
Motive, act as locus of, 64-9; courtly, 736; covering, 623-5; hierarchic, 808; Machiavelli's concern with, 689-90; money as motive, 93; national, 689; pecuniary, 651-3; sacrificial, 688-90; simple, complexity of, 101-8; suicide as, 529-30; universal, as substance, 43-6
Motivation, Christian totality of, 599-600
Mountain design, fecal meanings of, 832
Mountain-climbing, 826-7
Mourning Becomes Electra, 5-6, 9-10, 247
Murder, 432-3
Murder in the Cathedral, 263, 265, 298, 514, 536
Mussolini, Benito, 373
Mystery, 638-51; natural, 699; of social relations, 649-50, 699, 758; sources of, 704
Mystic state, composite portrait of, 853-4
Mysticism, 128, 855-6; and idealism, 299-300; and materialism, 291; and neuroticism, 288; nature of, 287-8; of means, 309-11; physiology of, 294
Mystification, as deception, 702-4; Carlyle on, 638-51; Karl Marx on, 625-38
Myth, esthetic, 727-8; Utopian, 724-6
Myth of the State, 565, 686
Myths of Plato, The, 724

Native Son, 339, 641, 718
Naturalism, 50, 53, 54, 55
Nature, 24-6; and God, 138-46; Mother, 283
Nature, 176, 263, 277
"Navaho Witchcraft," 564
Nazis, 408; "blood" philosophy of, 26
Necessity, 74-5
Negro in America, 717-19
Neo-Aristotelian School, problem of intrinsic reflected in, 465-84
Neo-Platonist pattern, 769
Neo-Platonists, 143, 293-4
Neurath, Otto, 410-11, 431, 510
Neurosis, social origins of, 804-6
Neuroticism, mysticism and, 288
Neutralization, 620-1
Neveu de Rameau, 142
New Deal, 367, 382, 383, 398
New Yorker, The, 587, 764
Newton, Sir Isaac, 138, 515
Nichomachean Ethics, 293
Nietzsche, 122, 298, 555, 617, 669, 692
Night Music, 83
Nominalism, 128, 129, 248
Nominalist aggregate, realist family and, 247-52
Notion, distinction between idea and, 180

Observations, 485
Occam, William of, 71, 80-1, 95, 98, 107, 138, 178, 248, 324
Occupational diversity, 110
"Ode on a Grecian Urn," 447-63, 728
Odets, Clifford, 83
Odyssey, 15
Offices, rhetorical, 597-602

Ogden, C. K., 615
Olson, Elder, 470ff.
"On First Looking Into Chapman's Homer," 457
On Methods of Inference, 695
On Style, 582
On the Imagination, 604
On the Improvement of the Understanding, 143-4, 145
On the Sublime, 598
One Mighty Torrent, the Drama of Biography, 266
O'Neill, Eugene, 5, 247
Oneness, 34-5
Operationalism, 55, 80, 279
Opinion, 150, 577-8; Aristotle on, 580-1
Oratory, styles of, 597
Oresteia, 20
Origin of Species, The, 153, 156-8
Ostrovitianov, K., 213
Othello, 413-14
Over-Soul, 277
Ovid, 650, 683, 684, 685, 695
Ownership, 557; roots of, 654

Pantheism, 75-7; and ontology, 72-4; defined, 72; Spinoza's, 75
Pantisocracy, 14; constitutional tactics of, 368-71
Pantomime, 667-8; positions of, 808
Papini, 275
Paradiso, 851
Pareto, 628
Parkes, H. B., 344, 349-50, 354-60
Pascal, Blaise, 225, 678-82
Passions, 134, 222
Past Recovered, The, 307
Pater, Walter, 534, 541
Pathetic Fallacy in the Nineteenth Century, 232-3
Paulsen, Friedrich, 131
Peace, 332, 337
Peer Gynt, 433-9, 757
Peirce, 275, 277
Peitho, 575-6, 801
Permanence and Change, 294, 504
Perry, Charles M., 53
Perry, Ralph, 62
Personality, pure, humanism cult of, 80
Persuasion, 700-3; competitive and public ingredient in, 578; Marxist, 713-21; pure, 791ff.; religious, 815-18; ultimate form of, 798
Phaedrus, 403, 419, 421, 426, 427, 428, 701, 754
Philodemus, 695
Philosophic schools: act, 227-4; agency and purpose, 275-320; agent in general, 171-226; terminology, 127-70 .
Philosophy of History, 39, 46, 200, 202, 267, 613
Philosophy of Literary Form, The, 108, 303, 480, 482, 510, 835
Philosophy of the Act, The, 236
Physical traits, and criminality, 256

Pico della Mirandola, 604, 607, 693
Pilgrim's Progress, 268
Plato, 28, 87, 94, 119, 197, 221, 230, 249, 250, 252, 253, 293, 317, 677, 712, 724, 754; as dialectician, 429; concept of Justice, 173; dialogues, 421, 724-5
Platonic love, 245
Plotinus, 30, 34, 293
Poe, Edgar Allan, 299
Poetics, 308
Poetry, 224, 233-4, 284-6, 347-9; lyric, 243-4; Marianne Moore's, 246, 485-502; Shelley's, 299
Poetry and Anarchism, 344
"Poetry and Philosophy in the Twelfth Century, the Renaissance of Rhetoric," 697
Poiema, pathema, mathema series, 264-5
Politics, 293
Portrait of a Lady, The, 171
Portrait of the Artist as a Young Man, A, 680, 838
Possessed, The, 793
Pragmatism, 128; nature of, 275-81; range of, 281-7
Pragmatism, 275
Pre-established harmony, 184, 193
Price system, 351, 353
Primal horde, theory of, 431-2
Prince, The, 682, 685-6, 689
Principles, 53; and reform, 356-7; conflict among, principles of, 373-6
Principles of Literary Criticism, 32, 235, 506
Principles of Nature and Grace, 225
Probability, 259-60
Procedures of Empirical Science, 415
Propaganda, 264, 267-8
Property, 167; identifying nature of, 547-8; mystery of, 788-9; private, 631-2
Proudhon, 676
Proust, Marcel, 307, 439
Provincial Letters, 678
Psychoanalysis, 269, 315, 316
Psychology (Aristotle), 232, 604
Psychopathia Sexualis, 808
Psychosis, hierarchic, 805-7
Psychosomatic medicine, 424
Pudd'nhead Wilson, 760
Purgatorio, 827, 831, 851
Purpose, 12, 186; modifications of, 292-311; Platonist and Neo-Platonist, 293-4

Quartets, 845-7
Quintilian, 575, 577, 583, 586, 594, 609; classification of rhetoric, 596-7; on persuasion, 573

Rabelais, 225, 687
Rackham, H., 592
Rage for Order, 820
Rationalism, 128, 129; and the verbal medium, 311-17; meanings of, 311-12
Rationality, 249-50
Ratios, 262; all, range of, 15-20; as principles of selectivity, 18; defined, 15, 151; instances of, 9-11; scene-agent, 7-9; ubiquity of, 11-15

Read, Herbert, 344-9, 359, 360, 362
Realism, 128, 248; scientific, contemporary, 251; Socialist, 210
Realist family and nominalist aggregate, 247-52
Realms of Being, 606
Reason, 12, 133-4; cunning of, 203; defined, 200; Spinoza's, 150
Red and the Black, The, 685, 828
Reduction, 503, 509; kinds of, 96-101; monetary, 91-6; to money, 110-11
Reflections, 432-3
Reich, Wilhelm, 168, 732
Relativism, 512-13, 722-3
Religion, 316; essence of, 790; money, a danger to, 112; universal, 44
Religious motive, money motive, substitute for, 94
"Religious Musings," 534
Representation, 503, 507-11
Representative anecdote, 59-61, 323-5
Republic, The, 87, 94, 173, 197, 427, 428, 676, 712
Res tegenda, 623, 697
Revolution, 348; Russian, 209-13
Rhetoric, 546-7; administrative, 682-90; basic function of, 565; classification of, 597-8; devices of, 590-1; epideictic, 594-6; in the Middle Ages, 693-8; magic in, 564-6; Marxist analysis of, 626-8; nature of as addressed, 563-4; realistic function of, 567-70; traditional kinds of, 594; traditional principles of, 613-14
Rhetoric (Aristotle), 292, 594, 777
"Rhetoric in the Middle Ages," 693, 730
Richards, I. A., 32, 235-6, 506, 614, 740
Rimbaud, Arthur, 667, 669
"Rime of the Ancient Mariner," 628
Road Through the Wall, The, 766
Robinson Crusoe, 268
Rodin, François, 327
Roosevelt, Franklin D., 391-2, 398, 586, 828; collectivism of, 393-4; death of, 433
Rosenberg, Harold, 36
Rougemont, Denis de, 398-400
Rousseau, Jean Jacques, 152, 270, 285, 303, 364, 555, 738
Ruskin, John, 233
Russell, George, 34
Russia, 16-17, 310, 315, 394; and sacrifice, 398
Russian Revolution, 209-13

Sacrifice: as essence of religion, 790; war and collective nature of, 394-8; willingness to, 775-7
Saint Ambrose, 316
Saint Augustine, 142-3, 576, 577, 590, 605, 625, 693, 817; on persuasion, 574; rhetoric of, 598-601
Saint John of the Cross, 833, 849
Saint Paul, 599, 600-1
Saint Teresa, 271, 845, 849
Saint Thomas, 227

Samson Agonistes, 527-30, 541, 552; suicidal motive in, 529
Santayana, George, 170, 214-33, 279, 299, 313, 606, 818
Santillana, George de, 131-2, 133, 429
Sappho, 732
Sartor Resartus, 614, 638-9, 642-5
Scapegoat, 336; dialectic of the, 406-8
Schelling, 177, 199
Schönberg, Arnold, 36
Schopenhauer, 199, 615
Science, 510; applied, purposive agents of, 286-7; autonomy of, 552-4; major aspects of, 214-15; possibilities of, 556-9; redemption in, 555-6
Science and Sanity, 238
Scientific realism, contemporary, 251
Scientist, 316; belief of, in personal God, 98-9
Scotus, Duns, 250, 483
Season in Hell, 667
"Secularization of the Devil, The," 836
Selected Poems (Marianne Moore), 485, 488, 493, 494, 495, 502
Self, 237, 238, 299-300
Self-deception, 559-61
Self-denial, 795-6
Self-expression, 148
Self-immolation, 531-4
Self-interference, 793-4, 803
Self-love, 671, 673
Self-sacrifice, 265
Semantics, Korzybskian, 240
Sense of the Past, 821
Sermon on the Mount, 343, 345
Seven Types of Ambiguity, 650
Sewanee Review, The, 224
Sex relations, mystery of, 639-41
Sex repression, 168
Shakespeare, William, 83-4, 133, 513, 560, 640, 717, 736
Shakespeare's Use of the Arts of Language, 590
Shaw, George Bernard, 657
Shelley, P. B., 174, 225, 226, 243-5, 660
Sic et Non, 730
Sir Gawain and the Green Knight, 738
Situation, 12-13; context of, 727-36
Situational approach, 130
Skepticism: of Hume, 182; of Santayana, 216-17
Smith, Adam, 397, 837
Social relations, mystery of, 645-50, 758
Socialism, 268, 310; as monetary system, 214; early Utopian, 207
Socialist realism, 210
Socrates, 230, 250, 403, 419, 579, 580, 710, 712, 754
"Sohrab and Rustum," 168, 531-3
Some Versions of Pastoral, 647
Sophist, The, 119
Sophists, 575, 584
Sorel, Julian, 560, 669, 828-9
Soul of Man Under Socialism, The, 640
Southey, Robert, 14
Speech, effective devices of, 603

Spencer, Herbert, 404
Spinoza, 69, 75, 81, 263, 265, 311, 413, 415, 468-9, 602, 611, 739, 813, 832; active and passive terms in, 148; alignment of terms in, 146-52; contextual paradox, 24-6; cult of Euclidean relations, 29; definition of substance, 50; negation formula, 295; on pantheism, 72; pantheism in, 75; philosophy of, 137-52
Spirit, 46-7, 203, 606
Spoils of Poynton, The, 489, 818-20
Stance family of words, 21, 341
Starlit Dome, The, 450
State, 132; modern, 328-9
State and Revolution, The, 13, 205
Stendhal, 285-6, 560, 561, 669, 685, 828
Stewart, J. A., 724
Stevens, Wallace, 224-6
Stoicism, 159-61, 163, 165-70, 271
Stoics, 575, 584
Strauss, Richard, 538
Stress, agnostic, 576-7
Striegel, 19
Suadere, 576
Suicide: as motive, 529-30; Existentialist notion of, 792
Sullivan, Sister Therese, 590
Summa Theologica, 744
Supernatural, 77; vocabularies, 120
Supernaturalism, 50, 53, 82
Surrealism, 348, 400, 429, 612
Suspense, 258-9
Swift, Jonathan, 8, 781, 832
Swords and Symbols, the Technique of Sovereignty, 87
Symbol, as enigma, 644
Symbolic, 36, 546-7; identities of, 551-2; of agency, 283-6
Symbolism, 612
Symonds, John Addington, 300
Symposium, 424
Synecdoche, 503, 507-9
Synusia, 411

Table of the Springs of Actions, 285, 615, 623
Tacitus, 266
Talmud, 343
Tate, Allen, 513-14
Technology, 116, 176
Tegumen, 623, 697
Tendency, 256-7
Teresa, Saint, 271
Terminology: Marxist, 585, 718-19; neutral, 620-1
Terms: dialectical, 708-11; featuring of, philosophic schools, 127-70; positive, 707-8; ultimate, 712-13
Thales, 118, 825
Theological reduction, 99-100
Theology, 694-5
Theophrastus, 266
Theory of Life, 411
Theory of the Leisure Class, 651-5, 658, 829
Thirteenth Amendment, 363
Thomas, Saint, 227

Thomas à Kempis, 311, 403
Thomist doctrine, 71, 102
Thought, 195; Hume's idea of, 182
Thought and Character of William James, The, 62
Tolstoy, 259, 288
Tonio Kröger, 757, 758
Topics, 580-1, 586-7
Totem and Taboo, 431
Toward a Dimensional Realism, 53
Tractatus Theologico-Politicus, 602
Transcendental, 189, 191, 192, 193,194, 198
Transcendentalism, 279, 281, 402
Transformation: imaging of, 634-7; tonal, 834
Treatise Concerning the Principles of Human Knowledge, 177
Trial, The, 758
Tribal definition, 26
Tristan, 539, 766
Trotsky, Leon 13-14, 347
Truman, Harry S., 549
Truth, 600-1; two principles of, in James, 282-3
Tugwell, Rexford Guy, 394
Turn of the Screw, The, 640-1, 739
Tuve, Rosemond, 596, 603
Twelfth Night, 303, 738
Tyler, Parker, 36, 37

Unconscious, the, 691-3
United States Constitution, 331, 343, 358, 361, 362, 372, 374
Universe, 87, 101-8
Upanishads, 845
Utopians, 207-8, 369
Utopian socialists, early, 207
Utopias, as ideologies, 723-6

Values, universal, external, 213
Variability, 155, 158
Varieties of Religious Experience, The, 288, 852
Veblen, Thorstein, 548, 560, 651-6, 748, 787, 829
Veitch, John, 55
Venus, 162, 164
Venus and Adonis, 233, 732, 736-45; explained in social terms, 739-44; homosexual implications in, 738
Venusberg, 827, 828
Verlaine, 850
View, 36
Virgil, 6
Virgin, and dynamo, 120-1
Virtue, 42; components of, 579; in Spinoza, 146; made inevitable, 14
Vocal gesture, language as, 236-7, 238
Volpone, 266-7

Wallace, Henry, 549
War: and collective nature of sacrifice, 394-8; as constitutive anecdote, 330-2; total, representativeness of, 328-30
War and Peace, 259
Warren, Austin, 820-1

Washington, Booker T., 717
Washington, George, 174, 390
"Waste Land, The," 513, 514, 843-4, 846
Weaning, 731-3
Wescott, Glenway, 553
What Is to Be Done?, 208, 719, 720
Wild Duck, The, 433
Wilde, Oscar, 534, 541, 640
Will, 71, 604-5
Williams, William Carlos, 486
Wilson, Thomas, 609
Windelband, 70, 255
Winspear, David, 552
Winters, Yvor, 481
Wisdom, of fools and children, 18

Wishes, 362, 378-9; generalizing of, 365-7
Wit and Its Relation to the Unconscious, 562
Witchcraft: Navaho, 564, 569; rhetoric of, 569
Wordsworth, 246; sonnets, 8, 475
Worker, 396-7
World history, 203-4
Wright, Richard, 339, 641, 718, 783

Yeats, William Butler, 303, 425, 459, 460, 461, 470, 820, 833, 840-1
Young, Stark, 83-4

Zeno, 260, 405, 419
Zilsel, Edgar, 429